THE
REQUEST
FOR
PROPOSAL
HANDBOOK

BY MICHAEL ASNER

A sourcebook of guidelines, best practices, examples,
laws, regulations and checklists from jurisdictions
throughout the United States and Canada

GOVERNMENT TECHNOLOGY. PRESS

Solutions for State & Local Government in the Information Age

The RFP Handbook

Michael Asner Consulting

Government Technology Press

9719 Lincoln Village Drive, Suite 500

Sacramento, CA 95827

916/363-5000 · fax 916/363-5197

— DISCLAIMER —

Great care has been taken to ensure that the information presented is accurate; however, this information is still subject to errors and subject to change. The examples have been obtained from many jurisdictions throughout North America and may not be applicable in every jurisdiction.

— RFPs AND THE LAW OF CONTRACTS —

The process of issuing an RFP and receiving proposals does, by design or accident, establish contractual rights and obligations. Each RFP and the associated process should be reviewed by your lawyer or legal department prior to issuing the RFP. The examples and sample RFPs used throughout this text have been used in many different jurisdictions in the past. The author makes no claim about the appropriateness, correctness or legal consequences of these examples or sample RFPs. Competent legal advice should be obtained to review your Request for Proposal and the associated process.

CONTENTS

CONTENTS CONT.

[1] Each one of these documents is in the public domain. The floppy disk provided with this book contains the documents in both MS Word and WordPerfect format.

Preface

Creating a Request for Proposal is a risky business! Public sector bodies and private sector corporations spend millions of dollars each year developing RFPs for a variety of products and services such as computer systems, land use studies, food services, and health care programs. Unfortunately, many of these RFPs have serious deficiencies. Sometimes, requirements are vague or incomplete. Sometimes, the RFP itself is poorly written and difficult to understand. Often, both the selection process and the evaluation criteria are ambiguous.

These RFPs are not effective. They do not promote the selection of the best proposal. At the same time, they are difficult to defend as being fair. They cannot stand up to public scrutiny.

This handbook — based on the knowledge and experience of a wide variety of public and private sector organizations — can help you create RFPs that are effective and that incorporate a proven evaluation methodology. The handbook has its origins in our workshops and six other reference publications developed since 1988. It contains explanations and examples of many important RFP issues.

Three objectives were kept in mind in creating this reference publication:

1. To provide guidance and reference material to construct an RFP and an evaluation process that can survive public scrutiny;

2. To identify the different approaches and "best practices" in jurisdictions throughout North America;

3. To facilitate the adoption of better practices and to avoid research costs by providing actual examples of policies, model RFPs, laws and regulations from different jurisdictions.

We believe that actual examples with commentaries are effective ways of informing readers about best practices. They are easy to understand and examples can be readily modified and adopted by any organization. This book provides valuable material, extensive examples and numerous ideas which can improve your next RFP. Examples are provided from many jurisdictions in the United States, including the states of Washington, New York, Alaska, New Mexico, California, South Dakota, Arizona, Florida and from several counties and cities. In Canada, there are examples from the provinces of Ontario, British Columbia, the Yukon Territory and from several local governments.

Many of the examples are taken from the state of Alaska. The reason for this is straightforward. Alaska has a lengthy Procurement Code, formal Purchasing Regulations, and an exemplary Model RFP. The editors believe that one complete set of examples of these documents from Alaska is more helpful than a variety of examples from different jurisdictions. Examples from other jurisdictions are used to provide different views and perspectives.

This handbook will be most useful to two specific groups:

1. All public sector buyers (other than the federal government) concerned about using the RFP process for a variety of procurements;

2. Public and private sector organizations acquiring information technology through the RFP process.

There are several items in this book which are not found in any other reference publication:

1. A description of the entire RFP process;

2. A detailed analysis of the Evaluation Process and its major components;

3. Actual examples of laws, regulations, and RFP documents from different jurisdictions.

This handbook is accompanied by a disk containing all of the documents provided in Part II. These documents — all in the public domain — may be imported to your word processor and used in constructing RFP policy, law, regulations, RFPs, and other related documents.

This is the first edition of *The RFP Handbook*. There are many other topics and issues which could have been included, and there are other perspectives which could have been presented. We welcome your comments and your criticism.

— *Michael Asner, Sacramento*
August, 1995

CHAPTER 1

Fundamental Issues

— CONTENTS —

1.1

What is a Request for Proposal (RFP)?

The decision to employ a Request for Proposal commits an organization to a formal process based on fair and open competition. This decision forces the organization to systematically define the acquisition process and the basis on which the proposals will be assessed. The RFP itself provides a standardized framework for vendor proposals and highlights the business, technical and legal issues that must be included in the final contract. By employing an RFP, an organization can obtain much information on which to base its decision. The RFP process — although arguably costly and time-consuming — increases the probability of success.

Our discussion of RFPs begins with the term itself. What is a Request for Proposal? There are many different definitions. Some are complex; others are simple. The one that I prefer is:

A Request for Proposal is a formal invitation from an organization to a supplier to submit an offer. The offer is to provide a solution to a problem or a need that the organization has identified. An RFP is a procurement process in which the judgment of the supplier's experience, qualifications and solution may take precedence over price.

There are several key concepts in this definition. First, an RFP is a document inviting suppliers to submit solutions to a stated problem. It is also a process in which the evaluators base the decision on more than price. Another concept is that of competition. The evaluation process is based on having several proposals from different vendors. A third concept is that the evaluation is based simply on a variety of factors as judged by the purchaser.

Stated another way, an RFP is a written request to suppliers inviting them to propose solutions (and prices) that satisfy functional requirements described in that document.[1] Proposals and suppliers are evaluated in terms of the ability of the solution to satisfy a stated requirement.

A comprehensive definition of the term RFP must include all of the following concepts:

• An RFP is a document with which an organization describes its requirements, asks suppliers for their proposed solutions, describes the key criteria which will be used in evaluating proposals, and outlines the terms and conditions under which the proponent will operate or supply goods or services. Chapter 4 discusses the RFP document in great detail.

• An RFP is also a process for obtaining offers from competing organizations, evaluating those proposals against stated requirements using a predefined evaluation process and a predefined set of evaluation criteria in which price is not the only factor. Most of this book deals with these issues.

For the sake of completeness, let's define the term "proposal" before leaving this section. A proposal is a formal offer by a supplier to provide certain goods and services. A proposal documents the response to the requirements of the RFP, describes the proposed solution, identifies the costs, and often indicates acceptance of the contractual terms and conditions stated in the RFP.

The state of Washington, Department of Information Services[2] has a good, but lengthy definition of information technology RFPs:

The RFP is used to acquire Information Technology Resources that may not have a fully described technical specification and/or for which there are competing functional solutions in the marketplace. The RFP is used to allow vendors the opportunity to propose solutions to a set of functional requirements and/or technical specifications. The RFP process gives the agency the opportunity to select the proposal which best meets agency needs over the expected life of the resource. Agencies should hold a pre-proposal conference when the RFP method is used.

The RFP is used to solicit a proposal and prices from the vendor for the vendor's best solution or solutions to the agency's information technology requirements.

In a few jurisdictions, such as the state of South Dakota[3], an RFP solicits only a technical solution:

(We) may utilize a Request for Proposal (commonly referred to as an "R.F.P.") for requirements which preclude the use of a specification. An RFP will contain functional specifications or a scope of work for which the offerer must respond with a sealed technical proposal. A formal proposal close date and time will be specified. Subjective evaluation criteria will be described and used to select a vendor. The vendor who responds to an R.F.P. with the offer of a technical proposal and is evaluated as acceptable will then be asked to submit a financial proposal which is usually in the form of a sealed quotation...

I.2

When is it Used?

In theory, a formal RFP is used whenever there is a need for obtaining goods and services as a solution to a stated problem. But if the anticipated solution is only $10,000, for example, for an evaluation of a technical design, then the RFP process must also be small.

The cost of preparing an RFP document can be small, especially if a similar one has previously been used by the organization. However, the cost of preparing the document is only one of many costs. Often, the costs of the RFP process far exceed the costs of the document. Costs are incurred in typing documents, having them reviewed, issuing them, answering suppliers' questions, defining evaluation procedures and criteria, evaluating proposals, and preparing reporting memos.

There is little sense in spending $5,000 worth of time and effort on an RFP document and process to acquire a $10,000 solution. A quicker route should be taken. However, the process for the $5,000 solution should still follow the principles of your purchasing policies and still must be fair. Even if your organization permits you to award small contracts on the strength of a telephone call or a letter, you must ensure that the process for asking or selecting vendors is fair and can be defended. You can't simply call the same supplier time after time, year after year, even if the individual contracts are minor.

As a principle, most public bodies and suppliers recognize that the effort must be commensurate with the amount to be spent. Formal RFPs are usually employed when there is a high visibility project or when the expenditures exceed a specified amount.

Many organizations have developed guidelines related to the level of effort and the value of the project. In some organizations, these guidelines are informal and individuals do not use identical rules. In other organizations, these guidelines have been adopted as policy. They have been written down and distributed to all managers to ensure that all suppliers are treated in the same way.

A brief review of the practices in many jurisdictions indicates that there are three different approaches to deciding when to use an RFP. In the first approach, an organization only uses an RFP as a last resort. In Alaska, for example, the Procurement Code[4] states that if you cannot award a contract by Competitive Sealed Bidding (known as a quotation in many jurisdictions), then you *must* use a Request for Proposal.

The second approach for deciding if an RFP is required is based on a set of conditions specifying when an RFP is *not* required. Policies[5] at BC Systems Corp. state that:

An RFP is not required when:

• **The expenditure is under $100,000.**

• **There is a proven sole source of supply.**

• **Changes to an existing License or Service Agreement are required.**

• **For release/version upgrades to products.**

• **For extensions to existing contracts (under specified circumstances).**

• **If an approved procurement agreement has been established from an earlier RFP process (standing offer).**

• **A similar requirement has been submitted to tender within the past six months and the same terms and conditions are applicable.**

The third approach for deciding if an RFP is required is based on a description of specific situations. For example, here's how one central agency defines the rules[6]:

The RFP process is to be used when:

• **The purchase is not solely a product or commodity but is more in the nature of a solution to a problem where the solutions are expected to be quite varied and/or difficult to evaluate; or**

• **Cost is not the only selection criterion; or**

• **There are economic development issues involved; or**

• **The final selection of a proponent is expected to be complex.**

"In practice, most purchases which meet these criteria will be major contracts for the supply of computer hardware, software development, systems maintenance, application support and end user support."

1.3

How Much Effort is Warranted?

There is a high cost associated with being "visibly fair" or holding a "fair and open" competition. Often there are dozens, if not hundreds, of potential suppliers for a specific service. How do you select an architect or a systems integrator to perform a $5,000 preliminary evaluation from 100 qualified firms?

Many organizations have defined a building-block approach to procurements using RFPs. With each increase in the level of expenditure, additional effort is justified and additional approvals are required.

A Specific Example

Here is how one government agency deals with this issue. As the estimated value of the procurement increases, the process becomes increasingly formal with additional documents, procedures and approvals required. All procurements based on factors other than lowest price require some form of RFP.

The manager initiating the procurement develops an estimate of the value of the procurement. This estimate determines the approach and the required approvals. As the expenditure level increases, the approach changes from phone calls, to letters, to a formal RFP. Similarly, the required approvals progress from one signature on a purchase order to a formal review of the project and the contract.

Managers are advised to ensure that all contract awards can stand up to public scrutiny, even those for less than $1,000. Here are the guidelines they use:

Estimated Value: less than $1,000

Approach:

Telephone one qualified supplier to identify the work, discuss the price and award the contract.

Approvals:

1. Approval of the project plan is not required.

2. Contract approval is required.

Estimated value: between $1,000 and $5,000

Approach:

Telephone at least three qualified suppliers to identify the work, discuss various approaches and request proposals in the form of letters. Evaluate the proposals, document your decision, and award a contract. Keep the letters.

Approvals:

1. Approval of the project plan is not required.

2. Contract approval is required.

Estimated value: between $5,000 and $20,000

Approach:

Issue a letter to at least five suppliers describing your requirements and the selection criteria. Request formal proposals but ensure that the evaluation process and RFP are kept as simple as possible. Evaluate the proposals, document your decision and award a contract.

Approvals:

1. Preliminary project approval.

2. Project approval.

3. Contract approval.

Estimated value: between $20,000 and $100,000

Approach:

Issue a formal RFP to known suppliers. Follow the RFP process described in our procedures manual. Use an evaluation committee. Advertise locally.

Approvals:

1. Preliminary project approval.

2. Project approval.

3. RFP Package.

4. Management approval of the winner.

5. Contract approval.

Estimated value: over $100,000

Approach:

Issue a formal RFP to known suppliers. Follow the RFP process described in our procedures manual. Use an evaluation committee. Advertise at least at the state level.

Approvals:

1. Preliminary project approval.

2. Project approval.

3. Finance Department approval.

4. RFP Package.

5. Management approval of winner.

6. Contract approval.

Within the guidelines, each type of approval was defined:

1. Preliminary project approval is required to initiate this process. The project's sponsor is advised to speak to the next level manager with contracting approval authority. The amount of work required to obtain this approval (and buy-in) from management will be commensurate with the size of the project. Small projects may require only a short conversation or memo. Larger projects may require many pages of justification, even at this preliminary level. Management will ensure that the proposed project complies with existing plans, budget commitments and restrictions. It is a good practice to document all requests for preliminary approval. This need not be elaborate. A short e-mail message is sufficient for small projects.

2. Project approval is required before preparing an RFP. Send the senior administrator a memo requesting approval for the project. Attach your project plan. In the memo, indicate the estimated total expenditure and the duration of the project.

A project plan details the tasks to be done, the timing for each, the relationships among tasks and the responsibility for completing each task.

3. Finance Department approval is required before issuing an RFP for a contract where the total potential cost is likely to exceed $100,000.

4. RFP Package approval is required before issuing an RFP. Approval by the manager, Finance Department and Administration must be obtained when the estimated contract value is more than $200,000.

The following documentation is to be sent to the manager, Finance Department and Administration for approval prior to issuing an RFP:

- Terms of reference
- Project plan
- Required approvals
- Business case
- The Request for Proposal
- Evaluation process and weights
- Method for identifying potential suppliers

5. Management approval of the winner is required before awarding a contract. Approval is given upon receipt and review of a memorandum identifying the recommended supplier and summarizing the evaluation results.

6. Contract approval is required prior to any contract being executed. It is a formalized procedure with levels of signing authority depending on the total contract value.

The complexity of the selection process and its importance increases with the dollar value of the project — as does the amount of work to be done. There is often great pressure on managers and project planners to break a large project into smaller pieces. While this is good project management practice, it can be viewed as a strategy to subvert these guidelines. For example, three $15,000 projects may be easier to get approved than one valued at $45,000.

Using the guidelines quoted above, the $15,000 projects only require that letters be sent to five suppliers. The $45,000 project requires both approval

of the RFP package by management and use of a local advertisement to publicize the competition.

Some Other Examples

In many jurisdictions, purchasing officials are given specific authority to ensure that the effort is commensurate with the value. In Alaska, for procurements under $25,000, there is more discretionary power granted to the commissioner to establish less formal procedures. In exercising this authority (to promote simple practices for small value contracts), the Procurement Code cautions about artificially dividing projects into small pieces[7]:

A procurement... that does not exceed an aggregate dollar amount of $25,000 may be made in accordance with regulations adopted by the commissioner for small procurements...

Small procurements need not be made through competitive sealed bidding or competitive sealed proposals but shall be made with competition that is practicable under the circumstances...

Procurement requirements may not be artificially divided or fragmented as to constitute a purchase under this section...

The procurement officer shall give adequate public notice of intent to make a procurement under this section...

In the Yukon, as in many comparable jurisdictions, dollar limits determine the RFP procedure. The language and limits are different than those used in Alaska, but the intent is similar[8]:

16.(2)(a) Below $25,000 estimated contract value, contracting authorities may enter into a contract or standing

offer agreement directly with a proponent.

(b) Between $25,000 and $50,000, contracting authorities will either invite proposals from three sources or issue publicly advertised Requests for Proposals.

(c) Above $50,000, contracting authorities will issue publicly advertised request for proposals, or invite proposals from all sources on an open source list.

The approach of increasing the level of for-mality, the required approvals, and the level of publicity is common and found in most jurisdictions. In some organizations, the "full-blown" process with major advertising occurs at $25,000 or $50,000. However, in large organizations making many large procurements each year, the most formal RFP process is not initiated until the estimated project cost is much higher — over $500,000 or in some places, over $1 million.

1.4

Advantages and Disadvantages

No reference book would be complete unless it presented some of the arguments for and against the RFP. Within the public sector, there is little choice. Organizations must use this process for certain specified procurements as a matter of public policy: to promote competition and to provide fair and open access to government buying activities. Remember that this process is also employed by private-sector firms not governed by public policy. Why do both public and private sector organizations use RFPs?

Advantages of an RFP

The use of RFPs is often based on law (in government), regulation (in agencies or local government bodies), or policy (in private sector firms). Regardless of the reason, RFPs are a legitimate and valuable management tool. Their use increases the probability of making a sound decision which will stand the test of time. An RFP is preferable to less formal methods of acquisition. Some of the advantages to organizations using RFPs are discussed below.

1. *Promotes competition*

The underlying strategy in employing competitive procedures is that competition promotes quality and generally results in lower prices, more value, greater flexibility in approaches, and more creative solutions.

2. *Better understanding*

The development of detailed requirements fosters a better understanding of the specific needs by all those involved within the organization. Generally, documentation for external use is more carefully prepared and more complete than internal documentation. As part of the preparation of an RFP, users are forced to identify their needs in enough detail for the vendors to propose realistic alternatives. This process often highlights misunderstandings between different user groups or stakeholders, and lack of corporate policies.

A well-managed RFP process gives the purchaser a psychological advantage. Vendors recognize that the purchasers have done their homework. The vendors, therefore, concentrate on structuring a proposal that addresses the users' specific needs.

3. Better information for the vendors

Communicating the organization's requirements to the vendors in writing ensures that all of the suppliers get the same information. In so doing, each vendor addresses the same problem — the one defined by your organization.

When requirements are communicated verbally to the vendors, there is an increased frequency of misunderstandings. Vendors can then innocently or intentionally misunderstand the information. This may become a major issue should the proposal, once accepted, not provide the results expected by the users.

A formal process is the only way the purchaser can document that each vendor has received the identical information.

4. Simplified evaluation

Insisting that each vendor provide similar information in a similar format has several advantages. It is obvious, in reading a proposal, that a vendor has deliberately chosen to avoid issues or direct answers. Having a fixed format for all proposals makes the job of comparing the various offerings easier as information is presented in the same sequence and format.

5. Less biased selection

Formalizing the requirements and the selection process often produces better results. Individual preferences or biases may prove difficult to defend in a process which incorporates predefined selection criteria, written evaluations and public scrutiny.

6. Improved quality of the proposals

The structuring of a formal proposal process elicits better, more complete information from a supplier. The process itself requires the active participation of users and management. This often improves the quality of the decision.

Disadvantages of an RFP

The adoption of a formal RFP process carries with it some significant disadvantages. Organizations issuing RFPs are quick to recognize the two major problem areas are related to time and cost. It is often argued that the apparent disadvantages in using an RFP are not real. The argument is that even if an RFP were not used, the same amount of time would have to be invested to identify requirements, investigate suppliers, and resolve differences among the various participants in the process. People familiar with the process claim that the only change imposed by an RFP on a major selection is the sequence and timing of certain events. Using an RFP, the homework must be done before the document is issued. Specifications must be precise, contract terms defined and project management strategies identified. When an RFP is not used, the definition of specifications, contract terms and project management strategies can be deferred until they are actually needed.

Some disadvantages to using an RFP include:

1. Increased time

One experienced person, working with a favoured supplier, can identify the "best solution" for an organization quickly. The adoption of an RFP process can add months — sometimes even years — to the date that an acceptable solution is implemented.

The RFP process requires extensive staff time — to define the requirements, prepare the RFP, set the evaluation process, perform the evaluations, and interact with several vendors.

The seemingly long delay between the decision to acquire a solution and its delivery often frustrates staff who must work with the existing system.

2. Increased costs

The time spent by staff on RFP tasks is expensive. Some organizations, not having much experience in this area, hire consultants to guide them through the process.

Often, there is an opportunity cost associated with not having a solution in place. Delays introduced by the RFP process carry a cost in terms of lost opportunities, reduced information or reduced service levels. These delays can bring into question the effectiveness of the entire organization.

1.5

Other Procurement Options

here are two issues concerning other purchasing options. First, there are no universally accepted definitions of terms. Even the simplest term such as "Request for Proposal" presents problems. Some organizations use the singular "proposal;" others, the plural "proposals." So, before you start any discussion of options, ensure that everyone agrees on definitions. Terms such as "Request for Information," "tender," "quotation" and "bid" must be defined and used consistently throughout your documentation and in dealing with colleagues and suppliers. Otherwise, confusion will reign.

It is becoming common practice to include a definition of terms in the RFP document. For example, one RFP I recently reviewed contained the following as the first paragraph on page two, immediately following the cover page:

Request for Proposal Definition

An RFP defines the situation or objective for which the goods and/or services are required, how they are expected to be used and/or problems that they are expected to ad- dress. Proponents are invited to propose solutions that will result in the satisfaction of the purchaser's objectives in a cost-effective manner. The proposed solutions are evaluated against a predetermined set of criteria of which price may not be the primary consideration.

Having dealt with the definition issue, we should recognize that there are many other ways of obtaining goods and services depending on the cost, the number of suppliers, the urgency of the need, the amount of risk you are prepared to take, your position within the organization, your organization's policies as well as applicable laws and regulations.

There are many other ways in which organizations can obtain goods and services. Most of these take less work than an RFP.

If the item being sought can be defined as a commodity — that is, a purchase with only mandatory requirements or specifications — then it can be acquired using something other than an RFP. Depending on circumstances and local definitions, a quotation, bid, tender, emergency purchase, small procurement or minor purchase may be used.

If the item being sought (either goods or services) is being selected on the basis of qualitative judgments where price is only one of the factors, then an RFP would normally be used in most jurisdictions. However, there are several circumstances in which many organizations simplify the process and do not require an RFP, or alternatively, require something less than a full-fledged RFP.

There are other competitive procurement options, supported by policy, that are sometimes used instead of an RFP[9]:

Standard acquisition processes include Request for Proposal, Request for Quotation, Master Agreements, Sole Source, Interagency Transfer, Strategic Partnerships and Corporate Agreements.

Typically, organizations have simplified procedures for small procurements and emergency purchases. Some organizations permit restricted competition using an RFP in which the number of vendors is limited. Most organizations have a process for awarding a contract without an RFP when there is an acknowledged sole source. These alternatives to RFPs are described more fully in Chapter 5.

If the organization has no intention of procuring goods and services, it should not issue an RFP. If it is interested in learning about products and services available in the marketplace, there are simpler and better procedures. The more formal, less effective approach is to use a Request for Information (RFI), in which the organization identifies the types of problems or types of services in which it is interested and invites suppliers to provide information. A better approach is to call up two or three vendors and invite them to present information about their products or solutions. Most vendors will gladly provide information about their products and services and will welcome the opportunity to learn more about an organization, including its problems and requirements. There is no conflict nor impropriety in inviting vendors to present their credentials. Inviting one supplier to present its credentials may raise some concerns about favoritism. Inviting several competing suppliers to brief you on their capabilities is not favoritism but good business — keeping up-to-date with a changing marketplace.

It is, however, highly unethical to issue an RFP when there is no intention of accepting any proposal.

[1] Page 4-2, Reference - 0 *1.
[2] Page 4.10, Reference - 1 *2.
[3] Page 4, Reference *3.
[4] Page 21, Reference *4.
[5] This policy is reproduced in Part II of this book. Also see Reference *5.
[6] Page 3-3, Reference *6.
[7] Page 28, Reference *4.
[8] Page 13, Reference *7.
[9] Page 4.5, Reference *2.

CHAPTER 2

Policy Issues

— CONTENTS —

CHAPTER 2

Policy Issues

— CONTENTS CONT —

2.1

Policy Issues

In this chapter we present different approaches to establishing and promulgating approved RFP policies and practices throughout an organization — policies and practices which will enable purchasers to understand and implement the organization's objectives.

Approaches vary greatly, from statements of principle to detailed "cookbooks" containing step-by-step instructions.

Some organizations only provide their buyers/suppliers with high-level statements of policy, broad statements incorporating high-level principles and general approaches; e.g., "All purchasing will be done in a visibly fair, ethical and prudent manner."

Other organizations develop detailed sets of guidelines, procedures or examples to be followed. Still others take the middle ground, providing buyers/vendors with handbooks such as "Preparing an RFP" or "The Request for Proposal Process," which contain a mixture of policy, principles, examples and rules.

One of the difficulties in trying to understand different approaches to establishing policy is that there are no agreed upon standardized terms used throughout North America. A "procedure" in one state is a "guideline" in another. A "policy" in a city government can be a "guideline" in a school system. A "policy" in a corporation can contain items that a different organization would classify as a "guideline," "directive" or "rule."

■ 2.1.1 Definitions

In analyzing these different types of documents, policies, directives, guidelines, etc., we recognized that there are two families of terms to be considered: first, those terms which convey, by their level of detail, the intended use of the document. Here is how these terms are defined[1]:

Principle: a rule or code of conduct.

Policy: a definite course or method of action selected from among alternatives and in the light of given conditions to guide and determine present and future decisions.

Rule: a prescribed guide for conduct or action, an accepted practice.

Guideline: an outline (as by a government) of policy or conduct.

Procedure: a series of steps followed in a regular, definite order; an established way of doing things.

Best Practice: This term, not defined in Webster's Dictionary, is composed of "best" (used in the sense of extremely productive or advantageous) and "practice" (used in the sense of a usual way of doing something.) Hence, an exemplary practice — one followed by an acknowledged leader in a field or endeavor.

Handbook: a concise reference book covering a particular subject.

Manual: a book capable of being conveniently handled; a handbook.

The second family of terms conveys not the use of the document, but the means by which compliance is sought. These terms include law, regulation and directive. Here is how these terms are defined:

Law: a rule of conduct or action prescribed or formally recognized as binding or enforced by a controlling authority.

Regulation: an authoritative rule dealing with details of procedure.

Directive: an authoritative instrument issued by a high-level official body or competent official.

Laws, regulations and directives often contain principles, policies, guidelines, procedures and rules.

■ 2.1.2 What is "Policy"?

In order to consider "policy," we have to agree on what it is. There are many definitions, but a useful definition of "policy" is "course or general plan of action adopted by government, party, person, etc." Policy is usually thought of as a guide to action which has been formulated by senior management. Policy is used to set goals and expectations. It is implemented using rules, instructions or procedures, but policy itself is simply a general expression of management intent. Policy furnishes broad guidelines for organizational behavior. It guides and determines future decisions.

Policy can provide important guidance on day-to-day decisions. This is especially true when an organization doesn't have procedures or rules, or when new situations arise. Each of the day-to-day decisions can be evaluated for its conformance to the policy.

■ 2.1.3 How Can Policies Differ?

Every public body has its own purchasing policy. In some organizations it's written down; in others it's simply part of the culture. Informal policies ("we know what it is so we don't have to write it down") are coming under severe scrutiny as being contrary to public policy. The rules of the game must be known by all.

Purchasing policies can differ widely. A few examples will illustrate some major differences.

In some jurisdictions, the purchasing policy requires that all suppliers be treated equally. This policy ensures that suppliers from other jurisdictions do not suffer a price penalty. In other places, the purchasing policy is designed to encourage local industry. So, suppliers from other jurisdictions are penalized by increasing their quoted prices for comparison with the prices from local suppliers.

Here's a specific example of this: Companies bidding on work in Alaska that do not have an office there are penalized 10 percent on price. Alternatively, the Western Procurement Initiative, an agreement among several Western provinces in Canada, prohibits price penalties for out-of-province Western suppliers competing in these provinces.

In some jurisdictions, the winning proposal is the one which satisfies all of the mandatory requirements and costs the least. In other jurisdictions, the winning proposal is the one judged as providing the greatest value for the money. These different policies will lead to the selection of different proposals as being the "best."

In Ontario, the policy regarding the procurement of information technology requires that government purchasers select the proposal with the least evaluated cost. In other jurisdictions, the practice is to award contracts to the vendor "which displays the best combination of product capabilities and cost effectiveness." The least-evaluated-cost alternative is almost always different than the best-combination-of-price-and-cost alternative.

◼ 2.1.4 What is an Effective Policy?

Before attempting to evaluate (and improve) your organization's purchasing policy, we should attempt to define effectiveness. How are we going to assess a policy and why is this important?

Many organizations believe that an effective policy has five important characteristics:

1. It is reasonable.

2. It is clearly stated.

3. It is available in writing.

4. It is known throughout the organization and by the public.

5. It is consistently applied in all appropriate situations.

Let's discuss the last point: "It (policy) is consistently applied in all appropriate situations." The RFP procedures manual and rules cover many situations and answer many questions which normally arise. For example, the RFP normally states that all questions will be answered in writing. The RFP rules usually identify the number of bidders that are required. Sometimes situations arise which are not covered. In these cases, your organization's policy can help you determine an appropriate response. For example, what happens if one of the firms that received the RFP calls you up and says "we want this job: tell us how much money you have and we'll do it for that amount." What is your response, and why? Using your policy of treating all suppliers the same, the response is obvious. If you tell this supplier your budget, you must tell all of the suppliers.

Within many organizations, a policy must not only be effective but enforceable, and consistent with existing laws and other public policies. The courts in many jurisdictions have influenced RFP practices. They have condoned some practices, prohibited others, and prescribed specific rules of conduct. An organization's ability to change the content of the RFP, and to deal with suppliers, is constrained by laws and court rulings.

Many jurisdictions now have freedom of information laws governing the release of information by public bodies. Using these laws, much information previously kept secret is now routinely released, released as part of the debriefing process, or released upon formal application by a vendor.

More and more jurisdictions are legislating public access to government information. Many public sector bodies are opening up their records even before these laws are passed. The release of information which was formerly unavailable can have a dramatic effect on public sector buyers and private sector companies. These laws often ensure that all vendors have equal access to government business. They go a long way toward ensuring that all suppliers, both large and small, get their fair share of business from the public sector. They can "level the playing field" by making public much more information about the specifics of the procurement process.

These information access laws can affect every business selling to the public sector in three ways.

First, it becomes easier for all companies to know the rules of the game. Every agency and department covered by the law must make its procurement policies and procedures available to any person or firm on demand.

Second, it becomes easier to see how these rules were applied in specific situations. Vendors will be able to review the selection criteria and the evaluators' notes for every competition. They will be able to obtain valuable information about the process, and insights into the purchaser's approaches and reasoning. No longer will vendors have to speculate about the relative importance of price, experience, and the proposed program. They will be able to obtain enough factual information to judge for themselves whether the entire process was carried out in a fair and open manner.

Finally, these laws often add another level of legislated protection for every firm's data. Some public bodies do not rigorously apply their own rules for ensuring that supplier's data is kept confidential. These laws, because they are laws and not simply internal policy, can decrease the amount of information which is inadvertently disclosed. These laws do not replace laws dealing with trade secrets or proprietary information. They simply protect certain corporate information in a different way.

Let's see how these laws can help vendors sharpen their marketing skills and obtain information which was never available before. Consider a major project that uses the Request for Proposals process to select the supplier in a jurisdiction with informal RFP practices.

The RFP process is quite straightforward and relatively simple. The agency in question defines the problem or situation in a "requirements document." This document, once approved, is combined with some administrative rules and conditions into a Request for Proposal (RFP). The RFP is released and a number of vendors then prepare proposals. Following the closing date for the competition, the proposals are evaluated, usually by a committee, using a predefined set of evaluation criteria and weights. Once a winner has been selected, a contract is completed by the parties. Companies not winning the competition are invited to a debriefing session. Finally, the program or project is undertaken by the supplier.

During the course of any major procurement — from inception, through the RFP process, to completion of the contract — a number of critical documents are developed. Project files can be extremely large and often contain much valuable information. Some of this information will be available, under the access to information law, simply by asking. Typically, a project file will include a project initiation document, the Request for Proposal, a description of the evaluation process and the weights, a list of proponents invited to prepare proposals, minutes of the proponents meeting, lists of proposals submitted, evaluators' notes and memos, a detailed evaluation of each proposal, a summary of the evaluations, a memo recommending the award, information related to negotiations and contract provisions, the signed contract, and correspondence with proponents.

Under many access to information laws, most of the information cited above is available for the asking. Other information requires some negotiation, and some information will not be released. The general approach, in many jurisdictions, is to release all information which has been prepared by the agency and which contains no information provided in confidence as part of a supplier's proposal.

Here is an item-by-item description of information which would typically be released under this sort of law:

Something Old:

The Request for Proposal document and the minutes of the proponents meeting can be released to anyone at anytime. This has been public policy for decades.

Something New:

After the contract has been signed with the successful proponent, documentation about the evaluation process and the weights used can be released. If suppliers were invited to submit proposals, the list of suppliers and any documents establishing the basis for inviting suppliers can be released. The list of all companies submitting proposals and the total price of the award can be released at this time.

More New Information:

The purchasing manager can release the evaluator's notes and memos, the evaluation of each proposal, the summary of all evaluations, the memo

recommending the award and the signed contract so long as these documents contain no information declared as being of a proprietary nature.

Some freedom of information laws prohibit disclosure of trade secrets, and almost any other information provided in a proposal. This broad prohibition applies to information that has been submitted in confidence and which, if released, could reasonably be expected to harm a firm's competitive position. Product features, prices, project management techniques, staff capabilities and many other items contained in many proposals cannot be released without permission.

Other freedom of information laws declare all information contained in a proposal as public after the contract has been awarded.

The implications of many different types of access to information laws are similar:

• *Procurements will be more "visibly fair."*

Much information will be available which was not previously available. Suppliers will be able to review the process, the evaluation, and the recommendation to ensure that their proposal was properly treated.

• *RFPs will be improved and the competitive process will be more fair.*

Since the weights and the detailed evaluation process are available after the fact, there will now be pressure to make them available as part of the actual Request for Proposal. (This is done in many jurisdictions already.) Once the weights are stated in the RFP, suppliers will be able to tailor their proposals accordingly.

• *Supplier debriefings will be abandoned.*

Since much more information is available under the act than was previously given at supplier briefings, the briefings will cease to have any value. Firms will simply write a letter to the purchasing manager after the competition and request the evaluator's assessment of their proposal and the winner's scores. In some jurisdictions, such as Florida, this information is automatically released once the contract is awarded.

A Sampling of Purchasing Policies:

Every purchase is made in the public interest. All vendors will receive a fair and equal opportunity...

– State of South Dakota

•

The State Purchasing Division is required by law to competitively bid and award contracts to the lowest responsible bidder... The lowest bidder is the one who: meets specifications, meets terms and conditions of the bid, formal or informal; and provides the lowest price.

– State of New Mexico

•

The cornerstone of the Public Sector Purchasing Policy is the principle of probity, which means that all activities are undertaken in a visibly fair, ethical and prudent manner.

– Province of British Columbia

•

The objectives of government contracting policy are to ensure that government contracting activities are carried out in a fair, fiscally responsible, accountable, open and competitive manner.

– Yukon Government

•

... to ensure the fair and equitable treatment of all persons who deal with the procurement system... (and to) foster effective broad-based competition within the free enterprise system.

– State of Alaska

•

Promote fair and open competition... (and to) provide maximum practical opportunity for participation by minority and women-owned businesses.

– State of Washington

•

To ensure that Arizona taxpayers are receiving the maximum value for every expenditure.

– State of Arizona

•

Competitive bidding is designed to benefit the public body and is not for the benefit of the bidders.

– State of California

■ 2.1.5 Implementing Policy

There are many different ways of implementing RFP policy. In some jurisdictions it's done simply with high-level statements such as "all procurements shall be made in an visibly fair, ethical and prudent manner."

In others, it's done by passing laws and regulations. Still others use guidelines and standardized documents. There seems to be no consistent approach. This is not surprising, because the requirements of each organization are different. There are vast differences in budgets, and in the influence of organizations. Clearly, the recognition of the need for stringent procedures is greater at the state and provincial level than at the local government level.

In reviewing many different organizations, it appears that there is no "best" approach to implementing RFP policy. To make matters worse, there is no simple way to illustrate how different organizations have dealt with this complex issue. Consequently, we've taken the approach of providing detailed examples for a representative group of organizations. These examples illustrate the diversity of approaches in current use, and the lack of standards related to definitions and procedures. The table below identifies the organizations that have been included and the different types of documents they have adopted.

There are many different approaches used to promote effective RFP practices: laws, regulations, administrative manuals, the use of standardized documents, policy statements and handbooks. The table below identifies the organizations that are discussed in this chapter, and the instruments that they use to encourage, to promote, and to enforce good RFP practices.

Section/Organization	Instruments						
	Law	Regulation	Directive	Administrative Manual	Standardized Documents	Policy	Handbook
2.2 State of Alaska	X	X		X	X		
2.3 State of Washington	X	X			X		
2.4 Yukon Territory		X	X				
2.5 BC Systems Corp.					X	X	X

2.2

State of Alaska

Use of RFPs in Alaska is prescribed by four instruments:

1. *Procurement Code*[2]: a state law which establishes the framework for all procurements. It requires, for example, that sole source procurements be used only after clear and compelling evidence is provided in writing.

2. *Purchasing Regulations*[3]: provide additional details to implement the law. For example, the regulations provide examples of circumstances in which sole source procurement might be appropriate and declare that written permission from the chief procurement officer is required.

3. *Administrative Manual*[4]: provides detailed, step-by-step procedures to ensure compliance with the law and regulations. The manual provides, for example, 21 pages of instructions and guidelines related to issuing a professional services contract.

4. *Standardized RFP Shell*[5]: provides a model of an RFP with all of the options. Use of this document is a time-saving approach to help purchasing officials generate consistent documents that comply

with policy, regulations, law and administrative requirements.

Each of these instruments is described in more detail in this section. Some of these documents are provided in their entirety in Part II — Documents From Selected Jurisdictions.

■ 2.2.1 State Procurement Code

This 74-page law has some interesting features. First, it is a law dealing with the details of the procurement process. This, in itself, is unusual. Many jurisdictions, including most provinces in Canada and local government bodies throughout North America, enshrine procurement rules not in law, but in policy documents. Those that don't have formal written published policies or procedures manuals run their procurement function by "established practices." Laws are rigid, and subject to review by the courts. They are typically more accessible to the public and more enforceable than policies or procedures.

Some of the features detailed in this law are noteworthy:

• The chief procurement officer must have procurement experience (this is not a political appointment).

• Specifications cannot be unduly restrictive.

• RFPs must allow vendors 21 days to develop a proposal.

• Proposals are public documents.

• "Best and final" offers are permitted.

• Sole source procurements must be justified in writing.

• There is a formal protest procedure.

While many of the topics and much of the content of each of this law's nine articles are similar to those found in other jurisdictions and certainly not exciting to read, there are some interesting features. A review of these features can help your organization improve its RFP practices.

The remainder of this section provides a brief description of the salient parts of this act and many of its noteworthy features. (Much of this descriptive material is provided in the language of the act itself. Extracts from the act are either enclosed in quotation marks or printed in bold.)

Organization of the Act

This law is more than 70 pages in length. It is organized into 13 sections:

- **Purpose**
- **Organization of State Procurement**
- **Competitive Sealed Bidding**
- **Competitive Sealed Proposals**
- **Other Procurement Methods:**
  - **Sole Source Procurements**
  - **Limited Competition Procurements**
  - **Emergency Procurements**
  - **Small Procurements**
- **Preference for Alaska Products**
- **Preference for Recycled Products**
- **Contract Formation and Modification**
- **Procurement Records and Reports**
- **Legal and Contractual Remedies**
- **Intergovernmental Relations**
- **General Provisions**
- **Procurement Statute Index**

Purpose

The act identifies nine "underlying purposes and policies" focusing on developing consistent practices throughout government, providing fair and equitable treatment for all, fostering broad-based competition, and safeguarding the integrity of the process. Here is the language of the act related to purpose:

1. Simplify, clarify and modernize the law governing procurement...

2. Establish consistent procurement principles for all branches of state government.

3. Provide for increased public confidence...

4. Ensure the fair and equitable treatment of all persons who deal with the procurement system...

5. Provide increased economy in state procurement activities...

6. Foster effective broad-based competition within the free enterprise system.

7. Provide safeguards for the maintenance of a procurement system of quality and integrity.

8. Permit the continued development of state procurement practices...

9. Eliminate and prevent discrimination in state contracting...

Article 1: Organization of State Procurement

This article deals with a wide range of organizational issues. It defines the responsibilities of the chief procurement officer and the right to establish regulations. It defines the use of bidders' lists and specifications to promote competition.

- *Centralized Authority*

This part of the act establishes the centralization of procurement authority and the roles and qualifications of the chief procurement officer. This officer must have purchasing experience.

The act requires that:

The chief procurement officer must have at least five years of prior experience in public procurement, including large-scale procurement of supplies, services or professional services, and must be a person with demonstrated executive and organizational skills. The chief procurement officer may be removed by the commissioner only for cause. The term of office of the chief procurement officer is six years.

- *Establish Regulations*

The act directs the chief procurement officer to establish regulations to manage the procurement function including bid protests, confidentiality of data, use of payment and performance bonds.

- *Bidders Lists*

The act requires that (a) "The Commissioner shall establish and maintain lists of person who desire to provide supplies, services, professional services, or construction services.... "and that (b) "to be on a list, a person must have a valid Alaska business license."

- *Specifications*

The act defines "specifications" and encourages careful definition to foster competition:

... specification means a description of the physical or functional characteristics, or of the nature of a supply, service, professional service or construction project...

... specifications must promote overall economy for the purposes intended and encourage competition in satisfying the state's needs, and may not be unduly restrictive...

Article 3: Competitive Sealed Proposals

This article states that if you can't award a contract by Competitive Sealed Bidding (known as a quotation in many jurisdictions), then you must use a Request for Proposal. This article then imposes some conditions on the RFP, proposals and the procurement officer:

- Subcontractors must be identified.
- Evaluation factors must be stated in the RFP.
- Adequate notice must be given.
- Proposals are public documents.
- "Best and final" offers can be used.
- Expressions of Interest can be used.

Subcontractors:

The request must require the offerer, no later than five working days after the proposal that is the most advantageous to the State is identified, to list subcontractors the offeror proposes to use in the performance of the contract...

Evaluation Factors:

A request for proposal must contain that information necessary for an offerer to submit a proposal or contain references to any information that cannot reasonably be included with the request. The request must provide a description of the factors that will be considered by the procure-

ment officer when evaluating the proposals received, including the relative importance of price and other evaluation factors...

Notice:

The procurement officer shall give adequate public notice... at least 21 days before [proposals are due]. If a determination is made in writing that a shorter notice period is necessary for a particular bid, the 21-day period may be shortened. The determination shall be made by the chief procurement officer...

Notice may include publication in a newspaper..., notices posted in public places within the area where the work is to be performed, notices mailed to all prospective contractors on the appropriate list...

Failure to comply with the notice requirements of this section does not invalidate a bid or the award of a contract. If the state fails to substantially comply with the requirements of this section, the state is liable for damages caused by that failure...

Disclosure of Proposals:

Proposals are public documents as are the names of the offerors:

The procurement officer shall open proposals so as to avoid disclosure of contents to competing offerors during the process of negotiation. A register of proposals... shall be prepared. The register and the proposals are open for public inspection after the notice of intent to award a contract is issued... To the extent that the offerer designates and the procurement officer concurs, trade secrets and other proprietary data contained in the proposal documents are confidential.

Best and Final Offers

Offerors are permitted to revise proposals based on discussions with the procurement officer prior to best and final offers:

As provided in the request for proposals, and under regulations adopted by the commissioner, discussions may be conducted with responsible offerors who submit proposals determined to be reasonably susceptible of being selected for award for the purpose of clarification to assure full understanding of, and responsiveness to, the solicitation requirements. Offerors reasonably susceptible of being selected for award shall be accorded fair and equal treatment with respect to any opportunity for discussion and revision of proposals, and revisions may be permitted after submissions and before the award of the contract for the purpose of obtaining best and final offers. In conducting discussions, the procurement officer may not disclose information derived from proposals submitted by competing offerors...

Award of Contract:

Selection must be based on only those factors identified in the RFP:

The procurement officer shall award a contract under competitive sealed proposals to the responsible and responsive offerer whose proposal is determined in writing to be the most advantageous to the state taking into consideration price and the evaluation factors set out in the request for proposals. Other factors and criteria may not be used in the evaluation. The contract file must contain the basis on which the award is made.

Expression of Interest:

The evaluation of unpriced technical proposals can be used to identify qualified firms. These firms can then be issued an RFP.

When it is considered impractical to initially prepare a definitive purchase description to support an award based on listed selection criteria, the procurement officer may issue an expression of interest requesting the submission of unpriced technical offers, and then later issue a request for proposals limited to the offerors whose offers are determined to be technically qualified under the criteria set out in the expression of interest.

Article 4: Other Procurement Methods

This article specifies four additional procurement methods — sole source, limited competition, emergency and small procurements — and when each may be used.

Sole Source Procurements:

This method may only be used when a responsible official has determined in writing that there is only one source for the required procurement.

A contract may be awarded... without competitive sealed bidding, competitive sealed proposals, or other competition in accordance with regulations adopted by the commissioner. A contract may be awarded... only when the chief procurement officer... determines in writing that there is only one source for the required procurement or construction. A sole source procurement may not be awarded if a reasonable alternative source exists. The written determination must include findings of fact that support by clear and convincing evidence the determination that only one source exists...

Limited Competition Procurements:

Under certain circumstances, the formal processes of competitive sealed bidding or competitive sealed proposals can be replaced with simpler, shorter processes.

A contract... under $100,000 may be awarded without competitive sealed bidding or competitive sealed proposals in accordance with regulations adopted by the commissioner. A contract may be awarded under this section only when the chief procurement officer... determines in writing that a situation exists that makes competitive sealed bidding or competitive sealed proposals impractical or contrary to the public interest. Procurements under this section shall be made with competition that is practicable under the circumstance...

Small Procurements:

For procurements under $25,000 there is more discretionary power granted to the commissioner to establish less formal procedures:

Article 7: Contract Formation and Modification

This article provides for a notice of intent to award a contract. During the notice period, suppliers who believe they have been aggrieved can initiate a formal protest.

At least 10 days before the formal award of a contract (from a competitive sealed proposals process), the procurement officer shall provide to each bidder or offerer notice of intent to award a contract...

Article 8: Procurement Records and Reports

This article defines the record-keeping required

for different types of procurements, the public's right to information, and the content of the commissioner's report to the legislature.

Records of Contracts Awarded Under Competitive Sealed Proposals:

Publicly accessible contract files must be kept by the commissioner and the contracting agency:

A contract file open for public inspection shall be kept by the commissioner and the contracting agency for each contract awarded under competitive sealed proposals. The file kept by the commissioner must contain a summary of the information in the file of the contracting agency. The file kept by the contracting agency must contain:

(1) a copy of the contract;

(2) the register of proposals prepared... and a copy of each proposal submitted; and

(3) the written determination to award the contract...

Records of Sole Source and Emergency Procurements:

All sole source procurements must be recorded in a listing by the commissioner:

The commissioner shall maintain for a minimum of five years a record listing all sole source procurements contracts... The record must contain:

(1) each contractor's name

(2) the amount and type of each contract; and

(3) a listing of the supplies, services, professional services, or construction procured under each contract.

Public Access To Procurement Information:

Many public sector bodies attempt to maintain as confidential as much information as possible. In Alaska, the law is clear — information is public.

Procurement information is public except as otherwise provided by law.

Report To Legislature:

Every two years, the commissioner must report to the legislature. The report must identify and summarize the procurement activity. Information is provided concerning all Sealed Competitive Proposals, procurements, sole source and emergency procurements, as well as a description of any matters that involved litigation.

Article 9: Legal And Contractual Remedies

This article describes the supplier complaint process. This topic is discussed at length in Chapter 8.

■ 2.2.2 Alaska Purchasing Regulations

These regulations provide additional details, rules, clarifications, and procedures related to the Procurement Code. The regulations are organized into 15 articles covering 44 pages.

Article 1: Source Selection

The most interesting paragraph of this article deals with conflict of interest where one supplier has "inside" information. This article anticipates the situation in which the person helping to create the RFP wants to submit a proposal:

Exclusion of Prospective Contractor From Competition:

A procurement officer may exclude a prospective contractor from submitting bid or proposal, or may reject a

prospective contractor's bid or proposal, after making a written determination that the prospective contractor assisted in drafting the invitation to bid or request for proposal, or gained substantial information regarding the invitation to bid or request for proposal that was not available to the public.

Article 2: Specifications

This article attempts to ensure that competition is fair and open by defining the purpose and nature of specifications.

Purpose of Specifications:

(a) The purpose of a specification is to serve as a basis for obtaining, in a cost effective manner, a supply, service, or construction item suitable for the state's needs.

(b) Specifications must, to the extent practicable, emphasize functional or performance criteria while limiting design or other detailed physical descriptions to those necessary to meet the needs of the state. Purchasing agencies should include as a part of their purchase requisitions the principal functional or performance needs to be met...

No Restrictive Specifications:

All specifications must describe the requirements to be met without having the effect of exclusively requiring a proprietary supply, service, or construction item, or procurement from a sole source, unless no other manner of description will suffice.

Article 4: Competitive Sealed Proposals

This article defines the evaluation process, information that must be contained in the RFP, and the rules regulating discussions with individual offerors to obtain best and final proposals.

Evaluation of Proposals:

(a) The procurement officer or an evaluation committee consisting of the procurement officer and at least two state employees or public officials shall evaluate proposals.

(b) The evaluation must be based only on the evaluation factors set out in the request for proposals. Numerical rating systems may be used, but are not required. If numerical rating systems are not used, the procurement officer, or each member of the evaluation committee, as applicable, shall explain his or her ranking determination in writing. Evaluation factors not specified in the request for proposals may not be considered. The weighting value or numerical system to be applied to each evaluation factor must be set out in the request for proposals.

(c) Cost must be an evaluation factor unless [the procurement is for architectural engineering or land surveying services] and if a numerical rating system is used, the request for proposals must state the value to be applied to cost.

(d) For the purposes of evaluating cost factors... the proposal with the lowest cost factor must receive the highest available rating allocated to cost. Each proposal that has a higher cost factor than the lowest must have a lower rating for cost. If a numerical rating system is used to evaluate the cost factor, the points allocated to higher-priced proposals must be equal to the lowest proposal price multiplied by the maximum points available for price, divided by the higher proposal price.

Only One Responsive Proposal Received:

If only one responsive and responsible proposal is received in response to a Request for Proposal, the procurement officer may either make an award..., reject the pro-

posal, or reject the proposal and resolicit proposals.

Proposal Discussions with Individual Offerors:

(a) Offerors of proposals reasonably susceptible for award as determined in the evaluation... may be offered the opportunity to discuss their proposals with the procurement officer or evaluation committee at the discretion of the procurement officer. The evaluation of a proposal may be adjusted as a result of a discussion under this section. The condition, terms, or price of the proposed contract may be altered or otherwise changed during the course of discussions.

(b) The procurement officer may limit discussions to specific sections of the request for proposals. If during discussions there is a need for any substantial clarification of or change in the request for proposals, the request must be amended to incorporate the clarification or change. Auction techniques that reveal one offeror's price to another, and disclosure of any information derived from competing proposals are prohibited. Any oral modification of a proposal shall be reduced to writing by the offerer.

(c) Following discussions, the procurement officer shall set a date and time for the submission of best and final proposals. Best and final proposals may be submitted only once. However, the chief procurement officer or the head of a purchasing agency may make a written determination that it is in the state's best interest to conduct additional discussions or change the state's requirements and require another submission of best and final proposals. Otherwise, discussion of or changes in the best and final proposals may not be allowed before award. If an offerer does not submit a best and final proposal or a notice of withdrawal, the offeror's immediately previous proposal is considered the offeror's best and final proposal.

(d) After best and final proposals are received, final evaluations will be conducted...

Article 7: Sole Source Procurement

This article describes when and how a sole source procurement can be made. The determination must be in writing and must be approved by the chief procurement officer.

Conditions For Use of Sole Source Procurement:

(a) A request by a purchasing agency that a procurement be restricted to one potential contractor must be accompanied by a written explanation as to why no other source is suitable or acceptable to meet the need. An agency may advertise an intent to make a sole source award for the purpose of determining if other sources are available or interested in a particular procurement. Award of a sole source procurement may not be made without prior written approval of the chief procurement officer or the commissioner of transportation and public facilities...

(b) The written determination... that there is only one source for the required procurement must specify the duration of its effectiveness.

(c) A procurement officer shall conduct negotiations, as appropriate, as to price, delivery, and terms of a sole source procurement.

(d) The following are some examples of circumstances in which sole source procurement might be appropriate:

(1) if the compatibility of equipment, accessories, or replacement parts is the main consideration;

(2) if a specific item is needed for trial use or testing, including testing of a prototype;

(3) if an item is to be procured for resale;

(4) public utility services are to be procured;

(5) if there exists a sole source of expertise re-

quired to perform a specific professional service;

(6) if the procurement is for operation of a concession contract on state property by a non-profit organization whose sole purpose is to operate the concession and provide other public services on the property;

(7) if the procurement is with government police agencies to provide investigative, enforcement, or support services in support of state law enforcement objectives;

(8) if the procurement is for the services of legal counsel for the purpose of advising or representing the state in specific civil or criminal proceedings or on specific matters before federal or state regulatory agencies, boards or commissions;

(9) if the procurement is by the Office of the Governor for lobbying, labor negotiation, consulting by a foreign national or employment of a foreign national.

Record of Sole Source Procurement:

A record of every sole source procurement shall be made and forwarded to the chief procurement officer and must include:

(1) the supplier's or contractor's name

(2) the amount and type of each contract

(3) a listing of the supplies, services, or construction procured under each contract; and

(4) the identification number of each procurement file.

Article 8: Limited Competition Procurements

This article ensures that competitions are open to all suppliers unless limitations or restrictions have been specifically justified in writing.

Conditions For Use Of Limited Competition Procurement:

(a) Any request by a purchasing agency that a procurement be restricted to several potential contractors must be accompanied by a written explanation as to why other sources are not suitable or available and why the open competitive sealed bidding or competitive sealed proposal processes are impractical or contrary to the public interest. An agency may advertise an intent to make a limited competition procurement for the purposes of determining if other sources are available or interested in a particular procurement...

Article 14: Miscellaneous Provisions

This article provides the chief procurement officer the authority to amend RFPs. It also identifies acceptable reasons for canceling an RFP, rejecting all proposals or rejecting a specific proposal.

Extension Of Solicitation; Cancellation of Solicitation; Amendment of Solicitation:

(a) Before the opening of bids or proposals, a solicitation may be amended, or the time for opening may be extended, upon the procurement officer's determination that the extension or amendment is in the state's best interest. All potential bidders or offerors known to have copies of the solicitation shall be advised of the extension or amendment.

(b) Before the opening of bids or proposals, a solicitation may be canceled in whole or in part if the chief procurement officer or the head of a purchasing agency issuing a solicitation determines that cancellation is in the state's best interest. Reasons for cancellation include the following:

(1) the state no longer requires the supplies, services, or construction;

(2) the state no longer can reasonably expect to pay for the procurement;

(3) proposed amendments to the solicitation would

be of such magnitude that a new solicitation is desirable; or

(4) the officer, after consultation with the attorney general, determines that a solicitation is in violation of the law.

Rejection Of All Proposals:

After the opening of bids or proposals or after notice of intent to award but before award, all bids or proposals may be rejected in whole or in part by the chief procurement officer or the head of a purchasing agency issuing the solicitation. Reasons for rejection include the following:

(1) the supplies, services, or construction being procured are no longer required;

(2) ambiguous or otherwise inadequate specifications were part of the solicitation;

(3) the solicitation did not provide for consideration of all factors of significance to the state;

(4) prices exceed available money and it would not be appropriate to adjust quantities to accommodate available money;

(5) all otherwise acceptable bids or proposals received are at unacceptable prices;

(6) there is reason to believe that the bids or proposals may not have been independently arrived at in open competition, may have been collusive, or may have been submitted in bad faith; or

(7) the award is not in the best interests of the state.

Rejection of Individual Proposals:

Reasons for rejecting an individual bid or proposal include the following:

(1) the business that submitted the bid or proposal is not responsible...

(2) the bid or proposal is nonresponsive;

(3) the supply, service, or construction item fails to meet the specifications or other acceptability criteria set out in the solicitation; or

(4) the bid or proposal fails to meet the goals or other provisions set out in the solicitation to eliminate and prevent in state contracting discrimination because of race, religion, color, national origin, sex, age, marital status, pregnancy, parenthood or handicap.

■ 2.2.3 Administrative Manual

The state law — called the Procurement Code — and the associated regulations provide that professional services contracts can be obtained using competitive sealed proposals (the RFP process). The State Administrative Manual describes the detailed procedures for procuring professional services. This 21-page section of a much larger manual identifies the requirements imposed by the law and regulations, and the procedure for satisfying them. It also serves as a repository for some best practices, helpful hints and checklists.

This document contains step-by-step instructions which, if followed, will (a) deliver professional services in an effective and efficient manner; and (b) ensure that the contract complies with the law and the Department of Administration's requirements. This procedure leads the reader through six steps:

1. Request and receive authority to seek professional services.

2. Solicit proposals.

3. Evaluate proposal and select contractor.

4. Prepare a contract and negotiate.

5. Evaluate contractor's performance.

6. Provide procurement report.

The Administrative Manual deals with six major topics:

1. Assessing the need for a contract

2. Obtaining authority to seek professional services

3. Soliciting proposals

4. Selecting a contractor

5. Preparing a contract

6. Contract accounting and control.

This procedure provides all the required essential information such as the specific form and timing of a public notice of the Request for Proposal.

This procedure also contains helpful information to assist the purchasing officer in creating the RFP. For example:

82.160(2) - Experience Factor

It may be of value to consider specific experience when evaluating proposals. If this criteria is used, you should task related experience, not agency-related experience. A description of the experience considered valuable should be limited to those specific characteristics necessary to accomplish the goals of the RFP.

A good example of necessary experience might be: Experience in designing and implementing ADABAS applications with COBOL II in an MVS environment...

A bad example of necessary experience might be: Previous experience working with department Y, division X.

This procedure contains additional reference material to help promote best practices and compliance with the law and regulations. It contains two checklists. The first deals with considerations when preparing an RFP and contains 48 items. Some of the items on this list reflect specific requirements

imposed by law or regulation. Other items are more generic and reflect good practices. Here are two typical items:

11. You may wish to advise offerors of your budget or estimated cost for the proposed contract.

36. Include a copy of the committee evaluation sheet which will be used by the Proposals Evaluation Committee. Indicate the weighting for each item including cost. The proposals must be evaluated using the same criteria set forth in the RFP. No other weighted criteria may be used.

The second checklist is for Professional Services Contracting. It contains 42 items and is designed to help the purchasing officer prepare an accurate, complete contract. Here are two representative items from this list:

2. Has your agency waited ten days, after sending out the Notice of Intent to Award before approving the contract?

29. Does the contract require or contain a clause stating the successful proposal is an integral part of the contract?

■ 2.2.4 Request for Proposal Shell

The state has developed a standardized document, some 50 pages in length, consisting of an RFP and the instructions to the procurement officer for modifying it as appropriate. The document is available both in hard copy and in computer-readable form.

This document, based on many years of experience, includes much valuable information to promote "best practices" and to ensure that the RFP and the related process comply with the law and regulations. For example, the document contains detailed sample calculations related to costing, and sample evaluation sheets for scoring proposals.

The document is an easy way to ensure that RFPs are kept up to date. Each time a change is made in the law, regulations, or administrative procedures, the document is revised. The document clearly reduces the time to prepare an RFP by providing the procurement officer with a standardized document. The officer needs only to ensure that the shell is appropriately modified to reflect the specific situation.

Below is a sample from the document. Section 1.14 deals with subcontractors. The procurement officer is required to specify whether subcontractors will be allowed. The procurement officer is not permitted to delete this section from the RFP. If no subcontractors are allowed, the officer selects the appropriate clause. If subcontractors are allowed, the procurement officer can include the sample clause either as is or appropriately modified.

1.14 Subcontractors

Procurement Officer Note: Revise as required.

Subcontractors will not be allowed.

– OR –

Subcontractors may be used to perform work under this contract. If a proposer intends to use subcontractors the proposer must identify, in their proposal, the names of the subcontractors and the portions of the work the subcontractors will perform.

If a proposal with subcontractors is selected, the proposer must provide the following information concerning each prospective subcontractor within five working days from the date of the state's request:

(a) complete name of the subcontractor,

(b) complete address of the subcontractor,

(c) type of work the subcontractor will be performing,

(d) percentage of work the subcontractor will be providing,

(e) evidence, as set out in the relevant section of this RFP, that the subcontractor holds a valid Alaska business license,

(f) a written statement, signed by each proposed subcontractor, that clearly verifies that the subcontractor is committed to render the services required by the contract.

A proposer's failure to provide this information within the time set may cause the state to consider their proposal non-responsive and reject the proposal.

The substitution of one subcontractor for another may be made only at the discretion of the project director and with prior written approval from the project director.

This RFP shell contains several noteworthy practices. These are discussed in Chapter 4, The RFP Document.

2.3

State of Washington

The use of RFPs in the state of Washington is prescribed by four instruments:

1. Legislation, specifically RCW Chapter 43.105[6] : provides for the coordinated planning of state information services.

2. State policy and procedure: Acquisition and Disposal of Information Technology Resources[7] defines the rules and regulations for RFPs.

3. Model Request for Proposal[8]: a document developed in conjunction with the policy and procedure to facilitate the development of better RFPs.

4. Contractual "Standard Clauses"[9] : a document developed in conjunction with the policy and procedure to assist purchasers in developing appropriate contracts.

■ 2.3.1 RCW Chapter 43.105

The state has created an Information Services Board (ISB) which is empowered to acquire and dispose of all information technology equipment, proprietary software, and purchased services for all agencies of state government. Specifically, RCW Chapter

43.105 gives the Board the authority:

To purchase, lease, rent, or otherwise acquire, dispose of, and maintain equipment, proprietary software, and purchased services; or to delegate to other agencies and institutions of state government, under appropriate standards, the authority to purchase, lease, rent, or otherwise acquire, dispose of, and maintain equipment, proprietary software, and purchased services. Agencies and institutions of state government are expressly prohibited from acquiring or disposing of equipment, proprietary software, and purchased services without such delegation of authority.

RCW Chapter 43.105 defines information technology equipment to include data processing, telecommunications and office automation. It specifically identifies machines, devices, and transmission facilities used in information processing such as computers, word processors, terminals, telephones and cables.

RCW Chapter 43.105 also gives the ISB the duty to provide a vendor protest process, as follows: "To develop and implement a process for the resolution of appeals by vendors concerning the conduct of an acquisition process by an agency or the Department of Information Services."

■ 2.3.2 State Policy and Procedures

This 18-page policy has several interesting features:

1. It deals exclusively with information technology.

2. It ensures that acquisitions are consistent with existing plans and approved strategic directions and provides policy direction in key areas.

3. It requires the production of an acquisition plan prior to developing the RFP.

4. It defines the content and rules for the RFP process.

5. It permits other procurement methods including strategic partnering.

6. As required by law, it defines the protest procedure.

In the remainder of this section, each of these features is discussed.

1. It deals exclusively with information technology:

This policy defines the roles and responsibilities of this central agency. It establishes the purpose "To provide a framework for the acquisition and disposal of information technology resources which most effectively meet the needs of agencies and the state."

It defines objectives that include the following:

Provide a process to be used in the acquisition and disposal of information technology resources that will ensure the best value for the state.

Ensure that the acquisition and disposal of information technology resources support agency strategic information technology plans and the state information technology standards.

Promote fair and open competition.

Provide an acquisition and disposal process that meets agency business needs.

Provide maximum practical opportunity for participation by minority and women-owned businesses.

It defines the roles and responsibilities of the Information Services Board, the Department of Information Services, and the agencies.

2. It ensures that acquisitions are consistent with existing plans and approved strategic directions and provides policy direction in key areas.

This policy applies to all information technology acquisitions and disposals within the executive and judicial branches, regardless of the source of funds, the intended use or purpose, or the source of supply. The policy is in accordance with the intent of RCW Chapter 43.105.

The following policy statements apply:

A. Information technology acquisitions shall be consistent with the agency's Information Technology Plan and the Information Services Board (ISB) Strategic Directions for Information Technology, and Information Technology policies and standards.

B. The ISB is responsible for all delegated authority. It may grant, reduce, or rescind delegations of authority.

The ISB may grant special delegated authority for disposal, academic computing, and/or strategic partnerships.

D. Acquisitions shall use a standard acquisition process.

Standard acquisition processes include Request for Proposal, Request for Quotation, Master Agreements, Sole Source, Interagency Transfer, Strategic Partnerships and Corporate Agreements.

F. Contractual terms and conditions shall be included in solicitation documents.

The provisions labeled "Standard Clauses" are mandatory in content. Agency contracts must include the titles of these clauses and language that accomplishes the same intent.

1. Vendors shall be provided a procedure to follow in order to protest acquisitions.

Protests shall be accepted only after the announcement of the apparently successful vendor.

It requires the production of an acquisition plan prior to developing the RFP for acquisitions exceeding certain specified amounts.

...For acquisitions above the agency delegated authority, request DIS or ISB approval by submitting a completed Acquisition Approval Request form (Appendix A), and an Acquisition Plan to DIS. The Acquisition Plan describes and documents the following:

A. Problem to be solved or opportunity to be gained.

B. Information technology resource to be acquired.

C. Alternatives considered: evaluation of existing state and agency resources as well as other alternatives which were considered.

D. Agency business justification: state how this acquisition shall help the agency meet its business needs, the estimated Acquisition Costs and Cost Benefit Analysis (CBA) Costs, and the tangible and intangible benefits.

E. CBA and risk analysis.

F. Project management plan.

G. Vendor participation: list the vendors including MWBE's who are to receive the solicitation document.

H. Relationship to the agency MWBE plan.

I. Relationship to the ISB information technology standards and strategic directions.

J. Acquisition method to be used including the rationale for the selection of this method.

K. Acquisition and implementation schedule.

L. Post implementation review (PIR), criteria and plan; include the date the PIR is to be completed.

It defines the content and rules for the RFP process.

The RFP is used to acquire Information Technology Resources that may not have a fully described technical specification and/or for which there are competing functional solutions in the marketplace. The RFP is used to allow vendors the opportunity to propose solutions to a set of functional requirements and/or technical specifications. The RFP process gives the agency the opportunity to select the proposal which best meets agency needs over the expected life of the resource. Agencies should hold a pre-proposal conference when the RFP method is used.

The RFP is used to solicit a proposal and prices from the vendor for the vendor's best solution or solutions to the agency's information technology requirements.

The RFP process allows consideration of such items as functional capability, including:

a. Expansion and upgrade capability.

b. Vendor support.

c. Integration of the resource into the agency architecture.

It also allows consideration of full cost; including but not limited to, costs to purchase, finance, install, operate, use, and maintain; plus trade-in, redeployment, or residual value.

3. Agencies conducting RFP's shall:

a. Provide vendors with the vendor protest procedure as outlined in the section titled Protest Procedure.

b. Use the "Standard Clauses" as contained in Appendix B, and other terms and conditions appropriate for the specific type of contract to be negotiated.

c. Include in the RFP the specific criteria that shall be used to evaluate vendor responses.

d. Advertise the acquisition in the Seattle Daily Journal of Commerce or other major regional publication upon or before release of the RFP. In addition, advertising in the Wall Street Journal or other national publications may be appropriate, depending on the nature of the acquisition. Issue the RFP to a minimum of three vendors where available. RFP's shall be issued to all vendors who have expressed an interest in providing the Information Technology Resources to be acquired.

e. Give vendors adequate time to prepare responses and submit their proposal.

f. Notify vendors that they may bring their complaints about the solicitation document to the attention of DIS. (See Protest Procedure).

g. Give full and fair consideration to all vendors responding to the RFP.

h. Select the apparently successful vendor based on the RFP evaluation criteria.

i. Offer vendor debriefing conferences to requesting vendors.

j. Sign vendor contracts only after the time to file vendor protests has elapsed.

It permits other procurement methods including strategic partnering. Strategic partnering is the joining together of two independent organizations for the purposes of finding technological solutions to a business problem, or a response to an opportunity for the state to realize cost savings, increased productivity or other tangible benefits. Partnerships are intended to facilitate the development of innovative technologies or applications.

As required by law, it defines the protest procedure.

■ 2.3.3 Model RFP

The state has developed a standardized document, some 50 pages in length, consisting of an RFP and limited instructions to the procurement officer for modifying it as appropriate. The document is available both in hard copy and in a computer-readable form.

As with the state of Alaska, this document, based on many years of experience, includes much valuable information to promote "best practices" and to ensure that the RFP and the related process comply with the law and regulations. For example, the document contains a six-page description of the evaluation process to be used in all RFPs.

The document is an easy way to ensure that RFPs are kept up to date. Each time a change is made in law, regulations, or administrative procedures, the document is revised. The document clearly reduces the time to prepare an RFP by providing the procurement officer with a standard starting point. The officer needs only to ensure that the model is appropriately modified to reflect the specific situation.

This model RFP contains several noteworthy practices. These are discussed in chapter 4, The RFP Document.

■ 2.3.4 Contractual "Standard Clauses"

Information technology contracts are complex. Their clauses mirror the technology. Standard terms and conditions relate to items such as proprietary rights, compatibility issues, compliance with standards, equipment configurations, interfacing equipment and escrow of source code.

The Department of Information Services has developed some documents to help purchasers develop appropriate contracts for information technology procurements.

Vendors always prefer using standard contracts that have been designed to protect the vendor's interests. Historically, some large, powerful vendor or-ganizations have refused to modify their contracts in all but exceptional cases. These days, competition has made most vendors less rigid.

This 61-page document was developed to assist purchasers in identifying their contract requirements, and in proposing specific contract terms. This document is described in detail in Chapter 7, Section 7.3.2.

2.4

Yukon Government

Use of RFPs in the Yukon Territory is prescribed by two instruments:

1. Contracting Regulations[10]: Issued pursuant to Section 24(3) of the Financial Administration Act, these regulations establish a framework for procurement.

2. Contracting Directive[11] : Issued pursuant to Section 24(3) of the Financial Administration Act, this directive applies to all departments defined in the Public-Sector Act and provide the specific rules and procedures to be followed.

■ 2.4.1 Contracting Regulations

These regulations have some interesting features. First, they are regulations enacted under a law (Section 24[3] of the Financial Administration Act, Yukon Government). This, in itself, is unusual. Many jurisdictions, including many provincial and most local government bodies, enshrine procurement rules not in law, but in policy documents. Some public bodies don't even have formal published policies or procedures manuals. Instead, they run their procure-

ment function by "established practices."

Laws are rigid, and subject to review by the courts. Regulations are typically more accessible to the public and much more enforceable than policies or procedures not supported by the force of law. Informal policies get interpreted in the light of changing circumstances.

The regulations establish a framework for procurement within Yukon. They are only six pages in length and establish the overall approach to procurement. (The directives provide the details.)

While many of the topics and much of the content of each of this Regulation's 17 articles are similar to those found in other jurisdictions and certainly not exciting to read, there are some interesting features. A review of these features can help your organization improve its RFP practices.

There are five key areas dealt with in this document. (Information taken directly from the contract regulations is contained in boxes.)

1. The objectives are identified for more reasons than to simply ensure that procurement is done in a

fair and open manner. The introduction of "fiscally responsible" and "accountable" sets a tone not usually found in procurement law.

2. The objectives of government contracting policy are to ensure that government contracting activities are carried out in a fair, fiscally responsible, accountable, open and competitive manner.

2. The regulations provide access to material in a non-discriminatory way.

6. Reasonable access will be provided to government policy documents and related contracting materials upon request. Materials available for distribution will be supplied in a non-discriminatory manner, and any fees charged for such distribution will be reasonable.

3. The key principles of competing for government contracts are identified: competition will be open to all; and the rules will be stated in terms of criteria and spending thresholds.

7. Prospective bidders and proponents will be registered on open source lists on request.

8. Prospective bidders and proponents will be given copies of requests for bids or proposals upon request.

10. Contracting authorities will not use standards, specifications, evaluation criteria or time limits to respond to requests for bids or proposals ... or other means to unfairly limit competition.

4. The evaluation process will be visibly fair. Key information will be provided in the RFP and proponents will be provided information about losing proposals.

11. Evaluation criteria and standards used to evaluate bids and proposals will be fully and clearly described in requests for bids or proposals, and only those evaluation criteria and standards will be used to evaluate bids or proposals received.

12. Subject to territorial access to information legislation, bidders and proponents will, upon request, be given access to information about their own bids or proposals and how these were evaluated ...

5. The final principle established in these regulations is the right of a proponent to challenge an award, to receive some compensation for moneys spent, and to change the procurement process:

13. There will be a formal bid challenge mechanism, based on the following:

(a) Bidders and proponents will be given a reasonable opportunity to register complaints.

(b) Complainants will have a responsibility to make all reasonable attempts to settle their disputes with the applicable contracting authority.

(c) There will be an opportunity for redress, including compensation for costs of complaining and bid/proposal preparation costs.

(d) A mechanism to change, where warranted, government contracting policies and procedures will be provided.

■ 2.4.2 Yukon Government Contracting Directive

This directive provides the specific rules and procedures embodying the policies and principles established in the Contract Regulations. The Contracting Directive is organized into 70 clauses covering 17 pages.

Some of the features detailed in the directive are noteworthy:

• A list of contemplated contracts over $50,000 is made public.

• Dollar limits determine the RFP procedure.

• A pre-qualification process is governed by RFP rules.

• The information in the RFP is defined explicitly.

• Reasons for rejecting a proposal are defined explicitly.

• Evaluations can only be done on the criteria in the RFP.

• Extended contracts must be identified to the public.

• The bid challenge process uses a committee that includes representatives from the public.

The remainder of this section provides a more detailed description of each of these features.

• A list of contemplated contracts over $50,000 is made public. The list is to be created on a quarterly basis. Publication of this list permits suppliers to identify upcoming opportunities before the RFP is announced.

12. (1) Contracting authorities will, before the end of each fiscal year quarter, provide to the Deputy Head, Government Services, or delegate a listing of contracts and standing offer agreements in excess of $50,000... contemplated to be awarded in the following quarter.

(3) The Deputy Head, Government Services, or delegate will make available to the public the information provided by contracting authorities in subsection (1)...

• Dollar limits determine the RFP procedure.

These limits are consistent with those in other comparable jurisdictions.

16. (2) (a) Below $25,000 estimated contract value, contracting authorities may enter into a contract or standing offer agreement directly with a proponent.

(b) Between $25,000 and $50,000, contracting authorities will either invite proposals from three sources... or issue publicly advertised requests for proposals.

(c) Above $50,000, contracting authorities will issue publicly advertised request for proposals, or invite proposals from all sources on an open source list.

• A pre-qualification process is governed by RFP rules. It is used to establish a qualified source list that is only valid for up to one year. No names can be added to the qualified source list except through the formal process. This is an excellent approach. In many jurisdictions, the pre-qualification process is less formal and, therefore, more subjective and more difficult to defend as being "fair and open."

29. (1) Where a contracting authority pre-qualifies bidders or proponents before issuing a request for bids or proposals for a contract, it will establish a qualified source list pursuant to this directive, which will be valid for up to one year.

(2) The contracting authority will define the scope of each qualified source list in terms of the specific contracts which are contemplated.

30. (1) A contracting authority will publicly advertise for bidders or proponents to submit their qualifications for qualified source lists.

(2) Such requests for submission of qualifications will be considered to be Requests for Proposals as defined by this

directive and will be conducted pursuant to this directive.

31. Responses to requests for proposals issued pursuant to section 30 will be considered proposals as defined by this directive and will be evaluated accordingly.

32. A contracting authority will not add the name of a bidder or proponent to qualified source lists except through the evaluation and acceptance of the proponent's qualifications submitted in response to the request for bids or proposals.

• The information to be contained in the RFP is defined explicitly. This type of information is found in many other organization's directives and policies. However, some organizations do not insist that the RFP contain the contract terms, nor a full description of the evaluation process.

40. A request for bids or proposals will include the following information:

(a) the essential terms of the contract(s)... to be awarded including:

(i) a full description of the goods or services...

(ii) the form, amount, and terms and conditions of any required performance security

(iii) the completion date or any other timing considerations...

(iv) other terms and conditions which would be relevant...

(b) terms and conditions for the submission of bids or proposals...

(c) a full description of the manner in which bids or proposals will be evaluated including:

(i) the method to be used to evaluate bids or proposals

(ii) the evaluation criteria, stated in such a manner as

to clearly identify all the information to be provided by the bidder or proponent which will be used to evaluate the bid or proposal...

• Reasons for rejecting a proposal are defined explicitly. In stating the formal reasons, the organization removes the appearance of arbitrary actions.

47. The contracting authority may reject a bid or proposal which has been received prior to the closing time only where:

(a) it is not submitted in the required form;

(b) there are significant omissions of required information;

(c) a bid or proposal is not signed as required in the request for bids or proposals;

(d) the required bid security in the required form is not provided;

(e) the bid or proposal has conditions attached which are not authorized by the request for bids or proposals;

(f) the bid or proposal fails to meet one or more standards specified in the request for bids or proposals; or

(g) there is substantial evidence that, pursuant to the evaluation criteria contained in the request for bids or proposals, a bidder or proponent would be unable to carry out the contract as specified.

• Evaluations can only be done on the criteria in the RFP.

50. The contracting authority will evaluate bids or proposals... solely on the basis of the evaluation criteria and requirements contained in the request...

• Extended contracts must be identified to the

public. Sole source contracts that are extended beyond the limit for sole sourcing must be identified; contracts resulting from restricted competition that exceed the corresponding limit must also be identified. In many jurisdictions, this information is not readily available. In some, it is only released to the public when an application is made under the access to information laws.

60. (1) In the case of a sole sourced contract (for under $25,000 when an RFP would normally be used) where a contracting authority increases the value of the contract past the limit for sole sourcing permitted by these paragraphs, the contracting authority will immediately identify the contract to the Deputy Head of Government Services or delegate.

(2) In the case of an invitationally sourced contract (for between $25,000 and $50,000 involving an RFP) where a contracting authority increases the value of the contract past the limit for invitational tendering permitted by these paragraphs, the contracting authority will immediately

identify the contract to the Deputy Head of Government Services or delegate.

(3) The Deputy Head, Government Services, or delegate, will identify all contacts under this section to the public at regular intervals.

• The bid challenge process uses a committee that includes representatives from the public. It is unusual to have members of the public participate in the challenge process.

61. (2) The (bid challenge) committee will be made up of a chair, an alternate who will act in the absence of the chair, five representatives from the Government of Yukon, and five representatives from the public.

64. (3) A complaint registered with the committee which is found by the chair to warrant a hearing will be heard by a panel of three members consisting of the chair and one member appointed by the chair from the representatives of the government and one member appointed by the chair from the representatives of the public.

2.5

British Columbia Systems Corp.

British Columbia Systems Corp.'s mission is to provide information technology solutions which assist public sector organizations in the province of British Columbia to maintain and fundamentally improve the quality of service to the public. BC Systems Corp. is owned by the provincial government and has over 400 employees. Its 1994 revenue was about $200 million.

Use of RFPs is prescribed by three instruments:

1. Policy[12]: a short document establishing key elements of the procurement process.

2. Handbook[13]: a small manual containing a description of the RFP process, sample forms and guidelines to assist the procurement officer.

3. RFP Shell[14]: a 17-page document standardizing the terms and conditions and providing a description of the contents of the Requirements Section.

■ 2.5.1 Policy

This five-page policy sets the tone and direction for procurement activities. It identifies key practices but does not contain step-by-step instructions.

The policy has several interesting features:

• It is available to all staff at their computer terminals through their local area network.

• Competitive bidding must be used whenever it is practical.

• While the organization does maintain lists of vendors, these lists are not relied upon to identify all suitable vendors.

• The role of the Contracts Department is "to ensure fair, ethical business practices" in an "environment of equity."

• The Request for Information is defined as a "fact gathering activity... without making a purchase commitment."

• Regardless of contract value, they use an RFP if there is any possibility of a conflict.

• For procurements in which the estimated value exceeds $100,000, they release the RFP in draft form (to identify potential problems and supplier complaints).

Their policy document also identifies some of the standard terms and conditions and those circumstances in which an RFP can be replaced by a directed contract (sending it to one vendor without a competitive process). The entire document is provided in Part II — Documents from Selected Jurisdictions.

■ 2.5.2 Handbook

The Guide To Tendering is a 25-page handbook identifying details of current recommended procurement practices. It includes a copy of the policy and the Standardized RFP Shell. The purpose of the handbook is:

• To guide an employee through the steps involved in the corporation's competitive bidding process;

• To define the responsibilities of all parties involved in the process; and

• To provide useful information that directly impacts anyone involved in such a process.

The guide provides the procurement officer with much necessary information:

• When to use an RFP

• Steps in the process

• Laws related to the process

• Services available from other departments such as Finance

• Checklists

• Examples of simple and complex evaluations

• A copy of the procurement policy

• Sample RFP

■ 2.5.3 Sample RFP

This 17-page document is available online and in hard-copy form. It is organized into two sections: Part A contains the administrative details and the standard terms and conditions. This part is maintained by the Contracts Department. Part B contains the statement of requirements and is prepared by the user group.

This standardized document is discussed in Chapter 4 — The RFP Document and contained both in Part II and on the diskette provided with this publication.

---

[1] Webster's Seventh New College Dictionary, 1972
[2] Reference *4. See also Part II - Documents From Selected Jurisdictions.
[3] Reference *8. See also Part II - Documents From Selected Jurisdictions.
[4] Section 82, Reference *9.
[5] Reference *10. See also Part II - Documents From Selected Jurisdictions.
[6] Chapter 43.105 RCW, Reference *11.
[7] Reference *2. This entire document is contained in Part II of this book and on the floppy diskette provided.
[8] Reference *12. This document originally was contained in Appendix C of Reference *2. The entire document is contained in Part II of this book.
[9] Reference *13. This document originally was contained in Appendix B of Reference *2. The entire document is contained in Part II of this book and on the floppy diskette provided with this publication.
[10] Reference *7.
[11] Reference *7.
[12] See Reference *5. This document is also in Part II.
[13] Reference *18.
[14] Reference *25. See also Chapter 4. The document is contained in Part II.

CHAPTER 3

The RFP Process

— CONTENTS —

CHAPTER 3

The RFP Process

– CONTENTS CONTD. –

3.1

Introduction

Acquiring a solution to a problem by using a Request for Proposal is a process. Not surprisingly, this process is similar in many different organizations. The basic approach of state and local government bodies is not radically different than that found in private sector firms: requirements are identified; offers are solicited; and proposals are evaluated.

But some differences do exist. They are usually related to the characteristics of the goods and services being acquired, and the culture and policies of the organization. The provision of food services to an educational institution requires different terms and conditions than supplying a production planning system to a manufacturing facility. Also, the requirements related to the amount of "fair and open competition" can be very different in the public and private sectors.

Using an RFP process to procure goods and services is always part of a larger organizational initiative. To design a new facility, you may need to engage an architect to provide a design. To run an institution, you may need to engage a maintenance firm. To improve an organization's cash flow, you may need to acquire a new financial software package, or engage a systems integration company to perform the work.

The RFP and the RFP process are only a small part of each of these projects, but a critical part nonetheless.

In recent times, RFPs have been used extensively to acquire computer systems and services since these are often large procurements with complex requirements. Many organizations acknowledge this emphasis in their administrative processes and documentation.

In Washington state, the RFP process is used by many state agencies for information technology procurements and the Department of Information Services issues guidelines for administering this process.

In the state of Alaska, the Administration Manual[1] contains a section related to contracting for software development (acquired through an RFP process).

In the state of California, the Procurement Division has developed Rules Governing Competition, a document describing their iterative RFP process.

The primary objective of the RFP process is to acquire a solution to a problem or need. If this were the only objective, the task would be simple and straightforward: you could call a supplier, discuss your requirements, and ask for a proposal. Alternatively, you could define your requirements and send them to one or more potential suppliers. Both of these approaches would produce solutions which could solve the problem in a reasonable manner.

In most organizations, especially public sector bodies, there are many more objectives than simply finding a solution — even one within budget. Some of these objectives result from simple business considerations. Others originate in public policy, law, or administrative requirements imposed by the organization on itself.

Here are some of the objectives which any procurement might be required to satisfy[2]:

• Ensure the fair and equitable treatment of all persons who deal with the procurement system.

• Foster effective broad-based competition within the free enterprise system.

• Provide safeguards for the maintenance of a procurement system of quality and integrity.

• Eliminate and prevent discrimination in state contracting.

• Identify the best solution to our stated requirements in terms of features, costs and risks.

There are many elements that contribute to a successful RFP process and to a successful project. The most important is to regard the RFP process as a project. It is not a part-time undertaking that can be scheduled "as time permits." It's a project requiring resources, staff and an appropriate amount of time. A successful RFP project requires:

• Formal definition of tasks

• Understanding of the requirements

• Sufficient time and budget

• An experienced procurement officer who understands the roles of different stakeholders

• Active support and involvement of the stakeholders

• Knowledge of best practices, including use of standardized documents and checklists

• Knowledge of major risks and problems.

In many organizations, much work must be done prior to the actual acquisition process. This work usually involves a clear articulation of the problem, the project and the risks. Here is an example of the type of planning that often precedes the acquisition process[3].

...For acquisitions above the agency delegated authority, request DIS or ISB approval by submitting a completed Acquisition Approval Request form (Appendix A), and an Acquisition Plan to DIS. The Acquisition Plan describes and documents the following:

A. Problem to be solved or opportunity to be gained.

B. Information technology resource to be acquired.

C. Alternatives considered: evaluation of existing state and agency resources as well as other alternatives which were considered.

D. Agency Business Justification: state how this acquisition shall help the agency meet its business needs, the estimated Acquisition Costs and Cost Benefit Analysis (CBA) Costs, and the tangible and intangible benefits.

E. CBA and risk analysis.

F. Project management plan.

G. Vendor participation: list the vendors including MWBE's who are to receive the solicitation document.

H. Relationship to the agency MWBE plan.

I. Relationship to the ISB information technology standards and Strategic Directions.

J. Acquisition method to be used including the rationale for the selection of this method.

K. Acquisition and implementation schedule.

L. Post Implementation Review (PIR) Criteria and Plan: include the date the PIR is to be completed.

This chapter deals with some of the elements of success for an RFP process through discussion of critical issues and by presenting examples from many jurisdictions.

3.2

Examples

In this section, we first provide a high-level view of the process and then present examples of the process as seen by three different organizations. You will note that the steps are similar. Only the emphasis and level of detail is different.

First, a high-level view of the process from an Arizona perspective[4]:

...a Request for Proposals (RFP)...is used for purchases exceeding $10,000. The competitive sealed proposal method may be used if the State Procurement Administrator determines that the use of competitive sealed bidding is either not practicable or not advantageous to the state. Proposals are opened publicly at the time and place designated in the RFP. Normally, only the name of each offeror is read publicly. All other information contained in the proposals is confidential so as to avoid disclosure of contents prejudicial to competing offerors. The proposals are open for public inspection after contract award.

As provided in the Request for Proposals, discussions may be conducted with responsible offerors who submit proposals determined by the state to be reasonably susceptible to being selected for award. Discussions are conducted for the purpose of clarification to ensure full understanding and responsiveness to the solicitation requirements. Offerors are accorded fair treatment with respect to any opportunity for discussion and revision of proposals and such revisions may be permitted after submissions and before award for the purpose of obtaining best and final offers. In conducting discussions, there shall be no disclosure of any information derived from proposals submitted by competing offerors.

The award shall be made to the responsible offeror whose proposal is determined in writing to be the most advantageous to the state taking into consideration the evaluation factors set forth in the RFP.

■ 3.2.1 Example 1: Ontario

Here is the process that the Management Board Secretariat in Ontario recommends to the ministries for procuring information technology goods and services[5]:

1. Define the problem or the needs that you

have. This definition becomes the requirements statement that will be the basis of the RFP and the suppliers' proposals.

2. Write down the requirements and how you will decide which combination of solution, product and supplier will best meet these needs. The resulting document is called the Request for Proposal, or RFP. The method for deciding which combination of solution, product, and supplier best meets these requirements is called your evaluation methodology.

3. Decide which suppliers you will ask to propose solutions and invite them to participate in this competition.

4. Issue the RFP to suppliers.

5. If appropriate, have a meeting with the suppliers to explain your RFP. This meeting is called a supplier briefing.

6. Accept all proposals from suppliers submitted before the deadline.

7. Compare each supplier's proposal with the requirements contained in the RFP, and use the evaluation methodology to select the best proposal. This step is the evaluation and selection of proposals.

8. Evaluate the various financing options for this procurement.

9. Negotiate contract terms and conditions with one or more of the top suppliers.

10. Inform unsuccessful suppliers why you didn't choose their proposal. This step is called the debriefing of suppliers.

11. Complete the contract.

12. Implement the solution.

■ 3.2.2 Example 2: Information Technology

Here's another description of the RFP process.

It was originally printed in a book dealing with RFPs for information technology products and services[6].

Steps to a Successful Project

The selection and implementation of a system can be thought of as a process consisting of six steps:

1. Initiate the project

2. Establish your requirements

3. Issue the Request for Proposal

4. Select the vendor

5. Negotiate an agreement

6. Implement the system

Before beginning any of the steps, the project manager should prepare a detailed plan consisting of a list of tasks, a timetable, a budget and a list of available staff. This plan should then be reviewed by the Steering Committee.

1. Initiate the Project

The purpose of this step is to establish whether a computer-based system is warranted. During this step, the project manager attempts to ensure that this project, if successful, will help the organization achieve a defined goal. In particular, the project manager should investigate three questions:

• What are our problems or requirements? Can a computer system help solve these problems?

• How are computers being used in other organizations, especially those of similar size?

• What companies offer software that addresses our needs?

2. Establish Your Requirements

The purpose of this step is for the organization to identify current procedures and practices which may be replaced by new systems; e.g., Payroll, Billing or Office Automation. More specifically:

• Document the current systems, their strengths and shortcomings, the flow of information and the processing volumes.

• Identify which systems are to be computerized.

This step often entails much work with little apparent progress. However, the information obtained during this step will simplify selecting the best system, ensure a good match with the organization's requirements, and provide good information for developing a report for management.

If you do solid work during this step, it will reduce two common problems affecting the selection and acceptance of a new system. First, incomplete definitions of user requirements make the selection process difficult and often cause drawn-out discussions with suppliers to define the specific requirements. Furthermore, a clear definition of your requirements, developed by a cross section of staff, will ensure that staff's expectations about the new system are realistic, and that staff has had a say in the determination.

In reviewing the current systems, examine the following performance characteristics: timeliness, accuracy, usefulness of information, efficiency, necessity, completeness, and reliability of information.

The volume of transactions identified during this step will be used by the suppliers to determine the amount of equipment required. (Some vendors have standard worksheets used to determine the information they require concerning volumes.) Don't depend on guesswork. Count the transactions for a month and adjust the counts to reflect your peak season or anticipated changes in your business. Be sure to in-

clude how much detailed information you want to keep on file and for how long. Also consider future growth and demands for information not met by the current system.

A typical statement of requirements for an application system, such as General Ledger or Production Scheduling, may be five to 10 pages long and would consist of the following information:

• A narrative of the current system

• Copies of forms and reports currently used

• Statement of volumes

• A description of the problems to be solved by the new system or identified enhancements

• A statement of expected benefits and priorities.

Often, these descriptions include information which the auditors have previously prepared, such as information flow diagrams.

3. Issue the Request for Proposal

During this step, the Request for Proposal is prepared, reviewed and approved by the Steering Committee and issued to qualified vendors.

The preparation of an RFP can be a major activity, especially the first time. It can take many months. The draft version is often shown to the organization's lawyers and auditors to ensure that their concerns are addressed by the document.

4. Select the Vendor

There are many different methods of evaluating proposals. Some methods assign points to each feature and award the contract on the basis of the most points per dollar.

Some organizations simply form an assessment group. Vendors failing to meet mandatory requirements are often eliminated during the initial review. Each evaluator attends the demonstrations and reviews all of the proposals. Following this, each member of the group assesses each vendor and its proposal based on four major criterion:

• Quality of the supplier and its proposal based on discussions and reference checks

• Quality of the applications programs and how closely they satisfy the organization's requirements

• Price as determined from a five-year cash flow analysis

• Quality of support offered by the supplier.

5. Negotiate an Agreement

In the public sector, negotiation is often only clarification since the RFP contained a contract or a description of key contractual issues. Once terms have been clarified, the contract is signed.

6. Implement the Systems

The management and planning of the implementation process is a major undertaking. During the implementation phase, the equipment is delivered and the application programs installed. It is during this step that most of the problems will surface — problems which will affect the success of the project.

New application systems should be installed one at a time. For example, the General Ledger system will be installed and tested. Following this, the system will be used for a sufficient length of time to validate its accuracy and to ensure that staff understand its complexities. Once this application has been formally accepted by the organization, the next system will be addressed. This way, should there be prob-

lems with one system, the problems can be isolated.

Under no circumstances should the new system be used for production work until it has functioned error-free to the satisfaction of staff.

■ 3.2.3 Example 3: State of Alaska

The state's Administrative Manual describes the steps to be completed to obtain professional services using an RFP process. Each of the six steps listed below is required to ensure compliance with laws and regulations. Each step is described in more detail in a separate section of the Administrative Manual[7].

1. Request and receive authority to seek professional services.

2. Solicit proposals for desired services.

3. Evaluate proposals submitted and select a contractor.

4. Prepare a contract and negotiate with selected contractor.

5. Evaluate contractor's performance.

6. Provide (statutory) Procurement Representative

■ 3.2.4 Example 4: State of California

Most RFP processes are built on the concept of preparing specifications, issuing the RFP, obtaining proposals, selecting a winner and awarding a contract. In many jurisdictions, these steps are rigid, providing little room for error. The process used by the state of California to obtain products and services is a good example of a much more flexible approach, one which facilitates the development of solutions based on discussions between suppliers and purchasers.

The common RFP process is both rigid and inflexible. Its success depends on two assumptions: first, that the RFP document and process are well-defined;

and, second, that the vendors understand the problem to be solved. Often, these assumptions are shown to be false.

In practice, there are many opportunities for purchasers to compromise the process:

- Specifications can be unduly restrictive;
- Requirements can be ambiguous or contradictory;
- Contractual terms can be unacceptable;
- Evaluation processes can favour one approach;
- Deadlines can be unrealistic.

There are also many opportunities for suppliers to compromise the process and produce a non-compliant or weak proposal:

- Requirements can be misinterpreted;
- Key features can be overlooked;
- Important issues and directions stated in the RFP can be neglected;

Many organizations believe that the normal RFP process is both inefficient and unforgiving. They also believe that it is often ineffective. In some jurisdictions, it is very difficult to change the RFP once it is issued; and it is illegal to waive non-compliance of any mandatory requirement.

In an attempt to offset some of the obvious shortcomings of the normal RFP process, some organizations have adopted less rigid practices :

- Draft RFPs are issued for comment prior to the official release;
- Formal protest procedures are established and publicized in the RFP;
- Amendments and clarifications to the original RFP are permitted.

The state of California has gone much further in restructuring the RFP process. Their process is much more conversational and incorporates a phased approach for producing proposals. Their process is designed to increase the likelihood that the final proposal not contain any disqualifying defects.

There are four key elements which support the development of responsive, compliant, and appropriate solutions by suppliers in dealing with the state of California. These elements, taken as a group, represent a significant innovation in this process.

1. Phased Development of the Proposal

The RFP process follows a phased approach which includes much discussion between the parties. Four key activities are:

a. Submission of conceptual proposals and discussions;

b. Submission of detailed technical proposals and discussions;

c. Submission of draft proposals;

d. Submission of final proposals.

2. Production of an Acceptable Contract Prior to Final Proposals

The state employs standard contracts; however, it recognizes the differing approaches of vendors to contract issues and permits the insertion of vendor-specific language. To ensure that the process does not stall during contract negotiations, contracts must be acceptable to the state prior to the vendor submitting its final proposal.

3. Full Disclosure of All Administrative Requirements

To facilitate the development of compliant final bids, the state takes great care to define all of the administrative requirements.

4. Full Disclosure of Key Procurement Issues

The proposal describes in detail the way in which cost elements will be determined and used to calculate the cost of bid. It also describes the evaluation process and the way in which points will be assigned and the winner determined.

In the remainder of this section, each of these four factors is discussed in more detail.

1. Phased Development of the Proposal

A list of key dates (see table) illustrates the usual steps in this process. These dates are published in the RFP. Several of these steps are unusual in any RFP process and will be discussed in more detail later in this section.

The RFP also contained a standardized clause describing the process:

This procurement will follow a phased approach designed to increase the likelihood that the final bid will be received without disqualifying defects. The objective of the additional steps is to ensure that the bidders clearly understand the state's requirements before attempting to develop their final solutions, to ensure that the state clearly understands what each bidder intends to propose before these bids are finalized and to give each bidder an opportunity to modify his/her bid to correct problems discovered by the state...

Vendors were admonished to follow the instructions for this phased approach:

If a Vendor expects to be afforded the benefits of the steps included in this RFP, the Vendor must

Event No/Description	Date
1. Release of Request for Proposal	
2. Last day to submit questions for clarification of RFP at the bidder's conference	
3. Bidder's conference	
4. Last day to submit proposed contract changes, intention to respond, signed Confidentiality Statement, and financial responsibility information	
5. Submission of Conceptual Proposal	
6. Confidential discussion with individual bidders	
7. Submission of detailed technical proposal	
8. Confidential discussions with individual bidders	
9. Last day to finalize proposed contract language	
10. Last day to submit final question for clarification of RFP prior to submittal of draft proposal	
11. Last day to request a change in the requirements of the RFP	
12. Last day to protest the RFP	
13. Submission of draft proposal	
14. Submission of final proposal	
15. Demonstration of requirements	
16. Notification of Intent to Award	
17. Last day to protest selection	
18. Contract award and execution	

take the responsibility to:

• **Carefully read the entire RFP;**

• **If clarification is necessary; ask appropriate questions in a timely manner;**

• **Submit all required responses, complete to the best of Vendor's ability, by the required dates and times;**

• **Make sure that all procedures and requirements of the RFP are accurately followed and appropriately addressed; and**

• **Carefully reread the entire RFP before submitting a bid.**

The RFP contained a set of Rules Governing Competition. These rules, developed by Procurement Division, Department of General Services, have been standardized and are included in all RFPs. Some of the key terms which contribute to this process are discussed below. The entire document, is contained in Part II of this book.

The bidding steps are organized into two phases: a compliance phase and a final phase. An RFP may include none, some, or all of the steps in the compliance phase. These steps are a Conceptual Proposal, Detailed Technical Proposal and revisions of either or both.

The final phase may include submission of a draft bid and revisions. It always includes submission of a compliant final bid.

Costs are only included in the final bid.

Compliance Phase

The compliance phase is an iterative, conversational mode of proposal and contract development. It requires the state, working together in confidence with each bidder, to assess and discuss the viability and effectiveness of the bidder's proposed methods of meeting the state's needs as reflected in the IFB/RFP. It is a departure from the rigid "either accept or reject" philosophy of traditional competitive bidding, yet it is highly competitive in nature. It provides the flexibility needed for the bidder to test a solution prior to formal submittal of the final bid. The steps may include the submission of a Conceptual Proposal and/or a Detailed Technical Proposal by the bidder, confidential discussions of the bidder's proposal(s) and, written discussion memorandum as to the correction of defects and the state's acceptance of such changes.

a. Conceptual Proposal

The conceptual proposal may be included for the purpose of allowing each bidder to provide a general concept of a proposal with just enough detail to enable the evaluators to determine if the bidder is on the right track toward meeting the functional requirements in the IFB/RFP; and if not, where the bidder must change a concept. This step invites the bidder to be as innovative as the IFB/RFP requirements allow in eliminating unnecessary constraints.

b. Detailed Technical Proposal

The detailed technical proposal may be included for the purpose of allowing each bidder to provide a detailed technical description of its proposal to determine at an early stage whether the proposal is totally responsive to all the requirements of the IFB/RFP, and if not, which elements are not responsive and what changes would be necessary and acceptable.

c. Evaluation of Proposals and Discussion Agenda

Upon receipt of the conceptual and detailed technical proposals, the evaluation team will review each proposal for the purpose of identifying areas in which the proposal is nonresponsive to a requirement, is defective, or which requires additional clarification so the state may fully understand the ramifications of an action proposed by the bidder. As a result of this evaluation, the evaluation team will prepare an agenda of items to be discussed with the bidder, and will normally transmit the agenda to the bidder at least two working days before the scheduled meeting. The agenda may also include, in addition to the identification of discovered defects, a discussion of the bidder's proposed vendor support, implementation plans, validation plan, demonstration plans and proposed contracts, as appropriate.

d. Confidential Discussion with Each Bidder

In accordance with the discussion agenda, the evaluation team will meet with each bidder for the purpose of discussing the conceptual proposal or detailed technical proposal (as the case may be) in detail. The bidder may bring to the discussion those persons who may be required to answer questions or commit to changes. As the first order of business, the bidder may be asked to give a short proposal overview presentation. To the maximum extent practical, the bidder will address the major concerns of the evaluation team, as expressed in the discussion agenda, and should be prepared to answer any questions that may arise as a result of the presentation. The participants will then proceed to discuss each of the agenda items.

The state will not make counter proposals to a bidder's proposed solution to the IFB/RFP requirements. The state will only identify its concerns, ask for clarification, and express its reservations if a particular requirement of the IFB/RFP is not, in the opinion of the state, appropriately satisfied. The primary purpose of this discussion is to ensure that the bidder's final bid will be responsive.

e. Discussion Memorandum

Throughout the confidential discussion, a written record will be kept of all items discussed, their resolution, any changes the bidder intends to make and the state's acceptance of such changes. If the bidder's proposal — with the agreed-to changes — is acceptable to the state, such acceptance shall be noted. If agreement has not been reached on all matters during the initial discussion, such will be noted with a specific plan for resolution before the next step. These resolutions and agreements will be prepared in final form as a discussion memorandum (which will be the official state documentation of the discussion), and will be mailed to the bidder normally within two working days of the discussion. If the discussion is not completed in one meeting and is continued in subsequent meetings, the discussion memoranda will follow the meeting at which the discussion is concluded. If a bidder discovers any discrep-

ancy, omission, or other error in the memorandum, the bidder shall immediately notify the state of such error in writing and request clarification or correction. Oral statements made by either party shall not obligate either party.

f. Rejection of Bidder's Proposal

If, after full discussion with a bidder, the state is of the opinion that the bidder's proposal (conceptual proposal or detailed technical proposal, as the case may be) cannot be restructured or changed in a reasonable time to satisfy the needs of the state, and that further discussion would not likely result in an acceptable proposal in a reasonable time, the bidder will be given written notice that the proposal has been rejected and that a final bid submission along such lines would be nonresponsive.

g. Submission of Amended Proposal

If, at the conclusion of the confidential discussion, the state determines that required and agreed-to changes can only be fully confirmed through the submission of an amended proposal (conceptual proposal or detailed technical proposal, as the case may be), the state may require the submission of an addendum consisting only of those pages which were in doubt or a complete resubmittal. Similarly, if the bidder wishes confirmation that the changes the bidder intends to make, in accordance with the discussion memorandum, are acceptable to the state, the bidder may request and receive permission, if time permits, to submit such addendum within a reasonable time after the conclusion of the confidential discussion. In either event, the state will advise the bidder as to the acceptability of the amended proposal, or my schedule another discussion period, if in the state's opinion, such a discussion is desirable.

Final Phase

The purpose of the final phase is to obtain bids that are responsive in every respect. This phase may include a draft bid and will always include a final bid, as described below:

a. Draft Bid

The purpose of the draft bid is to provide the state with an almost final bid in order to identify any faulty administrative aspect of the bid which, if not corrected, could cause the final bid to be rejected for ministerial reasons.

The draft bid should correspond to submittals and agreements of the compliance phase, if required, and must be complete in every respect as required by the IFB/RFP section on proposal and bid format, except cost. The inclusion of cost information in the draft bid may be a basis for rejecting the bid and notifying the bidder that further participation in the procurement is prohibited.

Review of the draft bid by the state may include confidential discussions with the individual bidders and will provide feedback to the bidder prior to submittal of the final proposal. If no such discussion step is included, the review of the draft bid does not include any assessment of the bid's responsiveness to the technical requirements of the IFB/RFP.

Regardless of the inclusion of a confidential discussion, the state will notify the bidder of any defects it has detected in the draft bid, or of the fact that it did not detect any such defects. Such notification is intended to minimize the risk that the final bid will be deemed defective; however, the state will not provide any warranty that all defects have been detected and the such notification will not preclude rejection of the final bid if such defects are later found.

If the state finds it necessary, it may call for revised draft bid submittals or portions thereof. The bidder will be notified of defects discovered in these submittals as well. Again, the state will not provide any warranty that all defects have been detected and that such notification will not preclude rejection of the final bid if such defects are later found.

b. Final Bid

The final bid must be complete, including all cost information, required signatures, contract language changes agreed to in writing and corrections to those defects noted by the state in its review of the draft bid. If required in the IFB/RFP, cost data (as identified in the above referenced section) must be submitted under separate, sealed cover. Changes that appear in the final bid, other than corrections of defects, increase the risk that the final bid may be found defective.

2. Production of an Acceptable Contract Prior to Final Proposals

Contract issues can derail the RFP process. Getting to "yes" for a contract can be a difficult, time-consuming, and frustrating process for both the vendors and the purchasers.

Some jurisdictions issue RFPs which only define the technical requirements. There is no mention of contracts in the RFP. In these jurisdictions, many months can pass between the selection of the winner and the signing of a contract. Sometimes, the contractual differences between the selected vendor and the purchasing organization are so great that a deal is never made.

Some jurisdictions include their contract with the RFP and make acceptance of this contract a mandatory condition. Sometimes, these contracts impose unacceptable terms on the supplier. For example, insisting on ownership rights for proprietary software or royalties on enhancements. In these cases, either the suppliers "no bid" or they submit a proposal which is judged to be non-compliant since it has changed the mandatory contract language.

Some jurisdictions include their proposed contracts and permit the supplier to suggest alternatives for unacceptable sections. This approach eliminates proposals from being non-compliant due to contract issues. However, using this approach, a contract is negotiated after the winner has been selected. Identifying contract issues in the RFP and discussing them in the proposal can lead to the early identification of sections unacceptable to the vendor or the purchaser. Even doing this, the final contract is still subject to negotiation after the winner has been selected. Consequently, either the project is delayed while negotiations take place, or the project is begun without a contract.

In California, the RFP process recognizes these problems and deals with them before the winner is selected. The state has model contract forms which are included in the RFP. However, as part of the discussion process, vendors can propose their own clauses, suggest changes to the standard clauses, and, in effect, negotiate their own terms. However, the time in which to accomplish this is determined by the published schedule. The contract must be fixed prior to final bids. Once the final bid has been submitted, no negotiation is permitted.

The state has defined both standard contracts and the process for modifying the terms to develop mutually agreeable final contracts.

D. Contractual Information

1. Contract Form

The state has model contract forms to be used by state agencies when contracting for EDP or telecommunications goods and services. The model contract(s) appropriate for the specific requirements of this IFB/RFP are included in the IFB/RFP.

2. Specific Terms and Conditions

In traditional competitive bidding, the contract to be awarded is included in the solicitation document in its final form, and any alteration by a bidder will result in rejection of its bid. The state recognizes, however, that the various suppliers of EDP goods and services have developed pricing structures and procedures that differ from each other, and that, if the state were to specify the exact language of the contract to be executed, if could result in firms being unwilling to do business with the state of California because of contract statements which are incompatible with their business methods. In recognition of the above, the form of the contract(s) contained in the attached Appendices permit, where appropriate, the substitution and/or insertion of vendor-specified language by the bidder. All such substitutions and insertions must be approved by the Department of General Services. The Department of General Services may request the Department of Finance's concurrence on the approval of changes involving significant issues. Terms and conditions which do not comply in substance with all material requirements of the IFB/RFP, which are contrary to the best interests of the state, or which are in opposition to state policy will not be accepted.

The state will prenegotiate repetitively used terms and conditions with vendors at their request. These prenegotiated terms and conditions will be kept on file and bidders may refer to them as their proposed contract language for individual solicitations.

3. Approval of Proposed Contracts

To comply with the requirement of competitive bidding procedures, the contract must be fixed prior to the submission of the final bids — no negotiation is permissible after that time. It is required, therefore, that any vendor who intends to bid on this IFB/RFP submit its proposed contract to the state in accordance with the schedule contained in Section I. If a bidder has prenegotiated language with the state, the bidder may indicate that this is the language proposed and submit only changes to any language that has not been prenegotiated. (For a particular IFB/RFP it is possible that prenegotiated language will not be acceptable due to special circumstances. The state will notify the bidder if this is the case and will renegotiate that language for this procurement.) For language that has not been prenegotiated, the proposed contract, or portions thereof, must be submitted in the form of the prescribed model(s), and deviations from the exact language contained in the model(s) must conform to the guidance therein stated.

The proposed contract must contain all proposed terms and conditions, but it must not contain (other than in sample form) any identification of the proposed good or cost data. (Note, however, that the draft bid must contain the approved contract with all the blanks filled in except for cost data, as specified in Paragraph II-C3 above.) The proposed contract must be clearly labeled "proposed contract" with the IFB/RFP identification from the IFB/RFP title page. The state will notify the bidder as to which, if any, terms and conditions are not acceptable to the state and will arrange an appropriate meeting at a mutually satisfactory time to resolve any differences.

Each appendix contains a set of instructions to guide the bidder through step-by-step procedures to develop proposed new language or changes to model contract language, negotiating contract language and securing state approval. Proposed contract language which is not prepared in accordance with these instructions may be returned to the bidder without review by the state.

It is essential that the bidder's proposed contract be acceptable to the state prior to the final bid submission date. Such acceptance does not relieve the bidder of providing other necessary information required in the contract. If a bid contains unapproved contract language the potential for bid rejection is substantially increased.

3. Full Disclosure of All Administrative Requirements

To facilitate the development of compliant final bids, the state takes great care to define all of the administrative requirements. Typically, this section of the RFP is more than 50 pages in length and contains all of the administrative issues the vendor must deal with. These include the following:

- Bidder responsibility
- Primary contractor
- Letter of Intent to Bid
- Financial statements
- Performance bond
- Confidentiality
- Productive use requirements
- Installation
- Implementation schedule
- Bidder references and staff capabilities
- Meetings
- Reports
- Maintenance requirements
- Data ownership
- Continuing standards of performance
- Other administrative requirements
- Special considerations
- Vendor data record
- Offset credits
- Drug free workplace
- Delivery
- Federal Employer Identification Number

4. Full Disclosure of Key Procurement Issues

There are two key issues which greatly influence each vendors' proposal strategy: cost and the evaluation process. The way in which cost is determined and the weight that it is given in the evaluation will influence a vendor's proposal. A solution in which cost is worth 75 percent of the points may suggest a very different approach to a vendor than a solution in which cost is only worth 10 percent.

Similarly, the details of how the evaluation will be performed, what factors are evaluated, how points are assigned, and the process for establishing compliance will all influence how each vendor develops its proposal.

In this RFP, the bidders were required to complete a prescribed Cost Summary Sheet. This sheet identified the required cost elements and identified the method that would be used to determine the "Cost of Bid." In this RFP, the evaluation process was defined. Vendors were informed of the sequence of steps in the evaluation and the details of each step. For example, they were informed that "only those bid that meet all mandatory requirements will be evaluated for the purposes of scoring points by meeting desirable requirements." They were then informed about the details of the scoring process: the number of points for each desirable feature and the way in which scores would be determined. Finally, they were informed as to the method for combining the cost point and the point earned for desirable features.

3.3

Winning Proposals and Successful Projects

■ 3.3.1 A Winning Proposal

It's often helpful to stop and consider the characteristics of a winning proposal and a successful RFP process prior to beginning the RFP itself. When planning the RFP process, it is helpful to consider the desirable results and ensure that your plan will promote the desired outcomes. This preliminary examination often introduces changes in the approach adopted, the detailed tasks, the RFP document, timing, and the requirements.

Let's first examine the output produced by the RFP — the actual proposals submitted for our consideration. What are we looking for? How do we define the proposal contents? What questions do we ask to help us determine the best supplier? How do we evaluate the proposals?

What is a proposal?

The first step is to agree on the definition of a proposal. A proposal is essentially a sales presentation. If it were simply a statement of prices and contract terms, it would not be a proposal but a quotation. A proposal can be thought of as serving three purposes:

1. It is a written attempt to persuade the evaluator to select the proposer and its product or services.

2. It is a response to an RFP supported by an array of credentials which attempt to convince the evaluator that the proposer is best qualified to provide the results the evaluator requires.

3. It is an offer to provide some specified goods or services; explaining the terms, the costs, and the suitability to satisfy the customer's needs.

What is a winning proposal?

Having defined a proposal, what is a winning proposal? What are the characteristics of the proposal, the organization, and the solution which make it attractive to the evaluators?

Obviously, a winning proposal is the one which receives the award. But why is it selected? The major reason for one supplier's proposal being selected over dozens of others is this: the proposal persuaded the reader that it was the best proposal and offered by the best organization for the job. The best proposal convinced the evaluators not simply that the supplier could do the job, but that the supplier could do the job better (and often at less risk) than any other organization.

Winning proposals have four characteristics in common. They convince the reader that:

1. The supplier fully understands the needs and problems.

2. The supplier knows how to satisfy the needs or solve the problems and offers a suitable plan.

3. The supplier is well qualified by virtue of experience and resources, including personnel, to carry out the proposed plan; and

4. The price asked is reasonable and is within the organization's budget.

This definition is not universal — it must conform to your organization's policy. So the "reasonable price" may become the "least cost" depending on your policy. In creating the RFP, we should ensure that we solicit enough specific information to evaluate these four characteristics. This evidence, in total, helps each evaluator assess the risk of failure (or the chances of success) associated with each proposal.

■ 3.3.2 Success in the RFP Process

Now that we've discussed the RFP, a proposal and a winning proposal, let's consider another important question. You can use this question to guide your efforts as you execute the Request for Proposal process. The question is: "What is success?"

When all of this is finished, how do we know if we have been successful? Some of the characteristics of a successful process are listed below.

• The procurement process was executed in a professional manner and was consistent with your organization's purchasing policy and the applicable laws and regulations.

• The procurement process was documented as you went along and could survive public scrutiny.

• No objections were raised by suppliers concerning the fairness of the process or the actual selection.

• The selected supplier performed as expected. The solution was implemented on time, within budget and satisfied the requirements.

Your organization (your boss) acknowledged that the project was a success.

3·4

Using Checklists

Checklists are valuable, easy-to-use, and help avoid mistakes. They are a simple yet effective way to provide guidance to managers, to help them organize their work, and to inform them of key issues and critical steps. They are a quality control tool and help ensure that all critical factors have been considered. Many organizations maintain checklists related to several aspects of the RFP process such as critical issues, contract terms, and the conduct of debriefing sessions.

■ 3.4.1 Checklist #1 — Organizing an RFP

This checklist was developed by a private-sector firm to review some of the organizational issues of the RFP process. Not all of the items apply in the public sector.

In studying real-life examples of RFPs, you can learn much about the management activities which determine the success of a project. Many of these activities are related to the process for issuing the Request for Proposal and evaluating the responses. This checklist identifies some of these success factors:

1. Pre-qualify the suppliers. Send the RFP only to vendors which you believe are capable of doing the job. Obtain sufficient information to ensure that each supplier satisfies the obvious mandatory requirements. For example, if you know that you will only deal with a firm having a local office, then ensure that each supplier has one before issuing the RFP.

2. Restrict the RFP to a limited number of suppliers. Preparation of a proposal by a supplier is a costly and time-consuming process. Responding to suppliers' questions and dealing with them during this process is also costly and time-consuming for your organization. Attempt to restrict the number of bidders to six or less.

3. Ensure that your choice of suppliers covers a range of alternatives. Don't prejudge the best solution.

4. Include a timetable in the RFP. Ensure that you provide adequate time for each vendor to prepare its proposal. Recognize that, for quite legitimate reasons, a vendor may wish to alter the schedule.

5. Quantify your requirements whenever possible. For example, if the selection of a system de-

pends on its response time, indicate the range of acceptable results.

6. Ensure that your senior management agrees with your list of potential vendors. Some senior managers, based on past experience, simply will not deal with certain suppliers.

7. Ensure that the process for developing and issuing the RFP and evaluating the proposals has been thought through, documented and approved by management.

8. Engage expert advice to assist you. If this is the first RFP for which you are responsible, talk to someone with experience in this area. Discuss the process, your expectations, and any risks you may have overlooked.

9. Ensure that the process for dealing with the vendors is fair and that each supplier is treated in a similar manner. Occasionally, an unsuccessful vendor will protest, often to senior management. Anticipating this, the issuer should carefully document the evaluation procedure, findings and conclusions.

10. Recognize that, unless there are surprises discovered during the process, or circumstances change, you have an implicit commitment to select one of the proposals. If you are not prepared at the outset to select one of the proposals, assuming it is a reasonable solution, then call your Request for Proposal a Request for Information.

11. Provide sufficient elapsed time and sufficient internal staff to do a good job. The process of preparing and issuing an RFP and evaluating the responses is expensive and time-consuming to both suppliers and your company.

12. Give suppliers as much information as possible. Tell them who the competitors are; ensure that answers are communicated to all suppliers; provide them with thorough information concerning your requirements and the selection process. Identify the evaluation criteria, your methodology, and the weights used in evaluating each major factor.

13. Ensure that your recommendations are consistent with your organization's approval processes and budget guidelines.

14. Document your requirements for confidentiality before releasing any information to the suppliers. Will you require each supplier to sign a non-disclosure agreement prior to receiving the RFP? Will you require information from each supplier prior to releasing the RFP?

■ 3.4.2 Checklist #2 – Project Manager's Checklist

This checklist was developed to help a project manager identify some key areas and potential sources of major problems.

Before Starting

1. Are the key users to be involved in preparing the RFP?

2. Have sufficient staff and time been allocated to this process?

3. Are the overall goals of the procurement process documented and understood?

Establishing Requirements

4. Did you quantify requirements whenever possible?

5. Is the requirements document precise, concise and easily understood?

6. Are the requirements large enough to warrant

a staged process calling for interim deliverables?

7. If you anticipate that some vendors will be unable to meet the mandatory requirements, can you justify the requirements from a business perspective?

8. Are the anticipated results of a successful solution stated clearly in objective terms?

9. Have the evaluation methodology and evaluation criteria been developed and used to ensure that the requirements are stated clearly?

Preparing the RFP Document

10. Are all of the requirements contained in one section of the RFP document?

11. Has each requirement been classified as "mandatory" or "desirable?"

12. Have you included an explanation of government and agency policies and legal requirements that may affect the outcome?

13. Are there sufficient funds available?

14. Have the evaluation methodology and criteria been documented as part of the RFP? Does the RFP describe all the requirements?

Inviting Suppliers

15. Has one person from the agency been assigned to deal with the suppliers?

16. Is your current supplier included? If not, have you documented the reasons and reviewed them with management?

17. Are you prepared to accept proposals from suppliers not on the suppliers list?

Evaluating Proposals

18. Do you have a strategy in place if none of the proposals is acceptable?

19. Does the evaluation include all related costs over the planned life of the technology?

20. Are all proposals failing to meet one or more mandatory requirement excluded from further consideration? Are the specific requirements then re-evaluated for clarity to ensure that all suppliers have understood each requirement in a similar way?

21. Are you prepared to accept one of the proposals if it satisfies the mandatory requirements but offers few "desirables?"

22. Have you selected the proposal that met all mandatory features and had the lowest evaluated cost?

23. During the evaluation process, did you contact suppliers to clarify their proposals, to ensure that your estimate of costs is based on a clear understanding of their proposal?

24. Has a compliance checklist been used to ensure that each supplier dealt with each requirement?

Completing the Contract

25. Is the proposal or any other information on which you are relying been incorporated into the contract?

Debriefing Suppliers

26. Once the winning supplier was selected, were the other competitors advised immediately?

27. Did the debriefing session uncover any potential problems?

28. Did the session provide the supplier with a clear understanding of why its proposal was unsuccessful and how to improve in the future?

29. Are you aware of the impact of freedom of information laws on the debriefing sessions?

3·5

Typical Timing

Most people involved in the RFP process for the first time underestimate how long it will take. There are many activities, many reviews and approvals, and many pitfalls. This section attempts to identify some of the factors influencing the estimate of the required time. If the timetable is too long, the organization suffers because the required solution is not available. If the timetable is too short, suppliers can and do claim that they are being treated unfairly. It is unreasonable to expect a supplier to prepare a creative proposal to a complex problem in a few days. It is also unreasonable to expect that all of the members of the evaluation committee will be available when required. Approvals often take longer than expected, especially if a key individual is unavailable. While contracts can be negotiated quickly, unusual terms can add weeks to the approval process. The evaluation of proposals may prove to be more complex than anticipated.

Don't underestimate the amount of your time the detailed, day-to-day management of this process will take. If you issue your RFP to 10 suppliers, their questions could cause much unexpected discussion and work. Be conservative and plan carefully.

Don't underestimate the amount of time the contract may be retained by your legal department.

With all of these caveats, let's discuss each of the major milestones in a typical process:

1. Complete the user requirements.

2. Construct the RFP.

3. Release the RFP.

4. Hold a suppliers' meeting.

5. Receive the proposals.

6. Complete the evaluations.

7. Finalize the contract.

Times vary radically. I have encountered situations in which the entire RFP process was executed in as little as four weeks or as much as one year. In the remainder of this section, each major task in a typical RFP process is discussed and some of the potential sources of delay are identified.

1. Complete the user requirements.

Often, the production of a clear, unified, cohesive statement of requirements by the user group takes much longer than the rest of the RFP process. Once the requirements have been given to the project manager, this manager must ensure that they are in a useful, easy-to-understand form. Often, the requirements must be rewritten for the RFP. Additional details concerning the organization and its structure must be added to the description. Requirements can be produced in a few days, or in the extreme, in several years.

When several departments are involved, the review and approval process may be delayed beyond any reasonable expectation. The requirements document can be a battleground for competing departmental objectives.

2. Construct the RFP.

Combining the user's statement of requirements, the administrative rules, and the terms and conditions into a cohesive, consistent RFP document can be completed in less than one week. But to do it quickly requires the time and energy of two people with different skills — one knowledgeable about the problem or requirements; the second, about RFPs. Even when these people are available, the pressures of other duties may make it impossible for them to devote sufficient attention to this work to complete it quickly.

In many organizations, the person responsible for the project is also responsible for creating the RFP. Often, this person has little experience with RFPs. Some organizations, as a quality control measure, insist that the RFP package be reviewed by management prior to its release. This review can identify deficiencies not apparent to the

project manager which may require additional time and energy to correct.

3. Release the RFP.

Once the RFP has been approved, it can be announced and released. In many jurisdictions, "release" is accomplished by sending notices to appropriate suppliers registered with the organization, and by placing advertisements in newspapers.

The process of obtaining approval for an advertisement is not always straightforward. Often, the advertisement will raise concerns about the description of the work. Do we really want to say we have a problem, or a deficiency in a system, or a requirement for yet another study? The announcements created by project mangers sometimes become the subject of senior management concerns and scrutiny. This always adds time to the process.

The placement of the ad may be the responsibility of a communications group within the organization. This group may have its own procedures and may introduce additional unanticipated delays.

4. Hold a suppliers' meeting.

Suppliers' meetings may or may not be mandatory. They are held sometime after the RFP has been released, after the suppliers have had sufficient time to review the RFP and identify their concerns and questions. If the RFP has only been distributed locally, then allowing one week between the receipt of the RFP and the meeting is appropriate. However, if the RFP has wide distribution, some additional time may be needed to permit organizations coming from remote locations to plan and schedule their attendance at the meeting.

5. Receive the proposals.

Most proposals, those for expenditures less than a few million dollars, are usually due two to four weeks after the RFP has been issued. Two weeks is the minimum time to digest an RFP and produce a proposal. Four weeks is reasonable for many proposals.

Timing is always a concern. In some organizations timing is set by policy, in others it's set by the project manager. In Alaska, timing is prescribed by law[8]:

The procurement officer shall give adequate public notice... at least 21 days before [proposals are due]. If a determination is made in writing that a shorter notice period is necessary for a particular bid, the 21-day period may be shortened. The determination shall be made by the chief procurement officer...

Notice may include publication in a newspaper,... notices posted in public places within the area where the work is to be performed, notices mailed to all prospective contractors on the appropriate list...

Failure to comply with the notice requirements of this section does not invalidate a bid or the award of a contract. If the state fails to substantially comply with the requirements of this section, the state is liable for damages caused by that failure...

Suppliers are suspicious when the time is too short to prepare a proposal. While "too short" is difficult to define, it is obvious when it happens. Recently, I saw a solicitation announced in a major newspaper by a multimillion dollar agency looking for a new financial package. The time permitted for response was five working days. Any responsible supplier learning about this solicitation for the first time couldn't possibly acquire the solicitation package and develop a proposal in only five days. It is hard to imagine how the issuing organization could argue that five days was reasonable or fair.

The classic question repeated at many supplier meetings is: Can the closing date be extended? Suppliers complain that they are not given sufficient time to prepare a reasonable offer.

If complaints are received before the competition's closing date and you believe that they are valid complaints, you can provide more time for all suppliers to respond.

When suppliers have been pre-selected and all suppliers agree to the extension, then simply adding a few weeks onto the deadline is an easy task. However, in many situations it is extremely difficult, if not impossible, to extend the deadline on an RFP. Some suppliers may have decided not to submit a proposal because the deadline was short. Informing those suppliers who did decide to submit a proposal that they have another month does nothing for the supplier who initially declined to participate. In fact, this supplier has been totally disadvantaged. In this situation, to extend the deadline requires you to cancel the original RFP and reissue a new RFP. In this way, all suppliers are treated in a fair manner.

Some purchasers intentionally keep the time short. Their argument is that they are testing the supplier's ability to manage a project. They believe that if a supplier is incapable of managing this small project — the development of a proposal in a month — how are they ever going to manage the actual project? There is some merit in this argument.

Some suppliers will initiate this complaint during the RFP process as a tactic for justifying a protest later if they do not win the competition. Having protested the timing during the process, they may, if they lose, request that the process be repeated since it was, in their opinion, unfair.

It is easier to get it right the first time. Consider key factors such as the complexity of the task, the timing of holidays, and the location of suppliers when deciding on the amount of time provided to prepare a proposal. However, even if you do "get it right," you may still receive complaints from suppliers.

6. Complete the evaluations

Suppliers require some notice before the presentations. Once presentations have been held, the evaluation team may decide to negotiate the contract with one or more suppliers, or call for "best and final" offers. These activities can add many additional weeks to the process.

7. Finalize the contract

Some organizations insist that suppliers sign their standard contract. This is accomplished in different jurisdictions in different ways. A contract can be imposed either as a condition in the RFP, by including the contract in the RFP, or during negotiations. This approach leads to quick conclusions since the supplier either accepts the standard contract or is considered "non-compliant" and eliminated from further consideration.

In other jurisdictions, or with other RFPs, contracts must be negotiated. To ensure that negotiations are completed quickly, some RFPs include a clause that restricts negotiations to five, 15 or 30 days. At the end of the stated time, negotiations are terminated with that supplier — presumably the one that scored highest on the evaluation — and begun with the second highest supplier.

Organizations with new types of clauses or nonstandard terms often require approval from lawyers before a contract can be signed. This can add significant amounts of time to the project start date.

3.6

People Issues

This section is written as if the purchaser and users were employees of a local government or municipality. Most projects in both the private and public sectors experience similar problems. However, projects within the public sector must satisfy an additional requirement: They must be easily defended by elected politicians and publicly-accountable administrators.

Some projects are technically successful but fail to help the organization as expected. Consider a typical information technology procurement for an application package, a custom-built tax collection system, or a local area network connecting all of the organization's personal computers. The system can do everything promised by the supplier: it has the right features and works well on the equipment. In short, it's a technical success. But the staff never accepted the system wholeheartedly. They complain that it's "not as good as the old system." Or the city administrator sees the system primarily as a source of complaint from council or managers. In these situations, the problem often lies not with the system

nor the supplier, but with the manner it which it was promoted and installed by management.

Negative reactions to systems features are often symptoms of people problems. Many systems projects fail because key issues related to roles and responsibilities of staff are neglected during the selection and implementation process. In many situations, problems are created because management does not understand the impact of the new system on relationships within the organization. Management often neglects or underestimates the stresses and uncertainties created by this type of project.

Projects fail because people resist change, or change is imposed on them without their involvement.

In this section, we will discuss each of the stakeholders involved in the process of selecting and installing a new system. Each has an interest in the success of the project, but their interests may be different. These differing interests are sometimes in conflict with one another. The emphasis in this section is not on the tasks but on the roles, expectations and relationships of these people. We will identify how each of the stakeholders can be involved in the process of change, how each helps shape the project and contributes to its success or failure.

In this discussion, we will assume that the project is to select and implement a packaged software solution for a major application such as a Geographic Information System. In doing this, the municipality follows a typical project methodology consisting of five steps:

1. Initiate the project.
2. Establish the requirements.
3. Issue the Request for Proposal.
4. Select the vendor/negotiate the contract.
5. Implement the system.

City Administrator and Council

The city administrator must be an enthusiastic supporter of the project. It is the city administrator who must provide the support for the project manager. It is this person who must deal with council and ensure that the project receives support and understanding.

There are many different styles of dealing with council. In some municipalities, the council gets deeply involved in the day-to-day activities; in other locations council acts as a Board of Directors in running the business. Some councilors get deeply involved in certain issues which reflect their own expertise. It is the city administrator who must initially decide how much information council is to be given and in what form. Following are responsibilities of the city administrator and council:

1. Initiate the project

Prior to project initiation, the city administra-

tor may wish to have an informal discussion with one or several members of council to advise them of the intentions and to seek their guidance on structuring the overall project. Do they wish formal reports at each phase? Does the council wish to be represented on the Steering Committee? It is extremely important to the overall success of the project that the city administrator be aware of each council members' view on computers and the project. It is often helpful to draw comparisons between a capital project, such as the selection of a contractor to build an addition to the facilities, and a computer project. It is also important that the city administrator understand each councilor's perspective on this project and attempt to deal with any misgivings.

Often, a lawyer on council will be concerned about the contract and potential cost overruns. In this situation, the city administrator or project manager might want to explain how they intend to deal with contract issues and see if their initial approach should be modified to deal with the lawyer's concerns.

Some councilors lack confidence in management's ability to deal with computers. These sorts of misgivings can only be mitigated by describing the detailed process for selection, involving the person at all stages of the project, and by meeting the timetable for each task.

In other cases, councilors have heard stories of computer projects which have failed. Some councilors may have firsthand experience with difficult systems. It is necessary to deal with each concern. The councilors' views and experience should be reflected in the city administrator's project plan.

One of the major goals in having the city administrator discuss this project with councilors on an informal basis is to identify those councilors who are most supportive of this project. By doing this, the city administrator can then enlist their help to gain the overall support of council.

At this stage of the project, prior to any homework being done, the city administrator should not attempt to define exact costs or timing for the project. The usual approach is to state that solid estimates will be available at the end of the first phase — Project Initiation.

The city administrator should not proceed with the initiation phase until the following events have occurred:

• Councilors have been made aware of this project and have identified their concerns and how they wish to be involved.

• A project manager has been selected and has agreed to undertake the project.

• Staff have been informed of the project and their concerns have been discussed with them.

• A Steering Committee has been formed.

Each of these stakeholders — councilors, project manager, staff and the Steering Committee — has an important role in dealing with people issues and generating a climate for enthusiastic support of the project.

Council's initial concerns usually relate to cost, time, need and the probability of success. Concerns about cost and timing are dealt with in the normal course of the project. Issues related to justification for the project and its ultimate success can be dealt with by providing council with related information. However, the underlying concern is usually related to confidence in management or fear of technology.

The project manager's initial concerns usually relate to lack of experience with similar projects, find-

ing sufficient time to devote to the new responsibilities, and fear of technology.

Staff's initial concerns usually center on job security and fear of change. Prior to speaking with staff, the city administrator should develop a policy to deal with the issues most likely to be raised, including job security, retraining, future promotions and expanded job definitions.

Once these initial concerns have been dealt with, the project manager should take over and develop an overall outline of the project. Once completed and reviewed with the Steering Committee, this plan can be formally presented to council. In doing this, council will be given the opportunity of discussing the matter and expressing their views.

Having completed the pre-initiation tasks, council can be presented with a formal request and a plan for the project itself. At the end of the initiation phase, council may be presented with a brief report outlining the findings, conclusions and recommendations for that phase.

As part of this phase, members of council or the entire council are sometimes interviewed to determine their views on the current system's shortcomings and new systems.

2. Establish the requirements

Once the project has been launched, the city administrator's role is reduced to the following:

• Participation in the Steering Committee.

• Informal discussions with the project manager about problems and issues.

• Discussions with staff about their concerns, and

• Dealing with council on this project.

The activities resulting from these responsibilities can be extremely time-consuming. It is important that the city administrator have sufficient time to deal with these issues. It is far better to slow down the pace of the project than to ignore people issues.

Both council and the city administrator are users of the information provided by systems. Hence, each will be interviewed during this phase.

3. Issue the Request for Proposal

A Request for Proposal can become a political issue. Firms left off the bidders list may complain to particular councilors or raise the issue publicly. The easiest way to deal with a supplier who wants to bid is to send it the Request for Proposal. It is easier to evaluate an additional proposal than to deal with this issue at a council meeting.

4. Select the vendor

It is important that the selection process and assessment be documented and the specific reasons for eliminating each supplier be recorded. It is not uncommon for a disgruntled supplier to suddenly appear at the council meeting the night the recommendation is being presented.

Often, municipalities will form a users group to evaluate the proposed systems. By having key users work together, acceptance of the selected system is promoted.

5. Implement the system

Implementation is the time when most problems surface. Great care should be taken to ensure that the implementation plans and expectations of all the stakeholders are realistic. Problems related to overtime, job descriptions, staff morale, and union demands can

be inflamed by an implementation process which is poorly executed. The city administrator should ensure that these issues are not permitted to boil over but rather are dealt with on a day-to-day basis.

The Project Manager

The city administrator must identify the person from the municipality who is best qualified to plan, manage and control this project on a day-to-day basis. It is important to ensure that this person is willing to be project manager and that the project manager will have sufficient time to do a good job. Often, organizations shift some of this person's regular duties to other staff. The project manager should be a senior person, respected by staff. In addition, the project manager should be someone who can be forthright and open about problems and who can communicate well with all levels of the organization, including council.

If the city administrator elects to manage this project, then great care must be taken to ensure that the timetable reflects the limited amount of time which may be available to move this project forward.

Before doing anything else, the project manager should take some time to think through the implementation process. Seasoned project managers recognize that the first steps taken establish a tone and a direction and have considerable influence on the project's overall success. The beginning of the project is the time to do some general systems thinking, not only about the computer aspects of the project, but the human, social and business systems as well. The project manager must not only think about how the new systems will be used, but also how the system will affect the people who use them and the nature of their jobs.

Following this, the project manager should develop the plan for the first step of the project and present it to the Steering Committee for review.

The project manager should consider engaging an outside expert to assist. (See Management Consultants section.)

A project schedule which keeps getting longer and longer is a major problem. Staff become demoralized and support for the project lessens. The project manager should be extremely generous in producing the initial schedule. It is far better to complete a two-year project in 14 months than to complete a 14-month project in two years.

In Phase 5, Implementation, systems are installed and put into production. Usually, systems are installed one at a time. While the supplier may suggest an implementation sequence (General Ledger, then Tax Rolls, etc.), this should not be accepted by the project manager without much thought and discussion. To the extent possible, the first system selected for implementation should be the one with the most enthusiastic group of users, for they will make it successful. Seeing and hearing about that initial success, other users will often modify their opposition to change. It is dangerous to initiate a new system with a group of disgruntled users, for they will ensure its failure.

Steering Committee

A Steering Committee is a useful forum for management to provide advice and policy decisions to the project manager and to ensure that there is a continuous flow of timely information about plans and progress throughout the organization.

The Steering Committee is usually composed of the city administrator, the project manager, and the department heads or key users. It may contain representation from council. It should meet on a regular basis to review plans and progress and to discuss concerns brought to the committee by its members.

Users
1. Team Building

Many people from the municipality will contribute to this project. Some of these people will spend considerable amounts of time on this work. The project manager should recognize that just assembling a group of good people doesn't make them a team. The project manager must "sell" the project to each person on the team and discuss their potential contribution to the project's success.

There are two significant issues that are often neglected. First, the project manager should reward success. There will be times when milestones are met or serious problems solved through the efforts of particular people. Remember that a successful project is made up of small victories. Recognize the efforts of individuals and praise people for a job well done.

The second most often neglected issue is overtime. Recognize that for some tasks and individuals, more than casual overtime is involved. Putting a person in a position where they will be expected to work 60-hour weeks for several months should not be done without the prior agreement of the individual. Providing special benefits to this person for doing the job is not a motivational issue, but an issue of fairness.

2. Resistance to Change

People generally do not like change. Change cannot be introduced successfully into an organization without paying special attention to the needs of people. People often resist change, even if the change will result in a superior system or produce a better, more interesting work environment. The project manager must attempt to understand the causes of resistance to change, and what can be done to gain the cooperation of staff. The project manager should ensure that the following tactics are part of the overall implementation strategy:

(a) Explain the need for change to all of the people in the organization. Do this in groups and in individual discussions. By providing staff with information about the planned changes, time to evaluate the effects of the changes on them, their jobs, and their relationships, staff will be less likely to oppose the changes.

(b) Gain the participation of each group which will be affected by the change. Let the staff participate in shaping the project. Often, staff can develop a better implementation sequence than that proposed by the supplier. However, if staff are involved, their ideas and input must be actually used, not ignored. When staff involvement is only a public relations gesture, it often backfires.

(c) Take advantage of the experience and know-how of staff. People familiar with the day-to-day practices can often spot flaws in the proposed changes or suggest creative solutions to problems overlooked by the experts involved.

(d) Avoid a preoccupation with the technical aspects of the project. Don't overlook the social and human aspects.

(e) Allow the organization, groups and individuals sufficient time to learn, to understand and to become familiar with the new system.

Many users greet the announcement of a computer project with fear. Clerks fear that the computer will make their jobs redundant or that, should their jobs survive, they may not be able to do them adequately. Middle level managers have their own set of fears related to job security, having to change long-standing practices, and loss of control. Senior managers are often intimidated by technology. They feel that they won't be able to apply their skills or that they must have detailed knowledge of computers to be successful.

Lawyers

Most municipalities insist that all contracts be approved by their lawyer. However, not all lawyers have dealt with computer contracts. Often, a project manager will seek guidance from the Steering Committee about the role of their lawyers in this project.

At a minimum, the lawyers should be briefed on the project plan. They should be asked if there are any special terms, conditions or approaches which should be identified in the Request for Proposal.

The municipality's lawyer may be a good resource for helping with the contract negotiations.

The project plan should provide adequate time for the municipality's lawyers to review the contracts and prepare their comments. Some lawyers have very little experience with computer contracts and find it helpful to discuss this matter informally with the project manager or management consultant.

Auditors

The auditors' legal responsibility is to ensure that the books of the corporation are kept according to standard accounting practices. Many auditing firms have expanded this definition to include a role in major systems projects. Many auditing firms, especially the ones with large management consulting practices, would like to review the system as part of the selection process. They would like to sit on the Steering Committee. Each of these activities, while potentially helpful, is time-consuming and expensive.

Sometimes it is very difficult to determine the motives of the auditor in recommending that you engage one of their consultants to help you. Are they speaking as auditors concerned about the soundness of the system, or as marketers for consulting services?

Unless there is a large amount of system development work involved, there is no need for the active involvement of the auditors with the day-to-day project.

As part of the project initiation, the municipality should inform the auditors about the project. The auditors can be very helpful in providing information about the current systems and their deficiencies.

During Step 2, Establish Your Requirements, the auditors can be very helpful. Information consisting of audit notes, reports, system descriptions and data flow charts may have been generated as part of the annual audit. This information should be provided at no cost to the municipality.

During Step 3, Issue the Request for Proposals, the municipality has identified the vendors and their experience with other municipalities. The project manager can ask the auditors if they have any clients using the proposed applications packages. If they do, then the auditors can furnish their opinion of the package as installed at another site. The auditors can also provide names of suppliers who have provided systems to their other municipal clients. This infor-

mation can be very helpful and should be provided by your auditors at no cost to the municipality.

Unions

Unions are primarily concerned with job losses. Other issues relate to the use of temporary help and retraining of staff. New computer systems and computer projects generate new work to be done. They also have the potential for generating large amounts of overtime, and the need for an abnormal number of temporary employees, sometimes for extended periods of time. Each of these factors, especially changes in job descriptions, are of interest to unions.

How these issues are dealt with is a matter of history within your municipality, the nature of the bargaining unit, and the style of management.

Some municipalities, anticipating changes in jobs, reassure their employees by guaranteeing that no jobs will be eliminated due to new technology. Some of these clauses identify various options employees have if, for example, a billing clerk's job description changes from primarily a manual task to one using a computer terminal.

Difficult situations arise when staff are afraid of the technology, implementation has bogged down, large amounts of overtime and temporary staff are being used, and negotiations are under way. The timing of contract negotiations should be considered when developing any implementation plan.

Unions often argue that a change in job descriptions to incorporate use of computer terminals represents an upgrading of the skills and should be accompanied by a change in job classification and pay.

An implementation project requiring many additional temporary employees for six months or more will generate demands from the union to make the jobs permanent.

Management Consultants

Many municipalities do not have enough experience with similar projects to be confident about the process or some of the technical decisions to be made. There are numerous consultants available who can help the municipality. However, it is important that the selected consultant be independent; that is, have no links with any of the products or companies being considered. The consultant can act as a resource. Ideally, the consultant will have experience in working with other municipalities and dealing with the products and vendors under consideration.

Some consultants specialize in helping organizations plan, select, and implement new computer systems. These consultants, having gone through the process before, can provide management with insights into people problems before they occur and suggestions for solving the problems if they do occur.

The consultant need not spend a lot of time or money to be of great value. Some municipalities bring in a consultant to act as a resource to the project manager and to sit on the Steering Committee. By structuring the consultant's role, the municipality can benefit greatly from the consultant's experience in similar situations at little cost.

Key roles for the consultant are:

- Participating in Steering Committee meetings.
- Identifying potential suppliers.
- Reviewing the selection process.
- Reviewing the final report.
- Providing assurance to management and council.

Suppliers

Suppliers play several different roles during the project. Initially, the supplier is one of the bidders. During this time, the municipality would have seen only the supplier's best side because it was trying to woo the organization.

During contract negotiations, both the supplier and the municipality may have shown a new face. Negotiations are, by their very nature, adversarial. During negotiations it is important to remember that the deal must be reasonable for both parties. It is unreasonable to expect the supplier to give up its profit on the project, or to give guarantees in areas not totally within its control.

Following negotiations, the municipality must work with the supplier to make the project a success. Often, the same people who dealt with the municipality during the proposal will negotiate the contract and then manage the project.

The project manager should recognize that the supplier and the municipality are likely to start off speaking different languages. Each will be using terminology based on their view of the world and their work environment. The project manager should meet with the supplier's representative to discuss the overall project and to begin to build bridges of understanding. The project manager should initiate regular review sessions with the supplier to discuss progress, plans and problems.

Communications with suppliers, even those with extremely amiable representatives, is difficult. Formal documentation should be the rule. Progress is reported in writing. Problems, changes, and plans should all be communicated in writing.

During implementation, the supplier's staff plays

a dual role: they are members of a project team and they are experts in the selected system. As experts, they should be consulted concerning systems matters. However, as members of a project team they are also subject to delays and problems.

When problems do occur as a result of the supplier's actions, or lack thereof, the project manager should deal with the supplier's project manager. The project manager should not attempt to identify the specific person responsible for the problem — that's the supplier's job. Be concerned only about the problem and its effects on the project.

If competence of supplier's staff is an issue, the project manager should deal with the supplier's project manager or the person who signed the contract. A municipality should insist on qualified, competent staff. It is better to halt a project pending new staff than to proceed using staff who are unacceptable to the municipality.

■ 3.6.1 Professional Procurement Adding Value to the Process[9]

Professional purchasers, particularly in the public sector, receive specific training in the area of proposal development and evaluation for the express purpose of ensuring best value in addition to fairness and accountability. This training is unique when compared with that of lawyers. It should be the lawyer's role to advise the stakeholders and the purchasing manager as to the likelihood of litigation. The purchasing manager, on the other hand, provides advice to the stakeholders in regard to evaluation based on utility, intangible value and costs. The purchasing manager also performs the requisite "match" of the process and documentation being contemplated against the particular corporation's policies, procedures and precedents.

Checklist #3: Value Added Through Professional Procurement

A Checklist of Important Tasks —

Needs Definition Phase:

1. Assists in defining the requirements.

2. Provides advice on alternative products/services.

3. Recommends different procurement approaches (e.g., obtaining the equipment and related maintenance services in the same RFP).

4. Advises on quality assurance alternatives.

5. Provides information on corporate standards, priorities, policies and in-house resources.

Planning Phase:

6. Provides advice on the time and nature of work required to conduct market research, research existing contracts, coordinate procurement with other users, source potential vendors, investigate solutions at other companies, prepare and issue the RFP, evaluate proposals, negotiate contracts, and secure all internal approvals.

7. Builds in process steps to ensure fairness and acceptability.

Research Phase:

8. Assesses economic and political environment to determine any impact on the planned procurement. For example, are tax laws changing? Is the value of the Canadian dollar rising? What are the transportation logistics?

9. Assesses internal information to determine if there have been vendor performance problems experienced by others.

10. Assesses external information in the indus-

try to determine what opportunities exist and the degree of competitiveness in the marketplace.

11. Determines the organization's relative position of strength and the factors that will maintain this, and considers the potential risks in the procurement.

12. Devises alternative acquisition methods when a creative solution is required and recommends a method consistent with policies, bylaws, best practices, etc.

13. Recommends changes to the plan to reflect mar-ket and internal conditions which may affect the results.

Sourcing Phase:

14. Assembles or creates suitable terms, conditions, instructions and special provisions which reflect the best approach after considering the research information. Considers life cycle and cost/benefit in determining price schedules.

15. Secures acceptance of all participants (other departments or cooperative partners) of the solicitation package and process.

16. Develops a list of potential bidders and issues and receives all public documents.

17. Receives and documents inquiries during the RFP or negotiation process, arranges vendor briefings as required and coordinates technical inquiries through the client.

18. Plans and conducts negotiations in accordance with standards for professional procurement.

19. Assesses critical information items for documenting in the corporate record in the event of a dispute or litigation.

Analysis Phase:

20. Conducts independent public openings and documents all official bid results.

21. Reviews all proposals received for irregulari-ties and develops spreadsheets of bid amounts, irregularities, and pertinent information for consideration by client. Also monitors results for compliance with internal and external policies and the Competition Act.

22. Conducts evaluation or provides assistance, determines treatment of irregularities and requests for additional information outside of the official process. (For example, pricing after the fact for missed items)

23. Coordinates all the parties and seeks consensus on the recommended vendor(s).

Awards Phase:

24. Regularly updates a standard award report form for senior management and prepares final reports for corporate-wide procurements or assists client in this.

25. Notifies unsuccessful bidders, conducts debriefings, and handles bid protests in accordance with standard policy and procedures.

26. Creates and communicates corporate standards for contracting utilizing the solicitation terms, conditions, as amended during contract negotiations.

27. Develops implementation and performance monitoring strategies and ensures expectations of both parties (client and vendor) are clear and that vendor delivery and billings are acceptable.

28. Implements automatic payments and payment discount procedures.

Contract Management Phase:

29. Handles performance disputes between client and vendor and takes appropriate action including holdbacks and other remedies to discharge the contract.

30. Establishes and maintains tickler files to begin new acquisition cycle upon expiration of established contracts.

3·7

Important Lessons

There are many different ways of improving the RFP process and document. Here are nine suggestions based on recent workshops given in a jurisdiction with few rules or guidelines concerning the amount of information to be included in the RFP document.

1. Disclose more information.

Most participants agreed that the more information provided in the RFP, the better the resulting proposals. It is very helpful to a supplier to have details about many factors including the budget, the number of companies invited to submit proposals, the evaluation process, criteria and weights, as well as any unusual contract terms.

If the RFP is based on a planning document or a feasibility study, then reference the earlier study and make it available to the suppliers.

With more information, some suppliers may decline to submit proposals. This will save all parties time and money. Alternatively, those proposals that are submitted will provide a closer fit with the requirements.

Some organizations, such as Yukon Government, issue a quarterly forecast of upcoming solicitations; others, such as BC Systems Corp. issue RFPs in draft form first.

2. Help the evaluators.

It is important that each of the evaluators deals with the process, the RFPs and the suppliers in a consistent and defensible manner. Often evaluators are inexperienced and welcome some direction on their role.

Some projects have an RFP officer who provides the project manager and evaluators with on-going advice, information about the evaluation process and scoring mechanisms, worksheets for conducting the evaluation, and guidance concerning best practices, policies and legal requirements, such as freedom of information.

3. Publish the budget.

This is a highly contentious issue which divided the participants. However, all agreed that it is critical for suppliers to submit proposals that are within budget. If every proposal exceeds the budget by 50 percent or more, the competence of the organization preparing the RFP becomes an issue.

Often, requirements are not specific enough to ensure that at least one proposal is within budget. Alternatively, the RFP may be asking for too much. In these cases, publishing the budget figure restricts the proposals developed by each supplier or leads the supplier to "no bid."

4. Manage the RFP process as a project.

Provide the project manager with sufficient time and resources to do a good job. Assign an experienced project manager. Use a standardized list of tasks. Identify the duration, deliverables, staff and skills required. Identify any approvals that are required and provide an appropriate amount of time.

5. Include weights in the RFP.

This approach was also contentious but there seemed to be more agreement than on the "publish the budget" issue.

Typically, an evaluation is based on criteria and weights. The criteria represent key characteristics such as price, ease of use of a new computer system, soundness of the project plan, experience of the vendor, and technical merit of the proposed solution.

The importance of each factor is reflected in its weight — the number of points assigned to that factor.

Many jurisdictions provide little or no information in the RFP about the weights. In some jurisdictions, the relative weight of each factor is described. For example, "technical merit is more important than each of the other factors." In other jurisdictions, the

actual weight is published: "technical merit is worth 70 (of 100) total points."

Suppliers will develop different proposals based on either their guesses about the points or the actual weight of each factor. The solution proposed when price is worth 30 points and technical merit is worth 70 will be very different than when price is worth 70.

6. Structure the proposals

Providing a rigid structure for the proposals as part of the RFP will simplify the evaluation. Some RFPs contain charts with each feature identified in the first column. Remaining columns are completed by the supplier identifying or qualifying its ability to comply. Some RFPs contain spreadsheets to standardize the financial comparison of proposals. Other RFPs identify the specific table of contents for the proposal and the detailed contents of each section.

Typically, it is a mandatory requirement that the proposal be completed to comply with the specified format.

7. Standardize the scoring.

Having a standard approach eliminates personal bias and takes some of the arbitrariness out of scoring. A good working definition of when to assign a five as opposed to an eight, for example, will ensure that evaluators can agree on a score rather than simply averaging the different scores.

8. Use risk as an evaluation criterion.

Some RFPs now ask each proponent to identify and discuss the risks associated with the project. This discussion will outline the proponent's experience on similar projects as well as provide valuable information for the project manager. Proponents are instructed to identify steps which can be taken to mitigate these risks.

9. Design the evaluation process to reflect the business needs.

The evaluation process determines the "winner." The same proposal can "win" in one process and not be a serious finalist in another. Consider these three different processes. In each, assume that the proposals considered satisfy the mandatory requirements of the RFP.

• If you are looking for a least-cost solution, then simply evaluate all proposals that satisfy your mandatory conditions and select the least expensive one.

• If you are looking for the proposal which provides the "best solution" within budget, then select the one with the highest point score that doesn't exceed the budget.

• If you are looking for the proposal which you believe can provide a sound solution and still costs less than the most expensive one, simply evaluate all proposals that satisfy your mandatory conditions. Then select all of those with a score more than some predetermined number (say 700 out of 1000 available points.) All of these proposals will be classified as "capable of providing a sound solution." Select the least expensive from this group.

3.8

Changing the RFP Process

How much change can you make in the RFP process once the RFP has been issued? Can you change the due date? Can you modify the requirements or other information contained in the RFP?

Before attempting to answer these questions, let's identify the types of changes that may be considered and their significance. The first category is that of "no change" or "minor change," including modifications to correct minor errors, ambiguities, and typos. Second, there is "changing the deadline." Finally, there are "material changes" — changes in the published evaluation criteria or weights; in the mandatory conditions, and major changes in the requirements or technical information provided in the RFP.

The rules regarding change are established by governing law, courts, policies, information contained in the RFP, and by established practices. The nature of permissible changes varies within and between jurisdictions. There is no established standard in this area. The discussion which follows deals with each type of change and how it is handled in different jurisdictions and organizations.

1. No Change

Obviously, change disrupts the smooth execution of the process. Too much change and suppliers will abandon their efforts to prepare an effective proposal. Ideally, there are no changes in the RFP as issued. This idealized situation does occur, but infrequently. Minor changes are common. However, even with minor changes, there is a limit to the amount of change that can be introduced while maintaining a managed process. Radical changes in RFPs after they are issued are unusual and will probably result in cancellation of the RFP. Some organizations, rather than suffering the embarrassment of canceling an RFP, simply let it run its course and then award no contract.

2. Minor Change

These changes are often identified by the issuer in reviewing the RFP that has been issued, or in response to phone calls from suppliers about obvious omissions, errors or ambiguities in the RFP. It is common practice for organizations to amend RFPs shortly after they have been issued. In some jurisdictions, this practice is sanctioned by law or by policy[10].

(a) Before the opening of bids or proposals, a solicitation may be amended, or the time for opening may be extended, upon the procurement officer's determination that the extension or amendment is in the state's best interest. All potential bidders or offerors known to have copies of the solicitation shall be advised of the extension or amendment.

3. Extension of the deadline

Sometimes, for quite legitimate reasons, the deadline for submission is extended. However, this change is, at best, awkward. At worst, it is unfair and may be challenged by a supplier.

In open competitions, some suppliers may receive the RFP and, on the basis of the deadline, decide to "no bid." In reviewing the document, they concluded that there wasn't sufficient time for them to prepare a proper proposal. If, two weeks later, the issuer announces an extension of the deadline by two weeks, they still may "no bid." The extension provided them with no additional time. Those firms, on the other hand, that had begun to create their proposal when they received the RFP, would have an extra two weeks to prepare. For these reasons, firms that initially decided to "no bid" may be aggrieved by the extension and complain about the fairness of the process.

In competitions where the suppliers were pre-qualified and therefore known to the issuer, the issuer could seek the agreement of all the potential bidders to the extension. In this case, if accepted by all, it would be implemented. If not, the original deadline would survive. To do otherwise would risk a challenge to the fairness of the process.

In competitions where all of the suppliers attend the suppliers meeting, the issuer could seek agreement as with the pre-qualified group.

In some jurisdictions, this practice is sanctioned by law or by policy.

4. Material Changes

Material changes involve important new data or substantial changes in the content of the RFP. For example, material changes would be: published weight of an evaluation factor was increased from 10 percent to 50 percent; a new mandatory condition was imposed; or 10 pages of new detailed requirements were added. All of these constitute material changes.

It is difficult to introduce major changes and still defend the process as being fair. Often, organizations are forced to cancel the RFP when these types of changes are identified. It is much easier to "get it right" the first time.

In some jurisdictions, the introduction of major changes after issuing the RFP is prohibited by law, by policy or by practice.

3.9

Certifying Compliance

A growing number of organizations require that an independent party certify the soundness of the RFP process. Some of these organizations provide an RFP officer to the project team; others simply audit the process after the award has been made.

Here is a typical audit letter that I would issue after having worked on a large procurement as the RFP officer:

Dear Project Director:

My mandate:

On July 15, 1995, I was engaged as the RFP Officer on the XXXXX Project. One of my tasks was to ensure that the selection process was "visibly fair" and "publicly defensible." Now that the selection process has been completed, I am submitting my report on this matter.

The standards I employed

In 1992, I wrote a book entitled "The RFP Process." In this book, I outlined those factors which I believe must be present to ensure that an RFP is both fair and defensible. Those factors are described on pages 4-1 to 4-3 of the book. (I have attached these pages to this letter.) Those factors were the criteria I used in forming my opinion.

My conclusions

I wish to commend you, your Steering Committee and your project team for the overall conduct of this process. It is my opinion that great care was taken by all to ensure that the integrity of the selection process was maintained from project planning through contract signing.

My reliance on specified events

While I was unable to observe each and every task associated with the process, I did observe many of the critical tasks:

1. I participated in the construction of the RFP. In so doing, I took great care to ensure that the requirements and various terms and conditions did not favor any particular supplier. The RFP itself contained much information about the project and was based on the principle of full disclosure.

2. The RFP was reviewed and approved by the project authority, the Management Steering Committee and legal counsel prior to its release.

3. The selection process was defined in writing and reviewed by the Project Authority prior to receipt of the proposals.

4. The proponents meeting was chaired by myself. A transcript was made available to all proponents at the same time.

5. All inquiries were handled via your office. All inquiries and responses thereto were in writing and were provided to all known proponents.

6. Prior to the evaluation process, the evaluation team was briefed on proper procedure by myself.

7. Separate evaluation teams dealt with functional specifications and costs.

8. The evaluation team attended the structured presentations and evaluated the proponents.

9. The recommended supplier was the unanimous choice of the evaluation team and was selected by employing the documented evaluation procedure.

Cumulatively, these observations demonstrate compliance with all the criteria identified in "The RFP Process."

Statement of compliance

To the extent that these tasks are a fair representation of the conduct of the project, I believe that the selection process was done in a visibly fair and ethical manner.

Yours sincerely ...

[1] Section 82.270, Reference *9.
[2] Section 82.270, Reference *4.
[3] Page 4.8, Reference *2.
[4] Page 6, Reference *24.
[5] See page 1-5, Reference *1.
[6] Pages 8-12, Reference *15.
[7] Section 82.010, Reference *9.
[8] Article 3, page 16, Reference *4.
[9] Issue #5, Reference *17.
[10] Article 14, page 40, Reference *8.

CHAPTER 4

The RFP Document

~ CONTENTS ~

CHAPTER 4

The RFP Document

— CONTENTS CONTD. —

4.1

How Much Information?

There are many types and sources of information about the RFP document:

1. Your organization's policies, rules and guidelines.

    2. Copies of old RFPs.

    3. Tables of contents of old RFPs.

    4. Standardized documents and contracts.

    5. Reference publications.

    6. Access to experienced people.

In this chapter, we focus on the RFP document by examining RFPs from many organizations in a number of different jurisdictions. We first discuss the role of specifications, then review the tables of contents for a variety of different types of RFPs, and discuss examples of complex RFPs. The final section of this chapter discusses different approaches to standardizing either the entire RFP document or specific sections.

How do you prepare an RFP? What must be included in the document? Suppose you are briefing a new manager with only limited experience in this process. What information and tools do you provide to promote the efficient production of an effective RFP?

Since the RFP document has a pivotal role in the purchasing and contracting process, it is extremely important that it be accurate, comprehensive, easily understood and complete. It must reflect your organization's policies and practices. It must provide sufficient information about the requirements and the evaluation process for an effective and practical proposal to be prepared.

One of the fundamental issues faced by most organizations is "how much information do we provide to suppliers?" In principle, the approach adopted by many jurisdictions is simple: provide suppliers with as much information as possible. These organizations reason that the more information suppliers have, the better the proposals. Creative solutions often require much detailed information about the specific issues and problems.

There are several other factors which also

support this approach. First, in many jurisdictions, there are access to information laws which permit suppliers to audit the RFP process. Under these laws, suppliers can obtain the evaluators' notes and details of the process. It is increasingly difficult, if not impossible, for purchasers to conceal details of their work.

A typical policy statement about information access follows[1]:

5. Reasonable access must be provided to government policy documents and related contracting materials upon request. Materials available for distribution are to be supplied in a non-discriminatory manner, and any fees charged for such distribution are to be reasonable.

Second, when suppliers are fully informed about the details of the procurement, the requirements and the process, they can make informed decisions related to producing a proposal. Suppliers can spend tens of thousands of dollars preparing a proposal. With more information, a supplier might be better able to determine beforehand that its approach will not succeed. It will, therefore, "no bid" and save itself much time and money.

Alternatively, a supplier might determine from the details in the RFP that it could win if it remedied one shortcoming. For example, the supplier identifies the need for an expert in geology, which it does not have. Rather than "no bid," the supplier could enlist the assistance of another organization with the required expertise either as a partner or as a subcontractor. In either case, the issuer would obtain a better proposal.

In this environment — one of a reasonably free exchange of information — there are fewer complaints from suppliers concerning the award.

Finally, in many jurisdictions, the courts have been called upon to enforce procurement and contract laws. Their decisions have caused organizations to include more, rather than less, information in the RFP. Some courts have declared that purchasing organizations have several duties toward the vendors submitting proposals. For example:

• Duty to treat all suppliers in a fair and equal manner.

• Duty not to misrepresent the situation.

• Duty of full disclosure of information.

• Duty to warn vendors of known dangers.

Important Lessons

There are many different ways of improving the RFP process and document. Adding specific information is easy to do and pays handsome dividends. Here are some suggestions based on recent workshops that were given in a jurisdiction with few rules or guidelines concerning the amount of information to be included in the RFP document. In some of the more highly regulated and structured jurisdictions, these suggestions are already implemented either by regulation, by policy, or as "best practices."

Disclose More Information

Most participants agreed that the more information provided in the RFP, the better the resulting proposals. It is very helpful to a supplier to have details about many factors including the budget, the number of companies invited to submit proposals, the evaluation process, criteria and weights, as well as any unusual contract terms.

If the RFP is based on a planning document or a feasibility study, then reference the earlier study and make it available to the suppliers.

With more information, some suppliers may decline to submit proposals. This will save all parties time and money. Alternatively, those proposals that are submitted will provide a closer fit with the requirements.

Publish the Budget

This was a highly contentious issue which divided the participants. Some thought that it was dangerous to give suppliers this information. Their fear was that once suppliers knew the budget, then all the resulting proposals would be for this amount. There would be no solutions at 50 percent of budget.

Others felt differently. They believed that suppliers, knowing the budget, would put in proposals which were acceptable. They believed that competition would still lead suppliers to submit solutions well under budget.

Both groups agreed that it is critical for suppliers to submit proposals that are within budget. If every proposal exceeds the budget by 50 percent or more, the competence of the organization preparing the RFP becomes an issue.

Often, stated requirements are not specific enough to ensure that at least one proposal is with-

in budget. Alternatively, the RFP may be asking for too much. In these cases, publishing the budget figure restricts the proposals developed by each supplier or leads the supplier to "no bid."

Often, organizations are underfunded. They require a solution, but they expect that the budget is inadequate. In this case, there is great advantage in publishing the budget. Some suppliers will "no bid" because the funding is inadequate. Other suppliers will take a more creative approach. They will examine the requirements and then investigate alternative approaches for satisfying some, if not all, of the needs.

Include Weights in the RFP

This approach was also contentious but there seemed to be more agreement than on the "publish the budget" issue. All agreed that a supplier's behaviour in terms of its approach to an RFP is greatly influenced by the evaluation criteria and weights.

Typically, an evaluation is based on criteria and weights. The criteria represent key characteristics such as price, ease of use of a new computer system, soundness of the project plan, experience of the vendor, and technical merit of the proposed solution. The importance of each factor is reflected in its weight, the number of points assigned to that factor.

Some jurisdictions provide little or no information in the RFP about the weights. In other jurisdictions, the relative weight of each factor is described. For example, "technical merit is more important than each of the other factors." In highly regulated jurisdictions, the actual weight is published: "technical merit is worth 70 (of 100) total points."

Suppliers will develop different proposals based on either their guesses about, or their knowledge of, the points or the actual weight of each factor. The solution proposed when price is worth 30 points and technical merit worth 70 points will be very different than when price is worth 70. A knowledge of the weights helps ensure that the suppliers focus on factors that are important to the purchaser.

Structure the Proposals

Providing a rigid structure for the proposals as part of the RFP will simplify the evaluation. Some RFPs contain charts with each feature identified in the first column. Remaining columns are completed by the supplier identifying or qualifying its ability to comply. Some RFPs contain spreadsheets to standardize the financial comparison of proposals. Other RFPs identify the specific table of contents for the proposal and the detailed contents of each section.

Typically, it is a mandatory requirement that the proposal be completed to comply with the specified format. Structured proposals are easier to evaluate.

4.2

What Goes in an RFP?

There are several ways to specify the contents of an RFP: by law, by policy, by guidelines or simply by example. At the operational level, all organizations use old RFPs to help prepare new ones. Later in this chapter, we will present sample RFPs and RFP templates.

First, let's see how RFPs are specified in law, or in policy. In Alaska, the State Procurement Code deals with the contents[2]:

A request for proposal must contain that information necessary for an offeror to submit a proposal or contain references to any information that cannot reasonably be included with the request. The request must provide a description of the factors that will be considered by the procurement officer when evaluating the proposals received, including the relative importance of price and other evaluation factors...

Many organizations, through their directives and policies, identify the specific pieces of information to be contained in the RFP. However, some organizations do not insist that the RFP contain the contract terms, nor a full description of the evaluation process. Here is an example from the Government of Yukon[3]:

40. A request for bids or proposals will include the following information:

(a) The essential terms of the contract(s)... to be awarded including:

(i) a full description of the goods or services ...

(ii) the form, amount, and terms and conditions of any required performance security...

(iii) the completion date or any other timing considerations...

(iv) other terms and conditions which would be relevant...

(b) terms and conditions for the submission of bids or proposals...

(c) a full description of the manner in which bids or proposals will be evaluated including:

(i) the method to be used to evaluate bids or proposals

(ii) the evaluation criteria, stated in such a manner as to clearly identify all the information to be provided by the bidder or proponent which will be used to evaluate the bid or proposal...

In Washington state, the policy takes special note of the RFP contents[4]:

3. Agencies conducting RFP's shall:

a. Provide vendors with the vendor protest procedure as outlined in the section titled Protest Procedure.

b. Use the "Standard Clauses" as contained in Appendix B, and other terms and conditions appropriate for the specific type of contract to be negotiated.

c. Include in the RFP the specific criteria that shall be used to evaluate vendor responses.

f. Notify vendors that they may bring their complaints about the solicitation document to the attention of DIS. (See Protest Procedure).

h. Select the apparently successful vendor based on the RFP evaluation criteria.

■ 4.2.1 The Role of Specifications or Requirements

The most important part of the RFP, in determining the quality of the solutions proposed by suppliers, is the specifications. Recognizing the critical role of specifications in shaping supplier responses, many organizations take great care to define their form and structure.

In Alaska, the Procurement Code first defines

"specifications," then identifies their purpose and scope, and, finally, cautions against overly restrictive requirements.

...specification means a description of the physical or functional characteristics, or of the nature of a supply, service, professional service or construction project...

...Specifications must promote overall economy for the purposes intended and encourage competition in satisfying the state's needs, and may not be unduly restrictive...

(a) The purpose of a specification is to serve as a basis for obtaining, in a cost effective manner, a supply, service, or construction item suitable for the state's needs.

(b) Specifications must, to the extent practicable, emphasize functional or performance criteria while limiting design or other detailed physical descriptions to those necessary to meet the needs of the state. Purchasing agencies should include as a part of their purchase requisitions the principal functional or performance needs to be met...

All specifications must describe the requirements to be met without having the effect of exclusively requiring a proprietary supply, service, construction item, or procurement from a sole source, unless no other manner of description will suffice.

The Model RFP developed by the state of Alaska[5] instructs the procurement officer to "be as specific and comprehensive as you possibly can." It goes on to state: Don't presume that they (vendors) will "get it" if you don't say it.

The sample RFP developed by BC Systems Corp. instructs the procurement officer concerning the requirements section[6]:

Requirement Definitions:

Indicate what the vendor needs to know about the overall approach you have selected for the project/ purchase.

Narrative of general goals and objectives of the project.

Scope and size of project.

Mandatory requirements.

Outline your requirements in respect of:

- **workplan, resource requirements, deliverables**
- **maintenance/enhancement**
- **development methodology**
- **programming standards**
- **experience/past performance/qualifications/ capabilities expected**
- **project management plan**
- **progress reporting and meetings**
- **structure of project team**

If the requirements are not stated accurately and clearly, poor proposals will be produced. If requirements are stated in a way which is perceived as being unnecessarily restrictive or favoring a particular supplier or approach, then you can expect to hear from the vendors, either informally or through the formal protest process or through the political process.

To ensure that there are no serious deficiencies in the requirements, some organizations invite vendors in to brief them on the particular area of expertise prior to writing the RFP. Other organizations release the RFP in a draft form for vendor comments. Others permit suppliers to identify apparent deficiencies between the time of issue and the closing date.

If your requirements are truly deficient and require major revisions, then it is better to withdraw the RFP. Alternatively, you could end up with inappropriate products or poorly defined solutions that could carry with them major political and legal consequences.

4.3

Sample Tables of Contents

There are many sources for good ideas which can improve your RFP. The table of contents of another organization's RFP can be used as a checklist against yours. It may help you to identify some areas or issues which you have not considered.

The next few pages describe five different RFPs. They progress from simple to more comprehensive. Only the tables of contents are provided. These tables offer insights into how organizations structure their RFPs and identify some of the critical issues. Tables of contents can be used as checklists for items and topics.

■ 4.3.1 Example #1: A Simple RFP

Table of Contents

I   Purpose

II   Evaluation Criteria

III   System Requirements

IV   Proposal Format

RFPs take many different forms. Each form reflects a different organization, culture, set of priorities, skills and requirements. In reviewing a variety of RFPs, you will see that many of them have four sections in common: Ground Rules, System Requirements, Evaluation Criteria, and Format of the Proposal.

Ground Rules

This first section typically identifies the purpose of the RFP, the name of the person to contact for further information, and the number of copies required. This section may include a timetable of dates relevant to the project. It may also address a wide variety of other issues and contain statements such as: "a corporate officer must sign the proposal"; "the issuer is not liable for costs"; and "the proposal will be incorporated in any resultant contract."

Requirements

This section deals with the specific requirements. It attempts to define the users' needs or problems. For example, if the RFP deals with acquiring a "turnkey" system — computer equipment, software, and applications packages from the same supplier — this section would contain a description of each of the current systems. It may also identify any known shortcomings or required enhancements. It would include a table of the volumes of each type of transaction both now, at the peak season, and for several years in the future.

Evaluation Criteria

This section identifies how the decision is to be made — how the best or most appropriate supplier and product will be selected. Many factors can influence the selection: cost, goodness of fit, support services available, and contractual conditions. At a minimum, this section should identify each of the factors which will be utilized. Some organizations only provide vague descriptions of the evaluation criteria; others go much further and identify not only each factor but its weight and the selection process itself.

Proposal Format

The final section of this simple RFP structures the proposal. It is important that each supplier provide its information in a comparable form. Imposing a sequence on all suppliers saves many hours of hunting through hundreds of pages of text.

A common organization for proposals is presented below:

1. Letter of Transmittal
2. Executive Summary
3. Our Understanding of the Requirements
4. Proposed Equipment, Software and Services
5. Costs
6. Physical Requirements
7. Training
8. Conversion Plan
9. Reliability and Backup
10. Project Plan and Timetable
11. Standard Agreements

■ 4.3.2 Example #2: Manufacturer

The previous section identified the minimum requirements for an RFP. But there are many variations on this theme. RFPs can be as short as three pages or as long as a collection of books. Examples #2 through #4 identify major improvements over the basic RFP (Example #1).

Table of Contents

1. Introduction
2. Possible Suppliers
3. Terms of Reference
4. Overall Goals
5. Current Environment
6. General Requirements
7. Specific Requirements
8. Appendices

Let's begin by examining an RFP only slightly more complex than the initial example. This RFP was issued by a large manufacturer with plants and distribution centers from coast to coast. The firm wanted to select a long-term supplier of an Integrated Office System supporting functions such as electronic mail, word processing, spreadsheets, graphics, office manager, communications and database.

You can see in the table of contents that the RFP contains a section titled "possible suppliers." This is unusual. Firms generally like to keep suppliers in the dark about the competition. However, for this organization, identifying the companies invited was part of the acquisition strategy. In fact, great care was taken to ensure that only those suppliers capable of doing the job were identified and spurious ones were eliminated. Each of the six suppliers identified in the RFP had been judged as able to satisfy the mandatory requirements. This initial screening — identifying the leaders in the field — took several months to complete. However, the size of the organization, the potential impact of the new systems and the long-term financial commitment warranted this approach.

■ 4.3.3 Example #3: State Agency

Table of Contents

Appendix C   Draft Agreement

This Request for Proposal was prepared by a state agency. The RFP reflected the investment of large amounts of time, money and experience. The approach to identifying requirements was especially well-done. In the requirements section, over 100 specific technical features were addressed. The accompanying compliance table listed each of the technical features and provided a space for the supplier to enter "yes" or "no." In addition, the compliance table identified whether each feature was mandatory, desirable or whether the question was simply for information purposes only.

Incorporation of this table in the RFP simplified the work of the evaluators and made it easy to highlight major weaknesses. The supplier then could address the specific shortcomings. In so doing, the quality and clarity of the proposals were improved.

■ 4.3.4 Example #4: Distributor

Table of Contents

This Request for Proposal, issued by a distributor, was for the replacement of its aging computer equipment and applications programs.

This RFP was well-organized and reflects a large amount of work by the distributor. The entire RFP process was centered on the use of an extensive vendor questionnaire. This questionnaire was over 130 pages in length and, as can be seen, is organized into six major areas (6.1 through 6.6).

Much of the success of this project could be attributed to the 83-page applications suitability section. This part of the questionnaire identified hundreds of specific requirements for each application program. Each vendor was required to "fill in the blanks."

The distributor categorized each requirement as mandatory or desirable. Each vendor was required to indicate how the proposed system would deal with this feature. This was done by putting a check mark in the appropriate column opposite this feature in the questionnaire. Columns were provided to categorize each feature as available as part of the standard system, to be added to the standard system at extra cost, to be added to the standard system at no extra cost, unavailable, or not required.

By delineating the specific requirements and organizing the vendors' responses into a standard form, the distributor was able to identify clearly the best two systems and suppliers. The final selection was made on the basis of demonstrations and track record.

■ 4.3.5 Example #5: Government Department

Table of Contents

Overview

This Request for Proposal (RFP) document is intended to assist vendors in the preparation of proposals to satisfy the stated requirements for the provision and support of computing equipment and software packages.

The Appendices contain specific details of this project's requirements which are to be satisfied by the vendor's proposed solutions.

1. Introduction

   1.1 Background

   1.2 Objective

   1.3 Functional Requirements

   1.4 System Capacity

   1.5 Initial Equipment Requirements

   1.6 Future Possible Equipment

2. Competitive Process

   2.1 Intent

   2.2 Goods and Services

   2.3 Rules for RFP Process

      2.3.1 Communications

      2.3.2 Treatment of Information

      2.3.3 General

   2.4 Schedule of Events

      2.4.1 Schedule

      2.4.2 Vendor Qualification

      2.4.3 Notice of Intent to Bid

      2.4.4 Receipt of Vendor Proposals

      2.4.5 Announcement of Successful Vendor

      2.4.6 Acceptance Testing

3. Proposal Selection

   3.1 Objectives

   3.2 Evaluation Process

      3.2.1 Qualification

      3.2.2 Viability of Implementation and Operation

      3.2.3 Credibility of Proposal

      3.2.4 Capacity of Equipment Proposed

      3.2.5 Service

      3.2.6 Technical Merit

      3.2.7 Effective Operating Cost

         3.2.7.1 Overview

         3.2.7.2 Late Delivery

         3.2.7.3 Other Costs

         3.2.7.4 Audit

4. Vendor Submissions

   4.1 General

      4.1.1 Reply Format

This Request for Proposal was for new equipment and applications software for four operating units in different locations. As can be seen from the table of contents, the document is a highly structured RFP, leaving few issues unidentified. The main body of the RFP itself was relatively short — under 20 pages.

The thoroughness and completeness of this RFP is reflected in its organization. The table of contents constitutes a reasonable checklist of issues and can by used by other organizations as a guideline when preparing an RFP.

4.4

Sample RFPs

Examples are an excellent way of transmitting detailed information about actual RFP documents and practices. This section contains an example of a relatively complex RFP, a discussion of some problems and features of a second RFP, and a description of some important RFP add-ons.

■ 4.4.1 Example of a Complex RFP

This section contains a discussion of key features of this large, complex RFP followed by an edited version of the actual RFP.

This RFP incorporates an evaluation process based on the following components:[7]

1. **Establish Compliance**
2. **Score the Proposals**
3. **Develop a Short-List**
4. **Interview Suppliers**
5. **Score the Proposals**
6. **Develop a Short-List**

7. **Demonstrate the Software**
8. **Score the Proposals**

Maintenance Management Systems

In 1990, Alaska issued this RFP for Automated Maintenance Management Systems. The RFP was to select a supplier for the purchase, modification and installation of systems (software and equipment) to meet the needs of both the State Equipment Fleet and the Alaska International Airport System.

The RFP (and its numerous attachments) was more than 140 pages long. An edited version of the RFP is contained in Part II.

There are many noteworthy features of this RFP. Some of these, such as the inclusion of the proposed project funding amount (Section 1.20 Proposed Project Funding) deal with fundamental issues. Others, such as the inclusion of the contract and the requirement for a demonstration of the software, are simply good practices which assist both the bidders and the evaluators.

This is a complex RFP. It encompasses a wide range of services. The project itself was large and highly visible. The creators of this RFP have included some features to help the vendors deal with its complexity and to ensure that the evaluation process was understood by the bidders and was seen as being open and fair.

The remainder of this chapter discusses some of these key features. The headings and section numbers used are those found in the actual RFP. Items are dealt with in the same sequence as they are presented in the RFP.

1.01 Intent

This section contains a high-level summary of key elements and mandatory requirements. Its inclusion helps bidders identify critical issues to be addressed.

1.10 Proposals

This section emphasizes certain mandatory features of the proposal. For example, failure to submit a proposal in the prescribed format will result in the rejection of that proposal.

1.12 Acceptance of Proposal Content

The creators of this RFP were obviously concerned about the RFP being challenged by a supplier. The challenges could arise in terms of the format, the legal requirements, or the process. To ensure that the process would go ahead even if challenged, the RFP required that suppliers review the RFP "without delay." If a supplier then objected

to part of the RFP, the supplier was instructed to inform the procurement officer in writing "no later than ten (10) working days" before the closing date. This would permit the procurement officer to issue any necessary amendments "in order to prevent the opening of a defective solicitation." The creators of this RFP go on to state that if a protest was not made in time, then the protest would be disallowed.

1.16 Subcontractors

Purchasers are often concerned about the use of subcontractors. In the past, suppliers have incorporated subcontractors into their proposals without identifying them as subcontractors. Clearly, the use of subcontractors affects the evaluation of the proposal. The greater the use of subcontractors, the greater the number of entities to be managed. Coordination of many different employees from five or six different firms is much more difficult than from one company.

Purchasers are also concerned about their legal recourse. They want to ensure that all companies and people working on a project are bound by the same legal agreement. This is not necessarily the case if subcontractors are used and they, in turn, use subcontractors.

To ensure that the evaluators are fully aware of the status of each person and company proposed on the project, the RFP requires corporate and individual resumes of all subcontractors and a statement of the legal relationship with the prime contractor.

1.19 Availability of Additional Technical Data

Complex projects are often based on a large

amount of information: existing systems, studies, reports, standards, etc. Rather than include all of these documents (which may run to thousands of pages) in the RFP, they are included by reference. This approach ensures that the state is making full disclosure of all known and available information to all suppliers on the same basis.

This RFP indicates the type and location of additional information which can assist the bidders in understanding the current systems and requirements.

1.20 Proposed Project Funding

For many proposals, suppliers spend a great deal of time speculating about the budget. If their proposal is too expensive, they will not survive the initial cut. On the other hand, if their proposal costs too little, they may have neglected or omitted certain highly desirable features or services. Knowledge of the budget helps focus the supplier's proposal on key issues. In many situations, the least cost solution can be less than 50 percent of the cost of a fully-featured, fully-supported or more sophisticated solution. Often, the levels of support, number of features, or basic approach (the proposal strategy) is determined, in part, or entirely by the budget.

Few RFPs contain the budget. Many purchasers believe by publishing the budget they have set the cost of all proposals. They believe that few suppliers will submit a proposal for only 50 percent or 60 percent of the announced funding limit. These purchasers believe that once the budget is known, highly creative and cheap

solutions will not be proposed.

On the other hand, some RFPs establish such a wide range of requirements and use terms which encourage suppliers to propose only comprehensive and expensive solutions. These RFPs may not have the budget to afford these expensive solutions.

It is highly embarrassing when all proposals exceed the budget. In many jurisdictions, there is no recourse but to revise the RFP (to reduce the requirements) and to issue it again.

This RFP is an example of the situation in which the requirements, including the legal undertaking, could lead suppliers to propose solutions far exceeding $500,000. To ensure that all proposals are within the approved budget, yet deal with these comprehensive requirements, the creators of the RFP have published the approved budget. The RFP indicates that "proposals in excess of $575,000 will be considered non-responsive."

1.24 Multiple or Alternative Proposals

Suppliers often have several different approaches, or several different options or techniques that they can propose. Each option or technique has its merits and may be viewed differently by the evaluation committee. For this reason, some suppliers like to provide options within their proposal and let the evaluators decide on the selection of a particular option. This approach can make the evaluation process extremely complicated and provide an unfair advantage to a supplier proposing a solution constructed of various options to be chosen by the customer.

To eliminate this problem, the RFP simply

states that multiple proposals shall be considered non-responsive.

2.05 Bid Bond and Performance Bond

To ensure that the supplier submitting the winning proposal signs the contract, the RFP asks for a $10,000 bid bond.

To ensure that the selected supplier completes the work to the satisfaction of the state, the RFP asks for a performance bond equal to the value of the contract.

3.04 Proposal Instructions

The instructions describing the organization and content of each proposal are described in nine pages. These instructions are clear, precise and detailed. They deal with both the format and content of each section of the proposal. These instructions go a long way in standardizing the responses from each bidder. In so doing, they make the competition fair by soliciting directly comparable information from each supplier. Furthermore, they provide each supplier with a lot of information about how the proposals will be evaluated, and they identify many specific pieces of information that must be submitted as part of the proposal.

Response Item 6: Pricing Proposal

Purchasers are always concerned about the budget. Many organizations have experienced surprises during the course of a project related to "extras." These are items not included in the original project plan or costs related to small changes in requirements. One method of con-

trolling costs is to insist on a fixed-fee contract.

All of the requirements related to the pricing proposal are mandatory. This ensures that all of the prices are directly comparable. Furthermore, the state requires a fixed-price contract with no price adjustments after the contract has been signed.

The RFP identifies the cost categories that must be used. It defines the components of each category.

Response Item 7. Project Management Plan

Many organizations know that project management is a critical success factor. However, it is often difficult to decide on the questions to be included in the RFP. If the questions are not detailed enough, then it is difficult to judge the soundness of the plans. The RFP reflects the belief that project management issues are critical to the success of the project. This belief is also reflected in the amount of detailed information requested in the RFP.

3.07 Evaluation of Proposals

This section of the RFP provided the vendors with much detail about the evaluation process and the importance of various criteria.

The RFP takes seven pages to describe the three-step evaluation process:

1. The written response to the RFP.
2. An oral interview.
3. A live system demonstration.

Step 1 was worth 1500 points based on seven categories:

1. Alaska Vendor Preference   250

2.	General Requirements	250
3.	Functional Requirements	500
4.	Technical Requirements	100
5.	Project Approach and Plan	50
6.	Qualifications & Experience	100
7.	Cost Proposal Evaluation	250

Those vendors submitting the highest rated proposals were scheduled for oral interviews.

Step 2 consisted of the oral interview and was worth 300 points. Step 3 was the live demonstration, worth 700 points.

Based on this section of the RFP, vendors were able to focus their attention on those factors which the state deemed as important. For example, the demonstration of the system was worth 700 points, or 28 percent of the total score. Of these points, 300 were assigned to demonstrations of structured examples of system transactions. From this, it was clear that the state valued seeing transactions being performed more than it valued the qualifications and experience of the firm, worth only 100 points.

4.07 Offeror Obligations

This section of the RFP identifies specific obligations which the state requires the offeror to undertake, including activities such as project management, compliance with standards and conversion of all master files. By explicitly identifying all major tasks and responsibilities, the state wishes to avoid major errors of omission.

Section 5. General Contact Information

This section of the RFP identifies specific items which the state will incorporate into the resulting contract. Many of these terms are common, such as the proposal becoming part of the contract (Item 5.02), or the requirement to sign the standard contract (Item 5.04).

5.29 Guarantee of Access to Software

One of these terms is uncommon. It relates to access to the software and declares that the "state shall have full and complete access to all source code, documentation, utilities, software tools and other similar items that are used to develop/install the proposed automated equipment and facilities management software/ hardware system or that may be useful in maintaining or enhancing the equipment and facilities management software/ hardware systems." This clause permits the state to employ the same techniques and tools used by the supplier should the supplier withdraw, withhold support, or go out of business.

Appendix D. Statement of Terms and Conditions Affirmation

This appendix is a legal affirmation of 19 specific conditions related to performance of the vendor. Three of the more interesting terms are:

1. The prices are binding for 180 days. While this may seem terribly long, software demonstrations can become 30-day tests, and contract negotiations can take much longer than anticipated.

2. Both bid and performance bonds will be required.

3. The supplier is required to guarantee uninterrupted access to all software tools and similar items not turned over upon completion or

installation.

Appendix H. Definitions

This section contains the definition of key terms. Inclusion of formal definitions is always a good idea to reduce the number of misunderstandings.

The complete RFP from the Alaska Department of Transportation is contained in Part II of this handbook.

■ 4.4.2 Problem-Solving Features of an RFP

Many problems occur from jurisdiction to jurisdiction and from RFP to RFP. Yet the fundamental issues are the same. I was recently given the opportunity to participate in a very exciting project — to select a systems integrator for a multi-million dollar project involving development, processing and support for a health care initiative.

The RFP which we constructed had a number of interesting features which, we believe, helped shape the project, and would contribute to its overall success. The RFP was some 220 pages in length, consisting of about 60 pages of administrative details and 160 pages of functional specifications for the systems.

In this section, we have identified some of the important features of our RFP and discuss the problems that each feature is intended to address.

Problem #1: Multiple Proposals are Difficult to Evaluate.

Suppliers often have several different approaches or several different options that they can propose. Each option or technique has its merits and may be viewed differently by the evaluation committee. For this reason, some suppliers like to provide options within their proposal and let the evaluators select a particular option. This approach can make the evaluation process extremely complicated and provide an unfair advantage to a supplier proposing a solution constructed of various options to be chosen by the customer.

To eliminate this problem, the RFP included the following paragraph:

Proponents are advised that the submission of multiple proposals, or alternative approaches to specific sections of the requirements, will be considered non-compliant and those proposals will be disqualified. We are relying on the proponent as expert, to identify in its proposal the approach which the proponent believes will be the most effective to produce the required systems and services on time and within budget.

Problem #2: Authority is Often Unclear.

On large projects, it is often unclear who can instruct the supplier to do some work. The project manager or director may not have spending authority or may not even be an employee of the purchaser.

To eliminate this problem, the RFP included the following paragraph:

3.0 PROJECT AUTHORITY

With respect to this RFP, only the Project Authority is empowered to:

- sign contracts or other commitments;

- commit the Province to the payment of any money pursuant to contracts signed;

- issue instructions to a successful proponent

- accept any deliverable.

Any specific delegation of this authority will be conveyed to the contractor in writing.

The Project Authority is: (name)

On large projects, payment is usually tied to "acceptance" of certain products or "completion" of certain tasks. But when does "acceptance" or "completion" occur? And who decides when it occurs?

To eliminate this problem, the RFP included the following paragraph:

4.0 ACCEPTANCE AUTHORITY

4.1 All work performed under any resultant contract or any extension thereof must be approved by the Project Authority.

4.2 The Project Authority will provide an Acceptance Testing Group with the responsibility to develop testing procedures, prepare test data, and perform acceptance tests of all equipment, software, applications programs, communications capabilities as well as documentation and training materials.

4.3 The Acceptance Testing Group will implement a testing methodology and standards and will provide these to the Systems Integrator and any other stakeholders.

4.4 The Acceptance Testing Group will identify all deficiencies in writing and provide this information to the Systems Integrator. The Acceptance Testing Group has no

authority to change any specifications, terms, or requirements.

4.5 The Acceptance Testing Group will inform the Project Authority of the test schedule, the status of each test when run.

4.6 Should the work or any portion thereof be deemed unacceptable or fail to pass an acceptance test, the Project Authority reserves the right of rejection or to request correction.

Problem #3: The Prime Contractor's Role is too Limited.

Systems integrators often include a list of responsibilities within their proposals. In fact, they are stating those activities, tasks, and items for which they will assume responsibility. Their usual approach is to ensure that all other tasks default to the purchaser. As new tasks are identified during the course of the actual project, the systems integrator increases the price. This approach can increase the cost of the project by 10 percent or more beyond the original budget.

Here's how it works: suppose both the systems integrator and the purchaser failed to identify "preparation of test data" as an activity defined in either the RFP or the proposal. Since the responsibility for this task was not identified in the proposal, the systems integrator would argue that it is an extra charge (to be paid by the purchaser).

To avoid this type of disagreement, the RFP stated that all tasks are the responsibility of the systems integrator except those few which were described in the RFP and assigned in the RFP to the purchaser. In this way, the argument was decided beforehand: if a new task arose, it was the responsibility of the systems integrator and it was, therefore, included in the original price.

Here is the wording used in the actual RFP:

4.1 Prime Contractor

The system integrator selected as a result of this RFP and the evaluation process will be the prime contractor responsible for all aspects of the development, installation, testing, and operation of the Pharmacy Network. All responsibilities and work, except that specifically excluded from the project within this document, is the responsibility of the system integrator.

Problem #4: Contract Provisions are "Deal Stoppers."

The purchasers wanted to ensure that all of the major contract terms were identified in the RFP and dealt with in the supplier's proposal. In this way, disagreements over key contract issues could be avoided, or at least identified and quickly resolved.

The RFP identified five pages of desirable clauses and approaches but none of these were declared as being mandatory. The proponents were instructed to identify (in the executive summary of their proposal) any contract terms that were not acceptable and to propose an alternative which would be acceptable.

7.9 Proposed Contract Terms

We have prepared a list of clauses and issues which we believe should be included in any contracts resulting from this RFP in order to ensure that there is a complete understanding of the business relationship between the parties. These terms are listed below.

The resulting contracts developed with the selected proponent should include, but not be limited to, these clauses.

Proponents must indicate acceptance of the contract clauses indicated in this section. Alternatively, if the proponent is unwilling to agree to a proposed clause or term, then your Executive Summary must reference an appendix, which identifies those clauses in dispute and should:

(a) suggest a specific alternative term, clause, or approach;

(b) provide an explanation of your reasons.

We anticipate that some proposals will have several alternative clauses.

Problem #5: Financial Data Biases the Evaluation.

From the outset, the project director recognized that there could be significant differences in the costs associated with each proposal. It was also felt that knowledge of the cost might influence the evaluators who were looking at functionality. To ensure that the process was fair, the people evaluating the proposed solution did so without any knowledge of the associated costs.

In preparing your proposal, the financial section should be completely separated from other sections, and should be provided under separate cover.

Problem #6: Project Management is Poorly Defined.

Many organizations know that project management is a critical success factor. However, it is often difficult to decide on the questions to be included in the RFP. If the questions are not detailed enough, then it is difficult to judge the soundness of the plans. We believed that project management issues would be critical to the success of the project. We, therefore, emphasized this factor.

(b) Project Management Information

The following information is required whenever project management issues are discussed in your proposal:

• Project Management Approach: Describe your project management approach including: (1) the method used in managing the project; and (2) the project management organizational structure including reporting levels and lines of authority.

• Project Control: Describe your approach to project control, including details of the methods used in controlling project activities.

• Project Schedule: A chart of project progression from beginning to completion that includes the achievement milestones upon which progress payments will be claimed.

• Status Reporting to the Project Authority: Describe your status reporting methodology including details of written and oral progress reporting.

• Interface with the Project Authority: Describe your contact points with the Project Authority including types of communications, level of interface, and identify by name those personnel who may commit your organization and to what extent.

Problem #7: Subcontractors Can Confuse Responsibilities, Roles and Risks

This was a large project which would, by its very nature, promote working partnerships among companies, the use of subcontractors and the formation of consortia. It was important, both in terms of legal agreements as well as working relationships, that the organization know the status of each person on the project and their skills. The RFP placed demands on the proponents in excess of those normally found in smaller RFPs. The organization wanted to know who was going to do the work, their corporate affiliation, and their skills and experience.

The organization was also concerned that key individuals with essential experience not be arbitrarily removed from the project.

Here is what the RFP stated:

(c) Subcontracted Work
Your proposal must include the following:

• A statement indicating the exact amount of work to be done by the prime contractor and each subcontractor, as measured by percentage of the total three-year cost.

• If a subcontractor is proposed, a statement on the subcontractor's letterhead should be included in the proposal. It should be signed by an authorized offer of the subcontracting firm, state the general scope of the work to be performed by the subcontractor and state the exact legal relationship between the prime contractor and subcontractor (distributor, agent, etc.)

• A statement identifying the linkage (that is, the

legal relationship) between the Prime Contractor and each person proposed on the project.

(d) Personnel

All proposed project personnel, including all subcontractor staff, must be identified with a resumé in the proposal. Each person's role in the project is to be identified and documented using the prescribed form. Pharmacare reserves the right to approve or disapprove any change in the successful proponents project team members whose participation is specifically offered in the proposal. This is to assure that persons with vital experience and skill are not arbitrarily removed from the project by the prime contractor.

Format of Resume —

Company Name:

Position with Company:

Role in the Project:

Experience with the Specific Tasks Being Proposed:

Work History on Similar Projects with the Company:

Legal Relationship of the Named Person with the Prime Contractor:

Problem #8: Risks are Left Intentionally Vague.

Often, RFPs require that the proponents state their understanding of the project, or state their experience on similar projects. Our project director decided to frame this question differently. The RFP would instruct each proponent to identify and discuss the risks associated with the project. This discussion would clearly indicate the proponent's experience on similar projects, as well as providing valuable information for the project director.

Here is what the RFP stated:

(e) Discussion of risks

The following information is required in response to the objective "to identify and mitigate risks."

Identify the potential risks and problems which, in your experience, occur on projects of this type. Identify steps which can be taken to avoid or mitigate these problems; and steps to be taken should the problem occur. Incorporate activities in the project plan to reduce the occurrence, severity and impact of events or situations which can compromise the attainment of any project objective;

Your discussion should deal, at least in part, with the degree of increased risk associated with levels of software development and customization imposed by the requirements, the degree of increased risk through levels of use of non-commercially available software, the degree of reduced risk associated with use of tools, techniques, and configurations similar to other existing, installed software, hardware, and network configurations.

Problem #9: Pricing is Not Sufficiently Structured.

The RFP structured the pricing information provided by each supplier. There were several interesting features of this section:

1. To assist in the determination of the estimated life-cycle cost of the project, suppliers were required to categorize each cost as fixed, estimated with a ceiling, estimated without a ceiling, etc.

2. To simplify the task of ensuring that the costing was complete, costs were to correspond to

the project plans. For every project task, there was a corresponding cost.

3. To simplify contract administration, payments were to be linked to specific project milestones.

4. To reduce the amount of work required to analyze each proposal's costs, proponents were required to submit costs in both hardcopy and electronic form. This permitted the financial analyst to standardize the analysis, using his own spreadsheet software.

Here is part of the RFP section dealing with costs:

8.2.8.1 Pricing Instructions

Your response should be submitted in a separate sealed package, clearly labeled on its exterior.

We are interested in obtaining financial data that is as precise as possible. We recognize that there are a variety of "prices" that can be quoted. Some are fixed, others depend on factors such as volume of processing, rate of inflation, or level of effort required.

We are interested in obtaining a fixed-price quotation for goods or services whenever possible. Clearly, the price of a specific piece of equipment can be stated precisely. Other prices, such as yearly maintenance or support, can be stated as fixed-price quotations or fixed-price subject to annual review or adjustment. There is a hierarchy of preferences regarding price evaluation. The best, from our perspective, is a fixed fee quotation. The worst, in terms of planning and evaluating, is an open-ended amount. It is quite acceptable to mix and match different pricing schemes on the different components or phases, as long as a single "best price" is submitted for any

unit of work.

Proposals will be preferred which avoid transaction based pricing, but rather deal with the provision of a stated capacity, with allowance for a 20 percent annual growth rate in business volumes.

Your response must be presented in the same sequence as the building blocks (major project components) identified as sections 5.3.1 through 5.3.6 of this RFP.

8.2.8 Requested Spreadsheets

Spreadsheets of costs must be submitted in hard copy as well as on diskette in either Lotus 1-2-3 or EXCEL format.

... provide a comprehensive schedule of costs that corresponds to plans presented in the "Proponent's Response" section of your proposal. Separate schedules are required for Development, Support, and Processing activities within each section.

Costs must be assigned to the time period in which they will be incurred:

(a) Development Phase — between the start of this project and the start of integration testing, scheduled for Feb. 1, 1994.

(b) Integration Testing Phase — scheduled for Feb. 1 through March 31, 1994.

(c) System Operations Phase — three one-year consecutive terms tentatively scheduled to begin on April 1, 1994.

Each cost schedule will, therefore, have 5 columns: (a), (b), (c-year 1), (c-year 2), (c-year 3).

Costs should be identified by project activity and by resources required. For example, one of the entries might be:

Completion of the design of sub-system XYZ: $10,000 (two system designers @ 10 days @ $400/day)

5. The far right column on each spreadsheet must identify the basis for the cost:

- Firm (fixed, no change);
- Subject to a ceiling of not more than x% greater in total;
- Subject to an annual adjustment of not more than x%;
- Subject to a specific assumption or rule which is stated in the accompanying notes.

This column should be sufficiently wide to contain the notes or this column can simply provide a note number. In the second case, the notes must be on the next page following the spreadsheet.

Personnel costs shall be identified by labor category for all personnel performing services during the Development Phase. The number of units shall be expressed in days and the unit price shall be the price per day for services to be provided. The sum of costs for each position shall equal the proposal costs for personnel for Development Phase tasks. These costs are required even if you are proposing a fixed fee amount for a specific task.

8.2.8.3 Payment Projections

The proponent must include a proposed schedule of payments (in both hard copy and electronic spreadsheet format). This schedule must include the total costs. The (basis, timing) trigger for payment for each cost must be identified. All Development Phase costs, including project management, must be based on milestones including final integrated system acceptance test. Ensure that these schedules take into account the hold-back of 10 percent for all development activities.

The final payment for Development Phase activities shall be withheld until completion of the related contract including the acceptance of all deliverables and services.

A spreadsheet is required for each of sections 3.3.1 through 3.3.6 as well as an aggregate spreadsheet totaling all costs.

Problem #10: Evaluation Process is Not Clearly Explained.

On every project and for every RFP, there is a debate over how much detail to provide about the evaluation process. Some want to publish as little as possible, thereby preserving an element of arbitrariness in the evaluation process. Others want each and every task identified, thereby removing most discretion from the evaluators.

This evaluation process incorporated a structured presentation by the top few proponents.

Here is what the RFP stated:

9.0 EVALUATION PROCESS

All proposals will be evaluated by an Evaluation Committee made up of Senior Management representatives, PNP Team members, a financial officer, and an independent consultant who is an RFP expert.

The Committee will evaluate and numerically score each proposal in accordance with the evaluation criteria driven by the content of the various sections of this RFP.

The Committee will arrive at a short list of the top proponents, and present those results to the Project Authority for review and approval.

The short-listed proponents will be scheduled for a structured oral presentation and interview. At the end of the oral interview the evaluation of the short listed proponents will be completed. The oral interview will be scheduled for a total of four hours, structured as follows:

• **1 hour and 45 minutes for the proponent to make a formal presentation to the Evaluation Committee;**

• **15 minute break**

• **2 hour interview of the proponents representatives by the Evaluation Committee.**

For the oral interview, the Proponent:

• **must have present for the entire session both the proposed Project Manager, and an executive empowered to make binding commitments on behalf of the organization;**

• **may have present such other personnel as may be required, with the maximum number of presenters in total not to exceed five.**

The session will be recorded and may be videotaped.

The Evaluation Committee will document all decisions in writing. Responses to any queries from the Evaluation Committee including those made during the oral interview, will be made part of the contract file.

Clarifications made during the interview will be appended to the written proposal as if they had been submitted with the proposal itself.

Problem #11: Contract Negotiations Become Stalled.

The organization was concerned that contract negotiations could drag on for weeks and delay the start of the project. The organization wanted to ensure that the selected company would enter into a formal contract quickly. For this reason, the organization stated that if, after 14 days, no contract had been signed, then the next best supplier would be selected. This was a powerful

lever designed to ensure that negotiations were initiated and concluded quickly.

Here is what the RFP stated:

2.5 Negotiation Delay

If an agreement cannot be negotiated within fourteen (14) days of notification to the designated proponent, the Purchasing Commission may, in its sole discretion, terminate negotiations with that proponent and negotiate an agreement with another proponent of its choice.

■ 4.4.3 Important RFP Add-Ons

Most RFPs share some common elements. However, there are some features found only in selected RFPs which can be valuable. These features, when appropriate, can help make the RFP much more effective and the selection of a supplier easier. This section identifies a few features which you many want to consider for inclusion in your next RFP.

1. Structure the RFP as a large questionnaire.

An RFP issued by a local government body consisted of 85 pages of requirements information organized as a questionnaire. Each requirement was identified as "minimum" or "desirable." Suppliers were required to indicate "yes" or "no" and provide a note containing additional information if necessary.

Here is a sample of a questionnaire used in an RFP to obtain information about work orders (used by a maintenance department):

REQUIREMENTS - WORK ORDERS

Work orders will be categorized as follows:

| 1. Received |
| 2. Diagnosed |
| 3. Estimated |
| 4. Waiting Approval |
| 5. In Progress |
| 6. Waiting For Parts |
| 7. Waiting For Labour |
| 8. Pending Outside Vendor Completion |
| 9. In Hold Pending Management Decision |
| 10. Completed |

2. Identify any industry-wide standards to be satisfied.

The inclusion of industry standards can both simplify your RFP and make it more precise.

There are some standards which can help define your requirements. These standards originate from several sources: industry associations, other systems which your organization may have implemented, and common industry practices.

One organization specified in its RFP that the supplier must comply with the Vehicle Maintenance Reporting Standard of the American Trucking Association. Their RFP explained that they wanted to adopt this standard, not because of its inventory control application, but because of its suitability for maintenance activity tracking.

3. Identify project management mechanisms

The success or failure of many projects is determined not by the technical merit of the solution, but by the supplier's project management

skills and structure. Many RFPs fail to request sufficient information to evaluate the suppliers' strengths and weaknesses in this area. Many fail to include project management experience, skills, and track record as part of the evaluation process.

Here is how this topic is dealt with in many RFPs:

"Suppliers must identify the project manager that would be assigned responsibility for the implementation of the systems. Suppliers must provide information as to the individual's appropriate experience in similar projects, experience with the proposed application packages, references and a brief statement of the manager's status within the supplier's organization including title, responsibilities, and years of service. We expect that, upon request, this person would be available for an interview prior to the selection of a supplier. In addition, suppliers must indicate the course of action that will be taken should this person terminate services with the supplier or be unacceptable to us."

Compare this with the more demanding, more formal and better organized document presented below:

"The offeror shall provide a project management plan that includes:

a. Project Management Approach. The offeror shall describe its project management approach including:

(1) the method used in managing the project; and

(2) the project management organizational structure including reporting levels and lines of authority.

b. Project control. The offeror shall describe its approach to project control including details of the methods used in controlling project activities.

c. Project schedule. A chart of project progression from beginning to completion that includes the achievement milestones upon which progress payments shall be claimed.

d. Status reporting. The offeror shall describe its status reporting methodology including details of written oral progress reporting. The state requires a minimum of weekly oral progress reporting and a minimum of monthly written progress reporting.

e. Interface with the state. The offeror shall describe its interface points with the state including types of interfaces, level of interface, and level of personnel who may commit the contractor and to what extent."

This document also required information about the project manager's experience, training and the use of subcontractors.

4. Require a structured demonstration

Many organizations incorporate this type of activity into the final stages of the evaluation process. Due to the time and cost involved, invitations are extended only to those suppliers still being considered. Here's how one organization handled this topic.

The demonstration took place over two days at the purchaser's site. It was attended by most stakeholders. It accounted for 28 percent of the evaluation score.

On day one, structured examples of system transactions were performed with no deviations allowed. Points were awarded based on (1) could the software perform the assigned tasks; (2) how well the tasks were performed by the software; and (3) a subjective assessment of the system's ease of use, logic and design.

On day two, the vendors were given 90 minutes to demonstrate key features of their applications. Points were awarded based on how well the demonstrated features applied to the users' requirements. Following the demonstration was a question and answer period with hands-on testing of the system by the users. Points were awarded on how well the system dealt with the users' specific requirements.

■ 4.4.4. Insist on "Most-Favoured Customer" Pricing

How do you ensure that you get the best price? How do you ensure that the supplier is not charging you more than another public body or private-sector firm for the same goods and services? Under Canadian law, the Competition Act prohibits a supplier from charging different prices for goods of like quality and quantity sold to two different organizations. If this occurs, the supplier is guilty of price discrimination, a criminal offense.

Purchasers can take some steps to ensure equal treatment from a supplier. First, they can enshrine a clause in the agreement reminding the supplier of its promise to provide prices and other terms at least as good as it offers to others. Second, the purchaser can provide for a retroactive adjustment if the supplier grants better terms to another organization. However, all of this is only theory if the purchaser never discovers that the "best price" it received was more than the supplier charged another organization. Discovery of major differences in terms and prices usually arises from discussions with colleagues in comparable organizations dealing with the same supplier.

Reproduced below is one of the standard clauses used by the New York City Board of Education to obtain "most-favoured customer" status.

New York City Bid Clarification

The first paragraph simply establishes that this deal is at least equal to the deal given to any other Board:

The bidder certifies that the entirety of the terms included herein, i.e. specifically and limited to prices, warranties, conditions and benefits, to the Board of Education of the City School District of the City of New York are at least equal to the same entirety of terms currently quoted by the bidder to any of its other Board of Education customers for the same or substantially similar quantity and type of item(s) and services as described herein. As used herein, the work "terms" shall include prices, warranties, conditions and benefits. This certification shall not apply to the terms under contracts in effect between the bidder and other customers at the date of submission of the within bid, except as provided herein.

The second paragraph applies if the bidder offers better terms to some other customer. If this occurs, these better terms are automatically applied to this contract.

The successful bidder (hereinafter called the

"Contractor") further certifies that during the period between the bid submission date and the completion of the term of this contract, should Contractor offer more favourable entirety of terms than those terms quoted herein under a contract in effect at the bid submission date with any other Board of Education customer, for the same or a substantially similar quantity and type of item(s) and services, then the Contractor shall immediately thereafter notify the Board of Education, Bureau of Supplies. Regardless of whether such notice is sent by the Contractor or received by the Board of Education, this contract shall be deemed amended retroactively to the effective date of the more favourable terms, to provide the more favourable terms. The Board of Education shall have the right and option to decline any such amendment.

The third paragraph requires the bidder to notify the Board if it offers better terms to another Board:

If the Contractor is of the opinion that apparently more favourable terms quoted, offered or provided to such other Board of Education customer is not more favourable treatment, the Contractor shall immediately notify the Director, Bureau of Supplies, of the Board of Education in writing setting forth in detail the reasons why the Contractor believes the apparently more favourable treatment is not in fact more favourable treatment. The Director, Bureau of Supplies, after consideration of the written explanation may, in his or her sole discretion, decline to accept the explanation and thereupon, the contract shall be deemed amended retroactively to the effective date of the more favourable terms, to provide the more favourable terms to the Board of Education of the City

School District of the City of New York.

The fourth paragraph ensures that any revisions requested by the bidder will be the best offer:

The Contractor further certifies that when the terms and conditions of the within contract provide for the written submission by the Contractor of a request for revision of terms, such requested revised terms will be at least equal to the Board of Education of the City School District to the City of New York than the same entirety of terms offered by the Contractor to any other Board of Education customer for the same or substantially similar quantity and type of item(s) and services as of the effective date of the revision.

The fifth paragraph permits the Board to inspect other contracts:

The Contractor hereby authorizes the inspection, review and copy of contracts and documents that pertain or relate to the performance of this clause of the contract.

The final paragraph requires the bidder to maintain the various contracts on file for this and other Boards for a specified time:

The Contractor shall be obligated to keep the contracts and documents referred to in the above paragraph during the effective period(s) of this contract and for a period of three years after the final payment of this contract.

4.5

Standardization

Why should you standardize? Why should an organization adopt and maintain a model RFP? What are the advantages of a readily available RFP "template?" It takes a lot of work to develop an RFP from scratch. To create a simple RFP, you need to know the process, the requirements, the organization's policies and guidelines, as well as applicable laws. The process often generates documents and is controlled by documents: review forms, approval forms, contracts, acceptance forms, etc.

Having created one RFP and completed the selection process, the second is a lot easier. In completing the first one, a person obtains real knowledge and experience. Having issued an RFP and evaluated proposals once or twice, organizations start to look for short cuts. How can they improve the results, simplify the process, and reduce the amount of knowledge needed?

There are a number of different responses to the question of standardization. Some organiza-

tions — typically those that issue few RFPs — start anew each time. However, if the same people are involved, then they build up a body of informal knowledge based on past experience. They have old project files, memos, a few examples, and their own prior work.

Other organizations go further. They recognize the costs and risks associated with this process. They attempt to extract some value from each effort which will improve the next RFP. These organizations introduce some level of standardization into the process or the document.

For most organizations, some level of standardization of the RFP makes sense. All RFPs must deal with the same two sets of issues. First, the rules for the process; second, the requirements or specifications.

Formalizing and standardizing the rules is relatively straightforward. Simply take the rules from your latest RFP and use these next time. If, in reviewing the new RFP, some of these rules no longer make sense, then change them. If a new situation arises and rules must be modified or added, then revise your standard.

It is difficult to standardize the detailed description of the requirements, for that is what makes each RFP unique. However, you can standardize the format and the type of information contained in your statement of requirements. You can standardize the format of the information that suppliers send back. You can standardize the questions which you ask suppliers to determine their experience, corporate capabilities, or references. You can have a pre-defined, standardized evaluation procedure (and forms).

Standardization makes it easier for new people to understand this process, it makes it easier for managers to direct and control this process, and it certainly makes it easier to defend the process as being "visibly fair."

Since the RFP is both a document and a process, there are many opportunities to introduce standardization. There are elements which can be used to simplify the process, reduce the risks, reduce the costs or reduce the amount of training required. For example:

1. Standardize the table of contents of the RFP document.

2. Standardize the terms and conditions which are included in the RFP document.

3. Standardize the contracts resulting from the process.

4. Standardize the process by identifying tasks and having a standard project plan.

5. Standardize the format of the RFP document.

6. Provide a standardized RFP shell.

7. Provide a standard checklist to monitor the tasks before the RFP is issued.

8. Provide a standard checklist to ensure that contracts deal with all required issues.

This section presents three examples of standardized RFPs. Other chapters deal with many of the other areas of standardization such as contracts, format, etc. The three examples are from Alaska, Washington and British Columbia. Each presents a different perspective on standardization. The complete documents are contained in Part II of this reference publication and on the diskette.

■ 4.5.1 State of Alaska

Many organizations produce some form of RFP shell — a template, model or sample which can be used as the basis for creating a new RFP. The intention is to reduce the work in preparing a new one and, at the same time, to capture the lessons learned in using the old one. Typically, following an RFP process, shortcomings and deficiencies in the RFP are identified and the "template" or sample revised accordingly.

Many of the samples have serious deficiencies — they lack instructions for their use. Without notes, instructions, text or commentary, it is difficult to know which parts of a sample RFP are mandatory and which are optional. It is also difficult to recognize the implications or importance of each specific feature or requirements.

The procurement officers in Alaska have less discretionary power than their colleagues in other jurisdictions. The detailed nature of the State Procurement Code and Regulations removes many options — there is no debate about publishing weights in an RFP or how to convert costs to points. These issues are prescribed by law and cannot be changed. This approach supports the development of a standardized RFP shell.

The RFP shell developed by the state has three groups of important features: (1) the structure and use of the document; (2) the instructions provided to the procurement officer; and (3) the terms included in the RFP itself. Each of these groups is discussed in the remainder of this section.

1. Structure and Use of the RFP Shell

The RFP Shell is noteworthy for several reasons:

• The document is easy-to-read and easy-to-follow.

• The document identifies the laws and regulations governing the content of each section.

• The document clearly identifies those sections in which the procurement officer has some discretion as well as those sections which must be included without alteration.

• The document is available to all government departments and agencies in both printed and electronic form. This makes it easy to modify with a minimum of effort.

• The document comes complete with attachments.

2. Instructions to the Procurement Officer

The document presents clear instructions to the procurement officer. Each section of the model RFP identifies the options available and the applicable section of the Procurement Code or Regulations which applies.

Instructions to Procurement Officers

Instructions to procurement officers are shaded and begin with "Procurement Officer Notes." Delete these instructions in the final draft of the RFP.

Procurement officer word choices in a section are in caps, bold print and italics. For example: WILL/WILL NOT. You should make the choice, then enter the word in regular style print, e.g., will not.

The location of unique names and numbers are identified like this: NAME or NUMBER. You should provide the correct name or number and enter that information in regular style print, e.g., 78492.

3. Items in the RFP Itself

Many of the detailed features of the actual RFP are also noteworthy. Here are some highlights. The actual document, some 50 pages in length, can be found in Part II. The following items, while not unique, do improve the process and quality of the document. They deal with issues, concerns and potential problems which are not always addressed in RFP documents in other jurisdictions:

• It is the vendor's responsibility to ensure that the RFP is not defective.

• The bidders meeting must be accessible to disabled people.

- Acceptable types of contracts are identified and discussed.

- Performance bonds may be required.

- The procurement officer is directed to describe the work to be done in detail — "Write it as if you were trying to explain it to a twelve year old child."

- The questions used to establish the scores are defined and published in the RFP.

In the remainder of this section, some of these key features are described:

1.07 Required Review

It is the vendor's responsibility to ensure that the RFP is not defective and does not inadvertently restrict competition. Protests must be made prior to the due date to permit time for revisions to be issued.

1.07 Required Review

Procurement Officer Note: This section should not be altered or deleted.

Proposers should carefully review this solicitation for defects and questionable or objectionable matter. Comments concerning defects and objectionable material must be made in writing and received by the contracting officer at least ten days before the proposal opening. This will allow issuance of any necessary amendments. It will also help prevent the opening of a defective solicitation and exposure of offeror's proposals upon which award could not be made. Protests based on any omission or error, or on the content of the solicitation, will be disallowed if these faults have not been brought to the attention of the contracting officer, in writing, at least ten days before the time set for opening.

2.02 Pre-Proposal Conference

The bidders meeting, if held, must be accessible to disabled people. Transcripts of questions and answers are issued.

2.02 Pre-proposal Conference

Procurement Officer Note: Enter appropriate information, alter, revise, or delete as required.

Any pre-proposal conference that is held must be accessible to prospective proposers with disabilities. This means that the location must be accessible. In addition, signing interpreters or other accommodations must be provided if required.

A pre-proposal conference will be held at TIME, Alaska Prevailing Time, on DATE in the PLACE conference room on the NUMBER floor of the NAME Building in CITY, Alaska. The purpose of the conference is to discuss the work to be performed with the prospective proposers and allow them to ask questions concerning the RFP. Questions and answers will be transcribed and sent to prospective proposers as soon as possible after the meeting.

Proposers with a disability needing accommodation should contact the procurement officer prior to the date set for the pre-proposal conference so that reasonable accommodation can be made.

2.07 Prior Experience

If certain levels of experience are required, they must be measurable and reasonable.

2.07 Prior Experience

Procurement Officer Note: alter, revise, or delete as required.

No specific minimums have been set for this RFP.

OR

In order for their offers to be considered responsive proposers must meet these minimum prior experience requirements.

Procurement Officer Note: Provide detail on the specific prior experience you require. State the minimum acceptable amount of time.

• Remember there must be some way for third-party independent verification of the experience you ask for.

• Be careful about what you ask for as you may set requirements so high that you disqualify good potential contractors.

• Specifications such as prior experience may not be unduly restrictive per AS 36.30.060 (c). Make sure that you have a reasonable basis for this and all other specifications.

Procurement Officer Note: This sentence should not be altered, but may be deleted if not required.

A proposer's failure to meet these minimum prior experience requirements will cause their proposal to be considered non-responsive and their proposal will be rejected.

3.01 Contract Type

The Model RFP serves as a tutorial document for procurement officers. It identifies the permissible types of contacts.

3.01 Contract Type

Procurement Officer Note: Identify appropriate type of contract. There are several different types of contracts which may be suitable for your project. Review the contract types listed below to determine which would be the most appropriate. The type of contract used is likely to have an impact on costs to the state. The procurement officer should select the type of contract that will best serve the state's needs at the most reasonable cost.

The following information is for preparer's information only and should not be printed in the final contract.

■ Fixed Price Contracts

Firm Fixed Price

The most common and easiest contract to administer is a firm fixed price contract. A fixed price contract is one which obligates the contractor to performance at a specified price.

Fixed Price With Adjustment

These contracts allow for price adjustments on the occurrence of specified changes in the cost or price factors set out in the contract. These types of contracts are most useful when the contractor's future prices are so uncertain as to make a firm proposal impossible, or if covering all probable risk, so high as to make the offer unattractive and possibly unfair to the state.

Fixed Price Incentive

A target price, ceiling price and a profit formula are used in this type of contract. When the contractor performs below the costs stipulated in the target price, the contractor and the state share in the savings. If costs exceed those estimated, the contractor's profit margin declines and the price ceiling is adhered to. In these types of contracts, performance can be quantified in terms of costs and services and/or deliverables.

■ Cost Reimbursement Contracts

Cost Plus Fixed Fee

Under these contracts, contractors are paid for all

allowable costs plus a predetermined fixed fee. These contracts have been found to be beneficial for research and development work.

Cost Plus Incentive Fee

Under this type of contract, a tentative fee based on estimated costs and a target price is established. If actual costs fall below estimated costs, the contractor and state share in the savings. The contractor can lose all or part of their fee, but they must be paid for all costs.

Cost Plus A Percentage Of Cost

These contracts are prohibited by statute. Under this type of contract the contractor receives payment for costs of performance plus a specified percentage of such actual costs as a fee. These contracts provide no incentive for efficient and economical contractor performance and must not be used.

■ **Other Types Of Contracts**

Time and Materials Contracts

In addition to a fixed labor rate, these contracts include separate costs for materials used under the contract.

Procurement Officer Note: Delete the previous contract information and include the following sentence with the appropriate information in the RFP.

This contract is an ENTER NAME OF TYPE contract.

3.07 It is within the authority of the procurement officer to require various types of performance bonds to ensure compliance with the RFP.

■ **Bid Bond - Performance Bond - Surety Deposit**

Procurement Officer Note: May be deleted. Bid bonds, performance bonds and surety deposits are not routinely required. Make sure you really need one before you specify it.

Procurement Officer Note: Do not alter or revise. Choose appropriate type(s) of bonds & enter appropriate information.

■ **Bid Bond**

Proposers must obtain a bid bond and submit it with their proposal. The amount of the bid bond for this contract is DOLLARS. If a proposer is selected to receive the contract and fails to negotiate, or fails to deliver a fully executed contract after negotiation, the bid bond will be immediately forfeited to the State. The time limit for negotiation or delivery of a contract is fourteen days from the date the proposer receives notice from the procurement officer. Proposals submitted without a bid bond will be rejected.

■ **Performance Bond**

Proposers must obtain a letter of commitment for a performance bond from a bonding company and submit it with their proposal. The amount of the performance bond must be equal to the entire dollar value of a proposer's offer, for the full term of the contract. If the contractor fails to satisfactorily perform the contract the bonding company which provided the performance bond will be required to obtain timely performance of the contract. The actual performance bond must be obtained from the bonding company and provided to the State within thirty days of the date of award of the contract. A proposer's failure to provide the performance bond, within the required time, will cause the State to reject the proposal.

■ **Surety Deposit**

In lieu of a performance bond, an irrevocable letter of credit, or cash, may be substituted. The amount of the surety deposit must be LIST DOLLAR AMOUNT OR

PERCENTAGE OF PROPOSAL PRICE. Substitution of a surety deposit must be approved by the Commissioner of the Department of NAME prior to its submittal. A proposer's failure to provide the surety deposit, within the required time, will cause the State to reject the proposal.

Procurement Officer Note: The amount of surety deposit should be what it would cost to pay the premium cost of a replacement contract.

5.01 Scope of Work

The purchasing officer is instructed to be as specific and as comprehensive as possible.

5.01 Scope of Work

Procurement Officer Note: Enter appropriate information — alter, revise or delete as required.

Information you provide in this section tells the Proposers what you want done.

Be as specific and comprehensive as you possibly can.

Let the proposer know exactly what you want.

Don't presume that they will "get it" if you don't say it.

Write it as if you were trying to explain it to a twelve year old child.

The Department of NAME, Division of NAME is soliciting proposals for WHAT KIND of services.

The department wants assistance to do WHAT .

The consultant will do WHAT .

The types of staff in State agencies that the contractor must interview are WHO .

Other helpful informational material that can be provided to the consultant includes WHAT .

The goal of this project is to WHAT .

5.02 Deliverables

The procurement officer is instructed to "list every deliverable you can think of."

5.02 Deliverables

Procurement Officers Note: Enter appropriate information. Alter, revise or delete as required. List every deliverable you can think of, even the ones that do not seem particularly important right now. Do not assume that the contractor will give you more than you ask for. You should be able to look through this list and be satisfied that the job will be finished when you get everything listed here.

The contractor will be required to provide the following deliverables;

    [a] WHAT

    [b] WHAT

    [c] WHAT

    [x] WHAT

    [y] WHAT

    [z] WHAT

5.03 Work Schedule

The procurement officer is instructed to list "every event and milestone you can think of."

5.03 Work Schedule

Procurement Officer Note: Enter appropriate information. Alter, revise or delete as required.

The contract term and work schedule set out herein represent the State's best estimate of the schedule that will be followed. If a component of this schedule, such as the opening date, is delayed, the rest of the schedule will likely be shifted by the same number of days.

The length of the contract will be from the date of award, approximately DATE, for approximately NUMBER calendar days until completion, approximately DATE .

The approximate contract schedule is as follows;

Procurement Officer Note: Enter appropriate information. Alter, revise or delete as required. List every item, event, milestone you can think of, beginning to end. Be as specific and comprehensive as you possibly can. Allow one or two reviews of each draft or redraft. Create multiple opportunities for interaction with the contractor. Don't just send the contractor away with some work to do and let them bring back something that may or may not suit you. Interact with the contractor to keep the project on track.

6.01 The state has standardized the proposal format.

Procurement Officer Note: The information you provide in this section should help proposers understand how you want their proposals structured and identify items you wan them to emphasize.

6.01 Proposal Format and Content

Procurement Officer Note: Alter, revise or delete as required.

The State discourages overly lengthy and costly proposals, however, in order for the State to evaluate proposals fairly and completely, proposers should follow the format set out herein and provide all of the information requested.

7.0 The state has standardized the evaluation process — the criteria, number of points or weights, and the evaluation questions. Five standard criteria are used: understanding of the project (15 percent), methodology used for the project (15 percent), management plan for the project (15 percent), experience and qualifications (15 percent), and contract cost (40 percent). Listed below is the explanation for one of the criterion: management plan for the project.

7.03 Management Plan for the Project 15%

Procurement Officer Note: Alter, revise or delete as required.

Proposals will be evaluated against the questions set out below.

[a] Does the management plan support all of the project requirements and logically lead to the deliverables required in the RFP?

[b] Is accountability completely and clearly defined?

[c] Is the organization of the project team clear?

[d] Does the management plan illustrate the lines of authority and communication?

[e] To what extent does the proposer already have the hardware, equipment, and licenses necessary to perform the contract?

[f] Does it appear that the proposer can meet the schedule set out in the RFP?

[g] Has the contractor offered alternate deliverables and gone beyond the minimum tasks necessary to meet the objectives of the RFP?

[h] Is the proposal practical, feasible, and within budget?

[i] Have any potential problems been identified?

[j] Is the proposal submitted responsive to all material requirements in the RFP?

Evaluation Form

The form used by the evaluators to record the scores contains the criteria and the evaluation questions. Here is the section of the form dealing with management plan for the project.

7.03 Management Plan for the Project: 15 percent

Maximum Point Value for this Section — 15 Points

100 Points x 15% = 15 Points

Proposals will be evaluated against the questions set out below.

[a] Does the management plan support all of the project requirements and logically lead to the deliverables required in the RFP?

[b] Is accountability completely and clearly defined?

[c] Is the organization of the project team clear?

[d] Does the management plan illustrate the lines of authority and communication?

[e] To what extent does the proposer already have the hardware, equipment, and licenses necessary to perform the contract?

[f] Does it appear that proposer can meet the schedule set out in the proposal?

[g] Has the contractor offered alternate deliverables and gone beyond the minimum tasks necessary to meet the objectives of the RFP?

[h] Is the proposal practical, feasible, and within budget?

[i] Have any potential problems been identified?

[j] Is the proposal submitted responsive to all material requirements in the RFP?

EVALUATOR'S POINT TOTAL FOR 7.03

■ 4.5.2 State of Washington Model Request For Proposal

The state of Washington, under the aegis of the Information Services Board, has developed a model RFP for hardware, software and related services. This model is intended to reflect recommended "best practices." It provides guidance and examples related to the types of provisions to be included in an information technology RFP.

This standardized RFP has many interesting features:

• The table of contents is extensive, containing more than 80 entries.

• The appendices add structure to the process by defining key items such as functional demonstration, benchmark, and proposal contents.

• The Acquisition Schedule contains 20 items.

• The process for dealing with supplier questions is defined.

• A letter of intent is required prior to submitting a proposal.

• Proposals are irrevocable for 120 days.

• Bid bonds up to 10 percent of the contract value can be required.

• Mandatory requirements are carefully defined.

• Multiple proposals are permitted.

• Minor irregularities can be waived.

• A single response may be insufficient.

• Proposal information is not necessarily confidential or proprietary.

• Travel costs can be paid for by suppliers.

• Functional demonstrations may be required.

• Disclosure of past contract performance is required.

• The evaluation procedure is defined explicitly.

In the remainder of this section, each of these features is described in more detail.

• The table of contents is extensive, containing more than 59 entries.

The table of contents is, in itself, useful. It can provide a checklist of items to be considered when creating an RFP for information technology resources.

• The appendices add structure to the process by defining key items such as functional demonstration, benchmark, and proposal contents.

Appendix A, Preliminary Evaluation Checklist, is two pages long and contains a list of the mandatory administrative requirements. For example: "Proposal received on time and at correct location (RFP Section 1.8.10)."

Appendix B, Standard Contract Terms, contains the proposed contract or a checklist of terms to be included.

Appendix C, Functional Demonstration, is a

one-page description of the intent and agenda for the demonstration.

Appendix D, Benchmark Requirements, contains the specific terms, conditions and steps to be followed during the benchmark process.

Appendix E, Evaluation Point Distribution, is a one-page description of the major criteria and the percentage of total points assigned to each.

Appendix F, Protest Procedures, contains the required description of the process.

Appendix G, Proposal Contents, is a five-page description of the required organization of a proposal.

Appendix H, Proposal Certification, is a one-page form to be completed by the vendor stating that all of the items being proposed have been installed at a customer site for at least 90 days.

• The Acquisition Schedule contains 20 items.

1.6 Acquisition Schedule

Letter to Vendors Soliciting Interest

Release Draft RFP to Vendors

Comments on Draft RFP Due

Release Final RFP to Vendors

Pre-proposal Conference

Letter of Intent to Propose Due

Issue Responses to Pre-proposal Conference Questions

Deadline for Complaints Regarding Technical Specifications

RFP Responses Due

Begin RFP Evaluations/Functional Demonstrations

Announce Finalists

Conduct Benchmarks

Customer Site Visits

Complete Evaluations

Announce Apparent Successful Vendor

Hold Vendor Debriefing Conferences

Negotiate Contract

Install and Test Equipment/Software

Begin Training

Conduct Acceptance Test

• The process for dealing with supplier questions is defined.

1.8 Administrative Requirements

1.8.1 Pre-proposal Conference

Specific questions concerning the RFP should be submitted in writing prior to the pre-proposal conference so that State representatives may prepare responses in advance of the conference.

Additional questions will be entertained at the conference; however, responses may be deferred and provided at a later date. Copies of all written questions and the State responses will be mailed to all vendors submitting a Letter of Intent to Propose. Only the written responses will be considered official.

The response to any question which is given orally at the conference is to be considered tentative. After the conference, questions will be researched and the official response published in writing. This will assure accurate, consistent responses to all vendors.

• A letter of intent is required prior to submitting a proposal.

1.8.2 Letter of Intent to Propose

A letter indicating the vendor's intent to respond to the RFP must be received by the RFP Coordinator at the address specified in the cover letter no later than 4:00 p.m. Pacific Time on the (date).

Failure to submit a Letter of Intent to Propose, by the deadline specified, will result in the rejection of the vendor's proposal.

Submission of the Letter of Intent to Propose constitutes the vendor's acceptance of the procedures, evaluation criteria, and other administrative instructions of the RFP.

Vendors may withdraw their Letters of Intent at any time before the deadline for proposal submission.

• Proposals are irrevocable for 120 days.

1.8.4 Proposal Certification

The vendor must certify in writing that all vendor proposal terms, including prices, will remain in effect for a minimum of 120 (number is optional depending on needs of agency) days after the Proposal Due Date, that all proposed hardware and system software has been operational at a non-vendor owned customer site for a period of 90 days prior to the Proposal Due Date, that all proposed capabilities can be demonstrated by the vendor, and that the proposed hardware and system software is currently marketed and sold.

• Bid bonds up to 10 percent of the contract value can be required.

1.8.5 Bid Bond

A Bid Bond of $_____, or ten (10) percent of the

proposed cost as submitted, (whichever is less) is required. Bonds must be payable to the State of Washington. Personal or company checks are not acceptable. Bonds will be retained by the State until a contract is executed or a vendor is disqualified. In the event the apparently successful vendor fails to enter into a contract with the Agency, in accordance with the terms of the RFP and the proposal, the bond may be retained and paid into the Washington State Treasury. In the event the State commences any action on the bond, the vendor agrees that venue shall lie in Thurston County. Bonds of qualified but unsuccessful vendors will be returned upon execution of the contract.

• Mandatory requirements are carefully defined.

1.8.7 Mandatory Requirement Defined

A mandatory requirement (MR) is a minimum need that must be met by the vendor. The state may eliminate from the evaluation process any vendor not fulfilling all mandatory requirements or not presenting an acceptable alternative.

Failure to meet a mandatory requirement (grounds for disqualification) shall be established by any of the following conditions:

1. The vendor states that a mandatory cannot be met.

2. The vendor fails to include information necessary to substantiate that a given mandatory requirement has been met (such as references to specific sections in technical documents).

Responses must indicate present capability; representations that future developments will satisfy the requirement are not sufficient.

3. The vendor fails to include information requested by a mandatory requirement (such as references to specific sections in technical documents, detailed explanations).

4. The vendor presents the information requested by this RFP in a manner inconsistent with the instructions stated by mandatory requirements in the RFP.

5. References report the vendor's inability to comply with one or more of the mandatory requirements.

6. The vendor fails to include the references required.

1.8.7 Acceptable Alternative Defined

An acceptable alternative is one which the State considers satisfactory in meeting a mandatory specification. The State, at its sole discretion, will determine if the proposed alternative meets the intent of the original mandatory requirement.

• Multiple proposals are permitted.

1.8.11 Multiple Proposals

Vendors interested in submitting more than one proposal may do so, providing each proposal stands alone and independently complies with the instructions, conditions and specifications of the RFP.

• Minor irregularities can be waived.

1.8.14 Waiver of Minor Administrative Irregularities

The State reserves the right, at its sole discretion, to waive minor administrative irregularities contained in any proposal.

• A single response may be insufficient.

1.8.15 Single Response

A single response (i.e., a proposal from only one vendor) to the RFP may be deemed a failure of competition and, at the sole option of the State, the RFP may be cancelled.

• Proposal information is not necessarily confidential or proprietary.

1.8.19 Proprietary Proposal Material

Any information contained in the proposal that is proprietary must be clearly designated. Marking the entire proposal as proprietary will be neither accepted nor honored. If a request is made to view a vendor's proposal, the State will comply according to the appropriate Public Disclosure Commission Procedures. If any information is marked as proprietary in the proposal, such information will not be made available until the affected vendor has been given an opportunity to seek a court injunction against the requested disclosure.

• Travel costs can be paid for by suppliers.

1.8.25 Performance and Demonstration Travel Costs

The State will bear all travel and associated per diem costs for evaluators to view functional demonstrations and performance benchmarks within the State of Washington. The vendor must bear all travel and associated per diem costs, not to exceed published State of Washington employees' reimbursement rates, for not more than (number) State employees to view functional demonstrations and performance benchmarks outside the State of Washington.

• Functional demonstrations may be required.

1.10 Functional Demonstration

A functional demonstration is necessary to gain a complete understanding of the vendor's proposal. The functional demonstration will provide an opportunity for vendors to further explain and/or demonstrate their responses to this RFP. Each vendor will be scheduled (number) days for the demonstration. Unless agreed to prior to scheduling the functional demonstration, the evaluation team will limit its time to normal working hours (8:00 AM to 5:00 PM). Specifics for the demonstration are explained in Appendix C.

• Disclosure of past contract performance is required.

4.3.4 Contract Performance

If the vendor has had a contract terminated for default during the past five years, all such incidents must be described. Termination for default is defined as notice to stop performance due to the vendor's non-performance or poor performance and the issue was either (a) not litigated; or (b) litigated and such litigation determined the vendor to be in default.

Submit full details of all terminations for default experienced by the vendor during the past five years including the other party's name, address and telephone number. Present the vendor's position on the matter. The Agency will evaluate the facts and may, at its sole discretion, reject the vendor's proposal if the facts discovered indicate that completion of a contract

resulting from this RFP may be jeopardized by selection of the vendor. If no such terminations for default have been experienced by the vendor in the past five years, so declare.

• The evaluation procedure is defined explicitly.

Six pages are devoted to this critical step. The evaluation is based on several teams working independently.

5 Evaluation Procedures

5.1 Basis for Evaluation

The Technical and Cost sections of the proposals will be evaluated on the basis of the vendor's proposals and demonstrations. The Management section of the proposals will be evaluated on the basis of references in addition to the information available in the vendor's proposal...

5.2 Evaluation Teams

The evaluation procedures will be performed by the RFP Coordinator and several teams formed by State staff. The team evaluations will progress independently of each other, without cross-dissemination of evaluation results (except in the event a proposal is rejected as non-responsive).

5.2.1 Technical Team

This team will conduct the technical evaluations using the technical proposals and functional demonstrations. It will also conduct the benchmark/performance demonstrations and evaluate the results. Financial and management data and evaluations thereof will not be available to the Technical Team.

5.2.2 Financial Team

This team will evaluate all the costs, instalment purchase terms, maintenance costs and supply costs, according to the financial evaluation criteria. The same criteria will be applied to all proposals. The Financial Team will also evaluate the participation level of Minority and Women Business Enterprises. Technical and benchmark/performance demonstration evaluation scores will not be available to the Financial Team.

5.2.3 Management Team

This team will evaluate the management portions of the response, and will contact references to verify the vendor's claims.

5.2.4 Selection Team

The Selection team will compile the scores, add the MWBE bonus for qualified vendors, and select the Apparently Successful Vendor on the basis of the final result.

• Scoring is performed by each team using a five-point scale.

5.4 Qualitative Review and Scoring

Proposals which pass the preliminary screening and mandatory requirements review will be evaluated and scored based on responses to requirements in the RFP. The evaluators will consider how well the vendor's proposed solution meets the needs of the Agency, as described in the vendor's response to each requirement. It is important that the responses be clear and complete, so that the evaluators can adequately understand all aspects of the proposal.

5.4.1 Scoring

Scoring will use pre-established evaluation criteria set out in Appendix (letter). Each scored item will be given a score by each evaluator. The evaluation teams will score independently of one another. Upon completion of this review, scores will be forwarded to the Selection team.

5.4.1.1 Technical Points

Points will be assigned based on the effectiveness and efficiency in the documented approach to supporting each of the technical items being rated. A scale of zero to five will be used, where the range is defined as follows:

0. Feature is non-responsive or wholly inadequate; if a mandatory requirement, it will result in the disqualification of the proposal.

3. Response indicates approach is effective and of average capability, performance, efficiency.

5. Feature or capability is clearly superior to that which is average or expected as the norm.

In addition to the point score assigned, each scored technical item is assigned a weighted value factor. The raw score given each item by the evaluators will be multiplied by the value for that item to give the weighted score.

• Cost is scored by comparing each proponent's cost with that of the lowest responsive proposal.

5.5 Evaluation of Cost Proposal

The score for the cost proposal will be computed by dividing the amount of lowest responsive bid the Agency receives by the vendor's total proposed cost. This sum will be multiplied by a weighting factor.

5.6 Total Weighted Score

The vendor's total weighted score is the sum of:

a) Total Technical weighted score;

b) **Total Management weighted score;**

c) **Total Benchmark/Performance Demonstration weighted score; and**

d) **Total Cost weighted score.**

Proposals obtaining a slightly different but comparable score are considered equal. The selection is then based on a predefined total of selected factors such as technical and benchmark scores.

5.8 Selection of Apparently Successful Vendor

The evaluation process is designed to award the acquisition not necessarily to the vendor of least cost, but rather to that vendor with the best combination of attributes based upon the evaluation criteria.

The Technical, Management, and the Financial Teams will separately present the results of their respective evaluations to the Selection Team. The Selection Team will compile the scores, add the MWBE bonus for qualified vendors and select the Apparently Successful Vendor on the basis of the final result.

Should any finalist vendor scores be within (number)% of the highest score, they will be considered equal and the selection of the Apparently Successful Vendor will be based on the proposal with the highest total of (cost, technical, management, and bench-mark/performance or whatever) points. If an Apparently Successful Vendor is identified, contract negotiations will begin. If, for any reason, a contract is not awarded to the first Apparently Successful Vendor, then the next highest ranking finalist vendor may be considered for contract negotiations.

Vendors eliminated from further competition will be mailed notification by the Agency as soon as practical.

■ 4.5.3 British Columbia Systems Corporation

BC Systems Corp. has developed a model RFP. As with the others contained in this section, this model is intended to reflect recommended "best practices" and identifies mandatory legal requirements. The BC System's model RFP is not as detailed as the others. However, it does go a long way toward ensuring that different managers produce comparable RFP documents.

The RFP document consists of two parts: Part A is the Administrative Section and is the same for all RFP Documents; Part B identifies the requirements and is unique to each situation. However, the format for Part B has been standardized to assist the users.

Part A always consists of a cover page with a summary of key information, a standard table of contents, and the Administrative Section.

Part A has some interesting features:

• The terms "mandatory," "desirable," and "optional" are defined and the phrase "proposals must meet all mandatory requirements" is included.

• Proposals must deal with contract issues. The RFP states that "All terms and conditions are deemed to be accepted by the bidder and incorporated in its proposal, except those conditions and provisions which are expressly excluded by the proposal.

• While debriefing sessions are offered, they are limited in scope: The debriefing is not to be seen as an opportunity to challenge the decision.

Once debriefing ends, the RFP process is finished and the RFP will not be discussed further with the bidder at any time.

• Subcontracting is defined and is acceptable "to remedy deficiencies in the prime bidder's product or service."

• Confidentiality and Security are discussed as is the impact of the Freedom of Information Act on proposals, trade secrets, and proprietary data.

Part B, Requirements Section, has a standardized format. It consists of eight sections:

• Purpose
• Requirements Definitions
• Evaluation Criteria
• Bidders Meeting
• Vendor Response Format For Pricing
• Detailed Costs
• Value-Added Considerations
• Company Profile.

The entire document is contained in Part II and on the floppy disk that accompanied this book.

---

[1] Page 4, Reference *7.
[2] Section AS 36.30.210 (b), page 22, Reference *4.
[3] Page 18, Reference *7.
[4] Page 4.11, Reference *2.
[5] Page 41, Reference *10.
[6] Page 12, Reference *25.
[7] Each of these components is described in the section "A Building Block Approach to the Process" found in Chapter 6.

CHAPTER 5

Dealing With Suppliers

– CONTENTS –

5.1

Introduction

Having prepared the RFP, the battle still isn't over. Some would argue that the worst is yet to come. Issuing the RFP carries with it a large number of questions, and many risks. For example:

- How do we identify suppliers?
- How many proposals do we need?
- If there are only one or two suppliers, can we award the contract without an RFP?

- If there are hundreds of suppliers, can we restrict the competition?
- Do we have to meet with the suppliers? Do we have to answer their questions?
- Are proposals confidential?

This chapter attempts to answer many of these questions and provides examples of the practices in different jurisdictions.

5.2

Inviting Suppliers to Compete

It's hard to know, without a lot of experience, how to invite suppliers to compete and which suppliers are capable of providing acceptable solutions. As always, there are competing objectives in this process:

• We want to ensure that the process is "fair and open" — that all suppliers have access to government procurement opportunities. (This often leads to a large number of suppliers submitting proposals.)

• We want lots of proposals to ensure that we evaluate a wide range of solutions.

• We want to ensure that the costs of preparing and evaluating proposals are commensurate with the money involved. (We really do not want to receive a lot of proposals except for very large projects.)

Underlying all of these objectives is the requirement that the project be successful. A successful project has the following characteristics:

• The procurement process was executed in a professional manner and was consistent with your purchasing policy.

• The procurement process was documented as you went along and could survive public scrutiny.

• No objections were raised by suppliers concerning the fairness of the process or the actual selection.

• The selected supplier performed as expected. The solution was implemented on time, within budget and satisfied the requirements.

• Your organization (your boss) acknowledged that the project was a success.

The process of inviting suppliers to compete is fraught with danger. Unsuccessful vendors, or those not even invited to compete, often claim that this step violates the spirit of "fair and open competition." These vendors will argue that this step was not conducted in a "visibly fair, ethical and prudent manner." Some of the frequently heard arguments are listed below:

• We weren't invited or selected so you didn't get the best solution.

• You invited only the top few suppliers who have dominated the market. But their days are over. The market has changed. You were either trying to limit the competition because you favored one of the top players, you weren't familiar with the marketplace, or you were trying to simplify and shorten the evaluation process.

• You invited too many suppliers and wasted our time and money. If we had known that there were 25 bidders, we would not have submitted a proposal. Why did you invite 25 firms to bid on $50,000 worth of work? The preparation of even a simple proposal cost our firm about $3,000 (that is, your $50,000 expenditure cost the invited firms a cumulative total of $75,000.) Your RFP process abused our industry.

• The process for selecting a company to submit a proposal appears to have been arbitrary. What were your selection criteria? Where did you get the list of potential suppliers? Why were we excluded? How old is your list?

There are two major ways suppliers are identified and invited to compete. Either all suppliers are invited through an open competition or some selected group of suppliers is informed of the RFP. Both of these approaches are discussed in the sections which follow.

■ 5.2.1 By Public Announcement

This approach does not require any prior knowledge of the marketplace by the purchasing organization. You simply advertise your intention to issue a Request for Proposal and wait for suppliers to respond. If advertisements only cost one dollar and evaluations were free, then this approach would be followed by every organization on every RFP.

Some public-sector bodies don't maintain vendor lists. They simply advertise every RFP in certain specified newspapers. The vendor community is aware of this practice and monitors these newspapers. This approach appears to work well and certainly ensures that all vendors have an equal opportunity of knowing about the RFP.

Advertising can be done in newspapers. But it can also be done electronically — making the RFP information available on an online system or bulletin board. In some jurisdictions this constitutes a public announcement, in others it does not.

The amount and location of the advertising usually depends on the nature of the procurement and the dollars involved. The larger the amount, the more widespread the advertising. If the procurement is for a service only available from large, national firms, then the advertisement may be in a national forum. If the procurement is highly political and subject to much debate, then the advertising may be national as well. Here is how the state of Washington prescribes its requirements[1]:

d. Advertise the acquisition in the Seattle Daily Journal of Commerce or other major regional publication upon or before release of the RFP. In addition, advertising in the Wall Street Journal or other national publications

may be appropriate, depending on the nature of the acquisition... Issue the RFP to a minimum of three vendors where available. RFP's shall be issued to all vendors who have expressed an interest in providing the Information Technology Resources to be acquired...

Often, public announcements of major procurements attract large numbers of vendors. Some organizations are committed, by their policies, to give each vendor a copy of the RFP. Typical regulations or policy documents state that: Prospective bidders and proponents will be given copies of requests for bids or proposals upon request.

To restrict the number of proposals received, and to impose some reasonable chance of success on each vendor, some organizations simply issue a pre-specified number of RFPs. They are released on a first-come, first-serve basis. For example, an organization might need an architect for a small design project. In announcing the RFP, they anticipate hundreds of responses. To reduce the amount of work, and the total cumulative marketing effort of the architectural industry, they indicate in their RFP that a reasonable number of RFPs have been printed and that RFPs will be issued on a first-come, first-served basis until supplies are exhausted.

■ 5.2.2 By Invitation

Inviting a selected group of suppliers is always a restrictive practice. If your organization's policy is based on open competition, then the restriction must be justifiable. Justification can take many forms: expediency, value of the contract, the cost of processing hundreds of proposals, etc. In some organizations, the justification must be made in writing and available to the public.

There are several different mechanisms for reducing the number of proposals by only inviting a selective group of suppliers to submit a proposal:

- Pre-Qualification
- Selection (of names on a list)
- Rotation (of names on a list)

Prequalification

Prequalification requires that a larger number of proponents provide only sufficient evidence of their ability to perform the contract to enable comparisons to be made and a smaller number (normally between five and ten) shortlisted. This process does not require a detailed response, for the objective is to reduce the proposal effort by proponents as a group. The request for a prequalification statement should contain mandatory questions carefully worded to enable conclusions to be drawn from the responses.

Some organizations insist that the prequalification process be run with the same set of rules as an RFP. They believe that since the process is used to restrict competition, it must be fully defensible. They also insist that the list of qualified vendors can then only be used for the intended purposes, and that the list expires after some pre-defined length of time, typically one year.

A prequalification phase adds time to the RFP process, but it saves time and effort during the proposal evaluation phase by reducing the number of proposals. It can generate more savings if more that one RFP will be issued to the same group over the next 12 months. This approach can save time and money spent by the vendor community in generating a larger number of proposals.

If you anticipate that a large number of suppliers will want to examine the RFP and submit a proposal, you may want to prequalify them to reduce numbers. Prequalification is usually performed on the basis of mandatory conditions and is regarded as a separate process.

Consider this example: suppose you wanted a new computer system designed. There are hundreds of system design firms in your city. How do you restrict the numbers? First, identify some of the mandatory requirements. For example, the new system may require specific skills or experiences such as a knowledge of local area networks, or specific brand-name computers or computer software. Using these factors, the list of several hundred could be reduced to several dozen. With some more thought, additional factors could be identified which would be mandatory and which would reduce the number of potential bidders to a reasonable number. The final process must be rational, easy to explain, and easy to justify.

Once these qualifications are known, they can be used to construct a list, to review your existing lists, or to construct an advertisement. The energy spent in searching for suppliers must be reasonable. There is an onus on suppliers that want to do business with organizations to register with them.

In many jurisdictions, the policy is to accept any proposal that is received before the closing

time so long as the vendor would have passed the prequalification screening.

Some jurisdictions only use this approach when other, more competitive approaches are ruled out. This is the case in Alaska, where the evaluation of unpriced technical proposals can be used to identify qualified firms. These firms can then be issued an RFP[2]:

When it is considered impractical to initially prepare a definitive purchase description to support an award based on listed selection criteria, the procurement officer may issue an expression of interest requesting the submission of unpriced technical offers, and then later issue a request for proposals limited to the offerors whose offers are determined to be technically qualified under the criteria set out in the expression of interest.

In some jurisdictions, to preserve the integrity of the RFP process, a prequalification process is governed by the same RFP rules. The process is often used to establish a qualified source list that is only valid for a specified time, such as a year. No names can be added to the qualified source list except through the formal process. This is an excellent approach.

In other jurisdictions, the pre-qualification process is less formal and, therefore, more subjective and more difficult to defend as being "fair and open."

Here is an example of a formal set of rules for this process[3]:

29. (1) Where a contracting authority prequalifies

bidders or proponents before issuing a request for bids or proposals for a contract, it will establish a qualified source list pursuant to this directive, which will be valid for up to one year.

(2) The contracting authority will define the scope of each qualified source list in terms of the specific contracts which are contemplated.

30.

(1) A contracting authority will publicly advertise for bidders or proponents to submit their qualifications for qualified source lists.

(2) Such requests for submission of qualifications will be considered to be requests for proposals as defined by this directive and will be conducted pursuant to this directive.

31. Responses to Requests for Proposals issued pursuant to section 30 will be considered proposals as defined by this directive and will be evaluated accordingly.

32. A contracting authority will not add the name of a bidder or proponent to qualified source lists except through the evaluation and acceptance of the proponent's qualifications submitted in response to the request for bids or proposals.

Selection

Many organizations maintain lists of suppliers for various commodities and services. Whenever a supplier contacts them regarding potential business, they encourage the supplier to register with them. Often, the related procurement law or regulations requires that the purchasing organization register vendors. These organizations usually have a registration package describing the types of procurements they make, their procedures and policies. There is wide variety in the quality of the lists maintained by organizations. Some lists are relatively complete; others only reflect those few suppliers known to the organization. List maintenance is an expensive undertaking and can become a major task. Obtaining new information from suppliers on an annual basis requires staff, computer resources and a budget. All are scarce commodities.

Some organizations have no choice — they are required by law or by policy to maintain and use supplier lists. Some organizations delete suppliers from the list if the suppliers do not send in a "no bid" for each RFP; others keep them on their list. Some charge for this service; others register all vendors at no cost.

In South Dakota[4], the State Purchasing Office must maintain "A list of prospective bidders, categorized by goods and services provided by each" to be used in the solicitation of bids. The registration fee was $50 as of July, 1992. In South Dakota, "A bidder may be removed from the bidders' list for failure to respond to or acknowledge two consecutive proposals, or for failure to pay the registration fee for each fiscal year..."

In New Mexico[5], state law requires that:

...the State Purchasing Agent shall send copies of the notice of Invitation for Bids involving the expenditure of more than five thousand dollars ($5,000) to those businesses who have signified in writing an interest in submitting bids for particular categories of items of

tangible personal property, construction and services, and have paid any required fees. Such fees shall be related to the actual direct cost of furnishing copies of the notice of Invitation to Bid to the prospective bidders.

Unlike other bid lists, failure to respond to bids received does not jeopardize a vendor's standing on the state of New Mexico's bidders' list. Your registration fee entitles you to receive bid information for one year. You are asked not to respond with a no-bid.

As of March, 1992 the registration fee was $75 per year.

The Procurement Code in Alaska[6] requires that (a) "The Commissioner shall establish and maintain lists of persons who desire to provide supplies, services, professional services, or construction services...." and that (b) "to be on a list, a person must have a valid Alaska business license."

Before an RFP is issued, the organization reviews its supplier list and selects those vendors providing the required services. The use of lists is dangerous. Lists are often incomplete or out of date. The costs of maintaining an accurate list often exceeds its value. Some purchasing organizations require that the users submit a list of suggested vendors. The theory is that the users are more familiar with the particular supplier community and should be able to ensure that the major players have been identified, even if they have not registered to be on the official suppliers list.

Large organizations may deal with thousands of suppliers, and may have lists exceeding 10,000 vendors. Keeping these lists up to date is a major

activity costing thousands of dollars each year.

Rotation

Lists create problems, but rotating the names on a list creates more problems. For each RFP, vendors are selected from the list according to a rotation system. Rotation of the names requires that the list be segmented into groups and each group is used in turn. For example, suppose you have the names of 100 different suppliers of cleaning services on your list. If the procurement is small and does not warrant inviting all 100 to submit proposals, you might divide the list into five groups of 20. For the first procurement, you would send the RFP to the first group of twenty. The next procurement would go to the second group. This would be repeated as required.

Simple questions are often asked that are difficult to answer. Remember that your selection may be challenged. Is your list accurate? Is it up to date? Would your procedure pass the test of being "visibly fair, ethical and prudent?" Is it fair to exclude a supplier if you only issue one RFP each year? Is it fair to exclude a supplier from future competitions because it submitted a proposal that did not win? Is it prudent to exclude any supplier?

This method is justified when the list is accurate and up-to-date, and it is unreasonable to invite all registered vendors to submit a proposal. Consider the impact of inviting all 100 vendors to submit proposals. Each vendor might spend $1,000 preparing a proposal, for a cumulative cost of $100,000 across all vendors. This is certainly disproportionate to the value of the contract.

This method can be extremely difficult to justify. Suppose a supplier is invited to submit a proposal and loses. The supplier is in the first group of 20 from the 100 suppliers cited above. Having been selected once, the supplier must now wait until all of the other groups have been used. The supplier is excluded from competing further until the balance of the 100 suppliers on the list has been invited. In some organizations, this may take more than a year! So, the reward for losing is being excluded from competition for a year.

Some organizations, through law, regulation, or policy do not permit restricted competitions. All suppliers must be allowed to submit proposals for any RFP. Others permit restricted competition in limited and special circumstances.

In Alaska, under certain circumstances, the formal processes of competitive sealed bidding or competitive sealed proposals can be replaced with simpler, shorter processes[7]:

A contract... under $100,000 may be awarded without competitive sealed bidding or competitive sealed proposals in accordance with regulations adopted by the commissioner. A contract may be awarded under this section only when the chief procurement officer... determines in writing that a situation exists that makes competitive sealed bidding or competitive sealed proposals impractical or contrary to the public interest. Procurements under this section shall be made with competition that is practicable under the circumstance...

In Alaska, competition can only be restricted under unusual circumstances and must be justified in writing and subject to public scrutiny[8]:

(a) Any request by a purchasing agency that a procurement be restricted to several potential contractors must be accompanied by a written explanation as to why other sources are not suitable or available and why the open competitive sealed bidding or competitive sealed proposal processes are impractical or contrary to the public interest. An agency may advertise an intent to make a limited competition procurement for the purposes of determining if other sources are available or interested in a particular procurement...

5.3

Some Important Numbers

How many suppliers constitute a reasonable number? How many suppliers are required to ensure "fair and open competition?" How many proposals are needed to select the "best" supplier?

Firm instructions, rules, or common practices on the number of vendors or proposals vary from organization to organization. However, the following guidelines are representative:

• The objective of the RFP process is to obtain detailed proposals from (typically) between five and ten qualified proponents.

• If the number of known and potentially qualified suppliers is less than five, reasonable efforts should be made to identify other suppliers, for example, by checking with the user group involved in the procurement, professional associations, or other organizations.

• If the number of known and potentially qualified suppliers is more than 15, it may be reasonable to attempt to reduce the number, depending on circumstances and the value of the contract. This may be done by rotation of qualified names (on your list) or by incorporating a prequalification phase in the RFP process.

The final number to be discussed is the number of proposals needed to award a contract. What happens if you only get one responsive and responsible proposal? Can you award the contract? The first question is "why did you only get one proposal?" Were the requirements restrictive? Was there some flaw in the process, or in the selection criteria? Many organizations will, upon receiving only one proposal, contact some of the suppliers who were expected to compete. These suppliers will be asked for their reasons. If this sort of informal investigation fails to uncover any flaw in the process or specifications, then there is no reason not to award the contract. Some organizations give the purchasing officer the option of cancelling the procurement or awarding a contract in this special situation.

Some organizations explicitly state in their policy documents that if only one proposal is received, the procurement officer need not award the contract and can cancel the competition. Cancellation may be justified, at least in the mind of the procurement officer, if the officer is concerned over the lack of competition, if the officer suspects that the specifications were poorly written or vague, or if the officer is concerned about the possibility of collusion between vendors to restrict competition.

5.4

When Can a Contract be Awarded without an RFP?

In most organizations, some form of competitive bidding must be used for all procurements. There are two exceptions to this rule of open competition: first, some organizations permit restrictive competitions which limit the number of vendors invited to propose. Second, in certain unusual situations occurring on an infrequent basis, a contract can be awarded without any competitive process.

These sole source procurements, or directed awards, can be highly contentious. They can cause serious problems. Questions may be raised concerning the reasons for the award. The integrity of the organization and the behavior of the procurement officer are often questioned. These procurements can become a media event orchestrated by a disgruntled supplier. Alternatively, sole source procurements are often a source of awkward and difficult questions in public forums, councils and legislatures.

Sole source procurements are a valid and sound business practice when done properly. There are two critical elements of a successful sole source procurement: justification and publicity.

■ 5.4.1 Justification

Awarding a contract on a sole source basis when legitimate competition exists is normally a bad business practice, and in some jurisdictions not simply unethical, but illegal.

Sole source procurements in the public sector must always be justified. The amount of justification depends on the organization and the value of the contract. In most organizations, a non-competitive procurement must be supported by market research to show that there is only one supplier that can meet the documented requirements. Obviously, the size of the search should be commensurate with the contract value. Large contracts awarded without a competitive process demand extensive market research, while smaller contracts require less.

Justification requires that the procurement officer seek companies capable of satisfying a set of requirements. As a "best practice," these requirements should be written down. Recognize that if the award is challenged, the documented requirements will be closely scrutinized. Solid, well-defined, non-restrictive requirements can support the award better than poorly written ones.

In Alaska, this process can only be used when a responsible official has determined in writing that there is only one source for the required procurement[9]:

A contract may be awarded... without competitive sealed bidding, competitive sealed proposals, or other competition in accordance with regulations adopted by the commissioner. A contract may be awarded... only when the chief procurement officer... determines in writing that there is only one source for the required procurement or construction. A sole source procurement may not be awarded if a reasonable alternative source exists. The written determination must include findings of fact that support by clear and convincing evidence the determination that only one source exists...

There are different circumstances in which this procurement method is justified: emergencies, when there is only one supplier, and when there isn't enough time for a proper RFP. Sometimes, there are situations where the requirements could be satisfied by more than one supplier, but unusual circumstances do not allow the competition to be carried out in time. For example, a current service contract expires in 90 days and management

estimates that the RFP process will take 120 days. In these situations, a contract could be awarded to the incumbent (or the current contract extended) but for as little time as possible (say 90 days).

In examining the rules, policies, regulations and laws related to sole sourcing in different jurisdictions, there are several obvious conclusions:

• There are two different approaches to identifying when sole sourcing can be used. In the first, the organization states that it may be used only in prescribed situations. In the second, the organization provides examples and leaves the actual determination to the procurement officer involved in each particular situation.

• Many of the reasons across these different jurisdictions are the same, although the language used is very different. Most organizations permit sole sourcing for emergencies, for reasons of technical compatibility and to permit the development of prototypes.

The remainder of this section contains the rules from several legal documents since these documents tend to be much more precise than internal policy memos. Two different documents are quoted. The North American Free Trade Agreement contains a good list in super-legal terms. The list in the state of Alaska Procurement Regulations contains some items specific to state government.

1. NAFTA[10]

Limited tendering procedures can be used:

(a) in the absence of tenders in response to an open or selective call for tenders, or where the tenders

submitted either have resulted from collusion or do not conform to the essential requirements of the tender documentation, or... on condition that the requirements of the initial procurement are not substantially modified in the contract as awarded;

(b) where, for works of art, or for reasons connected with the protection of patents, copyrights or other exclusive rights, or proprietary information, or where there is an absence of competition for technical reasons, the goods or services can be supplied only by a particular supplier and no reasonable alternative or substitute exists;

(c) in so far as is strictly necessary where, for reasons of extreme urgency brought about by events unforeseeable... the goods or services could not be obtained in time by means of open or selective tendering procedures;

(d) for additional deliveries by the original supplier that are intended either as replacement parts or continuing services for existing suppliers, services or installations, or as the extension of existing supplies, services or installations, where a change of supplier would compel (the purchaser) to procure equipment or services not meeting requirements of interchangeability with already existing equipment or services, including software...

(e) where (a purchaser) procures a prototype or a first good or service that is developed at its request in the course of and for a particular contract for research, experiment, study or original development...

(g) for purchases made under exceptionally advantageous conditions that only arise in the very short term, such as unusual disposals by enterprises that are not normally suppliers or disposal of assets of businesses

in liquidation or receivership, but not routine purchases from regular suppliers;

(h) for a contract to be awarded to the winner of an architectural design contents...

(i) where (a purchaser) needs to procure consulting services regarding matters of a confidential nature, the disclosure of which could reasonably be expected to compromise government confidences, cause economic disruption or similarly be contrary to the public interest.

3. (Each purchasing organization) shall prepare a report in writing on each contract awarded by it under paragraph two. Each report shall contain the name of the (purchasing organization), indicate the value and kind of goods or services procured, the name of the country of origin, and a statement indicating the circumstances and conditions described in paragraph two that justified the use of limited tendering...

2. State of Alaska

This article describes when and how a sole source procurement can be made. The determination must be in writing, and must be approved by the chief procurement officer[11].

(a) A request by a purchasing agency that a procurement be restricted to one potential contractor must be accompanied by a written explanation as to why no other source is suitable or acceptable to meet the need. An agency may advertise an intent to make a sole source award for the purpose of determining if other sources are available or interested in a particular procurement. Award of a sole source procurement may not be made without prior written approval of the chief procurement officer or the commissioner of transportation and public facilities...

(b) The written determination... that there is only one source for the required procurement must specify the duration of its effectiveness.

(c) A procurement officer shall conduct negotiations, as appropriate, as to price, delivery, and terms of a sole source procurement.

(d) The following are some examples of circumstances in which sole source procurement might be appropriate:

(1) if the compatibility of equipment, accessories, or replacement parts is the main consideration;

(2) if a specific item is needed for trial use or testing, including testing of a prototype;

(3) if an item is to be procured for resale;

(4) if public utility services are to be procured;

(5) if there exists a sole source of expertise required to perform a specific professional service;

(6) if the procurement is for operation of a concession contract on state property by a non-profit organization whose sole purpose is to operate the concession and provide other public services on the property;

(7) if the procurement is with government police agencies to provide investigative, enforcement, or support services in support of state law enforcement objectives;

(8) if the procurement is for the services of legal counsel for the purpose of advising or representing the state in specific civil or criminal proceedings or on specific matters before federal or state regulatory agencies, boards, or commissions;

(9) if the procurement is by the office of the Governor for lobbying, negotiation, consulting by a foreign national, or employment of a foreign national.

■ 5.4.2 Publicity

There are only a limited number of approaches to dealing with publicity about sole source procurements. First, an organization can keep it a secret. Second, an organization can publicize the award before the contract is signed. The third approach is to make public the award after the contract has been signed. All three approaches are in common practice.

No Publicity

Some organizations keep sole source procurements a secret, or try to. They believe that the awarding of contracts is an internal matter. They often believe that, because of exigencies, emergencies or special circumstances, their actions are justified. This is effective when it works. But with access to information laws and lots of disgruntled suppliers, secret deals are frequently discovered. Recently there was a feature story in a national newspaper about a government agency that awarded a contract for several million dollars without any competition. This agency was not subject to procurement laws or regulations, only an internal policy related to competitive practices. The senior official was quoted as saying that the policy is "only a guideline" and not always followed.

Pre-Award Publicity

The purpose of publicizing an intent to award a contract is to alert the supplier community and to identify any potential bidders who may have been overlooked. This approach reduces the number of supplier complaints. Here's how it works: First, an organization determines its requirements and documents them. It then surveys the marketplace to identify potential suppliers. Once an organization believes that there is only one supplier in a particular circumstance, it notifies other suppliers in the same industry that it intends to award a contract without a competitive process. It informs the industry of the size of the contract and the reasons that an RFP is not being used. If there are no objections, the contract is awarded. If a supplier objects, the situation is assessed and either the contract is awarded or an RFP is issued.

A Notice of Intent to Contract can be sent to other similar organizations on the supplier list or published in a newspaper.

This notice usually contains the following information:

- a brief description of the goods and services included in the proposed contract;
- the total value of the proposed contract;
- the name of the vendor selected;

- the reasons why this approach was taken.

Vendors that don't agree with the strategy of awarding the contract without an RFP are invited to discuss the issue with the purchasing organization. Based on the information provided by the vendor, or vendors, the purchasing organization may either complete the contract or issue an RFP.

This approach alerts a range of vendors to the existence of the proposed contract and averts many supplier complaints.

After Signing the Contract

It is better to announce a contract late then not at all. In some jurisdictions, all sole source contracts must be identified either to a senior executive, or to the governing political entity. Other jurisdictions go further and require publication of the information on a scheduled basis, usually not less than annually. The public record usually consists of at least the following information:

- the supplier's or contractor's name
- the amount and type of each contract
- a listing of the supplies, services, or construction procured under each contract.

5.5

Common Concerns

There are several issues which always arise related to issuing the RFP and vendor's questions. This section discusses some of these issues.

■ 5.5.1 Checklist #4 – Before Issuing the RFP

Before issuing the RFP, complete this checklist. Each "yes" indicates an increase in your chances of being successful. Three or more "nos" indicate that you should spend more time organizing the process before issuing the RFP. This checklist was developed by a private-sector firm.

1. Are you prepared to accept one of the proposals if it can satisfy the mandatory requirements or provide a reasonable solution to your needs?

2. Does the officer who must authorize the final expenditure know and approve of this project?

3. Have you finalized and documented the evaluation process?

4. If this is your first RFP, did you use consulting help?

5. Is the RFP being sent to at least three vendors? Fewer than six?

6. Were the key users involved in the preparation of the RFP?

7. Does each of the suppliers invited to submit a proposal have a chance of getting the contract?

8. Have you clearly identified those requirements which are mandatory as such in the RFP?

9. Are the overall goals of what you want to accomplish from the RFP process documented and understood by you? By your user community? By your management?

10. Do you have a strategy in place if none of the responses is acceptable?

11. Have you included your current supplier in the list of vendors?

12. Have you explained this RFP project to your staff?

13. Have you reviewed the short and long term implications of doing business with each of the vendors invited to respond to the RFP?

14. Have you included in the terms of reference an explanation of company policies and legal requirements that may affect the selection?

15. Before issuing the RFP to the various vendors, have you checked to see if each vendor wants to receive it?

16. Have you included in the RFP some background on your organization?

17. Have you documented your reasons for excluding certain vendors from this process?

18. Is there funding to implement the selected vendor's solution?

19. Have you taken the appropriate steps to protect the confidentiality of the information contained in the RFP?

20. Did you confirm the reputation and customer satisfaction levels for each vendor?

21. Do each of the vendors have a solid customer base in the required locations?

22. Has one person from your organization been assigned to deal with the vendors? Have you informed the vendors and people within your organization to direct all queries to this person?

■ 5.5.2 What Does it Mean to Release an RFP?

To issue or release an RFP is to have it ready and available for suppliers, to send it to the suppliers, or to inform suppliers that it is available.

The RFP must be released to all suppliers at the same time. While this is simple in theory, in practice it may be more difficult.

Suppose there is only one out-of-city supplier and your organization informs suppliers that the RFP is available using the mail service. It is quite possible that the out-of-city supplier may receive your notice several days after the local suppliers. Another two or three days may elapse until a courier service can pick up the RFP and deliver it to the out-of-city supplier. If the proposal due date is only a few weeks ahead, then this loss of five or more days may be significant, and may be interpreted as an unfair practice. Some organizations distribute notices via fax to ensure that all suppliers receive the material at the same time. It is then the supplier's responsibility to arrange delivery of their proposal using a courier service.

The time given to suppliers to prepare their proposals should be commensurate with the complexity of the requirements and take into account any time delays in dealing with suppliers in distant locations.

There is one situation related to this issue which often poses problems for the purchasing organization. What happens when a supplier hears about the competition and wants a copy of the RFP and the competition is still open? The supplier complains that it did not know about the competition or only heard of it late in the process.

There are two different situations to be considered — depending on whether it is an open competition or one based on a prequalification process or restricted source list.

Open Competition

For an open competition, where all suppliers are invited to submit proposals, give the supplier a copy of the RFP. You cannot extend the closing date without significant consequences. If the competition has closed, the supplier may think that your process is unfair, especially your process for announcing the RFP.

It is not the purchaser's responsibility to ensure that every supplier in the marketplace has been contacted. Your responsibility relates to providing publicity commensurate with the importance of the contract. It is not your responsibility to ensure that all eligible suppliers have registered with your purchasing department.

If the purchasing organization has restricted the number of suppliers in some arbitrary but justifiable manner, then the supplier should be provided with an explanation and assurances related to the next RFP. This often occurs in jurisdictions in which a set number of RFPs are released on a first-come, first-serve basis.

Pre-Qualification

The case involving pre-qualification is not as simple nor as straightforward as that for an open competition. If the pre-qualification process was formally defined, well-publicized, based on a set of justifiable mandatory conditions and held recently, then the list can be considered valid. Suppliers who didn't qualify, and suppliers who didn't know about the process can be refused an RFP.

Care must be taken in re-using a prequalification list for RFPs other than those for which the process was designed. It may be convenient to use the list of vendors who were prequalified as "systems integrators" for selecting a related but not identical "network designer." However, it may also be difficult to justify this action.

Care must be taken to ensure that the prequalification process was, in itself, fair and open. If the prequalification process cannot stand up to public scrutiny, then the contracts based on it can be successfully challenged.

Finally, care must be taken to ensure that the prequalification list is reasonably current. The "best practice" is that a prequalification list can only be used for its original purpose and for only 12 months. After that time, new vendors may have entered the market, or prequalified vendors may have changed their business practices.

■ 5.5.3 Do I Have to Explain the RFP to Suppliers?

Throughout this document, the approach taken is that suppliers should be given more information rather than less. The more clearly suppliers understand the RFP and the evaluation process, the better their proposals and the fewer protests that arise.

In many situations, since the RFP seeks solutions to problems, it is good practice to schedule a supplier briefing. The RFP timetable should indicate a meeting at which any supplier can ask questions regarding the RFP.

The meeting should be scheduled shortly after the RFP has been released (usually one or two weeks later). It should be open to all suppliers.

Attendance at the meeting should not be a condition of submitting a proposal unless the actual inspection of the site or some other justification warrants this stringent condition.

The purpose of the meeting is to ensure that the suppliers have a sound understanding of the requirements and other terms of the RFP. Many organizations believe that suppliers should be given as much information as possible. They should be told the names of all of the firms invited to compete. At a minimum, they should be told the number of firms invited to compete.

Infrequently, suppliers may ask questions during and following the suppliers' briefing which require significant modifications to the RFP. It is far better to discover weaknesses at this stage than during the evaluation process.

Typically, the proponents meeting will be chaired by the procurement officer or project manager and attended by project staff. Members of the project team are advised not to make specific commitments with regard to the timing of the final selection unless they are certain the commitment can be kept. This prevents calls from proponents the day after they expect an announcement.

Often, the meeting begins with the introduction of the players and a brief explanation of their roles. Following this, the project manager may give a brief overview of the work to be done.

Written questions, previously submitted, are then officially answered. Following this, questions are accepted from the suppliers present. In some cases, questions will be answered during the meeting. In other cases, the chair will indicate that a written response will be available with the transcript or minutes of the meeting.

Some type of record of the meeting is required. How this is handled varies from organization to organization. The most common practice is to produce minutes of the meeting which contain questions and answers. But minutes are subject to errors — either errors in fact or errors of omission. It is very easy to dismiss a question as trivial and not include it in the minutes. However, the answer to that question may cause a supplier to "no bid." To avoid making decisions about the importance of statements made during the meeting, some organizations produce an actual transcript. They hire a court reporter who records the meeting and issues a complete transcript. The procurement officer sends copies to all vendors having indicated an interest in submitting a proposal.

On occasion, some suppliers, anticipating that the RFP process was unfair or biased, have brought their own court reporters to the meeting. Clearly, this level of open conflict with suppliers is to be avoided.

■ 5.5.4 Do I Have to Keep a Record of Suppliers' Questions?

To treat all suppliers equally requires that all suppliers receive the same information.

What happens, then, when a supplier calls a member of the project team and asks some questions? If that member of the project team has not been designated as the official contact, then the supplier should be directed to the procurement officer. In addition, on some highly sensitive projects, the project person would be required to inform the procurement officer that a supplier had called.

RFPs always encourage supplier questions. The problem is ensuring that each supplier gets the same information. Discussions on the telephone are informal. People often forget their specific words. For example, consider the following situation: Three different suppliers each call up the procurement officer to discuss the requirements for a project plan as defined in the RFP. By the end of the third conversation, the procurement officer would probably be unable to recall which supplier was told "the June 3 deadline cannot be changed under any circumstances" and which one was told "I understand from the project manager that the June 3 deadline is important." Obviously, the

implications of each of these sentences could be different to each supplier. To avoid this level of informality, some organizations insist that all questions be submitted via fax "to ensure that we understand your specific questions." The answers are sent in writing via fax to all suppliers having received the RFP.

Some RFP timetables have a cut-off date for supplier questions. This date is usually a few days before proposals are due. This permits the purchaser to answer questions and send the answer to all suppliers.

This process, while seemingly too formal for many organizations, does ensure that suppliers received the same information. This is a critical requirement for a "fair and open" competition.

[1] Page 4.11, Reference *2.
[2] Page 24, AS 36.30.265, Reference *4.
[3] Paragraph 29, Page 15, Reference *7.
[4] Pages 3-4, Reference *3.
[5] Reference *26.
[6] AS 36.30.050, Reference *4.
[7] Article 4, Reference *4.
[8] Article 8, Reference *8.
[9] Article 4, Reference *4.
[10] Article 1016, Reference *27.
[11] Article 7, Reference *8.

The Evaluation Process

— CONTENTS —

The Evaluation Process

— CONTENTS CONTD. —

6.1

What is an Evaluation?

■ 6.1.1 Definition

The dictionary defines the word "evaluate" as "ascertain amount of; find numerical expression for; appraise, assess." Hence, an evaluation process is the means by which we appraise a proposal, in many cases by finding a numerical expression for its relative worth.

Most purchasing texts will inform you that evaluation is the process of comparing one vendor's proposal to your requirements. Proposals are compared using the process and criteria identified prior to issuing the RFP. Each proposal is evaluated using the same criteria.

Most texts emphasize that proposals are not directly compared with each other. They are always compared to requirements. In this way, we believe that it is easier to defend the process as being objective. Using this approach, we never say "We compared the two project plans — that of Company A and Company B — and Company A

had more details about the specific tasks, was more realistic in the schedule and was, therefore, a lot more convincing." What we say is "We evaluated both companies' plans against our requirements using the evaluation criteria and Company A scored higher because of the information they provided about the tasks and schedule."

The evaluation process establishes a ranking or a score for a proposal based not on our "real" requirements — for we might not have stated these completely or accurately — but on the requirements which we have written down in the RFP.

■ 6.1.2 Different Approaches

There are several different ways to evaluate proposals. Some are based on color coding of the responses; others on the use of adjectives (good, better, best); and still others on numerical scores.

Here's an example of an adjectival scoring system:

Rating	Evaluation Statements
Exceptional	The submission exceeds expectations, excellent probability of success and in achieving all objectives. Very innovative.
Good	Very good probability of success. Achieves all objectives in reasonable fashion.
Acceptable	Has reasonable probability of success. Some objectives may not be met.
Poor	Falls short of expectations and has a low probability of success.
Not acceptable	Submission fails to meet requirements and the approach has no probability of success.

While no method is perfect, some are better than others. One method that has been found satisfactory in many jurisdictions is a weighted point system in which points are awarded for each proposal's ability to meet predetermined criteria. Many organizations have found, through bitter experience, that it is harder to defend an evaluation based solely on words than one based on numbers. Scores seem easier to justify and to defined as being objective. Part of this is reality — often the detailed process for assigning scores is based on well-defined, measurable factors. For example: "The proposal will receive one point (to a maximum of four) for each full-time member of the project team with more than five years of directly related experience on similar projects." Part of the attraction of a numerical score is fiction: saying that a proposal received 230 points out of a maximum score of 400 is, to many people, much more concrete that saying that the proposal was "poor." Numbers imply objectivity and fairness.

Defending the Process

It is important that each of the evaluators deals with the process, the RFPs and the suppliers in a consistent and defensible manner. Often, evaluators are inexperienced and welcome some direction on their role.

Some projects have an RFP officer who provides the project manager and evaluators with on-going advice, information about the evaluation process and scoring mechanisms, worksheets for conducting the evaluation, and guidance concerning "best practices," policies and legal requirements such as freedom of information laws.

Having a standard approach eliminates personal bias and takes some of the arbitrariness out of scoring. A good working definition of when to assign a five versus an eight, for example, will ensure that evaluators can agree on a score rather than simply averaging the different scores. For example, "a score of five should be assigned only if the majority of the factors meet standards, the requirement is not overly difficult to meet, and the factors which are deficient are of a very minor nature."

In many organizations that use RFPs frequently, there is an unending debate over the evaluation process. At one extreme are those who want to make a choice without having to justify it. At the other extreme are those who want the decision to be an almost mechanical calculation of a score.

Some purchasers want to provide suppliers with as little information as possible. They'll begrudgingly identify the major selection criteria (usually price, proposed solution and quality of the proposal). They do not want to give the suppliers a lot of detail. Their argument is that the suppliers should know how to prepare a proposal. In fact, for many of these people — often senior purchasing officials — detailing the evaluation process or specific criteria is impractical. They don't know enough about the problem, the selection process or the alternative solutions. Their logic is that they will somehow "know" the best solution when they see it. In fact, what they are saying is that detailed selection criteria would restrict their choices. They want to be arbitrary and able to select whomever they wish.

Some purchasers want to provide suppliers with all of the selection details. For example, "in evaluating your company's capabilities, we will assign one point for each year in business." Provision of the detailed points ensures that each supplier understands the process, but invariably, the process comes under severe attack.

The best practice is to define the evaluation process, in summary form, in the RFP. Identify the major categories on which the proposal will be evaluated, and the weight assigned to each factor.

Unfortunately, some organizations do not publish the weights. Suppliers prepare very different proposals when the quality of the solution is worth 70 percent and cost 30 percent rather than cost being worth 70 percent and quality of the solution the remaining 30 percent.

It is good practice to ensure that the RFP explains the criteria that may result in the rejection of an offer, states that your evaluation will include both the purchase price and all one-time and ongoing costs that will be incurred, and states the relative importance of each major selection criterion.

Rather than relying on good practices alone, many jurisdictions specify in law, regulations, or directives the essential features of the evaluation process. In Alaska, the Procurement Regulations[1] specify the following:

(a) The procurement officer or an evaluation committee consisting of the procurement officer and at least two state employees or public officials shall evaluate proposals.

(b) The evaluation must be based only on the evaluation factors set out in the request for proposals. Numerical rating systems may be used, but are not required. If numerical rating systems are not used, the procurement officer, or each member of the evaluation committee, as applicable, shall explain his or her ranking determination in writing. Evaluation factors not specified in the request for proposals may not be considered. The weighting value or numerical system to be applied to each evaluation factor must be set out in the request for proposals.

(c) Cost must be an evaluation factor (unless the procurement is for architectural engineering or land surveying services) and if a numerical rating system is used, the request for proposals must state the value to be applied to cost.

(d) For the purposes of evaluating cost factors... the proposal with the lowest cost factor must receive the highest available rating allocated to cost. Each proposal that has a higher cost factor than the lowest must have a lower rating for cost. If a numerical rating system is used to evaluate the cost factor, the points allocated to higher-priced proposals must be equal to the lowest proposal price multiplied by the maximum points available for price, divided by the higher proposal price.

Here is the approach used in the state of Washington[2]:

The RFP process allows consideration of such items as functional capability, including:

> **a.   Expansion and upgrade capability.**
>
> **b.   Vendor support.**
>
> **c.   Integration of the resource into the agency architecture.**

It also allows consideration of full cost; including but not limited to, costs to purchase, finance, install, operate, use, and maintain; plus trade-in, redeployment, or residual value.

> •
>
> •

3.   Agencies conducting RFP's shall:

> •
>
> •

Include in the RFP the specific criteria that shall be used to evaluate vendor responses...

> •
>
> •

Give full and fair consideration to all vendors responding to the RFP.

In Yukon, care has been taken to ensure that the evaluation process will be visibly fair. Key information must be provided in the RFP and evaluations can only be done on the criteria in the RFP.

11[3]. Evaluation criteria and standards used to evaluate bids and proposals will be fully and clearly described in requests for bids or proposals, and only those evaluation criteria and standards will be used to evaluate bids or proposals received.

50[4]. The contracting authority will evaluate bids or proposals... solely on the basis of the evaluation criteria and requirements contained in the request...

Best and Final Offer

To complete our discussion of the evaluation process and permissible variations, we should mention "best and final offer." In some jurisdictions, the suppliers are provided with a second chance. If their initial proposal is capable of satisfying the requirements but has some deficiencies or shortcomings, then the purchasing organization can, in many jurisdictions, ask for a "best and final offer." This is a formal process designed to promote fair and open competition, yet permit proposals to be modified based on input from the purchasing organization.

Here is how it is structured in Alaska[5]

(a)   Offerors of proposals reasonably susceptible for award as determined in the evaluation... may be offered the opportunity to discuss their proposals with

the procurement officer or evaluation committee at the discretion of the procurement officer. The evaluation of a proposal may be adjusted as a result of a discussion under this section. The condition, terms, or price of the proposed contract may be altered or otherwise changed during the course of discussions.

(b)   The procurement officer may limit discussions to specific sections of the request for proposals. If during discussions there is a need for any substantial clarification of or change in the request for proposals, the request must be amended to incorporate the clarification or change. Auction techniques that reveal one offeror's price to another, and disclosure of any information derived from competing proposals, are prohibited. Any oral modification of a proposal shall be reduced to writing by the offeror.

(c)   Following discussions, the procurement officer shall set a date and time for the submission of best and final proposals. Best and final proposals may be submitted only once. However, the chief procurement officer or the head of a purchasing agency may make a written determination that it is in the state's best interest to conduct additional discussions or change the state's requirements and require another submission of best and final proposals. Otherwise, discussion of or changes in the best and final proposals may not be allowed before award. If an offeror does not submit a best and final proposal or a notice of withdrawal, the offeror's immediately previous proposal is considered the offeror's best and final proposal.

(d)   After best and final proposals are received, final evaluations will be conducted...

The state of California has adopted an iterative process which permits vendors to exchange information with the purchasing organization. This process provides suppliers the opportunity to modify their approaches based on discussions. (This process is described in Section 3.2.4 Example 4: State of California.)

Rejecting a Proposal

In many organizations, the reasons for rejecting a specific proposal are straightforward: either the proposal did not satisfy one or more of the mandatory conditions or the proposal failed to score sufficient points to be considered for the award. There are other reasons which can be invoked: the business that submitted the proposal was not responsible — the evaluators judged that there was a high risk that the business that submitted the proposal could not complete the work on time and within budget.

Some jurisdictions do more than provide examples. They define the specific reasons for rejecting a proposal. In stating the formal reasons, the organization removes the appearance of arbitrary actions[6]:

47.   The contracting authority may reject a bid or proposal which has been received prior to the closing time only where:

(a)   it is not submitted in the required form;

(b)   there are significant omissions of required information;

(c)   a bid or proposal is not signed as required in the request for bids or proposals;

(d)   the required bid security in the required form is

not provided;

    (e)   the bid or proposal has conditions attached which are not authorized by the request for bids or proposals;

    (f)   the bid or proposal fails to meet one or more standards specified in the request for bids or proposals; or

    (g)   there is substantial evidence that, pursuant to the evaluation criteria contained in the request for bids or proposals, a bidder or proponent would be unable to carry out the contract as specified.

Rejecting All Proposals

Occasionally, all proposals are rejected. This obviously should be a rare occurrence caused by unusual and unanticipated circumstances. The Alaska Procurement Code[7] contains a list of some reasons:

After the opening of bids or proposals or after notice of intent to award but before award, all bids or proposals may be rejected in whole or in part by the chief procurement officer or the head of a purchasing agency issuing the solicitation. Reasons for rejection include the following:

    (1)   the supplies, services, or construction being procured are no longer required;

    (2)   ambiguous or otherwise inadequate specifications were part of the solicitation;

    (3)   the solicitation did not provide for consideration of all factors of significance to the state;

    (4)   prices exceed available money and it would not be appropriate to adjust quantities to accommodate available money;

    (5)   all otherwise acceptable bids or proposals received are at unacceptable prices;

    (6)   there is reason to believe that the bids or proposals may not have been independently arrived at in open competition, may have been collusive, or may have been submitted in bad faith; or

    (7)   the award is not in the best interests of the state.

■ 6.1.3 What Are the Steps in an Evaluation?

Most evaluation processes are similar. The proposals are received, copies are produced, if required, and the proposals (or sections of the proposals) are distributed to the evaluators.

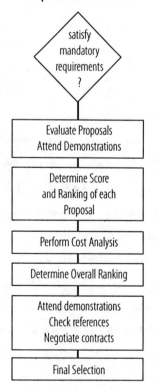

Receive and distribute Proposals to Evaluators

satisfy mandatory requirements ?

Evaluate Proposals
Attend Demonstrations

Determine Score and Ranking of each Proposal

Perform Cost Analysis

Determine Overall Ranking

Attend demonstrations
Check references
Negotiate contracts

Final Selection

The first determination by the project manager or RFP officer is whether the proposal has complied with each of the mandatory terms and conditions. If it has not, it may be eliminated from further consideration. In some jurisdictions, proposals that do not comply with each of the mandatory terms and conditions stated in the RFP must be eliminated from further consideration; in other jurisdictions, they may be eliminated at the discretion of the procurement officer.

If the organization is handling cost as a separate issue, then the cost proposal is separated from the technical proposal. If technical experts are being used to evaluate certain features, then they are given only those sections of the proposals which deal with their issues.

The proposals are then evaluated and a score is computed for each of the predefined criteria. Proposals may be ranked and only those capable of providing an acceptable solution are evaluated further.

More detailed evaluations may incorporate demonstrations or presentations, site visits, and reference checks. Once the evaluators have determined the best proposal, contract negotiation is started. Failure to negotiate an acceptable contract within a predefined time is reason to reject a proposal and consider the next best. In some jurisdictions, "best and final offer" is used to permit those few suppliers judged capable of satisfying the requirements the opportunity to revise their original proposal. In this way, deficiencies can be corrected and a better solution provided.

The main objective of this cumbersome process is to determine the winner, not to rank all the proposals in order. While careful attention must be given to the top two or three, it matters less whether a given proposal ends up fifth or seventh in ranking. Knowing this, some organizations only evaluate the most difficult areas of each proposal to see which suppliers are to be fully evaluated.

Methods of evaluating the proposals will differ based on the goods and services involved, the number of proposals received, and the complexity of the project. Some organizations have standardized the evaluation process. This topic is discussed in section 6.3 of this chapter.

Definition of A Winning Proposal

Whatever specific criteria a particular evaluation process may incorporate, most evaluators look for the following in a proposal:

• Clear evidence that the supplier fully understands the requirements.

• An approach which appears technically sound, achievable within constraints explained by the vendor, and offered in enough detail to provide evidence of these characteristics.

• Clear evidence that the supplier can deliver the expected results by mobilizing qualified staff, capable management, and an experienced organization.

Here are several examples of relatively simple evaluation procedures:

Sample Evaluation Procedure #1

One of the most common evaluation methodologies involves only five steps. These are illustrated below. Following supplier interviews, scoring is completed and the winner selected.

Prior to issuing the RFP, the project manager established the evaluation criteria and the corresponding weights. Once the proposals were received, the evaluation was begun. For those proposals judged as compliant, the evaluation team scored each using a scale of one to 10. Total scores were calculated by multiplying the criterion score by the weight. The highest ranking proposals were short-listed and those suppliers were then interviewed. Following this, additional scoring was done and the winner selected.

This method has been found to be practical in many situations. An example of the application of such a system is set out below.

Establish Compliance
Score the Proposals (including cost)
Develop a Short-List
Interview Suppliers
Score the Proposals

Step 1 – Establish Compliance.

First, we ensure that the proposal complies with each of the mandatory requirements. For example, suppose the RFP stated that a solution must run "on a Unix platform," or that the firm must provide 24-hour service and the proposal did not comply. In these cases, the proposal must be classified as "non-compliant" and disqualified.

The first thing that must be done is to examine each proposal to determine if it meets the mandatory requirements. Any proposal not meeting the mandatory requirements will be rejected immediately with no further consideration.

Step 2 – Score the Proposals.

If a large number of proposals is received, it is appropriate to determine a shortlist of a few proponents for in-depth evaluation.

We now evaluate each proposal and establish a score using the predefined evaluation criteria and weights. For example, suppose that the RFP required the provision of training. We might assign 10 points if the supplier ran regularly scheduled classes on a monthly basis in the same city but only five points if the classes were scheduled less frequently.

Step 3 – Develop a Short-list.

Each proposal must be evaluated independently by comparing it with the established evaluation criteria. Comparisons to other proposals may not be appropriate as bias can influence the scoring. If possible, each member of the evaluation committee should evaluate all the proposals. The committee as a whole may then meet to review each proposal and to achieve a consensus on its advantages and disadvantages. They identify the group of suppliers scoring highest and perform a more detailed investigation of their proposals.

Step 4 – Interview Suppliers.

We interview the short-listed suppliers to clarify the information in their proposals and meet their representatives. These interviews are often used to evaluate the inter-personal skills of the project manager and to clarify critical aspects of the proposal. This step could also be used to designate demonstrations and presentations.

Step 5 – Score the Proposals

Following this, the scoring is completed and the winner selected. A typical evaluation form follows.

The evaluation process just described is composed of a number of building blocks: Establish Compliance, Score the Proposals, Develop a Short-List, Interview Suppliers and Score the Proposals.

Evaluation Summary

Supplier: ABC Company

Criteria	Weight	Score	Weighted Score
(1)	(2)	(3)	(2x3)
Price response	20	8	160
Technical response			
Function	10	8	80
Performance	10	6	60
Service	10	8	80
Software Compatible	10	9	90
Qualifications & Experience			
Vendor Reputation	10	7	70
Experience	10	8	80
Project Team	5	7	35
Quality of the Proposal	15	6	90
TOTAL WEIGHTED POINTS			**745**

Sample Evaluation Procedure #2
A three-stage selection process:

Score the Proposals
Develop a Short-List
In-Depth Evaluations
Develop a Short-List
Demonstrations/Presentations
Evaluate Costs
Final Scoring

There are several distinct ways of evaluating proposals. This one, developed by a municipality, is based on a three-stage process and incorporates demonstrations. Presentations are becoming more popular as an integral part of any evaluation process. With many information technology products, including Geographic Information Systems, a picture is truly "worth a thousand words." Products are often differentiated by factors such as ease of use which can only be evaluated first-hand. The writeup which follows describes both the process and some of the major evaluation criteria.

PROPOSAL SELECTION

1.1 Selection Committee

The Selection Committee will measure each vendor using the evaluation process described below.

However, the Selection Committee reserves the right to reject proposals which, in its opinion, are clearly non-viable. In such a case, if the vendor has demonstrated a valid understanding of the requirement and is otherwise qualified, the municipality will inform the vendor of the reason for rejection and may allow an opportunity to rectify the problem.

1.2 Evaluation Process

1. The first stage in the evaluation process is intended to filter out those vendors considered not to have a viable corporate presence in our region (where local support is deemed necessary) or considered to be incapable of providing the necessary function in the identified environments or the necessary hardware and/or software maintenance. This is an assessment of the vendor's ability to meet the implementation, operational and maintenance requirements and the extent of compliance with the implementation schedule described previously.

The intent is to use the vendor as an expert and to encourage creative proposals. However, the Selection Committee reserves the right to reject proposals which, in its opinion, are clearly non-viable from an implementation, operational, environmental, scheduling, technological or other point of view. In such a case, if the vendor has demonstrated a valid understanding of the requirement and is otherwise qualified, the municipality will inform the vendor of the reason for rejection and may allow an opportunity to rectify the problem.

2. The second stage is a straightforward acceptable/unacceptable analysis of the vendors' responses to the mandatory requirements. A numerical score will be assigned based on how well these requirements were met. All qualified proposals will then be evaluated for completeness and suitability to the requirements. Suppliers will be contacted, if necessary, to clarify an item in question. A short-list will be prepared of suppliers considered most appropriate for the municipality, based on proposal responses.

3. During the third stage, short listed vendors will be asked to perform demonstrations and/or presentations. References for systems similar to the municipality's, supporting the performance claimed by the vendor, will be checked. In addition, the mandate and capability of the vendor to undertake the necessary commitments will be checked and assessed. This may include an inspection of the facilities of the vendor or vendor references prior to award of the contract, to verify claims made in the proposal. Interviews with key personnel would be conducted during the inspection. Shortlisted GIS vendors may be asked to demonstrate their capabilities with a sample of the municipality's mapping data.

The municipality will place a great deal of emphasis on the quality of the references and their similarity to the municipality's target environment.

A five-year effective operating cost will be calculated. The effective operating costs will include all one-time and continuing costs associated with meeting the mandatory and desirable requirements described in the Appendices.

The order of priority of the areas addressed by this RFP are:

The core components:

Processing Infrastructure

Application Environment, including GIS

The network components:

Network Infrastructure

LAN Operating System

Other Products and Services

Contract negotiations with the preferred supplier(s) will begin in priority order. The selected

vendors will be required to negotiate a contract in a format acceptable to the municipality, and based on the municipality's standard Corporate Systems contract.

■ 6.1.4 Evaluations Don't Always Work as Intended

Not all evaluation processes work well. Some don't work at all. They sometimes result in the obvious choice being overlooked, or out-scored. Let's examine the reasons, but first let's examine the evaluation process.

Here's how the evaluation process works. First, we define our needs as best we can. In fact, we are abstracting a "model" of what we think we need. (Often, we don't find out until later that our basic statement of requirements was incomplete, or inadequate.) Once we write down these requirements they take on a life of their own. For it is the requirements, as stated in the RFP, that are used in the evaluation process.

Second, we define an evaluation process — a way of assessing each proposal. In fact, we are looking for a simple way of taking each supplier's information and translating it into a score of some sort. By translating each proposal into a score, we make the process more objective, or at least we think so. The evaluation process can be thought of as a machine. In one end, we feed the proposals. At the other end comes out a score for each. We then simply compare the scores and the highest one is the winner.

Even a cursory examination reveals the fact that there is a lot of room for error in this process.

In the extreme, the proposal obtaining the highest score may be the least appropriate solution. In this case, either the requirements were not adequately defined or the evaluation process was flawed. There are several assumptions which can lead us to withdrawing or modifying the RFP, changing our requirements, changing the evaluation process, or selecting an inappropriate proposal.

In a sense, we've created a model of reality — we've used the RFP document to define the characteristics of the solution we want. We then compare the proposed solution with the requirements as specified using the evaluation process as defined to produce a score. The evaluation process is a "machine" that compares the proposal with the RFP's requirements and assigns a score based on the "goodness of fit." The fundamental assumption we make is that the model reflects our requirements accurately and that the highest scoring proposal will lead to the best solution. This is not always true!

Incomplete Requirements

The foundation for all of this work — the RFP, the proposals and the evaluation — is the Requirements Document. If this document is deficient, incomplete or ambiguous, the proposals will miss the mark. They will not offer viable solutions.

Even complete and clear documents can mislead the vendors and create major problems. Sometimes, organizations "over-design" their requirements. To use an automobile analogy, they identify the characteristics of the high performance car they would like, not the mid-range car they can afford. "Over-design" can lead to all proposals exceeding the budget.

Inappropriate Evaluation Process

Another assumption is that the evaluation process and the scoring mechanism we have created will work as we intended them to — they will identify the "best" proposal. Sometimes, scoring mechanisms, the weights used, or the factors themselves are not appropriate. For example, we may have neglected an important factor such as our assessment of the risk associated with each solution. In this case, the proposal with the highest score could, in theory at least, also carry with it the highest risk.

Another example may help illustrate this point. Suppose that cost is worth 40 percent of the score and technical merit of the proposed solution is worth 10 percent. In this case, a proposal having a poor technical solution but not costing much could score higher than one having a brilliant solution but costing somewhat more. This may not have been the intention of the project manager or executive director when the evaluation process was defined.

Many organizations first establish the evaluation process and then the scoring mechanisms. When these have been defined, they create scenarios to reflect different types of proposals they might get. They investigate how different types of proposals would be scored: a proposal with a brilliant technical solution but a high risk versus a proposal from an established vendor with a mediocre solution but costing only 50 percent as much as the competitions'. In this way, the evaluators test and modify the process and the scoring mechanism prior to issuing the RFP.

Costing Issues

The evaluation process determines the "winner." The same proposal can "win" in one process, and not even be a serious finalist in another. Consider these three different processes. In each, assume that the proposals considered satisfy the mandatory requirements of the RFP.

1. If you are looking for a least-cost solution, then simply evaluate all proposals that satisfy your mandatory conditions and select the least expensive one.

2. If you are looking for the proposal which provides the "best solution" within budget, then select the one with the highest point score that doesn't exceed the budget.

3. If you are looking for the proposal which you believe can provide a sound solution and still costs less than the most expensive one, simply evaluate all proposals that satisfy your mandatory conditions. Then select all of those with a score more than some predetermined number — say 700 out of 1000 available points. All of these proposals will be classified as "capable of providing a sound solution." Select the least expensive from this group.

6.2

A Building Block Approach to the Process

In this section, we'll examine the process itself. In reviewing a large number of RFPs, only six building types of building blocks were identified:

1.	Establish Compliance
2.	Score the Proposals
3.	Develop a Short-List
4.	Interview Suppliers
5.	Evaluate the Cost
6.	Impose Upset Levels

Many different evaluation processes can be constructed by combining some or all of these building blocks in different sequences. The example above used only four of these. More complex examples can use all six and repeat some of them two or three times. For example, one evaluation process commonly used is based on a three-step short-listing process. After each major type of analysis, the list of suppliers still being considered is reduced. This is repeated three times; once for each type of analysis.

Different processes formed by using different building blocks, different evaluation criteria and different weights will yield different results. Purchasers should test their evaluation process before using it on real proposals. Some organizations create hypothetical vendors and "walk through" the evaluation process. These purchasers are investigating the ability of their intended process to yield an acceptable result. They are seeing how small differences in process or weight can influence the results. For example, if "technical merit" receives 10 percent more weight, will the results change? Is this acceptable? If cost is included as an evaluation criterion, could a company win the competition but be $200,000 higher than a close competitor? Is this acceptable?

Often, by testing their evaluation process, organizations discover that the process will readily identify those firms capable of doing an acceptable job. The process will identify a group of companies that score high — say in the 80 to 90 percent range. The process may not, however, be very good at identifying which of the companies in this group is the best. Often, additional thought and more specific criteria have to be included to validate the winner.

For almost any proposal, a face-to-face presentation by the proponents adds value to the process. It is very difficult to determine by reading the proposal and references "the ability of the project manager to communicate effectively with a wide range of users." This attribute is readily determined in a two-hour presentation by the project manager. Presentations provide a quality control check on the selection process. They often reveal issues which have been overlooked or under-valued. While a firm cannot go from last place to first place on the basis of a presentation, the presentation can be useful in differentiating the skills of the top three proponents.

■ 6.2.1 Establish Compliance

Mandatory Requirements

Some organizations establish a set of mandatory requirements in the RFP. These requirements can be administrative, such as "Proposals are due by August 15 and must be received no later than 5:00 p.m. at the specified location." The requirements can also be technical in nature, identifying a critical feature or functional capability. For RFPs with mandatory requirements, the evaluation process is a two-step process. First,

the evaluators examine each supplier's ability to satisfy the mandatory requirements. Suppliers not able to do this are eliminated from further consideration. Second, the evaluators assign a score to each proposal based on the evaluation criteria (similar to the example presented earlier).

Typically, evaluators establish compliance before doing a more detailed analysis of a proposal. During this step, one or more evaluators review each proposal to ensure that all of the mandatory conditions have been met. A mandatory condition is a requirement that must be met without alteration. One example is the submission of the proposal by a specified time. If it is late, it is usually returned to the supplier unopened. Another example is a requirement that the supplier must provide 24-hour emergency service.

To simplify the analysis of the proposals, all of the mandatory requirements are often identified in one section of the RFP. The RFP then instructs the vendor to respond to each requirement in the same section of the proposal.

Many evaluators are uncomfortable eliminating a supplier from further consideration for failure to satisfy a mandatory condition — especially if the requirement is, in fact, only "highly desirable" and not really mandatory.

Mandatory requirements must be precisely defined and must be essential elements in the success of the project. For example, consider the following mandatory requirement: "Suppliers must have a local service office." Now, I presume that the concern of the purchasing organization was prompt service and travel time. As stated, this requirement is poorly defined and could cause a number of problems for the evaluators.

First, the RFP didn't state the type of service required. Was it for equipment repairs, software support, network support? Second, no service levels were given. Did they need eight-hour per day support? Or 24-hour support? Third, no mention was made of the level of expertise required locally. Did they require a very expensive technical expert who might only be found at the supplier's head office or development facility?

It is difficult to declare a proposal non-compliant when the mandatory requirement was not stated precisely and could be interpreted several ways. In these cases, evaluators often declare all proposals compliant, examine the actual requirement more closely, and seek clarification from the suppliers. Evaluators often ignore ambiguous mandatory requirements and evaluate each proposal on its merits.

As a result of this process, each proposal is declared to be either compliant or non-complaint. Compliant proposals are evaluated further. Non-compliant proposals are eliminated from the competition after preparing a memo for the project file.

To ensure that the suppliers identify which terms are mandatory, many RFPs define the term, indicating that it will be identified by use of the word "must." Here are the definitions used by the state of Arizona[8]:

5. Definition of Key Words Used in the RFP

5.1 Shall, Must: Indicates a mandatory requirement.

Failure to meet these mandatory requirements may result in the rejection of a proposal as non-responsive.

5.2 Should: Indicates something that is recommended but not mandatory. If the offeror fails to provide recommended information, the state may, at its sole option, ask the offeror to provide the information or evaluate the proposal without the information.

5.3 May: Indicates something that is not mandatory but permissible.

It is both a common practice and a "best practice" to summarize all of the mandatory terms on one page in the RFP and reference the pages which describe each of the requirements in more detail.

Often, "within budget" is a mandatory condition. However, suppliers are not always told the budget. There are several different approaches to handling this problem. Obviously, publishing the budget is the best but there are some compelling arguments raised against it in many jurisdictions. If your organization does not publish the budget, then it must include language in the RFP which indicates the type of solution you are seeking or the importance attributed to cost. For example, "we are looking for an economical solution" or "cost is the overriding consideration."

Here is what one jurisdiction tells its purchasers if all the proposals exceed the unpublished budget:

When this happens, your [organization] may appear to be incompetent and ill-prepared, but you can reduce the impact on your organization. You have two alternatives:

• cancel the procurement and perhaps also the project for which the procurement is being done; or,

• review your requirements and reduce them to the essential needs to be met. This will mean a new competition, with a new requirements documents and all the inherent delays and potential for complaints from the supplier community.

Some jurisdictions do not permit significant changes to the RFP or proposal through negotiation. For these, it is not proper, usually contrary to written policies, and sometimes illegal to identify the winning company and then approach them to determine how much of their solution they can deliver — not for their proposed price of (for example) $100,000 — but for your budgeted amount of $50,000.

Make sure you understand the business case for the project since a procurement is part of a project. Ensure the project plan is well thought through. Assure yourself that suitable technology products and services are available at the prices you anticipate before you finalize the project plan. This knowledge of products and services can be gained by talking to industry contacts, suppliers and other ministries about suitable products and services.

Ensure your requirements document contains only specifications that truly reflect program needs.

Include a tentative amount in the RFP. For example, a statement such as "we anticipate that the winning supplier will propose a solution whose total life-cycle present value cost is between $1 million and $1.3 million." This information will ensure that suppliers propose solutions which are

affordable, if those solutions exist.

Alternatively, structure the RFP so that the supplier proposes a solution which can be expanded as needed. For example, suppose you want to acquire services related to developing a complex training system. Your RFP could ask for a proposal to develop "up to" three training modules, or to provide training for "up to" 200 people, or a treatment program for "up to" 15 people. In this way, you can obtain a proposal for the product and select the quantity that is affordable.

■ 6.2.2 Score the Proposals

In most evaluation processes, scoring is performed as the first or second task immediately following the determination of compliance.

Most proposals require that the financial information be provided separately from the rest. This is to ensure that the technical evaluators have no knowledge of the pricing proposal and avoids the debate over whether knowledge of the pricing proposal influenced an evaluator's assessment of technical factors.

Upon receipt of the proposals, the financial section is removed and given to the analyst for evaluation. This person receives the information, establishes the costs to be used in the evaluation, and determines the score (if required). (Costing is dealt with as building block #5, Section 6.2.5.)

Copies of the remainder of each proposal are distributed to the evaluation team as required. For small proposals, each member of the evaluation team reads the entire proposal (except for cost) and performs the evaluation. On larger proposals, specific sections are usually assigned to individuals. For example, the communications expert on the evaluation team and the project manager would evaluate the proposed network.

The evaluators then meet to review each others evaluations to resolve differences and to ensure that they share the same understanding of each proposal. This process results in scores for each evaluation criterion. The purpose of the meeting, and the team effort for that matter, is to discuss, understand and resolve differences — not simply to average the scores. If two evaluators, both expert in the area, score the same proposal as a "two" and a "six" respectively, there is some fundamental difference in each evaluator's interpretation of the proposal. It is not good enough to give the proposal a "four" — the average of the two scores. Fairness dictates that the two evaluators discuss the issue, identify the differences in interpretation, and agree upon a score.

Three components are required to score a proposal: criteria, weights, and a scoring system. Each of these is discussed in the remainder of this section.

Evaluation Criteria

Evaluation criteria are as different as people. Some are very specific and easy to assess. Others are vague and highly subjective.

There are three major groups of critera: technical, management and cost.

Technical criteria usually include the following: understanding of the problem, soundness of the approach and solution, ability to satisfy the stated requirements, service and support capabilities, analysis of risks, and testing methodology.

Management criteria usually include the following: Project plans, management approach, qualifications of key people, project timetable, and corporate experience.

Cost is often evaluated in terms of the following critera: Total life cycle costs, cost controls, consistency with technical and management plans.

An Example of Detailed Selection Criteria

Here is how an RFP might set out the evaluation criteria in a well-detailed plan. This particular example is from an RFP for an integrated law office system.

Vendor proposals will be evaluated based upon the following criteria. Criteria are listed in order of importance:

(a) the ability of the vendor to propose a complete solution to the documented needs;

(b) the degree to which the proposed solution fully integrates the data processing, office automation, and word processing capabilities of the system, providing transparent access to all system functions via a single user terminal or work station;

(c) the seven-year present value of the total cost of the proposed solution, including initial front-end costs, recurring annual costs and incremental costs for upgrades and expansion;

(d) the financial stability and degree of established business presence of the vendor in the New York legal community;

(e) the success of the vendor in installing similar

systems of comparable size and complexity;

(f) the degree to which the proposed software, after modifications which the vendor is willing to perform, will meet the documented application needs;

(g) the amount of modification required to be performed on the application software;

(h) the hardware reliability, and the quality and availability of maintenance and support; and

(i) the quality of user training, implementation assistance, documentation and the application software support.

Proposals are evaluated by scoring them in each of the selection categories. The raw scores — usually out of "10" — are multiplied by the weight and totalled. The supplier with the highest score becomes the first choice.

For example, the first selection criterion deals with providing a complete solution to the customer's requirements. This selection criterion had a weight of 20 percent. The buyer had determined before issuing the RFP that there were 10 important elements to an integrated law office system. To determine the score for this section, a supplier would receive between zero and two points for each application or feature which they could provide. They would receive a zero if this feature was absent from their proposal. They would receive a one if the feature was there but at a rudimentary or unsophisticated level. Suppliers proposing a sophisticated version of a feature, such as an advanced word processing package, with a large, well-established user base would receive a score of two. There were 10 required features, which are listed below:

Applications

· accounting

· word processing

· work product retrieval

· internal databases

· external legal and non-legal databases

· client matter management

· electronic mail/office functions

Support

· hardware installation and support

· network design, installation and support

· user training and system documentation

Evaluation criteria are those factors which are used in the assessment of the proposals' merits. They are usually divided into three classifications: categories, major criteria and detailed criteria.

New Criteria

Once the evaluation criteria are stated it is difficult to deal with factors that have not been included. How do you handle the proposal from a supplier that suggests an unexpected approach, a new piece of technology, or provides information which changes the way you think about the project? How do you build this unknown into the RFP? You certainly cannot include a factor labelled "unexpected information." If you did, you would be accused of being arbitrary. One approach which seems to be gaining in popularity is to include "management of risk" as a factor. This permits the evaluators to take into account new, unexpected information. For all new information influences the evaluators' assessment of the risks of the project. Other criteria which permit the evaluators to reward suppliers for innovation and unexpected approaches is "assessment of the strategies proposed to minimize the risks associated with the project."

Weights

Weights are used to assign a relative importance to each evaluation criterion. They are usually determined by the project manager in consultation with the users and the steering committee prior to release of the RFP. Weights reflect the degree of importance of various criteria. Consider the following example:

(a)	Price response	20%
(b)	Technical response	40%
	• functionality and features	
	• delivery performance	
	• service	
	• use with ministry software	
(c)	Qualifications & Experience	25%
	• vendor reputation	
	• team experience	
(d)	Quality of proposal	15%

Scoring Systems

Scoring systems are used to establish a numerical value for the merits of the proposal in dealing with each evaluation criteria. Numerical scoring systems are easier to understand and explain.

Evaluators sometimes have a difficult time deciding on the specific score of a factor. Suppose

you were evaluating the plan for a project, or the project manager's experience. When is it worth five out of 10? Why isn't it worth a score of six? Or four?

The more general question is how do we eliminate personal bias and take some of the arbitrariness out of scoring? Can we ensure that each of the evaluators are using the same scheme?

Precise Rules Accompany Each Score

The following rules were taken from a U.S. government publication dealing with procurement policy in the U.S. Air Force (Air Force Regulation 70-15). They go a long way toward standardizing the rules for assigning scores. I certainly recommend their inclusion in your evaluation process.

1. If a requirement (objective) is particularly difficult to meet and the proposal offers an approach which, with little or no risk, will yield a result which exceeds requirements qualitatively, the item should score 8, 9 or 10, dependent upon the level of exceptional features offered.

2. If the requirement (objective) is relatively difficult to meet, the majority of the factors are acceptable, no major deficiencies or risks exist therein, and the collective approach yields a qualitative benefit beyond that which is minimal, a score of 6 or 7 should be assigned, dependent upon the benefits to be attained.

3. If the majority of the factors meet standards, the requirement is not overly difficult to meet, and the factors which are deficient are of a very minor nature or are susceptible to easy correction, the item should be scored five.

4. If the major number of important factors are

acceptable but one or more factors is deficient and some minor risk is involved in the correction thereof, the score for the item should be four.

The assignment of a score above five must reflect some qualitative achievement such as improved ease of maintenance effort through simplicity of design.

5. If a majority of the factors for the item are deficient and their correction, either collectively or individually, poses a serious problem in correction or has a "domino" effect on the other design features, or the approach poses a high risk without means for correction, or if the approach fails, a score of three, two or one should be assigned, with the lower score indicating a serious or severe condition.

6. If the major factors of the item are deficient to the extent that a major reorientation of the proposal is necessary, or if the approach taken is undesirable and correction would require a major and material change in the proposal, the item should be scored zero.

SCORING SYSTEM SUMMARY

10	EXCEPTIONAL
9	
8	EXCEEDS STANDARDS
7	
6	MEETS STANDARDS
5	
4	
3	FAILS TO MEET STANDARDS
2	
1	
0	UNACCEPTABLE

A score is established for each criterion. In some situations, each member of the evaluation team establishes a score for each criterion. In other situations, the team meets and, by consensus, establishes one score for the entire team.

The score is multiplied by the weight to determine the number of evaluation points awarded. This process is repeated for all of the criteria and a total evaluation score is calculated.

Guidelines Accompany Each Score

Many organizations publish guidelines to assist the evaluators. Recently, Ontario used the guidelines described in this section to identify the winner in an RFP[9] for reengineering the procurement function.

Each of 10 different factors was to be scored by each evaluator. The scores were then multiplied by the corresponding weights to determine the overall total score for each proposal.

The evaluators were instructed to use the following scoring system to assign an integer from zero to 10 for each factor:

Rating	Score
Perfect	10
Superior	8
Satisfactory	6
Unsatisfactory	4 or less

There were 10 factors. The evaluation guidelines contained both positive and negative indicators for each factor. Many organizations do not specifically identify these negative factors. The rest of this section contains the factors, the indicators and the weights assigned.

Factor 1: Bidder Capability (Weight = 10)

Positive Indicators:

1. Significant projects in three key areas

2. Organizational depth and scope

3. Established in the Ontario marketplace for three years or more

4. Previous government assignments

Negative Indicators:

1. Marginal projects

2. Extensive use of subcontractors

Factor 2: Project Team (Weight = 40)

Positive Indicators:

1. Project manager is experienced in all three key areas

2. Project manager has managed large, similar projects

3. Key assistants (two or three) are experienced in three key areas

4. Extra (contingency) resources are available

5. Two or more specialists to assist team

6. Experience with a similar system

7. Commitment/dedication of resources

Negative Indicators:

1. Limited experience of the project manager

2. Poor reference checks

3. Marginal projects to illustrate qualifications

4. "Bare bones" team

5. Part-time project manager

Factor 3: Project Plan (Weight = 15)

Positive Factors:

1. Clarity and rationality

2. Deliverables related to project steps

3. Quality checks/reviews

4. Workload data

5. Key issues for each deliverable are identified

6. Effective use of government personnel

Negative Factors:

1. Apparent anomalies

2. Illogical flow

Factor 4: Bid Price (Weight = 10)

Positive Factors:

1. Not more than 25 percent below the mean

Negative Factors:

1. More than 25 percent below the mean

2. Above the mean

Factor 5: Tools/Methodology (Weight = 15)

Positive Factors:

1. Proven existence of established methodology

2. Methodology used previously

3. Comprehensive software support

5. Integrated software tools

Negative Factors

1. Methodology unproven or unsubstantiated
2. Limited software

Factor 6: Approach (Weight = 15)

Positive Factors:

1. Emphasis on building support
2. Effective education and communication
3. Sensitivity for ministry concerns
4. Recognition of key stakeholders

Factor 7: Understanding of our Environment (Weight = 10)

Positive Factors

1. Evident understanding of diversity, control/service issues, ministry involvement
2. Previous government experience

Negative Factors

1. Absence of evident understanding

Factor 8: Risk Management (Weight = 15)

Positive Factors:

1. Thoughtful response
2. Innovative ideas
3. Apparent recognition of problem

Negative Factors:

1. Routine reply

Factor 9: Schedule (Weight = 10)

Positive Factors:

1. Meets deadline with a practical schedule
2. Complete by target date with good rationale

Negative Factors:

1. Not definitive
2. More than two months late

Factor 10: Implementation (Weight = 10)

Positive Factors

1. Firm has proven track record on systems integration, development and implementation management
2. Project personnel are experienced with development and implementation

Negative Factors

1. No track record

Other Scoring Techniques

There are many less precise techniques in common usage. In some RFPs, each proposal automatically receives five out of 10 for a given factor. This amount is then adjusted up or down based on a consensus of the evaluators' opinions. This technique is less precise and more arbitrary than the previous two.

In some jurisdictions, desirable features are evaluated as "yes" or "no." If the supplier proposes to satisfy the requirement, it receives all of the points assigned to the feature. It the supplier cannot satisfy the requirement, it receives no points.

Some organizations do not use a scoring system, but rather assign points for specific values of each factor. The maximum points represent the importance of the factor. For example, prior experience on similar projects could be worth a total of eight points. The proposal would receive two points for each previous project up to the maximum.

■ 6.2.3 Develop a Short-List

Once an evaluation score has been determined for each proposal, this step is used to reduce the number of proposals to be evaluated in subsequent steps.

Consider the following illustrative example. Eight proposals were evaluated and the following scores were assigned: 82, 80, 78, 72, 65, 63, 50, 48.

We now wish to develop a short list. Let's first divide the scores into groups. A group consists of proposals with similar scores. The first group could be 82, 80, 78. There is some question as to which group the proposal scoring 72 should be in. It is always easier to justify keeping a proposal in the competition than disqualifying it. Since 72 is mid-way between 78 and 65, let's put the proposal with 72 in the first group. The next two groups are easier: one being 65 and 63; the other, 50 and 48.

If we want to keep lots of proposals in the competition, we could eliminate only the lowest group: 50 and 48. If we want fewer proposals, we could eliminate the middle group: 65 and 63.

It is neither fair nor defensible to eliminate a proposal that scored better than one that has been kept in. For example, we cannot drop the proposal with the score of 72 if we keep the one with the score of 65.

In some jurisdictions, the evaluators are not strictly bound by the point scores. The project manager has the discretionary power to declare whether a one or two point difference in scores represents a significant difference in the quality of the proposed solution.

This short-listing process produces a reduced list of proposals to be evaluated further.

■ 6.2.4 Interview Suppliers

Presentations are often used to obtain additional information from the proponents or to see a product demonstrated. Presentations provide an opportunity to meet the supplier personnel, to assess their inter-personal skills, and to clarify the proposal. Often, face-to-face presentations confirm the evaluation process. Sometimes, the presentations provide critical information not readily available nor easily determined from a written proposal. For example, the project manager from one of the vendor's may, in discussing the details of the proposal, demonstrate a depth of knowledge and experience that far exceeds the description in the proposal. Alternatively, presentations provide some suppliers the opportunity to show how little they know about certain specific aspects of the project.

The procurement officer should prepare an agenda for the presentation outlining the objectives of the presentation and any specific requirements. All shortlisted proponents should be given a copy of the agenda far enough in advance to allow them to prepare properly. A set of evaluation criteria should be prepared (prior to issuing the RFP) in order to evaluate the presentations.

Notes should be taken during the presentations, and/or written responses obtained from the proponents. The notes may become part of the documentation supporting the final selection decision.

This process usually occurs after the initial evaluation. The interview may, in fact, be a presentation, or a demonstration of software, or a question and answer session.

During these sessions, information is obtained to clarify the supplier's proposal but not to modify the proposal. These sessions are not an opportunity for the purchaser to change the requirements or the RFP terms, or for the supplier to submit major modifications. They are not a negotiation session.

Often, the supplier's performance is rated by the evaluation team and used to complete the scoring.

■ 6.2.5 Evaluate the Cost

There are several different approaches for incorporating cost into an evaluation. Whichever approach is used must reflect the priorities and the business case related to the RFP. Cost is normally submitted as a separate section in a proposal or in a separate document. In this way, the evaluation team which has been formed to deal with functionality and other issues is not tainted by knowing the costs of various proposals.

While cost is usually analyzed separately, there is communication between the evaluation team and the financial team to ensure that the tasks underlying the costs are reasonable. Often, the financial officer will attend meetings of the evaluation team to obtain a better understanding of each proposal's approach and to ensure that all

cost items have been identified.

Cost usually means cumulative cost — a total cost of all related activities, goods and services. In some jurisdictions, they use life-cycle costing based on a nominal period of five years. In other jurisdictions, they determine the costs over the contract period. In still others, they use an "evaluated cost" based on features and requirements.

What are the different ways of handling costs?

There are different approaches to handling costs. Cost, as used in this section, means life-cycle costs: the total value of all costs associated with a proposal over the life of the contract or the life of the solution. Each approach could yield a different "winner" from the same set of proposals.

The different ways are:

1. Least cost

2. Greatest benefits per dollar

3. Cost as selection criteria

Least Cost

In the least cost approach, each proposal is evaluated and a score established for it. The evaluators eliminate any proposals which do not satisfy the organization's mandatory requirements. A mandatory requirement may be the ability to service 500 user terminals concurrently, or the ability to provide a particular set of third party applications programs. For those proposals which remain, the selection is made on the basis of least cost. That is, select the proposal which can satisfy all of the mandatory requirements and costs less than the others as determined by the life-cycle cost.

There is a fundamental problem with this approach. What if the next-to-the-cheapest proposal dramatically outperforms the cheapest one and costs only $100 more? Are you giving up $5,000 in additional benefits (or several hundred evaluation points in features and capabilities) for a $100 savings in total cost?

To deal with this problem, some organizations use a modified procedure. They first determine those firms capable of doing an excellent job as measured by their scores, excluding cost. For example, if there are 1000 total points available, the purchasing officer might declare that any firm obtaining more than 750 points is capable of doing an excellent job. For those firms, cost would be examined and the contract awarded to that firm with more than 750 points whose solution costs the least.

Greatest Benefits per Dollar

In greatest benefits, each proposal is evaluated and a score established for it. The score excludes any considerations of cost. Once this has been completed, the total score for each proposal is divided by the total cost to obtain a "points per dollar" measurement of the proposal. The proposal with the greatest "points per dollar" represents the greatest value and is selected. Cost is the life-cycle cost.

Cost as an Evaluation Category

In this method, cost is simply another factor which is included in the scoring scheme. For example, cost could be assigned 20 points. The lowest-cost proposal would receive all 20 points.

Other, more expensive proposals, would receive fewer points.

There are several ways of assigning these points. First, points could be deducted at the rate of one point for each $20,000 difference in cost. Using this method, if Proposal A costs $1,000,000 and Proposal B costs $1,200,000, Proposal A would receive 20 points and B would receive 10 points.

Second, points could be assigned on a pro rata basis. If the least cost was $200,000, then that proposal would receive 20 points. A proposal costing $250,000 would receive (200 out of 250) or 16 points.

Determining Cost

There are other ways of determining the cost of a proposal. Most organizations base their assessment on some type of cumulative cost over the useful life of the solution. Some organizations look at only "out of pocket" dollars; others offset costs with benefits to arrive at a net cost. The table below contains an example of how one organization[10] defined the costing process.

There are many different ways of evaluating proposals and selecting a supplier. In Ontario, government ministries must choose the proposal that meets all mandatory requirements and has the lowest evaluated cost. The policy extract presented below identifies the cost elements which must be included in any evaluation and the policy guidelines in use within one ministry:

EVALUATION AND SELECTION

Ministries must evaluate all relevant costs and benefits of bids/proposals.

Capabilities, functions and features that are proposed, but were not specified in the RFP can only be evaluated if they are relevant to the procurement and directly related to these stated objectives and requirements of the RFP. If taken into an evaluation, the proposed items imply additional requirements and must be justified on a cost/benefit basis. All suppliers whose proposals meet all mandatory requirements must be given the opportunity to amend their proposals in regards to these additional requirements.

Evaluation methodologies for bids/proposals must meet the following criteria:

• satisfy both users and suppliers;

• facilitate the establishment of meaningful and understandable values between all desirable features;

• permit disclosure of the desirable features and their relative values to suppliers;

• incorporate life-cycle costing (i.e., costs over the time period that the information technology will be used by a ministry).

The evaluated cost of a bid or proposal is the sum of its price and all other costs and benefits relevant to the evaluation, that the ministry expects to incur in using the proposed information technology.

Other costs in an evaluation of proposals must include, where relevant, at least the following costs:

• Total costs of hardware, software, facilities, maintenance, training, operations, and power, space and other environmental requirements. These costs must be calculated over the time frame that the ministry plans to use the proposed information technology;

• One time costs such as site preparation, delivery, installation, documentation, and conversion;

• An assessed cost for every desirable feature;

• Provincial and federal taxes and duties;

• Additional benefits such as ownership credit or residual value that the ministry expects the Government of Ontario to obtain after using the proposed information technology.

Ministries must comply with the directive on Supplies, Equipment and Services for directions on Canadian content and industrial development.

Ministries must choose the bid or proposal that meets all mandatory requirements and has the lowest evaluated cost.

1. assessed cost — an estimate of the lowest cost alternative (i.e. proposal cost, third-party purchase, in-house development, doing without, or a combination thereof) to meet all requirements specified for a feature.

Calculating Cost Points

If cost is included as one of the evaluation criteria, then we require some way of translating the dollar amount into a score. Suppose cost has been assigned 50 evaluation points out of a total possible score of 200. How many points does each proposal get? How are they calculated?

Here are three techniques I've seen used. The first is based on the actual cost of each proposal. The second is based on the relative differences in costs among the proposals. The third is based on an interval scale. In establishing a costing procedure care must be taken to ensure that an artificially low priced proposal can accommodate your organization, as some suppliers may submit a low bid simply to obtain the work.

1. Ratio of costs

Using the first method, the vendor with the lowest cost proposal (that was compliant) would receive all 50 available points. All other vendors would receive a smaller number of points as determined by the ratio of their costs. If the lowest cost proposal was for $400, and if vendor B's proposal cost $500, then Vendor B would receive 400 of 500, or 80 percent of the available points.

2. Differences in costs

Using the second method, the points are based on the differences in costs. Using the same data, we first determine the difference in cost between the two proposals. This is $100. We then express this as a percentage of the lowest cost proposal, that is, 100/400, or 25 percent. On this basis, B receives 75 percent of the available points.

3. Points per interval

In this method, all proposals within the same range of costs receive the same number of points. For example, those within 10 percent of the lowest price receive 100 percent of the points. Those proposals whose costs are between 10 and 25 percent greater than the lowest cost receive 90 percent of the points. Those proposals whose costs are between 25 and 50 percent greater than the lowest cost receive 70 percent of the points. Proposals costing more than 50 percent of the lowest cost are rejected.

■ 6.2.6 Impose Upset Levels

Upset levels are used to eliminate the possibility of a proposal obtaining the most points overall when it has serious deficiencies in one or more categories. It is quite possible that a proposal could receive very high marks in several categories and few in a critical area and still win the competition. An upset level is a minimum score that a proposal must receive, either in total or in a category, to remain in the evaluation.

Suppose that 40 evaluation points are available for the technical response. An upset level of 20 would indicate that, regardless of the scores in other categories, no supplier will be accepted with a score of only 20 in this area.

Upset levels ensure that a proposal with an unacceptably low score in one category cannot win the competition. The best practice is to announce in the RFP that "proposals must obtain 50 out of 75 technical points to be considered technically acceptable. Proposals with fewer points will be eliminated from further consideration."

6.3

Standardizing the Evaluation Process

There are two elements of standardization that are used. First, an organization can always use the same evaluation process, the same weights, and the same criteria. Second, the organization can always use the same form on which to record the evaluation score. Some organizations take these steps further and develop an Evaluators' Handbook to ensure that each evaluator receives the same instructions.

This section contains three examples of standardization. The first, based on Alaska, contains a standardized process and a worksheet for recording the scores. The second, from Washington, contains the standardized process. The third, developed by a consultant for use in various jurisdictions, contains an example of a standard document used in the evaluation — an Evaluators' Handbook.

■ 6.3.1 State of Alaska

The state of Alaska has created a Model RFP to be used by the procurement officer to construct a wide variety of RFPs. Section seven presents the five major evaluation criteria, their suggested weights, and the specific questions to be used to establish the score. The entire RFP is contained in Part II of this publication.

7.01 Understanding of the Project — 5 percent

Procurement Officer Note: Alter, Revise, or Delete as Required.

Proposals will be evaluated against the questions set out below.

[a] Has the proposer demonstrated a thorough understanding of the purpose and scope of the project?

[b] How well has the proposer identified pertinent issues and potential problems related to the project?

[c] Has the proposer demonstrated that it understands the deliverables the state expects it to provide?

[d] Has the proposer demonstrated that it understands the state's time schedule and can meet it?

One of the attachments to the Model RFP contains a form to be used by each evaluator to document the scoring and the evaluator's comments. The section of this form corresponding to 7.01 is set out below. The entire form is contained in the Alaska Model RFP in Part II of this handbook.

7.01 Understanding of the Project — 5 percent

Maximum Point Value for this Section — 5 Points

(100 Points x 5 percent = 5 Points)

Proposals will be evaluated against the questions set out below.

[a] Has the proposer demonstrated a thorough understanding of the purpose and scope of the project?

EVALUATOR'S NOTES

[b]   How well has the proposer identified pertinent issues and potential problems related to the project?

EVALUATOR'S NOTES

[c] Has the proposer demonstrated that it understands the deliverables the state expects it to provide?

EVALUATOR'S NOTES

[d] Has the proposer demonstrated that it understands the State's time schedule and can meet it?

EVALUATOR'S NOTES

EVALUATOR'S POINT TOTAL FOR 7.01

■ 6.3.2 State of Washington

The state of Washington has also created a model RFP. Section 5 describes the Proposal Evaluation Procedures to be used. It prescribes:

- the basis for evaluation
- the use of evaluation teams
- the evaluation process
- the use of criteria
- the scoring mechanism
- the selection of the apparently successful vendor.

Section 5 can be found in its entirety in Part II of this handbook.

■ 6.3.3 Evaluators' Handbook

An Evaluators' Handbook is a standardized document. It is produced immediately following the production of a draft RFP and prior to the RFP's release. It has four main uses:.

1. To obtain buy-in from management.

The Evaluators' Handbook is initially used to brief the steering committee or senior management on the details of the evaluation process, and to ensure that the procedure and weights reflect their views.

2. To validate the evaluation process.

The Evaluators' Handbook is also used by the procurement officer or project manager to ensure that the evaluation process will work — that it will differentiate between suppliers. It is used to test the process based on created sample scores for typical suppliers. In this way, the procurement officer can determine if the process will produce a winner. Sometimes, evaluation processes simply identify a group of suppliers capable of doing a credible job. By testing the process, the procurement officer can determine if most "typical" scores will be grouped together or if a "winner" will emerge. In testing the process, weights and factors are changed to reflect a better understanding of the requirements.

3. To instruct the evaluators.

Sometimes, this review of the process causes criteria and weights to be modified. Once this review is completed, the RFP can be issued.

The Evaluators' Handbook can then be used to brief the evaluators to ensure that there is a common understanding of the process. Often, evaluators are taken from line departments and have no formal training related to their roles and responsibilities. They may be unaware of the various laws, policies, and constraints imposed on their deliberations.

4. To document the evaluation.

Based on the Evaluators' Handbook, a set of evaluation sheets is prepared. Each evaluator uses this set to establish a score for each proposal. These sheets become part of the project file and can be used to defend the process from supplier complaints of bias or arbitrary behavior by the evaluators.

Description of the Contents

The Evaluators' Handbook consists of five sections. A brief description of each section follows. A sample Evaluators' Handbook for an actual RFP is contained in Part II of this handbook.

I. Principles

This section identifies the laws, regulations, policies and principles to be followed by evaluators.

II. Steps in the Process

This section identifies the steps to be followed between approval of the evaluation process and de-briefing suppliers. The sample document contains 17 different steps organized chronologically.

III. A Proposed Scoring System

This section contains the scoring system which the procurement officer is proposing to use.

IV. Evaluation Categories

This section identifies the evaluation process and categories as published in the RFP.

V. Evaluation Worksheets

This section identifies each of the evaluation criteria as published in the RFP and the detailed steps for scoring. Sometimes the RFP only identifies high-level factors such as "supplier experience." This section would then contain those sub-factors contributing to "supplier experience."

6.4

Other Approaches, Options and Practices

■ 6.4.1 Reference Checking – A Better Approach

Proponent references should normally be used to confirm the selection rather than as an evaluation criterion. In many cases, only the references of the winning proponent need be checked. If several proponents are close in the final evaluation, references may be used to help choose between them. The interview should be conducted using predetermined, consistent questions in order to receive reliable and objective information about service, support, reliability, etc.

References should only be checked if the RFP requested them.

If the evaluation committee has chosen not to request references, any provided by individual proponents should be ignored.

Most selection procedures require the bidders to identify reference accounts. The wording in many RFPs is similar:

"Proposals must include a list of references including names and telephone numbers for whom the bidder has performed similar work. These references might be contacted during the proposal evaluation phase to determine their satisfaction with the work carried out." Or "Provide three references, for work performed within the last two years, which you judge to be of similar scope and complexity."

Invariably, someone from the selection team makes the calls. If this is your job, what do you say? What questions do you ask? What is the purpose of the exercise? Clearly, you want to verify that the supplier did in fact do a very good job at that company. But only the most naive evaluator would assume that a supplier will submit the name of a bad reference. The existence of a few solid references only demonstrate that the bidder has the potential for excellent work. Obviously, a bidder will only submit the names of companies which they know will provide them with a wonderful reference.

There is another, more aggressive tactic. Phone the reference accounts not only to learn about the bidder, but to learn the names of other purchasers. Once this has been accomplished, call all of the purchasers who weren't listed as references.

The purpose of these calls to "non reference" accounts is to learn about the supplier from a broader range of customers. These customers will relate both good and bad stories about the bidder, and its products or services.

The purpose of contacting "non reference" accounts is not simply to identify problem situations (which may have been caused by the supplier or its products, the purchaser, third parties, etc.). The purpose is to learn what the supplier did when difficulties were encountered. What did the supplier do when its project leader left? What happened when the key user became ill? What did the supplier do when you required more product on short notice? Did the supplier act in the customer's best interest? Did the supplier simply disavow responsibility? Did the supplier and purchaser solve the problem by working as partners?

If these conversations cause you to be concerned about the risks in dealing with a particular supplier, then discuss the information with the supplier. Listen to the supplier's side before accepting the information.

Listed below is part of one organization's reference questionnaire. They used it in the telephone survey of current users (of a software supplier's financial modelling system).

1. Was an evaluation of various vendors carried out?

2. If yes, who was considered and why was this vendor/product chosen?

3. How long have you had this program?

4. What training was provided? Was it any good? Rate it one to 10.

5. Did you find many bugs or errors in the system?

6. How responsive was the vendor to your queries and problems? Did the vendor take an active role in solving any problems?

7. How would you rate the vendor's support on a scale of one to 10?

8. How have you used support?

9. What do you consider to be the major limitations of the system?

10. Are you considering an alternative at this time?

If you do decide to incorporate this approach to reference checking into your evaluation procedure, I suggest that you modify your RFP so that the bidders are aware of this process. Here's how one RFP informed the bidders that the reference checking would include a broad range of customers, not just the names they provided:

"Our evaluation will be made primarily via checks with the bidder-provided references and other industry sources and users known to the evaluation team."

■ 6.4.2 Judgment and the RFP Process[11]

One of the advantages of a full RFP process is that observers will see that decisions are fair, open and objective. One problem is that "objective" purchasing decisions are not always in the best interests of the buyer or the seller. The best decisions almost always include an element of judgment, and it's difficult to make "objective" judgments.

This can be a particularly thorny problem in the public sector. A few years ago, I was part of the rescue effort for the procurement of a major systems outsourcing contract. The first time around, the process came unglued in the premier's office. People from the winning vendor, under contract, played important client roles in the RFP process. This was not seen as fair, open or objective.

The second time around, everything had to be done properly. The level of interest, and scrutiny, came home to me at the first public bidders' meeting. One bidder came to the meeting with its own court reporter — they felt it important to capture every word spoken during the meeting. But we kept a role for judgment, developing a process that was fair, open, and unbiased.

Unbiased

An objective process is one that would yield the same outcome, regardless of who was responsible for the process. When judgment is allowed to play a significant role, it's practically impossible to have an objective RFP process. The losing bidders will claim that their people are qualified and they would not have reached the same conclusion. Fortunately, most RFP's do not need to be objective.

The critical substitution is to replace "objective" with "unbiased." Now there is no way for an individual to exercise judgment and avoid charges of bias from those who disagree with the conclusion. But a properly selected panel can exercise a collective judgment and avoid the charge. We used two panels to produce a fair, open and unbiased RFP process. The second time around was successful.

Structure

The client was interested in purchasing all of their system development services from the successful outsourcing bidder. They would undertake a kind of "partnership" with the winning vendor. It was difficult to see how the traditional requirements approach would capture all of the client's concerns. This RFP was not about requirements. It focused on concerns.

Proponents had to develop a proposal which addressed client concerns as laid out in the RFP. There were, in addition, some basic requirements, e.g., proponents had to have a local office and be large enough that this contract would not be more than 25 percent of their business. But the main emphasis in the RFP and in the bidders' meetings was on the client's concerns.

Outside consultants conducted the bidders' meetings and provided the basic connection between the client and possible proponents. I was one of the "outside consultants." Not everyone was happy with the rules that were established, but there was general acceptance that the process would be "fair and open." And the court reporter did not return after the first bidders' meeting.

Two panels were employed to keep the process unbiased, while admitting a measure of judgment. The first selection panel contained a majority of outside members. They were distinguished members of the local data processing community, with no direct connection to the client. This first panel was to determine which proposals were judged to be responsive to the RFP.

There were six proposals and three were judged by the outside selection panel to be responsive to the RFP. It is important to point out that using such a panel was a leap of faith. The client did not control the selection panel and had no political option but to live with whatever it decided. This initial panel did not make the same decisions the client would have made, but its decisions were reasonable.

Final Selection

The remaining proponents were assumed to have acceptable proposals. It became a question of which proposal was the best fit to the client's current and likely future concerns. There was no way to separate senior client management from this decision, but it did need to be an unbiased selection that would be recognized as such by outsiders.

Interviews were arranged between each of the three remaining proponents and senior client managers. Outside consultants were present during all of these interviews. Final presentations were made, by the remaining proponents, to a

selection panel that contained a majority of members from the client organization. Distinguished outsiders were present during all of the deliberations.

A clear winner emerged from the process. And the process, itself, was a winner. The accepted proposal went far to establish an effective "partnership." Indeed, it went further than could have been required by a conventional RFP. The focus on concerns in the RFP worked to the client's benefit. The client felt good about the outcome and even the losing proponents accepted its fairness.

Lessons

There is a role for judgment even in the most exposed of public sector procurement exercises. The use of selection panels provides an unbiased process that still allows for judgment. The first selection panel could be replaced with an objective determination of whether bids meet specified minimum conditions. But this would shift the emphasis from concerns to requirements.

The use of selection panels is an effective way to replace "objective" with "unbiased." In a wide range of RFP conditions, "unbiased" meets the need for a defensible process and allows judgment to play a role. The focus on concerns is an option worth serious consideration when services are being procured and when an initial selection panel can be employed.

[1] Page 11, 2AAC 12.260, Reference *8.

[2] Page 4.10, Reference *2.

[3] Clause 10, page 4, Reference *7.

[4] Clause 50, page 21, Reference *7.

[5] Page 13, 2AAC 12.290, Reference *8.

[6] Clause 47, Reference *7.

[7] Page 40, 2AAC 12.860, Reference *8.

[8] Page 22, Reference *19.

[9] Reference *20.

[10] This table was published in Issue #1 of Reference *17.

[11] This section was originally published in Issue #6, Reference *17. It was written by Robert Fabian, a management consultant based in Toronto.

CHAPTER 7

Ending the Process

— CONTENTS —

7.1

Introduction

By the time you actually get to these tasks — the end issues — much has already been accomplished: specifications were written; the RFP document was created and issued; proposals were received and evaluated; supplier presentations were held. In some jurisdictions, a second set of proposals was evaluated as the "best and final" offers. All that remains is the relatively simple process of confirming the winner, finalizing the contract, dealing with the losers and closing the project file. At this point, the end of the selection process is close at hand — only four tasks remain.

1. Confirm the Winner

This chapter begins, for all organizations, when they have selected the "winner" — the supplier and proposal judged best able to satisfy the organization's requirements. The specific set of tasks that remain depends on your organization's policies and procedures. Confirming the winner may involve nothing more than having the evaluation committee's choice confirmed by management.

2. Finalize the Contract

Before starting the project, the contract must be completed. If your organization included its standard contract as part of the RFP, then there is little contract negotiation because only minor issues remain unstated.

3. Dealing with the Losers

Dealing with the losers involves paperwork and politics: sending out the official notice of the winner or the Notice of Intent to Contract, returning bid bonds and, in many jurisdictions, meeting with vendors to review the selection process and the reasons why they didn't win.

4. Complete the RFP File

Completing the RFP file involves not only additional paperwork but also reviewing or auditing the just-completed selection process.

In the remainder of this chapter, these and other end issues are discussed. Not all of these issues apply to any one RFP. In fact, some of these tasks are mutually exclusive.

7.2

Confirm the Winner

After a winner has been chosen, the specific set of tasks that remains depends on your organization's policies and procedures. Confirming the winner may involve nothing more than having the evaluation committee's choice confirmed by management.

Often, the project manager or procurement officer is required to formally recommend a supplier/proposal to management. The purpose of this step is to seek final approval of the proposal based on the actual proposed costs, and to obtain permission to enter into contract negotiations with that supplier.

Once the evaluation team has completed its work, the leader usually constructs a memorandum identifying the winner, its score, the proposed cost, and the most important features of its proposal. The memo seeks approval of the selection, approval of the expenditures, and authority to enter into contract discussions or negotiations.

The recommendation is normally in the form of a memorandum. The supplier with the highest score may not always be declared the winner. In some jurisdictions, evaluators are permitted to declare that small differences in scores may not be material. In these cases, the selection is based on the proposal "providing the most benefits" or "in the best interests of the state."

In some jurisdictions, a Notice of Intent to Contract is published or distributed to all of the bidders. This notice provides a formal mechanism for any of the bidders to protest the award prior to a contract being signed. In Alaska, the Procurement Code provides that each bidder be informed of the intent at least 10 days before the formal award of a contract. During the notice period, suppliers who believe they have been aggrieved can initiate a formal protest. Protest procedures are dealt with extensively in Chapter 8.

7.3

Finalize the Contract

This section has a limited scope. It is not intended to be a guide to negotiation strategy or tactics. These issues are highly influenced by different laws and permissible practices in different jurisdictions. Some jurisdictions permit "best and final" offers; others do not. The amount of negotiation varies radically from none to all issues in the RFP and proposal being negotiated.

There are many books and courses focusing on contracts and the negotiation process. The remainder of this section contains some specific issues which frequently arise in discussions related to RFPs and contracts. These issues can be characterized as questions.

■ 7.3.1 Do We Include Contract Terms in the RFP?

The more information contained in the RFP, the better the proposal. If there are mandatory contractual requirements, these should be stated in the RFP. If your organization has a certain set of terms and conditions that must be used, then state this in the RFP. It is very frustrating and unproductive to have the "winner" declared unresponsive for failure to agree to contractual terms that were not contained in the RFP, and not identified until the negotiations began.

There are many different approaches to contracts and RFPs. At one extreme, the RFP includes the purchasing organization's standard contract and it is a condition of the RFP that the supplier accept this contract if selected as the winner. This approach is both simple and rigid. There is little room for negotiation and, in fact, negotiations occur only to clarify minor issues not dealt with in the draft contract. This is the case in South Dakota.[1]:

The state generally does not sign standard contract forms submitted by vendors. The bid with the vendor's signature affixed thereto shall constitute an offer to sell

to the state under the terms and conditions contained therein...

It is also the case in Arizona that no contract is actually signed — the proposal is simply accepted. All of the terms and conditions for the contract are included in the RFP. The state only needs to accept the supplier's offer by sending a notice of award in order to form a contract[2]:

A response to a Request for Proposals is an offer to contract with the state based upon the terms, conditions, scope of work and specifications contained in the state's Request for Proposals. Proposals do not become contracts unless and until they are accepted by an authorized procurement officer. A contract is formed when the procurement officer provides written notice of award(s) to the successful offeror(s). The contract has its inception in the award document, eliminating a formal signing of a separate contract. For that reason, all of the terms and conditions of the procurement contract are contained in the Request for Proposals; unless modified by a Solicitation Amendment (SPO Form 207) or a Contract Amendment (SPO Form 217) signed by the authorized procurement officer.

At the other extreme, some organizations do not deal with the specifics of the contract in the RFP. They first select the winner and then begin contract negotiations. This approach often takes much time and energy since there can be many significant issues not dealt with in the RFP or the proposal. For example, issues related to warranty, performance bonds, progress payments, and rules for accepting deliverables.

Few organizations leave contract issues totally out of the RFP. This gives the suppliers too much power during negotiations.

Between these two extremes are a number of commonly used approaches:

1. The RFP contains the purchasing organization's standard terms and conditions which form the basis for contract negotiation; or

2. The RFP contains a checklist of issues to be dealt with by the supplier in its proposals; or

3. The RFP identifies those few key contractual terms that the purchasing organization deems as mandatory; or

4. The RFP contains a draft contract but acceptance of all of its terms is not mandatory. The supplier is instructed in the RFP to review the draft contract, identify in its proposal those clauses which are unacceptable, and the reasons or problems, and to propose alternatives. In this way, the proposals identify those few contractual issues that must be resolved during contract negotiations.

Limiting Negotiations

If an organization does not put all of its contractual requirements in the RFP, then putting a time limit on negotiations can give the purchaser some needed leverage. If the contract language in the RFP is weak or vague, then announcing to a supplier that it has won creates problems. The supplier knows that you want its solution, that a contract must be executed and that the project has stringent deadlines. In this case, you have given the supplier a negotiating advantage. By simply delaying, the supplier can increase its pressure on you to sign the supplier's standard contract.

To counteract this situation, many organizations include a clause in the RFP stating that if negotiations cannot be concluded with the "winner" within 14 days, then the next highest supplier will be contacted and negotiations begun anew. This puts pressure on the "winner" to maintain a certain level of flexibility during negotiations.

■ 7.3.2 Should We Include the Proposal as Part of the Contract?

If there are special features or services offered in the proposal, they should be included in the contract. Many organizations do not want to take each and every proposal feature and transcribe it into the contract document. There are, therefore, two choices: transcribe the most important features from the proposal into the contract, or include the proposal as part of the contract. Many organizations, as a normal practice, include both the supplier's proposal and the RFP document as part of the contract.

The contract also includes a statement regarding the precedence arrangements. Typically, the contract takes precedence over the proposal and then the RFP. If the contract doesn't deal with an issue, then the terms in the proposal (or RFP) are used. The contract states that the attached proposal is part of the contract and that the contract terms take precedence over the attached proposal. In this way, all of the vendor's proposed features, terms, and deliverables are made part of the contract.

■ 7.3.3 If Negotiations are Not Permitted, Can We Change the Proposal?

Some jurisdictions do not permit negotiations, only minor clarifications of the proposal or RFP information. Having declared in the RFP that the selection will be on the basis of the stated criteria, you must stick with it. It is not "visibly fair" to use the negotiation process as a method of obtaining major changes to the vendor's proposal. Quite possibly, one of the other vendors would be willing to provide an even better deal on your modified requirements.

Once there is no flexibility in negotiating major changes to the winning vendor's proposal, there is not much left to do during this step. Typically, items and timings are clarified. Issues not previously dealt with in either the RFP or the proposal are resolved. These are usually small items involving logistics, minor contract terms, or timing. They are usually not major cost items or substantive issues. For example, the proposal may have identified a training program. The details of this program in terms of when, where, etc., may be part of the negotiation/clarification process.

■ 7.3.4 Can We Simplify Contract Negotiations?

Contracts are complex and require special skills to understand and negotiate. However, many procurement activities are being decentralized these days. To assist diverse groups in developing acceptable contracts and to assist these groups to deal with suppliers effectively, many organizations have developed some tools. These tools take several forms: a contract expert available from a central group to support the procurement officer, standardized terms and conditions, standardized checklists of features, compulsory terms and conditions, and contract handbooks.

In an ideal world, lawyers working for an organization or retained by it would be accessible on short notice and readily available to the procurement officer. It would then be a simple matter of a meeting or two between the procurement officer and the lawyer to ensure that a detailed contract was included in the RFP. The lawyer would also help ensure that the RFP incorporated best legal practices.

However, this is rarely the case. Usually, lawyers working for public sector bodies are busy with policy and major legal initiatives. They are difficult to access, their time is at a premium, and, in some cases they know little about procurement law. But procurements must still be done expeditiously, and procurement officers have to get on with their work. To compensate for the difficulties in getting on-going advice and assistance from lawyers before and during the RFP process, many organizations have developed standard terms and conditions, checklists, and handbooks to support the preparation of a contract by the procurement officer rather than a lawyer.

In many organizations, lawyers are simply not available. Other methods must be used to protect the organization's interests and to develop reasonable contracts. Checklists are the simplest tools; handbooks are the most complex.

■ 7.3.5 A Contract Checklist

A simple checklist contains terms and conditions to be considered for inclusion in a contract. Using this checklist requires a great amount of knowledge on behalf of the procurement officer. Often, this checklist is included in the RFP.

Here is a sample of a checklist developed by the author for use in an RFP for a systems integrator. While the checklist is a poor substitute for timely, competent legal assistance, it has its place. Using it, the procurement officer can at least ensure that important issues are address in the proposals or in discussions with the suppliers.

8.12 Contract Clauses and Issues

We expect that the following clauses and terms will, where relevant as determined by the objectives and workplan, be incorporated into the resulting contract(s):

1. Description of hardware and prices:

Include a list of all components and related documentation; identify unit prices and all applicable taxes separately; identify all related costs including transportation, shipping insurance and installation charges separately.

2. Description of software and prices:

Include a list of all software components and related documentation; identify unit prices and all applicable taxes separately; identify all related costs including transportation, shipping insurance and installation charges separately.

3. Project management

Designate the project manager by name; identify

key project team staff; provide for no transfer of such personnel without consent of the project authority; provide for removal of any staff at buyers request; provide firm dates for delivery, installation, education and training, and other key milestones.

4. Site preparation

Identify if this is a buyer's or supplier's responsibility. If it is supplier's, specify cost; if buyers, specify approval mechanism. Identify power and environmental specifications.

5. Delivery date

Specify the delivery date for each item and documentation by date or duration from previous contract milestone. State buyer's right to postpone; buyer's right to cancel. Provide a definition of acceptance (if delivery is phased, secure acknowledgement from supplier that acceptance will not occur until all items have been delivered and installed, and have passed acceptance test).

6. Transfer of title

Provide for risk of loss and insurance. Identify when title passes.

7. Installation

Identify the cost of this supplier responsibility.

8. Conversion of data

Identify level of supplier assistance and cost. Provide names of conversion tools and capabilities and any guarantees related to effectiveness.

9. Education and training

Provide names/qualifications of trainers; amount, timing, location, cost of training. Provide for buyer input into design of training; Identify training methodology, population. State how much is free, and the cost of additional units.

10. Hardware test

Distinguish between acceptance test and manufacturer's diagnostic tests for hardware; provide definition of acceptance.

11. Acceptance tests

Identify test, period, performance criteria, including documentation, specifications, proposal promises. Identify specific reliability standards including recovery times; identify problem notification mechanism.

12. Price and payment

Confirm that only prices and expenses identified in the contract will be paid for; provide price protection for future enhancements. Identify volume discounts. Guarantee most favoured customer pricing; identify a payment schedule based on milestones. Provide year-to-year price protection.

13. Taxes

Pass on customs rebates to buyer.

14. Warranties

Ensure that the warranty period is distinct from the acceptance test period and period during which system is under maintenance; provide warranty against defects in hardware commencing on acceptance. Scope of maintenance services included in warranty should be comparable to paid-for maintenance services; provide warranty as to new equipment. Warrant compatibility: that equipment works in conjunction with specified (software) applications systems, and that resulting system can interface with other specified equipment or software in a predetermined manner; warrant equipment as to capacity. Guarantee expansion capabilities and provide statement of upgrade costs; warrant that supplier either owns the intellectual property rights in the computer system (software) or is authorized to sell/license them;

warrant against defects in software commencing on acceptance.

15. Warranty disclaimers

Include all promises as express warranties.

16. Remedies

Provide for liquidated damages, supply of interim solution, termination for nondelivery; provide liquidated damages, repair all problems at no cost, or termination of agreement for inability of Provide for express preservation of all other remedies including claims for damages resulting from a system's inadequate performance. Available remedies are to include provision of additional equipment at no cost to meet performance criteria.

17. Patent/copyright indemnity

The buyer's scope of indemnity should cover patents, copyrights, trade secrets, and all other intellectual property rights. Buyers in Canada should be indemnified in regard to all patents or copyrights, but not just U.S.

Scope of indemnity should cover all damages, expenses, and settlement costs, including reasonable legal fees, not just damages awarded by courts.

18. Limitation of liability

Supplier is responsible for direct damages equal to purchase price or license fee or one year of maintenance, as appropriate. There should be no limits on liability for claims regarding intellectual property, unauthorized disclosure of buyer's confidential information, personal injury, or property damages.

19. Excusable delays

The supplier is to give notice of an excusable event and try to work around it; secure buyer's right to terminate agreement if delay continues beyond certain limit or right to solve problem directly; delays accepted without penalty at the sole discretion of the project authority.

20. Termination

Termination by buyer for cause, and without causes upon specified payments.

21. Buyer's confidential information; publicity

Agreement requires supplier to keep confidential buyer's confidential information. Nature of buyer's information may require all supplier's employees who have access to such buyer information to sign nondisclosure agreements with buyer; supplier must obtain buyer's permission to use buyer's name in supplier's marketing literature.

22. Upgrades and trade-in credits

Provide trade-in credits to assure market for buyer's used system.

23. Governing law

Province of British Columbia.

24. Assignment

Obtain ability to assign agreement to other crown agency.

25. Notices

Provide for deemed receipt five days after mailing.

26. Entire agreement

27. Amendment

Only by written agreement of parties.

28. License of software

Provide for institution license and ability to make modifications. Modify restrictions on transfer to permit assignment of license; provide permission to make back-up copy as exception to restriction on copying.

29. Escrow arrangements

Provide escrow arrangements for all applications

software not owned by the buyer.

30. Complete systems

Acknowledge that the supplier is providing a complete system: all necessary equipment, software, applications programs, procedures and processing capabilities.

31. Systems acceptance testing

Acknowledge that this is to be performed in conformance with standards and procedures established by the quality assurance group.

32. Back-up provisions

Identify the provision for recovering system when power outages or other short-term interruptions, such as a disk drive becoming disabled, occur.

33. Expiration

Acknowledge that the supplier will assist in transfer to other supplier/processing site at end of contact term.

34. Third-party maintenance

Provide for access to suppliers diagnostic/technical documents.

35. Processing

Provide a detailed description of services; identify service levels, performance guarantees; provide for liquidated damages or credits on processing; provide for express preservation of other remedies.

36. Ownership

Provide a clear statement of ownership for all software and applications programs. Provide for waiver of moral rights; warrant that supplier, employees of supplier, all subcontractors, and all subcontractors' employees will sign copyright assignments and waiver of moral rights.

37. Disaster recovery

Define any provision toward disaster recovery and the costs and levels of service.

38. Performance guarantees

Identify all performance guarantees including minimum up-time, response time for processing transactions, and for providing maintenance services, maximum recovery time, and any other performance measures.

■ 7.3.6 A Contract Handbook

Another approach is the use of a handbook to assist the procurement officer in developing a draft contract for inclusion in the RFP. The state of Washington has developed a publication which has been made available on disk to its agencies and departments. This contracting handbook is intended to help agencies specify appropriate contract terms in RFPs. It is provided as an appendix to their standardized RFP model[3]. Agencies are required to use this material in their contracts.

For every competitive acquisition or negotiated sole source acquisition, an agency is required to use the Terms and Conditions (together with appropriately tailored negotiable clauses) in the solicitation document (RFP or RFQ) when issued, and as a basis for negotiating the resulting contract.

This 63-page document contains instructions for building a proposed contract from three types of information: a list of standard terms and conditions, suggested terms and conditions containing approved wording, and six different checklists. The table of contents for this contracting handbook is presented below. The entire document is contained in Part II of this publication and on the disk which was included.

Information Technology Contract Terms and Conditions

Table of Contents

7.4

Release the Results[4]

When do you release results? Timing is everything! There is considerable debate and disagreement among public procurement officials as to when RFP results should be released. Public procurement agencies must take care in ensuring consistency in the application of general rules about the release of results. Any real or perceived inconsistency in the process can create an atmosphere of distrust by both management and the vendor community. Purchasing officials must ensure that the integrity and credibility of the RFP process and the resulting award are not compromised by the untimely or inconsistent release of results.

There are three steps in a typical RFP process when decisions are made and suppliers can be eliminated from further consideration:

1. Pre-Evaluation Step. A proposal will not be accepted because it is late, or not evaluated because it is incomplete.

2. Technical Evaluation Step. Proposals are evaluated and a short-list established. Proposals not on the short-list are eliminated from further consideration.

3. Contract Award Step. Short-listed proposals are evaluated and the winner is determined.

In some jurisdictions, suppliers eliminated from further consideration are informed of their status at each step. Others wait until after the final award.

This article considers the relative merits of informing proponents of their status at each step in the process.

1. Pre-Evaluation Step

Some suppliers will not make it to the Technical Evaluation Step. I recommend that those suppliers be informed as soon as possible. If a late or rejected proposal is retained by the purchasing organization, the proponent may erroneously expect that its proposal will be evaluated.

The primary reasons for eliminating suppliers from further consideration at this step are non-compliance with terms and conditions stated in the RFP, for example:

- proposal was received late
- proposal was not signed
- mandatory requirements were not met
- information provided in the proposal was lacking and the proposal could not be evaluated
- the proponent is currently disqualified from doing business with the purchaser.

Many organizations will inform the proponents by telephone, followed by written notice, and offer an in-person briefing.

When a proposal is rejected because it is late, it should be returned to the vendor. Proposals delivered late by hand should not be accepted. If received late through the mail or by courier, the envelope should be returned unopened with an explanatory note.

If the proposal package has no name and return address, the envelope should be opened in the presence of two people, the reason the envelope was opened should be noted on the face of the envelope and it should be returned with an explanatory letter.

2. Technical Evaluation Step

Informing proponents that they did not make the short-list (before the contract is awarded) causes problems and adds no value to the process. Vendors often look on this as an opportunity to provide more and better information, and an opportunity to correct deficiencies in their original proposal. In fact, if this is permitted, the vendor is receiving a second chance.

In some jurisdictions, the purchasing officials will actually provide the proponents an opportunity to challenge the decision about their qualifying for the short-list and will permit the proponent to submit additional information. This practice is justified by them on the basis of obtaining better proposals.

Proposals can only be short-listed based on the information provided in each proposal using the pre-defined evaluation criteria. New information cannot be introduced after a decision is reached to eliminate a proposal from further consideration. If the information was important, it should have been included in the original proposal.

Permitting suppliers to augment their original proposal in this way leaves the procurement officials open to claims of incompetence: they did not perform an adequate review and analysis before issuing the RFP or they are changing the rules as the process progresses to suit their own needs, or to favour a particular supplier.

To permit suppliers to augment their proposals, or to modify the evaluation process as it progresses is not permitted. These types of actions by a procurement official are clearly inappropriate, if not illegal. They will be seen as showing a lack of expertise in evaluating proposals, or an "easy out" in case a mistake or oversight occurred.

The results of a short-listing process should be kept confidential. Advising a proponent that it was unsuccessful at this stage should be delayed until a final selection and award has been made. If the award is then challenged by a disgruntled supplier, the challenge will not delay the commencement of work.

If you inform a proponent that its proposal did not make the short-list, you must live with that decision. You cannot go back to the proposals that were not on the short-list and subsequently chose one. Otherwise, you will most certainly be seen as "playing games." Your credibility within the supplier community will suffer.

The evaluators must be confident in their assessment of the proposals at each stage and be prepared to explain and defend their reasons to each proponent and their management.

Proposals failing to make the short-list should not be reconsidered in subsequent evaluation steps. If no proposal is found to be acceptable, a revised RFP should be issued or an alternative method of procurement used.

3. Contract Award Step

All short-listed proposals and suppliers should be evaluated in an identical manner. Once the award has been announced to the winner, then all proponents should be informed.

Proponents should be offered a formal debriefing to discuss their proposals' shortcomings. Debriefings should be presented as an opportunity to learn and thereby improve future proposals, rather than an opportunity to challenge the award.

Jurisdictions following the practices described in this article achieve recognition that their RFP process is open, fair and competitive. These jurisdictions experience fewer challenges of their procurement decisions.

7.5

Dealing with the Losers

A debriefing is often looked upon as the crumbs given to losers to offset, at least in the purchasers mind, the cost of submitting a losing proposal. It is an attempt by the purchasing organization to provide some value to the suppliers. It is also a means by which the purchaser can determine which suppliers are really mad and intend to challenge the results, either through senior management, the political process or the courts.

Some jurisdictions simply ignore the losers. Some not only ignore the losers but they offend them. Here is what one organization published in its RFP[5]:

> **The evaluation team will utilize specific criteria to rate various requirements for evaluation purposes. Such a rating will be confidential and no totals or scores will be released to any vendor...**

Most jurisdictions provide an opportunity for suppliers to obtain details about their proposals and why they didn't win. The suppliers are offered some information as a "thank you" for the cost and effort of preparing a proposal.

All commercial dealings are covered by a wide variety of laws related to commercial practices, discrimination, protection of trade secrets and proprietary information. In some jurisdictions, there are additional laws dealing with access to information or protection of privacy — laws which often expand the information given to suppliers about RFPs and evaluations.

No Access to Information Laws

In jurisdictions without access to information laws, there are a wide variety of practices dictated by policy or "common sense." Some jurisdictions give out as little information as possible; others provide reasonable levels through briefing sessions. Still others provide as much information as they can about the supplier's own proposal and its strengths and weaknesses.

Many jurisdictions have written policies related to supplier debriefings. Here is one example:

Once the award is announced, proponents may contact the procurement officer to find out why they lost and for details of the winning proposal. No other persons associated with the procurement are permitted to disclose information to the suppliers. The procurement officer in charge of the RFP will, if requested, schedule a formal debriefing with the supplier.

Debriefings are treated as an exchange of information which helps both the proponents and the agency. Adequate time must be allowed. It is important that the debriefing is not seen as an opportunity to challenge the decision.

Debriefing meetings will be chaired by the procurement officer. The intent of the debriefing is to aid the supplier in presenting a better proposal in subsequent RFPs. Where weights were used in the evaluation, each proponent will be given a list of the major evaluation criteria with the maximum weights and the vendor will be given an indication of how it scored relatively in each category. It is not necessary to disclose the actual scores. Using the range of proposals in each category of the evaluation as a benchmark, the proponent who is being debriefed will be provided with at least the winning supplier's evaluation rating as compared to the supplier being debriefed, with substantiation where appropriate.

The proponent must not be told how individual firms ranked or how they scored.

Access to Information Laws Exist

In jurisdictions where information laws exist, there is a wide variety of approaches. Some organizations give out little information and simply wait for the suppliers to use the procedure established under the access law. Other organizations are more proactive. They identify the information which will be available under the information access law and they make it available to suppliers either when asked or as a preemptive measure to avoid supplier complaints.

Under many different access to information laws in many jurisdictions, a large amount of information is available about an RFP and the proposals:

- Project authorization
- The RFP document
- The evaluation process
- The evaluator's notes
- Memo recommending the winner
- Supplier proposals, except for competitive information
- Evaluation summary sheets

Confidentiality and Disclosure

Many jurisdictions instruct their procurement people via laws, regulations and policies about debriefing and providing information to suppliers after the contract has been awarded. An entire book could be written about this topic. Detailed examination of these laws and practices is beyond the scope of this publication. Here is a limited selection of approaches:

Procurement information is public except as otherwise provided by law.

-State of Alaska

Subject to territorial access to information legislation, bidders and proponents will, upon request, be given access to information about their own bids or proposals and how these were evaluated...

-Yukon Government

After award and distribution, the bids and quotes of all bidders shall be open to public inspection...

-State of Washington

The head of a public body must refuse to disclose... information that would harm significantly the competitive position... of the third party.

-Province of British Columbia

Final bids are public upon opening.

- State of California

7.6

Complete the RFP File

Almost all the work has now been completed. What's left is the paperwork. This is usually thought of as a necessary evil. In fact, there is some value that can be gleaned from these few remaining activities. An organization can make the lessons and information obtained during the process readily available to others, ensuring that the lessons learned are integrated into future activities. To do so requires some energy and time, but the payback can be large. There are four tasks remaining — none of which are complex or expensive.

1. Complete the Project File

By now, the project file is bursting. It may in fact be several files kept by several different people. These files must be sorted to get rid of early drafts, telephone notes that were transcribed, and other non-essential documents. Sufficient information must be retained to satisfy the organization's retention practices and to support the validity of

the process and the contract if challenged in the courts. While it is not necessary to keep all of the files associated with each RFP process in the same physical location, it is very helpful to know what they are and where they are located.

Computer files residing on a network, a central computer, or a personal computer can be archived. They can be copied onto floppy disks and stored either with the hardcopy or in a central location.

Some organizations prepare an index of the files associated with each RFP. This index is available to other authorized people. Access to the actual files is controlled. In some organizations, the index is on a computer network. The index includes both hardcopy files and computer files.

These files are now accessible and can provide much valuable information to others performing similar activities in the future.

2. Complete the Official Records

Some organizations require that certain

contract information be recorded and made available to the public. Often, this information is reported to a governing body — a council, assembly, or legislature — on a periodic basis.

In Alaska, publicly accessible contract files must be kept by the commissioner and the contracting agency[6]:

A contract file open for public inspection shall be kept by the commissioner and the contracting agency for each contract awarded under competitive sealed proposals. The file kept by the commissioner must contain a summary of the information in the file of the contracting agency. The file kept by the contracting agency must contain:

    (1)   a copy of the contract;

    (2)   the register of proposals prepared... and a copy of each proposal submitted; and

    (3)   the written determination to award the contract...

3. Catalog Key Documents

Many organizations, in an attempt to obtain additional value from their collection of documents, organize an RFP library. This library can be an actual room with shelves. It can also be a virtual library — simply an index of RFPs which is made available on the organization's computer network. The index can be used by interested people to determine the location of different types of RFPs. These RFPs, in turn, can exist as computer files on the network, or as hardcopy or disks.

4. Audit the Process.

An audit of the RFP process when it has been completed can yield valuable information. Also, having an audit as a standard activity ensures that the procurement officer adheres to the organization's policies, guidelines and standards.

Every RFP project teaches some lessons: the evaluators learn about specifying mandatory requirements precisely; deficiencies in contract terms are identified; a new question is asked about supplier experience; a better way of analyzing costs is created. There is much value in documenting these lessons so they are readily available for the next RFP process.

There are several different ways to audit this process. First, the procurement officer can do it. This, to some people, represents a potential conflict. The individual responsible for running the process is now required to identify deficiencies in the process and lessons learned. While this is not the ideal situation, it is better to have the procurement officer review the process at the end than no one at all.

Some organizations have the RFP process reviewed by an internal auditor — a staff member who has functioned as a procurement officer. This audit tends to be more thorough and more formal than the first type.

Other organizations bring in an external auditor. They provide this person with all of the project files and access to the project team. Based on a review of these files, the auditor offers an opinion about the soundness of the process and potential improvements.

All of these audits identify improvements to be considered in the process and the documents used. All that is required is a process for evaluating these recommendations and introducing them as changes in policy, regulations, or best practices.

[1] Page 9, Reference *3.

[2] Reference *19.

[3] Reference *13.

[4] This section originally appeared in Issue #5, Reference *17. It was written by Ken Babich, ex-president of a chapter of the National Institute of Governmental Purchasers.

[5] Page 5-26, Reference *16.

[6] Article 8, page 41, Reference *4.

CHAPTER 8

Supplier Complaints and Protest

— CONTENTS —

8.1

Policy Requirements

Several months ago, one of my clients asked me to review a small paragraph which they planned on inserting into their published RFP Policy. This paragraph was designed to inform suppliers that the organization did indeed have a policy and a process for dealing with complaints and protests. While the paragraph was small, it caused a re-examination of the entire process. It raised several fundamental questions related to the RFP process and how to ensure that supplier complaints did not become political issues. This chapter examines these issues from the perspective of the public sector.

Supplier complaints, protests and appeals are a fact of life. There are always more losers than winners and some of the losers will feel aggrieved. They may believe that the requirements were too vague, that the time to complete the proposal was too short, that the selection process was arbitrary, or even worse, that the winner was selected before the RFP was issued. They may believe that the

incumbent was favoured by "insider information." There are hundreds of reasons why suppliers could feel aggrieved. And in many situations, complaints do have merit.

Supplier protests have serious implications. The evaluator's decision can be challenged by both senior management and the politicians. The process itself can be subjected to public scrutiny and found lacking. Often, the competence and objectivity of the purchasing officers is questioned.

Supplier complaints can be dealt with in many different ways. Some organizations recognize this situation and take steps to ensure that suppliers' concerns are dealt with in a fair and open manner. Some organizations fail to provide suppliers with any process for resolving concerns other than the political process. Some organizations go even further — they appear to dare the suppliers to question their decision. Imagine that you were a supplier, and you had just submitted your first proposal (which cost you $10,000 in staff time). You lost to a firm which you believed was inferior. In re-reading the RFP, you once again realized that the purchaser maintained the position that the entire evaluation process was confidential. The RFP stated:

The evaluation team will utilize specific evaluation criteria to rate various requirements for evaluation purposes. Such a rating will be confidential and no totals or scores will be released to any vendor.[1]

How would you feel? Would you think that the process was fair? Or would you think that the purchasing officer was hiding behind the language of the RFP? Would you, as a responsible member of the community, think that this statement was good policy? Since the RFP precluded any debriefing, your protests could only be directed to senior management, political masters or the courts. None of these provide for quiet resolution of the issue.

Some senior officials and politicians do not want any formalized approach. They prefer retaining the power to deal with supplier complaints as they see fit. Often, their actions are seemingly arbitrary and possibly contrary to public policy. However, these actions do deter all but the most resolute of suppliers from getting enough good information to understand the issue, resolve the complaint, or to warrant "going public."

This chapter discusses different approaches to supplier complaints, protests and appeals. It identifies ways to ensure that your process is publicly defensible, and that supplier protests do not become public issues. It provides examples (both good and poor) of how some organizations handle these issues in terms of policy and practices.

What are the requirements for a policy dealing with supplier protests? Before you need a policy, you have to recognize that complaints have some legitimacy. The basic element is to realize that some suppliers' complaints will have merit and substance and, therefore, suppliers should have some form of recourse. In considering this question further, we identified three major requirements. First, the competition must be fair and open, and therefore easily defended. Your fundamental approach must be based on accepted public policy. Second, the policy should include features designed to discourage supplier protests. And finally, there should be an effective dispute resolution mechanism. Ideally, the process should solve the problem quickly and quietly.

Promote Fair and Open Competition

The first requirement is to ensure that supplier protests evaporate once the facts are known. That is, your entire RFP process must be publicly defensible. If the process and your specific actions can survive close public scrutiny, then your decision will be upheld.

Your policy must provide for a fair and open competition. Your specific actions must be easily defended.

Discourage Supplier Protests

The minimum requirements related to

supplier protests are to ensure that the process is fair and easily defended, and to provide a dispute resolution mechanism. But can more be done? Can you, through your actions and policy, actively discourage suppliers from protesting your decisions?

Some organizations have taken a pro-active approach to ensure that few suppliers object to a decision. These organizations provide the supplier community with training and education about their policies and processes. They offer workshops on RFP process; they publish their policies, and they develop handbooks on how to submit a proposal. Others hire an RFP expert to ensure that high-visibility RFPs are properly executed. Some organizations provide losing suppliers with extensive debriefings. Others release their RFPs in draft form to obtain supplier acceptance of the RFP prior to the competition itself.

Your policy should incorporate features designed to convince suppliers of the fairness of the process and, thereby, deter them from a public protest.

Provide an Effective Dispute Resolution Mechanism

Even when a protest has no basis in fact, it can still cause a lot of damage. Suppliers can aggressively challenge all aspects of a decision, the requirements, the process, the competence of the staff, the analysis performed, the criteria and the weights. It is always better that this be done through an internal process, rather than in public. Hence, the second requirement of any policy is to promote the quiet resolution of disputes before they become public issues. Is there a way in which protests can be handled without making them public events? Can you avoid the questions by the politicians and the articles in the newspapers? Can you keep the protests out of court?

In the rest of this chapter, each of these three policy requirements is examined in more detail. The placement of an item in the first or second group (good public policy versus an approach which discourages supplier protests) is, to a certain extent, arbitrary. Common approaches and widely accepted practices were placed in the "good public policy" group. Unusual or innovative approaches, generally found in fewer than 10 percent of RFPs, were placed in the second group — the "discourage suppliers" category.

8.2

Promote Fair and Open Competition

Being in the public sector means that you have an obligation to suppliers, to your organization, and to the public. It means that you work in a fish-bowl environment and must often deal with conflicting objectives. Policy often conflicts with operational effectiveness. For example, you may be required to issue a formal RFP but you don't have the time or staff to prepare an adequate description of your requirements. It is unrealistic to prepare an RFP and issue it to 40 suppliers for a $10,000 project. Many organizations provide policy guidelines to assist staff in determining the amount of effort warranted by the expenditure. These guidelines serve several purposes. They ensure that different procurement officials adopt similar practices and they assure the supplier community that procurement is governed by a set of reasonable, defensible rules.

In the public sector, the pressure to justify each and every major purchase is increasing. State and provincial governments, cities, utilities, school boards, hospitals — in fact, all public sector bodies — are being subjected to more and more public scrutiny. Each of these organizations is required by law, by policy, or by regulation to conduct its procurement activities in a visibly fair manner.

The most obvious objectives in issuing an RFP are to solve a problem by selecting a proposal, and to obtain fair value. However, there are many other objectives imposed on this process by the courts, by law, by policy and by accepted practice.

Laws, regulations and courts in both the United States and Canada have established that the issuer of an RFP cannot act in an arbitrary manner. The issuer has certain obligations to all potential suppliers who receive or respond to the RFP, not only to the winner of the competition. These duties relate to disclosure of important information and fair treatment of suppliers. Furthermore, the RFP cannot be unduly restrictive in defining specifications.

The test of a policy is how it is reflected in

practice. All suppliers must be treated equally. The RFP process must be open and fair. These characteristics must be readily demonstrable both through your actions and by a review of project documents.

Many organizations have developed guidelines to help their staff comply with their RFP policy and the law. Here are some guidelines which can be used by an organization as a checklist to ensure that its RFP process is both visibly fair and publicly defensible.

• *Full Disclosure of Information*

You must fully disclose all relevant information to all suppliers. You have to provide suppliers with all information that you have which could affect their decision to submit a proposal, or the details of their proposal. You have to inform them of any known dangers which may not be obvious from the RFP documents. You must provide them with accurate information and not misrepresent the situation.

The specifications that you provide must be reasonable and not constructed so as to limit competition. In some jurisdictions, this is very important and is quoted in their information for suppliers. The examples which follow are from South Dakota[2] and Yukon, respectively[3]:

It is the intent of the SPO (State Purchasing Office) that specifications are provided in order to encourage free and open competition. The bidder has, however, a responsibility to advise the SPO if, in its opinion, the language of the specification inadvertently restricts or limits the procurement to a single source. Such notification must be submitted in writing at least twelve days prior to the official bid opening date. In addition, the SPO strives to use procedures that will accomplish its mission in accordance with the law and prudent business practices. Potential bidders are encouraged to notify the SPO whenever, in their judgement, specifications are not considered as permitting open competition, complying with standard trade practices or imposing and impractical or unreasonable burden.

Contracting authorities must not use standards, specifications, evaluation criteria or time limits to respond to requests for bids or proposals, contribution agreements, source lists, or other means to unfairly limit competition.

• *Fair Treatment of Suppliers*

You must treat all suppliers in a fair and equal manner. Each supplier must have the same chance of winning the competition based on the information in the RFP. Suppliers often argue that the incumbent is at an advantage because they are currently working for the organization. But the issue is whether you are treating the incumbent and other proponents the same. Is the person who deals with the incumbent on a day-to-day basis also evaluating the proposals? Has the manager been instructed to take care not to inadvertently disclose information about the RFP process, or the budget to the incumbent?

• *Inviting Suppliers to Compete*

The criteria for inviting suppliers to submit proposals must be reasonable and applied equally to all potential suppliers. Often, these criteria are not stated correctly. Consider the following illustrative example: A purchaser wanted to ensure that the supplier's service staff could reach their site within a few hours when needed. So, in deciding on which suppliers to invite, the procurement officer stated that "suppliers must have a service office in our city." This was unreasonable as several suppliers were located in another city, but only 90 minutes away by train or car. The requirement should have been "service staff must be available and able to reach our site within four hours."

• *Issuing the RFP*

The RFP must be released to all suppliers at the same time. While this measure seems obvious, favoured suppliers are sometimes telephoned to pick up the RFP. Other suppliers receive the RFP several days later by post or courier. A few days can be a significant advantage when the proposal is due only two or three weeks later.

• *Providing Information to Suppliers*

The same information must be communicated to all suppliers. It is often difficult to remember precisely the information which you convey to a supplier in a telephone conversation. For this reason, there is often one designated person who deals with all supplier inquiries. Furthermore, many organizations insist that all supplier questions be submitted in writing. These same organizations often answer these questions only in writing. Certainly, this has been made easier with the wide acceptance of fax machines.

In many organizations, it is standard procedure to provide all suppliers with copies of all questions received and answers issued. Most organizations take minutes at suppliers meetings and distribute the minutes to all suppliers who attended or who received an RFP. To avoid accusations that important information stated at the meeting was not included in the minutes, some organizations have a court reporter at the meetings. They distribute transcripts rather than minutes. This procedure costs only a few hundred dollars and works well, although there is sometimes a delay in producing the transcript.

• *Establishing the Rules*

The RFP rules must be contained in the RFP and must not be changed. This principle has been established by the courts in some jurisdictions. If you want to give preference to local companies, then it must be stated in the RFP. In many jurisdictions, local suppliers are afforded a 10 percent price advantage. This is quite proper so long as the specific rule is described in the RFP.

• *The Evaluation Process*

All proposals must be evaluated in the same manner, using the same process and the same people. The evaluation team often consists of specialists, including accountants, network designers, project managers, and user representatives. Typically, each member of the evaluation team reviews the same sections of all proposals and assigns each a score based on a predetermined method of scoring.

• *Debriefing Session*

Unsuccessful suppliers must have the opportunity of a debriefing session. This is a standard practice in almost all jurisdictions. The debriefing "provides an opportunity for a proposer to receive a critical review of the losing proposal, and be apprised of what, in the opinion of the evaluators, were its particular strengths and weaknesses. Simultaneously, the justification for the procurers' selection of the winner is likely to become apparent..."[4]

Access to information legislation exists in many jurisdictions. Under these laws, many of the documents normally found in a project file can be released upon application by a supplier. These documents could include evaluation criteria and weights, list of bidders invited, list of proposals received, evaluation committee members' notes, and summary of all evaluations. Armed with this information, suppliers can judge for themselves whether they believe the process was visibly fair.

So regardless of how little information a supplier is given at a debriefing, much information is readily available. In fact, you cannot guarantee that something will not be released under the terms of an Access to Information Act.

• *Compliance with Policies*

The process must comply with your organization's purchasing policy and established practices and laws. The policy must be reasonable, clearly stated, and available in writing.

• *The Evaluation Process Must be Documented*

Many organizations insist that the evaluation criteria and weights be established prior to opening the proposals. This avoids accusations that the evaluation criteria were established only after reviewing a specific supplier's proposal. While the process must be documented, often little of this information makes its way into the RFP.

• *Requests for an RFP*

Any suppliers requesting an RFP must be given one. Some organizations insist that only invited suppliers or registered suppliers can submit proposals. This often creates problems. There are always new suppliers in town, suppliers who haven't had the time to register, or suppliers from out-of-province or from another country who want to submit a proposal. Some jurisdictions refuse to issue RFPs to unknown firms. In other jurisdictions, RFPs are issued to anyone who requests one. The assumption is that the evaluation process will identify the best supplier, and if an unknown supplier wants to submit a proposal, it should be permitted. Some public sector organizations have discovered that it is easier to hand out an extra RFP and evaluate another proposal than to explain, at the political level, why an important company was not permitted to compete.

• *Publicizing the RFP*

The RFP must be publicized in a manner consistent with its value and importance. Minor competitions can be done using the telephone; major competitions may require ads in newspapers or official posting as prescribed by regulation.

• *Provide Information About the Evaluation in the RFP*

The RFP must contain some information about the evaluation process. At a minimum, it must sketch the evaluation process, identify the major categories of evaluation criteria, and indicate the most important criteria. Ideally, the RFP should describe the evaluation process, identify the major evaluation criteria and their weights.

Current practices vary radically. At one extreme, some RFPs provide no information about the evaluation process, and only hint at the evaluation criteria. At the other extreme, organizations provide several pages of descriptive information about the evaluation process, a detailed description of each of the major evaluation factors and its weight.

8.3

Discourage Supplier Protests

Your policy and procedures should incorporate features designed to convince suppliers of the fairness of the process and thereby discourage them from launching a public protest.[5] There are many ways of discouraging supplier protests since purchasers, in general, and most certainly public buyers, have great power to affect a supplier's economic well-being. This section identifies pro-active, positive tasks which will, by their very nature, provide suppliers with convincing evidence of the quality of the organization's RFP practices. None of these measures are punitive or designed to "win through intimidation" — a tactic still employed by some purchasing executives.

• *Provide Information to Suppliers*

Up-to-date, accurate information helps suppliers understand how to compete effectively, and reduces the demands on purchasers for explanations and presentations. There are three documents which, when available, benefit the suppliers in terms of supplying more information and benefit the purchasing organization in terms of its credibility and professionalism:

1. RFP Policy — a concise statement of your organization's principles and major policy items related to RFPs.

2. RFP Handbook — a book identifying your major procedures and practices. This handbook typically has sample RFPs and the forms used in the process.

3. "Doing Business With Us" — a booklet containing essential information about the organization's purchasing practices. These booklets typically include the following topics: role of the purchasing department, what we buy, who can tender, purchasing policies, how to be on our supplier list, preparing your tender, awarding contracts, payment, supplier assistance, and a telephone directory for purchasing staff. They often include the supplier registration forms as well.

All of this information can be made available in many different forms: books, online computer access, workshops, and via electronic mail.

• *Prepare an Evaluators' Guide*

An Evaluators' Guide is a handbook which contains key policy items, evaluation procedures, weights, criteria, and scoring mechanisms. It also contains the actual worksheets which will be used by the evaluators for the RFP under consideration and the detailed scoring instructions. While sections of this handbook are generic and apply to all RFPs, other sections are specific. Obviously, the evaluation criteria and weights change from RFP to RFP. Also, details of the evaluation process itself can be different.

Here are the contents for a typical Evaluators' Handbook[6]:

Table of Contents

Overall Approach

Evaluation Categories

Evaluation Process

Master Evaluation Table

Scoring Mechanism

Explanation of the Evaluation Criteria

Completing the Evaluation

The Scoring System

Evaluation Worksheet

Some jurisdictions have an evaluation planning meeting prior to opening the proposals. At that meeting, the RFP expert reviews the process, the procedure, and the specific worksheets with the team.

• *Include an RFP Officer in the Process*

Have an RFP officer — an expert — as part of the process. This person plays two major roles: to protect the integrity of the process and to assure suppliers of a fair and open competition (and thereby discourage complaints).

First, the RFP officer will protect the integrity of the process with the following actions: (1) by editing and reviewing the entire RFP document, particularly the terms and conditions section; (2) by briefing the project team on the process; (3) by answering questions; (4) by monitoring the process; (5) by attending the evaluation meetings; and (6) by producing an audit report once the contract has been signed.

Second, the officer will ensure that issues, as they arise, are addressed from the suppliers' perspective as well as the purchasers'. The RFP officer will maintain a log of key events, produce an audit report and attend debriefing meetings with suppliers.

Typically, this person's role is identified in the RFP. This person is introduced at the suppliers meeting and responds to questions about the process. Finally, the terms of reference for this work are stated at the suppliers' meeting and noted in the minutes.

• *Provide Debriefing Information to Suppliers*

Purchasers should identify both the information and documents which will be available after an award is made. Since much of this information is available under access to information legislation, the purchasing organization should be pro-active and release this information automatically.

Typically, the following information is available under the legislation after an award:

- evaluation criteria, weights, scoring mechanism
- evaluators' handbook
- names of bidders
- winner's total score
- each bidder's own scores
- each bidder's own evaluation
- RFP officer's terms, events log, final report

The state of Florida goes one step further. Their standard RFP contains a "Bidders Request for Notification of No Award" for suppliers who want to receive written notice that they didn't win. If the supplier wants to receive the actual bid tabulations, they can indicate this on the form and submit $5.00 to over the cost of mailing and copies.

• *Publish the Protest Policy in the RFP and Other Supplier Documents.*

The RFP should identify the existence of a policy and how a supplier can obtain a copy. In many jurisdictions the supplier has a specific legal right to protest actions related to public procurement. These rights are often identified in both the RFP and in booklets provided to the

supplier community by the organization. The state of New Mexico includes the following paragraph in their supplier reference booklet[7]:

In accordance with Section 13-1-172 NMSA 1978, any bidder or offeror who is aggrieved in connection with a solicitation or award of a contract may protest to the State Purchasing Agent. If, pursuant to Section 13-1-99 NMSA 1978, the procurement is excluded from procurement through the State Purchasing Agent, the protest shall be made to the central purchasing office having responsibility for initiating the solicitation. The protests must be submitted in writing within fifteen (15) calendar days after knowledge of the facts or occurrences giving rise to the protest. The protest shall include the name and address of the protestant; include the solicitation number; contain a statement of the grounds for protest; and specify the ruling requested from the State Purchasing Agent or the central purchasing office.

In Florida, they publish information about the protest procedure in the RFP. Suppliers not filing on time are deemed to have given up this right[8]:

Proposal tabulations with recommended awards will be posted for review by interested parties at the location where proposals were opened and will remain posted for a period of 72 hours. Failure to file a protest with the time prescribed in Section 120.53(5), Florida Statutes, shall constitute a wavier of proceedings under Chapter 120, Florida Statutes. Posting will be on or about (insert date here.)

8.4

Provide an Effective Dispute Resolution Mechanism

So far, this chapter has dealt with ways of avoiding protests through "best practices" or by introducing barriers to discourage suppliers from protesting. Regardless of how solid your policies are, and how thorough your procedures, there will be disgruntled suppliers. The reasons are straightforward:

First, there are always more losers than winners, so the odds favour protests being initiated.

Second, mistakes will occur, no matter how knowledgeable or well trained a procurement officer is. Suppliers will be aggrieved, and some of them will launch protests.

Third, awarding contracts based on political reasons or on seemingly arbitrary criteria has become unacceptable. Awards based on arbitrary criteria generate protests.

While a supplier can always seek relief in the courts, there should be some simple administrative process for resolving these differences. This remedy should not involve the courts; it should be fast, inexpensive and defensible. Furthermore, the administrative approach should be able to solve the problem quietly, without attracting the harsh glare of publicity.

Procurement officials can do much to mitigate complaints. They can offer explanations or clarifications to suppliers. They can remove ambiguities and resolve conflicts and errors in the RFP documents.

A supplier's first recourse should be a discussion with the procurement officer. Procurement officers must be accessible. They must be willing to at least listen to suppliers. They must exhibit some sensitivity to the supplier who feels aggrieved. Remember, it can cost a supplier tens of thousands of dollars to prepare a formal proposal. Suppliers do this because they believe that the business is potentially theirs. If they suspect that they have been treated unfairly, and they cannot get any level of information, empathy, explanation, or resolution from the procurement official, they may decide to protest. Suppliers do not protest an award without much thought and deliberation. Protests consume large amounts of corporate time and energy. And, in many jurisdictions, suppliers know that to protest is to forego future business. Procurement officials, both in the public and private sectors, are "only human" and are often influenced by past dealings with suppliers.

A protest can be formally defined as a written objection by an interested party to a solicitation for the acquisition of supplies or services, or a written objection by an interested party to a proposed award or to the actual award of the related contract.

There are many reasons cited for protesting an award:

1. The purchasing official fails to comply with rules or regulations.

2. The purchasing officials' actions unfairly limit a supplier's opportunity to win. For example, an arbitrary requirement to have an office in Omaha, or eight years of experience.

3. The RFP requirements were unduly restrictive and failed to promote fair and open competition. For example, features were identified but were not necessary to achieve reasonable functionality and were available from only one supplier.

4. One supplier was favoured by the requirements, evaluation process or criteria.

In these harsh economic times, protests will arise as suppliers compete more vigorously for fewer dollars. Shrinking budgets, more complex organizations and changing paradigms all contribute to the difficult environment in which procurement officers must work.

It would appear that there are three different approaches to dispute resolution. In the first approach, the purchasing organization is arrogant, insular or insensitive. It doesn't really want to deal with suppliers' concerns. Their attitude is basically "we're always right! You can talk to us, but we won't listen or do very much!" Organizations adopting this tactic usually have no published policy about RFPs or protests. They often offer suppliers a debriefing but then indicate that almost all of the information is confidential or protected by freedom of information legislation. They do not willingly provide evidence of their own shortcomings to suppliers feeling aggrieved. In extreme cases, the RFP actually contains a phrase excluding the possibility of a debriefing!

In the second approach, the organization does want to deal with suppliers' concerns. These organizations often provide suppliers with lots of information and genuinely try to deal with complaints in a business-like manner. Where these organizations fall short is that there is no appeal from the decision of the purchasing officer, other than the courts or the politicians. This approach is differentiated from the first by the attitude of the procurement officials, and, sometimes by the procedures themselves.

The final approach is based on the organization wanting to address suppliers' concerns to the satisfaction of the suppliers. These organizations provide suppliers as much information as possible. In addition, they provide the suppliers with a well-defined, publicized appeal process. These organizations have a written procedure as part of RFP policy which provides for an initial attempt to resolve disputes internally, then through an objective third party. In some of these organizations, the seriousness of this event is reflected in the policy and practice of not awarding the contract until the protest is resolved.

8.5

Some Examples of Policies and Practices

The examples which follow were collected in many forms. Some are based on public documents; some are based on correspondence. Others are anecdotal, based on interviews with officials in the organization.

These examples do not include any "horror stories" about organizations whose policies speak of "fair competition" but whose actions fail to demonstrate any such approach. Unfortunately, some public sector bodies still award contracts in arbitrary, improper and sometimes illegal ways. The examples which follow are for organizations whose practices correspond with their policies.

These examples, as with other topics throughout this book, do not deal with federal government or agencies in either the U.S. or Canada. At the federal level, in both countries, suppliers are encouraged to resolve the issue with the contracting officer. Failing this, a formal protest can be made. In Canada, the protest is to the issuing organization, usually Public Works and Government Services Canada. In the United States, the protest is made to the General Accounting Office, or the General Services Administration Board of Contract Appeal. Both of these agencies of the U.S. government have developed extensive procedures for handling protests.[9]

The recently signed North American Free Trade Agreement between Canada and the United States contains a section on supplier complaints. It is a good illustration of the principles underlying a complaint procedure and is included as an example.

The examples presented in this section are incomplete. Each example does not cover the same issues. The level of detail reflects the information collected, the source, and the time available for this survey.

The anecdotal descriptions are provided first; then the more formalized processes.

■ 8.5.1 Anecdotal Descriptions

Large City Government

This local government ensures that all suppliers who submitted a proposal are informed of an award prior to its public announcement. Suppliers are advised to direct all complaints to the Purchasing Department in writing. Each complaint is answered in writing.

If the supplier is still not satisfied, the complaint will be dealt with first by a commissioner and then by the elected council.

The purchasing manager believes that this approach is very effective. Each supplier's concerns are dealt with in a forthright manner. Awards and contracts are held in abeyance if a protest has been lodged pending resolution of the complaint.

Large, Urban Board of Education

This organization uses a multi-step complaint procedure.

Disgruntled suppliers first deal with the Purchasing Department. If the supplier is still not satisfied with the explanations given, then the supplier can request the opportunity to present its case to an internal Administration Committee. If the supplier complaint is still unresolved, then the supplier can present its case to the Board.

I have been informed that in the last four years, only one grievance has reached the Administration Committee or the Board. The manager of the Purchasing Department attributes this to two factors: clear, concise RFP documents, and open communication with the suppliers.

Where major contracts are involved, the Purchasing Department takes the time to contact each unsuccessful bidder and provide opportunities for feedback. In most cases, verbal communication is sufficient. When requested, they do not hesitate to provide unsuccessful suppliers with all the information they can within the parameters of the applicable Freedom of Information and Privacy Protection Act.

Part of their success is that they never play "hard to get" in providing information unless release of the information is prohibited by the Act.

Province of Ontario

One particular Ministry spends hundreds of million of dollars each year. They have no policy or procedure to handle disgruntled suppliers following an award announcement.

The do offer debriefing meetings with individual suppliers after the award has been made. During the meeting, they discuss the pros and cons of a supplier's proposal.

If a vendor is still dissatisfied, the procurement officer will respond in writing explaining how the evaluation criterion were used and why the vendor's proposal was not chosen.

Centralized Multi-Agency Purchasing Group

This organization is required to ensure that its procedures conform to the published rules. Their policy places great emphasis on the principle of fair and open competition.

If unsuccessful suppliers raise questions or express concerns about the award or the process, they are offered a debriefing session. If the briefing is deemed by the supplier as being unsatisfactory, then the supplier is advised to refer the matter to an administrative tribunal to request a review, or use the court system.

This group contends that the vast majority of questions and concerns are resolved to the satisfaction of the suppliers during the debriefing process. They state that a few complaints have been escalated to either the tribunal or the court system but the decisions have never resulted in a change to any award or damages being paid to any supplier.

This organization is constantly defending its actions in the press and through the political process.

■ 8.5.2 Examples of Formal Procedures

The state of Arizona provides a good overview of their formal process[10]:

An interested party may protest a solicitation, proposed award or the award of a contract. The protest must be in writing and must include the name, address and telephone number of the protestant; signature of the protestant, or (its) representative; identification of the purchasing agency and the solicitation or contract number; a detailed statement of the legal and factual grounds of the protests including copies of relevant documents; and the form of relief requests.

A protest of a solicitation must be filed within a reasonable time before bid opening or after the closing date for receipt of initial proposals. In other cases, a protest must be filed within ten days after the protestant knows, or should have known, the basis of the protests. The protestant must file the protests with the responsible procurement officer and notify the State Procurement Administrator of the protest. If a protest is filed prior to contract award, all interested parties will be notified; if the protest is filed after contract award, the successful contractor(s) will be notified.

The procurement officer will issue a written decision within fourteen days after a protest has been filed. If the procurement officer fails to issue a decision within fourteen days, the protestant may proceed with an appeal as if the procurement officer had issued an adverse decision. An appeal from a decision by the procurement officer must be filed with the Director of the Department of Administration within five days from the date the decision is received. Notice of the appeal will be given to successful contractors or, if no award has been made, to all interested parties. A decision on the appeal by the Director shall be final.

State of Alaska

The state of Alaska provides a good example of a rigorous approach to supplier protests. The state publishes its appeal procedure in its RFPs. A supplier can protest an award by filing a letter with the project procurement officer who then reviews the facts and renders a judgement. This decision can be appealed by the supplier to an outside agency — the Department of Administration — which will then investigate the issue and render an objective determination.

Here is a formal, legalistic example published in an RFP issued by the Department of Transportation1[11].

3.12 Aggrieved Respondents

3.12.1 Protests

An interested party may protest the award of a contract, the proposed award of a contract, or a solicitation for professional services by an agency. The protest shall be filed in writing with the Project Procurement Officer, Information Systems Division, Department of Transportation and Public Facilities, P.O. Box Z, Juneau, Alaska 99811, within 10 days after a Notice of Intent to Award the contract is issued and include the following information:

1. the name, address, and telephone number of the protester;

2. the signature of the protester or the protester's representative;

3. identification of the contracting agency and the solicitation or contract at issue;

4. a detailed statement of the legal and factual grounds of the protest, including copies of relevant documents; and

5. the form of relief requested.

The project procurement officer shall issue a written decision containing the basis of the decision within the statutory time lime set out in AS36.30.580. A copy of the decision shall be furnished to the protester by certified mail or other method that provides evidence of receipt.

3.12.2 Appeals

An appeal from the decision of the Project Procurement Officer on a protest may be filed by the protester with the Commission, Department of Administration, P.O. Box C, Juneau, Alaska 99811-0200. An appeal shall be filed within five (5) days after the decision is received by the protester. The protester shall also file a copy of the appeal with the issuing office. The appeal shall contain the information required in paragraph 3.12.1; as well as:

1. a copy of the decision being appealed; and

2. identification of the factual or legal errors in the decision that form the basis for the appeal.

If necessary, a hearing shall be held to determine whether the award of the contested contract was made in accordance with statues and prescribed procedures. The hearing shall be limited to the evaluation and solicitation process used in this Request for Proposals.

North American Free Trade Agreement[12]

The North American Free Trade Agreement describes the principles and key features of a supplier complaint process. This article can be used by any organization as a guide for preparing its own Supplier Complaint Procedure.

In reading this article, "party" refers to the governments of Canada, Mexico, and the U.S. "Entity" refers to a federal institution.

Article 1017: Bid Challenge

1. In order to promote fair and impartial procurement procedures, each Party shall adopt and maintain bid challenge procedures for procurement covered by this Chapter in accordance with the following:

(a) each Party shall allow suppliers to submit bid challenges concerning any aspect of the procurement process, which for the purposes of this Article begins after an entity has decided on its procurement requirement and continues through the contract award;

(b) a Party may encourage a supplier to seek a resolution of any complaint with the entity concerned prior to initiating a bid challenge;

(c) each Party shall ensure that its entities accord

fair and timely consideration to any complaint regarding procurement covered by this Chapter;

(d)   whether or not a supplier has attempted to resolve its complaint with the entity, or following an unsuccessful attempt at such a resolution, no Party may prevent the supplier from initiating a bid challenge or seeking any other relief;

(e)   a Party may require a supplier to notify the entity on initiation of a bid challenge;

(f)   a Party may limit the period within which a supplier may initiate a bid challenge, but in no case shall the period be less than 10 working days from the time when the basis of the complaint became known or reasonably should have become known to the supplier;

(g)   each Party shall establish or designate a reviewing authority with no substantial interest in the outcome of procurements to receive bid challenges and make findings and recommendations concerning them;

(h)   on receipt of a bid challenge, the reviewing authority shall expeditiously investigate the challenge;

(i)   a Party may require its reviewing authority to limit its considerations to the challenge itself;

(j)   in investigating the challenge, the reviewing authority may delay the awarding of the proposed contract pending resolution of the challenge, except in cases of urgency or where the delay would be contrary to the public interest;

(k)   the reviewing authority shall issue a recommendation to resolve the challenge, which may include directing the entity to re-evaluate offers, terminate or re-compete the contract in question;

(l)   entities normally shall follow the recommendations of the reviewing authority;

(m)   each Party should authorize its reviewing authority, following the conclusion of a bid challenge procedure, to make additional recommendations in writing to an entity respecting any facet of the entity's procurement process that is identified as problematic during the investigation of the challenge, including recommendations for changes in the procurement procedures of the entity to bring them into conformity with this Chapter;

(n)   the reviewing authority shall provide its findings and recommendations respecting bid challenges in writing and in a timely manner, and shall make them available to the Parties and interested persons;

(o)   each Party shall specify in writing and shall make generally available all its bid challenge procedures; and

(p)   each Party shall ensure that each of its entities maintains complete documentation regarding each of its procurements including a written record of all communications substantially affecting each procurement, for at least three years from the date the contract was awarded, to allow verification that the procurement process was carried out in accordance with this Chapter.

2.   A Party may require that a bid challenge be initiated only after the notice of procurement has been published or, where a notice is not published, after tender documentation has been made available. Where a Party imposes such a requirement, the 10-working day period described in paragraph 1(f) shall begin no earlier than the date that the notice is published or the tender documentation is made available.

Yukon Government

One of the principles established in the Yukon

Government's regulations[13] is the right of a proponent to challenge an award, to receive some compensation for monies spent, and to change the procurement process:

12. There must be a formal bid challenge mechanism based on the following:

(a) Bidders and proponents must be given a reasonable opportunity to register complaints.

(b) Complainants must have a responsibility to make all reasonable attempts to settle their disputes with the applicable contracting authority.

(c) There must be an opportunity for redress, including compensation for costs of complaining and bid/proposal preparation costs.

(d) As mechanism to change, where warranted, government contracting policies and procedures will be provided.

The bid challenge process uses a committee that includes representatives from the public. It is unusual to have members of the public participate in the challenge process[14].

PART VI - BID CHALLENGE PROCESS
Bid challenge committee

A. The Minister of Government Services will appoint a standing bid challenge committee to act on complaints registered pursuant to this directive.

B. The committee will be made up of a chair, an alternate chair who will act in the absence of the chair, five (5) representatives from the Government of the Yukon, and five (5) representatives from the public.

C. Each appointment will be for a term of up to

two (2) years, and may be renewed.

D. Within the policy laid out in this directive, the committee may establish its own rules of procedure.

Registering a complaint

E. The Deputy Head of Government Services will accept a complaint made in writing by a bidder or proponent or prospective bidder or proponent who has reason to believe that a Deputy Head, or a public servant to whom a Deputy Head has delegated contracting authority, has treated them unfairly or has not followed the process required by the Contract Regulations or this directive, provided that the complaint is received

(a) up to 60 days following the closing time, or up to 15 days following the award of the contract or standing offer agreement, whichever is later, or

(b) in the event of an extension of a standing offer agreement, up to 30 days following the date of the extension.

F. The bid challenge process described in this Part does not apply to decisions made under paragraphs (a) to (f) of this directive.

G. The Deputy Head, Government Services may require the complainant to provide full details related to the complaint, including their efforts to resolve the complaint directly with the contracting authority.

H. The Deputy Head, Government Services will, without undue delay, forward the complaint to the Deputy Head of the contracting authority and to the bid challenge committee established pursuant to section .

The registration of a complaint pursuant to section will not require the contracting authority to delay award of the contract.

Considering the complaint

I.   The contracting authority will provide a written report about the circumstances relating to the complaint to the chair without delay.

J.   The chair of the bid challenge committee without delay will conduct an initial review of the complaint to determine whether or not there will be an inquiry or hearing.

K.   A complaint registered with the committee which is found by the chair to warrant a hearing will be heard by a panel of three (3) members consisting of the chair and one (1) member appointed by the chair from the representatives of the government and one (1) member appointed by the chair from the representatives of the public.

L.   Where possible, the qualifications of the members selected by the chair to hear a complaint will be appropriate to the matter under consideration.

M.   The panel will hear and consider the complaint within a reasonable time following registration of the complaint.

N.   The panel will allow the complainant and the contracting authority against whom the complaint was registered to address the panel in person and in writing.

O.   The chair may call upon such advisors as the panel considers advisable to report to the panel.

P.   Complaints may be heard in any place in the Yukon.

Q.   The panel will not cancel, revoke, amend or alter a contract.

Unfounded complaints

I. (1) The panel may refuse to hear and consider, or may cease to consider a complaint on the grounds that

(a)   the complaint is trivial, frivolous, vexatious or not made in good faith, or

(b)   the complainant does not have a sufficient personal interest in the subject matter of the complaint.

(2)   Where the panel refuses to consider or ceases to consider a complaint, the chair will inform the complainant and the contracting authority against whom the complaint was registered and may state reasons therefor.

Access to information

II. A. Notwithstanding any restrictions on the disclosure of documents in this directive, the panel may examine any documents relating to the complaint.

B.   All information used by the panel in its deliberations, and which may be disclosed under territorial access to information legislation, will be disclosed to both parties to the complaint.

Redress

III. A.Where the panel considers that a complaint is valid, it may recommend that the contracting authority pay to the complainant compensation for:

1.   the complainant's reasonable costs in preparing a bid or proposal; and/or

2.   the complainant's reasonable costs for participating in the inquiry or hearing.

B.   In making its decision, the panel will consider all the circumstances relevant to the complaint, including:

1.   the seriousness of any deficiency in the procurement process found by the panel;

2.   the degree to which the complainant and all other interested parties were prejudiced;

3.   the degree to which the integrity and efficiency

of the competitive procurement system was prejudiced; and

4. whether the parties acted in good faith.

Panel to report

IV. The panel will make a report of its findings and recommendations, if any, to the Deputy Head of the contracting authority and to the complainant.

Duty to respond

V. A. Where the panel recommends a change to government policy or procedure, the Deputy Head of the contracting authority will, within a reasonable period of time, address the recommendation to the government body which has the authority to consider, and if warranted to act on, the recommendation.

B. The Deputy Head of the contracting authority will, within a reasonable period of time, provide to the chair a written response(s) which describe(s) progress being made in addressing the panel's recommendation(s). The Deputy Head will provide a copy of the response(s) to his or her Minister.

Distribution of response

VI. (1) The chair will forward a copy of the Deputy Head's response(s) to the complainant.

(2) On forwarding the copy of the Deputy Head's response(s) to the complainant pursuant to subsection (1), the chair will forward a copy of all material relating to the complaint to the Deputy Head of Government Services.

State of Washington

The state of Washington also includes its protest procedures and the allowable grounds for protest in the RFPs for information technology[15]:

PROTEST PROCEDURES

A. Procedure

This protest procedure is available to vendors responding to this RFP requesting a debriefing conference. Protests are made:

1. To the Department of _____ after the announcement of the apparently successful vendor. Vendor protests shall be received, in writing, by the Department of _____ within five business days after the vendor debriefing conference.

2. To DIS only after protesting first to the Department of _____ and its resolution is not satisfactory to the protesting party. Protests to DIS shall be received, in writing, within five business days after the vendor has received notification of a decision on the protest from the Department of _____.

3. To the ISB for acquisitions approved by the ISB, only after protesting first to DIS and DIS resolution is not satisfactory to either party. Protests to the ISB shall be made within five business days after the vendor has received notification of the DIS decision.

B. Grounds for protest are:

1. Errors were made in computing the score.

2. The state failed to follow procedures established in the RFP, the ISB policy: Acquisition and Disposal of Information Technology Resources, or applicable state or federal laws or regulations.

3. Bias, discrimination or conflict of interest on the part of an evaluator.

Protests not based on these criteria shall not be considered.

C. Format and Content

Protesting vendors shall include, in their written protest to the Department of _____ and DIS, all facts and arguments upon which they rely. Vendors shall, at a minimum, provide:

1. Information about the protesting vendor; name of firm, mailing address, phone number and name of individual responsible for submission of the protest.

2. Information about the acquisition and the acquisition method.

3. Specific and complete statement of the State action(s) protested.

4. Specific reference to the grounds for the protest.

5. Description of the relief or corrective action requested.

6. For protests to DIS or the ISB, a copy of the Department of _____'s written decision on the protest.

D. Review Process

Upon receipt of a vendor protest, the Department of _____ shall postpone further steps in the acquisition process until the vendor protest has been resolved.

The Department's internal protest review procedures consist of the following: (_____).

The Department of _____ shall perform an objective review of the protest by individuals not involved in the acquisition protested. The review shall be based on the written protest material submitted by the vendor.

A written decision will be delivered to the vendor within five business days after receipt of the protest, unless more time is needed. The protesting vendor shall be notified if additional time is necessary.

E. DIS Review Process

The vendor may protest to DIS in writing within five business days after the vendor has received notification of the agency decision.

DIS shall consider all the available facts and issue a decision in writing within five business days after receipt of the protest, unless more time is needed. The protesting vendor shall be notified if additional time is necessary. The DIS decision constitutes the final step of the protest process, except protests which may be reviewed by the ISB as outlined under Section I, "ISB Review Process."

DIS may choose to convene a Protest Review Board (Board). The Board shall be advisory to the DIS Director and its scope of review shall be limited to procedural issues raised by the protesting vendor.

F. Final Determination

The final determination shall:

1. Find the protest lacking in merit and uphold the agency's action; or

2. Find only technical or harmless errors in the agency's acquisition process conduct, determine the agency to be in substantial compliance, and reject the protest; or

3. Find merit in the protest and provide the agency options which may include:

Correct its errors and reevaluate all proposals, and/or

Reissue the vendor solicitation document; or

4. Make other findings and determine other courses of action as appropriate.

G.   ISB Review Process

Protests to the ISB may be made only for ISB approved acquisitions, and only after review by DIS. Protests of the decisions of DIS shall be made by letter to the Chair, ISB, who may establish procedures to resolve the protest. Protests shall be received by the Chair, ISB, within five business days after the decision of DIS in order to be considered. The resulting decision is final, with no further administrative appeal available.

[1] Page 5-26, Reference *16.

[2] Reference *3.

[3] Page 4, Reference *7.

[4] Page 102, Reference *28.

[5] Many of the items in this section could also be included in the first section, Promote Fair and Open Competition, or in both sections. The items described in this section are uncommon. They are not found in a majority of RFPs across the entire public sector.

[6] A sample Evaluators Handbook is contained in Part II of this publication.

[7] Page 11, Reference *26.

[8] Reference *21.

[9] See References *30 and *31.

[10] Page 10, Reference *24.

[11] The entire RFP is contained in Part II.

[12] Reference *27.

[13] Page 5, Reference *7.

[14] Pages 24-26, Reference *7.

[15] Reference *12.

CHAPTER 9

References and Notes

The following books, pamphlets, and government publications are referenced in the footnotes in Chapters 1 through 8.

Reference 1

Information Technology Procurement, A Managers Reference Notes, 80 pages, May, 1992

Contact: Management Board Secretariat, Information Technology Division, Government of Ontario

              4th Floor, 56 Wellesley St. West, Toronto, Ontario, Canada M7A 1Z6

              Phone: (416) 327-2121 · Fax: (416) 327-2088

This book presents an overview of the procurement process, a description of key issues, and detailed explanations of the main components of the process.

Reference 2

Acquisition and Disposal of Information Technology Resources in Washington State Government, 18 pages, Sept., 1989

Contact: Dept. of Information Services, Policy and Regulation Division

              State of Washington

              P.O. Box 42440, Olympia, WA 98504-244

Reference 3

Vendor's Manual, State of South Dakota, 18 pages, 1992.

Contact: Office of Purchasing & Printing, State of South Dakota

500 E. Capitol Ave., Pierre, SD 57501-3405

Phone: (605) 773-3405 · Fax: (605) 773-4840

Reference 4

State Procurement Code, AS 36.30, 74 pages, Aug. 22, 1994

Contact: Dept. of Administration, State of Alaska, Division of General Services

P.O. Box 110210, Juneau, AK 99811-0210

Phone: (907) 465-2250 · Fax: (907) 465-2189

Reference 5

Policy: Invitation to Quote and Request For Proposal, 4 pages, 1994.

Contact: Purchasing & Contracts Dept., B.C. Systems Corp.

4000 Seymour Place, Victoria, B.C. V8X 4S8, Canada

Phone: (604) 389-3944 · Fax: (604) 389-3916

Reference 6

The Request For Proposal Process, 143 pages, Aug., 1993.

Contact: Michael Asner Consulting

5951-237A Street, Langley, B.C., Canada V2Z 1A6

Phone: (604) 530-7881 · Fax: (604) 530-7881

Much of the content of this earlier publication has been reflected in the Request For Proposal Handbook.

Reference 7

Government of Yukon, Contracting Regulations and Contracting Directive, 26 pages, March 20, 1995

Contract: Contract Administration, Government Services, Yukon Government

P.O. Box 2703, Whitehorse, Yukon, Canada Y1A 2C6

Reference 8

Purchasing Regulations, AAC Title 2, Chapter 12, 51 pages, March 30, 1990.

Contact: Dept. of Administration, State of Alaska, Division of General Services

P.O. Box 110210, Juneau, AK 99811-0210

Phone: (907) 465-2250 · Fax: (907) 465-2189

Reference 9

State Administrative Manual

Contact: Dept. of Administration, State of Alaska, Division of General Services

P.O. Box 110210, Juneau, AK 99811-0210

Phone: (907) 465-2250 · Fax: (907) 465-2189

Section 82 of this manual is 23 pages long and deals with Professional Services Contracts.

Reference 10

RFP Shell, 56 pages.

Contact: Dept. of Administration, State of Alaska, Division of General Services

P.O. Box 110210, Juneau, AK 99811-0210

Phone: (907) 465-2250 · Fax: (907) 465-2189

Reference 11

Chapter 43.105 RCW, Department of Information Services, 16 pages, Feb., 1995.

Contact: Dept. of Information Services, State of Washington

P.O. Box 42440, Olympia, WA 98504-2440

This legislation creates the Department of Information Services.

Reference 12

Model Request For Proposal, 41 pages, 1992.

Contact: Dept. of Information Services, State of Washington

P.O. Box 42440, Olympia, WA 98504-2440

Reference 13

Contractual Standard Clauses, Additional Contractual Clauses, 61 pages, 1989.

Contact: Dept. of Information Services, State of Washington

P.O. Box 42440, Olympia, WA 98504-2440

Reference 14

THIS NUMBER WAS NOT USED.

Reference 15

How To Create An Effective M.I.S. Request For Proposals, 131 pages, 1990.

Contact: Michael Asner Consulting

5951-237A Street, Langley, B.C., Canada V2Z 1A6

Phone: (604) 530-7881 · Fax: (604) 530-7881

Much of the content of this earlier publication has been reflected in the Request For Proposal Handbook.

Reference 16

How To Evaluate Information Technology Proposals, 380 pages, 1994.

Contact: Michael Asner Consulting

5951-237A Street, Langley, B.C., Canada V2Z 1A6

Phone: (604) 530-7881 · Fax: (604) 530-7881

Much of the content of this earlier publication has been reflected in the Request For Proposal Handbook.

Reference 17

The RFP Report, 12 pages, printed quarterly since 1993

Contact: Michael Asner Consulting

5951-237A Street, Langley, B.C., Canada V2Z 1A6

Phone: (604) 530-7881 · Fax: (604) 530-7881

Much of the content of this earlier publication has been reflected in the Request For Proposal Handbook.

Reference 18

Guide To Tendering, page 46, 1993.

Contact: Purchasing & Contracts Dept., B.C. Systems Corp.

4000 Seymour Place, Victoria, B.C. V8X 4S8, Canada

Phone: (604) 389-3944 · Fax: (604) 389-3916

This handbook contains guidelines, their procurement policy and a model RFP.

Reference 19

State of Arizona, Request For Proposal A5-0036, 36 pages, March 2, 1995.

Contact: State Procurement Office, State of Arizona, Executive Tower

Suite 101, 1700 West Washington, Phoenix, AZ 85007

This RFP for interpreter services contains the Standardized Notice (Form SPO 201RFP), and standard terms and conditions (Form 202-A).

Reference 20

Strategic Procurement Management Request For Proposal Tender No. 93.PS.1, 128 pages, 1993.

Contact: Strategic Procurement Project, Management Board Secretariat, Government of Ontario

Room M1-57, Macdonald Block, 900 Bay Street, Toronto, Ontario, Canada M7A 1N3

Phone: (416) 327-4185 · Fax: (416) 327-3198

This is a 19-page RFP with 109 pages of attachments. Appendix A is a 91-page discussion of Strategic Procurement Management.

Reference 21

State of Florida, Request For Proposal, Contractual Services, Acknowledgement Form, PUR 7033, 2 pages, 1991.

Contact: Division of Purchasing, State of Florida, Koger Executive Center

Knight Building, Suite 216, Tallahassee, FL 32399-0950

Phone: (904) 488-8366

This is a standard form used as page one on RFPs and contains General Conditions applying to all RFPs.

Reference 22

Request for Proposal, DOJ-4024, Consolidated Firearms Information System, 275 pages, April 17, 1995.

Contact: State of California, Department of Justice

Contains standardized Rules Governing Competition. Provides a good example of an iterative RFP process.

Reference Number: 23

NOT USED

Reference 24

How to do Business with the State of Arizona, 4th edition, 12 pages, Pct. 1989.

Contact: Dept. of Administration, Finance Division, State of Arizona, State Procurement Office

Executive Tower, Suite 101, 1700 West Washington, Phoenix, AZ 85007

Reference 25

Standardized RFP, 17 pages.

Contact: Purchasing & Contracts Dept., B.C. Systems Corp.

4000 Seymour Place, Victoria, B.C. V8X 4S8, Canada

Phone: (604) 389-3944 · Fax: (604) 389-3916

Reference 26

How To Do Business With The State of New Mexico, 11 pages, 1991.

Contact: State of New Mexico, General Services Dept., Purchasing Division

1100 St. Francis Drive, Santa Fe, NM 87503

Phone: (505) 827-0472

Reference 27

North American Free Trade Agreement, 450 pages, 1992.

Contact: U.S.Government Printing Office

Reference 28

The Procurers, 240 pages, 1991.

Contact: McGraw-Hill Ryerson

A discussion of public sector procurement in Canada.

Reference 29

Proposals That Win Federal Contracts, 334 pages, 1990.

Contact: Panoptic Enterprises

P.O. Box 1099, Woodbridge, Virginia 22193-0099

Phone: (703) 670-2812

Author: Barry L. McVay

While written for the supplier community, this book deals with many topics of interest to purchasers. Chapter 1 contains a description of the government's rules and the different roles and responsibilities of the many players. Other chapters deal with RFPs, contract types, and costing.

Reference 30

Bid Protests at GAO: A Descriptive Guide, 44 pages, 1991.

Contact: General Accounting Office

441 G Street, N.W., Washington, DC 20548

The federal government has extensive supplier complaint procedures. These detailed procedures can provide much information and many ideas on which to base your own process.

Reference 31

Rules of Procedure, 58 pages, Jan. 1994.

Contact: General Services Administration, Board of Contract Appeals

18th and F Streets, N.W., Washington, DC 20405

The federal government has extensive supplier complaint procedures. These detailed procedures can provide much information and many ideas on which to base your own process.

9.1

Selected Bibliography

1. Software Selection Takes Teamwork

Arvai, Ernest Stephen

Today's Office v20n5, pp16-19, Oct 1985, ISSN 0744-2815

A description of the membership of the selection team, the selection process, contents of the RFP, and the contract.

2. Developing an Effective RFP

Asner, Michael

Data Processing Management, section 1-05-25, Auerbach Publishers, 1987

This article examines a sample request for proposal to demonstrate how to write one and evaluate its responses.

3. RFPs - Doing it the Right Way

Asner, Michael

Canadian Datasystems, v 19, n1, pages 112-3, Jan. 1987, ISSN 0008-3364

4. Computer Contract Negotiations

Auer, Joseph and Harris, Charles Edison

Van Nostrand Reinhold, 1984, 423 p, ISBN: 0-442-20369-1

5. Negotiating Computer Contracts: Balancing the Risks,

Bandman, Marc. B.

Commercial Law Bulletin, v 2, n 6, pp 20-24, Nov/Dec 1987

Major topics include: A discussion of commonly used terms, and the negotiation process; Formation of an inter-disciplinary team to negotiated; Vendor accountability.

6. Next time you're buying, try the RFI process

Berkowitz, Charles F.

Communications News, v29, n6, p35, June, 1992, ISSN: 0010-3632

Discusses the merits of Requests for Information (RFIs), and Requests for Recommendation (RFRs) when used in conjunction with RFPs.

7. Bernacchi on Computer Law (2 Volumes)

Bernacchi, Frank and Statland,

Little, Brown and Company, 1986

8. Rx for Successful RFPs

Bex, Michael

Computers in Healthcare, v 8, n 11, pp 31-34, Sept 1987, ISSN: 0274-631X

Suggested key contract issues including indemnification, product defects, installation tests, hardware failure.

9. Rx for successful RFPs

Bex, M.

Computers in Healthcare, v8n11, pp 31-2,34, Sept. 1987, ISSN 0274-631X

10. Successful RFPs are No Accident!

Bex, Michael

Computers in Healthcare, v 8, n 3, pp 84, March 1987, ISSN 0274-631X

11. Financial and Clinical Systems Procurement

Biddle, Mark H.

Computers in Healthcare, v 9, n 9, p 74, Sept 1988

Questions to ask.

12. Computer Contracts, Negotiation, Drafting (3 volumes)

Bigelow, Robert P.

Matthew Bender, 1987

13. Request for Proposals for Library Automation

Bolef, D. and Gardner, T.

Bulletin of the Medical Library Association, v 76, n 2, pp 141-145,

April 1988

14. Shaking up the foundation

Braly, Damon

Health Management Technology, v16, n9, p16(4), August 1995

Describes a structured process for selecting vendors based on a qualifications matrix, ability to meet requirements, remote-site management capabilities and willingness to act as prime contractor.

15. The RFR: winning the race of technology

Buchman, Matthew L.

Journal of Systems Management, v41, n9, p64(4), Sept. 1990, ISSN: 0022-4829

This article discusses Request for Recommendations in which vendors are asked to make an abbreviated proposal.

16. Proposal Project Management

Burnap, C.F.

Proceeding of the 20th Annual Seminar - Project Management Institute, pp 315-321, 1988

17. Evaluating Vendor Proposals

Canning, B.

Journal of Institute of Management Consultants, v 23, n 3, pp 9-14, May 1987, ISSN 0019-0012

18. The Request for Proposal: Is it Just a Paper Chase?

Ciotti, V.

Healthcare Financial Management, v 42, n 6, pp 48-50, June 1988

19. Advanced Legal Strategies for Buying and Selling Computers and Software

Davidson, Duncan M. and Davidson, Jean A.

John Wiley & Sons, 1986

20. A Process of Selection of a Geographic Information System by the City of Boston

Distefano, J.M.

Proceedings of NCGA's mapping and geographic information systems Conference in 1987

Published by National Computer Graphics Association, 1987

21. The Consultants' Corner

Drabenstott, Jon

Library High Technology, v 5, n 1, p 99, Spring, 1987

The RFP in the automation procurement process.

22. Software aids in drafting RFPs, evaluating responses

Eckerson, Wayne

Network World, v8, n46, p2(2), Nov. 18, 1991, ISSN: 0887-7661

23. The Consultant's Corner

Epstein, S.B. et al

Library High Technology, v 5, n 1 , pp 99-112, Spring 1987

The RFP in the automation procurement process.

24. An RFP Can Do Your Bidding

Fennell, William

Trial, v 22, n 1, Jan.1986

Using an RFP to choose a computer system

25. Personal Computers and the Practice of Law

Flannery, William J., Jr.

Legal Economics, v 11, n 2, pp 35-44, Mar/Apr 1985, ISSN 0360-1439

A description of the RFP process in a law firm including types of software currently available.

26. Selecting an information system without an RFP

Gibson, Reginald P.; Berger, Steven; Ciotti, Vincent G.

Healthcare Financial Management, v46, n6, pp48-54, June 1992, ISSN: 0735-0732

This article describes how one hospital adopted a more efficient process by using a Request For Quotation, involving end users extensively, and scripting site visits.

27. The Computer Law Annual 1985

Gilburne, Hohnston and Grogan, editors

Harcourt Brace Jovanovich, 1985

28. 10 things to consider before making an outsourcing decision

Golden, Kathleen

Insurance & Technology, v20, p38(2), Feb., 1995, ISSN: 1054-0733

This article suggests that an RFP must reflect management goals and that the in-house IS department should be allowed to respond to the RFP.

29. You Will Find the Software Package You Need

Goldman, B.

Small Systems World, v 12, n 6, p 16-19, June 1984

A description of the software selection process. Discusses definition of needs, development of RFP, evaluation process, contract negotiation, and system conversion responsibilities.

30. Eliminating the Surprise Factor in Software Contracts

Gruenfeld, Lee

Computerworld, v 23, n 41, p 27, Oct. 9 1989

Purchasing a software package with custom modifications. Discusses how to handle changes in scope as the project proceeds.

31. How to Develop Effective RFPs

Guerrieri, John A., Jr.

Journal of Information Systems Management, v 1, n 4, pp 40-47, ISSN: 0739-9014

Role of the systems manager. The RFP as a tool to organize and formalize vendor negotiations. Structure and content of the RFP.

32. Advanced RFP Writing, The Quick Way to Lose Your Health and Sanity

Hawthorne, Judy A.

Conference paper 23, Jun 83

Available from NTIS

The acquisition process for Army libraries. Documentation requirements.

33. About to Make a Purchase? It's Buyer Beware: Duffy

Hilbourn, Cathy

Computing Canada, v 13, n 7, p 17, Apr 2 1987, ISSN: 0319-1061

Tips for computer buyers. The acquisition process.

34. Coming to Terms

Horak, Ray and Goleniewski, Lillian

Network World, v 6, n 38, p 63, Sept. 25 1989

Building a harmonious long-term relationship with your software vendor begins at the RFP stage.

35. How to Choose a Vendor (Part 3)

Johnson, Eugene

Credit Union Magazine, v 54, n 2, pp 58-62, Feb 1988, ISSN: 0011-1066

Use of weights to make evaluations more objective. Discussion of contract issues.

36. "Debugging" the information system contracting process

Kalyvas, James R.

Health Systems Review, v28, n2, pp42-46, Mar/Apr 1995, ISSN: 0891-0200

Provides guidance on negotiating contracts. Suggests that a purchaser should, from the outset, identify the key contractual provisions which it wants the vendor to adopt.

37. Giving Vendors a Fair Shake

Karten, Naomi

Computerworld, v 23, n 49, p 137, Dec. 4 1989

To get the best deal, try conducting a methodical review of all proposals. Discusses compilation of evaluation criteria.

38. Preparing a Training Request

Karten, Naomi

Computerworld, v 23, n 17, p 112, Apr 24 1989, ISSN: 0010-4841

A description of the process (using an RFP) to select a supplier of training services.

39. Responding to an RFP: a Vendor's Viewpoint

Kingston, Robert A.

Library High Technology, v 5, n 1 , pp 61-65, Spring 1987, ISSN 0737-8831

40. All You Ever Wanted to Know Concerning System Acquisition

LaBell, T.

Communications News, v 22, n 4, pp 30-35, April 1985

41. The Vendor's Corner

Lewis, N. et al

Library High Technology, v 5, n 1, pp 87-97, Spring 1987, ISSN 0737-8831

42. Designing an Effective Request For Proposal

Lowe, Gary Wayne

Small Systems World, v 12, n 5, pp 34-39, May 1984, ISSN: 0272-5444

Description of a 6-step computer selection process. Discussion of evaluating vendor proposals.

43. Designing an Effective Request For Proposal

Loew, Gary Wayne

Systems/3X World, v 15, n 2, pp 52-60, Feb 1987, ISSN: 0272-5444

The acquisition process. Suggested organization and content for an RFP.

44. The RFP - Request for Punishment

Matthews, Joseph R. and Williams, Joan Frye and Salmon, Stephen R.

Library High Technology, v 5, n 1, p 15, Spring 1987

A tool for selecting an automated library system.

45. Learning the ABCs of RFPs

Merrill, Lynn

World Wastes, v37, n9, pp45-48, Sept. 1994, ISSN: 0745-6921

A view of the process for acquiring a solid-waste consultant using RFPs.

46. RFP alternatives can help speed decisions

Molloy, Maureen

Network World, v7, n40, p23(2), Oct. 1, 1990, ISSN: 0887-7661

The need for faster ways to acquire and implement network solutions is making the RFP outdated.

47. The Law of Computer Technology

Nimmer, Raymond T.

Warren, Gorham & Lamont, 1986

48. Icons dull the pain of RFPs

Olsen, Florence

Government Computer News, v13, n3, p28(1), Feb. 7, 1994, ISSN: 0738-4300

This article describes a Windows-based RFP system that includes icons to ease the tasks of preparing an RFP.

49. Computer Contracts

Pearson, Hilary E.

Routledge Chapman & Hall, 1984, $70.50 ISBN 90-6544-198-0

This 312-page book is an international guide to agreements and software protection.

50. Administering Contracts & Managing Vendors

Polis, R.

Infosystems, v 32, n 11, pp 72-74, Nov. 1985

Discusses the path to successful procurement.

51. Office of Federal Procurement Policy suggest ways to rate past performance

Power, Kevin

Government Computer News, v13, n11, p65(1), May 30, 1994, ISSN: 0738-4300

This article discusses past performance, past experience, and ways to evaluate these factors.

52. The Second Time Around

Predmore, L.G.

Information Technology and Libraries, v 7, n 4, pp 394-400, Dec. 1988

Preparing the RFP for a second-generation (Library) system.

53. You Better Shop Around

Rampt, Bradford D.

Association Management, v 40, n 5, pp. 55-59, May 1988, ISSN: 0004-5578

Guidelines to direct an association executive through a computer acquisition process. Determine the required applications software before deciding on the hardware.

54. Ask and Receive

Rao, Anand

LAN Magazine, v7, n2, 129(4), Feb., 1992, ISSN: 0898-0012

Provides guidelines for creating an effective RFP for the network.

55. Negotiating (and Litigating) Computer Contracts

Raysman and Zammit

Law Journal Seminars Press, 1988

56. An RFP Guides a 'Right' Buy

Romei, Lura K.

Modern Office Technology, v 34 p 82, May 1989, ISSN 0026-8208

Description of the RFP for the City of Denver related to Local area network purchases.

57. Computer System RFPs and Contracts

Rondeau, E.P.

International Facility Management Association, Proceedings from 1989 Computer and High-Tech Systems Conference, pp 63-74, 1989

58. National Institute of Standards and Technology's Model RFP helps unravel mystery of contracts

Schwartz, Karen D.

Government Computer News, v12, n13, p64(1), June 21, 1993, ISSN: 0738-4300

Describes development of a Model RFP which demonstrates how to structure open systems RFPs. Also provides advice on how to evaluate RFPs.

59. Nineteen Eighty-Nine Computer Law Forms Handbook: A Legal Guide to Drafting & Negotiating

Schwartz, Laurens R.

Clark Boardman, 1988 ($67.50) ISBN: 0-87632-601-7

60. RFPs Go On-Line

Semilof, Margie

Network World, v 3, n 23, p 17, Aug 11 1986

A description of an automated request for proposal system to handle vendor bids for a telephone system for American Edwards Laboratories.

61. Even the odds

Shultz, Dana

LAN Magazine, v9, n5, p79(5), May 1994, ISSN: 0898-0012

Discusses negotiating contracts with systems supplier and includes a list of ten steps to achieving a successful network contract.

62. Science and Engineering Workstation Procurement Contract goes to Internet

Sikorovsky, Elizabeth

Federal Computer Week, v9, n12, p1(2), May 29, 1995, ISSN: 0893-052X

This project represents a growing trend towards use of Internet for maintaining government contracts. The draft contract proposal is only available on the Internet.

63. Consultant Evaluation and Selection

Sirosky, Dennis S.

Journal of Systems Management, v 40, n 11, p 10, Nov. 1989

A client perspective on selecting a consultant.

64. Saga of an RFP for an Automated System (library)

Smorch, Tom

American Libraries, v 15, n 2, p 397, June 1984

65. Acquiring and Protecting Computer Information Technology

Sookman, Barry B.

Carswell, 1988 ISBN: 0-459-32911-1

This 600-page looseleaf reference book deals extensively with contracting issues, copyright protection, trade secret protection, and trade-marks, patents, and criminal law primarily from a Canadian perspective.

66. Don't bomb out when preparing RFPs

Stein, Murray

Computerworld, v27, n7, p102, Feb. 15, 1993, ISSN: 0010-4841

This article contains numberous tips for avoiding common pitfalls in designing an effective RFP.

67. Manufacturing: Hardware and Software

Stickler, Michael J.

Systems/3X World, v 16, n 5, pp 96,98, May 1988, ISSN: 0885 7806

10 steps in the selection process for MRPII software. Evaluation of proposals.

68. The Municipal Computer Systems Handbook

Strock, Barry and Adkins, Dave

RST Ctr, 1989 ($29.95), 300 p., ISBN: 0-9623460-0-4

A 300-page guide to computer systems planning, procurement, vendor negotiations, contracts and implementation for Local Government officials.

69. The Vendors' Corner - the Request for Proposal (libraries)

Sugnet, Chris

Library High Technology, v 5, n 1, p 87, Spring 1987

70. Preparing RFPs, RFQs and Negotiating Contracts Requires Meticulous Attention to Many Details

Tate, Lemuel

Communications News, v 24, n 12, p 46, Dec 1987

71. The Objective Request-for-Proposal

Taylor, James B.

Library High Technology, v 4, n 1, pp 37-39, Spring 1986, ISSN 0737-8831

72. Defining Computer Information Needs for Small Business: A Delphi Method

Taylor, Raymond E. & Meinhardt, David J.

Journal of Small Business Management, v 23, n 2, pp 3-9, Apr 1985, ISSN: 0047-2778

A description of definition of information needs using a Delphi technique and its benefits in terms of cost, involvement, and accuracy.

73. RFP Writer's Combat Manual

Vezmar, John, Editor

Venture Communications, 1988, ISBN 0-929646-04-5, 135p., $59.

74. RFPs: the Risk of Shady Tactics

Wallace, Bob

Network World, v 5, n 8, p 13, Feb. 22 1988

75. The Computer Consultant is an Insurance Policy

Yonda, Marguerite M.

Office, v 101, n 5, pp 78-81, May 1985, ISSN 0030-0128

The role of a consultant in reducing risks during the planning, selection and implementation process.

76. Negotiating Computer Contracts

Yonda, Marge

Computerworld, v 20, n 7A, pp 25-26, Feb 19 1986, ISSN: 0010-4841

Common contractual pitfalls. Clauses which should be included to protect the purchaser's interests.

77. American Bar Association Software Contract Forms 1987 Collection, The Law of Computer Related Technology: Compendium of Software Licensing Provisions

Anonymous

Butterworths, American Intellectual Property Association, Jan. 1988

78. Computer Selection: Evaluation Process Is Key to Success

Anonymous

Small Business Report, v 13, n 3, pp 22-25, Mar 1988, ISSN: 0164-5382

Investigation of available systems. Selection criteria. Contract negotiation.

79. RFP Responses Perplexing

Anonymous

Computerworld, v 19, n 8, p 23, Feb. 25 1985

80. Tender Thoughts Prove Rewarding

Anonymous

Computer Weekly, p 8, June 8 1989

Computer buyers' invitations to tender guidelines.

81. Tips on Preparing a Request For Proposal (Part 2)

Anonymous

Modern Materials Handling, v 42, n 5, pp 68-72, Apr 1987, ISSN: 0026-8038

A discussion of the items which should be included in the functional requirements as part of the RFP: volumes, inventory levels, etc.

PART 2

DOCUMENTS FROM SELECTED JURISDICTIONS

DOCUMENT I

Acquisition and Disposal of Information Technology Resources in Washington State Government

September 1989

. . . a framework for the acquisition and
disposal of information technology resources
which most effectively meet the needs of the
agency and the state."

Prepared by: Department of Information Services

Adopted by: Washington State Information Services Board

George Lindamood, Director

Len McComb, Chair

Policy and Regulation Division

PO Box 42440

Olympia, WA 98504-244

— TABLE OF CONTENTS —

Introduction

The Washington State Information Services Board (ISB), at its September 28, 1989, meeting, adopted a new state policy and standard procedure for the Acquisition and Disposal of Information Technology Resources. This policy and standard procedure is took effect upon adoption.

The policy and standard procedure provide additional authority to the agencies to manage their own acquisitions through higher levels of delegated authority. These higher levels of delegated authority are contingent on agency director's requesting delegated acquisition authority, agencies having submitted their internal acquisition policies and procedures for review, and compliance with the state policy, *Agency Planning for Information Technology.*

In addition, all agencies were given delegated acquisition authority for single acquisitions with an acquisition cost of $10,000 or less.

The new delegated acquisition authority does not include delegated authority for the acquisition of:

- private branch exchanges (PBX's),

- central exchange services,

- video telecommunications, or

- resources subject to Department of Information Services (DIS) monitoring and approval as the result of a legislative budgetary proviso.

Enabling Legislation

The ISB is empowered to acquire and dispose of all information technology equipment, proprietary software, and purchased services for all agencies of the executive and judicial branches of state government. Specifically, RCW Chapter 43.105 gives the Board the authority:

"To purchase, lease, rent, or otherwise acquire, dispose of, and maintain equipment, proprietary software, and purchased services; or to delegate to other agencies and institutions of state government, under appropriate standards, the authority to purchase, lease, rent, or otherwise acquire, dispose of, and maintain equipment, proprietary software, and purchased services. Agencies and institutions of state government are expressly prohibited from acquiring or disposing of equipment, proprietary software, and purchased services without such delegation of authority".

RCW Chapter 43.105 defines information technology equipment to include data processing, telecommunications, and office automation. It specifically identifies machines, devices, and transmission facilities used in information processing, such as computers, word processors, terminals, telephones, and cables.

RCW Chapter 43.105 also gives the ISB the duty to provide a vendor protest process, as follows:

"To develop and implement a process for the resolution of appeals by vendors concerning the conduct of an acquisition process by an agency or the Department of Information Services".

Purpose

To provide a framework for the acquisition and disposal of information technology resources which most effectively meets the needs of agencies and the state.

Objectives

Objectives for this information technology acquisition and disposal policy and standard procedure include:

• Provide a process to be used in the acquisition and disposal of information technology resources that will ensure the best value for the state.

• Ensure that the acquisition and disposal of information technology resources support agency strategic information technology plans and the state information technology standards.

• Promote fair and open competition.

• Provide an acquisition and disposal process that meets agency business needs.

• Provide maximum practical opportunity for participation by minority and women owned businesses.

The accomplishment of these objectives is the mutual responsibility of DIS and the agencies.

Policy

Scope

This policy applies to all information technology acquisitions and disposals within the executive and judicial branches, regardless of the source of funds, the intended use or purpose, or the source of supply. The policy is in accordance with the intent of RCW Chapter 43.105.

Policy Statements

The following policy statements apply:

A. Information technology acquisitions shall be consistent with the agency's Information Technology Plan and the Information Services Board (ISB) Strategic Directions for Information Technology, and Information Technology policies and standards.

B. The ISB is responsible for all delegated authority. It may grant, reduce, or rescind delegations of authority.

- Agencies have no authority for acquisition and/or disposal other than what is specifically delegated by the ISB.
- The ISB has granted a minimum acquisition and disposal approval level of $10,000 to all agencies.
- The ISB has granted all agencies general delegated authority to:
  - *Pay monthly bills for previously approved and established telephone service.*
  - *Pay bills for existing services under previously approved and established contracts.*
  - *Acquire process control equipment.*
- The Department of Information Services (DIS) is delegated authority to approve acquisitions when the acquisition cost is under $3 million and the Cost Benefit Analysis (CBA) cost is under $7 million.
- The ISB may annually review and may grant delegated approval authority for acquisitions up to 2% of agency annual information technology expenditures.
- The ISB may grant special delegated authority for disposal, academic computing, and/or strategic partnerships.

C. The information technology acquisition process shall:

- Normally be competitive.
- Ensure the best value for the state.
- Provide the maximum practicable opportunity for participation by Minority and Women's Business Enterprises (MWBE).
- Require agencies to evaluate the use of existing state resources.

D. Acquisitions shall use a standard acquisition process.

- Standard acquisition processes include Request For Proposal, Request For Quotation, Master Agreements, Sole Source, Interagency Transfer, Strategic Partnerships and Corporate Agreements.

E. DIS may establish Master Agreements and Corporate Agreements.

F. Contractual terms and conditions shall be included in solicitation documents.

- The provisions labeled "Standard Clauses" are mandatory in content. Agency contracts must include the titles of these clauses and language that accomplishes the same intent.
- Additional contractual clauses shall have the approval as to form of the agency assistant attorney general.

G. Agencies shall obtain approval from the State Finance Committee for all lease/purchase finance arrangements over $10,000 and comply with other provisions of chapter 356 laws of 1989.

H. Agencies shall obtain approval from the Office of Financial Management for all financial systems acquisitions.

I. Vendors shall be provided a procedure to follow in order to protest acquisitions.

   • Protests shall be accepted only after the announcement of the apparently successful vendor.

J. DIS shall be responsible to identify unplanned, high risk, or high impact acquisitions for ISB review.

K. DIS shall be responsible for the interpretation of this policy and its implementing standards.

Standard Procedure

Overview of Agency Responsibilities

Responsibilities

A. Request delegated authority.

B. Ensure that funds for information technology resources are expended in a prudent manner and the resulting technology meets the business needs of the agency.

C. Ensure acquisitions are consistent with the agency's Information Technology Plan and conform to the approved Information Services Board (ISB) policies and standard procedures.

D. Determine and document the functional and technical requirements for the information technology resources to be acquired.

E. Obtain Department of Information Services (DIS) or ISB approval consistent with the agency's delegated authority.

F. Plan acquisitions, provide management review, conduct acquisitions, contract with vendors, and report acquisitions in accordance with the approved ISB policies and standard procedures.

G. Provide an opportunity for Minority and Women's Business Enterprises (MWBE) to participate in the acquisition process.

H. Conduct Post Implementation Reviews (PIR).

I. Dispose of information technology resources in accordance with the approved ISB policy and standard.

DIS Responsibilities:

A. Review and provide recommendations to the ISB regarding requests for Delegated Authority from the agency director.

B. Review and approve planned acquisitions when:

   • the Acquisition Cost exceeds an agency's Delegated Acquisition Authority,
   • is under three million dollars, and

- the Cost/Benefit Analysis Cost is under seven million dollars.

C. May submit to the ISB for approval acquisitions which have significant agency or statewide impact, have a high degree of risk, or are not consistent with agency Information Technology Plans.

D. Develop, maintain, and distribute acquisition and disposal policies, standard procedures, and guidelines which are consistent with other ISB policies and standards.

E. Instruct agency personnel in the use of the acquisition policy and standards.

F. Interpret the acquisition and disposal policy and standard, and determine an agency's compliance with them.

G. Act as the final administrative appeal for vendor protests of agency conducted acquisitions, except for acquisitions conducted by and for DIS or approved by the ISB.

H. Establish Master and Corporate Agreements for information technology resources.

ISB Responsibilities

A. Review requests for Delegated Authority from agency directors and either grant or deny the requests.

B. Review and approve planned acquisitions when the Acquisition Cost is estimated to be three million dollars or more, or the Cost/Benefit Analysis Cost is estimated to be seven million dollars or more. Acquisitions may also be reviewed if they are not consistent with the agency Information Technology Plan, or involve significant impact or high risk.

C. Act as final administrative appeal for vendor protests of acquisitions conducted by and for DIS or approved by the ISB.

Delegation of Authority

Delegated Authority

Delegated Authority is the authorization granted by the ISB to an agency director to acquire and/or dispose of Information Technology Resources. Unconditional Delegated Acquisition Authority may be granted for academic computing. Other Delegated Acquisition Authority may be granted for up to two (2) percent of the annual agency expenditures for information technology, as reported in compliance with the ISB policy titled: Agency Planning for Information Technology.

Delegated Authority does not exempt the agency from using the acquisition or disposal processes specified by the ISB; it only exempts the agency from securing ISB or DIS approval prior to conducting the acquisition. Delegated Authority shall be reviewed annually and may be rescinded at the discretion of the ISB.

All agencies are granted a minimum acquisition and disposal approval level of $10,000. The ISB may grant Delegated Acquisition Authority above the $10,000 level on the recommendation of DIS. DIS will use the following as key criteria for continuation of delegated authority:

A. A request from the agency director for Delegated Acquisition Authority.

B. An agency Information Technology Plan as specified in the ISB policy titled: Agency Planning for Information Technology.

C. Internal agency policies and procedures for the management of information technology acquisitions.

The ISB shall grant or deny the request(s) for Delegated Authority and notify the agency director of the rationale for its decision.

Acquisition Procedure

Acquisitions or Disposals within Delegated Authority

The agency shall conduct the acquisition or disposal in compliance with the ISB policy and standard procedure for: Acquisition and Disposal of Information Technology Resources, and consistent with its own acquisition policy and procedure. This may be done without additional approval of DIS.

Acquisition Plan

For acquisitions above the agency delegated authority, request DIS or ISB approval by submitting a completed Acquisition Approval Request form (Appendix A), and an Acquisition Plan to DIS. The Acquisition Plan describes and documents the following:

A. Problem to be solved or opportunity to be gained.

B. Information technology resource to be acquired.

C. Alternatives considered: evaluation of existing state and agency resources, as well as other alternatives which were considered.

D. Agency Business Justification; state how this acquisition shall help the agency meet its business needs, the estimated Acquisition Costs and Cost Benefit Analysis (CBA) Costs, and the tangible and intangible benefits.

E. CBA and risk analysis.

F. Project management plan.

G. Vendor Participation; list the vendors including MWBE's who are to receive the solicitation document.

H. Relationship to the agency MWBE plan.

I.   Relationship to the ISB information technology standards and Strategic Directions.

J.   Acquisition method to be used including the rationale for the selection of this method.

K.   Acquisition and implementation schedule.

L.   Post Implementation Review (PIR) Criteria and Plan; include the date the PIR is to be completed.

M.   Other relevant information.

(NOTE: If a feasibility study has been prepared in accordance with Revised Feasibility Study Guidelines, May 1992, it may be acceptable in place of items A through F of this list.)

Acquisition Process

A.   Acquisition Methods

Acquisitions shall be conducted in accordance with one of the acquisition methods identified in the Acquisition and Disposal of Information Technology Resources Policy. If the acquisition process involves vendor solicitations, the agency shall use either a Request for Quotation (RFQ) or a Request for Proposal (RFP).

1. RFQ

a.   The RFQ is used to acquire information technology resources that can be fully described in a technical specification and can be delivered by a specified date. RFQ's list only specific requirements, often in the form of technical specifications, and are always awarded to the vendor who can meet the requirements and the delivery date with the lowest price. RFQ's are only used for currently deliverable Information Technology Resources.

b.   The RFQ document shall contain sufficient information to enable the vendor to provide price information to satisfy all technical, functional, performance, maintenance, and delivery requirements.

c.   The RFQ document shall state the agency's MWBE participation goals for this acquisition. When MWBE participation goals are established for the acquisition, final selection of an apparently successful vendor will be based upon evaluation rules published by the Office of Women's Business Enterprises (OMWBE). Such evaluations shall be independent of and subsequent to the technical and financial evaluation process.

d.   Agencies conducting RFQ's shall:

(1) Provide vendors with the vendor protest procedure as outlined in the section titled Protest Procedure.

(2) Use the "Standard Clauses" as contained in Appendix B, and other terms and conditions appropriate for the specific type of contract to be negotiated.

(3) Send the RFQ to a minimum of three vendors, when available.

(4) Conduct an objective evaluation of the responses and select the apparently successful vendor meeting the requirements and providing the lowest price response.

(5) Offer vendor debriefing conferences to requesting vendors.

(6) Sign vendor contracts only after the time to file vendor protests has elapsed.

e.   Telephone RFQ's

When telephone RFQ's are used, the agency is required to document the vendor, the bid, the date and time of the bid, and the individual soliciting and recording the bid. Telephone quotes are limited to ten percent of an agency's Delegated Authority (not to exceed $75,000), or $10,000, whichever is more. DIS has the authority, on a case by case basis, to authorize increases at the request of the agency director.

2. RFP

The RFP is used to acquire Information Technology Resources that may not have a fully described technical specification and/or for which there are competing functional solutions in the marketplace. The RFP is used to allow vendors the opportunity to propose solutions to a set of functional requirements and/or technical specifications. The RFP process gives the agency the opportunity to select the proposal which best meets agency needs over the expected life of the resource. Agencies should hold a pre-proposal conference when the RFP method is used.

The RFP is used to solicit a proposal and prices from the vendor for the vendor's best solution or solutions to the agency's information technology requirements.

The RFP process allows consideration of such items as functional capability, including:

a.   Expansion and upgrade capability.

b.   Vendor support.

c.   Integration of the resource into the agency architecture.

It also allows consideration of full cost; including but not limited to, costs to purchase, finance, install, operate, use, and maintain; plus trade in, redeployment, or residual value.

The RFP document shall state the agency's MWBE participation goals for this acquisition. When MWBE participation goals are established for the acquisition, final selection of an apparently successful vendor will be based upon evaluation rules published by the OWMBE. Such evaluations shall be independent of and subsequent to the technical and financial evaluation process.

Agencies conducting RFP's shall:

a.   Provide vendors with the vendor protest procedure as outlined in the section titled Protest Procedure.

b.   Use the "Standard Clauses" as contained in Appendix B, and other terms and conditions appropriate for the specific type of contract to be negotiated.

    c.   Include in the RFP the specific criteria that shall be used to evaluate vendor responses.

    d.   Advertise the acquisition in the Seattle Daily Journal of Commerce or other major regional publication upon or before release of the RFP. In addition, advertising in the Wall Street Journal or other national publications may be appropriate, depending on the nature of the acquisition. Issue the RFP to a minimum of three vendors where available. RFP's shall be issued to all vendors who have expressed an interest in providing the Information Technology Resources to be acquired.

    e.   Give vendors adequate time to prepare responses and submit their proposal.

    f.   Notify vendors that they may bring their complaints about the solicitation document to the attention of DIS. (See Protest Procedure).

    g.   Give full and fair consideration to all vendors responding to the RFP.

    h.   Select the apparently successful vendor based on the RFP evaluation criteria.

    i.   Offer vendor debriefing conferences to requesting vendors.

    j.   Sign vendor contracts only after the time to file vendor protests has elapsed.

3. Sole Source

The sole source method is used only when there is a clear technological or economic advantage to the state. The criteria to determine if an acquisition should be made through the sole source process includes, but is not limited to:

    a.   Compatibility with the current installed base; or

    b.   A law requires a single source; or

    c.   If grant funded and the funding source has stipulated a sole source; or

    d.   The Acquisition Cost of a product is under $2000; or

    e.   Recovery from a disaster; or

    f.   The product is a gift or donation; or

    g.   Only one source of supply.

4. Interagency Transfer

Interagency transfer occurs when the ownership or license of equipment or proprietary software is transferred from one agency to another agency.

5. Strategic Partnership

The use of Strategic Partnerships are limited to higher education institutions and may only be entered into with the approval of the ISB.

6. Master Agreement

Master Agreements are established by DIS for often purchased Information Technology Resources. Agencies should determine if the resource to be acquired is on a Master Agreement before proceeding with the acquisition. Master Agreements are always established through a competitive process, and acquiring from a Master Agreement satisfies the competition requirement.

7. Corporate Agreement

Corporate Agreements are agreements competitively negotiated and administered by DIS with the original manufacturer or provider of a product or service. It will provide significant advantages to the state resulting from DIS's leverage as a corporate buyer. The resulting products and services shall be available to state agencies and political subdivisions through DIS Leasing and Brokering.

Approvals

DIS or ISB approval shall be obtained:

A. Prior to conducting the acquisition, unless the acquisition is within the agency's Delegated Authority.

B. Prior to the release of any Request for Proposal (RFP) or Request for Quotation (RFQ) documents unless the acquisition is within the agency's Delegated Authority.

The ISB or DIS may delegate any or all subsequent steps in the acquisition process to the agency director.

Reporting

A. Report completed acquisitions.

Report the acquisition of all computers, including personal computers (PC's), and all other Information Technology Resources with an Acquisition Cost over $10,000 to DIS, using the Monthly Acquisition Report form contained in Appendix A. Resources acquired from another state government organization are exempt from the reporting requirement.

B. Report Post Implementation review (PIR).

Conduct and report the PIR as outlined in the Agency Acquisition Plan. PIR's shall be submitted to DIS for acquisitions approved by the ISB or as requested by the DIS.

Exceptions to the Legislative Branch Acquisition Process

These procedures do not apply to information technology acquisitions within the Legislative Branch.

Emergency Acquisitions

Agencies may acquire equipment and services valued above their levels of delegated authority without prior approval when it is necessary to restore existing levels of operation following a disaster such as fire, flood, earthquake, vandalism, or theft. Such acquisitions are limited to the purchase of services and equipment to restore operations. Acquisitions are limited to replacement equipment of the same class as the inoperative equipment. These acquisitions may be made without regard to acquisition costs, but shall be reported immediately to DIS.

Budget Provisos

Certain information technology resource acquisitions may be associated with or included under Legislative Budget Provisos. When such Budget Provisos are the result of an Information Technology Project Feasibility Study, or otherwise require DIS monitoring and approval of a project, the agency delegated authority is automatically rescinded for all associated acquisitions.

Supplies

This procedure includes the acquisition of supplies only when they are included as part of the initial acquisition. Supplies used for continuing operation are purchased under the policies of the Department of General Administration, Office of State Procurement.

Personal Services

This procedure excludes the acquisition of personal services, which are acquired under the policies of the Office of Financial Management.

Protest Procedure

This protest procedure is available to vendors who have submitted a response to the agency's vendor solicitation and have requested a debriefing conference. Protests are made:

A. To the agency conducting the acquisition after the agency has announced the apparently successful vendor. Vendor protests shall be received, in writing, by the agency within five business days after the vendor debriefing conference.

B. To DIS only after protesting first to the agency and the agency resolution is not satisfactory to the protesting party. Protests to DIS shall be received, in writing, within five (5) business days after the vendor has received notification concerning the protest from the agency.

C. To the ISB for acquisitions conducted for DIS or for acquisitions approved by the ISB, only after protesting first to DIS and the DIS resolution is not satisfactory to the protesting party. Protests to the ISB shall be made within five (5) business days after the vendor has received notification of the DIS decision.

Grounds for protest are:

A. Errors were made in computing the score.

B. The agency failed to follow procedures established in the solicitation document, the ISB policy and standard: Acquisition and Disposal of Information Technology Resources, or applicable state or federal laws or regulations.

C. Bias, discrimination or conflict of interest on the part of an evaluator. Protests not based on these criteria shall not be considered.

Format and Content

Vendors shall include in their written protest to the agency and DIS, all facts and arguments upon which the vendor relies. Vendors shall, at a minimum, provide:

A. Information about the protesting vendor; name of firm, mailing address, phone number and name of individual responsible for submission of the protest.

B. Information about the acquisition; issuing agency, acquisition method.

C. Specific and complete statement of the agency action(s) protested.

D. Specific reference to the grounds for the protest.

E. Description of the relief or corrective action requested.

F. For protests to DIS or the ISB, a copy of the agency's written decision on the protest.

Agency Review Process

Agencies conducting competitive acquisitions of information technology resources shall provide the protest process to the vendor. The agency review shall precede all other reviews.

Upon receipt of a vendor protest, the agency is required to notify DIS that they have received a vendor protest, and to postpone further steps in the acquisition process until the vendor protest has been resolved.

The agency is required to perform an objective review of the protest by individuals not involved in the acquisition process protested. The review shall be based on the written protest material submitted by the vendor and all other facts known to the agency.

The agency is required to render a written decision to the vendor within five (5) business days after receipt of the vendor protest, unless more time is needed. The protesting vendor shall be notified if additional time is necessary.

DIS Review Process

The vendor shall protest to DIS in writing within five (5) business days after the vendor has received notification of the agency decision.

DIS shall consider all the available facts, and issue a decision in writing within ten (10) business days after receipt of the protest, unless more time is needed. The protesting vendor shall be notified if additional time is necessary. The DIS decision constitutes the final step of the protest process, except protests which may be reviewed by the ISB as outlined under a subsequent paragraph titled "ISB Review Process".

Final Determination

The final determination shall:

A. Find the protest lacking in merit and uphold the agency's action; or

B. Find only technical or harmless errors in the agency's acquisition process, determine the agency to be in substantial compliance, and reject the protest; or

C. Find merit in the protest and provide the agency options which may include:

- Correct its errors and reevaluate all proposals; and/or

- Reissue the vendor solicitation document; or

D. Make other findings and determine other courses of action as appropriate; and

ISB Review Process

Protests to the ISB may be made only for acquisitions conducted for DIS or ISB approved acquisitions, and only after review by DIS. Protests of the decisions of DIS shall be made by letter to the Chair, ISB, who may establish procedures to resolve the protest. Protests shall be received by the Chair, ISB, within five (5) business days after the decision of DIS in order to be considered. The resulting decision is final, with no further administrative appeal available.

Vendor Complaints

Vendors may submit their complaint to the agency prior to responding to the vendor solicitation document if the vendor believes the solicitation document unduly constrains competition, or contains inadequate or improper criteria. These complaints shall be made in writing before bid submission. A copy of the complaints shall be forwarded to DIS, which may take steps to intervene. These complaints shall not be handled through the Protest Procedure.

Contract Clauses

Contract Clauses

Contract terms and conditions for an acquisition shall be included in the RFQ or RFP documents. A set of suggested contractual provisions appears in Appendix B. Each term labeled "Standard Clause" (SC) is mandatory in content, meaning that agency contracts must cover the subject of the provision, but need not necessarily use the exact language recommended in Appendix B. Other terms and conditions may be negotiated between the agency and the vendor and shall be approved by the agency Assistant Attorney General.

Disposal Procedure

Disposals Within Agency's Delegated Disposal Authority

For disposals within the agency's delegated disposal authority, conduct the disposal in compliance with the agency's acquisition and disposal policy and procedures, without additional review by DIS.

Disposals Without Delegated Disposal Authority

Agencies without specific delegated disposal authority may dispose of equipment with an estimated residual value of $10,000 or less. For equipment with $10,000 or more residual value, contact DIS. A Property Disposal Approval Request form is contained in Appendix A.

Approval and specific procedures for each disposal shall be provided on a case-by-case basis.

References

Reference to other policies, standards and applicable documents

The following policies, standards and applicable documents issued by DIS shall be reviewed in relation to the individual acquisition:

A. Agency Planning for Information Technology, January 1989.

B. Revised Feasibility Study Guidelines, May 1992.

C. Strategic Directions for Information Technology in Washington State Government, June 1988.

DOCUMENT 2

State of Alaska Procurement Code

STATE PROCUREMENT CODE

PURPOSE: This Act shall be construed and applied to promote its underlying purposes and policies. The underlying purposes and policies of this Act are to:

(1) simplify, clarify, and modernize the law governing procurement by the State;

(2) establish consistent procurement principles for all branches of State government;

(3) provide for increased public confidence in the procedures followed in State procurement;

(4) ensure the fair and equitable treatment of all persons who deal with the procurement system of the State;

(5) provide increased economy in State procurement activities and maximize to the fullest extent practicable the purchasing value of State funds;

(6) foster effective broad-based competition within the free enterprise system;

(7) provide safeguards for the maintenance of a procurement system of quality and integrity;

(8) permit the continued development of State procurement practices and policies; and

(9) eliminate and prevent discrimination in State contracting because of race, religion, color, national origin, sex, age, marital status, pregnancy, parenthood, handicap, or political affiliation.

ARTICLE 1

ORGANIZATION OF STATE Procurement

Sec. 36.30.005. CENTRALIZATION OF PROCUREMENT AUTHORITY.

(a) Except as otherwise provided, all rights, powers, duties, and authority relating to the procurement of supplies, services, and professional services, and the control over supplies, services, and professional services vested in or exercised by an agency on January 1, 1988, are transferred to the commissioner of administration and to the chief procurement officer. Authority granted under this subsection shall be exercised in accordance with this chapter.

(b) Except as otherwise provided, all rights, powers, duties, and authority relating to the procurement of construction and procurements of equipment or services for the state equipment fleet and the control over construction of state facilities and the state equipment fleet vested in or exercised by an agency on January 1, 1988, are transferred to the commissioner of transportation and public facilities, subject to regulations adopted by the commissioner of administration. Notwithstanding AS 44.68.110, authority relating to disposals from the state equipment fleet is vested in the commissioner of transportation and public facilities, subject to regulations adopted by the commissioner of administration. Authority granted under this subsection shall be exercised in accordance with this chapter.

(c) Notwithstanding other provisions of law, all rights, powers, duties, and authority relating to the procurement of supplies, services, professional services, and construction and the disposal of supplies for the University of Alaska are transferred to the Board of Regents. To the maximum extent possible, authority granted under this subsection shall be exercised in accordance with this chapter. The Board of Regents shall adopt regulations under this subsection that are substantially equivalent to the regulations adopted by the commissioner of administration to implement this chapter. For the purposes of this subsection, unless the context otherwise requires, in this chapter

(1) "agency" means a subunit of the University of Alaska;

(2) "attorney general" means the president of the University of Alaska;

(3) "chief procurement officer" means a person designated by the president of the University of Alaska whose qualifications are substantially equivalent to those provided in AS 36.30.010(a);

(4) "commissioner," "commissioner of administration," or "commissioner of transportation and public facilities" means the Board of Regents or the president of the University of Alaska if so designated by the Board of Regents by regulations adopted under this subsection; and

(5) "department" means the University of Alaska.

Sec. 36.30.010. CHIEF PROCUREMENT OFFICER.

(a) The commissioner shall appoint to the partially exempt service the chief procurement officer of the state. The chief procurement officer must have at least five years of prior experience in public procurement, including large scale procurement of supplies, services, or professional services, and must be a person with demonstrated executive and organizational ability. The chief procurement officer may be removed by the commissioner only for cause. The term of office of the chief procurement officer is six years.

(b) Except as otherwise specifically provided in this chapter, the chief procurement officer shall

(1) procure or supervise the procurement of all supplies, services, and professional services needed by an agency;

(2) exercise general supervision and control over all inventories of supplies belonging to an agency and prescribe the manner in which supplies shall be purchased, delivered, stored, and distributed;

(3) prescribe the time, manner, authentication, and form of making requisitions for supplies and services;

(4) sell, trade, transfer between agencies, or otherwise dispose of surplus, obsolete, or unused supplies and make proper adjustments in the accounts of agencies concerned;

(5) establish and maintain programs for the inspection, testing, and acceptance of supplies and services and the testing of samples submitted with bids;

(6) prescribe standard forms for bids and contracts; and

(7) provide for other matters that may be necessary to carry out the provisions of this chapter and the regulations adopted under this chapter.

(c) While a person performs the duties of the chief procurement officer under this chapter, the person may not be employed in or appointed to another position with the state.

(d) The annual salary of the chief procurement officer is range 23 of the salary schedule established in AS 39.27.011.

Sec. 36.30.015. EXECUTIVE BRANCH AGENCIES.

(a) The commissioner of transportation and public facilities may delegate to another agency the authority to contract for construction. Before delegating authority to an agency under this subsection, the commissioner of transportation and public facilities shall make a written determination that the agency is capable of implementing the delegated authority. Notwithstanding delegation of authority under this subsection, contracts for construction are governed by this chapter and regulations adopted by the commissioner of administration under this chapter.

(b) The commissioner of administration may delegate to an agency the authority to contract for and manage services, professional services, and supplies. Notwithstanding delegation of authority under this subsection, an agency's exercise of the authority is governed by this chapter and regulations adopted by the commissioner under this chapter. Before delegating authority to an agency under this subsection, the commissioner shall make a written determination that the agency is capable of implementing the delegated authority.

(c) The commissioner of administration may not delegate the authority to dispose of supplies or the authority to adopt regulations under this chapter.

(d) An agency may not contract for the services of legal counsel without the approval of the attorney general.

(e) The board of directors of the Alaska Railroad Corporation and the board of directors of the Alaska Aerospace Development Corporation shall adopt procedures to govern the procurement of supplies, services, professional services, and construction. The procedures must be substantially equivalent to the procedures described in this chapter and in regulations adopted under this chapter.

(f) The board of directors of the Alaska Housing Finance Corporation, notwithstanding AS 18.56.088, shall adopt regulations under AS 44.62 (Administrative Procedure Act) and the board of trustees of the Alaska State Pension Investment Board shall adopt regulations under AS 37.10.240 to govern the procurement of supplies, services, professional services, and construction for the respective public corporation and board. The regulations must

> (1) reflect competitive bidding principles and provide vendors reasonable and equitable opportunities to participate in the procurement process; and
>
> (2) include procurement methods to meet emergency and extraordinary circumstances.

(g) The Department of Transportation and Public Facilities shall adopt regulations to manage the procurement of supplies, services, professional services, and construction for the repair, maintenance, and reconstruction of vessels, docking facilities, and passenger and vehicle transfer facilities of the Alaska marine highway system. The regulations must be based on principles of competitive procurement consistent with this chapter to satisfy the special requirements of the Alaska marine highway system as determined by the Department of Transportation and Public Facilities.

Sec. 36.30.020. LEGISLATURE.

The Legislative Council shall adopt and publish procedures to govern the procurement of supplies, services, professional services, and construction by the legislative branch. The procedures must be based on the competitive principles consistent with this chapter and must be adapted to the special needs of the legislative branch as determined by the Legislative Council. The procedures must be consistent with the provisions of AS 36.30.080(c) - (e) and 36.30.085.

Sec. 36.30.030. COURT SYSTEM.

The administrative director of courts shall adopt and publish procedures to govern the procurement of supplies, services, professional services, and construction by the judicial branch. The procedures must be based on the competitive principles consistent with this chapter and must be adapted to the special needs of the judicial branch as determined by the administrative director of courts. The procedures must be consistent with the provisions of AS 36.30.080(c) - (e) and 36.30.085.

Sec. 36.30.040. PROCUREMENT REGULATIONS.

(a) The commissioner shall adopt regulations governing the procurement, management, and control of supplies, services, professional services and construction by agencies. The commissioner may audit and monitor the implementation of the regulations and the requirements of this chapter with respect to using agencies.

(b) The commissioner shall adopt regulations pertaining to

(1) suspension, debarment, and reinstatement of prospective bidders and contractors;

(2) bid protests;

(3) conditions and procedures for the procurement of perishables and items for resale;

(4) conditions and procedures for the use of source selection methods authorized by this chapter, including sole source procurements, emergency procurements, and small procurements;

(5) the opening or rejection of bids and offers, and waiver of informalities in bids and offers;

(6) confidentiality of technical data and trade secrets submitted by actual or prospective bidders or offerors;

(7) partial, progressive, and multiple awards;

(8) storerooms and inventories, including determination of appropriate stock levels and the management of agency supplies;

(9) transfer, sale, or other disposal of supplies;

(10) definitions and classes of contractual services and procedures for acquiring them;

(11) providing for conducting price analysis;

(12) use of payment and performance bonds in connection with contracts for supplies, services, and construction;

(13) guidelines for use of cost principles in negotiations, adjustments, and settlements;

(14) conditions under which an agency may use the services of an employment program;

(15) a bidder's or offeror's duties under AS 36.30.115 and 36.30.210; and

(16) the elimination and prevention of discrimination in state contracting because of race,

religion, color, national origin, sex, age, marital status, pregnancy, parenthood, handicap, or political affiliation.

Sec. 36.30.050. LISTS OF CONTRACTORS.

(a) The commissioner shall establish and maintain lists of persons who desire to provide supplies, services, professional services, or construction services to the state.

(b) A person who desires to be on a list shall submit to the commissioner evidence of a valid Alaska business license. A biennial fee may be established by regulation in an amount reasonably calculated to pay the costs of administering this section. A construction contractor shall also submit a valid certificate of registration issued under AS 08.18. The commissioner, by regulation, may require submission of additional information.

(c) The lists may be used by the chief procurement officer or an agency when issuing invitations to bid or requests for proposals under this chapter. The lists may be used by the legislative council, the court system, and the Alaska Railroad Corporation.

(d) Repealed, Sec. 24 ch 65 SLA 1987.

Sec. 36.30.060. SPECIFICATIONS.

(a) The commissioner shall adopt regulations governing the preparation, revision, and content of specifications for supplies, services, professional services, and construction required by an agency. The commissioner shall monitor the use of these specifications.

(b) Specifications for construction of highways must conform as closely as practicable to those adopted by the American Association of State Highway and Transportation Officials.

(c) The commissioner may obtain expert advice and assistance from personnel of using agencies in the development of specifications. Specifications must promote overall economy for the purposes intended and encourage competition in satisfying the state's needs, and may not be unduly restrictive. The requirements of this subsection regarding the purposes and nonrestrictiveness of specifications apply to all specifications, including those prepared by architects, engineers, designers, and other professionals.

(d) In this section, "specification" means a description of the physical or functional characteristics, or of the nature of a supply, service, professional service, or construction project; it may include requirements for licensing, inspecting, testing, and delivery.

Sec. 36.30.070. SUPPLY MANAGEMENT.

The commissioner shall adopt regulations governing the

(1) management of supplies during their entire life cycle;

(2) sale, lease, or disposal of surplus supplies by public auction, competitive sealed bidding, or other appropriate method;

(3) purchase of surplus supplies by an employee of the using or disposing agency; and

(4) transfer of excess supplies.

Sec. 36.30.080. LEASES.

(a) The department shall lease space for the use of the state or an agency wherever it is necessary and feasible, subject to compliance with the requirements of this chapter. A lease may not provide for a period of occupancy greater than 40 years. An agency requiring office, warehouse, or other space shall lease the space through the department.

(b) Repealed, Sec. 11 ch 75 SLA 1994.

(c) If the department, the Board of Regents of the University of Alaska, the legislative council, or the supreme court intends to enter into or renew a lease of real property with an annual rent to the department, University of Alaska, legislative council, or supreme court that is anticipated to exceed $500,000, or with total lease payments that exceed $2,500,000 for the full term of the lease, including any renewal options that are defined in the lease, the department, the Board of Regents, the legislative council, or supreme court shall provide notice to the legislature. The notice must include the anticipated annual lease obligation amount and the total lease payments for the full term of the lease. The department, the Board of Regents, the legislative council, and the supreme court may not enter into or renew a lease of real property

> (1) requiring notice under this subsection unless the proposed lease or renewal of a lease has been approved by the legislature by law; an appropriation for the rent payable during the initial period of the lease or the initial period of lease renewal constitutes approval of the proposed lease or renewal of a lease for purposes of this paragraph;
>
> (2) under this subsection if the total of all optional renewal periods provided for in the lease exceeds the original term of the lease exclusive of the total period of all renewal options.

(d) When the department is evaluating proposals for a lease of space, the department shall consider, in addition to lease costs, the life cycle costs, function, indoor environment, public convenience, planning, design, appearance, and location of the proposed building.

(e) When the department is considering leasing space, the department should consider whether leasing is likely to be the least costly means to provide the space.

Sec. 36.30.085. LEASE-PURCHASE AGREEMENTS.

(a) To perform its duties and statutory functions, the department, the Board of Regents of the University of Alaska, the legislative council, or the supreme court may enter into lease-purchase agreements.

The department, the Board of Regents, the legislative council, or the supreme court may enter into a lease-purchase agreement only if the department, the Board of Regents, the legislative council, or the supreme court is the lessee under the agreement.

(b) When evaluating proposals to acquire real property under a lease-purchase agreement, the department, the Board of Regents, the legislative council, or the supreme court shall consider

(1) in addition to lease costs, the life cycle costs, function, indoor environment, public convenience, planning, design, appearance, and location of the real property proposed for acquisition; and

(2) whether acquisition of the real property by lease-purchase agreement is likely to be the least costly means to provide the space.

(c) A lease-purchase agreement

(1) may not provide for a period of occupancy under the full term of the lease-purchase agreement that is greater than 40 years;

(2) must provide that lease payments made by the department, the Board of Regents, the legislative council, or the supreme court are subject to annual appropriation.

(d) If the department, Board of Regents, legislative council, or supreme court intends to enter into or renew a lease-purchase agreement for real property, the department, Board of Regents, legislative council, or supreme court shall provide notice to the legislature. The notice must include the

(1) anticipated total construction, acquisition, or other costs of the project;

(2) anticipated annual amount of the rental obligation; and

(3) total lease payments for the full term of the lease-purchase agreement.

(e) The department, the Board of Regents, the legislative council, or the supreme court may not enter into a lease-purchase agreement to acquire real property unless the agreement has been approved by the legislature by law.

(f) The provisions of (d) and (e) of this section do not apply to a lease-purchase agreement

(1) related to the refinancing of an outstanding balance owing on an existing lease-purchase agreement; or

(2) by the University of Alaska if the lease-purchase agreement is secured by student fees or university receipts as defined in AS 14.40.491.

(g) In this section,

(1) "full term of the lease-purchase agreement" includes all renewal options that are defined within the lease-purchase agreement;

(2) "lease-purchase agreement" includes a lease-financing agreement.

Sec. 36.30.090. DELIVERY OF SUPPLIES.

Supplies purchased under this chapter shall be delivered at a location within the state unless the department determines that a point of delivery outside the state would be in the best interest of the state. A bid or proposal involving the procurement of supplies shall specify the delivery location and shall state that the price is the delivered price at that location.

Sec. 36.30.095. PROCUREMENT OF PAPER.

Except as otherwise required under AS 36.15.050 or AS 36.30.322 - 36.30.338, when a state agency purchases paper, at least 25 percent of the quantity purchased must be recycled paper unless the commissioner of the department in which the agency is located makes a written finding that recycled paper is not available for the purchase or that, after application of the procurement preference under AS 36.30.339, the recycled paper is more expensive than the nonrecycled paper. If the agency is not located in a department, the procurement officer for the agency shall make the written finding. If the agency is located in the Office of the Governor, the governor shall make the written finding.

ARTICLE 2

COMPETITIVE SEALED BIDDING

Sec. 36.30.100. GENERAL POLICY.

(a) Except as otherwise provided in this chapter, or unless specifically exempted by law, an agency contract shall be awarded by competitive sealed bidding.

(b) Competitive sealed bidding is not required

(1) when the commissioner determines in writing that food, clothing, or medical supplies, or supplies for use in laboratory or medical studies may be purchased otherwise to the best advantage of the state;

(2) for the purchase of products or services manufactured or provided by an employment program; or

(3) for the purchase of products or services provided by the correctional industries program established under AS 33.32.

(c) Repealed, Sec. 20 ch 102 SLA 1989.

Sec. 36.30.110. INVITATION TO BID.

(a) When competitive sealed bidding is used, the procurement officer shall issue an invitation to bid. It must include a time, place, and date by which the bid must be received, purchase description, and a description of all contractual terms and conditions applicable to the procurement.

(b) The bidder must have a valid Alaska business license at the time designated in the invitation to bid for bid opening. A bidder for a construction contract shall also submit evidence of the bidder's registration under AS 08.18.

(c) If the commissioner of transportation and public facilities makes a written finding that the release of the estimated cost of a construction contract would adversely affect the state's ability to obtain the best competitive bid, the estimated cost is confidential information and may not be released to the public before bid opening.

Sec. 36.30.115. SUBCONTRACTORS.

(a) Within five working days after the identification of the apparent low bidder, the apparent low bidder shall submit a list of the subcontractors the bidder proposes to use in the performance of the contract. The list must include the name and location of the place of business for each subcontractor and evidence of the subcontractor's valid Alaska business license. A bidder for a construction contract shall also submit evidence of each subcontractor's registration under AS 08.18. If a subcontractor on the list did not have a valid Alaska business license and a valid certificate of registration under AS 08.18 at the time the bid was opened, the bidder may not use the subcontractor in the performance of the contract, and shall replace the subcontractor with a subcontractor who had a valid Alaska business license and a valid certificate of registration under AS 08.18 at the time the bid was opened.

(b) A bidder may replace a listed subcontractor if the subcontractor

(1) fails to comply with AS 08.18;

(2) files for bankruptcy or becomes insolvent;

(3) fails to execute a contract with the bidder involving performance of the work for which the subcontractor was listed and the bidder acted in good faith;

(4) fails to obtain bonding;

(5) fails to obtain insurance acceptable to the state;

(6) fails to perform the contract with the bidder involving work for which the subcontractor was listed;

(7) must be substituted in order for the prime contractor to satisfy required state and federal affirmative action requirements;

(8) refuses to agree or abide with the bidder's labor agreement; or

(9) is determined by the procurement officer not to be a responsible subcontractor.

(c) If a bidder fails to list a subcontractor or lists more than one subcontractor for the same portion of work and the value of that work is in excess of half of one percent of the total bid, the bidder shall be considered to have agreed to perform that portion of work without the use of a subcontractor and to have represented the bidder to be qualified to perform that work.

(d) A bidder who attempts to circumvent the requirements of this section by listing as a subcontractor another contractor who, in turn, sublets the majority of the work required under the contract violates this section.

(e) If a contract is awarded to a bidder who violates this section, the purchasing officer may

(1) cancel the contract; or

(2) after notice and a hearing, assess a penalty on the bidder in an amount that does not exceed 10 percent of the value of the subcontract at issue.

Sec. 36.30.120. BID SECURITY.

(a) Bid security shall be required for all competitive sealed bidding for construction contracts when the price is estimated by the procurement officer to exceed an amount established by regulation of the commissioner. Bid security on construction contracts under the amount set by the commissioner may be required when the circumstances warrant. Bid security may be required for competitive sealed bidding for contracts for supplies, services, or professional services in accordance with regulations of the commissioner when needed for the protection of the state.

(b) Bid security must be a bond provided by a surety company authorized to do business in the state or otherwise supplied in a form satisfactory to the commissioner. Bid security must be in an amount equal to at least five percent of the amount of the bid.

(c) When the invitation to bid requires security, the procurement officer shall reject a bid that does not comply with the bid security requirement unless, in accordance with regulations, the officer determines that the bid fails to comply in a nonsubstantial manner with the security requirements.

Sec. 36.30.130. PUBLIC NOTICE OF INVITATION TO BID.

(a) Effective until August 22, 1998. The procurement officer shall give adequate public notice of the invitation to bid at least 21 days before the date for the opening of bids. If a determination is made in writing that a shorter notice period is necessary for a particular bid, the 21-day period may be shortened. The determination shall be made by the chief procurement officer for bids for supplies, services, or professional services. The determination shall be made by the commissioner of transportation and public facilities for bids for construction or acquisition of property for the state equipment fleet. Notice shall be published in the Alaska Administrative Journal. The time and manner of notice must be in accordance with regulations adopted by the commissioner of administration. When practicable, notice may include

(1) publication in a newspaper calculated to reach prospective bidders located in the state;

(2) notices posted in public places within the area where the work is to be performed or the material furnished; and

(3) notices mailed to all active prospective contractors on the appropriate list maintained under AS 36.30.050

(A) if the contractors are located in the state;

(B) upon request, if the contractors are not located in the state.

(b) Failure to comply with the notice requirements of this section does not invalidate a bid or the award of a contract. If the state fails to substantially comply with the requirements of (a) of this section, the state is liable for damages caused by that failure.

Sec. 36.30.140. BID OPENING.

(a) The procurement officer shall open bids at the time and place designated in the invitation to bid. All bid openings are open to the public. The amount of each bid and other relevant information that is specified by regulation of the commissioner, together with the name of each bidder, shall be recorded.

(b) The information recorded under (a) of this section is open to public inspection as soon as practicable before the notice of intent to award a contract is given under AS 36.30.365. The bids are not open for public inspection until after the notice of intent to award a contract is given. To the extent the bidder designates and the procurement officer concurs, trade secrets and other proprietary data contained in a bid document are confidential.

Sec. 36.30.150. BID ACCEPTANCE AND BID EVALUATION.

(a)   Bids shall be unconditionally accepted without alteration or correction, except as authorized in AS 36.30.160. The procurement officer shall evaluate bids based on the requirements set out in the invitation to bid, which may include criteria to determine acceptability such as inspection, testing, quality, delivery, and suitability for a particular purpose. The criteria that will affect the bid price and be considered in evaluation for award must be objectively measurable, such as discounts, transportation costs, and total or life cycle costs. The invitation to bid must set out the evaluation criteria to be used. Criteria may not be used in bid evaluation if they are not set out in the invitation to bid.

(b)   Repealed, Sec. 11 ch 37 SLA 1993.

Sec. 36.30.160. LATE BIDS; CORRECTION OR WITHDRAWAL OF BIDS; CANCELLATION OF AWARDS.

(a)   Bids received after the bid due date and time indicated on the invitation to bid may not be accepted unless the delay was due to an error of the contracting agency.

(b)   Correction or withdrawal of inadvertently erroneous bids before or after bid opening, or cancellation of awards or contracts based on bid mistakes may be permitted in accordance with regulations adopted by the commissioner. After bid opening, changes in bid prices or other provisions of bids prejudicial to the interest of the state or fair competition may not be permitted. Except as otherwise provided by regulation, a decision to permit the correction or withdrawal of a bid, or to cancel an award or contract based on bid mistake, shall be supported by a written determination made by the procurement officer. If a bidder is permitted to withdraw a bid before award, an action may not be maintained against the bidder or the bid security.

Sec. 36.30.170. CONTRACT AWARD AFTER BIDS.

(a)   Except as provided in (b) - (h) of this section, the procurement officer shall award a contract based on the solicited bids with reasonable promptness by written notice to the lowest responsible and responsive bidder whose bid conforms in all material respects to the requirements and criteria set out in the invitation to bid.

(b)   The procurement officer shall award a contract based on solicited bids to the lowest responsive and responsible bidder after an Alaska bidder preference of five percent, an Alaska products preference as described in AS 36.30.322 - 36.30.338, and a recycled products preference under AS 36.30.339 have been applied. In this subsection, "Alaska bidder" means a person who

> (1) holds a current Alaska business license;

> (2) submits a bid for goods, services, or construction under the name as appearing on the person's current Alaska business license;

> (3) has maintained a place of business within the state staffed by the bidder or an employee of the bidder for a period of six months immediately preceding the date of the bid;

> (4) is incorporated or qualified to do business under the laws of the state, is a sole proprietorship and the proprietor is a resident of the state, or is a partnership and all partners are residents of the state; and

> (5) if a joint venture, is composed entirely of ventures that qualify under (1) - (4) of this subsection.

(c) Except as otherwise provided under (e) or (f) of this section, if a bidder qualifies under (b) of this section as an Alaska bidder, is offering services through an employment program, and is the lowest responsible and responsive bidder with a bid that is not more than 15 percent higher than the lowest bid, the procurement officer shall award the contract to that bidder. This subsection does not give a bidder who would otherwise qualify for a preference under this subsection a preference over another bidder who would otherwise qualify for a preference under this subsection.

(d) The procurement officer shall award an insurance-related contract based on solicited bids to the lowest responsive and responsible bidder after an Alaska bidder preference of five percent. In this subsection, "Alaska bidder" means a person who meets the criteria set out in (b) (1) - (5) of this section and who is an Alaska domestic insurer.

(e) If a bidder qualifies under (b) of this section as an Alaska bidder, is a sole proprietorship owned by an individual who is a person with a disability, and is the lowest responsible and responsive bidder with a bid that is not more than 10 percent higher than the lowest bid, the procurement officer shall award the contract to that bidder. This subsection does not give a bidder who would otherwise qualify for a preference under this subsection a preference over another bidder who would otherwise qualify for a preference under this subsection or (f) of this section.

(f) If a bidder qualifies under (b) of this section as an Alaska bidder, if 50 percent or more of the bidder's employees at the time the bid is submitted are persons with a disability, and if the bidder is the lowest responsible and responsive bidder with a bid that is not more than 10 percent higher than the lowest bid, the procurement officer shall award the contract to that bidder. The contract must contain a promise by the bidder that the percentage of the bidder's employees who are persons with a disability will remain at 50 percent or more during the contract term. This subsection does not give a bidder who would otherwise qualify for a preference under this subsection a preference over another bidder who would otherwise qualify for a preference under this subsection or (e) of this section.

(g)   The division of vocational rehabilitation in the Department of Education shall add to its current list of qualified employment programs a list of individuals who qualify as persons with a disability under (e) of this section and of persons who qualify under (f) of this section as employers with 50 percent or more of their employees being persons with disabilities. A person must be on this list at the time the bid is opened in order to qualify for a preference under (e) or (f) of this section.

(h)   A preference under (c), (e), or (f) of this section is in addition to any other preference for which the bidder qualifies, including the preference under (b) of this section; however, a bidder may not receive a preference under both (e) and (f) of this subsection for the same contract.

(i)   This section applies to all insurance contracts involving state money. In this subsection, "state money" includes state grants and reimbursement to municipalities, school districts, and other entities.

(j)   In this section, "person with a disability" means an individual

(1)   who has a severe physical or mental disability that seriously limits one or more functional capacities in terms of employability; in this paragraph, "functional capacities" means mobility, communication, self-care, self-direction, interpersonal skills, work tolerance, or work skills;

(2)   whose physical or mental disability

(A)   results from amputation, arthritis, autism, blindness, burn injury, cancer, cerebral palsy, cystic fibrosis, deafness, head injury, heart disease, hemiplegia, hemophilia, respiratory or pulmonary dysfunction, mental retardation, mental illness, multiple sclerosis, muscular dystrophy, musculo-skeletal disorders, neurological disorders, paraplegia, quadriplegia, other spinal cord conditions, sickle cell anemia, specific learning disability, or end stage renal disease; in this subparagraph, "neurological disorders" include stroke and epilepsy; or

(B)   is a disability or combination of disabilities that are not identified in (A) of this paragraph and that are determined on the basis of an evaluation of rehabilitation potential to cause substantial functional limitation comparable to a disability identified in (A) of this paragraph; and

(3)   whose vocational rehabilitation can be expected to require multiple vocational rehabilitation services over an extended period of time.

Sec. 36.30.180.   PURPOSE.

The legislature finds that there exists in the state continuing high unemployment, underutilization of resident construction and supply firms, and high costs unfavorable to the welfare of Alaskans and to the economic health of the state. The purpose of bidder preference for resident firms when the state acts as a market participant is to encourage local industry, strengthen and stabilize the economy, decrease unemployment, and strengthen the tax and revenue base of the state.

Sec. 36.30.190. MULTI-STEP SEALED BIDDING.

When it is considered impractical to initially prepare a definitive purchase description to support an award based on price, the procurement officer may issue an invitation to bid requesting the submission of unpriced technical offers to be followed by an invitation to bid limited to the bidders whose offers are determined to be technically qualified under the criteria set out in the first solicitation.

ARTICLE 3
COMPETITIVE SEALED PROPOSALS

Sec. 36.30.200. CONDITIONS FOR USE.

(a) Except as otherwise provided in this chapter, or unless specifically exempted by law, an agency contract shall be awarded by competitive sealed proposals if it is not awarded by competitive sealed bidding. Construction may only be procured by competitive sealed proposals if the conditions under (c) of this section are met.

(b) The commissioner may provide by regulation that it is either not practicable or not advantageous to the state to procure specified types of supplies, services, or construction by competitive sealed bidding that would otherwise be procured by that method. When the chief procurement officer, or for construction contracts or procurements for the state equipment fleet, the commissioner of transportation and public facilities, determines in writing that the use of competitive sealed bidding is either not practicable or not advantageous to the state, a contract may be entered into by competitive sealed proposals in accordance with the regulations. When it is determined that it is practicable but not advantageous to use competitive sealed bidding, the chief procurement officer or commissioner of transportation and public facilities shall specify with particularity the basis for the determination.

(c) When the chief procurement officer determines that it is advantageous to the state, a procurement officer may issue a request for proposals requesting the submission of offers to provide construction in accordance with a design provided by the offeror. The request for proposals shall require that each proposal submitted contain a single price that includes the design/build.

Sec. 36.30.210. REQUEST FOR PROPOSALS.

(a) A request for competitive sealed proposals must contain the date, time, and place for delivering proposals, a specific description of the supplies, construction, services, or professional services to be provided under the contract, and the terms under which the supplies, construction, services, or professional services are to be provided. The request must require the offeror, no later than five working days after the proposal that is the most advantageous to the state is identified, to list subcontractors the offeror proposes to use in the performance of the contract. The list must include the name and location of the place of business for each subcontractor, the work to be subcontracted to each subcontractor, and evidence of the subcontractor's valid Alaska business license. An offeror for a construction contract shall also submit evidence of the offeror's registration under AS 08.18 and evidence of registration for each listed subcontractor.

(b) A request for proposals must contain that information necessary for an offeror to submit a proposal or contain references to any information that cannot reasonably be included with the request. The request must provide a description of the factors that will be considered by the procurement officer when evaluating the proposals received, including the relative importance of price and other evaluation factors.

(c) Notice of a request for proposals shall be given in accordance with procedures under AS 36.30.130. The procurement officer may use additional means considered appropriate to notify prospective offerors of the intent to enter into a contract through competitive sealed proposals.

(d) The provisions of AS 36.30.115(b) - (e) apply to competitive sealed proposals.

(e) The offeror must have a valid Alaska business license at the time designated, in the request for proposals, for opening of the proposals.

Sec. 36.30.220. STANDARD OVERHEAD RATE.

(a) An agency that provides services to another agency under a contract covered by this chapter shall establish a standard overhead rate. If an agency submits a proposal in response to a request for competitive sealed proposals, the agency must include its standard overhead rate within its proposal.

(b) In this section, "standard overhead rate" means a charge established for services and professional services from an agency that is designed to compensate the agency for administration and support services incidentally provided with the services contracted for.

Sec. 36.30.230. DISCLOSURE OF PROPOSALS.

The procurement officer shall open proposals so as to avoid disclosure of contents to competing offerors during the process of negotiation. A register of proposals containing the name and address of each offeror shall be prepared in accordance with regulations adopted by the commissioner. The register and the proposals are open for public inspection after the notice of intent to award a contract is issued under AS 36.30.365. To the extent that the offeror designates and the procurement officer concurs, trade secrets and other proprietary data contained in the proposal documents are confidential.

Sec. 36.30.240. DISCUSSION WITH RESPONSIBLE OFFERORS AND REVISIONS TO PROPOSALS.

As provided in the request for proposals, and under regulations adopted by the commissioner, discussions may be conducted with responsible offerors who submit proposals determined to be reasonably susceptible of being selected for award for the purpose of clarification to assure full understanding of, and responsiveness to, the solicitation requirements. Offerors reasonably susceptible of being selected for award shall be accorded fair and equal treatment with respect to any opportunity for discussion and revision of proposals, and revisions may be permitted after submissions and before the award of the contract for the purpose of obtaining best and final offers. In conducting discussions, the procurement officer may not disclose information derived from proposals submitted by competing offerors. AS 44.62.310 does not apply to meetings with offerors under this section.

Sec. 36.30.250. AWARD OF CONTRACT.

(a) The procurement officer shall award a contract under competitive sealed proposals to the responsible and responsive offeror whose proposal is determined in writing to be the most advantageous to the state taking into consideration price and the evaluation factors set out in the request for proposals. Other factors and criteria may not be used in the evaluation. The contract file must contain the basis on which the award is made.

(b) In determining whether a proposal is advantageous to the state, the procurement officer shall take into account, in accordance with regulations of the commissioner, whether the offeror qualifies as an Alaska bidder under AS 36.30.170(b), is offering the service of an employment program, or qualifies for a preference under AS 36.30.170(e) or (f).

Sec. 36.30.260. CONTRACT EXECUTION.

A contract awarded under competitive sealed proposals must contain

(1) the amount of the contract stated on its first page;

(2) the date for the supplies to be delivered or the dates for construction, services, or professional services to begin and be completed;

(3) a description of the supplies, construction, services, or professional services to be provided; and

(4) certification by the project director for the contracting agency, the head of the contracting agency, or a designee that sufficient funds are available in an appropriation to be encumbered for the amount of the contract.

Sec. 36.30.265. MULTI-STEP SEALED PROPOSALS.

When it is considered impractical to initially prepare a definitive purchase description to support an award based on listed selection criteria, the procurement officer may issue an expression of interest requesting the submission of unpriced technical offers, and then later issue a request for proposals limited to the offerors whose offers are determined to be technically qualified under the criteria set out in the expression of interest.

Sec. 36.30.270. ARCHITECTURAL, ENGINEERING, AND LAND SURVEYING CONTRACTS.

(a) Notwithstanding conflicting provisions of AS 36.30.100 - 36.30.260, a procurement officer shall negotiate a contract for an agency with the most qualified and suitable firm or person of demonstrated competence for architectural, engineering, or land surveying services. The procurement officer shall award a contract for those services at fair and reasonable compensation as determined by the procurement officer, after consideration of the estimated value of the services to be rendered, and the scope, complexity, and professional nature of the services. When determining the most qualified and suitable firm or person, the procurement officer shall consider the

> (1) proximity to the project site of the office of the firm or person unless federal law prohibits this factor from being considered in the awarding of the contract; and
>
> (2) employment practices of the firm or person with regard to women and minorities.

(b) If negotiations with the most qualified and suitable firm or person under (a) of this section are not successful, the procurement officer shall negotiate a contract with other qualified firms or persons of demonstrated competence, in order of public ranking. The procurement officer may reject all or part of a proposal.

(c) This section does not apply to contracts awarded in a situation of public necessity if the procurement officer certifies in writing that a situation of public necessity exists.

(d) Notwithstanding the other provisions of this section, a procurement officer may include price as an added factor in selecting architectural, engineering, and land surveying services when, in the judgment of the procurement officer, the services required are repetitious in nature, and the scope, nature, and amount of services required are thoroughly defined by measurable and objective standards to reasonably enable firms or persons making proposals to compete with a clear understanding and interpretation of the services required. In order to include price as a factor in selection, a majority of the persons involved by the procurement officer in evaluation of the proposals must be registered in the state to perform architectural, engineering, or land surveying services.

(e) This section does not apply to a contract that incorporates both design services and construction.

ARTICLE 4
OTHER PROCUREMENT METHODS

Sec. 36.30.300. SOLE SOURCE PROCUREMENTS.

(a) A contract may be awarded for supplies, services, professional services, or construction without competitive sealed bidding, competitive sealed proposals, or other competition in accordance with regulations adopted by the commissioner. A contract may be awarded under this section only when the chief procurement officer or, for construction contracts or procurements for the state equipment fleet, the commissioner of transportation and public facilities determines in writing that there is only one source for the required procurement or construction. A sole source procurement may not be awarded if a reasonable alternative source exists. The written determination must include findings of fact that support by clear and convincing evidence the determination that only one source exists. Except for procurements of supplies, services, professional services, or construction that do not exceed the amount for small procurements under AS 36.30.320(a) or (b), as applicable, the authority to make the determination required by this subsection may not be delegated.

(b) The using agency shall submit written evidence to support a sole source determination. The commissioner of administration or the commissioner of transportation and public facilities, as appropriate, may also require the submission of cost or pricing data in connection with an award under this section.

(c) The procurement officer shall negotiate with the single supplier, to the extent practicable, to obtain a contract advantageous to the state.

(d) Procurement requirements may not be artificially divided, fragmented, aggregated, or structured so as to constitute a purchase under this section or to circumvent the source selection procedures required by AS 36.30.100 - 36.30.270.

Sec. 36.30.305. LIMITED COMPETITION PROCUREMENTS.

(a) A contract for supplies, services, professional services, or a construction contract under $100,000, may be awarded without competitive sealed bidding or competitive sealed proposals, in accordance with regulations adopted by the commissioner. A contract may be awarded under this section only when the chief procurement officer, or, for construction contracts under $100,000 or procurements for the state equipment fleet, the commissioner of transportation and public facilities, determines in writing that a situation exists that makes competitive sealed bidding or competitive sealed proposals impractical or contrary to the public interest. Procurements under this section shall be made with competition that is practicable under the circumstance. Except for procurements of supplies, services, professional services, or construction that do not exceed the amount for small procurements under AS 36.30.320(a) or (b), as applicable, the authority to make a determination required by this section may not be delegated.

(b) The using agency shall submit written evidence to support a determination under this section.

(c) Procurement requirements may not be artificially divided, fragmented, aggregated, or structured so as to constitute a purchase under this section or to circumvent the source selection procedures required by AS 36.30.100 - 36.30.270.

(d) Sole source procurements may not be made under this section.

(e) Architectural, engineering, and land survey contracts under AS 36.30.270 may not be made under this section.

Sec. 36.30.310. EMERGENCY PROCUREMENTS.

Procurements may be made under emergency conditions as defined in regulations adopted by the commissioner when there exists a threat to public health, welfare, or safety, when a situation exists that makes a procurement through competitive sealed bidding or competitive sealed proposals impracticable or contrary to the public interest, or to protect public or private property. An emergency procurement need not be made through competitive sealed bidding or competitive sealed proposals but shall be made with competition that is practicable under the circumstances. A written determination by the chief procurement officer of the basis for the emergency and for the selection of the particular contractor shall be included in the contract file. The written determination must include findings of fact that support the determination. Except when there is insufficient time for the chief procurement officer to make the written determination required by this section, the chief procurement officer may not delegate the authority to make the determination.

Sec. 36.30.315. DETERMINATIONS BY CHIEF PROCUREMENT OFFICER; CRIMINAL PENALTY.

(a) In a determination made by the chief procurement officer under AS 36.30.300 - 36.30.310, the chief procurement officer shall independently examine the material facts of the procurement and independently determine whether the procurement is eligible for the procurement method requested.

(b) If the chief procurement officer knowingly makes a false statement in a determination made by the chief procurement officer under AS 36.30.300 - 36.30.310, the chief procurement officer is guilty of a class A misdemeanor.

Sec. 36.30.320. SMALL PROCUREMENTS.

(a) A procurement for supplies, services, or construction that does not exceed an aggregate dollar amount of $25,000 may be made in accordance with regulations adopted by the commissioner for small procurements.

(b) A contract for professional services that does not exceed $25,000 may be made under regulations adopted by the commissioner for small procurements, except that an agency may not contract for the services of legal counsel without the approval of the attorney general.

(c) Small procurements need not be made through competitive sealed bidding or competitive sealed proposals but shall be made with competition that is practicable under the circumstances.

(d) Procurement requirements may not be artificially divided or fragmented so as to constitute a purchase under this section or to circumvent the source selection procedures required by AS 36.30.100 - 36.30.270.

(e) The procurement officer shall give adequate public notice of intent to make a procurement under this section in accordance with regulations adopted by the commissioner.

ARTICLE 5
PREFERENCE FOR ALASKA PRODUCTS

Sec. 36.30.322. USE OF LOCAL FOREST PRODUCTS.

(a) Only timber, lumber, and manufactured lumber products originating in this state from Alaska forests may be procured by an agency or used in construction projects of an agency unless the manufacturers and suppliers who have notified the commissioner of commerce and economic development of their willingness to manufacture or supply Alaska forest products

(1) have been given reasonable notice of the forest product needs of the procurement or project; and

(2) are unable to supply the products at a cost that is within seven percent of the price offered by a manufacturer or supplier of non-Alaska forest products.

(b) The provisions of AS 36.30.326 - 36.30.332 do not apply to procurements of timber, lumber, and manufactured lumber products or the use of those items in construction projects of an agency.

(c) During the period of performance of a state contract, the contractor shall maintain records showing efforts made in using Alaska forest products or evidence of Alaska forest products not being available or reasonably competitive. The contractor shall provide the records to the procurement officer on a periodic basis, as required by regulations adopted by the commissioner of commerce and economic development.

Sec. 36.30.324. USE OF ALASKA PRODUCTS AND RECYCLED ALASKA PRODUCTS.

Alaska products shall be used whenever practicable in procurements for an agency. Recycled Alaska products shall be used when they are of comparable quality, of equivalent price, and appropriate for the intended use.

Sec. 36.30.326. CONTRACT SPECIFICATIONS.

Contract specifications for a procurement for an agency must include a provision that a bidder or offeror that designates in a bid or proposal the use of Alaska products identified in the specifications will receive the preference granted under AS 36.30.328 in the evaluation of the bid or proposal if the designated Alaska products meet the contract specifications.

Sec. 36.30.328. GRANT OF ALASKA PRODUCTS PREFERENCE.

In the evaluation of a bid or proposal for a procurement for an agency, a bid or offer that designates the use of Alaska products identified in the contract specifications and designated as Class I, Class II, or

Class III state products under AS 36.30.332 is decreased by the percentage of the value of the designated Alaska products under AS 36.30.332.

Sec. 36.30.330. PENALTY FOR FAILING TO USE DESIGNATED PRODUCTS.

(a) If a successful bidder or offeror who designates the use of an Alaska product in a bid or proposal for a procurement for an agency fails to use the designated product for a reason within the control of the successful bidder or offeror, each payment under the contract shall be reduced according to the following schedule:

(1) for a Class I designated Alaska product - four percent;

(2) for a Class II designated Alaska product - six percent;

(3) for a Class III designated Alaska product - eight percent.

(b) A person is not a responsible bidder or offeror if, in the preceding three years, the person has twice designated the use of an Alaska product in a bid or proposal for a procurement for an agency and has each time failed to use the designated Alaska product for reasons within the control of the bidder or offeror.

(c) The procurement officer shall report to the commissioner of commerce and economic development each contractor penalized under (a) of this section. The commissioner of commerce and economic development shall maintain a list of contractors determined not to be responsible bidders under (b) of this section.

Sec. 36.30.332. CLASSIFICATION OF ALASKA PRODUCTS.

(a) The commissioner of commerce and economic development shall adopt regulations establishing the value added in the state for materials and supplies produced or manufactured in the state that are used in a state procurement and establishing whether a product qualifies as a recycled Alaska product. The commissioner shall publish a list of the products annually. A supplier may request inclusion of its product on the appropriate list.

(b) Materials and supplies with value added in the state that are

(1) more than 25 percent and less than 50 percent produced or manufactured in the state are Class I products;

(2) 50 percent or more and less than 75 percent produced or manufactured in the state are Class II products; and

(3) 75 percent or more produced or manufactured in the state are Class III products.

(c) In a bid or proposal evaluation a

(1) Class I product is given a three percent preference;

(2) Class II product is given a five percent preference;

(3) Class III product is given a seven percent preference.

Sec. 36.30.334. IDENTIFICATION OF ALASKA PRODUCTS.

An agency may identify specific Alaska products for use in making a procurement.

Sec. 36.30.336. APPLICATION.

Notwithstanding other provisions of this chapter, AS 36.30.322 - 36.30.338 apply to all procurements subject to this chapter, except as provided in AS 36.15.050 and AS 36.30.322(b).

Sec. 36.30.338. DEFINITIONS.

In AS 36.30.322 - 36.30.338

(1) "Alaska product" means a product of which not less than 25 percent of the value, as determined in accordance with regulations adopted under AS 36.30.332(a), has been added by manufacturing or production in the state;

(2) "produced or manufactured" means processing, developing, or making an item into a new item with a distinct character and use through the application within the state of materials, labor, skill, or other services;

(3) "product" means materials or supplies but does not include gravel and asphalt;

(4) "recycled Alaska product" means an Alaska product of which not less than 50 percent of the value of the product consists of a product that was previously used in another product, if the recycling process is done in the state.

ARTICLE 6

PREFERENCE FOR RECYCLED PRODUCTS

Sec. 36.30.339. PROCUREMENT PREFERENCE FOR RECYCLED PRODUCTS.

(a) In the evaluation of a bid or proposal for an agency procurement of products, the agency shall decrease the bid or proposal by five percent if the bid or proposal indicates that the products being purchased will be recycled products.

(b) A decrease made under (a) of this section is in addition to other preferences allowed for the procurement.

(c) The department shall establish the minimum percentage of recycled content that will qualify a product as a recycled product under (a) of this section.

ARTICLE 7
CONTRACT FORMATION AND MODIFICATION

Sec. 36.30.340. REVIEW AND APPROVAL BY THE ATTORNEY GENERAL.

If a contract contains a term that is in conflict with a state standard form contract term or if a standard term is deleted or modified by a term that is not standard, the contract must be reviewed by the Attorney General and approved as to form.

Sec. 36.30.350. BID CANCELLATION, REJECTION.

An invitation to bid, a request for proposals, or other solicitation may be canceled or any or all bids or proposals may be rejected in whole or in part or the date for opening bids or proposals may be delayed when it is in the best interests of the state in accordance with regulations adopted by the commissioner. The reasons for cancellation, rejection, or delay in opening bids or proposals shall be made part of the contract file.

Sec. 36.30.360. DETERMINATION OF RESPONSIBILITY.

(a) A written determination of nonresponsibility of a bidder or offeror shall be made by the procurement officer in accordance with regulations adopted by the commissioner. The unreasonable failure of a bidder or offeror to promptly supply information in connection with an inquiry with respect to responsibility is grounds for a determination of nonresponsibility with respect to the bidder or offeror.

(b) Information furnished by a bidder or offeror under (a) of this section is confidential and may not be disclosed without prior written consent by the bidder or offeror.

Sec. 36.30.362. DETERMINATION TO AWARD A CONTRACT TO A NONRESIDENT. Except for awards made under AS 36.30.170, if the procurement officer awards a contract to a person who does not reside or maintain a place of business in the state and if the supplies, services, professional services, or construction that is the subject of the contract could have been obtained from sources in the state, the procurement officer shall issue a written statement explaining the basis of the award. The statement required under this section shall be kept in the contract file.

Sec. 36.30.365. NOTICE OF INTENT TO AWARD A CONTRACT.

At least 10 days before the formal award of a contract that is not for construction, and at least five days before the award of a construction contract, under this chapter, except for a contract awarded under AS

36.30.300 - 36.30.320, the procurement officer shall provide to each bidder or offeror notice of intent to award a contract. The notice must conform to regulations adopted by the commissioner.

Sec. 36.30.370. TYPES OF CONTRACTS.

Any type of contract that will promote the best interests of the state may be used, except that the use of a cost-plus-a-percentage-of-cost contract is prohibited.

Sec. 36.30.380. APPROVAL OF ACCOUNTING SYSTEM.

REPEALED, Sec. 24 CH 65 SLA 1987. Repealed or Renumbered

Sec. 36.30.390. MULTI-TERM CONTRACTS.

(a) Unless otherwise provided by law, a contract for supplies, services, or professional services may be entered into for any period of time considered to be in the best interests of the state provided the term of the contract and conditions of renewal or extension, if any, are included in the solicitation and funds are available for the first fiscal period at the time of contracting. Payment and performance obligations for succeeding fiscal periods shall be subject to the availability and appropriation of funds for them.

(b) Before using a multi-term contract, the procurement officer shall determine in writing that

(1) estimated requirements cover the period of the contract and are reasonably firm and continuing; and

(2) the contract will serve the best interests of the state by encouraging effective competition or otherwise promoting economies in state procurement.

(c) When funds are not appropriated or otherwise made available to support continuation of performance in a subsequent fiscal period, the contract shall be canceled. The contractor may only be reimbursed for the reasonable value of any nonrecurring costs incurred but not amortized in the price of the supplies, services, or professional services delivered under the contract that are not otherwise recoverable. The cost of cancellation may be paid from any appropriations available for these purposes.

Sec. 36.30.400. COST OR PRICING DATA.

(a) Before an award of a contract or a change order or contract modification, the contractor or prospective contractor shall submit cost and pricing data. The contractor or prospective contractor shall certify that, to the best of the contractor's or prospective contractor's knowledge and belief, the data submitted is accurate, complete, and current as of a mutually determined specified date and will continue to be accurate and complete during the performance of the contract.

(b) When a contractor becomes aware of a situation that may form the basis of a claim for compensation that exceeds the amount designated as the base amount of the contract and before performing additional work or supplying additional materials, the contractor shall submit cost and pricing data on the additional work or materials. The contractor shall certify that, to the best of the contractor's knowledge and belief, the data submitted is accurate, complete, and current and is the actual cost to the contractor of performing the additional work or supplying the additional materials.

(c) A contract, change order, or contract modification under which a certificate is required under (a) or (b) of this section must contain a provision that the price to the state, including the contractor's profit or fee, will be adjusted to exclude any significant sums by which the state finds that the price is increased because the cost or pricing data furnished by the contractor or prospective contractor is inaccurate, incomplete, or not current as of the date agreed upon by the parties.

(d) The requirements of (a) of this section do not apply when

(1) the contract price is based on adequate price competition;

(2) the contract price is set by law or regulation; or

(3) it is determined by the procurement officer in writing and in accordance with regulations adopted by the commissioner that the requirements of (a) of this section may be waived, and the reasons for waiver are stated.

Sec. 36.30.410. RIGHT TO INSPECT PLANT.

The state may, at reasonable times, inspect the part of the plant or place of business of a contractor or subcontractor that is related to the performance of a contract awarded or to be awarded by an agency.

Sec. 36.30.420. RIGHT TO AUDIT RECORDS.

(a) The state may, at reasonable times and places, audit the books and records of a person who has submitted cost or pricing data under AS 36.30.400 to the extent that the books and records relate to the cost or pricing data. A person who receives a contract, change order, or contract modification for which cost or pricing data is required, shall maintain books and records that relate to the cost or pricing data for three years after the date of final payment under the contract, unless a shorter period is authorized in writing by the commissioner.

(b) The state may audit the books and records of a contractor or a subcontractor to the extent that the books and records relate to the performance of the contract or subcontract. Books and records shall be maintained by the contractor for a period of three years after the date of final payment under the prime contract and by the subcontractor for a period of three years after the date of final payment under the subcontract, unless a shorter period is authorized in writing by the commissioner.

Sec. 36.30.430. STANDARD MODIFICATION CLAUSES FOR CONTRACTS.

(a) The commissioner shall adopt regulations permitting the inclusion of clauses providing for adjustments in prices, time of performance, or other contract provisions as appropriate.

(b) The commissioner shall adopt regulations permitting or requiring the inclusion in state contracts of clauses providing for appropriate remedies and covering the following subjects:

    (1) liquidated damages;

    (2) specified excuses for delay or nonperformance;

    (3) termination of the contract for default; and

    (4) termination of the contract in whole or in part for the convenience of the state.

Sec. 36.30.460. MODIFICATION OF STANDARD CLAUSES.

The procurement officer or the head of a contracting agency may vary the clauses adopted under AS 36.30.430 for inclusion in a particular state contract if the

    (1) variations are supported by a written determination that states the circumstances justifying the variation; and

    (2) approval required by AS 36.30.340 is obtained.

Sec. 36.30.470. FISCAL RESPONSIBILITY.

A contract modification, change order, or contract price adjustment under a construction contract in excess of an amount established by regulation of the commissioner is subject to prior written certification by the fiscal officer of the agency responsible for funding the project or the contract, or other official responsible for monitoring and reporting upon the status of the costs of the total project budget or contract budget, as to the effect of the contract modification, change order, or adjustment in contract price on the total project budget or the total contract budget. If the certification of the fiscal officer or other responsible official discloses a resulting increase in the total project budget or the total contract budget, the procurement officer may not approve the contract modification, change order, or adjustment in contract price unless sufficient funds are available, or the scope of the project or contract is adjusted to permit the degree of completion that is feasible within the total project budget or total contract budget as it existed before the contract modification, change order, or adjustment in contract price under consideration. A contract modification change order, or adjustment in contract that is signed by both parties and has been reasonably relied on by a contractor, is presumed to be valid even if the provisions of this section have not been met.

Sec. 36.30.480. COST PRINCIPLE REGULATIONS.

The commissioner shall adopt regulations setting out cost principles that shall be used to determine the allowability of incurred costs for the purpose of reimbursing costs under contract provisions that provide for the reimbursement of costs. If a written determination is approved at a level above the procurement officer, the cost principles may be modified by contract.

ARTICLE 8
PROCUREMENT RECORDS AND REPORTS

Sec. 36.30.500. RETENTION OF PROCUREMENT RECORDS.

Procurement records shall be retained and disposed of in accordance with records retention guidelines and schedules approved by the state archivist. Retained documents shall be made available to the attorney general or a designee upon request and proper receipt.

Sec. 36.30.510. RECORDS OF CONTRACTS AWARDED UNDER COMPETITIVE SEALED PROPOSALS.

A contract file open for public inspection shall be kept by the commissioner and the contracting agency for each contract awarded under competitive sealed proposals. The file kept by the commissioner must contain a summary of the information in the file of the contracting agency. The file kept by the contracting agency must contain

(1) a copy of the contract;

(2) the register of proposals prepared under AS 36.30.230 and a copy of each proposal submitted; and

(3) the written determination to award the contract prepared under AS 36.30.250.

Sec. 36.30.520. RECORDS OF SOLE SOURCE AND EMERGENCY PROCUREMENTS.

(a) The commissioner shall maintain for a minimum of five years a record listing all sole source procurement contracts made under AS 36.30.300 and emergency procurements made under AS 36.30.310. The record must contain

(1) each contractor's name;

(2) the amount and type of each contract; and

(3) a listing of the supplies, services, professional services, or construction procured under each contract.

(b) The Department of Transportation and Public Facilities and any agency to whom the commissioner of administration or the commissioner of transportation and public facilities has delegated procurement authority under AS 36.30.015 shall, by October 1 of each year, submit to the commissioner of administration records of the type specified in (a) of this section. The commissioner of administration shall maintain these records as required by (a) of this section.

Sec. 36.30.530. PUBLIC ACCESS TO PROCUREMENT INFORMATION.

Procurement information is public except as otherwise provided by law.

Sec. 36.30.540. REPORT TO LEGISLATURE.

The commissioner shall biennially report to the legislature concerning procurements by agencies. The report must include

(1) the records maintained by the commissioner under AS 36.30.510 and the records maintained under as 36.30.520(a) for the previous two fiscal years;

(2) recommendations for changes in this chapter or other laws based on implementation of this chapter in the previous two fiscal years;

(3) a description of any matters that involved litigation concerning this chapter in the previous two fiscal years;

(4) a list of procurements made under this chapter from out-of-state sources during the previous two fiscal years together with the total number of procurement contracts entered into during that period with out-of-state contractors and the total value of these contracts; this paragraph does not apply to procurements made under AS 36.30.320; and

(5) a list of procurements made under this chapter from state sources during the previous two fiscal years together with the total number of procurement contracts entered into during that period with state contractors and the total value of these contracts; this paragraph does not apply to procurements made under AS 36.30.320;

(6) the number of bidders and offerors that bid on or made proposals for procurements under this chapter, the number of these bidders and offerors that were located in the state, and the number of these bidders and offerors that were located outside the state; this paragraph does not apply to procurements made under AS 36.30.320.

ARTICLE 9
LEGAL AND CONTRACTUAL REMEDIES

Sec. 36.30.560. FILING OF A PROTEST.

An interested party may protest the award of a contract, the proposed award of a contract, or a solicitation for supplies, services, professional services, or construction by an agency. The protest shall be filed with the procurement officer of the contracting agency in writing and include the following information:

(1) the name, address, and telephone number of the protester;

(2) the signature of the protester or the protester's representative;

(3) identification of the contracting agency and the solicitation or contract at issue;

(4) a detailed statement of the legal and factual grounds of the protest, including copies of relevant documents; and

(5) the form of relief requested.

Sec. 36.30.565. TIME FOR FILING A PROTEST.

(a) A protest based upon alleged improprieties in an award of a contract or a proposed award of a contract must be filed within 10 days after a notice of intent to award the contract is issued by the procurement officer.

(b) If the protester shows good cause, the procurement officer of the contracting agency may consider a filed protest that is not timely.

Sec. 36.30.570. NOTICE OF A PROTEST.

The procurement officer shall immediately give notice of a protest filed under AS 36.30.565 to the contractor if a contract has been awarded or, if no award has been made, to all interested parties.

Sec. 36.30.575. STAY OF AWARD.

If a protest is filed the award may be made unless the procurement officer of the contracting agency determines in writing that a

(1) reasonable probability exists that the protest will be sustained; or

(2) stay of the award is not contrary to the best interests of the state.

Sec. 36.30.580. DECISION BY THE PROCUREMENT OFFICER.

(a) The procurement officer of the contracting agency shall issue a written decision containing the basis of the decision within 14 days after a protest has been filed. A copy of the decision shall be furnished to the protester by certified mail or other method that provides evidence of receipt.

(b) The time for a decision may be extended up to 26 days for good cause by the commissioner of administration, or for protests involving construction or procurements for the state equipment fleet, the commissioner of transportation and public facilities. If an extension is granted, the procurement officer shall notify the protester in writing of the date of the decision is due.

(c) If a decision is not made by the date it is due, the protester may proceed as if the procurement officer had issued a decision adverse to the protester.

Sec. 36.30.585. PROTEST REMEDIES.

(a) If the procurement officer sustains a protest in whole or in part, the procurement officer shall implement an appropriate remedy.

(b) In determining an appropriate remedy, the procurement officer shall consider the circumstances surrounding the solicitation or procurement including the seriousness of the procurement deficiencies, the degree of prejudice to other interested parties or to the integrity of the procurement system, the good faith of the parties, the extent the procurement has been accomplished, costs to the agency and other impacts on the agency of a proposed remedy, and the urgency of the procurement to the welfare of the state.

Sec. 36.30.590. APPEAL ON A PROTEST.

(a) An appeal from a decision of a procurement officer on a protest may be filed by the protester with the commissioner of administration, or for protests involving construction or procurements for the state equipment fleet, the commissioner of transportation and public facilities. An appeal shall be filed within 10 days after the decision is received by the protester. The protester shall file a copy of the appeal with the procurement officer.

(b) An appeal must contain the information required under AS 36.30.560. In addition, the appeal must include

    (1) a copy of the decision being appealed; and

    (2) identification of the factual or legal errors in the decision that form the basis for the appeal.

Sec. 36.30.595. NOTICE OF A PROTEST APPEAL.

(a) The procurement officer shall immediately give notice of an appeal filed under AS 36.30.590 to the contractor if a contract has been awarded or, if no award has been made, to all interested parties.

(b) The commissioner of administration or the commissioner of transportation and public facilities, as appropriate, shall, on request, furnish a copy of the appeal to a person notified under (a) of this section, except that confidential material shall be deleted from the copy.

Sec. 36.30.600. STAY OF AWARD DURING PROTEST APPEAL.

If a protest appeal is filed before a contract is awarded and the award was stayed under AS 36.30.575, the filing of the appeal automatically continues the stay until the commissioner of administration or the commissioner of transportation and public facilities, as appropriate, makes a written determination that the award of the contract without further delay is necessary to protect substantial interests of the state.

Sec. 36.30.605. PROTEST REPORT.

(a) The procurement officer of the contracting agency shall file a complete report on the protest and decision with the commissioner of administration or the commissioner of transportation and public facilities, as appropriate, within seven days after a protest appeal is filed. The procurement officer shall furnish a copy of the report to the protester and to interested parties that have requested a copy of the appeal under AS 36.30.595(b).

(b) The procurement officer may request an extension of time to prepare the protest report. The request must be in writing listing the reasons for the request. The commissioner of administration or the commissioner of transportation and public facilities, as appropriate, shall respond to the request in writing. If an extension is granted, the commissioner shall list the reasons for granting the extension and indicate the date the protest report is due. The commissioner shall notify the protester in writing that the time for submission of the report has been extended and the date the report is due.

(c) The protester may file comments on the protest report with the commissioner of administration or the commissioner of transportation and public facilities, as appropriate, within seven days after the report is received. The protester shall provide copies of the comments to the procurement officer and to interested parties that have requested a copy of the appeal under AS 36.30.595(b).

(d) The protester may request an extension of time to prepare the comments on the protest report. The request must be in writing listing the reasons for the request. The commissioner of administration or the commissioner of transportation and public facilities, as appropriate, shall respond to the request in writing. If an extension is granted, the commissioner shall list the reasons for granting the extension and indicate the date the comments are due. The commissioner shall notify the procurement officer in writing that the time for submission of the comments has been extended and the date the comments are due.

Sec. 36.30.610. DECISION WITHOUT HEARING.

(a) The commissioner of administration or the commissioner of transportation and public facilities, as appropriate, shall dismiss a protest appeal before a hearing is held if it is determined in writing that the appeal is untimely under AS 36.30.590(a).

(b) The commissioner of administration or the commissioner of transportation and public facilities, as appropriate, may issue a decision on an appeal without a hearing if the appeal involves questions of law without genuine issues of fact.

(c) The commissioner of administration or the commissioner of transportation and public facilities, as appropriate, shall, within 15 days from the date the appellant's comments on the protest report are due under AS 36.30.605(c) and (d), notify the appellant of the acceptance or rejection of the appeal and, if rejected, the reasons for the rejection.

Sec. 36.30.615. HEARING ON PROTEST APPEAL.

A hearing on a protest appeal shall be conducted in accordance with AS 36.30.670 and regulations adopted by the commissioner.

Sec. 36.30.620. CONTRACT CONTROVERSIES.

(a) A contractor shall file a claim concerning a contract awarded under this chapter with the procurement officer. The contractor shall certify that the claim is made in good faith, that the supporting data are accurate and complete to the best of the contractor's knowledge and belief, and that the amount requested accurately reflects the contract adjustment for which the contractor believes the state is liable.

(b) If a controversy asserted by a contractor concerning a contract awarded under this chapter cannot be resolved by agreement, the procurement officer shall, after receiving a written request by the contractor for a decision, issue a written decision. The decision shall be made no more than 90 days after receipt by the procurement officer of all necessary information from the contractor. Failure of the contractor to furnish necessary information to the procurement officer constitutes a waiver of the claim. Before issuing the decision the procurement officer shall review the facts relating to the controversy and obtain necessary assistance from legal, fiscal, and other advisors.

(c) The time for issuing a decision under (b) of this section may be extended for good cause by the commissioner of administration, or for a controversy involving a construction contract or procurement for the state equipment fleet, the commissioner of transportation and public facilities, if the controversy concerns an amount in excess of $50,000. The procurement officer shall notify the contractor in writing that the time for the issuance of a decision has been extended and of the date by which a decision shall be issued.

(d) The procurement officer shall furnish a copy of the decision to the contractor by certified mail or other method that provides evidence of receipt. The decision must include a

    (1) description of the controversy;

(2) reference to the pertinent contract provisions;

(3) statement of the agreed upon and disputed facts;

(4) statement of reasons supporting the decision; and

(5) statement substantially as follows:

"This is the final decision of the procurement officer. This decision may be appealed to the commissioner of (administration transportation and public facilities). If you appeal, you must file a written notice of appeal with the commissioner within 14 days after you receive this decision."

(e) If a decision is not made by the date it is due, the contractor may proceed as if the procurement officer had issued a decision adverse to the contractor.

(f) If a controversy asserted by the state concerning a contract awarded under this chapter cannot be resolved by agreement the matter shall be immediately referred to the commissioner of administration or the commissioner of transportation and public facilities, as appropriate.

Sec. 36.30.625. APPEAL ON A CONTRACT CONTROVERSY.

(a) An appeal from a decision of the procurement officer on a contract controversy may be filed by the contractor with the commissioner of administration, or for a controversy involving a construction contract or procurement for the state equipment fleet, the commissioner of transportation and public facilities. The appeal shall be filed within 14 days after the decision is received by the contractor. The contractor shall file a copy of the appeal with the procurement officer.

(b) An appeal must contain a copy of the decision being appealed and identification of the factual or legal errors in the decision that form the basis for the appeal.

Sec. 36.30.630. HEARING ON A CONTRACT CONTROVERSY.

(a) Except as provided in (b) of this section, a hearing shall be conducted according to AS 36.30.670 and regulations adopted by the commissioner of administration on a contract controversy appealed to the commissioner of administration or the commissioner of transportation and public facilities or referred to either commissioner under AS 36.30.620(f).

(b) Within 15 days after receipt of an appeal on a contract controversy the commissioner of administration or the commissioner of transportation and public facilities, as appropriate, may adopt the decision of the procurement officer as the final decision without a hearing.

Sec. 36.30.632. DELEGATION.

The commissioner of administration and the commissioner of transportation and public facilities may delegate responsibilities under AS 36.30.590 and 36.30.630 to the head of the contracting agency.

Sec. 36.30.635. AUTHORITY TO DEBAR OR SUSPEND.

(a) After consultation with the using agency and the attorney general and after a hearing conducted according to AS 36.30.670 and regulations adopted by the commissioner of administration, the commissioner of administration or the commissioner of transportation and public facilities may debar a person for cause from consideration for award of contracts. Notice of a debarment hearing shall be provided in writing at least seven days before the hearing. The debarment may not be for a period of more than three years.

(b) The commissioner of administration or the commissioner of transportation and public facilities, after consultation with the using agency and the attorney general, may suspend a person from consideration for award of contracts if there is probable cause for debarment and compelling reasons require suspension to protect state interests. The suspension may not be for a period exceeding three months.

(c) The authority to debar or suspend shall be exercised in accordance with regulations adopted by the commissioner of administration.

Sec. 36.30.640. CAUSES FOR DEBARMENT OR SUSPENSION.

The causes for debarment or suspension include

(1) conviction for commission of a criminal offense as an incident to obtaining or attempting to obtain a public or private contract or subcontract, or in the performance of the contract or subcontract;

(2) conviction under state or federal statutes of embezzlement, theft, forgery, bribery, falsification or destruction of records, receiving stolen property, or other offense indicating a lack of business integrity or business honesty that currently and seriously affects responsibility as a state contractor;

(3) conviction or civil judgment finding a violation under state or federal antitrust statutes;

(4) violation of contract provisions of a character that is regarded by the commissioner to be so serious as to justify debarment action, such as

(A) knowing failure without good cause to perform in accordance with the specifications or within the time limit provided in the contract; or

(B) failure to perform or unsatisfactory performance in accordance with the terms of one or more contracts, except that failure to perform or unsatisfactory performance caused by acts beyond the control of the contractor may not be considered to be a basis for debarment;

(5) for violation of the ethical standards set out in law or regulation;

(6) for a violation of this chapter punishable under AS 36.30.930(2); and

(7) any other cause listed in regulations of the commissioner determined to be so serious and compelling as to affect responsibility as a state contractor, including debarment by another governmental entity for a cause listed in the regulations.

Sec. 36.30.645. WRITTEN DETERMINATIONS.

(a) The commissioner of administration or the commissioner of transportation and public facilities shall issue a written decision to debar or suspend. The decision must

(1) state the reasons for the action taken; and

(2) Inform the debarred person of rights to judicial appeal or inform the suspended person of rights to administrative and judicial appeal.

(b) A copy of the decision under (a) of this section shall be mailed or otherwise furnished immediately to the debarred or suspended person and any other intervening party.

Sec. 36.30.650. HEARING ON A SUSPENSION.

(a) A person suspended under AS 36.30.635 is entitled to a hearing conducted according to AS 36.30.670 and regulations adopted by the commissioner of administration if the person files a written request for a hearing with the commissioner of administration or the commissioner of transportation and public facilities, as appropriate, within seven days after receipt of the notice of suspension under AS 36.30.645.

(b) If a suspended person requests a hearing the commissioner of administration or the commissioner of transportation and public facilities, as appropriate, shall schedule a prompt hearing unless the attorney general determines that a hearing at the proposed time is likely to jeopardize an investigation. A hearing may not be delayed longer than six months after notice of the suspension is provided under AS 36.30.645.

Sec. 36.30.655. LIST OF PERSONS DEBARRED OR SUSPENDED.

The commissioner shall maintain a list of all persons debarred or suspended from consideration for award of contracts.

Sec. 36.30.660. REINSTATEMENT.

(a) The commissioner of administration or the commissioner of transportation and public facilities may at any time after a final decision to debar a person from consideration for award of contracts reinstate the person after determining that the cause for which the person was debarred no longer exists or has been substantially mitigated.

(b) A debarred person may request reinstatement by submitting a petition to the commissioner of administration or the commissioner of transportation and public facilities supported by evidence showing that the cause for debarment no longer exists or has been substantially mitigated.

(c) The commissioner of administration or the commissioner of transportation and public facilities may require a hearing on a reinstatement petition. A decision on reinstatement shall be made in writing within seven days after a reinstatement petition is submitted. The decision must specify the factors on which it is based. A decision under this section is not subject to judicial appeal.

Sec. 36.30.665. LIMITED PARTICIPATION.

The commissioner of administration or the commissioner of transportation and public facilities may permit a debarred person to participate in a contract on a limited basis during the debarment period if the commissioner determines in writing that the participation is advantageous to the state. The determination shall specify the factors on which it is based and the limits imposed on the debarred person.

Sec. 36.30.670. HEARING PROCEDURES.

(a) The commissioner of administration or the commissioner of transportation and public facilities shall act as a hearing officer or appoint a hearing officer for a hearing conducted under this chapter. The hearing officer shall arrange for a prompt hearing and notify the parties in writing of the time and place of the hearing. The hearing shall be conducted in an informal manner. The provisions of AS 44.62 (Administrative Procedure Act) do not apply to a hearing conducted under this chapter.

(b) The hearing officer may

(1) hold prehearing conferences to settle, simplify, or identify the issues in a proceeding, or to consider other matters that may aid in the expeditious disposition of the proceeding;

(2) require parties to state their positions concerning the various issues in the proceeding;

(3) require parties to produce for examination those relevant witnesses and documents under their control;

(4) rule on motions and other procedural matters;

(5) regulate the course of the hearing and conduct of the participants;

(6) establish time limits for submission of motions or memoranda;

(7) impose appropriate sanctions against a person who fails to obey an order of the hearing officer, including

(A) prohibiting the person from asserting or opposing designated claims or defenses or introducing designated matters into evidence;

(B) excluding all testimony of an unresponsive or evasive witness; and

(C) excluding a person from further participation in the hearing;

(8) take official notice of a material fact not appearing in evidence, if the fact is among the traditional matters subject to judicial notice;

(9) administer oaths or affirmations.

(c) A transcribed record of the hearing shall be made available at cost to a party that requests it.

Sec. 36.30.675. RECOMMENDATION BY THE HEARING OFFICER.

(a)   If the commissioner of administration or the commissioner of transportation and public facilities is not acting as hearing officer, the hearing officer shall recommend a decision to the commissioner based on the evidence presented. The recommendation must include findings of fact and conclusions of law.

(b)   The commissioner of administration or the commissioner of transportation and public facilities may affirm, modify, or reject the hearing officer's recommendation in whole or in part, may remand the matter to the hearing officer with instructions, or take other appropriate action.

Sec. 36.30.680. FINAL DECISION BY THE COMMISSIONER.

A decision by the commissioner of administration or the commissioner of transportation and public facilities after a hearing under this chapter is final. A decision shall be sent within 20 days after the hearing to all parties by personal service or certified mail, except that a decision by the commissioner of transportation and public facilities involving procurement of construction shall be sent within 90 days after the hearing to all parties by personal service or certified mail.

Sec. 36.30.685. JUDICIAL APPEAL.

(a)   A final decision of the commissioner of administration or the commissioner of transportation and public facilities under AS 36.30.610, 36.30.635(a), 36.30.650, or 36.30.680 may be appealed to the superior court in accordance with the Alaska Rules of Appellate Procedure.

(b)   A final decision of the commissioner of administration or the commissioner of transportation and public facilities under AS 36.30.630(b) may be appealed to the superior court for a trial de novo.

Sec. 36.30.687. MISREPRESENTATIONS AND FRAUDULENT CLAIMS.

(a)   A person who makes or uses in support of a contract claim under this chapter, a misrepresentation, or who practices or attempts to practice a fraud, at any stage of proceedings relating to a procurement or contract controversy under this chapter

    (1)   forfeits all claims relating to that procurement or contract; and

    (2)   is liable to the state for reimbursement of all sums paid on the claim, for all costs attributable to review of the claim, and for a civil penalty equal to the amount by which the claim is misrepresented.

(b)   The procurement officer, commissioner or court shall make specific findings of misrepresentation, attempted fraud, or fraud before declaring a forfeiture under (a) (1) of this section.

(c)   Suits to recover costs and penalties under (a) (2) of this section must be commenced within six years after the discovery of the misrepresentation, fraud, or attempted fraud.

(d) A person who in a matter relating to a procurement or a contract controversy or claim under this chapter makes a misrepresentation to the state through a trick, scheme, or device is guilty of a class C felony.

(e) In this section, "misrepresentation" means a false or misleading statement of material fact, or conduct intended to deceive or mislead concerning material fact, whether it succeeds in deceiving or misleading.

Sec. 36.30.690. EXCLUSIVE REMEDY.

Notwithstanding AS 44.77 or other law to the contrary, AS 36.30.560 - 36.30.699 and regulations adopted under those sections provide the exclusive procedure for asserting a claim against an agency arising in relation to a procurement under this chapter.

Sec. 36.30.695. OTHER RULES OF PROCEDURE.

The commissioner may adopt by regulation additional rules of procedure providing for the expeditious administrative review of all contract claims or controversies, both before the contracting agency and through an appeal heard de novo.

Sec. 36.30.699. DEFINITION.

In AS 36.30.560 - 36.30.695, "interested party" means an actual or prospective bidder or offeror whose economic interest may be affected substantially and directly by the issuance of a contract solicitation, the award of a contract, or the failure to award a contract; whether an actual or prospective bidder or offeror has an economic interest depends on the circumstances.

ARTICLE 10
INTERGOVERNMENTAL RELATIONS

Sec. 36.30.700. COOPERATIVE PURCHASING AUTHORIZED.

A public procurement unit may either participate in, sponsor, conduct, or administer a cooperative purchasing agreement for the procurement of supplies, services, professional services, or construction with one or more public procurement units or external procurement activities in accordance with an agreement entered into between the participants. Cooperative purchasing may include joint or multi-party contracts between public procurement units and open-ended state public procurement units contracts that are made available to local public procurement units.

Sec. 36.30.710. SALE, ACQUISITION, OR USE OF SUPPLIES BY A PUBLIC PROCUREMENT UNIT.

(a) A public procurement unit may sell to, acquire from, or use any supplies belonging to another public procurement unit or external procurement activity independent of the requirements of AS 36.30.060 and 36.30.100 - 36.30.260.

(b) A public procurement unit may enter into an agreement, independent of the requirements of AS 36.30.060 and 36.30.100 - 36.30.260, with another public procurement unit or external procurement activity for the cooperative use of supplies or services under the terms agreed upon between the parties.

Sec. 36.30.720. JOINT USE OF FACILITIES.

A public procurement unit may enter into agreements for the common use or lease of warehousing facilities, capital equipment, and other facilities with another public procurement unit or an external procurement activity under the terms agreed upon between the parties.

Sec. 36.30.730. SUPPLY OF PERSONNEL, INFORMATION, AND TECHNICAL SERVICES.

(a) A public procurement unit may, upon written request from another public procurement unit or external procurement activity, provide personnel to the requesting public procurement unit or external procurement activity. The public procurement unit or external procurement activity making the request shall pay the public procurement unit providing the personnel the direct and indirect cost of furnishing the personnel, in accordance with an agreement between the parties.

(b) The informational, technical, and other services of a public procurement unit may be made available to another public procurement unit or external procurement activity except that the requirements of the public procurement unit tendering the services has precedence over the requesting public procurement unit or external procurement activity. The requesting public procurement unit or external procurement activity shall pay for the expenses of the services so provided, in accordance with an agreement between the parties.

(c) Upon request, the commissioner may make available to public procurement units or external procurement activities the following services, among others:

(1) standard forms;

(2) printed manuals;

(3) product specifications and standards;

(4) quality assurance testing services and methods;

(5) qualified products lists;

(6) source information;

(7) common use commodities listings;

(8) supplier performance ratings;

(9) lists of persons debarred or suspended from consideration for award of state contracts;

(10) forms for invitations for bids, requests for proposals, instructions to bidders, general contract provisions, and other contract forms; and

(11) contracts or published summaries of them, including price and time of delivery information.

(d) The commissioner may provide the following technical services, among others:

(1) development of product specifications;

(2) development of quality assurance test methods, including receiving, inspection, and acceptance procedures;

(3) use of product testing and inspection facilities; and

(4) use of personnel training programs.

(e) The commissioner may enter into contractual arrangements and publish a schedule of fees for the services provided under (c) and (d) of this section.

(f) Repealed, Sec. 28 ch 90 SLA 1991.

Sec. 36.30.735. RESTRICTION ON CONTRACTING WITH OR EMPLOYING EXPERTS ON RADIATION HAZARDS.

(a) Except for the Department of Health and Social Services, the Department of Labor, the Department of Environmental Conservation, and the Department of Military and Veterans' Affairs, a state agency may not

(1) contract, other than with the Department of Health and Social Services, to have services performed that require expertise in determining or reducing the hazards of radiation; or

(2) employ a person whose duties require expertise in determining or reducing the hazards of radiation.

(b) In this section, "state agency"

(1) means a state department or agency, whether in the legislative, judicial, or executive branch;

(2) does not include the University of Alaska, a municipality, or an agency of a municipality.

(c) In this section, "radiation" does not include radiation emitted from a Federal Communications Commission licensed facility emitting radiation of a wave length longer than one centimeter and an average power output not exceeding two kilowatts.

Sec. 36.30.740. REVIEW OF PROCUREMENT REQUIREMENTS.

To the extent possible, the commissioner may collect information concerning the type, cost, quality, and quantity of commonly used supplies, equipment for the state fleet, services, or construction being procured or used by state public procurement units. The commissioner may also collect this information from local public procurement units. The commissioner may make this information available to a public procurement unit upon request.

Sec. 36.30.750. CONTRACT CONTROVERSIES.

(a) Under a cooperative purchasing agreement, controversies arising between an administering public procurement unit and its bidders, offerors, or contractors shall be resolved in accordance with AS 36.30.560 - 36.30.699.

(b) A local public procurement unit that is not subject to AS 36.30.560 - 36.30.699 may enter into an agreement with another local public procurement unit or external procurement activity to establish procedures or use that unit's or activity's existing procedures to resolve controversies with contractors, whether or not the controversy arose under a cooperative purchasing agreement.

Sec. 36.30.790. DEFINITIONS. In AS 36.30.700 - 36.30.790

(1) "cooperative purchasing" means procurement conducted by, or on behalf of, more than one public procurement unit, or by a public procurement unit with an external procurement activity;

(2) "external procurement activity" means a buying organization not located in this state that, if located in this state, would qualify as a public procurement unit; an agency of the United States is an external procurement activity;

(3) "local public procurement unit" means a municipality or other subdivision of the state or other entity that expends public funds for the procurement of supplies, services, professional services, and construction, and any nonprofit corporation operating a charitable hospital;

(4) "public procurement unit" means either a local public procurement unit or a state public procurement unit;

(5) "state public procurement unit" means the Department of Administration and any other contracting agency of the state.

ARTICLE 11
GENERAL PROVISIONS

Sec. 36.30.850. APPLICATION OF THIS CHAPTER.

(a) This chapter applies only to contracts solicited or entered into after January 1, 1988, unless the parties agree to its application to a contract solicited or entered into before that date.

(b) This chapter applies to every expenditure of state money by the state, acting through an agency, under a contract, except that this chapter does not apply to

(1) grants;

(2) contracts for professional witnesses to provide for professional services or testimony relating to existing or probable lawsuits in which the state is or may become a party;

(3) contracts of the University of Alaska where the work is to be performed substantially by students enrolled in the university;

(4) contracts for medical doctors and dentists;

(5) acquisitions or disposals of real property or interest in real property, except as provided in AS 36.30.080 and 36.30.085;

(6) disposals under AS 38.05;

(7) contracts for the preparation of ballots under AS 15.15.030;

(8) acquisitions or disposals of property and other contracts relating to airports under AS 02.15.070, 02.15.090, 02.15.091, and AS 44.88;

(9) disposals of obsolete property under AS 19.05.060;

(10) disposals of obsolete material or equipment under AS 35.20.060;

(11) agreements with providers of services under AS 44.47.250; AS 47.07; AS 47.08; AS 47.10; AS 47.17; AS 47.24; AS 47.25.195, and 47.25.310;

(12) contracts of the Department of Fish and Game for flights that involve specialized flying and piloting skills and are not point-to-point;

(13) purchases of income-producing assets for the state treasury or a public corporation of the state;

(14) operation of the state boarding school established under AS 14.16, if the State Board of Education or the commissioner of education adopts regulations for use by the state boarding school in procurement and contracting;

(15) a contract that is a delegation, in whole or in part, of investment powers held by the commissioner of revenue under AS 14.40.400, AS 14.42.200, 14.42.210, AS 18.56.095, AS 37.10.070, 37.10.071, or AS 37.14;

(16) a contract that is a delegation, in whole or in part, of investment powers or fiduciary duties

of the Board of Trustees of the Alaska Permanent Fund Corporation under AS 37.13;

(17) the purchase of books, book binding services, newspapers, periodicals, audio-visual materials, network information services access, approval plans, professional memberships, archival materials, objects of art, and items for museum or archival acquisition having cultural, historical, or archaeological significance; in this paragraph

> (A) "approval plans" means book selection services in which current book titles meeting an agency's customized specifications are provided to the agency subject to the right of the agency to return those books that do not meet with the agency's approval;

> (B) "archival materials" means the noncurrent records of an agency that are preserved after appraisal because of their value;

> (C) "audio-visual materials" means nonbook prerecorded materials, including records, tapes, slides, transparencies, films, filmstrips, cassettes, videos, compact discs, laser discs, and items that require the use of equipment to render them usable;

> (D) "network information services" means a group of resources from which cataloging information, holdings records, inter-library loans, acquisitions information, and other reference resources can be obtained;

(18) contracts for the purchase of standardized examinations for licensure under AS 08;

(19) Effective January 1, 1995. Contracts for home health care provided under regulations adopted by the Department of Health and Social Services and for adult residential care services provided under regulations adopted by the Department of Health and Social Services or by the Department of Administration;

(20) contracts for supplies or services for research projects funded by money received from the federal government or private grants;

(21) guest speakers or performers for an educational or cultural activity;

(22) contracts of the Alaska Industrial Development and Export Authority for a clean coal technology demonstration project that

> (A) is attempting to develop a coal-fired electric generation project;

> (B) uses technology that is capable of commercialization during the 1990's; and

> (C) qualifies for federal financial participation under P.L. 99-190 as amended;

(23) disposals of supplies acquired through foreclosure of loans issued under AS 03.10;

(24) purchases of curatorial and conservation services to maintain, preserve, and interpret

> (A) objects of art; and

> (B) items having cultural, historical, or archaeological significance to the state;

(25) acquisition of confidential seismic survey data necessary for pre-sale oil and gas lease analyses under AS 38.05.180;

(26) contracts for village public safety officers;

(27) purchases of supplies and services to support the operations of the Alaska state troopers or the division of fish and wildlife protection if the procurement officer for the Department of Public Safety makes a written determination that publicity of the purchases would jeopardize the safety of personnel or the success of a covert operation;

(28) expenditures when rates are set by law or ordinance;

(29) construction of new vessels by the Department of Transportation and Public Facilities for the Alaska marine highway system;

(30) contracts entered into with a regional development organization; in this paragraph, "regional development organization" has the meaning given in AS 44.33.026;

(31) contracts that are to be performed in an area outside of the country and that require a knowledge of the customs, procedures, rules, or laws of the area; or

(32) contracts that are between the Department of Law and attorneys who are not employed by the state and that are for the review or prosecution of possible violations of the criminal law of the state in situations where the attorney general concludes that an actual or potential conflict of interest makes it inappropriate for the Department of Law to review or prosecute the possible violations.

(c) Except for AS 36.30.085 and 36.30.700 - 36.30.790, this chapter does not apply to contracts between two or more agencies, the state and its political subdivisions, or the state and other governments.

(d) Nothing in this chapter or in regulations adopted under this chapter prevents an agency or political subdivision from complying with the terms and conditions of a grant, gift, bequest, cooperative agreement, or federal assistance agreement.

(e) Renumbered as AS 36.30.170(e) .

Sec. 36.30.860. SUPPLEMENTARY GENERAL PRINCIPLES OF LAW APPLICABLE.

Unless displaced by the particular provisions of this chapter, the principles of law and equity, including AS 45.01 - AS 45.09, AS 45.12, and 45.14 (Uniform Commercial Code), the law merchant, and law relative to capacity to contract, agency, fraud, misrepresentation, duress, coercion, mistake, or bankruptcy shall supplement the provisions of this chapter.

Sec. 36.30.870. ADOPTION OF REGULATIONS.

(a) Regulations under this chapter shall be adopted in accordance with AS 44.62

(Administrative Procedure Act).

(b) Regulations under this chapter applicable to procurements of construction or procurements for or disposal of property of the state equipment fleet shall be adopted by the commissioner of administration only after consultation with the commissioner of transportation and public facilities.

Sec. 36.30.880. REQUIREMENT OF GOOD FAITH.

All parties involved in the negotiation, performance, or administration of state contracts shall act in good faith.

Sec. 36.30.890. FEDERAL ASSISTANCE.

If a procurement involves the expenditure of federal funds or federal assistance and there is a conflict between a provision of this chapter or a regulation adopted under a provision of this chapter and a federal statute, regulation, policy, or requirement, the federal statute, regulation, policy, or requirement shall prevail.

Sec. 36.30.900. PRODUCT PREFERENCES.

This chapter does not modify AS 36.15.010 and 36.15.020 regarding preference for Alaska forest products, or AS 36.15.050 and 36.15.060 regarding preference for Alaska agricultural and fisheries products, except as provided in AS 36.30.170(b), (c), and (e) - (h), and 36.30.339.

Sec. 36.30.910. PURCHASES THROUGH GENERAL SERVICES ADMINISTRATION.

This chapter does not prevent purchasing through the general services administration as provided by law.

Sec. 36.30.920. REPORTING OF ANTICOMPETITIVE PRACTICES.

When for any reason collusion or other anticompetitive practices are suspected among bidders or offerors, a notice of the relevant facts shall be transmitted to the attorney general by the person who suspects the collusion or other anticompetitive practices.

Sec. 36.30.930. CIVIL AND CRIMINAL PENALTIES.

The following penalties apply to violations of this chapter:

(1) a person who contracts for or purchases supplies, equipment for the state fleet, services, professional services, or construction in a manner the person knows to be contrary to the requirements of

this chapter or the regulations adopted under this chapter is liable for all costs and damages to the state arising out of the violation;

(2) a person who intentionally or knowingly contracts for or purchases supplies, equipment for the state fleet, services, professional services, or construction under a scheme or artifice to avoid the requirements of this chapter is guilty of a class C felony.

Sec. 36.30.940. ENFORCEMENT.

The attorney general on behalf of the state shall enforce the provisions of this chapter.

Sec. 36.30.950. SEVERABILITY.

If any provision of this chapter or any application of this chapter to any person or circumstance is held invalid, the invalidity does not affect other provisions or applications of this chapter that can be given effect without the invalid provision or application, and to this end the provisions of this chapter are declared severable.

Sec. 36.30.990. DEFINITIONS.

In this chapter, unless the context in which a term is used clearly requires a different meaning or a different definition is prescribed for a particular provision,

(1) "agency"

(A) means a department, institution, board, commission, division, authority, public corporation, the Alaska Pioneers' Home, or other administrative unit of the executive branch of state government;

(B) does not include

(I) the University of Alaska;

(ii) the Alaska Railroad Corporation;

(iii) the Alaska Housing Finance Corporation;

(iv) a regional Native housing authority created under AS 18.55.996 or a regional electrical authority created under AS 18.57.020;

(v) the Department of Transportation and Public Facilities, in regard to the repair, maintenance, and reconstruction of vessels, docking facilities, and passenger and vehicle transfer facilities of the Alaska marine highway system;

(vi) the Alaska Aerospace Development Corporation;

(vii) the Alaska State Pension Investment Board;

(2) "change order" means a written order signed by the procurement officer, directing the contractor

to make changes that the changes clause of the contract authorizes the procurement officer to order without the consent of the contractor;

(3) "commissioner" means the commissioner of administration;

(4) "competitive sealed bidding" means the procedure under AS 36.30.100 - 36.30.190;

(5) "competitive sealed proposals" means the procedure under AS 36.30.200 - 36.30.260;

(6) "construction" means the process of building, altering, repairing, maintaining, improving, or demolishing a public highway, structure, building, or other public improvement of any kind to real property other than privately owned real property leased for the use of agencies; it includes services and professional services relating to planning and design required for the construction; it does not include the routine operation of a public improvement to real property nor does it include the construction of public housing;

(7) "contract" means all types of state agreements, regardless of what they may be called, for the procurement or disposal of supplies, equipment for the state fleet, services, professional services, or construction;

(8) "contract modification" means a written alteration in specifications, delivery point, rate of delivery, period of performance, price, quantity, or other provisions of a contract accomplished by mutual action of the parties to the contract;

(9) "department" means the Department of Administration;

(10) "employment program " means a nonprofit program to increase employment opportunities for individuals with physical or mental disabilities that constitute substantial handicaps to employment;

(11) "grant" means property furnished by the state, whether real or personal, designated by law, including an appropriation Act, as a grant;

(12) "lease-financing agreement" means a lease-purchase agreement that secures or is related to financing instruments of the lessor, including revenue bonds or certificates of participation;

(13) "lease-purchase agreement" means a lease that

(A) transfers ownership of the property to the lessee by the end of the lease term;

(B) contains a purchase option at a price less than the fair market value of the property on the date the option is exercisable;

(C) has a term, at inception, equal to 75 percent or more of the economic life of the property; or

(D) contains minimum lease payments, including minimum lease payments during a renewal provided for in the agreement, whose present value at the inception of the agreement equals 90 percent or more of the fair market value at the inception of the agreement of the real property that is the subject of the agreement; the present value shall be determined by using as a discount rate the most recent Bond Buyer 20-Bond G.O. Index;

(14) "person" means a business, individual, union, committee, club, other organization, or group of individuals;

(15) "procurement" means buying, purchasing, renting, leasing, or otherwise acquiring supplies, equipment for the state fleet, services, or construction; it also includes functions that pertain to the obtaining of a supply, equipment for the state fleet, service, or construction, including description of requirements, selection and solicitation of sources, preparation and award of contract, and all phases of contract administration;

(16) "procurement officer" means a person authorized to enter into and administer contracts for an agency and make written determinations with respect to them; it also includes an authorized representative of a procurement officer acting within the limits of authority;

(17) "professional services" means professional, technical, or consultant's services that are predominantly intellectual in character, result in the production of a report or the completion of a task, and include analysis, evaluation, prediction, planning, or recommendation;

(18) "public building" means improved real property leased to the state for governmental, public, or educational use, but does not include improved real property owned by the University of Alaska Heating Corporation and leased to the University of Alaska for a purpose within the scope, as of July 1, 1986, of the heating corporation's charter;

(19) "services" means the furnishing of labor, time, or effort by a contractor, not involving the delivery of a specific end product other than reports that are merely incidental to the required performance; it does not include employment agreements or collective bargaining agreements;

(20) "state money" means any money appropriated to an agency or spent by an agency irrespective of its source, including federal assistance except as otherwise specified in AS 36.30.890, but does not include money held in trust by an agency for a person;

(21) "supplies" means all property of an agency, including equipment, materials, and insurance; it includes privately owned real property leased for the use of agencies, such as office space, but does not include the acquisition or disposition of other interests in land.

Sec. 36.30.995. SHORT TITLE.

This chapter may be cited as the State Procurement Code.

Purchasing Policy — BC Systems Corp.

Policy: Invitation to Quote and Request For Proposal

BC Systems Corporation shall use competitive bidding wherever practical to ensure that all qualified bidders are afforded an equal opportunity to offer their goods and services. Lowest or any quotation will not necessarily be accepted.

Contracts and Purchasing Dept. will maintain a vendors list for all requirements. Vendors are encouraged to apply for registration. An Information Data Base will be developed for Managers or designates to review.

BEFORE YOU BEGIN, PLEASE REVIEW YOUR REQUIREMENTS WITH THE CONTRACTS AND PURCHASING DEPARTMENT. A Guide is available which contains useful information, ideas, examples and best practices.

All Invitations to Quote and Request For Proposals must be reviewed and processed by the Contracts and Purchasing Department to ensure fair, ethical business practice is maintained.

A sample RFP document is available in the Contracts and Purchasing Department to use as a guide to prepare new Request For Proposals. The environment of equity provided by the Corporation is accomplished through two main purchasing processes, the formal REQUEST FOR PROPOSAL process and the INVITATION TO QUOTE process. The Corporation also uses the Request For Information process as a fact gathering activity when a need to test the marketplace without making a purchase commitment exists.

Invitation to Quote

Contracts and Purchasing Staff will obtain final confirmation of all quotes and prices when a purchase requisition is issued and before a purchase order commitment is made.

The following guideline will be followed whenever practical:

Through an informal Invitation to Quote process, quotations will be obtained from the market place for a given product or service through direct communication with a minimum of three vendors. Vendors are asked via telephone, facsimile, or ITQ Form to provide quotes on low risk procurements where the dollar value is the main determining factor.

- estimated expenditure up to $25,0000 requires one vendor.

- estimated expenditure from $25,000 to $100,000 requires three vendors.

- formal quotations will be obtained for commodity hardware within the approved levels of the signing authority.

While these are the mandatory expense guidelines, either process can be used at expense levels lower than these. Use prudence when initiating a purchase. If the possibility for real conflict exists, use one of these processes even if not required.

Request for Proposal (RFP)

All RFPs which are in excess of $100,000 must be released to vendors in DRAFT format prior to the formal release of the RFP. The purpose of this is to have the market place comment on and addresses any concerns about the actions being taken by the Corporation before they are required to make a formal proposal. Estimated expenditure over $100,000 requires a minimum of five vendors.

Note: Contracts and Purchasing Department requires three to five days for RFP administration and mailing.

AN RFP IS NOT REQUIRED WHEN:

- The expenditure is under $100,000.

- There is a proven sole source of supply.

- Changes to an existing License or Service Agreement are required.

- For release/version upgrades to products.

- For extensions to existing contacts (provided the extension is not issued when a new contract should be done.)

- If Lease price is less than $35,000 per year.

- If an approved procurement agreement has been established from an earlier RFP process by ourselves or our customers.

- Goods or Services are covered by a standing offer by the Purchasing Commission.

- A similar requirement has been submitted to tender within the past six (6) months and the same terms and conditions are applicable.

- Emergency Purchases (if approved by Contract Manager).

- Approval by Vice President or president within signing authority.

THE FOLLOWING INFORMATION MUST BE PROVIDED TO THE VENDOR FOR "INVITATION TO QUOTE" AND "REQUEST FOR PROPOSALS":

- What we require or purpose and scope of proposal

- Unit or lot pricing

- Terms and conditions

- Contact for inquiries

- Selection criteria

- Firm pricing

- Currency and taxes

- When delivery/completion date is required

- Closing date and time

- How and when the bid or quote is to be submitted

- Indicate name and address for delivery

VENDORS ARE NOTIFIED ABOUT KEY TERMS AND CONDITIONS:

When issuing a Request for Proposal document or an Invitation to Quote form, the following terms and conditions are covered:

Note: *LOWEST OR ANY QUOTATION WILL NOT NECESSARILY BE ACCEPTED.*

- BC Systems is not responsible for any costs incurred in the preparation and presentation of the proposal

- Price Validation will be ensured by confirming that the evaluation committee has completed a price analysis/comparison, when price analysis cannot be performed, a cost analysis/examination of elemental cost data is to be completed.

- Quotations as first received are considered final. If an error has been made, another quotation sheet Form may be forwarded to a supplier on request up to date of closing.

- BC Systems reserves the right to award this order in part of in full, on the basis of quotation received, unless the supplier specifies that its quotation is valid only for the complete order.

- No charge for crating, boxing or cartage will be allowed on an invoice unless previously accepted with the quotation.

- The Manager of Contracts and Purchasing is responsible for communicating the awarding and the results of all Requests for Proposals and Invitations to Quote issued by the contracts department.

- When quotations have been received and an award made, the successful bidder will be held to their quotation, irrespective of subsequent representation that mistakes have been made in the quotations originally submitted.

- If it appears that an error has been made in the quotations before awarding of order, Contracts and Purchasing may communicate with the bidder to ascertain if the bidding company wishes to confirm price or withdraw quotations. Freight must not be shown in a lump sum.

- The G.S.T. Certification Clause is provided in the RFP and ITQ documents.

- BC Systems payment terms are to be brought to the Vendors attention.

- When the award has been made and the Purchase Order has been sent, the Vendor is to be aware that the PO may be cancelled if the products, services, facilities do not meet mutually agreeable acceptance tests.

RFP - Advice to Unsuccessful Bidders and Debriefing

- The Manager of Contracts and Purchasing is responsible to notify unsuccessful bidders following award of all RFPs and ITQs issued by the Contracts and Purchasing Department.

- Upon written request from an unsuccessful bidder, the Manger of Contracts and Purchasing will arrange for a debriefing session. The debriefing is not to be seen as an opportunity to challenge the decision.

- Debriefing sessions will be chaired by the Manager, Contracts and Purchasing or by a Vice President or President, one or two members of the evaluation committee will also attend.

- Debriefing meetings are treated as an exchange of information, vendors are permitted to take notes. The intent of the debriefing is to aid the vendor in presenting a better proposal in subsequent RFPs. The response of the unsuccessful vendor will be compared to the successful response only.

- Any request for information from vendors which does not relate directly to their own submission is to be directed to the Corporation's Freedom of Information Officer and is subject to the policies of that office.

Disqualification

- Responses that fail to meet mandatory requirements specified in tender will be disqualified.

- Responses received after the closing time and date will be disqualified.

- Responses which the Corporation considers contain other than normal ethical business practices will be disqualified.

DOCUMENT 4

Contracting Regulations and Contracting Directive, Yukon

Government of Yukon

CONTRACT REGULATIONS
and
CONTRACTING DIRECTIVE

This is an office consolidation of the Government of Yukon
Contract Regulations and Contracting Directive.

This text is published solely as a convenience and is not an authoritative
text of which judicial notice must be taken.

March 20, 1995

CONTENTS

CONTRACT REGULATIONS

PART I - INTERPRETATION

Definitions

1.   The following definitions apply in these regulations.

Bid - An offer, submitted in response to a request for bids, to supply goods or services or to purchase assets at a specific price or price formula, under stated terms and conditions.

Bidder - A person, partnership or corporation who submits a bid.

Contract - An agreement between a contracting authority and a contractor to provide a good, perform a service, construct a public work, or to lease real property, for consideration.

Contracting authority - Any government body or government employee having authority pursuant to the Financial Administration Act to enter into a contract on behalf of the Government of the Yukon.

Contractor - Any person, partnership or corporation which supplies goods or services or constructs a public work under a contract with the government.

Contribution agreement - An agreement between a donor and a recipient of a contribution which describes the obligations of each party and the conditions of payment.

Department - A department as defined in the Financial Administration Act.

Employment contract - A contract of service which establishes an employer - employee relationship.

Evaluation criteria - Criteria against which proposals are evaluated for purposes of determining:

a)   which proposals qualify for consideration; and

b)   how to rank valid proposals.

The selection of the successful proposal is based on factors which may include the effectiveness of the proposed solution, and the experience, qualifications, and financial capabilities of the proponents, rather than on price alone.

Goods contract - A contract for the purchase of articles, commodities, equipment, goods, materials or supplies, which may include installation.

Open source list - A list of persons, partnerships and/or companies which have indicated their willingness to respond to requests for bids or proposals.

Price-driven contract - A contract entered into as the result of a bid.

Proposal - An offer, either unsolicited or in response to a request for proposals, to propose a solution to a problem, need or objective, under stated terms and conditions, or to establish a qualified source list.

Proponent - A person, partnership or corporation who submits a proposal.

Public work - A project involving the expenditure of public funds for building construction, heavy construction or road, sewer or water main construction as specifically defined in the request for bids or proposals for the project.

Request for bids - A document defining the minimum standards to be met by bidders and the requirements of the contract so as to permit the evaluation of bids on the basis of price.

Request for proposals - A document inviting suppliers to propose a solution to a problem, need or objective.

Standing offer agreement - A method of supply used to provide direct access to sources of supply for goods and/or services, on an as-required basis, for specific periods of time, at prearranged prices and delivery conditions.

Subcontractor - A corporation, partnership or individual who has been awarded a contract by a contractor of the government and under that contract supplies goods or services or performs work on a public work for which the contractor was engaged.

Value-driven contract - A contract entered into as the result of a proposal.

PART II - GENERAL

Objectives

2.   The objectives of government contracting policy are to ensure that government contracting activities are carried out in a fair, fiscally responsible, accountable, open and competitive manner.

Scope

3.   These regulations apply to all contracts except:

(a)   employment contracts;

(b)   contracts relating to projects funded by the Government of the Yukon and carried out by another party under a contribution agreement for its own use; and

(c)   contracts for the practice of law as defined in the Legal Professions Act.

Application

4.

(1) Subject to the terms of any agreement between the Government of the Yukon and the Government of Canada, these regulations apply to projects carried out by the Government of the Yukon on behalf of the Government of Canada.

(2) These regulations apply to all departments which have deputy heads as defined in the Public Service Act.

PART III - PRINCIPLES

Access to policy documents and related materials

5. Reasonable access must be provided to government policy documents and related contracting materials upon request. Materials available for distribution are to be supplied in a non-discriminatory manner, and any fees charged for such distribution are to be reasonable.

Opportunity to compete for government contracts

6. Prospective bidders and proponents must be registered on open source lists on request.

7. Prospective bidders and proponents must be given copies of requests for bids or proposals upon request.

8. Contracting authorities must encourage competition for contracts, but must respect the following:

(1) There must be specific criteria for sole sourcing contracts, and specific sourcing thresholds to determine the level of competition for price-driven contracts, value-driven contracts and goods contracts.

(2) Contracting activities must be carried out in full compliance with all applicable Yukon land claims agreements.

(3) Contracting authorities must make best efforts to contract for goods and services in the community in which they are used, to the extent that doing so reasonably conforms to the objectives of these regulations, and to the extent that their needs can be met by community-based businesses.

9. Contracting authorities must not use standards, specifications, evaluation criteria, time limits to respond to requests for bids or proposals, standing offer agreements, contribution agreements, source lists, or other means to unfairly limit competition.

Open evaluation of bids and proposals

10. Evaluation criteria and standards used to evaluate bids and proposals must be fully and clearly described in requests for bids or proposals, and only those evaluation criteria and standards must be used to evaluate bids or proposals received.

11. Subject to the Access to Information Act, bidders and proponents must, upon request, be given access to information about their own bids or proposals and how these were evaluated, within a reasonable

time after the procurement competition.

Bid challenge mechanism

12. There must be a formal bid challenge mechanism, based on the following terms of reference:

(a) Bidders and proponents must be given a reasonable opportunity to register complaints.

(b) Complainants must have a responsibility to make all reasonable attempts to settle their disputes with the applicable contracting authority.

(c) There must be an opportunity for redress, including compensation for costs of complaining and bid/proposal preparation costs.

(d) A mechanism to change, where warranted, government contracting policies and procedures will be provided.

PART IV - FINANCIAL PROTECTION FOR SUBCONTRACTORS

Application

13. This part applies only to contracts for a public work.

Claim by unpaid subcontractors

14.

(1) The Deputy Head, Government Services or delegate must receive a claim for unpaid labour, material, equipment, or services, filed by a subcontractor on a contract for a public work, who has not been paid by the contractor for labour, material, equipment, or services rendered to the contractor for that contract.

(2) The Deputy Head, Government Services, or delegate shall process a claim pursuant to subsection (1) provided the claim is made after the payment for the labour, material, equipment, or services under his or her contract with the contractor becomes due, but not later than 90 days following the performance of the labour or services or the provision of the material or equipment, as the case may be, by the subcontractor.

Processing of claim

15.

(1) The Deputy Head, Government Services, or delegate must notify the contractor and contracting authority of the claim.

(2) The contracting authority must retain from monies remaining to be paid to the contractor on

the contract a sum equal to the amount of the claim.

(3) If the subcontractor and contractor have not reached settlement within 30 days of the receipt of notice of the claim by the contracting authority, the contracting authority must transfer the amount retained to the Deputy Head, Justice, or delegate, for disposition.

Discharge of obligation

16.

(1) Payment by the Government of the Yukon into a trust account or to the Supreme Court of Yukon is sufficient discharge by the government of any obligation it may have to pay the money to the contractor.

(2) The Government of the Yukon has no liability to the contractor or to the subcontractor if payment pursuant to section is in an amount greater or less than the amount lawfully payable by the contractor to the subcontractor.

CONTRACTING DIRECTIVE

PART I - INTERPRETATION

Definitions

1. The following definitions apply in this directive.

Award of contract or standing offer agreement - Refers to the decision to award the contract or the standing offer agreement to the selected bidder or proponent.

Bid - An offer, submitted in response to a request for bids, to supply goods or services or to purchase assets at a specific price or price formula, under stated terms and conditions.

Bidder - A person, partnership or corporation who submits a bid.

Bid security - Security given by a bidder or proponent to guarantee entry into a contract.

Change order - A document issued by the contracting authority to change a contract.

Closing time - The time and date on which bids or proposals must be received at the designated place.

Contract - An agreement between a contracting authority and a contractor to provide a good, perform a service, construct a public work, or to lease real property, for consideration.

Contracting authority - Any government body or government employee having authority pursuant to the Financial Administration Act to enter into a contract on behalf of the Government of the Yukon.

Contractor - Any person, partnership or corporation which supplies goods or services or constructs a public work under a contract with the government.

Contract price - The price or price formula stipulated in a contract.

Contract security - A deposit of securities by the contractor which the contracting authority may convert to carry out the contractor's obligations under the contract.

Contribution agreement - An agreement between a donor and a recipient of a contribution which describes the obligations of each party and the conditions of payment.

Crown Corporation - Yukon Housing Corporation, Yukon Liquor Corporation, Workers' Compensation Health and Safety Board, Yukon Development Corporation, and Yukon Lotteries Commission.

Department - A department as defined in the Financial Administration Act.

Employment contract - A contract of service which establishes an employer - employee relationship.

Estimated contract value - The total estimated value of the contract or standing offer agreement prior to issuing the request for bids or proposals.

Evaluation criteria - Criteria against which proposals are evaluated for purposes of determining:

a) which proposals qualify for consideration; and

b) how to rank valid proposals.

The selection of the successful proposal is based on factors which may include the effectiveness of the proposed solution, and the experience, qualifications, and financial capabilities of the proponents, rather than on price alone.

Expression of interest - A publicly advertised invitation to respond with identification and qualifications, to a particular category of work or anticipated project, for the establishment of a specific source list category.

Goods contract - A contract for the purchase of articles, commodities, equipment, goods, materials or supplies, which may include installation.

Invitational tender - A request for bids or proposals on a contract or standing offer agreement given to a number of identified bidders or proponents.

Open source list - A list of persons, partnerships and/or companies which have indicated their willingness to respond to requests for bids or proposals.

Price-driven contract - A contract entered into as the result of a bid.

Proposal - An offer, either unsolicited or in response to a request for proposals, to propose a solution to a problem, need or objective, under stated terms and conditions, or to establish a qualified source list.

Proponent - A person, partnership or corporation who submits a proposal.

Public tender - A request for bids or proposals made by public advertisement.

Public work - A project involving the expenditure of public funds for building construction, heavy construction or road, sewer or water main construction as specifically defined in the request for bids or proposals for the project.

Qualified source list - A list of bidders or proponents who meet the evaluation criteria specified for the award of a proposed contract.

Real property lease - A lease or agreement whereby the Government of the Yukon acquires a leasehold interest in or a licence to occupy real property.

Rejection of bid or proposal - The determination that a bid or proposal will not be evaluated on the basis that it does not meet the requirements specified in the request for bids or proposals.

Request for bids - A document defining the requirements of the contract and the minimum standards to be met by bidders so as to permit the evaluation of bids on the basis of price.

Request for proposals - A document inviting a supplier(s) to propose a solution to a problem, need or objective.

Standing offer agreement - A method of supply used to provide direct access to sources of supply for goods and/or services, on an as-required basis, for specific periods of time, at prearranged prices and delivery conditions.

Subcontractor - A corporation, partnership or individual who has been awarded a contract by a contractor of the government and under that contract supplies goods or services or performs work on a public work for which the contractor was engaged.

Unit price - A method of pricing in which the total amount payable is calculated by multiplying the number of identical units of work or items delivered by a fixed price per unit or item.

Utility - A corporation which provides electrical, water, telecommunications, municipal services, or transportation services to the public.

Valid bid or proposal - A bid or proposal which has not been rejected for failing to meet the requirements set out in the request for bids or proposals.

Value-driven contract - A contract entered into as the result of a proposal.

PART II - GENERAL

Objectives

2.   This document, in conjunction with the Contract Regulations, expresses the policy of the Government of the Yukon on the process by which the government will select contractors to supply goods and services. The objectives of this directive are to ensure that government contracting activities are carried out in a fair, fiscally responsible, accountable, open and competitive manner.

Authority

3. This directive was reviewed and approved as a Management Board Directive by Management Board on March 2, 1995 by M.B.M. #95-05-02, and can be revised only with the approval of Management Board.

Scope

4. This directive applies to all contracts except:

(a) employment contracts;

(b) contracts relating to projects funded by the Government of the Yukon and carried out by another party under a contribution agreement for its own use; and

(c) contracts for the practice of law as defined in the Legal Professions Act

Application

5. Subject to the terms of any agreement between the Government of the Yukon and the Government of Canada, this directive applies to projects carried out by the Government of the Yukon on behalf of the Government of Canada.

6.

(1) Subject to subsection (2), this directive applies to all departments which have deputy heads as defined in the Public Service Act.

(2) Where a crown corporation adopts a contracting bylaw which adheres to the Contract Regulations and is substantially consistent with this directive, and where Management Board so approves, that bylaw will apply in place of this directive.

Contracts of employment not authorized

7. Nothing in this directive authorizes the appointment or employment of any person as an employee of the government.

Overpayment not authorized

8. Nothing in this directive authorizes the making of a payment in excess of the amount payable under the terms of the contract.

Incentives

9. Nothing in this directive prohibits a contracting authority from offering incentives to prospective bidders or proponents, provided that:

(a) the availability of such incentives is clearly identified in the request for bids or proposals; and

(b) the incentives do not arbitrarily or unnecessarily limit the number of bidders or proponents.

Deemed delivery

10. Notification of any matter pursuant to this directive will be deemed to be delivered at the time transmitted by facsimile, or at the time delivered to a courier, or at the time delivered to Canada Post, as the case may be.

Contracts and standing offer agreements in excess of three years

11.

(1) No contract or standing offer agreement will be entered into without the approval of Management Board if the contract or standing offer agreement contains:

    (a) a stated initial term in excess of three (3) years; or

    (b) a stated initial term of three (3) years or less, but containing provision for renewal so that the aggregate of the initial term and the renewals may exceed three (3) years; or

    (c) a probable time of performance in excess of three (3) years.

(2) Contracts or standing offer agreements entered into pursuant to subsection (1) will be identified in the contract registry(ies) maintained pursuant to section .

Tendering forecast

12.

(1) Contracting authorities will, before the end of each fiscal year quarter, provide to the Deputy Head, Government Services, or delegate a listing of contracts and standing offer agreements in excess of $50,000, or in the case of goods contracts, in excess of $25,000, contemplated to be awarded in the following quarter.

(2) Where a department acquires goods or services through a contracting authority outside the department, the department will provide the required information to the Deputy Head, Government Services, or delegate.

(3) The Deputy Head, Government Services, or delegate will make available to the public the information provided by contracting authorities in subsections (1) and (2).

Community contracting

13.

(1) Contracting authorities, when contracting for goods and services for use in the communities, will

make best efforts to support community-based businesses within the context of existing contracting policy by:

(a) ensuring that community-based businesses have the opportunity to submit bids or proposals on contracts, and that they are competing on an equitable basis with contractors from outside the community,

(b) putting community-related contracting decisions into the hands of community-based employees, to the maximum extent possible,

(c) developing communications channels with local business organizations and contractors that will enable them to anticipate government needs in the community, and to develop their businesses to meet those needs, and

(d) taking into account the full cost of contracting outside the community when the goods and services are to be utilized within the community.

PART III - COMPETITIVE BIDDING REQUIREMENTS

Request for bids or proposals required

14. Except as provided in section , the contracting authority will invite bids or proposals in accordance with this directive prior to entering into any contract or standing offer agreement.

Issuing a request for bids or proposals package where other parties have been invited to submit bids or proposals

15. Except for bids or proposals requested pursuant to section , upon request, the contracting authority will, without delay, issue a request for bids or proposals to any prospective bidder or proponent.

Sourcing thresholds

16.

(1) For price-driven contracts:

(a) Below $10,000 estimated contract value, contracting authorities may enter into a contract or standing offer agreement directly with a bidder.

(b) Between $10,000 and $50,000, contracting authorities will either invite bids from three sources (or fewer if three sources can not be identified), or issue publicly advertised requests for bids.

(c) Above $50,000, contracting authorities will issue publicly advertised requests for bids, or invite bids from all sources on an open source list.

(2) For value-driven contracts:

(a) Below $25,000 estimated contract value, contracting authorities may enter into a contract or standing offer agreement directly with a proponent.

(b) Between $25,000 and $50,000, contracting authorities will either invite proposals from three sources (or fewer if three sources can not be identified), or issue publicly advertised requests for proposals.

(c) Above $50,000, contracting authorities will issue publicly advertised requests for proposals, or invite proposals from all sources on an open source list.

(3) For goods procurement:

(a) Below $10,000 estimated contract value, contracting authorities may enter into a contract or standing offer agreement directly with a bidder or proponent.

(b) Between $10,000 and $25,000, contracting authorities will either invite bids or proposals from three sources (or fewer if three sources can not be identified), or issue publicly advertised requests for bids or proposals.

(c) Above $25,000, contracting authorities will issue publicly advertised requests for bids or proposals, or invite bids or proposals from all sources on an open source list.

When request for bids or proposals not required

17. The contracting authority may enter into a contract or standing offer agreement directly with a bidder or proponent:

(a) as provided in paragraphs 16 (1)a, 16(2)a, and 16(3)a;

(b) in the event of an emergency as defined in the Civil Emergency Measures Act or its regulations;

(c) where immediate action is required to prevent or respond to injury or death to persons or animals or livestock, or damage to property;

(d) where the contract is to extend the existing occupancy of substantially the same real property leased by the contracting authority;

(e) for an agreement with a utility for work on the utility's facilities;

(f) in special cases authorized by the Minister of the contracting authority;

(g) where the contract relates to the protection of exclusive rights, such as patents, or where the existing equipment compels the contracting authority to purchase specific equipment from a specific supplier for reasons of compatibility; or

(h) where the contract will be awarded pursuant to a standing offer agreement entered into pursuant to this directive.

Publicly advertised requests for bids or proposals through Deputy Head, Government Services, or delegate

18. Publicly advertised requests for bids or proposals for the supply of goods and services and

responses to these solicitations will be issued and received by the Deputy Head, Government Services, or delegate.

Effect of bids higher than estimated contract value

19. Subject to section 20, where all bids or proposals submitted in response to a request for bids or proposals are higher than the estimated contract value, the request for bids or proposals will not necessarily be invalidated for this reason.

20.

(1) Except in the case of a goods contract, the contracting authority will not award a contract in excess of $55,000 where the bids or proposals were solicited by inviting only a limited number of sources on an open source list.

(2) In the case of a goods contract, the contracting authority will not award a contract in excess of $27,500 where the bids or proposals were solicited by inviting only a limited number of sources on an open source list.

(3) In the event that all valid bids or proposals received in response to an invitational request for bids or proposals are in excess of the dollar limits specified in subsections (1) and (2), the contracting authority will cancel the request for bids or proposals and may only reissue the request for bids or proposals by issuing a publicly advertised request for bids or proposals, or by inviting all sources on an open source list.

Non-disclosure of estimated contract value

21. Subject to subsection 66(1), the contracting authority may refuse to disclose the estimated contract value.

Open source lists

22.

(1) A contracting authority may maintain any number of open source lists for use in implementing the provisions of this directive.

(2) Where contracting authorities create new open or qualified source lists, or add to or delete names from open source lists, they will immediately inform the Deputy Head, Government Services, or delegate.

23. A contracting authority will define the scope of each open source list in terms of types of goods and services, and will use the open source list only for requests for bids or proposals within the defined scope.

24. The Deputy Head, Government Services, or delegate will issue public invitations to register on open source lists in April and October each year and at other times at the request of contracting authorities.

25. The Deputy Head, Government Services, or delegate will establish, maintain and make available a current register of all open and qualified source lists.

26. Upon request, the name of a prospective bidder or proponent will be added to open source lists at any time.

27. Subject to section 15 , a contracting authority may decide the method by which names are selected from the open source list for any given request for bids or proposals.

28. Contracting authorities may remove from open source lists the names of prospective bidders and proponents who, within the 12 month period immediately preceding, have not responded to a publicly advertised invitation to confirm or renew their listing on the open source list.

Prequalifying bidders or proponents

29.

(1) Where a contracting authority pre-qualifies bidders or proponents before issuing a request for bids or proposals for a contract, it will establish a qualified source list pursuant to this directive, which will be valid for up to one year.

(2) The contracting authority will define the scope of each qualified source list in terms of the specific contracts which are contemplated.

30.

(1) A contracting authority will publicly advertise for bidders or proponents to submit their qualifications for qualified source lists.

(2) Such requests for submission of qualifications will be considered to be requests for proposals as defined by this directive and will be conducted pursuant to this directive.

31. Responses to requests for proposals issued pursuant to section will be considered proposals as defined by this directive, and will be evaluated accordingly.

32. A contracting authority will not add the name of a bidder or proponent to qualified source lists except through the evaluation and acceptance of the proponent's qualifications submitted in response to the request for bids or proposals.

33. All available bidders or proponents on a qualified source list will be invited to submit bids or proposals for the specific contract or contracts for which they were pre-qualified.

Standing offer agreements

34. Contracting authorities who are authorized to enter into contracts for goods and services, may create, maintain and use standing offer agreements in accordance with this directive.

Discussion of request for bids or proposals

35. No information released by the contracting authority to one bidder or proponent may be withheld from another bidder or proponent.

Contract registry

36.

(1) The Deputy Head, Government Services, or delegate, will maintain a registry(ies) of all contracts, contract change orders and standing offer agreements.

(2) The registry(ies) maintained pursuant to subsection (1) will be public document(s).

Contracting information for Yukon First Nations

37. Based upon the obligations of the Government of the Yukon arising out of the Umbrella Final Agreement, the Deputy Head, Government Services, or delegate will:

(a) Upon request, provide to Yukon First Nations and First Nations corporations information on:

   (i) how to compete for contracts and standing offer agreements; and

   (ii) how to register on open source lists and submit proposals for qualified source lists.

(b) Inform all Yukon First Nations of invitations to register on open source lists issued under section

(c) Notify Yukon First Nations which have indicated the wish to be so advised of all publicly advertised requests for bids or proposals related to contracts, standing offer agreements, and prequalification of bidders or proponents.

(d) Inform Yukon First Nations on a regular basis of contracts awarded in excess of $50,000, or in the case of contracts for goods, in excess of $25,000, in the First Nations' traditional territories for which requests for bids or proposals were not publicly advertised.

38. Where a contracting authority invites bids or proposals from a limited number of prospective bidders or proponents pursuant to paragraphs 16(1)(b), 16(2)(b), and 16(3)(b), the contracting authority will give notice of the invitation to all Yukon First Nations which have registered on open source lists maintained under this directive.

PART IV - THE COMPETITIVE BIDDING PROCESS

Request for bids or proposals inclusive

39. All terms and conditions of the request for bids or proposals must be stated in the request for bids or proposals.

Information in request for bids or proposals

40. A request for bids or proposals will include the following information:

(a) the essential terms of the contract(s) or standing offer agreement(s) to be awarded, including:

    (i) a full description of the goods or services to be delivered, including estimated quantities where applicable;

    (ii) the form, amount, and terms and conditions of any required performance security, or any performance penalty permitted by law, if any;

    (iii) the completion date or any other timing considerations which are to be terms of the contract(s) or standing offer agreement(s);

    (iv) other terms and conditions which would be relevant in setting a price for the goods or services; and

    (v) indication that the request for bids or proposals is for a qualified source list, or a standing offer agreement, if this is the case.

(b) terms and conditions for the submission of bids or proposals, including:

    (i) the form in which bids or proposals are to be submitted;

    (ii) the information required to be provided in the bid or proposal;

    (iii) the place to which bids or proposals must be submitted; and

    (iv) the closing time.

(c) a full description of the manner in which bids or proposals will be evaluated, including:

    (i) the method to be used to evaluate bids or proposals;

    (ii) the evaluation criteria, stated in such a manner as to clearly identify all the information to be provided by the bidder or proponent which will be used to evaluate the bid or proposal; and

    (iii) in the case of proposals, the weighting assigned to each evaluation criterion.

(d) the tax-exempt status of the Government of the Yukon under the Goods and Services Tax (GST);

(e) a provision that bids or proposals do not contain an amount for the GST;

(f) the name and title of the designated contact person; and

(g) in the case of publicly advertised requests for bids or proposals, the time and place of tender opening.

Content of public notice

41. When public notice of a request for bids or proposals is given, the public notice need not contain the full request for bids or proposals, but must state where prospective bidders or proponents may pick up the full request for bids or proposals.

Form of evaluation criteria

42.

(1) Evaluation criteria will take the form of one or both:

    (a) minimum standards to be met;

    (b) ranking criteria.

(2) Where ranking criteria are used, they may include:

    (a) the experience of the bidder or proponent with similar contracts or standing offer agreements;

    (b) knowledge of local technical conditions and culture;

    (c) the dollar amount of the bid or proposal submitted;

    (d) the qualifications of the bidder or proponent for the contract or standing offer agreement;

    (e) the means proposed by the bidder or proponent to carry out the contract or standing offer agreement;

    (f) the schedule proposed by the bidder or proponent; or

    (g) any other criteria relevant to the particular request for proposals.

Use of specific product trade names

43. Requests for bids or proposals may refer to specific product trade names/brands only to establish a standard of performance expected, except where the requirement for a specific product has been explicitly justified, in which case the request for bids or proposals will clearly stipulate the requirement for the product.

Availability of requests for bids or proposals

44. The contracting authority will use its best effort to make requests for bids or proposals, or addenda to requests for bids or proposals, available to all bidders or proponents at the same time.

Opening of bids or proposals

45. Where the value of the contract or standing offer agreement is estimated at $50,000 or greater, or in the case of a goods contract is estimated at $25,000 or greater, or the request for bids or proposals was publicly advertised, then:

    (a) all bids or proposals will be opened at a designated time and place in the presence of at least one witness;

    (b) anyone who wishes to be present at the bid or proposal opening will be permitted to attend; and

    (c) upon opening each bid or proposal, the following will be recorded in a written log and announced to those present:

(i)   the name of the bidder or proponent;

(ii)   the amount and form of bid security provided with the bid or proposal, if applicable; and

(iii)   in the case of a bid, the amount of the bid, where practicable.

Late bids or proposals

46.

(1)   The contracting authority will reject any bids or proposals received after the closing time.

(2)   Late bids or proposals will be returned to the bidder or proponent.   In the case of sealed bids or proposals, they will be returned unopened.

Rejection of timely bids or proposals

47.   The contracting authority may reject a bid or proposal which has been received prior to the closing time only where:

(a)   it is not submitted in the required form;

(b)   there are significant omissions of required information;

(c)   a bid or proposal is not signed as required in the request for bids or proposals;

(d)   the required bid security in the required form is not provided;

(e)   the bid or proposal has conditions attached which are not authorized by the request for bids or proposals;

(f)   the bid or proposal fails to meet one or more standards specified in the request for bids or proposals; or

(g)   there is substantial evidence that, pursuant to the evaluation criteria contained in the request for bids or proposals, a bidder or proponent would be unable to carry out the contract as specified.

Notice of rejection

48.

(1)   Where a contracting authority rejects a bid or proposal, the contracting authority will notify the bidder or proponent, by the quickest means available, that the bid or proposal was rejected. In the case of a written bid or proposal, this will be confirmed in writing.

(2)   The contracting authority will, upon request, provide to rejected bidders or proponents a full explanation why their bid or proposal has been rejected.

Two stage evaluations of proposals

49.   When evaluating proposals, contracting authorities will evaluate and score non-price factors before

taking price into account.

Contracting authority to rank bids or proposals

50. The contracting authority will evaluate and rank bids or proposals not rejected pursuant to sections or solely on the basis of the evaluation criteria and requirements contained in the request for bids or proposals.

Award of contract or standing offer agreement

51.

(1) Subject to subsection (3), when a single contract or standing offer agreement is awarded, it will be awarded to the bidder who submitted the lowest bid or to the proponent who submitted the highest ranking proposal.

(2) Subject to subsection (3), where more than one contract or standing offer agreement is awarded pursuant to a request for bids or proposals, they will be awarded to:

> (a) bidders in the sequence in which their bids were received, from lowest price bid to highest, or

> (b) proponents in the sequence in which their proposals were ranked, from highest to lowest.

(3) Only Management Board may authorize bypassing the lowest price bid or the highest ranking proposal.

Placement on qualified source list

52. If the purpose of the request for proposals was to establish a qualified source list, the contracting authority will place all bidders or proponents who meet the qualifications on the qualified source list and notify them.

Form of bid security

53. Where required by the contracting authority, bid security will be in the amount specified by the contracting authority and in the form of

(a) a bid bond, or

(b) cash, bank draft, certified cheque, Canadian postal money order, assignable redeemable term deposit, bearer or assignable bonds of the Government of Canada or of the government of a province, or irrevocable letter of guaranteed credit acceptable to the Government of the Yukon.

Errors in contract value

54. Where unit prices are requested and the bid or proposal contains an error in calculating the estimated contract value, the unit price will prevail.

PART V - ADMINISTRATION OF THE CONTRACT

Form of contract security

55. Contract security, where required, will be in the amount specified by the contracting authority and in the form of

(a)   a security bond acceptable to the Government of the Yukon, or

(b)   cash, bank draft, certified cheque, Canadian postal money order, assignable redeemable term deposit, bearer or assignable bonds of the Government of Canada or of the government of a province, or irrevocable letter of guaranteed credit acceptable to the Government of the Yukon.

Change in contract security

56. Where the amount payable under a contract is increased or decreased, the contracting authority may require a corresponding change in contract security.

Replacement of contract security

57. At any time during the contract period or warranty period for the contract, the contractor may replace the form of contract security provided to the contracting authority by another form of contract security listed in section 55 .

Contract insurance

58. The form and amount of any insurance required will be defined in the request for bids or proposals.

Change orders permitted

59. Contracting authorities may issue change orders to accommodate changes in the scope, schedule or price of the contract that could not have been reasonably foreseen when the request for bids or proposals was issued.

Disclosure of extended contracts

60.

(1) In the case of a sole sourced contract pursuant to paragraphs , , and , where a contracting authority increases the value of the contract past the limit for sole sourcing permitted by these paragraphs, the contracting authority will immediately identify the contract to the Deputy Head of Government Services, or delegate.

(2) In the case of an invitationally sourced contract pursuant to paragraphs 16(1)(a), 16(2)(a), and 16(3)(a), where a contracting authority increases the value of the contract past the limit for invitational tendering permitted by these paragraphs, the contracting authority will immediately identify the contract to the Deputy Head, Government Services, or delegate.

(3) The Deputy Head, Government Services, or delegate, will identify all contracts under this section to the public at regular intervals.

PART VI - BID CHALLENGE PROCESS

Bid challenge committee

61.

(1) The Minister of Government Services will appoint a standing bid challenge committee to act on complaints registered pursuant to this directive.

(2) The committee will be made up of a chair, an alternate chair who will act in the absence of the chair, five (5) representatives from the Government of the Yukon, and five (5) representatives from the public.

(3) Each appointment will be for a term of up to two (2) years, and may be renewed.

(4) Within the policy laid out in this directive, the committee may establish its own rules of procedure.

Registering a complaint

62.

(1) The Deputy Head of Government Services will accept a complaint made in writing by a bidder or proponent or prospective bidder or proponent who has reason to believe that a Deputy Head, or a public servant to whom a Deputy Head has delegated contracting authority, has treated them unfairly or has not followed the process required by the Contract Regulations or this directive, provided that the complaint is received

(a) up to 60 days following the closing time, or up to 15 days following the award of the contract or standing offer agreement, whichever is later, or

(b) in the event of an extension of a standing offer agreement, up to 30 days following the date of the extension.

(2) The bid challenge process described in this Part does not apply to decisions made under paragraphs (a) to (f) of this directive.

(3) The Deputy Head, Government Services may require the complainant to provide full details related to the complaint, including their efforts to resolve the complaint directly with the contracting authority.

(4) The Deputy Head, Government Services will, without undue delay, forward the complaint to the Deputy Head of the contracting authority and to the bid challenge committee established pursuant to section 61.

63. The registration of a complaint pursuant to section 62 will not require the contracting authority to delay award of the contract.

Considering the complaint

64.

(1) The contracting authority will provide a written report about the circumstances relating to the complaint to the chair without delay.

(2) The chair of the bid challenge committee without delay will conduct an initial review of the complaint to determine whether or not there will be an inquiry or hearing.

(3) A complaint registered with the committee which is found by the chair to warrant a hearing will be heard by a panel of three (3) members consisting of the chair and one (1) member appointed by the chair from the representatives of the government and one (1) member appointed by the chair from the representatives of the public.

(4) Where possible, the qualifications of the members selected by the chair to hear a complaint will be appropriate to the matter under consideration.

(5) The panel will hear and consider the complaint within a reasonable time following registration of the complaint.

(6) The panel will allow the complainant and the contracting authority against whom the complaint was registered to address the panel in person and in writing.

(7) The chair may call upon such advisors as the panel considers advisable to report to the panel.

(8) Complaints may be heard in any place in the Yukon.

(9) The panel will not cancel, revoke, amend or alter a contract.

Unfounded complaints

65.

(1) The panel may refuse to hear and consider, or may cease to consider a complaint on the grounds that

(a) the complaint is trivial, frivolous, vexatious or not made in good faith, or

(b) the complainant does not have a sufficient personal interest in the subject matter of the complaint.

(2) Where the panel refuses to consider or ceases to consider a complaint, the chair will inform the complainant and the contracting authority against whom the complaint was registered and may state reasons therefor.

Access to information

66.

(1) Notwithstanding any restrictions on the disclosure of documents in this directive, the panel may examine any documents relating to the complaint.

(2) All information used by the panel in its deliberations, and which may be disclosed under territorial access to information legislation, will be disclosed to both parties to the complaint.

Redress

67.

(1) where the panel considers that a complaint is valid, it may recommend that the contract authority pay to the complainant compensation for:

(a) the complainant's reasonable costs in preparing a bid or proposal; and/or

(b) the complainant's reasonable costs for participating in the inquiry or hearing.

(2) In making its decision, the panel will consider all the circumstances relevant to the complaint, including:

(a) the seriousness of any deficiency in the procurement process found by the panel;

(b) the degree to which the complainant and all other interested parties were prejudiced;

(c) the degree to which the integrity and efficiency of the competitive procurement system was prejudiced; and

(d) whether the parties acted in good faith.

Panel to report

68. The panel will make a report of its findings and recommendations, if any, to the Deputy Head of the contracting authority and to the complainant.

Duty to respond

69.

(1) Where the panel recommends a change to government policy or procedure, the Deputy Head of the contracting authority will, within a reasonable period of time, address the recommendation to the government body which has the authority to consider, and if warranted to act on, the recommendation.

(2) The Deputy Head of the contracting authority will, within a reasonable period of time, provide to the chair a written response(s) which describe(s) progress being made in addressing the panel's recommendation(s). The Deputy Head will provide a copy of the response(s) to his or her Minister.

Distribution of response

70.

(1) The chair will forward a copy of the Deputy Head's response(s) to the complainant.

(2) On forwarding the copy of the Deputy Head's response(s) to the complainant pursuant to subsection (1), the chair will forward a copy of all material relating to the complaint to the Deputy Head of Government Services.

State of Alaska, Purchasing Regulations

PURCHASING REGULATIONS

AAC Title 2, Chapter 12

(Revised 6/29/95)

ARTICLE 01
SOURCE SELECTION

02 AAC 012.0010

NONDISCRIMINATION IN SOURCE SELECTION.

Source selection may not be based on discrimination because of race, religion, color, national origin, sex, age, marital status, pregnancy, parenthood, disability, or political affiliation.

History -

Eff. 1/1/88, Register 104; am 6/29/95, Register 134

Authority -

AS 36.30.040

02 AAC 012.0020

EXCLUSION OF PROSPECTIVE CONTRACTOR FROM COMPETITION.

A procurement officer may exclude a prospective contractor from submitting a bid or proposal, or may reject a prospective contractor's bid or proposal, after making a written determination that the prospective contractor assisted in drafting the invitation to bid or request for proposal, or gained substantial information regarding the invitation to bid or request for proposal that was not available to the public.

    History -

    Eff. 1/1/88, Register 104

    Authority -

    AS 36.30.040

    AS 36.30.050

02 AAC 012.0030

PROCURING STATE-PRODUCED SUPPLIES OR SERVICES FROM INDUSTRIES OF ALASKA CORRECTIONAL INSTITUTIONS.

Purchasing requirements of an agency may be fulfilled by procuring supplies produced or services performed by industries of Alaska correctional institutions. The commissioner of administration will determine whether such supplies or services meet the state's requirements and whether the price represents a reasonable cost for such supplies or services. If a procurement is to be made from the state correctional industries program, the private sector may not be solicited to compete.

    History -

    Eff. 1/1/88, Register 104

    Authority -

    AS 33.32.030

    AS 36.30.040

    AS 36.30.100

02 AAC 012.0040

PROCUREMENT OF LEGAL COUNSEL.

An agency may not contract for the services of legal counsel without the prior written approval of the attorney general. Contracts for the services of legal counsel may incorporate clauses for adjustments in prices, time of performance, and total dollar amount.

    History -

    Eff. 1/1/88, Register 104

    Authority -

    AS 36.30.015

    AS 36.30.040

02 AAC 012.0050

PROCURING SUPPLIES OR SERVICES FROM EMPLOYMENT PROGRAMS.

(a) The chief procurement officer shall maintain a list of employment programs that qualify under AS 36.30.990(10).

(b) A procurement officer may fulfill agency requirements by procuring supplies produced or services performed by an eligible employment program.

(c) Before procuring supplies or services from an employment program, the procurement officer shall determine whether the supplies or services meet the state's requirements and whether the price represents a reasonable cost for the supplies or services. If it is determined that the requirements cannot be met by supplies or services produced by an employment program, or the price is not reasonable, the procurement may be made from the private sector in accordance with AS 36.30 and this chapter. If a procurement is made from an employment program, it is not necessary that the private sector be solicited.

History -

Eff. 1/1/88, Register 104; am 3/30/90, Register 113

Authority -

AS 36.30.040

AS 36.30.100

02 AAC 012.0060

CONTRACTORS LISTS.

(a) A person who wishes to be on a contractors list must submit to the commissioner of administration

(1) evidence of a valid Alaska business license;

(2) a biennial fee of $25 if required; and

(3) for construction contractor lists, a valid certificate of registration issued under AS 08.18.

(b) The commissioner of administration or the chief procurement officer may require other information for contractors lists.

(c) A business that is debarred or suspended under AS 36.30 shall be removed from the contractors list during the period of debarment or suspension.

(d) If a solicitation is returned to a state agency by the U.S. Postal Service as undeliverable, the returned solicitation shall be forwarded to the Department of Administration for removal of the bidder or offeror from the contractors list. The state will not pursue correction of incorrect addresses.

History -

Eff. 1/1/88, Register 104; am 3/30/90, Register 113

Authority -

AS 36.30.040

AS 36.30.050

ARTICLE 02
SPECIFICATIONS

02 AAC 012.0070

AUTHORITY TO PREPARE SPECIFICATIONS.

The chief procurement officer may prepare and approve specifications for supplies or services. The commissioner of transportation and public facilities may prepare and approve specifications for construction and purchases for the state equipment fleet.

History -

Eff. 1/1/88, Register 104

Authority -

AS 36.30.040

AS 36.30.060

02 AAC 012.0080

PURPOSE OF SPECIFICATIONS.

(a) The purpose of a specification is to serve as a basis for obtaining, in a cost effective manner, a supply, service, or construction item suitable for the state's needs.

(b) Specifications must, to the extent practicable, emphasize functional or performance criteria while limiting design or other detailed physical descriptions to those necessary to meet the needs of the state. Purchasing agencies should include as a part of their purchase requisitions the principal functional or performance needs to be met. The preference for functional or performance specifications is primarily applicable to the procurement of supplies and services. This preference is often not practicable in construction, apart from the procurement of supply type items for a construction project.

(c) It is state policy to procure standard commercial products if practicable. In developing specifications, unique requirements should be avoided.

History -

Eff. 1/1/88, Register 104

Authority -

AS 36.30.040

AS 36.30.060

02 AAC 012.0090

NO RESTRICTIVE SPECIFICATIONS.

All specifications must describe the requirements to be met without having the effect of exclusively requiring a proprietary supply, service, or construction item, or procurement from a sole source, unless no other manner of description will suffice.

History -

Eff. 1/1/88, Register 104

Authority -

AS 36.30.040

AS 36.30.060

02 AAC 012.0100

BRAND NAME SPECIFICATION.

A specification that limits the procurement of items to a specific manufacturer's name or catalog numbers may be used only if the procurement officer makes a written determination that only the identified brand name item or items will satisfy the state's needs.

History -

Eff. 1/1/88, Register 104

Authority -

AS 36.30.040

AS 36.30.060

02 AAC 012.0110

QUALIFIED PRODUCTS LIST.

(a) A qualified products list may be developed with the approval of the chief procurement officer, or the commissioner of transportation and public facilities, if testing or examination of the supplies or construction items before issuance of the solicitation is desirable or necessary in order to best satisfy state requirements.

(b) When developing a qualified products list, a representative group of potential suppliers must be solicited, in writing, to submit products for testing and examination to determine acceptability for inclusion on a qualified products list. Any potential supplier, even though not solicited, may offer its products for consideration.

(c) Inclusion on a qualified products list must be based on results of tests or examinations conducted in accordance with state requirements. Test results may be made public in a manner that protects the confidentiality of the identity of the competitors, such as using numerical designations. Except as otherwise provided by law, trade secrets, test data, and similar information provided by the supplier will be kept confidential if requested in writing by the supplier.

(d) The existence of a qualified products list does not constitute prequalification of any prospective supplier of prequalified products.

History -

Eff. 1/1/88, Register 104

Authority -

AS 36.30.040

AS 36.30.060

ARTICLE 03
COMPETITIVE SEALED BIDDING; MULTISTEP BIDDING

02 AAC 012.0120

INVITATIONS FOR COMPETITIVE SEALED BIDS.

(a) An invitation to bid must include the following:

(1) instructions and information to bidders concerning the bid submission requirements, the time and date set for receipt of bids, the address of the office to which bids are to be delivered, the maximum time for bid acceptance by the state, and any other special information;

(2) a purchase or project description, evaluation factors, delivery or performance schedule, and the inspection and acceptance requirements that are not included in the purchase or project description;

(3) a description of all applicable contract terms and conditions, including warranty and bonding or other security requirements;

(4) a requirement for certification by the bidder that it complies with the applicable provisions of 42 U.S.C. 1981 and 42 U.S.C. 2000e through 2000e-17 (Civil Rights Act), 42 U.S.C. 12001 - 12213 (Americans with Disabilities Act of 1990), AS 18.80, and regulations adopted under those statutes;

(5) a requirement for certification by the bidder that, by submitting a bid, the bidder certifies

that the price submitted was independently arrived at without collusion; and

(6) provisions, such as goals or financial incentives, established to eliminate and prevent discrimination in state contracting because of race, religion, color, national origin, sex, age, marital status, pregnancy, parenthood, or disability.

(b) An invitation to bid may incorporate documents by reference.

(c) An invitation to bid may require the receipt of all amendments issued by the using agency to be acknowledged by bidders.

(d) An invitation to bid may require the submission of bid samples, descriptive literature, technical data, or other material. An invitation to bid may provide for any of the following before award:

(1) inspection or testing of a product for such characteristics as quality or workmanship;

(2) examination of such elements as appearance, finish, taste, or feel; or

(3) other examinations to determine whether a product conforms with other purchase requirements.

(e) An invitation to bid must require the bidder to submit evidence that the bidder's subcontractor work will be allocated to meet provisions, such as goals or financial incentives, established in the bid to eliminate and prevent discrimination in state contracting because of race, religion, color, national origin, sex, age, marital status, pregnancy, parenthood, or disability.

History -

Eff. 1/1/88, Register 104; am 5/16/88, Register 106; am 6/29/95, Register 134

Authority -

AS 36.30.040

AS 36.30.110

02 AAC 012.0130

PUBLIC NOTICE.

(a) Notice of an invitation to bid, except for small purchases made under 2 AAC 12.400, shall be published in the Alaska Administrative Journal as required by AS 36.30.130(a) and by at least one of the following methods:

(1) in mailings to those on contractors lists compiled under 2 AAC 12.060;

(2) in a newspaper of general circulation;

(3) in a newspaper of local circulation in the area pertinent to the procurement;

(4) in other appropriate media.

(b) Nothing in this section limits the additional forms of public notice that may be used by the procurement officer.

(c)   The procurement officer may require payment of duplication costs or a deposit for the supplying of the invitation to bid.

History -

Eff. 1/1/88, Register 104; am 3/30/90, Register 113

Authority -

AS 36.30.040

AS 36.30.130

02 AAC 012.0140

PRE-OPENING CORRECTION OR WITHDRAWAL OF BIDS.

(a)   A bid may be corrected or withdrawn by written request received in the office designated in the invitation for bids before the time and date set for opening.

(b)   A request under (a) of this section must provide authorization for the person making the correction or withdrawal to do so.

(c)   If a bid is withdrawn, the bid security, if any, shall be returned to the bidder.

(d)   All documents relating to the correction or withdrawal of a bid shall be included in the appropriate procurement file.

History -

Eff. 1/1/88, Register 104

Authority -

AS 36.30.040

AS 36.30.160

02 AAC 012.0150

RECEIPT, OPENING, AND RECORDING OF BIDS.

(a)   A bid must be submitted in a sealed envelope with the invitation to bid number identified on the outside of the envelope. Upon receipt, a bid correction shall be stored in a secure place until the time and date set for bid opening.

(b)   Bids and corrections shall be opened at the time, date, and place designated in the invitation to bid. The name of each bidder, the bid price, and other information deemed appropriate by the procurement officer shall be tabulated.

History -

Eff. 1/1/88, Register 104

Authority -

AS 36.30.040

AS 36.30.140

02 AAC 012.0160

LATE BIDS, LATE CORRECTIONS, AND LATE WITHDRAWALS.

A bid received after the time and date set for receipt of bids is late. A correction or withdrawal of a bid received after the time and date set for opening of bids at the place designated for opening is late. A late bid correction, or withdrawal, may not be accepted unless the delay was due to an error of the contracting agency.

History -

Eff. 1/1/88, Register 104

Authority -

AS 36.30.040

AS 36.30.160

02 AAC 012.0170

INADVERTENT ERRORS DISCOVERED AFTER OPENING BUT BEFORE AWARD.

(a)   Inadvertent errors discovered after opening but before award, other than minor informalities, may not be corrected. If a bidder submits proof that clearly and convincingly demonstrates that an inadvertent error other than a minor informality was made, the bidder may withdraw the bid.

(b)   If, before award, a procurement officer knows of an error in a bid, the officer shall notify the bidder of the error.

History -

Eff. 1/1/88, Register 104

Authority -

AS 36.30.040

AS 36.30.160

02 AAC 012.0180

BID EVALUATION AND AWARD.

(a)   Award of a bid may not be based on discrimination due to the race, religion, color, national origin, sex, age, marital status, pregnancy, parenthood, disability, or political affiliation of the bidder. A bid shall be evaluated to determine whether the bidder responds to the provisions, such as goals or financial incentives, established in the invitation to bid in order to eliminate and prevent discrimination in state contracting because of race, religion, color, national origin, sex, age, marital status, pregnancy, parenthood, or disability.

(b)   An evaluation of product acceptability shall be conducted to determine whether a bidder's offering is acceptable as set out in the invitation to bid. A bid that does not meet the acceptability requirements shall be rejected as nonresponsive.

(c)   Bids may be evaluated to determine which bid offers the lowest cost to the state in accordance with the evaluation criteria set out in the invitation to bid. Evaluation factors need not be precise predictors of actual future costs, but to the extent possible the evaluation factors must

(1)   be reasonable estimates based upon information the state has available concerning future use; and

(2)   treat all bids equitably.

(d)   Nothing in this section permits contract award to a bidder submitting a higher quality item than that designated in the invitation for bids if the bidder is not also the lowest bidder as determined under (c) of this section. This section does not permit negotiations with a bidder.

History -

Eff. 1/1/88, Register 104; am 5/16/88, Register 106; am 6/29/95, Register 134

Authority -

AS 36.30.040

AS 36.30.150

02 AAC 012.0190

ONLY ONE RESPONSIVE BID RECEIVED.

If only one responsive bid is received in response to an invitation to bid, including multi-step bidding, an award may be made to the single bidder if the bidder is responsible and if the procurement officer finds that the price submitted is fair and reasonable and that either other prospective bidders had reasonable opportunity to respond or there is not adequate time for resolicitation. Otherwise the bid may be rejected and

(1)   new bids or offers may be solicited;

(2)   the proposed procurement may be canceled; or

(3)   if the procurement officer determines in writing that the need for the supply or service continues, but that the price of the one bid is not fair and reasonable, and there is no time for resolicitation or it is unlikely that resolicitation would increase the number of bids, the procurement may be conducted under 2 AAC 12.410 (sole source procurement), 2 AAC 12.430 (limited competition procurement), or 2 AAC 12.440 (emergency procurements), as appropriate.

History -

Eff. 1/1/88, Register 104

Authority -

AS 36.30.040

AS 36.30.350

02 AAC 012.0200

DOCUMENTATION OF AWARD.

Following award, a record showing the basis for determining the successful bidder shall be made a part of the procurement file.

History -

Eff. 1/1/88, Register 104

Authority -

AS 36.30.040

AS 36.30.500

02 AAC 012.0210

NOTICE OF INTENT TO AWARD.

Notice of intent to award does not constitute a formal award of a contract. The notice of intent to award must include

(1)   a statement of the bidder's right under AS 36.30 to protest the award, including the time within which the protest must be received; and

(2)   the name of the successful bidder.

History -

Eff. 1/1/88, Register 104; am 3/30/90, Register 113

Authority -

AS 36.30.040

AS 36.30.365

AS 36.30.565

ARTICLE 04
COMPETITIVE SEALED PROPOSALS

02 AAC 012.0215

EXCEPTIONS TO COMPETITIVE SEALED BIDDING.

The following types of supplies and services, for which the use of competitive sealed bidding is either not practicable or not advantageous to the state, may be procured by competitive sealed proposals without written findings by the chief procurement officer:

(1) professional services;

(2) supplies and services for clean up of oil and hazardous substances;

(3) telephone systems and telephone system maintenance;

(4) concessions in state parks;

(5) helicopter charter services for geological field research conducted by the Department of Natural Resources;

(6) a lease of office space in excess of 10,000 square feet.

History -

Eff. 3/30/90, Register 113; am 6/29/95, Register 134

Authority -

AS 36.30.040

AS 36.30.200

02 AAC 012.0220

PUBLIC NOTICE OF COMPETITIVE SEALED PROPOSALS.

Public notice shall be given by distributing the request for proposals or notice of requests for proposals in the manner provided in 2 AAC 12.130.

History -

Eff. 1/1/88, Register 104

Authority -

AS 36.30.040

AS 36.30.210

02 AAC 012.0230

CORRECTION, MODIFICATION, OR WITHDRAWAL OF PROPOSALS.

A proposal may be corrected, modified, or withdrawn before the time and date set for receipt of proposals, in the manner described in 2 AAC 12.140, 2 AAC 12.160, or 2 AAC 12.170.

History -

Eff. 1/1/88, Register 104; am 3/27/93, Register 125

Authority -

AS 36.30.040

02 AAC 012.0240

RECEIPT AND REGISTRATION OF PROPOSALS.

Proposals, modifications, and corrections shall have the date and time of receipt noted on the envelope upon receipt, and shall be held in a secure place. After the date set for receipt of proposals, a register of proposals must be prepared. The register must include the name of each offeror and a description of the supply, service, or construction item offered.

History -

Eff. 1/1/88, Register 104

Authority -

AS 36.30.040

AS 36.30.230

02 AAC 012.0250

LATE PROPOSALS, LATE CORRECTIONS, LATE MODIFICATIONS, AND LATE WITHDRAWALS.

Unless otherwise provided in the request for proposals, a proposal, correction, modification, or withdrawal received after the date and time set for receipt of proposals is late, and may not be accepted unless the delay is due to an error of the contracting agency.

History -

Eff. 1/1/88, Register 104; am 3/27/93, Register 125

Authority -

AS 36.30.040

AS 36.30.210

02 AAC 012.0260

EVALUATION OF PROPOSALS.

(a) The procurement officer, or an evaluation committee consisting of the procurement officer and at least two state employees or public officials, shall evaluate proposals.

(b) The evaluation must be based only on the evaluation factors set out in the request for proposals. Numerical rating systems may be used, but are not required. If numerical rating systems are not used, the procurement officer, or each member of the evaluation committee, as applicable, shall explain his or her ranking determination in writing. Evaluation factors not specified in the request for proposals may not be considered. The weighting value or numerical system to be applied to each evaluation factor must be set out in the request for proposal.

(c) Cost must be an evaluation factor unless the services or supplies sought are selected in accordance with AS 36.30.270(a) and (b). If a numerical rating system is used, the request for proposals must state the value to be applied to cost.

(d) For the purposes of evaluating cost factors, the proposed costs of an offeror who qualifies as an Alaska bidder under AS 36.30.170(b) shall be reduced by five percent. The proposal with the lowest cost factor must receive the highest available rating allocated to cost. A proposal that has a higher cost factor than the lowest must have a lower rating for cost.

(e) An evaluation factor must be included which takes into consideration whether an offeror qualifies as an Alaska bidder under AS 36.30.170(b). If the procurement officer uses a numerical rating system, at least 10 percent of the rating system value or weighting value that is used must be assigned to the Alaska bidder evaluation factor. This factor may be prorated based on the amount of the contract performed in Alaska. The following are some additional evaluation factors that may be considered:

(1) the offeror's experience in Alaska performing work similar to that sought in the request for proposals;

(2) the percent of work that will be performed in Alaska;

(3) the location of the office of the offeror where the work will be performed.

(f) A proposal from a debarred or suspended offeror shall be rejected.

(g) Evaluation meetings may be held by an evaluation committee to discuss the request for proposals, the evaluation process, the weighting of evaluation factors, and proposals received, before evaluation.

(h) If the evaluation is performed by an evaluation committee, each member shall exercise independent judgment and no member's vote may be weighted more than any other.

(i) An evaluation may not be based on discrimination due to the race, religion, color, national origin, sex, age, marital status, pregnancy, parenthood, disability, or political affiliation of the offeror. A proposal shall be evaluated to determine whether the offeror responds to the provisions, including goals and financial incentives, established in the request for proposals in order to eliminate and prevent discrimination in state contracting because of race, religion, color, national origin, sex, age, marital status, pregnancy, parenthood, or disability.

History -

Eff. 1/1/88, Register 104; am 5/16/88, Register 106; am 7/2/88, Register 106; am 3/30/90, Register 113; am 3/27/93, Register 125; am 6/29/95, Register 134

Authority -

AS 36.30.040

AS 36.30.210

AS 36.30.250

02 AAC 012.0265

EVALUATION FACTORS FOR HEAVY TRUCKS AND EQUIPMENT.

If a state agency uses competitive sealed proposals to procure heavy trucks and heavy equipment, the state agency may use other evaluation factors in addition to the evaluations factors set out in 2 AAC 12.260(e), including

(1) the price;

(2) the quality of the article offered;

(3) the performance capabilities of the offerors and the manufacturers;

(4) the suitability of the article offered;

(5) the service requirements, including warranty, parts availability, and parts locations;

(6) durability as measured by projected operating and maintenance costs;

(7) the resale value;

(8) the transportation charges;

(9) the date of delivery and performance; and

(10) other factors determined to be pertinent or peculiar to the procurement.

History -

Eff. 3/27/93, Register 125

Authority -

AS 36.30.040

AS 36.30.250

02 AAC 012.0270

ONLY ONE RESPONSIVE PROPOSAL.

If after evaluation under 2 AAC 12.260 and discussion under 2 AAC 12.290 only one responsive and responsible proposal is available for award, the procurement officer may make an award in accordance with AS 36.30.250, may reject the proposal, or may reject the proposal and resolicit proposals.

History -

Eff. 1/1/88, Register 104; am 6/29/95, Register 134

Authority -

AS 36.30.040

AS 36.30.350

02 AAC 012.0280

DUTY OF OFFERORS

Repealed or Renumbered Repealed.

History -

Eff. 1/1/88, Register 104; repealed 6/29/95, Register 134

02 AAC 012.0290

PROPOSAL DISCUSSIONS WITH INDIVIDUAL OFFERORS.

(a) Offerors of proposals reasonably susceptible for award as determined in the evaluation conducted under 2 AAC 12.260, may be offered the opportunity to discuss their proposals with the procurement officer or evaluation committee at the discretion of the procurement officer. The evaluation of a proposal may be adjusted as a result of a discussion under this section. The conditions, terms, or price of the proposed contract may be altered or otherwise changed during the course of the discussions.

(b) The procurement officer may limit discussions to specific sections of the request for proposals. If during discussions there is a need for any substantial clarification of or change in the request for proposals, the request must be amended to incorporate the clarification or change. Auction techniques that reveal one offeror's price to another, and disclosure of any information derived from competing proposals, are prohibited. Any oral modification of a proposal shall be reduced to writing by the offeror.

(c) Following discussions, the procurement officer shall set a date and time for the submission of best and final proposals. Best and final proposals may be submitted only once. However, the chief procurement officer or the head of a purchasing agency may make a written determination that it is in the state's best interest to conduct additional discussions or change the state's requirements and require another submission of best and final proposals. Otherwise, discussion of or changes in the best and final proposals may not be allowed before award. If an offeror does not submit a best and final proposal or a notice of withdrawal, the offeror's immediately previous proposal is considered the offeror's best and final proposal.

(d) After best and final proposals are received, final evaluations will be conducted as described in 2 AAC 12.260.

History -

Eff. 1/1/88, Register 104

Authority -

AS 36.30.040

AS 36.30.240

02 AAC 012.0300

DOCUMENTATION OF CONTRACTOR SELECTION.

When a contractor has been selected by competitive sealed proposal, the procurement officer shall enter into the procurement file a written record of the basis on which the selection was found to be most advantageous to the state.

History -

Eff. 1/1/88, Register 104

Authority -

AS 36.30.040

AS 36.30.250

02 AAC 012.0310

NOTICE OF INTENT TO AWARD.

Notice of intent to award shall be issued in accordance with 2 AAC 12.210.

History -

Eff. 1/1/88, Register 104

Authority -

AS 36.30.040

AS 36.30.365

ARTICLE 05

COMPETITIVE SEALED PROPOSALS FOR ARCHITECT, ENGINEER, OR LAND SURVEYING SERVICES

02 AAC 012.0320

PROCUREMENT OF ARCHITECT, ENGINEER, OR LAND SURVEYING SERVICES.

(a) Except as provided otherwise in this section, architect, engineer, or land surveyor services must be procured under 2 AAC 12.220 - 2 AAC 12.310, 2 AAC 12.320 - 2 AAC 12.390, and 2 AAC 12.400. In the case of inconsistency, the provisions of 2 AAC 12.320 - 2 AAC 12.390 control.

(b) Procurement of minor or incidental architect, engineer, or land surveying work associated with and performed during construction, is not subject to 2 AAC 12.320 - 2 AAC 12.390.

History -

Eff. 1/1/88, Register 104

Authority -

AS 36.30.040

AS 36.30.270

02 AAC 012.0330

DETERMINATIONS REQUIRED BEFORE PROCUREMENT OF SERVICES.

Before announcing the need for architect, engineer, or land surveying services, the head of the purchasing agency must determine

(1) that the services to be acquired are services subject to AS 36.30.270;

(2) that a reasonable inquiry has been conducted and it has been determined that state personnel are unable or unavailable to perform the services required under the proposed contract;

(3) that the purchasing agency has developed, and fully intends to implement, a written plan for using the services.

History -

Eff. 1/1/88, Register 104

Authority -

AS 36.30.040

AS 36.30.270

02 AAC 012.0340

PUBLIC ANNOUNCEMENT OF REQUIRED ARCHITECT, ENGINEER, OR LAND SURVEYING SERVICES.

(a) Notice of the need for architect, engineer, or land surveying services shall be given as described in 2 AAC 12.130.

(b) A solicitation must be prepared which describes the state's requirements, sets out the evaluation criteria, and includes notice of any conference to be held.

(c) The procurement officer may require a payment of a fee or deposit to supply a solicitation.

History -

Eff. 1/1/88, Register 104

Authority -

AS 36.30.040

AS 36.30.270

02 AAC 012.0350

ARCHITECT, ENGINEER, OR LAND SURVEYOR SELECTION COMMITTEE.

(a) If a contract for architect, engineer, or land surveying services is expected to exceed $25,000, the chief procurement officer, commissioner of transportation and public facilities, or commissioner of natural resources, as appropriate, shall designate a minimum of three individuals to serve as members of an architect, engineer, and land surveying selection committee for that contract. The committee must consist of

(1) a majority of registered persons if registration is required under AS 36.30.270(d), or, if registration is not required under AS 36.30.270(d), a majority of state employees who are well qualified in architecture, engineering, or land surveying, as appropriate; and

(2) a procurement officer representing the purchasing agency requiring the services, and preferably qualified in architecture, engineering or land surveying, and other members as appropriate.

(b) The chief procurement officer, commissioner of transportation and public facilities, or commissioner of natural resources, as appropriate, shall designate one member to chair the committee and to negotiate a contract with the most qualified and suitable firm or person in accordance with AS 36.30.270.

History -

Eff. 1/1/88, Register 104; am 3/27/93, Register 125

Authority -

AS 36.30.040

AS 36.30.270

02 AAC 012.0360

EVALUATION OF STATEMENTS OF QUALIFICATIONS AND PERFORMANCE DATA; SELECTION OF FIRMS OR PERSONS FOR DISCUSSIONS.

(a) The selection committee shall evaluate

(1) statements submitted in response to the solicitation for architect, engineer, or land surveying services, including proposals for joint ventures; and

(2) supplemental statements of qualifications and performance data, if submission of such statements was required.

(b) All statements and supplemental statements of qualifications and performance data shall be evaluated in light of the criteria set out in the solicitation.

(c) Criteria to be used in evaluating the statement of qualifications and performance data may include

(1) experience in providing the required services;

(2) the qualifications and competence of persons who would be assigned to perform the services,

as reflected by technical training and education;

(3) ability to perform the services, as reflected by workload and the availability of adequate personnel, equipment, and facilities to perform the services expeditiously; and

(4) past performance, as reflected by the evaluations of private persons and officials of other government entities that have retained the services of the firm or person, with respect to such factors as control of costs, quality of work, and ability to meet deadlines.

(d) The selection committee may select firms or persons evaluated as being professionally and technically qualified for discussions and reasonably susceptible for award of a contract. The procurement officer shall notify each firm or person in writing of the date, time, and place of discussions, and, if necessary, shall provide each firm or person with additional information on the project and the services required. The notice may provide that a representative of a firm or person must attend discussions in order for the firm or person to be considered further.

History -

Eff. 1/1/88, Register 104

Authority -

AS 36.30.040

AS 36.30.270

02 AAC 012.0370

DISCUSSIONS.

The selection committee may hold discussions regarding the proposed contract with the firms or persons selected. The purpose of such discussions is to explore the scope and nature of the required services and the relative utility of alternative methods of approach. The conditions, terms, or price of the proposed contract may be altered or otherwise changed during the course of the discussions.

History -

Eff. 1/1/88, Register 104

Authority -

AS 36.30.040

AS 36.30.270

02 AAC 012.0380

SELECTION OF THE MOST QUALIFIED AND SUITABLE FIRMS OR PERSONS.

After discussions, if held under 2 AAC 12.370, the selection committee shall reevaluate and select, in order of preference, no fewer than three firms or persons that the committee considers to be the most highly qualified and suitable to provide the required services. The selection committee shall prepare a memorandum of the selection process which indicates how the evaluation criteria were applied to determine the ranking of the three most highly qualified and suitable firms or persons. The memorandum shall be included in the procurement file.

History -

Eff. 1/1/88, Register 104; am 3/27/93, Register 125

Authority -

AS 36.30.040

AS 36.30.270

02 AAC 012.0390

NEGOTIATION AND AWARD OF CONTRACT.

(a)   The procurement officer shall negotiate with the most qualified and suitable offerors in the order in which they are ranked. Contract negotiations shall be directed toward

(1)   making certain that the offeror has a clear understanding of the scope of the work and the requirements involved in providing the required services;

(2)   determining that the offeror will make available the necessary personnel and facilities to perform the services within the required time; and

(3)   agreeing upon compensation that is fair and reasonable, taking into account the estimated value, scope, complexity, and nature of the required services.

(b)   The offeror selected for award shall submit and certify cost and pricing data.

(c)   Upon failure to negotiate a contract with the most qualified and suitable offeror, the procurement officer shall enter into negotiations with the next most qualified and suitable offeror.

(d)   If the procurement officer is unable to negotiate a contract with any of the offerors initially selected as the most highly qualified and suitable offerors, additional offerors may be selected in preferential order based on their respective qualifications.

(e)   Written notice of the intent to award must comply with 2 AAC 12.310 and must be sent to each offeror. Notice of intent to award must be made available to the public.

(f)   After award of the contract, a memorandum setting out the principal elements of the negotiation shall be prepared by the procurement officer. The memorandum shall be included in the procurement file and be available to the public upon request.

History -

Eff. 1/1/88, Register 104; am 3/27/93, Register 125

Authority -

AS 36.30.040

AS 36.30.270

ARTICLE 06
SMALL PURCHASES

02 AAC 012.0400

AUTHORITY TO MAKE SMALL PURCHASES.

(a) Purchasing agencies shall use procedures adequate and reasonable to provide competition, and to make records to facilitate auditing of the purchasing agency, for contracts for

(1) purchases of supplies, services, or construction estimated to cost less than $1,000;

(2) procurements of replacement parts and services estimated to cost not more than $1,500 for aircraft, automotive, marine, construction, laboratory, scientific, office, or industrial equipment;

(3) advertising, troll onboard observer services, or point-to-point air travel on scheduled airlines estimated to cost no more than $5,000;

(4) professional services estimated to cost no more than $5,000;

(5) legal or hearing officer services estimated to cost no more than $25,000;

(6) concessions estimated to have gross receipts of less than $5,000;

(7) chartered air travel for the office of the governor estimated to cost no more than $10,000;

(8) professional services for the office of the governor estimated to cost no more than $25,000;

(9) procurements of supplies or services while on travel status with, or on behalf of the governor estimated to cost no more than $10,000; and

(10) fish food for hatchery use estimated to cost no more than $10,000.

(b) For procurement of supplies, services, or construction estimated to cost between $1,000 and $5,000, other than procurements described in (a) of this section, the following procedures shall be followed, except that, if the following procedures are not practicable under the circumstances, the procedures required by (a) of this section shall be followed:

(1) at least three firms or persons shall be contacted for written quotations; the procurement officer shall include as part of the procurement file a list of firms and persons contacted, a summary of the responses, and copies of all quotations received;

(2) the award shall be made to the lowest responsive and responsible respondent, taking into account applicable Alaskan bidder and Alaskan products preferences, and shall be made in accordance with the specifications and award criteria in the solicitation.

(c) For a procurement of supplies, services, or construction estimated to cost between $5,000 and

$25,000, other than a procurement described in (a) of this section, the following procedures shall be followed:

(1) at least three firms or persons shall be contacted for written quotations; the procurement officer shall include as part of the procurement file a list of firms and persons contacted, a summary of the responses, and copies of all quotations received;

(2) the award shall be made to the lowest responsive and responsible respondent, taking into account applicable Alaskan bidder and Alaskan product preferences, and shall be made in accordance with the specifications and award criteria in the solicitation.

(d) For procurement of professional services estimated to cost between $5,000 and $25,000, other than procurements described in (a) of this section, or concession services estimated to bring in gross receipts between $5,000 and $25,000 annually, the following procedures shall be followed:

(1) at least three firms or persons shall be solicited for informal proposals, orally or in writing; if oral solicitation is used, oral proposals shall be followed up with written proposals that are made a part of the procurement file, and in that file the procurement officer shall record who made the solicitation, the specifications of the services solicited, the date the solicitation took place, the name of the firms or persons contacted, the name of the person in a firm that is contacted, the response of each firm or person contacted, and a justification for the award; for written proposals, the procurement officer shall include as part of the procurement file a list of firms or persons contacted, a copy of the solicitation used, a summary of the responses, copies of all proposals received, and a justification for the award;

(2) the award shall be made to the most qualified responsive and responsible offeror, taking into account applicable Alaskan bidder and Alaskan product preferences, and shall be made in accordance with the specifications and award criteria in the solicitation.

(e) The procurement officer may use the appropriate contractors list. It is not necessary to solicit all vendors on the contractors list. If used, the list shall be rotated to the extent necessary to give all interested prospective contractors opportunity to compete. Nothing in this section limits the procurement officer from contracting additional firms or persons not on the list.

History -

Eff. 1/1/88, Register 104; am 3/30/90, Register 113; am 3/27/93, Register 125; am 6/29/95, Register 134

Authority -

AS 36.30.040

AS 36.30.320

ARTICLE 07
SOLE SOURCE PROCUREMENT

02 AAC 012.0410

CONDITIONS FOR USE OF SOLE SOURCE PROCUREMENT.

(a)   A request by a purchasing agency that a procurement be restricted to one potential contractor shall be accompanied by a written explanation as to why no other source is suitable or acceptable to meet the need. The agency shall include with the written explanation the evidence necessary for the independent examination and determination, as required under AS 36.30.315, of the material facts of the procurement. To determine if other sources are available or interested in a procurement, an agency may advertise an intent to make a sole source award. Except for a procurement that does not exceed the amount for small procurements under AS 36.30.320, the award of a sole source procurement may not be made without the prior written approval of the chief procurement officer or the commissioner of transportation and public facilities, as appropriate under AS 36.30.300(a).

(b)   The written determination, required under AS 36.30.300(a), that there is only one source for the required procurement must specify the duration of the determination's effectiveness.

(c)   A procurement officer shall conduct negotiations, as appropriate, as to the price, delivery, and terms of a sole source procurement.

(d)   The following are examples of circumstances in which sole source procurement might be appropriate:

(1)   if the compatibility of equipment, accessories, or replacement parts is the main consideration;

(2)   if a specific item is needed for trial use or testing, including testing of a prototype;

(3)   if an item is to be procured for resale;

(4)   repealed 6/29/95;

(5)   if there exists a sole source of expertise required to perform a specific professional service;

(6)   if the procurement is for operation of a concession contract on state property by a nonprofit organization whose sole purpose is to operate the concession and provide other public services on the property;

(7)   if the procurement is with a government police agency to provide investigative, enforcement, or support services in support of state law enforcement objectives;

(8)   if the procurement is for the services of legal counsel for the purpose of advising or representing the state in specific civil or criminal proceedings or on a specific matter before a federal or state regulatory agency, board, or commission;

(9)   if the procurement is by the office of the Governor for lobbying, labor negotiation, or

consulting by a foreign national.

History -

Eff. 1/1/88, Register 104; am 6/29/95, Register 134

Authority -

AS 36.30.040

AS 36.30.300

AS 36.30.315

02 AAC 012.0420

RECORD OF SOLE SOURCE PROCUREMENT.

A record of every sole source procurement shall be made and forwarded to the chief procurement officer, and must include

(1) the supplier's or contractor's name;

(2) the amount and type of each contract;

(3) a listing of the supplies, services, or construction procured under each contract; and

(4) the identification number of each procurement file.

History -

Eff. 1/1/88, Register 104

Authority -

AS 36.30.040

AS 36.30.300

ARTICLE 08
LIMITED COMPETITION PROCUREMENTS

02 AAC 012.0430

CONDITIONS FOR USE OF LIMITED COMPETITION PROCUREMENT.

(a) A request by a purchasing agency that a procurement be restricted to several potential contractors must be accompanied by a written explanation as to why other sources are not suitable or available and why the competitive sealed bidding and competitive sealed proposal processes are impractical or contrary to the public interest. The agency must include with the written explanation the evidence necessary for the independent examination and determination, as required under AS 36.30.315, of the material facts of the procurement. To determine if other sources are available or interested in a procurement, an agency may advertise an intent to make a limited competition procurement.

(b) A procurement for construction under this section must be for less than $100,000.

(c) A procurement officer shall conduct negotiations, as appropriate, as to price, delivery, and terms, equally with each potential contractor for a limited competition procurement.

History -

Eff. 1/1/88, Register 104; am 3/30/90, Register 113; am 6/29/95, Register 134

Authority -

AS 36.30.040

AS 36.30.305

ARTICLE 09
EMERGENCY PROCUREMENTS

02 AAC 012.0440

DETERMINATION OF EMERGENCY CONDITIONS.

(a) For the purposes of AS 36.30.310, emergency conditions include

    (1) fire, flood, epidemic, riot, environmental accident, or a similarly compelling reason;

    (2) equipment failure, if the need for timely repair is essential;

    (3) a situation in which procurement through competitive sealed bidding or competitive sealed proposals is impracticable or contrary to the public interest; or

    (4) a need to protect public or private property.

(b) Before a procurement may be made under this section, a written determination of emergency is required from the chief procurement officer, or from the commissioner of transportation and public facilities for a construction contract or a procurement for the state equipment fleet. An agency requesting a determination of emergency shall provide a written explanation as to why emergency conditions exist. The agency shall include with its explanation the evidence necessary for the independent examination and determination, as required under AS 36.30.315, of the material facts of the procurement.

(c) The agency official at the site of an emergency condition may make a determination of emergency under this section if

    (1) immediate action is necessary to protect public health, welfare, or safety, or to protect public or private property; and

    (2) insufficient time exists for

        (A) the agency to provide the explanation and evidence required under (b) of this section; and

        (B) the chief procurement officer or the commissioner of transportation and public facilities to make the written determination of emergency required under AS 36.30.310 and (b) of this section.

History -

Eff. 1/1/88, Register 104; am 3/30/90, Register 113; am 6/29/95, Register 134

Authority -

AS 36.30.005

AS 36.30.040

AS 36.30.310

02 AAC 012.0450

PROCUREMENT METHODS FOR EMERGENCY CONDITIONS.

(a) Emergency procurement is limited to the supplies, services, professional services, or construction necessary to meet the emergency.

(b) An agency may make an emergency procurement by any reasonable means. If practical, approval by the head of the agency must be obtained before an emergency procurement of $5,000 or more is made.

(c) A procurement by the Department of Natural Resources during a fire suppression emergency shall be made in accordance with the procedures established by that department.

History -

Eff. 1/1/88, Register 104

Authority -

AS 36.30.040

AS 36.30.310

02 AAC 012.0460

RECORD OF EMERGENCY PROCUREMENT.

The procurement officer or the agency official responsible for procurement shall make and promptly forward to the chief procurement officer a record of each emergency procurement. The record must set out

(1) the contractor's name;

(2) the amount and type of the contract;

(3) a listing of the supplies, services, or construction procured under the contract; and

(4) the identification number of the procurement file.

History -

Eff. 1/1/88, Register 104

Authority -

AS 36.30.040

AS 36.30.310

ARTICLE 10
CONTRACT FORMATION AND MODIFICATION

02 AAC 012.0470

STANDARD CONTRACT CLAUSES.

The chief procurement officer and the commissioner of transportation and public facilities, in consultation with the attorney general, may establish standard contract clauses for state contracts. A procurement officer may modify a standard clause only with the prior written approval of the attorney general as to form.

History -

Eff. 1/1/88, Register 104

Authority -

AS 36.30.040

AS 36.30.340

02 AAC 012.0480

NOVATION OR CHANGE OF NAME.

(a) A state contract or subcontract may not be transferred or otherwise assigned without the prior written consent of the chief procurement officer or the head of a purchasing agency.

(b) If the chief procurement officer or the head of a purchasing agency determines it is in the best interests of the state, a successor in interest may be recognized in a novation agreement in which the transferor and the transferee agree that

(1) the transferee assumes all of the transferor's obligations under the contract;

(2) the transferor waives any and all rights it has under the contract as against the state; and

(3) the transferee furnishes satisfactory performance and payment bonds, if required by the procurement officer.

(c) If a contractor requests to change the name in which it holds a contract with the state, the procurement officer responsible for the contract may, when it is in the best interests of the state, enter into an agreement with the requesting contractor to effect the change of name. The agreement changing the name must specifically indicate that no other terms and conditions of the contract are changed.

History -

Eff. 1/1/88, Register 104; am 3/30/90, Register 113

Authority -

AS 36.30.040

02 AAC 012.0490

RESPONSIBILITY OF PROSPECTIVE CONTRACTORS

Repealed or Renumbered Repealed 3/27/93.

02 AAC 012.0500

STANDARDS OF RESPONSIBILITY.

(a) Factors that may be considered in determining whether a prospective contractor is responsible include whether the prospective contractor

(1) has a satisfactory record of performance;

(2) is qualified legally to contract with the state; and

(3) has supplied all necessary information in connection with the inquiry concerning responsibility.

(b) The procurement officer may require the prospective contractor to demonstrate the availability of necessary financing, equipment, facilities, expertise, and personnel, by submitting

(1) evidence that the contractor possesses the necessary items;

(2) acceptable plans to subcontract for the necessary items;

(3) a documented commitment from, or explicit arrangement with, a satisfactory source to provide the necessary items; or

(4) other information required by the procurement officer.

(c) The state's determination of responsibility does not relieve the contractor from the requirements for performance under the contract.

History -

Eff. 1/1/88, Register 104

Authority -

AS 36.30.040

AS 36.30.360

02 AAC 012.0510

ACCESS TO PLANT OR PLACE OF BUSINESS.

(a) If an inspection is made in the plant or place of business of a contractor or subcontractor, the contractor or subcontractor shall provide without charge all reasonable facilities and assistance for the safety and convenience of the person performing the inspection or testing.

(b) On-site inspection of construction shall be performed in accordance with the terms of the contract.

History -

Eff. 1/1/88, Register 104

Authority -

AS 36.30.040

AS 36.30.410

02 AAC 012.0520

INSPECTION AND TESTING OF SUPPLIES AND SERVICES.

(a) The state will, in its discretion, inspect supplies and services at the contractor or subcontractor's facility, and perform tests to determine whether they conform to solicitation requirements, or, after award, to contract requirements, and are therefore acceptable. Inspections and tests will be conducted at any reasonable time.

(b) The chief procurement officer may establish operational procedures governing the testing and trial use of equipment, materials, and other supplies by a state agency, and the application of resulting information and data to specifications or procurements.

History -

Eff. 1/1/88, Register 104

Authority -

AS 36.30.040

AS 36.30.410

02 AAC 012.0530

RETENTION OF BOOKS AND RECORDS.

Books and records that relate to a state contract or subcontract shall be retained in such a manner that all actual costs related to the contract or subcontract can be easily determined.

History -

Eff. 1/1/88, Register 104

Authority -

AS 36.30.040

AS 36.30.420

02 AAC 012.0540

PRICE ANALYSIS.

The chief procurement officer and the commissioner of transportation and public facilities may establish procedures for price analysis in the bid evaluation process.

> History -
>
> Eff. 1/1/88, Register 104
>
> Authority -
>
> AS 36.30.040

02 AAC 012.0550

COST AND PRICING DATA.

A procurement officer may not waive the requirements of AS 36.30.400(a) concerning submission of cost and pricing data.

> History -
>
> Eff. 1/1/88, Register 104
>
> Authority -
>
> AS 36.30.040
>
> AS 36.30.400

02 AAC 012.0560

GUIDELINES FOR COST PRINCIPLES.

(a) The commissioner of administration, the commissioner of transportation and public facilities, or the chief procurement officer may establish guidelines for cost principles that may be used to determine allowability of incurred costs for the purpose of reimbursement under contract provisions that provide for the reimbursement of costs.

(b) Cost principles may be modified by contract upon approval of the head of the using agency.

> History -
>
> Eff. 1/1/88, Register 104
>
> Authority -
>
> AS 36.30.040

02 AAC 012.0570

USE OF FEDERAL COST PRINCIPLES.

In dealing with contractors operating according to federal cost principles, such as Defense Acquisition

Regulations, Section 15, or Federal Procurement Regulations, Part 1-15, the procurement officer may use the federal cost principles as guidance in contract negotiations.

> History -
> Eff. 1/1/88, Register 104
> Authority -
> AS 36.30.040
> AS 36.30.480

ARTICLE 11
SUPPLY MANAGEMENT

02 AAC 012.0580

INVENTORIES.

The chief procurement officer, the commissioner of transportation and public facilities, and the head of a purchasing agency may establish procedures to determine appropriate stock levels and the management of agency supplies.

> History -
> Eff. 1/1/88, Register 104
> Authority -
> AS 36.30.040

02 AAC 012.0590

SUPPLIES INVENTORY RECORDS.

(a) At the end of each fiscal year or other period as required by the chief procurement officer, each state agency shall submit to the chief procurement officer an inventory report, verified by a physical count and certified by the agency's head, listing the following:

    (1) all nonconsumable supplies with a unit acquisition cost of more than $500;

    (2) supplies determined by the chief procurement officer to be sensitive, regardless of cost;

    (3) supplies with a unit acquisition cost exceeding $200, determined to be sensitive by an agency property officer; and

    (4) lease purchase or installment purchase equipment.

(b) Theft of supplies shall be immediately reported to the appropriate law enforcement agency. All lost, stolen, or destroyed supplies shall be reported to the chief procurement officer by the agency.

> History -

Eff. 1/1/88, Register 104; am 3/30/90, Register 113

Authority -

AS 36.30.040

AS 36.30.070

AS 37.05.160

02 AAC 012.0600

SURPLUS SUPPLIES.

(a)   The chief procurement officer may act on behalf of the state in all matters pertaining to the disposition of surplus supplies. No purchasing agency, except the University of Alaska, the Alaska Court System or the Alaska Legislature, may transfer or otherwise dispose of supplies owned by the state without authorization of the chief procurement officer. Purchasing agencies shall notify the chief procurement officer of all surplus supplies on the forms and at the times that the officer prescribes. The chief procurement officer shall determine the fair market value of surplus supplies if necessary.

(b)   Surplus supplies shall be offered through spot bids, competitive sealed bids, public auction, established markets, or posted prices. If unusual circumstances render the above methods impractical, the chief procurement officer may employ other disposition methods, including appraisal or barter.

(c)   Unless approved by the chief procurement officer in advance in writing, only United States Postal Money Orders, certified checks, cashiers' checks, or cash may be accepted for sales of surplus property.

(d)   Notice of sale of surplus supplies by competitive sealed bidding must be publicly available from the chief procurement officer at least 10 days before the date set for opening bids.

(e)   An employee of the owning or disposing agency may not directly or indirectly purchase or agree with another person to purchase surplus supplies if the employee is, or has been, directly or indirectly involved in the disposal, maintenance, or preparation for sale of the surplus supplies.

History -

Eff. 1/1/88, Register 104; am 3/30/90, Register 113

Authority -

AS 36.30.040

AS 36.30.070

02 AAC 012.0610

FEDERAL SURPLUS MATERIAL PROGRAM.

The Department of Administration will, in its discretion, acquire and distribute from the United States Government surplus property that may be usable and necessary for public purposes by a state agency or a political subdivision of the state. The chief procurement officer may

(1)   prepare and file a state plan of operation with the United States General Services Administration;

(2)   act on behalf of the state with federal agencies or other surplus property agencies regarding federal surplus property; and

(3)   distribute federal surplus property to eligible entities.

History -

Eff. 1/1/88, Register 104

Authority -

AS 36.30.040

AS 36.30.070

ARTICLE 12
LEGAL AND CONTRACTUAL REMEDIES

02 AAC 012.0615

PROTEST OF PROVISIONS AND CANCELLATION OF SOLICITATION.

(a)   An interested party may protest provisions of an invitation to bid or request for proposals by filing with the procurement officer a written protest that includes the information required by AS 36.30.560 no less than 10 days before the date of bid opening or proposal opening, or by the date set out in the invitation to bid or request for proposals for filing of the protest.

(b)   An interested party may protest the cancellation of an invitation to bid or request for proposals by filing with the procurement officer a written protest that includes the information required by AS 36.30.560 no more than 10 days after a notice of cancellation is issued by the procurement officer.

History -

Eff. 3/30/90, Register 113; am 3/27/93, Register 125

Authority -

AS 36.30.040

02 AAC 012.0620

DECISION TO SUSPEND.

(a)   If a determination to suspend a contractor or prospective contractor is made under AS 36.30.635, the written decision shall be sent to the person to be suspended. The decision must state that

(1)   the suspension is for the period it takes to complete an investigation into possible debarment, but not for a period in excess of three months;

(2) bids or proposals will not be solicited from the suspended person, and, if they are received, they will not be considered during the period of suspension; and

(3) if a hearing has not been held, the suspended person may request a hearing.

(b) A contractor or prospective contractor is suspended upon issuance of the written decision to suspend. The suspension remains in effect during an appeal. The suspension may be ended by the officer who issued the written decision to suspend or by a court. Otherwise, the suspension ends when it has been in effect for three months or when a debarment decision takes effect.

History -

Eff. 1/1/88, Register 104

Authority -

AS 36.30.040

AS 36.30.635

02 AAC 012.0630

INITIATION OF DEBARMENT ACTION.

(a) Written notice of a proposed debarment action shall be sent by certified mail, return receipt requested, to the last known address of the contractor or prospective contractor. This notice must

(1) state that debarment is being considered;

(2) set out the reasons for the action;

(3) state that the contractor or prospective contractor may be represented by counsel.

(b) Notice of proposed debarment must also be sent to the attorney general and the purchasing agency.

History -

Eff. 1/1/88, Register 104

Authority -

AS 36.30.040

AS 36.30.635

02 AAC 012.0640

EFFECT OF DEBARMENT DECISION.

A debarment decision takes effect upon issuance of the written decision. After the debarment decision takes effect, the contractor remains debarred until a court or the commissioner of the department that issued the decision orders otherwise, or until the debarment period specified in the decision expires.

History -

Eff. 1/1/88, Register 104

Authority -

AS 36.30.040

AS 36.30.635

02 AAC 012.0650

REQUEST FOR HEARING.

A person entitled to a hearing under AS 36.30 must request in writing that a hearing be held. The request must be received by the commissioner of administration or the commissioner of transportation and public facilities, as appropriate, within the applicable time period set out in AS 36.30 and must set out specific grounds for the hearing.

History -

Eff. 1/1/88, Register 104

Authority -

AS 36.30.040

AS 36.30.695

02 AAC 012.0660

NOTICE OF TIME AND PLACE OF HEARING.

The hearing officer shall send a written notice of the time and place of a hearing to the last known addresses of the person requesting the hearing and other affected persons. A copy shall be sent to the purchasing agency.

History -

Eff. 1/1/88, Register 104

Authority -

AS 36.30.040

AS 36.30.670

02 AAC 012.0670

HEARING PROCEDURES.

(a) A hearing shall be as informal as is reasonable and appropriate under the circumstances. The weight to be attached to evidence presented is within the discretion of the hearing officer. Stipulations of fact agreed upon by the parties may be regarded and used as evidence at the hearing. The hearing officer may require evidence in addition to that offered by the parties.

(b) A hearing may be recorded. All evidence produced at a hearing shall be preserved.

(c) Opening statements may be made at the hearing at the discretion of the hearing officer.

(d) The particular principles of law listed in AS 36.30.860 will be considered by the hearing officer if they are specifically argued by a party.

(e) A witness must testify under oath or affirmation. A witness may be cross-examined.

History -

Eff. 1/1/88, Register 104

Authority -

AS 36.30.040

AS 36.30.670

02 AAC 012.0680

REPORTING SUSPECTED ANTICOMPETITIVE PRACTICES.

The chief procurement officer, in consultation with the attorney general, shall develop procedures, including forms, for reporting suspected anticompetitive practices. A procurement officer who suspects that an anticompetitive practice has occurred or may be occurring shall follow these procedures.

History -

Eff. 1/1/88, Register 104

Authority -

AS 36.30.040

AS 36.30.635

AS 36.30.920

02 AAC 012.0690

FRAUD OR BAD FAITH BY THE CONTRACTOR.

Upon finding that a solicitation or award is in violation of law and that the recipient of the contract acted fraudulently or in bad faith, the chief procurement officer or the head of a purchasing agency shall, after consulting with the attorney general, declare the contract void.

History -

Eff. 1/1/88, Register 104

Authority -

AS 36.30.040

AS 36.30.687

ARTICLE 13

INTERGOVERNMENTAL RELATIONS

02 AAC 012.0700

REQUESTS FOR PERSONNEL, INFORMATION, AND SERVICES.

(a) A request made to a public procurement unit by another public procurement unit to provide or make available personnel, services, information, or technical services under AS 36.30.730 must be complied with only to the extent that is mutually agreed upon.

(b) A request made to a state public procurement unit by another state public procurement unit to provide or make available personnel, services, information, or technical services under AS 36.30.730 must comply with the procedures established by the office of management and budget.

(c) A request made to a state public procurement unit by another public procurement unit to provide or make available personnel, services, information, or technical services under AS 36.30.730 must comply with AS 37.07, the Executive Budget Act.

> History -
> Eff. 1/1/88, Register 104
> Authority -
> AS 44.17.030
> Art. III, sec. 1, Ak. Const.
> Art. III, sec. 16, Ak. Const.
> Art. III, sec. 24, Ak. Const.

02 AAC 012.0710

DEFINITION.

In AS 36.30.790(5), "agency" means the same as in AS 36.30.990.

> History -
> Eff. 1/1/88, Register 104
> Authority -
> AS 44.17.030
> Art. III, sec. 1, Ak. Const.
> Art. III, sec. 16, Ak. Const.
> Art. III, sec. 24, Ak. Const.

ARTICLE 14
MISCELLANEOUS PROVISIONS

02 AAC 012.0720

APPLICABILITY.

This chapter applies to every transaction to which AS 36.30 applies.

History -

Eff. 1/1/88, Register 104

Authority -

AS 36.30.040

AS 36.30.850

02 AAC 012.0730

FEDERAL ASSISTANCE.

If a procurement involves the expenditure of federal money or requires federal assistance and there is a conflict between a provision of this chapter and a federal statute, regulation, policy, or requirement, the procurement officer shall comply with the federal statute, regulation, policy, or requirement.

History -

Eff. 1/1/88, Register 104

Authority -

AS 36.30.040

AS 36.30.890

02 AAC 012.0740

AUTHORITY TO DELEGATE.

(a) Except as otherwise provided by AS 36.30 or this chapter, the chief procurement officer, commissioner of administration, commissioner of transportation and public facilities, or the commissioner of commerce and economic development will, in their discretion, delegate their authority under AS 36.30 to an employee in a department or agency. Authority conferred on the head of a purchasing agency by AS 36.30 may be delegated by that officer to an employee in that purchasing agency. A delegation of authority must be in writing.

(b) The chief procurement officer, commissioner of administration, commissioner of transportation and public facilities, commissioner of commerce and economic development, or the head of a purchasing agency may revoke authority that the officer has delegated.

(c) An employee delegated authority by the chief procurement officer, commissioner of administration, commissioner of transportation and public facilities, commissioner of commerce and economic development, or the head of a purchasing agency, may exercise that authority only in accordance with the delegation, AS 36.30, and this chapter.

History -

Eff. 1/1/88, Register 104

Authority -

AS 36.30.040

AS 36.30.015

02 AAC 012.0750

PURCHASE REQUESTS BY AGENCIES.

(a) If the chief procurement officer believes that a purchase request is not in the best interests of the state or that further review is needed, the officer shall return the purchase request to the requesting agency.

(b) The chief procurement officer may decide when a procurement will be initiated.

History -

Eff. 1/1/88, Register 104

Authority -

AS 36.30.040

02 AAC 012.0760

PURCHASE OF ITEMS SEPARATELY FROM CONSTRUCTION CONTRACT.

The commissioner of transportation and public facilities is authorized to determine whether a supply item or group of supply items will be included as a part of, or procured separately from, a contract for construction.

History -

Eff. 1/1/88, Register 104

Authority -

AS 36.30.005

AS 36.30.040

02 AAC 012.0770

TRADE SECRETS AND CONFIDENTIAL TECHNICAL DATA.

The chief procurement officer and the commissioner of transportation and public facilities may establish procedures to protect the confidentiality of trade secret and confidential technical data.

History -

Eff. 1/1/88, Register 104

Authority -

AS 36.30.040

AS 36.30.140

AS 36.30.230

02 AAC 012.0780

DETERMINATION OF CONTRACTUAL TERMS AND CONDITIONS.

(a)   The chief procurement officer may determine the contractual provisions, terms, and conditions of solicitations and contracts, if the provisions, terms, and conditions are not contrary to statutory or regulatory requirements governing the procurement and if all standard contract terms have been reviewed and approved as to form by the attorney general.

(b)   The commissioner of transportation and public facilities may determine the contractual provisions and conditions of solicitations and contracts for construction and procurement of equipment or services for the state equipment fleet if the provisions, terms, and conditions are not contrary to statutory or regulatory requirements governing the procurement, and if all standard contract terms have been reviewed and approved as to form by the attorney general.

History -

Eff. 1/1/88, Register 104

Authority -

AS 36.30.040

AS 36.30.340

02 AAC 012.0790

NO RESTRICTIVE TERMS AND CONDITIONS.

Contractual terms and conditions may not have the effect of unnecessarily limiting competition or exclusively requiring a proprietary supply, service, or construction item or procurement from a sole source unless no other requirements will suffice.

History -

Eff. 1/1/88, Register 104

Authority -

AS 36.30.040

AS 36.30.060

02 AAC 012.0800

NON-COLLUSION CERTIFICATION.

Solicitations must provide that by submitting a bid or offer, the bidder or offeror certifies under penalty of perjury that the price submitted was independently arrived at without collusion.

History -

Eff. 1/1/88, Register 104

Authority -

AS 36.30.040

02 AAC 012.0810

BID, PAYMENT, AND PERFORMANCE BONDS FOR CONTRACTS.

Bid, payment, and performance bonds or other security shall be required for all construction contracts over $100,000, and may be required for contracts as the chief procurement officer, the head of a purchasing agency, or the officer's designee deems advisable to protect the interests of the state. Any such requirements must be set out in the solicitation. Irrevocable letters of credit may be substituted for the required bond at the discretion of the head of the purchasing agency.

History -

Eff. 1/1/88, Register 104

Authority -

AS 36.30.040

AS 36.30.120

02 AAC 012.0820

INSTALLMENT PURCHASE CONTRACTS.

Supply contracts may provide for installment purchase payments, including interest charges, over a period of time. If the procurement is made by competitive sealed bid or competitive sealed proposal, an installment payment agreement may not be used unless provision for installment payments is included in the solicitation.

History -

Eff. 1/1/88, Register 104

Authority -

AS 36.30.040

02 AAC 012.0830

ALTERNATE BIDS OR PROPOSALS.

Alternate bids or proposals are nonresponsive unless the solicitation states that such bids or proposals may be accepted.

History -

Eff. 1/1/88, Register 104; am 3/27/93, Register 125

Authority -

AS 36.30.040

AS 36.30.110

AS 36.30.210

02 AAC 012.0840

CONDITIONING BIDS OR PROPOSALS ON OTHER AWARDS NOT ACCEPTABLE.

A bid or proposal that is conditioned upon receiving award of both the particular contract being solicited and another state contract is nonresponsive unless conditioned bids are specifically authorized in the invitation to bid.

History -

Eff. 1/1/88, Register 104

Authority -

AS 36.30.040

AS 36.30.110

AS 36.30.210

02 AAC 012.0850

EXTENSION OF SOLICITATION OPENING TIME; CANCELLATION OF SOLICITATION; AMENDMENT OF SOLICITATION.

(a)   Before the opening of bids or proposals, a solicitation may be amended, or time for opening may be extended, upon the procurement officer's determination that the extension or amendment is in the state's best interest. All potential bidders or offerors known to have copies of the solicitation shall be advised of the extension or amendment.

(b) Before the opening of bids or proposals, a solicitation may be canceled in whole or in part if the chief procurement officer or the head of a purchasing agency issuing a solicitation determines that cancellation is in the state's best interest. Reasons for cancellation include the following:

(1) the state no longer requires the supplies, services, or construction;

(2) the state no longer can reasonably expect to pay for the procurement;

(3) proposed amendments to the solicitation would be of such magnitude that a new solicitation is desirable; or

(4) the officer, after consultation with the attorney general, determines that a solicitation is in violation of the law.

History -

Eff. 1/1/88, Register 104

Authority -

AS 36.30.040

AS 36.30.350

02 AAC 012.0860

REJECTION OF ALL BIDS OR PROPOSALS.

After the opening of bids or proposals or after notice of intent to award but before award, all bids or proposals may be rejected in whole or in part by the chief procurement officer or the head of a purchasing agency issuing the solicitation. Reasons for rejection include the following:

(1) the supplies, services, or construction being procured are no longer required;

(2) ambiguous or otherwise inadequate specifications were part of the solicitation;

(3) the solicitation did not provide for consideration of all factors of significance to the state;

(4) prices exceed available money and it would not be appropriate to adjust quantities to accommodate available money;

(5) all otherwise acceptable bids or proposals received are at unacceptable prices;

(6) there is reason to believe that the bids or proposals may not have been independently arrived at in open competition, may have been collusive, or may have been submitted in bad faith; or

(7) the award is not in the best interests of the state.

History -

Eff. 1/1/88, Register 104

Authority -

AS 36.30.040

AS 36.30.350

02 AAC 012.0870

REJECTION OF INDIVIDUAL BIDS OR PROPOSALS.

Reasons for rejecting an individual bid or proposal include the following:

(1) the business that submitted the bid or proposal is not responsible as determined under 2 AAC 12.490;

(2) the bid or proposal is nonresponsive;

(3) the supply, service, or construction item fails to meet the specifications or other acceptability criteria set out in the solicitation; or

(4) the bid or proposal fails to meet the goals or other provisions set out in the solicitation to eliminate and prevent in state contracting discrimination because of race, religion, color, national origin, sex, age, marital status, pregnancy, parenthood, or disability.

> History -
>
> Eff. 1/1/88, Register 104; am 5/16/88, Register 106; am 6/29/95, Register 134
>
> Authority -
>
> AS 36.30.040
>
> AS 36.30.350

02 AAC 012.0880

DISPOSITION OF BIDS OR PROPOSALS.

If bids or proposals are rejected, the bids or proposals that have been opened must be retained in the procurement file.

> History -
>
> Eff. 1/1/88, Register 104
>
> Authority -
>
> AS 36.30.040
>
> AS 36.30.350

02 AAC 012.0890

APPLICATION OF PREFERENCES.

In a solicitation to which both the Alaska bidder's preference (AS 36.30.170(b)) and the Alaska products preference (AS 36.30.328) apply, a procurement officer shall apply the bidder's preference first and the products preference second.

> History -
>
> Eff. 1/1/88, Register 104
>
> Authority -

AS 36.30.040

AS 36.30.170

AS 36.30.328

AS 36.30.336

02 AAC 012.0900

LOW TIE BIDS OR PROPOSALS.

Low tie bids or proposals are low responsive bids or proposals from responsible bidders or offerors which are identical in price after application of preferences under AS 36.30.170(b), 36.30.250, and 2 AAC 12.890. If low tie bids or proposals exist, award shall be made through a random drawing. Award may not be made by dividing the procurement among identical bidders.

> History -
>
> Eff. 1/1/88, Register 104
>
> Authority -
>
> AS 36.30.040
>
> AS 36.30.150

02 AAC 012.0910

EXTENSION OF TIME FOR BID OR PROPOSAL ACCEPTANCE.

After opening bids or proposals, a procurement officer may request bidders or offerors to extend the time during which the state may accept a bid or proposal.

> History -
>
> Eff. 1/1/88, Register 104
>
> Authority -
>
> AS 36.30.040

02 AAC 012.0920

MULTIPLE AWARD.

A multiple award may be made if award to two or more bidders or offerors of similar products is necessary for adequate delivery, service, or product compatibility. A multiple award shall be made in accordance with the provisions relating to competitive sealed bidding, competitive sealed proposals, small purchases, and emergency procurements, as applicable. Multiple awards may not be made if a single award will meet the state's needs without sacrifice of economy or service. Awards may not be made for the purpose of dividing the procurement, or to allow for user preference unrelated to utility or economy.

History -

Eff. 1/1/88, Register 104

Authority -

AS 36.30.040

02 AAC 012.0990

DEFINITIONS

(a)   In this chapter

(1) 'business license' means a license required under the Alaska Business License Act (AS 43.70) by the division of occupational licensing and, for a person engaging in a business subject to licensing provisions of a regulatory nature, a license, certificate, permit, registration, or similar evidence of authority issued for an occupation by competent legal authority;

(2) 'chief procurement officer' means the officer appointed under AS 36.30.010 as the chief procurement officer;

(3) 'concession contracts' means contracts entered into by the Department of Natural Resources under AS 41.21;

(4) 'cost analysis' means the evaluation of cost data for the purpose of arriving at costs actually incurred or estimates of costs to be incurred, prices to be paid, and costs to be reimbursed;

(5) 'cost data' means information concerning the actual or estimated cost of labor, material, overhead, and other cost elements that have been actually incurred or that are expected to be incurred by the contractor in performing the contract;

(6) 'employment agreement' means an agreement or contract between an employer and an employee in which the terms and conditions of employment are set out, and includes a contract with a citizen of a foreign country for services to be performed primarily in the foreign country, if the contract provides for such matters as state control of the work performed, the hours of work, the benefits that will be provided to a person who performs work under the contract, and the state's right to discharge a person who performs work under the contract;

(7) 'interested party' means an actual or prospective bidder or offeror whose economic interest might be affected substantially and directly by the issuance of a contract solicitation, the award of a contract, or the failure to award a contract;

(8) 'minor informalities' means matters of form rather than substance which are evident from the bid document, or are insignificant matters that have a negligible effect on price, quantity, quality, delivery, or contractual conditions and can be waived or corrected without prejudice to other bidders;

(9) 'nonresponsive' means a bid or proposal that does not conform in all material respects to the solicitation;

(10) 'price analysis' means the evaluation of price data, without analysis of the separate cost components and profit as in cost analysis, which may assist in arriving at prices to be paid and costs to be reimbursed;

(11) 'price data' means factual information concerning offered or proposed selling prices, historical selling prices, and current selling prices, including profit, for supplies, services, or construction substantially similar to those being procured;

(12) 'responsive bidder' means a firm or person who has submitted a bid that conforms in all material respects to the solicitation;

(13) 'soliciatation' means an invitation to bid, a request for proposals, a request for quotations, or any other document issued by the state for the purpose of soliciting bids or proposals to perform a state contract.

(b) In AS 36.30,

(1) 'medical doctor' means a person who is licensed to practice medicine in the state under AS 08.64; a person who is authorized to practice in the state as an advanced nurse practitioner because of specialized education and experience and who is certified to perform acts of medical diagnosis and to prescribe medical, therapeutic, or corrective measures under regulations adopted by the Board of Nursing (12 AAC 44.400); or a physician assistant as defined in 12 AAC 40.990;

(2) 'protestor' means an actual or prospective bidder, offeror, or contractor who is aggrieved in connection with the solicitation or the award of a contract and who files a protest.

(c) In the definition of 'procurement officer' set out in AS 36.30.990(13), 'authorized' means authorized by a written delegation under 2 AAC 12.740 by the head of an agency that has a delegation of procurement authority based on a written determination of capability under AS 36.30.015.

History -

Effective 1/1/88, Register 104; am 3/30/90, Register 113; am 3/27/93, Register 125

Authority -

AS 36.30.040

DOCUMENT 6

Model Request for Proposals
State of Alaska

S T A T E   O F   A L A S K A
Department Of *Name*
Division Of *Name*
Physical Address

Request For Proposals
RFP *Number*
Date Of Issue: *Date*

Title And Purpose Of RFP:
*Procurement Officer Note: Provide a brief statement
that summarizes RFP; Who, What, Where, When, Why*

Proposers Are Not Required To Return This Form.

Name
Procurement Officer
Department Of *Name*

Name
Project Director
Department Of *Name*

TABLE OF CONTENTS

SECTION ONE

Introduction and Instructions   *Page*

Procurement Officer Note: REMEMBER TO REVISE PAGE NUMBERS TO MATCH YOUR RFP

SECTION FOUR

Background Information

SECTION FIVE

Scope and Schedule

SECTION SIX

Proposal Format and Content

SECTION SEVEN

Evaluation Criteria and Contractor Selection

SECTION EIGHT

Attachments

Attachments

Standard Agreement Form

Appendix A

Appendix B1 or B2

Notice of Intent to Award

Proposal Evaluation Form

Contractor Evaluation Form

Checklist

Instructions to Procurement Officers

- Instructions to procurement officers are shaded and begin with "Procurement Officer Notes." Delete these instructions in the final draft of the RFP.

- Procurement officer word choices in a section are in caps, bold print and italics. For example: WILL/WILL NOT. You should make the choice, then enter the word in regular style print, e.g., will not.

- The location of unique names and numbers are identified like this: NAME or NUMBER. You should provide the correct name or number and enter that information in regular style print, e.g., 78492.

- Delete this instruction page in the final draft.

Section One

Introduction And Instructions

1.01

Return Mailing Address, Contact Person, Telephone & Fax Numbers,

Deadline for Receipt of Proposals

Procurement Officer Note: Enter Appropriate Information - Alter, Revise, Or delete As Required.

Proposers must submit one copy of their proposal, in writing, to the procurement officer in a sealed envelope. It must be addressed as set out below.

Department of NAME

Division of NAME

Attention: PROCUREMENT OFFICER NAME

RFP Number: NUMBER

Project name: NAME

MAILING ADDRESS

CITY, ALASKA, ZIP CODE

Proposals must be received no later than 1:30 PM, Alaska prevailing time on DATE. Fax proposals are acceptable but not encouraged. Oral proposals are not acceptable.

A proposer's failure to submit their proposal prior to the deadline will cause their proposal to be disqualified. Late proposals or amendments will not be opened or accepted for evaluation.

Procurement Officer Note: Enter Appropriate Information - Alter, Revise, Or delete As Required.

PROCUREMENT OFFICER: NAME - PHONE # 907-NUMBER - FAX # 907-NUMBER - TDD # 907-NUMBER

PROJECT DIRECTOR: NAME - PHONE # 907-NUMBER - FAX # 907-NUMBER - TDD # 907-NUMBER

CONTACT PERSON: NAME - PHONE # 907-NUMBER - FAX # 907-NUMBER - TDD # 907-NUMBER

Procurement Officer Note: If Reproduction Cost Is Less Than Five Dollars delete The Following Two Sentences.

One RFP is provided by the State. Additional RFP's may be purchased for the cost of reproduction, $.25 per page.

1.02

Contract Term & Work Schedule

Procurement Officer Note: Enter Appropriate Information - Alter, Revise, Or delete As Required.

The contract term and work schedule set out herein represent the State's best estimate of the schedule that will be followed. If a component of this schedule, such as the opening date, is delayed, the rest of the schedule will be shifted by the same number of days.

The length of the contract will be from the date of award, approximately DATE , for approximately NUMBER calendar days until completion, approximately DATE .

The approximate contract schedule is as follows;

Procurement Officer Note: Enter All Critical Activities, Dates, & Milestones. Account For All Of The Time From The Beginning To The End Of The Project. Enter Appropriate Information - Alter, Revise, Or Delete As Required.

[a] Issue RFP DATE ,

(Minimum 21 days circulation period between issue and open date, also requires publication in the Alaska Administrative Journal.)

[b] Open RFP DATE ,

[c] Proposal Evaluation Committee complete evaluation by DATE ,

[d] State issues Notice of Intent to Award a Contract DATE ,

(Minimum period between issuing notice of intent and issuing contract is 10 days - to allow time for protests.)

[e] State issues contract DATE ,

[f] Contract start DATE,

[g]   First contractor work period DATE to DATE ,

[h]   Contractor submit first draft DATE ,

[i]   First draft review by State DATE to DATE ,

[j]   Draft back to contractor for revision as required DATE to DATE , Contractor submit final report DATE.

1.03

Purpose of the Request for Proposal (RFP)

Procurement Officer Note: Enter Appropriate Information - Alter, Revise, Or delete As Required.

The Department of NAME, Division of NAME is soliciting proposals for Insert A brief Description Of The Purpose Of The RFP Consistent With Cover Page; A more Detailed Description Including Scope Of Work Is To Be Provided Later In the Document.

1.04

Budget

Procurement Officer Note: Enter Appropriate Information - Alter, Revise, Or delete As Required.

Department of NAME, Division of NAME, estimates a budget of between LOW RANGE and HIGH RANGE dollars for completion of this project. Proposals priced at more than DOLLARS will be considered non-responsive.

1.05

Location of Work

Procurement Officer Note: Enter Appropriate Information - Alter, Revise, Or delete As Required.

The location(s) the work is to be performed, completed and managed IS / ARE at LOCATION(S) .

The State WILL / WILL NOT provide work-space for the contractor. The contractor must provide its own work-space.

The contractor should include in their price proposal: transportation, lodging and per diem costs sufficient to pay for NUMBER person(s) to make NUMBER trip(s) to LOCATION. Travel to other locations will not be required.

1.06

Assistance to Proposers With a Disability

Procurement Officer Note: This Section Should Not Be Altered Or Deleted.

Proposers with a disability may receive accommodation regarding the means of communicating this

RFP or participating in the procurement process. For more information contact the procurement officer no later than ten days prior to the deadline set for receipt of proposals.

1.07

Required Review

Procurement Officer Note: This Section Should Not Be Altered Or Deleted.

Proposers should carefully review this solicitation for defects and questionable or objectionable matter. Comments concerning defects and objectionable material must be made in writing and received by the contracting officer at least ten days before the proposal opening. This will allow issuance of any necessary amendments. It will also help prevent the opening of a defective solicitation and exposure of offeror's proposals upon which award could not be made. Protests based on any omission or error, or on the content of the solicitation, will be disallowed if these faults have not been brought to the attention of the contracting officer, in writing, at least ten days before the time set for opening.

1.08

Questions Received Prior to Opening of Proposals

Procurement Officer Note: Alter, Revise, Or Delete As Required.

All questions must be in writing and directed to the issuing office, addressed to the procurement officer. Telephone conversations must be confirmed in writing by the interested party.

Two types of questions generally arise. One may be answered by directing the questioner to a specific section of the RFP. These questions may be answered over the telephone. Other questions may be more complex and may require a written amendment to the RFP. The procurement officer will make that decision.

1.09

Amendments

Procurement Officer Note: THIS SECTION SHOULD NOT BE ALTERED OR DELETED.

If an amendment is issued it will be provided to all who were mailed a copy of the RFP.

1.10

Alternate Proposals

Procurement Officer Note: Alter or Revise As Required. 2 AAC 12.830 makes alternate proposals non-responsive unless the solicitation specifically permits them.

In accordance with 2 AAC 12.830 alternate proposals (proposals that offer something different than what is asked for) will be rejected.

1.11

Right of Rejection

Procurement Officer Note: Alter, Revise, Or Delete As Required.

Proposers must comply with all of the terms of the RFP, the State Procurement Code (AS 36.30), and all applicable local, state, and federal laws, codes, and regulations. The procurement officer may reject any proposal that does not comply with all of the material and substantial terms, conditions, and performance requirements of the RFP.

Proposers may not restrict the rights of the State or qualify their proposal. If a proposer does so, the procurement officer may determine the proposal to be a non-responsive counter-offer and the proposal may be rejected.

Minor informalities, that do not affect responsiveness; that are merely a matter of form or format; that do not change the relative standing or otherwise prejudice other offers; that do not change the meaning or scope of the RFP; that are trivial, negligible, or immaterial in nature; that do not reflect a material change in the work; or, that do not constitute a substantial reservation against a requirement or provision may be waived by the procurement officer.

The State reserves the right to refrain from making an award if it determines that to be in its best interest.

1.12

State Not Responsible for Preparation Costs

Procurement Officer Note: this section should not be altered or deleted.

The State will not pay any cost associated with the preparation, submittal, presentation, or evaluation of any proposal.

1.13

Disclosure of Proposal Contents

Procurement Officer Note: This section should not be altered or deleted.

All proposals and other material submitted become the property of the State of Alaska and may be returned only at the State's option. AS 09.25.110 requires public records to be open to reasonable inspection. All proposal information, including detailed price and cost information, will be held in confidence during the evaluation process and prior to the time a Notice of Intent to Award is issued.

Thereafter, proposals will become public information.

Trade secrets and other proprietary data contained in proposals may be held confidential if the proposer requests, in writing, that the procurement officer does so, and if the procurement officer agrees, in writing, to do so. Material considered confidential by the proposer must be clearly identified and the proposer must include a brief statement that sets out the reasons for confidentiality.

1.14

Subcontractors

Procurement Officer Note: REVISE as REQUIRED.

Subcontractors will not be allowed.

OR

Subcontractors may be used to perform work under this contract. If a proposer intends to use subcontractors the proposer must identify, in their proposal, the names of the subcontractors and the portions of the work the subcontractors will perform.

If a proposal with subcontractors is selected, the proposer must provide the following information concerning each prospective subcontractor within five working days from the date of the State's request:

[a]   complete name of the subcontractor,

[b]   complete address of the subcontractor,

[c]   type of work the subcontractor will be performing,

[d]   percentage of work the subcontractor will be providing,

[e]   evidence, as set out in the relevant section of this RFP, that the subcontractor holds a valid Alaska business license,

[f]   a written statement, signed by each proposed subcontractor, that clearly verifies that the subcontractor is committed to render the services required by the contract.

A proposer's failure to provide this information, within the time set, may cause the State to consider their proposal non-responsive and reject the proposal.

The substitution of one subcontractor for another may be made only at the discretion of the project director and with prior written approval from the project director.

1.15

Joint Ventures

Procurement Officer Note: Revise As Required.

Joint ventures will not be allowed.

OR

Joint ventures are acceptable. If submitting a proposal as a joint venture, the proposer must submit a copy of the joint venture agreement which identifies the principles involved, and their rights and responsibilities regarding performance and payment.

1.16

Proposer's Certification

Procurement Officer Note: Alter, Revise, Or Delete As Required

By signature on their proposal, proposers certify that they comply with;

[a]   the laws of the State of Alaska,

[b]   the applicable portion of the Federal Civil Rights Act of 1964,

[c]   the Equal Employment Opportunity Act and the regulations issued thereunder by the federal government,

[d]   the Americans with Disabilities Act of 1990, and the regulations issued thereunder by the federal government,

[e]   all terms and conditions set out in this RFP, and,

[f]   a condition that the proposal submitted was independently arrived at, without collusion, under penalty of perjury, and

[g]   that their offers will remain open and valid for at least 90 days.

By signature on their proposal, proposers also certify that programs, services, and activities provided to the general public under the resulting contract are in conformance with the Americans with Disabilities Act of 1990, and the regulations issued thereunder by the federal government.

If any proposer fails to comply with [a] through [g] of this paragraph, the State reserves the right to disregard the proposal, terminate the contract, or consider the contractor in default.

1.17

Conflict of Interest

Procurement Officer Note: Alter, Revise, Or delete As Required.

Each proposal shall include a statement indicating whether or not the firm or any individuals working on the contract has a possible conflict of interest (e.g., employed by the State of Alaska) and, if so, the nature of that conflict. The Commissioner, Department of NAME , reserves the right to cancel the award if any interest disclosed from any source could either give the appearance of a conflict or cause speculation as to the objectivity of the program to be developed by the offeror. The Commissioner's determination regarding any questions of conflict of interest shall be final.

1.18

Right to Inspect Place of Business

Procurement Officer Note: Alter, Revise, Or Delete As Required.

At reasonable times, the State may inspect those areas of the contractor's place of business that are related to the performance of a contract. If the State makes such an inspection, the contractor must provide reasonable assistance.

1.19

Solicitation Advertising

Procurement Officer Note: Alter, Revise, Or Delete As Required. Look Up 2 Aac 12.220 And Comply With Its Public Notice Requirements.

Public notice has been provided in accordance with 2 AAC 12.220.

1.20

News Releases

Procurement Officer Note: Enter Appropriate Information - Alter, Revise, Or delete As Required.

News releases related to this RFP will not be made without prior approval of the Commissioner of NAME, and then only in coordination with the project director.

1.21

Assignment

Procurement Officer Note: THIS SECTION SHOULD NOT BE ALTERED OR DELETED.

Per 2 AAC 12.480, the contractor may not transfer or assign any portion of the contract without prior written approval from the chief procurement officer or the head of the purchasing agency.

1.22

Disputes

Procurement Officer Note: This Section Should Not Be Altered Or Deleted.

Any dispute arising out of this agreement will be resolved under the laws of Alaska. Any appeal of an administrative order or any original action to enforce any provision of this agreement or to obtain relief from or remedy in connection with this agreement may be brought only in the superior court for the First Judicial District of Alaska.

1.23

Severability

Procurement Officer Note: This Section Should Not Be Altered Or Deleted.

If any provision of the contract or agreement is declared by a court to be illegal or in conflict with any law, the validity of the remaining terms and provisions will not be affected; and, the rights and obligations of the parties will be construed and enforced as if the contract did not contain the particular provision held to be invalid.

1.24

Federal Requirements

Procurement Officer Note: Alter, Revise, Or Delete As Required.

The proposer must identify all known federal requirements that apply to the proposal, the evaluation, or the contract.

SECTION TWO

STANDARD PROPOSAL INFORMATION

2.01

Authorized Signature

Procurement Officer Note: This Section Should Not Be Altered Or Deleted.

All proposals must be signed by an individual authorized to bind the proposer to the provisions of the RFP. Proposals must remain open and valid for at least ninety (90) days from the opening date.

2.02

Pre-proposal Conference

Procurement Officer Note: Enter Appropriate Information - Alter, Revise, Or delete As Required. Any Pre-Proposal Conference That Is Held Must Be accessible To prospective proposers With Disabilities. This Means That The Location Must be Accessible. In Addition, Signing Interpreters Or Other Accommodations must Be Provided If Required.

A pre-proposal conference will be held at TIME, Alaska Prevailing Time, on DATE in the PLACE conference room on the NUMBER floor of the NAME Building in CITY , Alaska. The purpose of the conference is to discuss the work to be performed with the prospective proposers and allow them to ask questions concerning the RFP. Questions and answers will be transcribed and sent to prospective proposers as soon as possible after the meeting.

Proposers with a disability needing accommodation should contact the procurement officer prior to the date set for the pre-proposal conference so that reasonable accommodation can be made.

2.03

Site Inspection

Procurement Officer Note: Alter, Revise, Or Delete As Required.

The State may conduct on-site visits to evaluate the proposer's capacity to perform the contract. Proposers must agree, at risk of being found non-responsive and having their proposal rejected, to provide the State reasonable access to relevant portions of their work sites. Site inspection will be made by individuals designated by the procurement officer at the State's expense.

2.04

Amendments to Proposals

Procurement Officer Note: Alter, Revise, Or Delete As Required.

Amendments to or withdrawals of proposals will only be allowed if acceptable requests are received prior to the deadline set for receipt of proposals. No amendments or withdrawals will be accepted after the deadline unless they are in response to State's request in accordance with 2 AAC 12.290.

2.05

Supplemental Terms and Conditions

Procurement Officer Note: this section should not be altered or deleted.

Proposals including supplemental terms and conditions will be accepted, but supplemental conditions that conflict with those contained in this RFP or that diminish the State's right's under any contract resulting from the RFP will be considered null and void. The State is not responsible for identifying conflicting supplemental terms and conditions before issuing a contract award. After award of contract:

[a] if conflict arises between a supplemental term or condition included in the proposal and a term or condition of the RFP, the term or condition of the RFP will prevail; and

[b] if the State's rights would be diminished as a result of application of a supplemental term or condition included in the proposal, the supplemental term or condition will be considered null and void.

2.06

Discussions with Proposers

Procurement Officer Note: Alter, Revise, Or Delete As Required.

Discussions Held Must Be Accessible To prospective proposers With Disabilities. This Means that The Location Must Be Accessible.

In Addition, Signing Interpreters Or other Accommodations Must Be Provided If Required.

The State may conduct discussions with proposers for the purpose of clarification in accordance with AS 36.30.240 and 2 AAC 12.290. The purpose of these discussions will be to ensure full understanding of the requirements of the RFP and proposal. Discussions will be limited to specific sections of the identified by the procurement officer. Discussions will only be held with proposers who have submitted a proposal deemed reasonably susceptible for award by the procurement officer. Discussions, if held, will be after initial evaluation of proposals by the PEC. If modifications are made as a result of these discussions they will be put in writing. Following discussions, the procurement officer may set a time for best and final proposal submissions from those proposers with whom discussions were held. Proposals may be reevaluated after receipt of best and final proposal submissions.

Proposers with a disability needing accommodation should contact the procurement officer prior to the date set for discussions so that reasonable accommodation can be made.

2.07

Prior Experience

Procurement Officer Note: Alter, Revise, Or Delete As Required.

No specific minimums have been set for this RFP.

OR

In order for their offers to be considered responsive proposers must meet these minimum prior experience requirements.

Procurement Officer Note: Provide Detail On The specific Prior Experience You Require.

State The Minimum Acceptable Amount Of Time

• Remember There Must Be Some Way For Third-Party Independent Verification Of The Experience You Ask For

• Be Careful About What You Ask For As You May Set Requirements So High That You Disqualify Good Potential Contractors

• Specifications such as prior experience may not be unduly restrictive per AS 36.30.060 (c). Make sure that you have a reasonable basis for this and all other specifications.

Procurement Officer Note: This Sentence Should Not Be Altered, But May Be deleted If Not Required.

A proposer's failure to meet these minimum prior experience requirements will cause their proposal to be considered non-responsive and their proposal will be rejected.

2.08

Evaluation of Proposals

Procurement Officer Note: REVISE AS REQUIRED. Cost Must Be An Evaluation Factor Unless The service Sought Is An Architectural, Engineering, Or Land Surveying Contract, That Is Selected In Accordance With As 36.30.270 (A)

The procurement officer, or an evaluation committee made up of the procurement officer and at least two State employees, will evaluate proposals. The evaluation will be based solely on the evaluation factors set out in section seven of this RFP.

2.09

Vendor Tax ID

Procurement Officer Note: This section should not be altered or deleted.

A valid Vendor Tax ID must be submitted to the issuing office with the proposal or within five days of the State's request.

2.10

F.O.B. Point

Procurement Officer Note: Delete if goods will not be PURCHASED as a result of this contract.

All goods purchased through this contract will be F.O.B. final destination. Unless specifically stated otherwise, all the prices offered must include the delivery costs to any location within the State of Alaska.

2.11

Alaska Business License & Other Required Licenses

Procurement Officer Note: This Section Should Not Be Altered Or Deleted.

At the time the proposals are opened, all proposers must hold a valid Alaska business license and any necessary applicable professional licenses required by Alaska Statute. Proposers should contact the Department of Commerce and Economic Development, Division of Occupational Licensing, P.O. Box 110806, Juneau, Alaska 99811-0806, for information on these licenses. Proposers must submit evidence of a valid Alaska business license with their proposal. A proposer's failure to submit this evidence with their proposal will cause their proposal to be determined non-responsive. Acceptable evidence that the proposer possesses a valid Alaska business license may consist of any one of the following:

[a]   copy of an Alaska business license with the correct SIC code;

[b]   certification on the proposal that the proposer has a valid Alaska business license and has included the license number in the proposal;

[c]   a canceled check for the Alaska business license fee;

[d]   a copy of the Alaska business license application with a receipt stamp from the State's occupational licensing office; or

[e]   a sworn and notarized affidavit that the proposer has applied and paid for the Alaska business license.

2.12

Application of Preferences

Procurement Officer Note: THIS Section Should Not Be Altered Or Deleted.

Certain preferences apply to all contracts for professional services, regardless of their dollar value. The following sections contain excerpts from the relevant statutes and codes; explain when they apply; and, provide examples of how to calculate the preferences.

2.13

5% Alaskan Bidder Preference

2 AAC 12.260. & AS 36.30.170

Procurement Officer Note: This Section Should Not Be Altered Or Deleted.

An Alaska Bidder Preference of five percent will be applied prior to evaluation. The preference will be given to a person who: (a) holds a current Alaska business license; (b) submits a proposal for goods or services under the name on the Alaska business license; (c) has maintained a place of business within the State staffed by the proposer, or an employee of the proposer, for a period of six months immediately preceding the date of the proposal; (d) is incorporated or qualified to do business under the laws of the State, is a sole proprietorship, and the proprietor is a resident of the State or is a partnership, and all partners are residents of the State; (e) if a joint venture, is composed entirely of entities that qualify under (a)-(d) of this subsection.

Alaska Bidder Preference Affidavit

In order to receive the Alaska Bidder Preference, proposals must include an affidavit certifying that the proposer is eligible to receive the Alaska Bidder Preference.

EXAMPLE

Sample Application

5% Alaska Bidder Preference

[STEP 1]

List the raw proposal prices and identify those eligible for preference.

Proposer #1	-	Non-Alaskan Proposer	$40,000
Proposer #2	-	Alaskan Proposer	$45,000
Proposer #3	-	Alaskan Proposer	$50,000

[STEP 2]

Calculate the amount of the 5% Alaska Bidder Preference by multiplying the Alaskan proposals by .05 and deducting that amount from the price(s).

| Proposer #2 | - | $45,000 x .05 = $2,250 | $45,000 - $2,250 = $42,750 |
| Proposer #3 | - | $50,000 x .05 = $2,500 | $50,000 - $2,500 = $47,500 |

[STEP 3]

List all proposal prices, adjusted where appropriate, by the application of the Alaska Bidder Preference.

Proposer #1	-	Non-Alaskan Proposer	$40,000
Proposer #2	-	Alaskan Proposer	$42,750
Proposer #3	-	Alaskan Proposer	$47,500

[STEP 4]

Identify the lowest priced proposal. In the example, Proposer #1 ($40,000) is lowest and would get the benefits allotted to the lowest priced proposal, provided it is a responsive and responsible proposal.

2.14

15% Employment Program Preference

AS 36.30.250. & AS 36.30.170

Procurement Officer Note: This Section Should Not Be Altered Or Deleted.

If a proposer qualifies for the Alaska Bidder Preference; is offering services through a qualified employment program; and, offers a proposal that is not more than fifteen percent higher than the lowest proposal, the procurement officer will award the maximum number of points allocated for cost to that proposer.

EXAMPLE

5% Employment Program Preference

[STEP 1]

List the raw proposal prices and identify those eligible for preference.

Proposer #1 -   Non-Alaskan Proposer $40,000

    No Employment Program

Proposer #2 -   Alaskan Proposer $45,000

    No Employment Program

Proposer #3 -   Alaskan Proposer $50,000

    With Employment Program

[STEP 2]

Calculate the amount of the 5% Alaska Bidder Preference by multiplying the Alaskan proposals by .05 and deducting that amount from the price(s).

Proposer #2 - $45,000 x .05 = $2,250 $45,000 - $2,250 = $42,750

Proposer #3 - $50,000 x .05 = $2,500 $50,000 - $2,500 = $47,500

[STEP 3]

List all proposal prices, adjusted where appropriate, by the application of the Alaska Bidder Preference.

Proposer #1 -   Non-Alaskan Proposer $40,000

    No Employment Program

Proposer #2 -   Alaskan Proposer $42,750

    No Employment Program

Proposer #3 -   Alaskan Proposer $47,500

    With Employment Program

[STEP 4]

Calculate the amount of the 15% Employment Program Preference by multiplying the lowest priced proposal by .15.

Proposer #1 - $40,000 x .15 = $6,000

[STEP 5]

List all proposal prices, adjusted, where appropriate, by the application of the Alaska Bidder Preference, and, where appropriate, deduct the employment program preference.

Proposer #1 -   Non-Alaskan Proposer $40,000

    No Employment Program

Proposer #2 -   Alaskan Proposer $42,750

    No Employment Program

Proposer #3 -   Alaskan Proposer $47,500 - $6,000 = $41,500

   With Employment Program

[STEP 6]

Identify the lowest priced proposal. In the example, Proposer #1 ($40,000)is lowest and would get the benefits allotted to the lowest priced proposal, provided, it is a responsive and responsible proposal.

2.15

10% Alaskans with Disabilities Preference

AS 36.30.250. & AS 36.30.170

Procurement Officer Note: This Section Should Not Be Altered Or Deleted.

If a proposer qualifies for the Alaska Bidder Preference; is a sole proprietorship owned by a person with a disability; and, offers a proposal that is not more than ten percent higher than the lowest proposal, the procurement officer will award the maximum number of points allocated for cost to that proposer.

EXAMPLE

10% Alaskans With Disabilities Preference

[STEP 1]

List the raw proposal prices and identify those eligible for preference.

Proposer #1 -   Non-Alaskan Proposer $40,000

   Not Disabled

Proposer #2 -   Alaskan Proposer $45,000

   Not Disabled

Proposer #3 -   Alaskan Proposer $50,000

   Disabled Alaskan

[STEP 2]

Calculate the amount of the 5% Alaska Bidder Preference by multiplying the Alaskan proposals by .05 and deducting that amount from the price(s).

Proposer #2 - $45,000 x .05 = $2,250 $45,000 - $2,250 = $42,750

Proposer #3 - $50,000 x .05 = $2,500 $50,000 - $2,500 = $47,500

[STEP 3]

List all proposal prices, adjusted where appropriate, by the application of the Alaska Bidder Preference.

Proposer #1 -   Non-Alaskan Proposer $40,000

   Not Disabled

Proposer #2 -   Alaskan Proposer $42,750

   Not Disabled

Proposer #3 -   Alaskan Proposer $47,500

   Disabled Alaskan

[STEP 4]

Calculate the amount of the 10% Alaskans with Disabilities Preference by multiplying the lowest priced proposal by .10.

Proposer #1 - $40,000 x .10 = $4,000

[STEP 5]

List all proposal prices, adjusted, where appropriate, by the application of the Alaska Bidder Preference, and, where appropriate, deduct the Alaskans with Disabilities Preference.

Proposer #1 -   Non-Alaskan Proposer $40,000

   Not Disabled

Proposer #2 -   Alaskan Proposer $42,750

   Not Disabled

Proposer #3 -   Alaskan Proposer $47,500 - $4,000 = $43,500

   Disabled Alaskan

[STEP 6]

Identify the lowest priced proposal. In the example, Proposer #1 ($40,000) is lowest and would get the benefits allotted to the lowest priced proposal, provided it is a responsive and responsible proposal.

2.16

10% Employers of People with Disabilities Preference
AS 36.30.250. & AS 36.30.170

Procurement Officer Note: This Section Should Not Be Altered Or Deleted.

If a proposer qualifies for the Alaska Bidder Preference; employs a staff that is made up of fifty percent or more people with disabilities; and, offers a proposal that is not more than ten percent higher than the lowest proposal, the procurement officer will award the maximum number of points allocated for cost to that proposer.

EXAMPLE

10% Employers Of People With Disabilities Preference

[STEP 1]

List the raw proposal prices and identify those eligible for preference.

Proposer #1 -   Non-Alaskan Proposer $40,000

    Not Employer of Disabled

Proposer #2 -   Alaskan Proposer $45,000

    Not Employer of Disabled

Proposer #3 -   Alaskan Proposer $50,000

    Employer of Disabled

[STEP 2]

Calculate the amount of the 5% Alaska Bidder Preference by multiplying the Alaskan proposals by .05 and deducting that amount from the price(s).

Proposer #2 - $45,000 x .05 = $2,250 $45,000 - $2,250 = $42,750

Proposer #3 - $50,000 x .05 = $2,500 $50,000 - $2,500 = $47,500

[STEP 3]

List all proposal prices, adjusted where appropriate by the application of the Alaska Bidder Preference.

Proposer #1 -   Non-Alaskan Proposer $40,000

    Not Employer of Disabled

Proposer #2 -   Alaskan Proposer $42,750

    Not Employer of Disabled

Proposer #3 -   Alaskan Proposer $47,500

    Employer of Disabled

[STEP 4]

Calculate the amount of the 10% Employers of People with Disabilities Preference by multiplying the lowest priced proposal by .10.

Proposer #1 - $40,000 x .10 = $4,000

[STEP 5]

List all proposal prices adjusted, where appropriate, by the application of the Alaska Bidder Preference and, where appropriate, deduct the Employers of People with Disabilities Preference.

Proposer #1 -　　　Non-Alaskan Proposer　　　$40,000

　　Not Employer of Disabled

Proposer #2 -　　　Alaskan Proposer　　　$42,750

　　Not Employer of Disabled

Proposer #3 -　　　Alaskan Proposer　　　$47,500 - $4,000 = $43,500

　　Employer of Disabled

[STEP 6]

Identify the lowest priced proposal. In the example, Proposer #1($40,000) is lowest and would get the benefits allotted to the lowest priced proposal, provided, it is a responsive and responsible proposal.

2.17

Qualifying for Disability Related Preferences
AS 36.30.170.

Procurement Officer Note: This Section Should Not Be Altered Or Deleted.

The Division of Vocational Rehabilitation in the Department of Education keeps a list of qualified employment programs; a list of individuals who qualify as persons with a disability; and a list of persons who qualify as employers with 50 percent or more of their employees being persons with disabilities. A person must be on this list at the time the bid is opened in order to qualify for a preference under this section.

As evidence of an individual's or a business' right to a certain preference, the Division of Vocational Rehabilitation will issue a certification letter. To take advantage of the employment program or disabilities preferences described above, an individual or business must be on the appropriate Division of Vocational Rehabilitation list at the time the bid is opened, and must provide the procurement officer a copy of their certification letter. Bidders must attach a copy of their certification letter to their bid. The bidder's failure to provide the certification letter mentioned above with their bid, will cause the State to disallow the preference.

2.18

Formula used to Convert Cost to Points
AS 36.30.250 & 2 AAC 12.260.

Procurement Officer Note: This Section Should Not Be Altered Or Deleted.

The distribution of points based on cost will be determined as set out in 2 AAC 12.260 (d). The lowest cost proposal will receive the maximum number of points allocated to cost. The point allocations for cost on the other proposals will be determined through the method set out below.

EXAMPLE

Formula Used To Convert Cost To Points

[STEP 1]

List the raw proposal prices and identify those eligible for preference.

Proposer #1   -   Non-Alaskan Proposer $40,000

Proposer #2   -   Alaskan Proposer $45,000

Proposer #3   -   Alaskan Proposer $50,000

[STEP 2]

Calculate the amount of the 5% Alaska Bidder Preference by multiplying the Alaskan proposals by .05 and deducting that amount from the price(s).

Proposer #2 - $45,000 x .05 = $2,250 $45,000 - $2,250 = $42,750

Proposer #3 - $50,000 x .05 = $2,500 $50,000 - $2,500 = $47,500

[STEP 3]

List all proposal prices, adjusted where appropriate, by the application of the Alaska Bidder Preference.

Proposer #1   -   Non-Alaskan Proposer $40,000

Proposer #2   -   Alaskan Proposer $42,750

Proposer #3   -   Alaskan Proposer $47,500

[STEP 4]

Convert cost to points using this formula.

[(Price of Lowest Cost Proposal)   x   (Maximum Points for Cost)]

    (Divided by) _____

(Cost of Each Higher Priced Proposal) = Points

The RFP allotted 40% (40 points) of the total of 100 points for cost.

Proposer #1 receives 40 points.

The reason they receive that amount is because the lowest cost proposal, in this case $40,000, receives the maximum number of points allocated to cost, 40 points.

Proposer #2 receives 37.4 points.

$40,000	x	40	=	1,600,000	—	42,750	=	37.4
LOWEST COST		MAX POINTS				PROPOSER #2		POINTS
				ADJUSTED BY				
				ALASKA BIDDER				
				PREFERENCE				

Proposer #3 receives 33.7 points.

$40,000	x	40	=	1,600,000	—	47,750	=	33.7
LOWEST COST		MAX POINTS				PROPOSER #3		POINTS
				ADJUSTED BY				
				ALASKA BIDDER				
				PREFERENCE				

2.19

Alaska Offeror's Preference

AS 36.30.250. & 2 AAC 12.260.

Procurement Officer Note: This Section Should Not Be Altered Or Deleted.

2 AAC 12.260 (e) provides Alaska offeror's a 10 percent overall evaluation point preference. Alaska Bidders, as defined in AS 36.30.170(b), are eligible for the preference. This preference will be added to the overall evaluation score of each Alaska offeror. Each Alaska offeror will receive 10% of the total available points, added to their evaluation score as a preference.

EXAMPLE

Alaska Offeror's Preference

[STEP 1]

Determine the number of points available to Alaskan offerors under the preference.

Total number of points available - 100 Points

| 100 x | 10% | = | 10 |
| Total Points | Alaskan Offerors | | Number of Points |

Available   Percentage Preference   Given to Alaskan Offerors

Under

the Preference

[STEP 2]

Add the preference points to the Alaskan offers. There are three offerors; Proposer #1, Proposer #2, and Proposer #3. Proposer #2 and Proposer #3 are eligible for the Alaskan Preference. For the purpose of this example presume that all of the proposals have been completely evaluated based on the evaluation criteria in the RFP. Their scores at this point are;

Proposer #1 - 89 points

Proposer #2 - 80 points

Proposer #3 - 88 points

Proposer #2 and Proposer #3 each receive 10 additional points. The final scores for all of the offers are;

Proposer #1 - 89 points

Proposer #2 - 90 points

Proposer #3 - 98 points

Proposer #3 is awarded the contract.

2.20

Contract Negotiations

Procurement Officer Note: This Section Should Not Be Altered Or Deleted.

After completion of the evaluation, including any discussions held with offerors during the evaluation, the State may elect to initiate contract negotiations. The option of whether or not to initiate contract negotiations rests solely with the State. If the State elects to initiate contract negotiations, these negotiations cannot involve changes in the State's requirements or the contractor's proposal which would, by their nature, affect the basis of the source selection and the competition previously conducted. If contract negotiations are commenced, they may be held in the PLACE conference room on the NUMBER floor of the NAME Building in CITY, Alaska.

If the contract negotiations take place in CITY, Alaska, the offeror will be responsible for their travel and per diem expenses.

2.21

Failure to Negotiate

Procurement Officer Note: Alter, Revise, Or Delete As Required.

If the selected contractor fails to provide the information required to begin negotiations in a timely manner; or, if the contractor fails to negotiate in good faith; or, if the contractor indicates they cannot perform the contract within the budgeted funds available for the project; or, if the contractor and the State, after a good faith effort, simply can not come to terms, the State may terminate negotiations with the contractor initially selected and commence negotiations with the next highest ranked proposer.

2.22

Notice of Intent to Award (NIA) — Proposer Notification of Selection
Procurement Officer Note: This Section Should Not Be Altered Or Deleted.

After the completion of contract negotiations the procurement officer will issue a written Notice of Intent to Award (NIA) and send copies to all proposers. The NIA will set out the names and addresses of all proposers and identify the proposal selected for award. The scores and placement of other proposers will not be part of the NIA.

2.23

Protest

Procurement Officer Note: This Section Should Not Be Altered Or Deleted.

AS 36.30.560, provides that an interested party may protest the content of a solicitation (RFP).

An interested party is defined in 2 AAC 12.990(a)(7) as "an actual or prospective bidder or offeror whose economic interest might be affected substantially and directly by the issuance of a contract solicitation, the award of a contract, or the failure to award a contract."

If an interested party wishes to protest the content of a solicitation, the protest must be received, in writing, by the procurement officer at least ten days prior to the deadline for receipt of proposals.

AS 36.30.560 also provides that an interested party may protest the award of a contract or the proposed award of a contract.

If a proposer wishes to protest the award of a contract or the proposed award of a contract, the protest must be received in writing by the procurement officer within ten days of the date the Notice of Intent to Award the contract is issued.

A protester must have submitted a proposal in order to have sufficient standing to protest the proposed award of a contract. Protests must include the following information;

[a] the name, address, and telephone number of the protester,

[b] the signature of the protester or the protester's representative,

[c] identification of the contracting agency and the solicitation or contract at issue,

[d] a detailed statement of the legal and factual grounds of the protest including copies of relevant

documents, and,

[e] the form of relief requested.

Protests filed by telex or telegram are not acceptable because they do not contain a signature. FAX copies containing a signature are acceptable.

The procurement officer will issue a written response to the protest. The response will set out the procurement officer's decision and contain the basis of the decision within the statutory time limit in AS 36.30.580. A copy of the decision will be furnished to the protester by certified mail, FAX or another method that provides evidence of receipt.

All proposers will be notified of any protests. The review of protests, decisions of the procurement officer, appeals, and hearings, will be conducted in accordance with the State Procurement Code (AS 36.30), Article 8 " Legal and Contractual Remedies".

SECTION THREE
STANDARD CONTRACT INFORMATION

3.01

Contract Type

Procurement Officer Note: IDENTIFY APPROPRIATE TYPE OF CONTRACT.

THERE ARE SEVERAL DIFFERENT TYPES OF CONTRACTS WHICH MAY BE SUITABLE FOR YOUR PROJECT.

REVIEW THE CONTRACT TYPES LISTED BELOW TO DETERMINE WHICH WOULD BE THE MOST APPROPRIATE.

THE TYPE OF CONTRACT USED IS LIKELY TO HAVE AN IMPACT ON COSTS TO THE STATE. THE PROCUREMENT OFFICER SHOULD SELECT THE TYPE OF CONTRACT THAT WILL BEST SERVE THE STATE'S NEEDS AT THE MOST REASONABLE COST.

The following information is for preparer's information only and should not be printed in the final contract

Fixed Price Contracts

Firm Fixed Price

The most common and easiest contract to administer is a firm fixed price contract. A fixed price contract is one which obligates the contractor to performance at a specified price.

Fixed Price With Adjustment

These contracts allow for price adjustments on the occurrence of specified changes in the cost or price factors set out in the contract. These types of contracts are most useful when the contractor's future prices are so uncertain as to make a firm proposal impossible, or if covering all probable risk, so high as to make the offer unattractive and possibly unfair to the state.

Fixed Price Incentive

A target price, ceiling price and a profit formula are used in this type of contract. When the contractor performs below the costs stipulated in the target price, the contractor and the state share in the savings. If costs exceed those estimated, the contractor's profit margin declines and the price ceiling is adhered to. In these types of contracts, performance can be quantified in terms of costs and services and/or deliverables.

Cost Reimbursement Contracts

Cost Plus Fixed Fee

Under these contracts, contractors are paid for all allowable costs plus a predetermined fixed fee. These contracts have been found to be beneficial for research and development work.

Cost Plus Incentive Fee

Under this type of contract, a tentative fee based on estimated costs and a target price is established. If actual costs fall below estimated costs, the contractor and state share in the savings. The contractor can lose all or part of their fee, but they must be paid for all costs.

Cost Plus A Percentage Of Cost

These contracts are prohibited by statute. Under this type of contract the contractor receives payment for costs of performance plus a specified percentage of such actual costs as a fee. These contracts provide no incentive for efficient and economical contractor performance and must not be used.

Other Types Of Contracts

Time And Materials Contracts

In addition to a fixed labor rate, these contracts include separate costs for materials used under the contract.

Procurement Officer Note: Delete the previous contract information and include the following sentence with the appropriate information in the RFP.

This contract is a ENTER NAME OF TYPE contract.

3.02

Contract Approval

Procurement Officer Note: ENTER APPROPRIATE INFORMATION - ALTER, REVISE, OR DELETE AS REQUIRED.

This RFP does not, by itself, obligate the State. The State's obligation will commence when the contract is approved by the Commissioner of the Department of NAME, the commissioner's designate, or the procurement officer. Upon written notice to the contractor, the State may set a different starting date for the contract. The State will not be responsible for any work done by the contractor, even work done in good faith, if it occurs prior to the contract start date set by the State.

3.03

Standard Contract Provisions

Procurement Officer Note: THIS SECTION SHOULD NOT BE ALTERED OR DELETED.

The contractor will be required to sign and submit the attached State's Standard Agreement Form for Professional Services Contracts (form 02-093/Appendix A). The contractor must comply with the contract provisions set out in this attachment. No alteration of these provisions will be permitted without prior written approval from the Department of Law. If a proposer objects to any of the provisions in Appendix A they must set out their objections in their proposal.

3.04

Proposal as a Part of the Contract

Procurement Officer Note: ALTER, REVISE, OR DELETE AS REQUIRED.

Part or all of this RFP and the successful proposal may be incorporated into the contract.

3.05

Additional Terms and Conditions

Procurement Officer Note: ALTER, REVISE, OR DELETE AS REQUIRED.

The State reserves the right to add terms and conditions during contract negotiations. These terms and conditions will be within the scope of the RFP and will not affect the proposal evaluations.

3.06

Insurance Requirements

Procurement Officer Note: THIS SECTION SHOULD NOT BE ALTERED OR DELETED.

The successful proposer must provide proof of workers' compensation insurance prior to contract approval.

The successful proposer must secure the insurance coverage required by the State. The coverage must be satisfactory to the Division of Risk Management. A proposer's failure to provide evidence of such insurance coverage is a material breach and grounds for withdrawal of the award or termination of the contract.

Procurement Officer Note: APPENDIX B2 REQUIRES PROFESSIONAL LIABILITY COVERAGE AND SHOULD BE USED WHEN CONTRACTING FOR PHYSICIANS, DENTISTS, ATTORNEYS, ARCHITECTS, ENGINEERS, ACCOUNTANTS, INSURANCE AGENTS AND BROKERS, APPRAISERS, LOSS CLAIMS ADJUSTERS, TAX CONSULTANTS, RISK MANAGEMENT & INSURANCE CONSULTANTS, INVESTMENT BROKERS, AND INVESTMENT & DIVESTITURE CONSULTANTS.

APPENDIX B1 SHOULD BE USED IN ALL OTHER APPLICATIONS.

FOR ASSISTANCE ON INSURANCE REQUIREMENTS, CONTACT THE DEPARTMENT OF ADMINISTRATION, DIVISION OF RISK MANAGEMENT.

CHOOSE APPROPRIATE FORM.

Proposers must review form APPENDIX B1 / APPENDIX B2 , attached, for details on required coverages.

3.07

Bid Bond - Performance Bond - Surety Deposit

Procurement Officer Note: MAY BE DELETED. BID BONDS, PERFORMANCE BONDS AND SURETY DEPOSITS ARE NOT ROUTINELY REQUIRED. MAKE SURE YOU REALLY NEED ONE BEFORE YOU SPECIFY IT.

Procurement Officer Note: DO NOT ALTER OR REVISE. CHOOSE APPROPRIATE TYPE(S) OF BONDS & ENTER APPROPRIATE INFORMATION.

Bid Bond

Proposers must obtain a bid bond and submit it with their proposal. The amount of the bid bond for this contract is DOLLARS . If a proposer is selected to receive the contract and fails to negotiate, or fails to deliver a fully executed contract after negotiation, the bid bond will be immediately forfeited to the State. The time limit for negotiation or delivery of a contract is fourteen days from the date the proposer receives notice from the procurement officer. Proposals submitted without a bid bond will be rejected.

Performance Bond

Proposers must obtain a letter of commitment for a performance bond from a bonding company and submit it with their proposal. The amount of the performance bond must be equal to the entire dollar value of a proposer's offer, for the full term of the contract. If the contractor fails to satisfactorily perform the contract the bonding company which provided the performance bond will be required to obtain timely performance of the contract. The actual performance bond must be obtained from the bonding company and provided to the State within thirty days of the date of award of the contract. A proposer's failure to provide the performance bond, within the required time, will cause the State to reject the proposal.

Surety Deposit

In lieu of a performance bond, an irrevocable letter of credit, or cash, may be substituted. The amount of the surety deposit must be list dollar amount OR percentage of proposal price. Substitution of a surety deposit must be approved by the Commissioner of the Department of NAME prior to its submittal. A proposer's failure to provide the surety deposit, within the required time, will cause the State to reject the proposal.

Procurement Officer Note: The amount of surety deposit should be what it would cost to pay the premium cost of a replacement contract.

3.08

Contract Funding

choose paragraph REVISE AS REQUIRED.

If a contract is expected to cross fiscal years, you must include the 2nd statement.

[a] Payment for the contract is subject to funds already appropriated and identified.

OR

[b] Approval or continuation of a contract resulting from this is contingent upon legislative appropriation.

3.09

Proposed Payment Procedures

Procurement Officer Note: CHOOSE PARAGRAPH - REVISE AS REQUIRED.

Preparers should be as specific as possible regarding payment provisions. You may want to consider retaining a percentage of the contract amount until THE CONTRACT IS successfully completed.

The State will make a single payment when all of the deliverables are received and the contract is completed and approved by the project director.

OR

The State will make payments based on a negotiated payment schedule. Each billing must consist of an invoice and progress report. No payment will be made until the progress report and invoice have been approved by the project director.

OR

The State will pay the entire contract amount in NUMBER equal payments. Each incremental payment will be made after NAME SPECIFIC TASKS OR REPORTS have been completed and approved by the project director. The final payment will not be made until the entire contract, including NAME SPECIFIC TASKS OR REPORTS are completed and approved by project director.

3.10

Contract Payment

Procurement Officer Note: ENTER APPROPRIATE INFORMATION - ALTER, REVISE OR DELETE AS REQUIRED.

No payment will be made until the contract is approved by the Commissioner of the Department of NAME the commissioner's designate or the procurement officer. Under no conditions will the State be liable for the payment of any interest charges associated with the cost of the contract.

The State is not responsible for and will not pay local, state, or federal taxes. All costs associated with the contract must be stated in U.S. currency.

3.11

Informal Debriefing

Procurement Officer Note: ALTER, REVISE, OR DELETE AS REQUIRED.

When the contract is completed, an informal debriefing may be performed at the discretion of the project director. If performed, the scope of the debriefing will be limited to the work performed by the contractor.

3.12

Contract Personnel

Procurement Officer Note: ALTER, REVISE, OR DELETE AS REQUIRED.

Any change of the project team members named in the proposal must be approved, in advance and in writing, by the project director. Personnel changes that are not approved by the State may be grounds for the State to terminate the contract.

3.13

Inspection & Modification - Reimbursement for Unacceptable Deliverables

Procurement Officer Note: ALTER, REVISE, OR DELETE AS REQUIRED.

The contractor is responsible for the completion of all work set out in the contract. All work is subject to inspection, evaluation, and approval by the project director. The State may employ all reasonable means to ensure that the work is progressing and being performed in compliance with the contract. Should the project director determine that corrections or modifications are necessary in order to accomplish its intent, the project director may direct the contractor to make such changes. The contractor will not unreasonably withhold such changes.

Substantial failure of the contractor to perform the contract may cause the State to terminate the contract. In this event, the State may require the contractor to reimburse monies paid (based on the identified portion of unacceptable work received) and may seek associated damages.

3.14

Termination for Default

Procurement Officer Note: ALTER, REVISE, OR DELETE AS REQUIRED.

If the project director determines that the contractor has refused to perform the work or has failed to perform the work with such diligence as to ensure its timely and accurate completion, the State may, by providing written notice to the contractor, terminate the contractor's right to proceed with part or all of the remaining work.

This clause does not restrict the State's termination rights under the contract provisions of Appendix A, attached.

3.15

Liquidated Damages

Procurement Officer Note: ENTER APPROPRIATE INFORMATION - ALTER, REVISE, OR DELETE AS REQUIRED.

LIQUIDATED DAMAGES CLAUSES ARE NOT GENERALLY REQUIRED

MAKE SURE YOU REALLY NEED IT BEFORE YOU SPECIFY IT

IF YOU DECIDE TO INCLUDE A LIQUIDATED DAMAGES CLAUSE YOU MUST INDICATE THE AMOUNT

The amount of liquidated damages must be reasonable, you must have a reasonable method to determine what amount will be used

EXPLAIN HOW YOU ARRIVED AT THAT AMOUNT

SPECIFY THE CONDITIONS UNDER WHICH YOU WILL INVOKE THE PROVISION

The State will include liquidated damages in this contract to assure its timely completion. The amount of actual damages will be difficult to determine. For the purposes of this contract the State has set the rate of liquidated damages at DOLLARS per day. This amount is based on PROVIDE BACKGROUND INFORMATION ON HOW YOU ARRIVED AT THAT NUMBER . If the contractor fails to DO SOMETHING the State will begin to collect liquidated damages on DATE and will continue to collect them until SOMETHING ELSE HAPPENS .

3.16

Contract Changes - Unanticipated Amendments

Procurement Officer Note: ENTER APPROPRIATE INFORMATION - ALTER, REVISE, OR DELETE AS REQUIRED.

During the course of this contract, the contractor may be required to perform additional work. That work will be within the general scope of the initial contract. When additional work is required, the project director will provide the contractor a written description of the additional work and request the contractor to submit a firm time schedule for accomplishing the additional work and a firm price for the additional work. Cost and printing data must be provided to justify the cost of such amendments per AS 36.30.400.

The contractor will not commence additional work until the project director has secured any required State approvals necessary for the amendment and issued a written contract amendment, approved by the Commissioner of the Department of NAME ; the Commissioner's designate; or, the project director.

3.17

Contract Invalidation

Procurement Officer Note: THIS SECTION SHOULD NOT BE ALTERED OR DELETED.

If any provision of this contract is found to be invalid, such invalidation will not be construed to invalidate the entire contract.

SECTION FOUR

BACKGROUND INFORMATION

4.01

Background Information

Procurement Officer Note: ALTER, REVISE, OR DELETE AS REQUIRED. GIVE THE PROSPECTIVE proposers AS CLEAR A PICTURE AS YOU CAN OF HOW YOU GOT WHERE YOU ARE

AT. THE MORE THEY UNDERSTAND THE BACKGROUND, THE BETTER THEY WILL BE ABLE TO ZERO IN ON WHAT YOU WANT.

Background information concerning this project is as follows; PROVIDE PERTINENT BACKGROUND INFORMATION .

SECTION FIVE

SCOPE OF WORK

5.01

Scope of Work

Procurement Officer Note: ENTER APPROPRIATE INFORMATION - ALTER, REVISE, OR DELETE AS REQUIRED.

INFORMATION YOU PROVIDE IN THIS SECTION TELLS THE Proposers WHAT YOU WANT DONE

BE AS SPECIFIC AND COMPREHENSIVE AS YOU POSSIBLY CAN

LET THE PROPOSER KNOW EXACTLY WHAT YOU WANT

DON'T PRESUME THAT THEY WILL "GET IT" IF YOU DON'T SAY IT

WRITE IT AS IF YOU WERE TRYING TO EXPLAIN IT TO A TWELVE YEAR-OLD CHILD

The Department of NAME , Division of NAME is soliciting proposals for WHAT KIND of services.

The department wants assistance to do WHAT .

The consultant will do WHAT .

The types of staff in State agencies that the contractor must interview are WHO .

Other helpful informational material that can be provided to the consultant includes WHAT .

The goal of this project is to WHAT .

5.02

Deliverables

ENTER APPROPRIATE INFORMATION. ALTER, REVISE, OR DELETE AS REQUIRED.

LIST EVERY DELIVERABLE YOU CAN THINK OF, EVEN THE ONES THAT DO NOT SEEM PARTICULARLY IMPORTANT RIGHT NOW.

DO NOT assume THAT THE CONTRACTOR WILL GIVE YOU MORE THAN YOU ASK FOR. YOU SHOULD BE ABLE TO LOOK THROUGH THIS LIST AND BE SATISFIED THAT THE JOB WILL BE FINISHED WHEN YOU GET EVERYTHING LISTED HERE.

The contractor will be required to provide the following deliverables;

[a] WHAT

[b] WHAT

[c] WHAT

[x] WHAT

[y] WHAT

[z] WHAT

5.03

Work Schedule

Procurement Officer Note: ENTER APPROPRIATE INFORMATION. ALTER, REVISE, OR DELETE AS REQUIRED.

The contract term and work schedule set out herein represent the State's best estimate of the schedule that will be followed. If a component of this schedule, such as the opening date, is delayed, the rest of the schedule will likely be shifted by the same number of days.

The length of the contract will be from the date of award, approximately DATE , for approximately NUMBER calendar days until completion, approximately DATE .

The approximate contract schedule is as follows;

Procurement Officer Note: ENTER APPROPRIATE INFORMATION. ALTER, REVISE, OR DELETE AS REQUIRED.

LIST EVERY ITEM, EVENT, MILESTONE YOU CAN THINK OF, BEGINNING TO END. BE AS SPECIFIC AND COMPREHENSIVE AS YOU POSSIBLY CAN.

ALLOW ONE OR TWO REVIEWS OF EACH DRAFT OR REDRAFT.

CREATE MULTIPLE OPPORTUNITIES FOR INTERACTION WITH THE CONTRACTOR.

DON'T JUST SEND THE CONTRACTOR AWAY WITH SOME WORK TO DO AND LET THEM BRING BACK SOMETHING THAT MAY OR MAY NOT SUIT YOU.

INTERACT WITH THE CONTRACTOR TO KEEP THE PROJECT ON TRACK.

SECTION SIX

PROPOSAL FORMAT AND CONTENT

Procurement Officer Note: THE INFORMATION YOU PROVIDE IN THIS SECTION SHOULD HELP proposers UNDERSTAND HOW YOU WANT THEIR PROPOSALS STRUCTURED AND

IDENTIFY ITEMS YOU WANT THEM TO EMPHASIZE.

6.01

Proposal Format and Content

Procurement Officer Note: ALTER, REVISE, OR DELETE AS REQUIRED.

The State discourages overly lengthy and costly proposals, however, in order for the State to evaluate proposals fairly and completely, proposers should follow the format set out herein and provide all of the information requested.

6.02

Introduction

Procurement Officer Note: ALTER, REVISE, OR DELETE AS REQUIRED.

Proposals must include the complete name and address of their firm and the name, mailing address, and telephone number of the person the State should contact regarding the proposal.

Proposals must confirm that the firm will comply with all of the provisions in this RFP; and, if applicable, provide notice that the firm qualifies as an Alaskan bidder. Proposals must be signed by a company officer empowered to bind the company. A proposer's failure to include these items in their proposals may cause their proposal to be determined to be non-responsive and the proposal may be rejected.

6.03

Understanding of the Project

Procurement Officer Note: ALTER, REVISE, OR DELETE AS REQUIRED.

Proposers must provide a comprehensive narrative statement that illustrates their understanding of the requirements of the project and the project schedule..

6.04

Methodology Used for the Project

Procurement Officer Note: ALTER, REVISE, OR DELETE AS REQUIRED.

Proposers must provide a comprehensive narrative statement that sets out the methodology they intend to employ and that illustrates how their methodology will serve to accomplish the work and meet the State's project schedule.

6.05

Management Plan for the Project

Procurement Officer Note: ALTER, REVISE, OR DELETE AS REQUIRED.

Proposers must provide a comprehensive narrative statement that sets out the management plan they intend to follow and illustrates how their plan will serve to accomplish the work and meet the State's project schedule.

6.06

Experience and Qualifications

Procurement Officer Note: ALTER, REVISE, OR DELETE AS REQUIRED.

Provide an organizational chart specific to the personnel assigned to accomplish the work called for in this RFP; illustrate the lines of authority; designate the individual responsible and accountable for the completion of each component and deliverable of the RFP.

Provide a narrative description of the organization of the project team.

Provide a personnel roster that identifies each person who will actually work on the contract and provide the following information about each person listed;

[a] title,

[b] resume,

[c] location(s) where work will be performed,

[d] itemize the total cost and the number of estimated hours for each individual named above.

Provide reference names and phone numbers for similar projects your firm has completed.

6.07

Cost Proposal

Procurement Officer Note: ALTER, REVISE, OR DELETE AS REQUIRED.

Proposer's cost proposals must include an itemized list of all direct and indirect costs associated with the performance of this contract, including, but not limited to, total number of hours at various hourly rates, direct expenses, payroll, supplies, overhead assigned to each person working on the project, percentage of each person's time devoted to the project, and profit.

6.08

Evaluation Criteria

Procurement Officer Note: ALTER, or revise as necessary

All proposals will be reviewed to determine if they are responsive. They will then be evaluated using the criteria set out in section seven.

SECTION SEVEN

EVALUATION CRITERIA AND CONTRACTOR SELECTION

THE TOTAL NUMBER OF POINTS USED
TO SCORE THIS CONTRACT IS 100

7.01

Understanding of the Project—5%

Procurement Officer Note: ALTER, REVISE, OR DELETE AS REQUIRED.

Proposals will be evaluated against the questions set out below.

[a]   Has the proposer demonstrated a thorough understanding of the purpose and scope of the project?

[b]   How well has the proposer identified pertinent issues and potential problems related to the project?

[c]   Has the proposer demonstrated that it understands the deliverables the State expects it to provide?

[d]   Has the proposer demonstrated that it understands the State's time schedule and can meet it?

7.02

Methodology Used for the Project—15%

Procurement Officer Note: ALTER, REVISE, OR DELETE AS REQUIRED.

Proposals will be evaluated against the questions set out below.

[a]   Does the methodology depict a logical approach to fulfilling the requirements of the RFP?

[b]   Does the methodology match and contribute to achieving the objectives set out in the RFP?

[c]   Does the methodology interface with the time schedule in the RFP?

7.03

Management Plan for the Project—15%

Procurement Officer Note: ALTER, REVISE, OR DELETE AS REQUIRED.

Proposals will be evaluated against the questions set out below.

[a]   Does the management plan support all of the project requirements and logically lead to the deliverables required in the RFP?

[b]   Is accountability completely and clearly defined?

[c]   Is the organization of the project team clear?

[d]   Does the management plan illustrate the lines of authority and communication?

[e]   To what extent does the proposer already have the hardware, equipment, and licenses necessary to

perform the contract?

[f]   Does it appear that the proposer can meet the schedule set out in the RFP?

[g]   Has the contractor offered alternate deliverables and gone beyond the minimum tasks necessary to meet the objectives of the RFP?

[h]   Is the proposal practical, feasible, and within budget?

[i]   Have any potential problems been identified?

[j]   Is the proposal submitted responsive to all material requirements in the RFP?

7.04

Experience and Qualifications—15%

Proposals will be evaluated against the questions set out below.

Questions regarding the personnel.

Procurement Officer Note: ALTER, REVISE, OR DELETE AS REQUIRED.

[a]   Do the individuals assigned to the project have experience on similar projects?

[b]   Are resumes complete and do they demonstrate backgrounds that would be desirable for individuals engaged in the work the project requires?

[c]   How extensive is the applicable education and experience of the personnel designated to work on the project?

[d]   How knowledgeable are the proposer's personnel of the local area and how many individuals have worked in the area previously?

Questions regarding the firm:

Procurement Officer Note: ALTER, REVISE, OR DELETE AS REQUIRED.

[e]   Has the firm demonstrated experience in completing similar projects on time and within budget?

[f]   How successful is the general history of the firm regarding timely and successful completion of projects?

[g]   Has the firm provided letters of reference from previous clients?

[h]   How reasonable are the firm's cost estimates?

[i]   If a subcontractor will perform work on the contract, how well do they measure up to the evaluation used for the proposer?

7.05

Contract Cost—40%

Procurement Officer Note: Alter and revise as required

Overall, a minimum of 40% of the total evaluation points will be assigned to cost. The cost amount used for evaluation may be affected by one or more of the preferences set out below.

5% Alaskan Bidder Preference—See section 2.13

15% Employment Program Preference—See section 2.14

10% Alaskans with Disabilities Preference—See Section 2.15

10% Employers of People with Disabilities Preference—See section 2.16

Converting Cost to Points

Procurement Officer Note: THIS SECTION SHOULD NOT BE ALTERED OR DELETED.

The lowest cost proposal will receive the maximum number of points allocated to cost. The point allocations for cost on the other proposals will be determined through the method set out in Section 2.18.

7.06

Alaska Offeror's Preference (10%)

Procurement Officer Note: THIS SECTION SHOULD NOT BE ALTERED OR DELETED.

If a proposer qualifies for the Alaska Bidder Preference, the proposer will receive an Alaska Offeror's Preference. The preference will be 10% of the total available points. This amount will be added to the overall evaluation score of each Alaska offeror.

SECTION EIGHT

ATTACHMENTS

8.01

Attachments

ALTER, REVISE, OR DELETE AS REQUIRED.

Attachments

Standard Agreement Form

Appendix A

Appendix B1 or B2

Notice of Intent to Award

Proposal Evaluation Form

Contractor Evaluation Form

Checklist

SAMPLE EVALUATION FORM

All proposals will be reviewed for responsiveness and then evaluated using the criteria set out herein.

Person or Firm Name

Name of PEC Member

Date of Review

RFP Number

EVALUATION CRITERIA AND SCORING

THE TOTAL NUMBER OF POINTS USED TO SCORE THIS CONTRACT IS 100

Procurement Officer Note: ALTER, REVISE, OR DELETE AS REQUIRED.

7.01 Understanding of the Project—5%

• Maximum Point Value for this Section — 5 Points

100 Points x 5% = 5 Points

Proposals will be evaluated against the questions set out below.

[a] Has the proposer demonstrated a thorough understanding of the purpose and scope of the project?

EVALUATOR'S NOTES

[b] How well has the proposer identified pertinent issues and potential problems related to the project?

EVALUATOR'S NOTES

[c] Has the proposer demonstrated that it understands the deliverables the State expects it to provide?

EVALUATOR'S NOTES

[d] Has the proposer demonstrated that it understands the State's time schedule and can meet it?

EVALUATOR'S NOTES

EVALUATOR'S POINT TOTAL FOR 7.01

Procurement Officer Note: ALTER, REVISE, OR DELETE AS REQUIRED.

7.02 Methodology Used for the Project—15%

• Maximum Point Value for this Section — 15 Points

100 Points x 15% = 15 Points

Proposals will be evaluated against the questions set out below.

[a]   Does the methodology depict a logical approach to fulfilling the requirements of the RFP?

EVALUATOR'S NOTES

[b]   Does the methodology match and contribute to achieving the objectives set out in the proposal?

EVALUATOR'S NOTES

[c]   Does the methodology interface with the time schedule in the proposal?

EVALUATOR'S NOTES

EVALUATOR'S POINT TOTAL FOR 7.02

Procurement Officer Note: ALTER, REVISE, OR DELETE AS REQUIRED.

7.03 Management Plan for the Project—15%

• Maximum Point Value for this Section — 15 Points

100 Points x 15% = 15 Points

Proposals will be evaluated against the questions set out below.

[a]   Does the management plan support all of the project requirements and

logically lead to the deliverables required in the RFP?

EVALUATOR'S NOTES

[b]   Is accountability completely and clearly defined?

EVALUATOR'S NOTES

[c]   Is the organization of the project team clear?

EVALUATOR'S NOTES

[d]   Does the management plan illustrate the lines of authority and

communication?

EVALUATOR'S NOTES

[e]   To what extent does the proposer already have the hardware, equipment, and licenses necessary to perform the contract?

EVALUATOR'S NOTES

[f]   Does it appear that proposer can meet the schedule set out in the proposal?

EVALUATOR'S NOTES

[g]   Has the contractor offered alternate deliverables and gone beyond the minimum tasks necessary to meet the objectives of the RFP?

EVALUATOR'S NOTES

[h]   Is the proposal practical, feasible, and within budget?

EVALUATOR'S NOTES

[i]   Have any potential problems been identified?

EVALUATOR'S NOTES

[j   Is the proposal submitted responsive to all material requirements in the RFP?

EVALUATOR'S NOTES

EVALUATOR'S POINT TOTAL FOR 7.03

Procurement Officer Note: ALTER, REVISE, OR DELETE AS REQUIRED.

7.04 Experience and Qualifications—15%

• Maximum Point Value for this Section — 15 Points

100 Points x 15% = 15 Points

Proposals will be evaluated against the questions set out below.

Questions regarding the personnel.

[a]   Do the individuals assigned to the project have experience on similar projects?

EVALUATOR'S NOTES

[b]   Are resumes complete and do they demonstrate backgrounds that would be desirable for individuals engaged in the work the RFP requires?

EVALUATOR'S NOTES

[c]   How extensive is the applicable education and experience of the personnel designated to work on the project?

EVALUATOR'S NOTES

[d]   How knowledgeable are the proposer's personnel of the local area and how many individuals have worked in the area previously?

EVALUATOR'S NOTES

Questions regarding the firm.

[e]   Has the firm demonstrated experience in completing similar projects on time and within budget?

EVALUATOR'S NOTES

[f]   How successful is the general history of the firm regarding timely and successful completion of projects?

EVALUATOR'S NOTES

[g]   Has the firm provided letters of reference from previous clients?

EVALUATOR'S NOTES

[h]   How reasonable are the firm's cost estimates?

EVALUATOR'S NOTES

[i]   If a subcontractor will perform work on the project, how well do they measure up to the evaluation used for the proposer?

EVALUATOR'S NOTES

EVALUATOR'S POINT TOTAL FOR 7.04

Procurement Officer Note: THIS SECTION SHOULD NOT BE ALTERED OR DELETED.

7.05 Contract Cost —40%

• Maximum Point Value for this Section — 40 Points

100 Points x 40% = 40 Points

Overall, a minimum of 40% of the total evaluation points will be assigned to cost. The cost amount used for evaluation may be affected by one or more of the following preferences.

5% Alaskan Bidder Preference

15% Employment Program Preference

10% Alaskans with Disabilities Preference

10% Employers of People with Disabilities Preference

Converting Cost to Points

Procurement Officer Note: THIS SECTION SHOULD NOT BE ALTERED OR DELETED.

The lowest cost proposal will receive the maximum number of points allocated to cost. The point allocations for cost on the other proposals will be determined through the method set out in Section 2.

EVALUATOR'S POINT TOTAL FOR 7.05

Procurement Officer Note: THIS SECTION SHOULD NOT BE ALTERED OR DELETED.

7.06 Alaska Preference 10%

• Alaska Bidders receive a 10% overall evaluation point preference.

• Point Value for Alaska Bidders in this Section — 10 Points

100 Points x 10% = 10 Points

Procurement Officer Note: THIS SECTION SHOULD NOT BE ALTERED OR DELETED.

If a proposer qualifies for the Alaska Bidder Preference, the proposer will receive an Alaska Offeror's Preference. The preference will be 10% of the total available points. This amount will be added to the overall evaluation score of each Alaska offeror.

EVALUATOR'S POINT TOTAL FOR 7.06 (either 0 or 10)

EVALUATOR'S COMBINED POINT TOTAL FOR ALL SECTIONS

Model Request for Proposal, State of Washington

WASHINGTON STATE

DEPARTMENT OF (_____)

SPECIFIC TITLE FOR THIS RFP

optional RFP "Number"

MODEL REQUEST FOR PROPOSALS

for the selection of (_____)

(date)

TABLE OF CONTENTS

Appendix C   *Functional Demonstration*
Appendix D   *Benchmark Requirements*
Appendix E   *Evaluation Point Distribution*
Appendix F   *Protest Procedures*
Appendix G   *Proposal Contents*
Appendix H   *Proposal Certification*

1 Introduction (Summary of the problem to be addressed through the acquisition)

1.1 General Information

(Background on the agency, current data processing environment, description of present systems and applications, physical environment and logical environment)

1.2 Scope

(Summary of products and services to be acquired)

1.3 Objective

(A clear statement of what the acquisition is intended to accomplish, or provide to, the agency)

1.4 RFP Coordinator

Upon release of this Request for Proposal (RFP), all vendor communications concerning this acquisition must be directed to the RFP Coordinator listed below. Unauthorized contact regarding the RFP with other state employees may result in disqualification. Any oral communications will be considered unofficial and non-binding on the Agency. Vendors should rely only on written statements issued by the RFP Coordinator.

Name

Agency

Address

City/State

Mailstop

Telephone

Fax

1.5 Acquisition Authority, Conduct, and Statewide Implications

This RFP is in compliance with the policies and procedures of the Department of Information Services (DIS) and the Information Services Board (ISB). The (Agency) has obtained previous approval from DIS/ISB for this acquisition (or "the acquisition is within it's delegated authority").

The (agency) conducts this acquisition under Chapter 43.105 of the Revised Code of Washington (RCW). This includes compliance with the statewide policies issued under the authority of the ISB, the guidelines approved by the ISB and published by DIS, and other applicable laws and regulations.

Because this RFP will result in a competitive procurement, other state agencies and local government units may qualify to purchase items under the subsequent contract. Approval to purchase will require agreement of both participating agencies and possibly the Planning and Policy Division of DIS. Vendors must be prepared to offer these agencies the right to purchase under this contract.

SEE FOLLOWING PAGE FOR ACQUISITION SCHEDULE

1.6 Acquisition Schedule (Optional items in italics)

Event	Completed by
Letter to vendors soliciting interest	
Release Draft RFP to Vendors	
Comments on Draft RFP Due	
Release Final RFP to Vendors	
Pre-proposal Conference	
Letter of Intent to Propose Due (FAX OKAY)	
Issue Responses to Pre-proposal Conference Questions	
Deadline for complaints regarding technical specifications	
RFP Responses Due (FAX NOT ACCEPTABLE)	
Begin RFP Evaluations/Functional Demonstrations	
Announce Finalists	
Conduct Benchmarks	
Customer Site Visits	
Complete Evaluations	
Announce Apparent Successful Vendor	
Hold Vendor Debriefing Conferences	
Negotiate Contract	
Install and Test Equipment/Software	
Begin Training	
Conduct Acceptance Test	

1.7 Acquisition Funding and Expenditure Limit

(Listing of sources of funds and amount available)

1.8 Administrative Requirements

1.8.1   Pre-proposal Conference

A (mandatory or optional) pre-proposal conference for all participating vendors is scheduled on the date identified in the acquisition schedule (Section 1.6) at (location). Each vendor may send a maximum of (number) representatives. Vendors may request that optional pre-proposal conferences be conducted by telephone or video conferencing but the vendor shall be responsible for any and all costs relating to such method of conferencing.

Specific questions concerning the RFP should be submitted in writing prior to the pre-proposal conference so that Agency representatives may prepare responses in advance of the conference. Additional questions will be entertained at the conference; however, responses may be deferred and provided at a later date. Copies of all written questions and the Agency responses will be mailed to all vendors submitting a Letter of Intent to Propose. Only the written responses will be considered official.

The response to any question which is given orally at the conference is to be considered tentative. After the conference, questions will be researched and the official response published in writing. This will assure accurate, consistent responses to all vendors.

1.8.2   Letter of Intent to Propose

A letter indicating the vendor's intent to respond to the RFP must be received by the RFP Coordinator at the address specified in the cover letter no later than 4:00 p.m. Pacific Time on the date identified in the acquisition schedule (Section 1.6).

Failure to submit a Letter of Intent to Propose, by the deadline specified, will result in the rejection of the vendor's proposal.

Submission of the Letter of Intent to Propose constitutes the vendor's acceptance of the procedures, evaluation criteria, and other administrative instructions of the RFP.

The Agency assumes no responsibility for delays caused by the U.S. Postal Service, state mail delivery systems, or any delivery or courier service the vendor may select. Time extensions will not be granted. Letters of Intent may be delivered by facsimile transmission.

Each vendor must appoint an individual to officially represent the vendor for this acquisition. Include the following information in the Letter of Intent to Propose:

Name of Vendor Representative

Title

Name of Company

Address

Telephone Number

Fax Number

Statement of Intent to Propose

Vendors may withdraw their Letters of Intent at any time before the deadline for proposal submission.

1.8.3   RFP Amendments

The Agency reserves the right to change the acquisition schedule or issue amendments to the RFP at any time. The Agency also reserves the right to cancel or reissue the RFP.

1.8.4   Proposal Certification

The vendor must certify in writing that all vendor proposal terms, including prices, will remain in effect for a minimum of 120 (number is optional depending on needs of agency) days after the Proposal Due Date, that all proposed hardware and system software has been operational at a non-vendor owned customer site for a period of 90 days prior to the Proposal Due Date, that all proposed capabilities can be demonstrated by the vendor, and that the proposed hardware and system software is currently marketed and sold. (A form is provided for certification - see Appendix H)

1.8.5   Bid Bond

A Bid Bond of $_____, or ten (10) percent of the proposed cost as submitted, (whichever is less) is required. Bonds must be payable to the State of Washington. Personal or company checks are not acceptable. Bonds will be retained by the Agency until a contract is executed or a vendor is disqualified. In the event the apparently successful vendor fails to enter into a contract with the Agency, in accordance with the terms of the RFP and the proposal, the bond may be retained and paid into the Washington State Treasury. In the event the Agency commences any action on the bond, the vendor agrees that venue shall lie in Thurston County. Bonds of qualified but unsuccessful vendors will be returned upon execution of the contract.

1.8.6   Performance Bond

1.8.7   Mandatory Requirement Defined

A mandatory requirement (MR) is an essential (agency) need that must be met by the vendor. The Agency will eliminate from the evaluation process any vendor not fulfilling all mandatory requirements or not presenting an acceptable alternative.

Failure to meet a mandatory requirement (grounds for disqualification) shall be established by any of the following conditions:

1.   The vendor states that a mandatory cannot be met.

2.   The vendor fails to include information necessary to substantiate that a given mandatory requirement has been met (such as references to specific sections in technical documents). A response of "will comply" is not sufficient

Responses must indicate present capability; representations that future developments will satisfy the requirement are not sufficient.

3. The vendor fails to include information requested by a mandatory requirement (such as references to specific sections in technical documents, detailed explanations). A response of "will comply" is not sufficient

4. The vendor presents the information requested by this RFP in a manner inconsistent with the instructions stated by any portion of this RFP.

5. Customer references, or site visits, report the vendor's inability to comply with one or more of the mandatory requirements.

6. The vendor fails to include the customer references required.

1.8.8 Acceptable Alternative Defined

An acceptable alternative is one which the Agency considers satisfactory in meeting a mandatory specification. The Agency, at its sole discretion, will determine if the proposed alternative meets the intent of the original mandatory requirement.

1.8.9 Desirable Option Defined

Desirable options (DO) are specifications for features and functions which the Agency would like to acquire but which are not absolutely necessary. Vendors that provide desirable options will be awarded additional points as part of the total available points in the overall evaluation.

1.8.10 Vendor Complaints Regarding Specifications

The Agency will consider vendor complaints regarding any requirements before the deadline for proposal submission. All complaints must be in writing and submitted to the RFP Coordinator by the date specified in the acquisition schedule (Section 1.6. The Agency reserves the right to modify requirements should a vendor complaint identify a change that is in the best interest of the Agency.

1.8.11 Proposal Response Date and Location

The vendor's proposal, in its entirety, must be received by the RFP Coordinator not later than 4:00 p.m., Pacific time in (City), Washington, on the date specified in the acquisition schedule (Section 1.6). Proposals arriving after the deadline will be returned, unopened, to their senders . All proposals and accompanying documentation will become the property of the Agency and may not be returned.

Vendors assume the risk of the method of dispatch chosen. The Agency assumes no responsibility for delays caused by any delivery service. Postmarking by the due date will not substitute for actual proposal receipt. Late proposals will not be accepted nor will additional time be granted to any vendor. Proposals may not be delivered by facsimile transmission or other telecommunication or electronic means.

1.8.12 Multiple Proposals

Vendors interested in submitting more than one proposal may do so, providing each proposal stands alone and independently complies with the instructions, conditions and specifications of the RFP.

1.8.13   Proposal Presentation and Format Requirements

1.8.13.1   Proposals are to be prepared on standard 8 1/2" x 11" paper. Foldouts containing charts, spread sheets, and oversize exhibits are permissible. The pages should be placed in a binder with tabs separating the major sections of the proposal. Manuals and other reference documentation may be bound separately. All responses, as well as any reference material presented must be written in english.

1.8.13.2   Proposals must respond to the RFP requirements by restating the number and text of the requirement in sequence and writing the response immediately after the requirement statement. This RFP is available in electronic format (specify) upon request to the RFP Coordinator. All responses to the requirements in Section 2.0 of this RFP must include cross-references to a specific page and paragraph in the vendor technical specification manuals (not sales brochures). Cross referencing an entire chapter or section consisting of numerous pages is not acceptable.   If vendors' cross referencing techniques are inadequate, they run the risk of failing a mandatory requirement.

1.8.13.3   Figures and tables must be numbered and referenced in the text by that number. They should be placed as close as possible to the referencing text. Pages must be numbered consecutively within each section of the proposal showing proposal section number and page number.

1.8.13.4   Proposals shall be based only on the material contained in this RFP. The RFP includes official responses to pre-proposal conference questions, amendments, addenda, and other material published by the (Agency) pursuant to the RFP. The vendor is to disregard any previous draft material and any oral representations it may have received. All responses to the requirements in Sections 2.0, 3.0, and 4.0 of this RFP must clearly state whether the proposed system will satisfy the referenced requirements, and the manner in which the requirement will be satisfied, including but not limited to cross-references to specific sections in the vendor technical specification manuals (not sales brochures). Each proposal must include all referenced manuals, including but not limited to manual(s) which cover the following: system, installation planning, and specifications for each type of equipment and software. Vendors must identify any restrictions in concurrent use of proposed hardware and software.

1.8.13.5   Financial and contractual responses are to be bound separately from the technical part of the proposal. No pricing information shall appear in the vendor proposal except in the financial section (Volume 2 outlined in Appendix G).

1.8.14   Waiver of Minor Administrative Irregularities

The State reserves the right, at its sole discretion, to waive minor administrative irregularities contained in any proposal.

1.8.15   Single Response

A single response to the RFP may be deemed a failure of competition and in the best interest of the

State, the RFP may be cancelled.

1.8.16   Proposal Rejection

The Agency reserves the right to reject any or all proposals at any time without penalty.

1.8.17   Withdrawal of Proposals

Vendors may withdraw a proposal which has been submitted at any time up to the proposal closing date and time. To accomplish this, a written request signed by an authorized representative of the vendor must be submitted to the RFP Coordinator. After withdrawing a previously submitted proposal, the vendor may submit another proposal at any time up to the proposal closing date and time.

1.8.18   Non-endorsement

As a result of the selection of a vendor to supply products and/or services to the Agency, the Agency is neither endorsing nor suggesting that the vendor's product is the best or only solution. The vendor agrees to make no reference to the Agency in any literature, promotional material, brochures, sales presentation or the like without the express written consent of the Agency.

1.8.19   Proprietary Proposal Material

Any information contained in the proposal that is proprietary must be clearly designated. Marking the entire proposal as proprietary will be neither accepted nor honored. If a request is made to view a vendor's proposal, the Agency will comply according to the Open Public Records Act, Chapter 42.17 RCW and the agencies applicable procedures. If any information is marked as proprietary in the proposal, such information will not be made available until the affected vendor has been given an opportunity to seek a court injunction against the requested disclosure.

Vendor should identify clearly any materials which constitute "(valuable) formulae, designs, drawings, and research data" so as to be exempt from public disclosure under RCW 42.27.310, or any materials otherwise claimed to be exempt, along with a statement of the basis for such claim of exemption. The state's sole responsibility shall be limited to maintaining the above data in a secure area and to notify bidder of any request(s) for disclosure within a period of five (5) years from date of award. Failure to so label such materials or failure to timely respond after notice of request for public disclosure has been given shall be deemed a waiver by the vendor of any claim that such materials are, in fact, so exempt.

1.8.20   Response Property of the Agency

All materials submitted in response to this request become the property of the Agency. Selection or rejection of a response does not affect this right.

1.8.21   No Obligation to Buy

The Agency reserves the right to refrain from contracting with any vendor. The release of this RFP does not compel the Agency to purchase.

1.8.22 Cost of Preparing Proposals

The Agency is not liable for any costs incurred by vendors in the preparation and presentation of proposals, demonstrations, and benchmarks (reference to section "Performance and Demonstration Travel Costs") submitted in response to this RFP.

1.8.23 Number of Proposal Copies Required

Vendors are to submit the following numbers of copies of their proposals:

(number) copies of Volume 1 (Technical Response).

(number) copies of Volume 2 (Financial Response).

(number) sets of technical manuals for the proposed configuration.

1.8.24 Errors in Proposal

The Agency will not be liable for any errors in vendor proposals. Vendors will not be allowed to alter proposal documents after the deadline for proposal submission.

The Agency reserves the right to make corrections or amendments due to errors identified in proposals by the Agency or the vendor. This type of correction or amendment will only be allowed for such errors as typing, transposition or any other obvious error. Any changes will be date and time stamped and attached to proposals. All changes must be coordinated in writing with, authorized by, and made by the RFP Coordinator. Vendors are liable for all errors or omissions contained in their proposals.

1.8.25 Performance and Demonstration Travel Costs

The Agency will bear all travel and associated per diem costs for evaluators to view functional demonstrations and performance benchmarks within the State of Washington. The vendor must bear all travel and associated per diem costs, not to exceed published State of Washington employees' reimbursement rates, for not more than (number) evaluators to view functional demonstrations and performance benchmarks outside the State of Washington.

1.8.26 Third Party Vendor

The Agency will accept proposals which include third party equipment and/or software only if the proposing vendor agrees to act as prime contractor and guarantor for all proposed equipment and software. Vendors must disclose the use of any third party vendor equipment or software and indicate willingness to assume prime contractor responsibility.

1.8.27 Necessary Ancillary Equipment and Software

Unless specifically excepted by the terms of the RFP, all parts, software, or accessories (i.e. cables, power converters, display devices) ordinarily furnished or required to make the proposed equipment a complete operating unit shall be furnished by the vendor, at no additional cost to the Agency. These items must be listed in the cost proposal.

1.8.28   Condition of Proposed Equipment

All equipment proposed must be new equipment or refurbished and warranted as new equipment.

1.8.29   Configuration Adjustment with Contract

The Agency reserves the right to select and exclude any equipment or software for the actual acquisition regardless of the configuration proposed by the vendor. The vendor will be consulted on any such adjustments whenever it is determined that the configuration adjustment may adversely impact the system performance.

1.8.30   Equipment Delivery

Vendors must certify that the proposed equipment can be delivered, installed and operationally ready within (number) days of each written order issued under the resulting contract.

1.9 Minority and Women Business Enterprises Consideration

In accordance with Chapter 39.19, Revised Code of Washington, Minority and Women Owned Business Enterprise goals have been established for this acquisition and are as follows: the Minority Business Enterprise (MBE) goal is (number) percent of the total cost and Women Business Enterprise (WBE) goal is (number) percent of the total cost. Final selection of an apparently successful vendor will be based upon the evaluation rules published by the Office of Minority and Women's Business Enterprises (OMWBE). Such evaluation shall be independent of and subsequent to the technical and financial evaluation process.

1.10 Functional Demonstration

A functional demonstration is necessary to gain a complete understanding of the vendor's proposal. The functional demonstration will provide an opportunity for vendors to further explain and/or demonstrate their responses to this RFP. Each vendor will be scheduled (number) days for the demonstration. Unless agreed to prior to scheduling the functional demonstration, the evaluation team will limit its time to normal working hours (8:00 AM to 5:00 PM). Specifics for the demonstration are explained in Appendix C.

1.11 Benchmark/Performance Demonstration

A Benchmark is necessary to assure that the configuration proposed is capable of performing the required workload under the performance requirements. Each finalist vendor will have (number) days to benchmark performance of the proposed system. Unless agreed to before scheduling the benchmark, the evaluation team will limit its time to normal working hours (8:00 AM to 5:00 PM). Specifics for the benchmark/performance demonstration are explained in Appendix D.

The successful vendor will be required to run the same benchmark described in Appendix D after installation on the agency's premises. The results of the second benchmark must equal or exceed the performance of the test benchmark. Failure to reproduce the results may be grounds for contract termination.

1.12 Agency Reservation of Right to Adjust Proposed Configuration During Evaluation

The Agency may, at its sole discretion, select or reject individual items of equipment and/or software proposed by the vendor. As part of the evaluation process, the Agency may find it necessary to add or delete hardware, software and/or services from the vendor's proposal to make equivalent evaluation comparisons.

2 Functional Requirements

2.1   Mandatory Requirements

2.2   Optional/Desirable Requirements

2.3   Performance Requirements

2.4   Configuration Requirements

3 Vendor Support Requirements

3.1 Delivery

3.1.1   The vendor assumes responsibility for the delivery, installation, maintenance, and initial adjustment of all vendor supplied equipment, software, and support services proposed.

3.1.2   The vendor must contractually commit to have equipment delivered, installed, and operationally ready within (number) days of each written order issued under the resulting contract. Anticipated installation date is shown on the acquisition schedule (Section 1.6).

3.2 Documentation

3.2.1   The vendor must provide documentation for all proposed hardware and software. The successful vendor must provide (number) complete sets of operating manuals for each item of equipment and software installed.

3.2.2   Describe method of updating manuals. Costs of updating manuals on a continuing basis must be included in the financial section.

3.3 Installation Assistance

3.3.1   Installation and initial adjustment is required for any hardware and software acquired from the vendor.

3.3.2   The vendor must submit an Installation Support Plan which delineates what support will be provided in meeting the installation requirements. The following specific areas must be addressed:

- Site preparation assistance.

- Duration of setup and testing period.

- Number of Agency personnel required during installation.

- Extent of initial adjustment services.

- Conversion assistance.

3.4 Maintenance Support

3.4.1   Local (defined by user) customer engineering support must be available for all hardware and software packages acquired from the vendor.

3.4.2   The vendor must describe the ongoing system analyst support program.

3.4.3   The vendor must provide a description of its maintenance organization capable of maintaining the installed equipment and software consistent with the RFP's requirements. If the organization is not already operational, describe when and how it will become operational.

3.4.4   The vendor must provide a Maintenance Support Plan which delineates the maintenance service that will be provided. The following must be provided by vendor and addressed in the Maintenance Support Plan:

- On-call hardware and software maintenance at the installed office in (city), Washington.

- Logging of maintenance and enhancement activities.

- Prime shift maintenance in (hours) required Monday through Friday.

- Non-prime shift maintenance (hours).

- The maximum elapsed time between notification of equipment malfunction and arrival on-site by maintenance personnel cannot exceed (number) hours Monday through Friday, excluding Washington state holidays, whenever malfunction requires on-site maintenance.

- Malfunctioning equipment must be repaired or replaced by the maintenance technician no later than the close of business on the workday following notification of equipment malfunction.

3.4.5   Describe any preventive maintenance practices required and estimate the number of hours per month that the equipment will be inoperable for preventive maintenance.

3.5 System Availability

The vendor must contractually agree to maintain a 95 percent continuous equipment availability level during prime shift on all installed equipment and software. A survey of vendor references will be made to determine the availability of vendor hardware and software currently installed at those sites. If availability levels are found to be less than those contracted for at any of the sites, the proposal may be eliminated from further consideration.

3.6 Performance Levels

The vendor must contractually agree to maintain equipment to minimum performance levels, such as response time. A survey of vendor references will be made to determine the quality levels at those sites. If they are less than those contracted for at any of the sites, the proposal may be eliminated from further consideration.

3.7 Training

3.7.1   The vendor must supply training for (number of employees) staff in the operation of the equipment proposed. Training should be completed in time for the staff to operate the equipment in the required fashion with minimum vendor aid immediately after installation and testing of equipment. Any training costs must be included in Volume 2.

3.7.2   The vendor must supply a list of courses offered.

3.7.3   The vendor must provide a description of the proposed training program and the location of the training site(s). If the location is not Olympia, the Agency will add the appropriate travel and per diem costs to the vendor's proposal.

3.8 Facilities Requirements

The vendor must separately itemize all installation and environmental requirements for all proposed hardware, including:

- Air conditioning.
- Electrical requirements.
- Raised flooring.
- Cabling requirements.
- Weight (floor loading).
- Space requirements.
- Humidity and temperature limits.
- Noise level.

- Special handling for chemicals and toxic fumes.
- Other environmental considerations.

3.9 Configuration Alteration

Upgrading of the system and/or peripherals must be available. Trade-in credits must be available for system upgrading. The vendor must describe how it handles upgrades and trade-ins.

4 Vendor Information Requirements

4.1 Customer References

The vendor must submit a minimum of (number) non-vendor owned customer references presently using the proposed equipment and software of comparable size to the issuing agency's volume requirements. The vendor must also submit a minimum of (number) non-vendor owned customer references presently using the vendor's maintenance program. The same references can be used for each of the above requirements. All hardware and software proposed and referenced must be installed at a customer site for 90 days prior to the Proposal Due Date. Include the following for each reference:

Company Name

Business Address

Name of Contact

Title of Contact

Telephone Number of Contact

Description of Installation

Date Installed

The state may, at it's option, contact other known vendor customers for references.

4.2 User Groups

The vendor must provide the User Group name, address, phone number, and contact person for vendor User Group (if any).

4.3 Vendor Background and Financial Responsibility

4.3.1   The vendor must provide a brief description of the corporation including history. The vendor must supply the same information for parent corporations, if applicable.

4.3.2   The vendor must submit a copy of its most recent audited, or compiled, financial statement with the name, address, and telephone number of a contact in the company's principal financing or banking organization. The financial statement must have been completed by a Certified Public Accountant.

4.3.3   If the vendor is not a publicly held corporation, it may comply with section 4.3 by providing the following information:

Describe the proposing organization, including size, longevity, client base, areas of specialization and expertise, and any other pertinent information in such a manner that the proposal evaluator may reasonably formulate an opinion about the stability and financial strength of the organization; and

Provide a banking reference; and

Provide a credit rating and name the rating service; and

Disclose any and all judgments, pending or expected litigation, or other real or potential financial reversals which might materially affect the viability or stability of the proposing organization; or warrant that no such condition is known to exist.

4.3.4   Contract Performance

If the vendor has had a contract terminated for default during the past five years, all such incidents must be described. Termination for default is defined as notice to stop performance due to the vendor's non-performance or poor performance and the issue was either (a) not litigated; or (b) litigated and such litigation determined the vendor to be in default.

Submit full details of all terminations for default experienced by the vendor during the past five years including the other party's name, address and telephone number. Present the vendor's position on the matter. The Agency will evaluate the facts and may, at its sole discretion, reject the vendor's proposal if the facts discovered indicate that completion of a contract resulting from this RFP may be jeopardized by selection of the vendor.

If no such terminations for default have been experienced by the vendor in the past five years, so indicate.

4.4 Pricing Information

The vendor must provide purchase prices and installation costs for each equipment item, software product, and service proposed (Volume 2, Section 2 outlined in Appendix G). All elements of recurring and nonrecurring costs which must be borne by the Agency must be identified. This includes, but is not limited to, hardware maintenance, system engineering, manuals and documentation, consultation, training, conversion, shipping charges, installation costs, testing and taxes.

4.5 Taxes

4.6 Contract Award and Execution

4.6.1   The Agency reserves the right to make an award without further discussion of the proposal submitted; there will be no best and final offer procedure. Therefore, the proposal should be initially submitted on the most favorable terms the vendor can offer. The vendor shall specifically stipulate in the Cover Letter that the proposal is predicated upon the acceptance of all the terms and conditions stated in the Request for Proposal. It is understood that the proposal will become a part of the official file on this matter without obligation to the Agency.

4.6.2   The general conditions and specifications of the RFP and the successful vendor's response will become part of the contract. Additionally, the Agency will verify vendor representations which appear in the proposal with respect to system performance (e.g., response time). Failure of the vendor to produce results promised in the proposal in demonstrations may result in elimination of the vendor from competition or in contract cancellation or termination.

4.6.3   The Apparently Successful Vendor will be expected to enter into an agreement with the Agency which is substantially the same as the contract included with this RFP as Appendix B.

In no event is a vendor to submit its own standard contract terms and conditions as a response to this RFP. The vendor needs to address the specific language in Appendix B and submit whatever exceptions or exact contract modifications that their firm may have to the proposed T's and C's. The standard clauses (SC), are mandatory in content and must be included verbatim in the contract.

4.6.4   The foregoing should not be interpreted to prohibit either party from proposing additional contract terms and conditions during negotiation of the final contract.

If the contract negotiation period exceeds 30 days or if the selected vendor fails to sign the final contract within five (5) business days of delivery of it, the Agency may elect to cancel the award and award the contract to the next-highest-ranked vendor.

4.6.5   (Titles) are the only individuals who may legally commit the Agency to the expenditure of funds for this procurement. No cost chargeable to the proposed contract may be incurred before receipt of a fully executed contract.

5 Evaluation Procedures

5.1 Basis for Evaluation

The Technical and Financial sections of the proposals will be evaluated on the basis of the vendor's proposals and demonstrations. The Management section of the proposals will be evaluated on the basis of references in addition to the information available in the vendor's proposal. The evaluation point distribution is shown under Appendix (letter).

5.2 Evaluation Teams

The evaluation procedures will be performed by the RFP Coordinator and several teams formed by State staff. The team evaluations will progress independently of each other, without cross-dissemination of evaluation results (except in the event a proposal is rejected as non-responsive).

5.2.1 Technical Team

This team will conduct the technical evaluations using the technical proposals and functional demonstrations. It will also conduct the benchmark/ performance demonstrations and evaluate the results. Financial and management data and evaluations thereof will not be available to the Technical Team.

5.2.2 Financial Team

This team will evaluate all proposal hardware, software, and services costs, maintenance costs, and other costs, according to the financial evaluation criteria. The same criteria will be applied to all proposals. The Financial Team will also evaluate the participation level of Minority and Women Business Enterprises. Technical and benchmark/performance demonstration evaluation scores will not be available to the Financial Team.

5.2.3 Management Team

This team will evaluate the management portions of the response, and will contact references to verify the vendor's claims.

5.2.4 Selection Team

The Selection team will compile the scores, add the MWBE bonus for qualified vendors, and select the Apparently Successful Vendor on the basis of the final result.

5.3 Evaluation Process

The evaluation process is described below.

5.3.1 Administrative Screening

All proposals will be reviewed by the RFP Coordinator to determine compliance with administrative requirements as specified in the RFP. Only proposals meeting all of the administrative requirements will be further evaluated.

5.3.2 Mandatory Screening

Proposals meeting all of the administrative requirements will be reviewed on a pass-fail basis by the Technical Team to determine if they meet mandatory response requirements as specified in Sections (fill in appropriate numbers) of this RFP. The Financial Team will determine if Volume 2 meets the mandatory response requirements as specified in this RFP. Proposals found not to be in substantial compliance will be rejected from further consideration. If all responding vendors fail to meet any single mandatory item, the Agency reserves the following options:

a. Cancel the procurement.

b. Delete the mandatory item.

Proposals meeting the mandatory requirements will progress to the next step of the evaluation.

The evaluation team may contact the vendor for clarification of any portion of the vendor's proposal.

5.4 Qualitative Review and Scoring

Proposals which pass the preliminary screening and mandatory requirements review will be evaluated and scored based on responses to requirements in the RFP. The evaluators will consider how well the vendor's proposed solution meets the needs of the Agency, as described in the vendor's response to each requirement. It is important that the responses be clear and complete, so that the evaluators can adequately understand all aspects of the proposal.

5.4.1   Evaluation Criteria and Scoring Techniques

Scoring will use pre-established evaluation criteria set out in Appendix (letter). Each scored item will be given a score by each evaluator. The evaluation teams will score independently of one another. Upon completion of this review, scores will be forwarded to the Selection team.

5.4.2   Evaluation Points

Points will be assigned based on the effectiveness and efficiency in the documented approach to supporting each of the items being rated. A scale of zero to four will be used, where the range is defined as follows:

0.   Feature is non-responsive or wholly inadequate; if a mandatory requirement, it will result in the disqualification of the proposal.

1.   Below Average - Feature or capability is substandard to that which is average or expected as the norm.

2.   Average (This will be the baseline score for each item with adjustments based on evaluation teams interpretation of proposal)

3. Above Average - Feature or capability is better than that which is average or expected as the norm.

4. Exceptional - Feature or capability is clearly superior to that which is average or expected as the norm.

In addition to the point score assigned, each scored technical item is assigned a weighted value factor. The raw score given each item by the evaluators will be multiplied by the value for that item to give the weighted score.

5.4.3   Technical Evaluation

Proposals that complete the steps above will be evaluated by the Technical Team and scored based on the vendors' response to mandatory and desirable requirements contained in Section 2.1 and 2.2.

5.4.4   Functional Demonstration

Vendors will perform a functional demonstration to further explain responses. (The following sentences are optional and only one should be used). The functional demonstration will be scored as shown in 5.4.2. The functional demonstration will not be separately scored but evaluators will be allowed, based on their response to the functional demonstration, to adjust scores given during the technical evaluation.

5.4.5   Management Evaluation

Proposals that complete the preceding steps will be evaluated by the Management Team and scored based on the vendors' response to requirements contained in sections 3 and 4.

5.4.6   Selection of Finalists

The (number) vendors with the highest combined (technical, management, or whatever) scores will be selected as the finalist vendors.

5.4.7   Benchmark/Performance Demonstration

The finalist vendors will be evaluated by the Technical team on a Benchmark/Performance Demonstration as required in Appendix D. Vendors failing to successfully execute a benchmark/performance demonstration will be eliminated from further evaluation.

5.4.8   Financial Evaluation

Proposals that have met the administrative requirements as specified in the RFP will be evaluated by the Financial Team. The Financial Team will determine the total cost of the vendors' proposals to the Agency over a (number)-year period.

5.5 Evaluation of Cost Proposal

The score for the cost proposal will be computed by dividing the amount of lowest responsive bid the Agency receives by the vendor's total proposed cost. This sum will be multiplied by a weighting factor.

5.6 Total Weighted Score

The vendor's total weighted score is the sum of:

a)   Total Technical weighted score;

b)   Total Management weighted score;

c)   Total Benchmark/Performance Demonstration weighted score; and

d)   Total Cost weighted score.

5.7 MWBE Preference

If the vendor has met the requirements for MWBE preference, a bonus of (number) percent of the achieved total weighted score for the Management and Financial sections will be added to the total weighted score upon tabulation. a bonus of (number) percent of the achieved total weighted score for the Financial will be added to the total weighted score upon tabulation.

5.8 Selection of Apparently Successful Vendor

The evaluation process is designed to award the acquisition not necessarily to the vendor of least cost, but rather to that vendor with the best combination of attributes based upon the evaluation criteria.

The Technical, Management, and the Financial Teams will separately present the results of their respective evaluations to the Selection Team. The Selection Team will compile the scores, add the MWBE bonus for qualified vendors and select the Apparently Successful Vendor on the basis of the final result.

Should any finalist vendor scores be within (number)% of the highest score, they will be considered equal and the selection of the Apparent Successful Vendor will be based on the proposal with the highest total of (cost, technical, management, and benchmark/performance or whatever) points. If an Apparently Successful Vendor is identified, contract negotiations will begin. If, for any reason, a contract is not awarded to the first Apparently Successful Vendor, then the next highest ranking finalist vendor may be considered for contract negotiations.

Vendors eliminated from further competition will be mailed notification by the Agency as soon as practical.

5.9 Vendor Debriefing

Vendors which submitted an unsuccessful bid may, within five (5) business days of mailing of the notice of intended contract award, request a meeting for debriefing and discussion of their proposals. The request must be in writing addressed to the RFP Coordinator. The debriefing must be held within five (5) working days of the request.

Debriefing will not include any comparisons of the vendor's unsuccessful proposal with any other vendor's proposal. The Agency will attempt to respond to questions and concerns in this debriefing.

5.10 Protest by Unsuccessful Vendor

Upon completion of the debriefing conference, a vendor is allowed five (5) business days to file a formal protest of the acquisition with the Agency. Further information regarding the filing and resolution of protests is contained in Appendix F, Protest Procedures.

Addendum A

PRELIMINARY EVALUATION CHECKLIST

VENDOR'S NAME _____

REVIEWER'S NAME _____

YES/NO

___ 1. Letter of Intent received on time and with all required content/information (RFP Section 1.8.2).

___ 2. Vendor attended mandatory pre-proposal conference (RFP Section 1.8.1).

___ 3. Proposal received on time and at correct location (RFP Section 1.8.10).

___ 4. Proposal is in effect for necessary number of days (RFP Section 1.8.4).

___ 5. Proposal format meets RFP preparation requirements (RFP Section 1.8.12).

___ 6. Proposal bound correctly in two volumes (RFP Section 1.8.12.5).

___ 7. No cost data included in Volume 1 (RFP Section 1.8.12.5).

___ 8. Hardware and software meet installation requirements (RFP Section 4.1).

___ 9. (Number) copies of technical proposal received (RFP Section 1.8.23).

___ 10. (Number) copies of financial proposal received (RFP Section 1.8.23).

___ 11. (Number) copies of reference documentation received (RFP Section 1.8.23).

___ 12. Vendor agrees to comply with contract provisions (RFP Section 4.5.3 and Addendum B).

___ 13. Vendor agrees to demonstration and benchmark travel arrangements (RFP Section 1.8.25).

___ 14. Proposal Volume 2 - Section 1 contains most recent audited financial statement (RFP Section 4.3.2).

___ 15. Proposal Volume 2 - Section 1 contains vendor background description (RFP Section 4.3.1).

___ 16. Proposal Volume 2 - Section 2 contains financial and cost data for RFP Sections 2.0 and 3.0 (RFP Section 4.4).

___ 17. Maintenance references are provided (RFP Section 3.4.6).

___ 18. Customer references provided (RFP Section 4.1).

___ 19. Vendor agrees to meet proposed delivery time schedule (RFP Section 1.8.30).

___ 20. Vendor provides information on local maintenance organization (RFP Section 3.4.3).

___ 21. Vendor provides user group information (RFP Section 4.2).

___ 22. Vendor agrees to all delivery support requirements (RFP Section 3.1).

___ 23. Vendor agrees to all documentation support requirements (RFP Section 3.2).

___ 24. Vendor agrees to all installation assistance requirements (RFP Section 3.3).

___ 25. Vendor agrees to all maintenance support requirements (RFP Section 3.4).

___ 26. Vendor agrees to equipment reliability maintenance contract (RFP Section 3.5).

___ 27. Vendor agrees to provide all training required (RFP Section 3.7).

___ 28. Vendor agrees to provide all facilities requirements information as required (RFP Section 3.8).

Addendum B

STANDARD CONTRACT TERMS

Note: For standard contract terms and conditions, see "Appendix B: Contractual 'Standard Clauses' and Additional Contractual Clauses" in the policy titled "Acquisition and Disposal of Information Technology Resources in Washington State Government," September 1989, contained after the tab "Acquisitions" in the "Information Technology Policy Manual."

Addendum C

FUNCTIONAL DEMONSTRATION REQUIREMENTS

The intent of the functional demonstration is to allow the State to gain a complete understanding of the vendor's proposal.

The State will schedule (number) days for the demonstration at a location selected by the vendor. The following topics will be covered: general information on the vendor, its products and its proposal; discussion and demonstration of the specific features identified as mandatory requirements in the RFP.

The presentation agenda will include:

1. Introduce participants.

2. Present corporate history.

3. Present range of products/services.

4. Describe all hardware and software proposed.

5. Explain how the proposed solution meets State needs.

6. Discuss vendor's support capabilities.

7. Present expansion capabilities for proposed configurations.

8. Question and answer period.

After this introduction, the hardware, software and procedural functions should be demonstrated using the mandatory requirements from sections 2.0 and 3.0 as a guideline. Areas to be covered include:

description of the hardware and software proposed and how it works; and demonstration of the proposed system and its functions. Every effort should be made to demonstrate all hardware and software proposed. In some cases, if it is not practical to demonstrate an item during the functional demonstration, the product must be explained as completely as possible. If a vendor chosen as a finalist has not demonstrated all hardware and software proposed, then the functional demonstration requirements not completed will become part of the benchmark requirements.

Addendum D

BENCHMARK REQUIREMENTS

The purpose of the benchmark is to assure that the proposed equipment and software can perform as specified in the RFP and as represented in the proposal. The benchmark requirements will be the minimum performance accepted. The State will schedule (number) days for the benchmark at a location selected by the vendor. Following are the benchmark steps.

Addendum E

EVALUATION POINT DISTRIBUTION

(This addendum provides the vendor with a detailed break down of evaluation points. The point distribution aids vendors in developing responsive proposals because it shows the relative importance to the State of various requirements and features.)

The evaluation criteria reflect a wide range of considerations. While purchase price is important, other factors are equally significant. Careful selection among the variety of products available depends on assessment of features, their design, their impact on State staff and numerous additional qualitative and quantitative considerations. Consequently, the State may not select the lowest cost solution. The objective is to choose a reliable and experienced vendor capable of providing an effective solution within a reasonable budget and timeframe.

The evaluation will consider three basic types of criteria:

1. Cost (_____% of total points);
2. Vendor's Management Characteristics and Stability (_____% of total points);
3. Functional Requirements (_____% of total points):
   a. Satisfaction of itemized specifications.
   b. Overall quality, flexibility, and ease of use.

Addendum F

PROTEST PROCEDURES

A.   Procedure

This protest procedure is available to vendors responding to this RFP requesting a debriefing conference. Protests are made:

1.   To the Department of _____ after the announcement of the apparently successful vendor. Vendor protests shall be received, in writing, by the Department of _____ within five business days after the vendor debriefing conference.

2.   To DIS only after protesting first to the Department of _____ and its resolution is not satisfactory to the protesting party. Protests to DIS shall be received, in writing, within five business days after the vendor has received notification of a decision on the protest from the Department of _____.

3.   To the ISB for acquisitions approved by the ISB, only after protesting first to DIS and DIS resolution is not satisfactory to either party. Protests to the ISB shall be made within five business days after the vendor has received notification of the DIS decision.

B.   Grounds for protest are:

1.   Errors were made in computing the score.

2.   The State failed to follow procedures established in the RFP, the ISB policy: Acquisition and Disposal of Information Technology Resources, or applicable state or federal laws or regulations.

3.   Bias, discrimination or conflict of interest on the part of an evaluator.

Protests not based on these criteria shall not be considered.

C.   Format and Content

Protesting vendors shall include, in their written protest to the Department of _____ and DIS, all facts and arguments upon which they rely. Vendors shall, at a minimum, provide:

1.   Information about the protesting vendor; name of firm, mailing address, phone number and name of individual responsible for submission of the protest.

2.   Information about the acquisition and the acquisition method.

3.   Specific and complete statement of the State action(s) protested.

4. Specific reference to the grounds for the protest.

5. Description of the relief or corrective action requested.

6. For protests to DIS or the ISB, a copy of the Department of _____'s written decision on the protest.

D. Review Process

Upon receipt of a vendor protest, the Department of _____ shall postpone further steps in the acquisition process until the vendor protest has been resolved.

The Department's internal protest review procedures consist of the following: (_____).

The Department of _____ shall perform an objective review of the protest by individuals not involved in the acquisition protested. The review shall be based on the written protest material submitted by the vendor.

A written decision will be delivered to the vendor within five business days after receipt of the protest, unless more time is needed. The protesting vendor shall be notified if additional time is necessary.

E. DIS Review Process

The vendor may protest to DIS in writing within five business days after the vendor has received notification of the agency decision.

DIS shall consider all the available facts and issue a decision in writing within five business days after receipt of the protest, unless more time is needed. The protesting vendor shall be notified if additional time is necessary. The DIS decision constitutes the final step of the protest process, except protests which may be reviewed by the ISB as outlined under Section I, "ISB Review Process".

DIS may choose to convene a Protest Review Board (Board). The Board shall be advisory to the DIS Director and its scope of review shall be limited to procedural issues raised by the protesting vendor.

F. Final Determination

The final determination shall:

1. Find the protest lacking in merit and uphold the agency's action; or

2. Find only technical or harmless errors in the agency's acquisition process conduct, determine the agency to be in substantial compliance, and reject the protest; or

3. Find merit in the protest and provide the agency options which may include:

   - Correct its errors and reevaluate all proposals, and/or

   - Reissue the vendor solicitation document; or

4. Make other findings and determine other courses of action as appropriate.

G. ISB Review Process

Protests to the ISB may be made only for ISB approved acquisitions, and only after review by DIS. Protests of the decisions of DIS shall be made by letter to the Chair, ISB, who may establish procedures to resolve the protest. Protests shall be received by the Chair, ISB, within five business days after the decision of DIS in order to be considered. The resulting decision is final, with no further administrative appeal available.

Addendum G

PROPOSAL CONTENTS

Vendor proposals in response to this RFP must be submitted in the format specified below. Proposals must include:

VOLUME I

Cover Letter: Signed by vendor representative authorized to make contractual obligations

Table of Contents

Executive Summary: A high level overview of your approach and the distinguishing characteristics of your proposal.

Section 1 - Introduction:

Statement of problem; identification of the State's needs; and general description of proposed solution and associated purchase price

1.1 Vendor Background Including:

Name and address of legal entity submitting the proposal.

Names of the principal officers.

Legal status of vendor organization, i.e., corporation, partnership, sole proprietor.

Federal Employer ID number.

Washington State Department of Revenue registration number.

1.2 Overview of Proposed Hardware/Software.

1.3 Proposal Certification (1.8.4).

1.4 Vendor Certifications including:

Performance demonstration and benchmark travel cost commitments (1.8.25).

Equipment delivery certification (1.8.30).

Proposed configurations satisfy all the mandatory requirements in this RFP and vendor can demonstrate the stated capabilities.

Proposed configurations and supporting software is in operation at customer sites by the Proposal Due Date (1.8.4).

Third Party Vendor commitment (1.8.26).

1.5 This section may be used by the vendor to present information of importance not otherwise provided for in the required proposal format.

Section 2 - Proposed Configuration(s)

2.1 The vendor must provide an itemized list and diagram of the all proposed hardware and software.

2.2 The vendor must provide a technical description of each hardware and software item proposed.

2.3 Explain how the proposed configuration will meet the State's needs.

Section 3 - Responses to Hardware and Software Requirements;

Section 4 - Responses to Vendor Support Requirements; and Section 5 - Responses to Vendor Information Requirements

Proposals must address, in sequence, each requirement of Sections 3, 4, and 5. Please respond in the following manner:

a. Restate the number and requirement as it appears in the RFP.

b. Indicate whether the product offered satisfies the requirement by stating one of the following:

- "Supported as described" meaning that the product offered completely meets the requirement;

- "Not supported" meaning that the product offered clearly does not satisfy the requirements; or

- "Partially supported" meaning that the product satisfies some portion of the requirement, but leaves the remainder unsatisfied.

- "Equivalent available" meaning that while the vendor does not fully satisfy the requirement as stated, it provides some of the required functionality. If functional equivalency is available through enhancement or modification, describe the necessary effort and associated costs.

c. Explain how the requirement is addressed. (Failure to provide this description will result in disqualification.)

VOLUME 2: Financial and Contractual Proposal

Section 1 - Vendor Background and Financial Responsibility

1.1 Corporate History (4.3.1)

1.2 Financial Report (4.3.2)

Section 2 - Financial and Cost Data

2.1 Provide itemized costs of hardware and software components, including the costs listed below. Detail and separate one-time and recurring costs where appropriate.

1. Applications Software - For each application or module list:

    a. Initial purchase price;

    b. Annual license fees;

    c. Annual maintenance fee; and

    d. Cost of hotline support.

2. Hardware - For the hardware and operating system software on which the proposed applications run, list the necessary devices and their unit costs and maintenance cost, such as:

    a. CPU;

    b. Operating System/System Utility Software;

    c. Disk Drives;

    d. Terminals/Workstations;

    e. Printers;

    f. Tape Drives; and

    g. Teleprocessing Monitor/Network.

3. Commercial Software - List and price commercially available software necessary to support or augment the application software proposed such as:

    a. Database management system;

    b. Data dictionary;

    c. 4 GL;

    d. Query language; and

    e. Other.

4. Services

    a. Modifications to application software;

    b. Standard and optional levels of conversion assistance and support;

    c.   Testing; and

    d.   Training.

5.   Other Costs - Itemize all other costs not listed in the preceding categories, such as:

    a.   Freight;

    b.   Cable supplies;

    c.   Travel;

    d.   Training; and

    e.   Taxes.

6.   Total Proposal Costs - Provide your total proposal costs, which includes all expenditures through conversion and implementation.

Section 3 - Contract Requirements

3.1 If the vendor takes exception to the terms and conditions that appear in Addendum B, it may propose, for state consideration, alternate language as section 3.

Supplemental Material

The vendor may submit materials such as reference manuals, brochures, articles, specifications, report samples, and the like which may be helpful, subject to the following:

    a.   Such supplemental materials will not qualify as substitutes for direct responses to the RFP's requirements.

    b.   Supplemental materials must not be combined with a required component of the proposal (included in a proposal binder, for example).

    c.   The Management Proposal may make reference to supplemental materials if submitted. However, the response must be stated in such a way within the Management Proposal that it is not necessary to refer to the supplemental material to evaluate the response (except specifically requested material, such as the vendor's financial statements).

    d.   The Technical and Cost proposals may not make reference to supplemental materials. Note that any such materials submitted will have no effect on the independent evaluation process. Such materials will in fact be withheld from the evaluators until the evaluation, scoring and selection of the Apparently Successful vendor has been completed.

Contractual "Standard Clauses," State of Washington

APPENDIX B

INFORMATION TECHNOLOGY

CONTRACT TERMS AND CONDITIONS

PURPOSE

Appendix B provides information technology sample contract check lists and Terms and Conditions (Ts&Cs). These are for use by state agencies in developing agency Requests for Proposals (RFPs), Requests for Quotations (RFQs), and as a basis for both competitive and negotiated contracts. The use of these Terms and Conditions meets the requirement of the Information Services Board (ISB) Information Technology Acquisition Policy and Standards for the Department of Information Services (DIS) Planning and Policy Division (PPD) contract approvals.

Ts&Cs

Ts&Cs consist of two types: 1) a set of Standard Clauses (SC) which are mandatory in content, meaning that agency contracts must cover the subject of the provision, but need not necessarily use the exact language recommended here; and 2) the remaining Ts&Cs with language which may be negotiated between agency and contractor. Provisions marked with an asterisk (*) are routine use clauses; they contain language typically found in such contracts and their use is encouraged.

Contracts intended for use as Master Agreements must be approved by DIS PPD staff.

TYPES OF CONTRACTS

Contract checklists and sample contract Terms and Conditions are included for a variety of contracts, including: Equipment Purchase; Equipment Lease; Installment Purchase/Lease Purchase; Equipment Maintenance; Software License; and a Short Form Purchase Order.

Not included are checklists for "turnkey" (combined hardware, software and applications systems), software development or personal services contracts. These contracts normally require careful tailoring to include specific and unique performance and work expectations, and the Ts&Cs in Appendix B are not intended to satisfy these kinds of contracts.

USE

Every acquisition of information technology resources from a vendor requires a contract (except for verbal orders over the telephone, within the dollar limits permitted by the ISB Acquisition Standard). The contract may be as simple as a one-time purchase order, or it may require complex provisions covering ongoing relations with the vendor.

For every competitive acquisition or negotiated sole source acquisition, an agency is required to use the Terms and Conditions (together with appropriately tailored negotiable clauses) in the solicitation document (RFP or RFQ) when issued, and as a basis for negotiating the resulting contract.

For simple acquisitions agencies may, in lieu of developing a contract, use the short form standard purchase order version.

Resources may be acquired through the use of state developed or vendor contracts. While vendor standard form contracts provide protection for the vendor, they do not necessarily provide adequate protection for the State. With either, it is desirable for agencies to develop a contract which specifies resources to be acquired and protects both vendor and agency interests. This Appendix provides a starting point.

APPENDIX B
INFORMATION TECHNOLOGY CONTRACT
TERMS AND CONDITIONS
TABLE OF CONTENTS

I. HOW TO USE THE APPENDIX

A. Build a Contract Using Sample Contract Terms and Conditions

If a sample contract using Appendix B Terms and Conditions is included in the contracting requirements of an RFP or RFQ, it provides the basis for subsequent negotiation with the apparently successful vendor.

If negotiating with a sole source vendor, or if no sample contract was used in the solicitation document, it is still recommended that a sample contract using Appendix B Terms and Conditions be developed and used to open contract discussions. Using these Terms and Conditions should provide an adequate degree of protection and clarity for the agency and the State.

1. Use the "Contract Checklists" in Section II of the Appendix to identify applicable Terms and Conditions. Use all Terms and Conditions that apply (for example, a single contract may include hardware purchase, some leased equipment, licensed software, and maintenance services). Note that the content and intent of Standard Clauses must be included in every acquisition (except where the Standard Short Form Purchase Order will suffice).

The remaining clauses may be tailored to fit the contract with specific language negotiated with the vendor.

2. The "Contract Checklists" provide a brief description of the provisions, together with comments on their use, as an aid in selection.

3. If a sample contract has not been included in a solicitation document, select Terms and Conditions from Section III. DIS PPD staff can provide sample contracts and Terms and Conditions on PC diskettes in WordPerfect format on request.

4. Modify the wording of selected provisions as appropriate.

5. Add any provisions necessary to complete the contract.

6. Construct a draft of the contract and review it with the agency Assistant Attorney General for completeness. Attach any referenced schedules, exhibits, etc., at the end of the contract.

7. Negotiate the contract.

8. Obtain agency Assistant Attorney General review and approval as to form.

9. Obtain DIS PPD approval, if required.

10. If possible, obtain the vendor's signature on the contract before you sign.

11. Sign two copies of the contract. Give one to the vendor, keep the other copy.

B. Build Terms and Attach a Vendor Contract

Often the standard vendor contract will contain provisions that are satisfactory for the final contract.

If so, the agency may wish to include the appropriate vendor provisions by reference in the "Opening Paragraph" of the contract, and by attachment. Be sure to indicate the hierarchy of the provisions — that is, the State's language takes precedence over vendor's language in the event of a conflict.

The steps to be followed are the same as outlined in A. above, except that the vendor contract should be attached to the draft produced from the sample contract Terms and Conditions.

Strike out any provisions in the vendor contract that are inappropriate.

C. Attach Terms to a Vendor Contract

Should a vendor contract include most of the provisions that may be satisfactory for the final contract, the agency may choose to utilize the vendor contract and attach appropriate supplemental or amending provisions.

The checklists contained in Section II should be used to ensure the appropriate Standard Clauses and other necessary provisions are included.

Modifications to vendor language and any required provisions not contained in the vendor contract should be attached and referenced as inclusions in the "Opening Paragraph."

Be sure that vendor provisions do not give inappropriate advantage to the vendor. As with all contracts, a review by the agency Assistant Attorney General, and DIS PPD when required, is necessary before signatures are affixed.

D. Standard Purchase Order

Many times a purchase may not require negotiation or the longer form set of purchase Terms and Conditions. Generally, these types of acquisitions are of low volume and/or off the shelf or small dollar magnitude and do not involve continuing payments or ongoing relationships with the vendor. Here, it is acceptable to use an agency purchase order. However, the purchase order should contain the general Terms and Conditions shown in the Short Form Purchase Order in Section III, or a set of agency purchase order Terms and Conditions that have been approved by the agency Assistant Attorney General.

II.   CONTRACT CHECKLISTS

The following checklists give the titles of the Terms and Conditions (provisions) and can be used with Section III of the Appendix to select the appropriate provisions for each contract. The provisions have been assembled in sample contract format. They contain Standard Clauses (SC) and other clauses which may be modified and used as needed. Those clauses which should routinely be included in any given contract (both Standard Clauses and others) are identified with an asterisk (*).

All SC provisions must be included in a contract for information technology resources. In most situations they may be used as written here, but occasionally rewording may be necessary. In all cases, their titles or captions and basic content must be included.

A. CHECKLIST FOR SAMPLE EQUIPMENT PURCHASE CONTRACT

1   Table of Contents: To list and identify the provisions contained within the contract.

2   *Contracting Parties, Equipment, Software, Services Schedule/Price Schedule: Every contract must 1) identify the parties of the contract, 2) show what is being contracted for (through the attachments), and 3) provide the terms of the transaction. If the contract results from an RFP or RFQ, it is appropriate to include a recitation as to the basis for the contract by reference in this section. Any schedules of equipment, software or services to be acquired together with prices/discounts should be incorporated by reference and attached to the contract.

3   *Advance Payment: To comply with State law that no advance payments shall be made to the Contractor.

4   *Affirmative Action: To ensure that the Contractor takes affirmative action with regard to employment, promotion, rates of pay, etc.

5   *Anti-Trust Violations: To establish that the Contractor assigns claims for overcharges resulting from antitrust violations to the State.

6   *Assignment: To establish that neither party shall assign, sublicense nor transfer its rights, duties, or obligations without written consent of the other party. If Contractor performance or financial condition is a problem, it may be necessary to keep Contractor assignment at the Customer's sole option.

7   Attorneys' Fees and Costs: General clause for payment of attorneys' fees.

8   Backup Availability: To provide a means for obtaining replacement system equipment upon a permanently disabling disaster for mission essential equipment. This or similar disaster recovery requirements should be specified in functional requirements in the solicitation documents.

9   Compatibility: To ensure that hardware, software or other products delivered are compatible with Customer's currently installed systems, or with other hardware, software or products also manufactured and/or available from Contractor. This clause should be tailored to Customer's specific operational needs as identified in functional requirements in the acquisition solicitation documents.

10   Compliance with Standards: To cause Contractor to comply with specified hardware and software standards (Customer's, American National Standards Institute (ANSI), International Standards Organization (ISO), or other).

11   *Compliance with Civil Rights Laws: (SC) To establish that the Contractor shall not discriminate against any person for reason of age, sex, race, creed, color, or national origin according to Title VII of the

Civil Rights Act.

12 Confidentiality: Provides for Contractor maintaining Confidentiality of Customer material.

13 Conflict of Interest: Prohibits Conflict of Interest, and provides for termination upon breach.

14 *Contractor Commitments, Warranties and Representations: To assure that written commitments by the Contractor within the scope of this contract shall be binding upon the Contractor. Documents containing written warranties should be incorporated by reference.

15 Counterparts: To provide for duplicate originals of the contract.

16 Covenant Against Contingent Fees: Prohibits contingent fees, permits termination for violation.

17 Cross Guarantees: To ensure that a contract signed by a subsidiary has the support of the parent organization and vice versa.

18 Definition of Terms: To establish specific definitions for terms used within the contract.

19 Discounts and Purchase Options: To establish any special discounts for volume or long-term lease and to define conditions for any lease/rental credits toward purchase.

20 Disputes: Dispute arbitration clause limits arbitration to determinations of fact. Should only be used if negotiating away a more onerous clause, as it limits agency rights and freedom of action to resolve a problem, by putting the issue in the hands of an arbitration team.

21 *Engineering Changes: To establish both parties' responsibilities for scheduling equipment engineering changes.

22 *Entire Agreement: To establish that the contract constitutes the entire agreement and supersedes all previous discussions, bid processes, and agreements, except as provided in Contractor Commitments, Warranties, and Representations. Specific documentation such as Contractor proposals, equipment and software specifications, communications regarding goods and services to be provided, etc. should be included in the contract by reference or attachment, where Contractor assurances and performance questions are concerned.

23 Equipment Configurations: Equipment conformance to specifications. Includes specific listings of equipment and interface and connectibility requirements, which should be included in acquisition solicitation documents.

24 Equipment Warranties: To establish specific Contractor warranties for performance of equipment and to define remedies in the event of failure of warranted products.

25 *Equipment Condition: To establish that the Contractor warrants that the equipment is newly manufactured or identified as refurbished.

26 Exchange Provisions: To establish conditions for upgrade, downgrade, trade-ins, etc., for exchange of leased or purchased equipment or licensed software.

27 *Failure to Perform: To establish that the State may withhold monies, beginning 30 days after

written notification that the Contractor has failed to perform any obligation in the contract.

28 *Governing Law: The contract will be governed by the law and statutes of the State of Washington, with venue set in the Superior Court in the county in which Customer has its headquarters — if other than Thurston County, so indicate.

29 Hold-back for Entire Contract Compliance: To provide for holdback of payment for products pending performance of entire contract. Other options include per diem liquidated damages for non-completion, or inclusion of a requirement for a Contractor's performance bond to be held in escrow by Customer pending full contract compliance.

30 *Independent Status of Contractor: (SC) The parties to the contract will be acting in their individual capacities and not as agents or associates of one another.

31 Industrial Insurance Coverage: Requires Contractor to have industrial insurance coverage.

32 *Installation (Site) Security: To assure Contractor conformance to State premise security regulations.

33 *Installation and Delivery Dates: To establish the terms, dates, and conditions for equipment delivery and installation.

34 Interface of Equipment: To provide assurance that contractor provided products will interface with specified telecommunications equipment, listed terminals and peripherals, as previously identified in the acquisition solicitation documents.

35 Licensing Standards: Establishes Contractor's requirement to be licensed to do business in Washington.

36 *Limitation of Liability: (SC) To establish that State is not liable to Contractor for consequential damages, or lost profits. In addition, Customer shall not be liable for damages or delay caused by acts of God or other circumstances beyond its control (Force Majeure clause).

37 Limitation of Authority: Identifies agency Contracting Officer as Customer authorized signatory, provides for other prior written delegation.

38 *Liquidated Damages: To establish the General Terms and Conditions for damages because of Contractor performance delays or State site preparation delays.

39 *Maintenance of Equipment: To establish the terms, conditions, and provisions for maintenance of the equipment.

40 Maintenance Surcharges: To establish costs for extraordinary maintenance situations.

41 *Maintenance Documentation: To assure that the Contractor shall provide appropriate documentation for maintenance of purchased equipment upon request.

42 Minority & Women's Business Enterprise Participation: Contracts with Minority or Women's Business Enterprise participation should include specific language covering required participation and

remedies upon breach of contract. Contact the Office of Minority and Women's Business Enterprises (OMWBE) for specific language.

43 *Non-Allocation of Funds: (SC) Often called the "Funding Out" clause, this provision allows termination for lack of funds, when the State fails to appropriate, allot, or allocate necessary funds to continue the contract into subsequent fiscal periods. If no periodic or future payments are required under the contract, this clause may be omitted.

44 *Notices: To define official addresses for formal notifications.

45 *OSHA/WISHA: To establish that the Contractor warrants that its products are designed to meet federal and State safety and health regulations.

46 *Patent and Copyright Indemnification - Equipment/Licensed Software: To establish responsibility of both parties in event of infringement of a U.S. or foreign Patent or Copyright.

47 *Payment and Invoice Provisions: To establish provisions for the timing of payments and establish conditions for delinquency and penalties.

48 Price Protection - Lease Rates/Purchase Prices/Maintenance Rates: To establish conditions for price increases, reductions, escalation, and notices thereof.

49 Price Protection - General: To guarantee state agencies the vendors most favored customer prices.

50 Protection of Proprietary Information: To establish protection of Contractor's rights and interests in technical information, software products, copyrights, etc.

51 Publicity: To establish that the Contractor will not use any advertising, sales promotion, or any other publicity materials wherein the State's name may be stated, implied, or inferred without the consent of the State.

52 *Quiet Possession and Usage: (SC) To confirm State's right to peaceful use of the product upon payment of the amounts due as specified in the contract.

53 *Risk of Loss (Purchased): To allocate risk and name the point in time at which the risk of loss of the equipment shifts from the Contractor to the Customer.

54 *Save Harmless: (SC) To indemnify the State from injury to persons or property caused by any acts or omissions of the Contractor.

55 *Severability: (SC) To establish that if any term or condition is invalid, the other terms or conditions are not affected.

56 Site and Installation Planning: To establish responsibility for site specifications and preparation.

57 Specifications: To provide for including technical equipment specifications by reference and attached to the contract.

58 *Standard of Performance and Acceptance of Equipment: To establish provisions for a standard of performance which must be met before any equipment is accepted by the State.

59 *Subcontractors: (SC) To establish the conditions under which the Contractor may enter into subcontracts with third parties.

60 *Taxes: To identify tax liability and exemptions for the contract.

61 *Term of Agreement: To establish the period of performance, conditions for extensions and termination, and the survivability of certain clauses.

62 Termination, Cancellation, and Repossession: To establish conditions for termination or cancellation of the lease or purchase contract by either party, and the requirement for notices.

63 Termination: Alternative termination clause, with Termination for Default, Termination for Convenience, and termination following arbitration under the optional disputes clause.

64 *Title (Purchased): To assure that the Contractor shall convey clear title of purchased equipment upon completion of acceptance testing.

65 Training: To establish Contractor responsibilities for training on equipment or software.

66 Transportation: To establish responsibility for cost of transportation, transit insurance, risk of loss, and title of equipment during shipment to the installation site.

67 *Waiver: (SC) To establish that a term or condition of the contract may be waived only by the written consent of both parties.

68 *Signature Blocks: To provide a statement of understanding and agreement followed by signature blocks.

B. CHECKLIST FOR SAMPLE EQUIPMENT LEASE CONTRACT

1 Table of Contents: To list and identify the provisions contained within the contract.

2 *Contracting Parties, Equipment, Software, Services Schedule/Price Schedule: Every contract must 1) identify the parties of the contract, 2) show what is being contracted for (through the attachments), and 3) provide the terms of the transaction. If the contract results from an RFP or RFQ, it is appropriate to include a recitation as to the basis for the contract by reference in this section. Any schedules of equipment, software or services to be acquired together with prices/discounts should be incorporated by reference and attached to the contract.

3 *Advance Payment: To comply with State law that no advance payments shall be made to the Contractor.

4 *Affirmative Action: To ensure that the Contractor takes affirmative action with regard to employment, promotion, rates of pay, etc.

5 *Alterations and Attachments: To establish that alterations or attachments to leased or rented machines may be made upon prior consent of the Contractor.

6 *Anti-Trust Violations: To establish that the Contractor assigns claims for overcharges resulting

from antitrust violations to the State.

7 *Assignment: To establish that neither party shall assign, sublicense nor transfer its rights, duties, or obligations without written consent of the other party. If Contractor performance or financial condition is a problem, it may be necessary to keep Contractor assignment at the Customer's sole option.

8 Attorneys' Fees and Costs: General clause for payment of attorneys' fees.

9 Backup Availability: To provide a means for obtaining replacement system equipment upon a permanently disabling disaster for mission essential equipment. This or similar disaster recovery requirements should be specified in functional requirements in the solicitation documents.

10 Compatibility: To ensure that hardware, software or other products delivered are compatible with Customer's currently installed systems, or with other hardware, software or products also manufactured and/or available from Contractor. This clause should be tailored to Customer's specific operational needs as identified in functional requirements in the acquisition solicitation documents.

11 Compliance with Standards: To cause Contractor to comply with specified hardware and software standards (Customer's, American National Standards Institute (ANSI), International Standards Organization (ISO), or other).

12 *Compliance with Civil Rights Laws: (SC) To establish that the Contractor shall not discriminate against any person for reason of age, sex, race, creed, color, or national origin according to Title VII of the Civil Rights Act.

13 Confidentiality: Provides for Contractor maintaining Confidentiality of Customer material.

14 Conflict of Interest: Prohibits Conflict of Interest, and provides for termination upon breach.

15 *Contractor Commitments, Warranties and Representations: To assure that written commitments by the Contractor within the scope of this contract shall be binding upon the Contractor. Documents containing written warranties should be incorporated by reference.

16 Counterparts: To provide for duplicate originals of the contract.

17 Covenant Against Contingent Fees: Prohibits contingent fees, permits termination for violation.

18 Cross Guarantees: To ensure that a contract signed by a subsidiary has the support of the parent organization and vice versa.

19 Definition of Terms: To establish specific definitions for terms used within the contract.

20 Discounts and Purchase Options: To establish any special discounts for volume or long-term lease and to define conditions for any lease/rental credits toward purchase.

21 Disputes: Dispute arbitration clause limits arbitration to determinations of fact. Should only be used if negotiating away a more onerous clause, as it limits agency rights and freedom of action to resolve a problem, by putting the issue in the hands of an arbitration team.

22 *Engineering Changes: To establish both parties' responsibilities for scheduling equipment

engineering changes.

23 *Entire Agreement: To establish that the contract constitutes the entire agreement and supersedes all previous discussions, bid processes, and agreements, except as provided in Contractor Commitments, Warranties, and Representations. Specific documentation such as Contractor proposals, equipment and software specifications, communications regarding goods and services to be provided, etc. should be included in the contract by reference or attachment, where Contractor assurances and performance questions are concerned.

24 Equipment Configurations: Equipment conformance to specifications. Includes specific listings of equipment and interface and connectibility requirements, which should be included in acquisition solicitation documents.

25 Equipment Warranties: To establish specific Contractor warranties for performance of equipment and to define remedies in the event of failure of warranted products.

26 *Equipment Condition: To establish that the Contractor warrants that the equipment is newly manufactured or identified as refurbished.

27 Exchange Provisions: To establish conditions for upgrade, downgrade, trade-ins, etc., for exchange of leased or purchased equipment or licensed software.

28 *Failure to Perform: (SC) To establish that the State may withhold monies, beginning 30 days after written notification that the Contractor has failed to perform any substantial obligation in the contract.

29 *Governing Law: (SC) The contract will be governed by the law and statutes of the State of Washington, with venue set in the Superior Court in the county in which Customer has its headquarters— if other than Thurston County, so indicate.

30 *Independent Status of Contractor: (SC) The parties to the contract will be acting in their individual capacities and not as agents or associates of one another.

31 Industrial Insurance Coverage: Requires Contractor to have industrial insurance coverage.

32 *Installation (Site) Security: To assure Contractor conformance to State premise security regulations.

33 *Installation and Delivery Dates: To establish the terms, dates, and conditions for equipment delivery and installation.

34 Insurance: To establish both parties' insurance responsibilities.

35 Interface of Equipment: To provide assurance that Contractor provided products will interface with specified telecommunications equipment, listed terminals and peripherals, as previously identified in the acquisition solicitation documents.

36 Licensing Standards: Establishes Contractor's requirement to be licensed to do business in

Washington.

37 *Limitation of Liability: (SC) To establish that State is not liable to Contractor for consequential damages, or lost profits. In addition, Customer shall not be liable for damages or delay caused by acts of God or other circumstances beyond its control (Force Majeure clause).

38 Limitation of Authority: Identifies agency Contracting Officer as Customer authorized signatory, provides for other prior written delegation.

39 *Liquidated Damages: To establish the general Terms and Conditions for damages because of Contractor performance delays or State site preparation delays.

40 *Maintenance of Equipment: To establish the terms, conditions, and provisions for maintenance of the equipment.

41 Maintenance Surcharges: To establish costs for extraordinary maintenance situations.

42 Minority & Women's Business Enterprise Participation: Contracts with Minority or Women's Business Enterprise participation should include specific language covering required participation and remedies upon breach of contract. Contact the Office of Minority and Women's Business Enterprises (OMWBE) for specific language.

43 *Non-Allocation of Funds: (SC) Often called the "Funding Out" clause, this provision allows termination for lack of funds, when the State fails to appropriate, allot, or allocate necessary funds to continue the contract into subsequent fiscal periods. If no periodic or future payments are required under the contract, this clause may be omitted.

44 *Notices: To define official addresses for formal notifications.

45 *OSHA/WISHA: To establish that the Contractor warrants that its products are designed to meet federal and state safety and health regulations.

46 *Patent and Copyright Indemnification: Equipment/Licensed Software: To establish responsibility of both parties in event of infringement of a U.S. or foreign Patent or Copyright.

47 *Payment and Invoice Provisions: To establish provisions for the timing of payments and establish conditions for delinquency and penalties.

48 Price Protection - Lease Rates/Purchase Prices/Maintenance Rates: To establish conditions for price increases, reductions, escalation, and notices thereof.

49 Price Protection - General: To guarantee state agencies the vendors most favored customer prices.

50 Protection of Proprietary Information: To establish protection of Contractor's rights and interests in technical information, software products, copyrights, etc.

51 Publicity: To establish that the Contractor will not use any advertising, sales promotion, or any other publicity materials wherein the State's name may be stated, implied, or inferred without the consent of the State.

52 *Quiet Possession and Usage: (SC) To confirm State's right to peaceful use of the product upon payment of the amounts due as specified in the contract.

53 *Relocation (Leased Equipment): To provide reasonable notice for movement of leased equipment.

54 *Risk of Loss (Lease or Rental): To relieve the State of responsibility for risks of loss or damage when leasing or renting equipment.

55 *Save Harmless: (SC) To indemnify the State from injury to persons or property caused by any acts or omissions of the Contractor.

56 *Severability: (SC) To establish that if any term or condition is invalid, the other terms or conditions are not affected.

57 Site and Installation Planning: To establish responsibility for site specifications and preparation.

58 Specifications: To provide for including technical equipment specifications by reference and attached to the contract.

59 *Standard of Performance and Acceptance of Equipment. To establish provisions for a standard of performance which must be met before any equipment is accepted by the State.

60 *Subcontractors: (SC) To establish the conditions under which the Contractor may enter into subcontracts with third parties.

61 *Taxes: To identify tax liability and exemptions for the contract.

62 *Term of Agreement: To establish the period of performance, conditions for extensions and termination, and the survivability of certain clauses.

63 Termination, Cancellation, and Repossession: To establish conditions for termination or cancellation of the lease or purchase contract by either party, and the requirement for notices.

64 Termination: Alternative termination clause, with Termination for Default, Termination for Convenience, and termination following arbitration under the optional disputes clause.

65 *Title (Leased): To establish that the Contractor retains title of all leased equipment, to assure that Customer does not impair same, and to assure Contractor retains clear title for equipment with purchase option.

66 Training: To establish Contractor responsibilities for training on equipment or software.

67 Transportation: To establish responsibility for cost of transportation, transit insurance, risk of loss, and title of equipment during shipment to the installation site.

68 *Waiver: (SC) To establish that a term or condition of the contract may be waived only by the written consent of both parties.

69 *Signature Blocks: To provide a statement of understanding and agreement followed by signature blocks.

C. CHECKLIST FOR SAMPLE EQUIPMENT INSTALLMENT PURCHASE/LEASE PURCHASE CONTRACT

1   Table of Contents: To list and identify the provisions contained within the contract.

2   *Contracting Parties, Equipment, Software, Services Schedule/Price Schedule: Every contract must 1) identify the parties of the contract, 2) show what is being contracted for (through the attachments), and 3) provide the terms of the transaction. If the contract results from an RFP or RFQ, it is appropriate to include a recitation as to the basis for the contract by reference in this section. Any schedules of equipment, software or services to be acquired together with prices/discounts should be incorporated by reference and attached to the contract.

3   *Advance Payment: To comply with State law that no advance payments shall be made to the Contractor.

4   *Affirmative Action: To ensure that the Contractor takes affirmative action with regard to employment, promotion, rates of pay, etc.

5   *Anti-Trust Violations: To establish that the Contractor assigns claims for overcharges resulting from antitrust violations to the State.

6   *Assignment: To establish that neither party shall assign, sublicense nor transfer its rights, duties, or obligations without written consent of the other party. If Contractor performance or financial condition is a problem, it may be necessary to keep Contractor assignment at the Customer's sole option.

7   Attorneys' Fees and Costs: General clause for payment of attorneys' fees.

8   Backup Availability: To provide a means for obtaining replacement system equipment upon a permanently disabling disaster for mission essential equipment. This or similar disaster recovery requirements should be specified in functional requirements in the solicitation documents.

9   Compatibility: To ensure that hardware, software or other products delivered are compatible with Customer's currently installed systems, or with other hardware, software or products also manufactured and/or available from Contractor. This clause should be tailored to Customer's specific operational needs as identified in functional requirements in the acquisition solicitation documents.

10   Compliance with Standards: To cause Contractor to comply with specified hardware and software standards (Customer's, American National Standards Institute (ANSI), International Standards Organization (ISO), or other).

11   *Compliance with Civil Rights Laws: (SC) To establish that the Contractor shall not discriminate against any person for reason of age, sex, race, creed, color, or national origin according to Title VII of the Civil Rights Act.

12   Confidentiality: Provides for Contractor maintaining Confidentiality of Customer material.

13   Conflict of Interest: Prohibits Conflict of Interest, and provides for termination upon breach.

14   *Contractor Commitments, Warranties and Representations: To assure that written commitments by the Contractor within the scope of this contract shall be binding upon the Contractor. Documents containing written warranties should be incorporated by reference.

15   Counterparts: To provide for duplicate originals of the contract.

16   Covenant Against Contingent Fees: Prohibits contingent fees, permits termination for violation

17   Cross Guarantees: To ensure that a contract signed by a subsidiary has the support of the parent organization and vice versa.

18   Definition of Terms: To establish specific definitions for terms used within the contract.

19   Discounts and Purchase Options: To establish any special discounts for volume or long-term lease and to define conditions for any lease/rental credits toward purchase.

20   Disputes: Dispute arbitration clause limits arbitration to determinations of fact. Should only be used if negotiating away a more onerous clause, as it limits agency rights and freedom of action to resolve a problem, by putting the issue in the hands of an arbitration team.

21   *Engineering Changes: To establish both parties' responsibilities for scheduling equipment engineering changes.

22   *Entire Agreement: To establish that the contract constitutes the entire agreement and supersedes all previous discussions, bid processes, and agreements, except as provided in Contractor Commitments, Warranties, and Representations. Specific documentation such as Contractor proposals, equipment and software specifications, communications regarding goods and services to be provided, etc. should be included in the contract by reference or attachment, where Contractor assurances and performance questions are concerned.

23   Equipment Configurations: Equipment conformance to specifications. Includes specific listings of equipment and interface and connectibility requirements, which should be included in acquisition solicitation documents.

24   Equipment Warranties: To establish specific Contractor warranties for performance of equipment and to define remedies in the event of failure of warranted products.

25   *Equipment Condition: To establish that the Contractor warrants that the equipment is newly manufactured or identified as refurbished.

26   Exchange Provisions: To establish conditions for upgrade, downgrade, trade-ins, etc., for exchange of leased or purchased equipment or licensed software.

27   *Failure to Perform: (SC) To establish that the State may withhold monies, beginning 30 days after written notification that the Contractor has failed to perform any substantial obligation in the contract.

28   *Governing Law: (SC) The contract will be governed by the law and statutes of the State of

Washington, with venue set in the Superior Court in the county in which Customer has its headquarters — if other than Thurston County, so indicate.

29 Hold-back for Entire Contract Compliance: To provide for holdback of payment for products pending performance of entire contract. Other options include per diem liquidated damages for non-completion, or inclusion of a requirement for a Contractor's performance bond to be held in escrow by Customer pending full contract compliance.

30 *Independent Status of Contractor: (SC) The parties to the contract will be acting in their individual capacities and not as agents or associates of one another.

31 Industrial Insurance Coverage: Requires Contractor to have industrial insurance coverage.

32 *Installation (Site) Security: To assure Contractor conformance to State premise security regulations.

33 *Installation and Delivery Dates: To establish the terms, dates, and conditions for equipment delivery and installation.

34 Installment Financing Provisions: A clause or set of clauses which Contractor may require to protect its security interests. Any installment purchase, lease with purchase option, or third party financing contract may need prior approval of the State Finance Committee, and/or use of specified Terms and Conditions as may be required by the Committee, the Office of Financial Management, or DIS PPD.

35 Insurance: To establish both parties' insurance responsibilities.

36 Interface of Equipment: To provide assurance that Contractor provided products will interface with specified telecommunications equipment, listed terminals and peripherals, as previously identified in the acquisition solicitation documents.

37 Licensing Standards: Establishes Contractor's requirement to be licensed to do business in Washington.

38 *Limitation of Liability: (SC) To establish that State is not liable to Contractor for consequential damages, or lost profits. In addition, Customer shall not be liable for damages or delay caused by acts of God or other circumstances beyond its control (Force Majeure clause).

39 Limitation of Authority: Identifies agency Contracting Officer as Customer authorized signatory, provides for other prior written delegation.

40 *Liquidated Damages: To establish the general Terms and Conditions for damages because of Contractor performance delays or State site preparation delays.

41 *Maintenance of Equipment: To establish the terms, conditions, and provisions for maintenance of the equipment.

42 Maintenance Surcharges: To establish costs for extraordinary maintenance situations.

43 *Maintenance Documentation: To assure that the Contractor shall provide appropriate

documentation for maintenance of purchased equipment upon request.

44 Minority & Women's Business Enterprise Participation: Contracts with Minority or Women's Business Enterprise participation should include specific language covering required participation and remedies upon breach of contract. Contact the Office of Minority and Women's Business Enterprises (OMWBE) for specific language.

45 *Non-Allocation of Funds: (SC) Often called the "Funding Out" clause, this provision allows termination for lack of funds, when the State fails to appropriate, allot, or allocate necessary funds to continue the contract into subsequent fiscal periods. If no periodic or future payments are required under the contract, this clause may be omitted.

46 *Notices: To define official addresses for formal notifications.

47 *OSHA/WISHA: To establish that the Contractor warrants that its products are designed to meet federal and state safety and health regulations.

48 *Patent and Copyright Indemnification: Equipment/Licensed Software: To establish responsibility of both parties in event of infringement of a U.S. or foreign Patent or Copyright.

49 *Payment and Invoice Provisions: To establish provisions for the timing of payments and establish conditions for delinquency and penalties.

50 Price Protection - Lease Rates/Purchase Prices/Maintenance Rates: To establish conditions for price increases, reductions, escalation, and notices thereof.

51 Price Protection - General: To guarantee state agencies the vendors most favored customer prices.

52 Protection of Proprietary Information: To establish protection of Contractor's rights and interests in technical information, software products, copyrights, etc.

53 Publicity: To establish that the Contractor will not use any advertising, sales promotion, or any other publicity materials wherein the State's name may be stated, implied, or inferred without the consent of the State.

54 *Quiet Possession and Usage: (SC) To confirm State's right to peaceful use of the product upon payment of the amounts due as specified in the contract.

55 *Risk of Loss (Purchased): To allocate risk and name the point in time at which the risk of loss of the equipment shifts from the Contractor to the Customer.

56 *Save Harmless: (SC) To indemnify the State from injury to persons or property caused by any acts or omissions of the Contractor.

57 Security Interest - Financed Equipment: Provides Contractor a security interest in property acquired under an installment purchase or third party financing contract. Any installment purchase, lease with purchase option, or third party financing contract may need prior approval of the State Finance Committee, and/or use of specified Terms and Conditions as may be required by the Committee, the Office

of Financial Management, or DIS PPD.

58   *Severability: (SC) To establish that if any term or condition is invalid, the other terms or conditions are not affected.

59   Site and Installation Planning: To establish responsibility for site specifications and preparation.

60   Specifications: To provide technical equipment specifications by reference and attachment to the contract.

61   *Standard of Performance and Acceptance of Equipment: To establish provisions for a standard of performance which must be met before any equipment is accepted by the State.

62   *Subcontractors: (SC) To establish the conditions under which the Contractor may enter into subcontracts with third parties.

63   *Taxes: To identify tax liability and exemptions for the contract.

64   *Term of Agreement: To establish the period of performance, conditions for extensions and termination, and the survivability of certain clauses.

65   Termination, Cancellation, and Repossession: To establish conditions for termination or cancellation of the lease or purchase contract by either party, and the requirement for notices.

66   Termination: Alternative termination clause, with Termination for Default, Termination for Convenience, and termination following arbitration under the optional disputes clause.

67   *Title (Purchased): To assure that the Contractor shall convey clear title of purchased equipment upon completion of acceptance testing.

68   Training: To establish Contractor responsibilities for training on equipment or software.

69   Transportation: To establish responsibility for cost of transportation, transit insurance, risk of loss, and title of equipment during shipment to the installation site.

70   *Waiver: (SC) To establish that a term or condition of the contract may be waived only by the written consent of both parties.

71   *Signature Blocks: To provide a statement of understanding and agreement followed by signature blocks.

D. CHECKLIST FOR SAMPLE EQUIPMENT MAINTENANCE CONTRACT

1   Table of Contents: To list and identify the provisions contained within the contract.

2   *Contracting Parties, Equipment, Software, Services Schedule/Price Schedule. Every contract must 1) identify the parties of the contract, 2) show what is being contracted for (through the attachments), and 3) provide the terms of the transaction. If the contract results from an RFP or RFQ, it is appropriate to include a recitation as to the basis for the contract by reference in this section. Any schedules of equipment, software or services to be acquired together with prices/discounts should be incorporated by

reference and attached to the contract.

3   *Advance Payment: To comply with State law that no advance payments shall be made to the Contractor.

4   *Affirmative Action: To ensure that the Contractor takes affirmative action with regard to employment, promotion, rates of pay, etc.

5   *Anti-Trust Violations: To establish that the Contractor assigns claims for overcharges resulting from antitrust violations to the State.

6   *Assignment: To establish that neither party shall assign, sublicense nor transfer its rights, duties, or obligations without written consent of the other party. If Contractor performance or financial condition is a problem, it may be necessary to keep Contractor assignment at the Customer's sole option.

7   Attorneys' Fees and Costs: General clause for payment of attorneys' fees.

8   Compliance with Standards: To cause Contractor to comply with specified hardware and software standards (Customer's, American National Standards Institute (ANSI), International Standards Organization (ISO), or other).

9   *Compliance with Civil Rights Laws: (SC) To establish that the Contractor shall not discriminate against any person for reason of age, sex, race, creed, color, or national origin according to Title VII of the Civil Rights Act.

10   Confidentiality: Provides for Contractor maintaining Confidentiality of Customer material.

11   Conflict of Interest: Prohibits Conflict of Interest, and provides for termination upon breach.

12   *Contractor Commitments, Warranties and Representations: To assure that written commitments by the Contractor within the scope of this contract shall be binding upon the Contractor. Documents containing written warranties should be incorporated by reference.

13   Counterparts: To provide for duplicate originals of the contract.

14   Covenant Against Contingent Fees: Prohibits contingent fees, permits termination for violation.

15   Cross Guarantees: To ensure that a contract signed by a subsidiary has the support of the parent organization and vice versa.

16   Definition of Terms: To establish specific definitions for terms used within the contract.

17   Disputes: Dispute arbitration clause limits arbitration to determinations of fact. Should only be used if negotiating away a more onerous clause, as it limits agency rights and freedom of action to resolve a problem, by putting the issue in the hands of an arbitration team.

18   *Engineering Changes: To establish both parties' responsibilities for scheduling equipment engineering changes.

19   *Entire Agreement: To establish that the contract constitutes the entire agreement and supersedes all previous discussions, bid processes, and agreements, except as provided in Contractor Commitments,

Warranties, and Representations. Specific documentation such as Contractor proposals, equipment and software specifications, communications regarding goods and services to be provided, etc. should be included in the contract by reference or attachment, where Contractor assurances and performance questions are concerned.

20 Equipment Warranties: To establish specific Contractor warranties for performance of equipment and to define remedies in the event of failure of warranted products.

21 *Failure to Perform: (SC) To establish that the State may withhold monies, beginning 30 days after written notification that the Contractor has failed to perform any substantial obligation in the contract.

22 *Governing Law: (SC) The contract will be governed by the law and statutes of the State of Washington, with venue set in the Superior Court in the county in which Customer has its headquarters — if other than Thurston County, so indicate.

23 *Independent Status of Contractor:(SC) The parties to the contract will be acting in their individual capacities and not as agents or associates of one another.

24 Industrial Insurance Coverage: Requires Contractor to have industrial insurance coverage.

25 *Installation (Site) Security: To assure Contractor conformance to State premise security regulations.

26 Licensing Standards: Establishes Contractor's requirement to be licensed to do business in Washington.

27 *Limitation of Liability: (SC) To establish that State is not liable to Contractor for consequential damages, or lost profits. In addition, Customer shall not be liable for damages or delay caused by acts of God or other circumstances beyond its control (Force Majeure clause).

28 Limitation of Authority: Identifies agency Contracting Officer as Customer authorized signatory, provides for other prior written delegation.

29 *Liquidated Damages: To establish the general Terms and Conditions for damages because of Contractor performance delays or State site preparation delays.

30 *Maintenance of Equipment: To establish the terms, conditions, and provisions for maintenance of the equipment.

31 Maintenance Surcharges: To establish costs for extraordinary maintenance situations.

32 *Maintenance Documentation: To assure that the Contractor shall provide appropriate documentation for maintenance of equipment.

33 Minority & Women's Business Enterprise Participation: Contracts with Minority or Women's Business Enterprise participation should include specific language covering required participation and remedies upon breach of contract. Contact the Office of Minority and Women's Business Enterprises

(OMWBE) for specific language.

34   *Non-Allocation of Funds: (SC)   Often called the "Funding Out" clause, this provision allows termination for lack of funds, when the State fails to appropriate, allot, or allocate necessary funds to continue the contract into subsequent fiscal periods. If no periodic or future payments are required under the contract, this clause may be omitted.

35   *Notices: To define official addresses for formal notifications.

36   *Payment and Invoice Provisions: To establish provisions for the timing of payments and establish conditions for delinquency and penalties.

37   Price Protection - Lease Rates/Purchase Prices/Maintenance Rates: To establish conditions for price increases, reductions, escalation, and notices thereof.

38   Protection of Proprietary Information: To establish protection of Contractor's rights and interests in technical information, software products, copyrights, etc.

39   Publicity: To establish that the Contractor will not use any advertising, sales promotion, or any other publicity matters wherein the State's name may be specifically stated, implied, or inferred without the consent of the State.

40   *Save Harmless:(SC) To indemnify the State from injury to persons or property caused by any acts or omissions of the Contractor.

41   *Severability: (SC) To establish that if any term or condition is invalid, the other terms or conditions are not affected.

42   Specifications: To provide technical equipment specifications by reference and attachment to the contract.

43   *Subcontractors: (SC) To establish the conditions under which the Contractor may enter into subcontracts with third parties.

44   *Taxes: To identify tax liability and exemptions for the contract.

45   *Term of Agreement: To establish the period of performance, conditions for extensions and termination, and the survivability of certain clauses.

46   Termination: Alternative termination clause, with Termination for Default, Termination for Convenience, and termination following arbitration under the optional disputes clause.

47   Training: To establish Contractor responsibilities for training on equipment or software.

48   *Waiver: (SC) To establish that a term or condition of the contract may be waived only by the written consent of both parties.

49   *Signature Blocks: To provide a statement of understanding and agreement followed by signature blocks.

E. CHECKLIST FOR SAMPLE SOFTWARE LICENSING CONTRACT

1   Table of Contents: To list and identify the provisions contained within the contract.

2   *Contracting Parties, Equipment, Software, Services Schedule/Price Schedule: Every contract must 1) identify the parties of the contract, 2) show what is being contracted for (through the attachments), and 3) provide the terms of the transaction. If the contract results from an RFP or RFQ, it is appropriate to include a recitation as to the basis for the contract by reference in this section. Any schedules of equipment, software or services to be acquired together with prices/discounts should be incorporated by reference and attached to the contract.

3   *Advance Payment: To comply with State law that no advance payments shall be made to the Contractor.

4   *Affirmative Action: To ensure that the Contractor takes affirmative action with regard to employment, promotion, rates of pay, etc.

5   *Anti-Trust Violations: To establish that the Contractor assigns claims for overcharges resulting from antitrust violations to the State.

6   *Assignment: To establish that neither party shall assign, sublicense nor transfer its rights, duties, or obligations without written consent of the other party. If Contractor performance or financial condition is a problem, it may be necessary to keep Contractor assignment at the Customer's sole option.

7   Attorneys' Fees and Costs: General clause for payment of attorneys' fees.

8   Business or Support Termination Rights: To give Customer a perpetual license in event of business termination, or termination of support of the licensed software regardless of term of license.

9   Compatibility: To ensure that hardware, software or other products delivered are compatible with Customer's currently installed systems, or with other hardware, software or products also manufactured and/or available from Contractor. This clause should be tailored to Customer's specific operational needs as identified in functional requirements in the acquisition solicitation documents.

10   Compliance with Standards: To cause Contractor to comply with specified hardware and software standards (Customer's, American National Standards Institute (ANSI), International Standards Organization (ISO), or other).

11   *Compliance with Civil Rights Laws: (SC) To establish that the Contractor shall not discriminate against any person for reason of age, sex, race, creed, color, or national origin according to Title VII of the Civil Rights Act.

12   Confidentiality: Provides for Contractor maintaining Confidentiality of Customer material.

13   Conflict of Interest: Prohibits Conflict of Interest, and provides for termination upon breach.

14   *Contractor Correction of Software Malfunction: To establish that the Contractor will provide correction to Contractor supplied software.

15   *Contractor Commitments, Warranties and Representations: To assure that written commitments by the Contractor within the scope of this contract shall be binding upon the Contractor. Documents containing written warranties should be incorporated by reference.

16   Counterparts: To provide for duplicate originals of the contract.

17   Covenant Against Contingent Fees: Prohibits contingent fees, permits termination for violation.

18   Cross Guarantees: To ensure that a contract signed by a subsidiary has the support of the parent organization and vice versa.

19   Definition of Terms: To establish specific definitions for terms used within the contract.

20   Disputes: Dispute arbitration clause — optional clause — limits arbitration to determinations of fact. Should only be used if negotiating away a more onerous clause, as it limits agency rights and freedom of action to resolve a problem, by putting the issue in the hands of an arbitration team.

21   *Entire Agreement: To establish that the contract constitutes the entire agreement and supersedes all previous discussions, bid processes, and agreements, except as provided in Contractor Commitments, Warranties, and Representations. Specific documentation such as Contractor proposals, equipment and software specifications, communications regarding goods and services to be provided, etc. should be included in the contract by reference or attachment, where Contractor assurances and performance questions are concerned.

22   Escrow of Source: Protects users right to continuity of use and access to source code for package programs. Clause is not intended for routine coverage of all software, rather for mission critical software, where Contractor's business cessation would gravely impact agency systems performance. Should be accompanied by an attached escrow agreement with Contractor, third party and Customer signatures.

23   Exchange Provisions: To establish conditions for upgrade, downgrade, trade-ins, etc., for exchange of leased or purchased equipment or licensed software.

24   *Failure to Perform: (SC) To establish that the State may withhold monies, beginning 30 days after written notification that the Contractor has failed to perform any substantial obligation in the contract.

25   Freedom of Use - Software: To insure that users of a computer service center have the right to use the center's software without interference or additional licenses.

26   *Governing Law: (SC) The contract will be governed by the law and statutes of the State of Washington, with venue set in the Superior Court in the county in which Customer has its headquarters — if other than Thurston County, so indicate.

27   Hold-back for Entire Contract Compliance: To provide for holdback of payment for products pending performance of entire contract. Other options include per diem liquidated damages for non-completion, or inclusion of a requirement for a Contractor's performance bond to be held in escrow by

Customer pending full contract compliance.

28 *Independent Status of Contractor: (SC) The parties to the contract will be acting in their individual capacities and not as agents or associates of one another.

29 *Installation (Site) Security: To assure Contractor conformance to State premise security regulations.

30 Licensing Standards: Establishes Contractor's requirement to be licensed to do business in Washington.

31 *Limitation of Liability: (SC) To establish that State is not liable to Contractor for consequential damages, or lost profits. In addition, Customer shall not be liable for damages or delay caused by acts of God or other circumstances beyond its control (Force Majeure clause).

32 Limitation of Authority: Identifies agency Contracting Officer as Customer authorized signatory, provides for other prior written delegation.

33 Minority & Women's Business Enterprise Participation: Contracts with Minority or Women's Business Enterprise participation should include specific language covering required participation and remedies upon breach of contract. Contact the Office of Minority and Women's Business Enterprises (OMWBE) for specific language.

34 *Non-Allocation of Funds: (SC) Often called the "Funding Out" clause, this provision allows termination for lack of funds, when the State fails to appropriate, allot, or allocate necessary funds to continue the contract into subsequent fiscal periods. If no periodic or future payments are required under the contract, this clause may be omitted.

35 *Notices: To define official addresses for formal notifications.

36 *Patent and Copyright Indemnification - Equipment/Licensed Software: To establish responsibility of both parties in event of infringement of a U.S. or foreign Patent or Copyright.

37 Protection of Proprietary Information: To establish protection of Contractor's rights and interests in technical information, software products, copyrights, etc.

38 Price Protection - General: To guarantee state agencies the vendors most favored customer prices.

39 Publicity: To establish that the Contractor will not use any advertising, sales promotion, or any other publicity materials wherein the State's name may be stated, implied, or inferred without the consent of the State.

40 *Quiet Possession and Usage: (SC) To confirm State's right to peaceful use of the product upon payment of the amounts due as specified in the contract.

41 *Save Harmless: (SC) To indemnify the State from injury to persons or property caused by any acts or omissions of the Contractor.

42 *Severability: (SC) To establish that if any term or condition is invalid, the other terms or

conditions are not affected.

43   Software Ownership: To warrant that Contractor is the owner of software and/or has unrestricted right to license it to Customer.

44   Software Maintenance, Upgrade, Enhancement: To establish the Contractor's responsibility to provide software updates, upgrades and enhancements. Specific requirements should be included in the solicitation document and be reflected in this clause.

45   *Software Documentation: To establish that the Contractor will provide appropriate software documentation.

46   Source Availability and Access: Provides Customer with source code to programs when Contractor warranty or Contractor maintenance expires.

47   Specifications: To provide technical software specifications by reference and attachment to the contract.

48   *Subcontractors: (SC) To establish the conditions under which the Contractor may enter into subcontracts with third parties.

49   *Taxes: To identify tax liability and exemptions for the contract.

50   *Term of Agreement: To establish the period of performance, conditions for extensions and termination, and the survivability of certain clauses.

51   Termination: Alternative termination clause, with Termination for Default, Termination for Convenience, and termination following arbitration under the optional disputes clause.

52   Training: To establish Contractor responsibilities for training on equipment or software.

53   *Waiver: (SC) To establish that a term or condition of the contract may be waived only by the written consent of both parties.

54   *Signature Blocks: To provide a statement of understanding and agreement followed by signature blocks.

F. CHECKLIST FOR SAMPLE SHORT FORM PURCHASE ORDER

1   Standard Terms and Conditions, Request for Quotation, Purchase & Field Order contracts: Standard disclaimer and heading for Short Form Purchase Order — incorporates by reference Washington Law, RCW 43.105 and DIS acquisition policy and procedure.

2   Acceptance: Integration clause-rejects vendor clauses without prior concurrence in writing.

3   Anti-trust: Assigns any overcharges due to anti-trust activity to Purchaser.

4   Assignments: Requires prior permission for assignment of proceeds due vendor.

5   Brands: Provides for Purchaser inspection of alternate products prior to acceptance.

6   Changes: Requires prior written consent to change purchase order conditions.

7   Default and Governing: Combines recovery of attorney fees and governing law in Washington.

8   Delivery: Establishes that time is of the essence, and makes order subject to termination for late performance.

9   Handling: Prohibits handling charges, unless specified in the order.

10   Identification: Instructions on including purchase order number in shipments, packages, invoices, etc.

11   Infringements: Indemnifies Purchaser against patent and copyright, trade secret, or franchising violations on part of the Vendor.

12   Liens, Claims and Encumbrances: Assures Purchaser of free and clear title.

13   Non-waiver by Acceptance of Variation: Assures that waiver of one term does not waiver other contract terms.

14   Nondiscrimination and Affirmative Action: Commits Vendor to affirmative action.

15   Off-Shore Items: Off-shore reporting requirement.

16   Payments, Cash Discount, Late Payment Charges: Provides for discounts and thirty day payment period; prohibits advance payments.

17   Prices and Price Warranty for Commercial Items: Combines Price Protection Clause and price warranty - or "most favored nation" clause.

18   Rejection: Reserves Purchaser's right to inspect and reject goods for nonconformity to the order and sets a time limit of two weeks on Purchaser's rejection.

19   Risk of Loss: Gives vendor risk of loss during shipment.

20   Safety and Health Requirements: Commits vendor to OSHA/WISHA.

21   Save Harmless: Indemnification clause protecting Purchaser from personal or property damage due to Vendor acts or omissions.

22   Shipping Instructions: Provides standard shipping instructions.

23   Taxes: Standard tax language, incorporating federal exemption if required.

24   Termination: Provides for termination on notice of Vendor breach.

25   Warranties: Vendor warrants conformance to specifications, provides for fitness for a particular purpose, when appropriate.

III. CONTRACT TERMS AND CONDITIONS

Contract Codes are:

    All = All contracts except Purchase Order Short Form

    EP = Equipment Purchase

EL = Equipment Lease

IP/LP = Installment Purchase/Lease Purchase

EM = Equipment Maintenance

SL = Software License

SF = Purchase Order Short Form

A. LONG FORM CONTRACT TERMS AND CONDITIONS - STANDARD CLAUSES

This section contains Standard Clauses (SC) which, when required in a contract, must be worded as follows:

1 *Compliance with Civil Rights Laws (SC) (Used in Contracts: All)

(Comments: To establish that the Contractor shall not discriminate against any person for reason of age, sex, race, creed, color, or national origin according to Title VII of the Civil Rights Act.)

The Contractor hereby assures that it will comply with Title VII of the Civil Rights Act to the end that no person shall, on the grounds of age, race, creed, color, sex or national origin be excluded from participation in, be denied the benefits of, or be otherwise subjected to discrimination under this contract or under any project, program or activity supported by this contract.

2 *Failure to Perform: (SC)

(Used in Contracts: All)

(Comments: To establish that the State may withhold monies, beginning 30 days after written notification that the Contractor has failed to perform any substantial obligation as stipulated in the contract.)

In the event Contractor has failed to perform any substantial obligation to be performed by the Contractor under this agreement and 30 days after written notice of said failure to perform is provided to Contractor said failure has not been cured, then the Customer may withhold all monies due and payable to Contractor, without penalty, until such failure to perform is cured or otherwise adjudicated.

3 *Governing Law: (SC)

(Used in Contracts: All)

(Comments: The contract will be governed by the Law and statutes of the State of Washington, with venue set in the Superior Court in the county in which Customer has its headquarters - if other than Thurston County, so indicate.)

This contract shall be governed in all respects by the law and statutes of the State of Washington. The venue of any action hereunder shall be in the Superior Court for Thurston County, Washington.

4 *Independent Status of Contractor (SC)

(Used in Contracts: All)

(Comments: The parties of the contract will be acting in their individual capacities and not as agents or associates of one another.)

The parties hereto, in the performance of this contract, will be acting in their individual capacities and not as agents, employees, partners, joint venturers or associates of one another. The employees or agents of one party shall not be deemed or construed to be the employees or agents of the other party for any purpose whatsoever.

5 *Limitation of Liability: (SC)

(Used in Contracts: All)

(Comments: To establish that State is not liable to Contractor for consequential damages, or lost profits. In addition, Customer shall not be liable for damages or delay caused by acts of God or other circumstances beyond its control (Force Majeure clause).)

5.1 The parties agree that neither the Contractor nor the Customer shall be liable to each other, regardless of the form of action, for consequential damages. The parties further agree that neither shall be liable to the other for any lost profits or any demand or claim, regardless of the form of action, against either party by any other person except a claim or demand based on patent or copyright infringement, in which case liability shall be as set forth elsewhere in this contract. This provision does not modify any provisions regarding liquidated damages, retainages or any other such conditions as are elsewhere agreed to herein between the parties.

5.2 Neither the Contractor nor the Customer shall be liable for damages arising from causes beyond the reasonable control and without the fault or negligence of either the Contractor, the Customer or their respective subcontractors.

5.3 Such causes may include, but are not restricted to, acts of God or of the public enemy, acts of any governmental body acting in either its sovereign or contractual capacity, war, explosions, fires, floods, epidemics, quarantine restrictions, strikes, freight embargoes, and unusually severe weather; but in every case the delays must be beyond the reasonable control and without fault or negligence of the Contractor, the Customer, or their respective subcontractors.

5.4 If delays are caused by the default of a subcontractor without its fault or negligence, neither the Contractor nor the Customer shall be liable for damages for delays, unless the supplies or services to be furnished by their subcontractors were obtainable on comparable terms from other sources in sufficient time to permit the Contractor or the Customer to meet its required performance schedule.

5.5 Neither party shall be liable for personal injury or damage to tangible property except personal injury or damage to tangible property proximately caused by each party's respective fault or negligence.

6 *Non-Allocation of Funds: (SC)

(Used in Contracts: All)

(Comments: Often called the "Funding Out" clause, this provision allows termination for lack of funds, when the State fails to appropriate, allot, or allocate necessary funds to continue the contract into subsequent fiscal periods. If no periodic future payments are required under the contract, this clause may be omitted.)

If funds are not allocated for this contract for periodic payment in any future biennial fiscal period, the Customer will not be obligated to pay the net remainder of agreed to consecutive periodic payments remaining unpaid beyond the end of the then-current biennium. The Customer agrees to notify the Contractor of such nonallocation at the earliest possible time. No penalty shall accrue to the Customer in the event this provision shall be exercised. This provision shall not be construed so as to permit the Customer to terminate this contract in order to acquire similar equipment, software or services from a third party.

7 *Quiet Possession and Usage: (SC)

(Used in Contracts: EP EL IP\LP SL)

(Comments: To confirm State's right to peaceful use of the product upon payment of the amounts due as specified in the contract.)

The Customer upon paying the amounts due hereunder and performing all other covenants, terms, and conditions on its part to be performed hereunder, may and shall peacefully and quietly have, hold, possess, and enjoy the equipment/software for the term provided without suit, molestation, or interruption.

8 *Save Harmless: (SC)

(Used in Contracts: All)

(Comments: To indemnify the State from injury to persons or property caused by any acts or omissions of the Contractor.)

Contractor shall protect, indemnify and save the Customer harmless from and against any damage, cost or liability for any or all injuries to persons or tangible property arising from acts or omissions of Contractor, its officers, employees, agents, or subcontractors howsoever caused.

9 *Severability: (SC)

(Used in Contracts: All)

(Comments: To establish that if any term or condition is invalid, the other terms or conditions are not affected.)

If any term or condition of this contract or the application thereof to any person(s) or circumstances is held invalid, such invalidity shall not affect other terms, conditions or applications which can be given effect without the invalid term, condition or application; to this end the Terms and Conditions of this contract are declared severable.

10 *Subcontractors: (SC)

(Used in Contracts: All)

(Comments: To establish the conditions under which the Contractor may enter into subcontracts with third parties.)

Contractor means any firm, provider, organization, individual, or other entity performing services under this Contract. It shall include any subcontractor retained by the prime Contractor as permitted under the terms of this Contract. Subcontractor means one not in the employment of the Contractor who is performing all or part of the services under this Contract under a separate contract with the Contractor. The Contractor may, with prior written permission from the Customer enter into subcontracts with third parties for its performance of any part of the Contractor's duties and obligations. In no event shall the existence of a subcontract operate to release or reduce the liability of the Contractor to the Customer for any breach in the performance of the Contractor's duties. The Contractor agrees that all subcontractors shall be agents of the Contractor, and the Contractor further agrees to hold the Customer harmless omissions of the Contractor's subcontractors, their agents, or employees. The Customer shall not be liable for any loss or damage resulting from personal injury, physical loss, harassment of employee, or violations of the PATENT AND COPYRIGHT INDEMNIFICATION provisions of this Contract occasioned by the acts or omissions of the Contractor's subcontractors, their agents or employees. The PATENT AND COPYRIGHT INDEMNIFICATION provisions of this Contract shall apply to all subcontractors.

11 *Waiver: (SC)

(Used in Contracts: All)

(Comments: To establish that a term or condition of the contract may be waived only by the written consent of both parties.)

Waiver of any breach of any term or condition of this contract shall not be deemed a waiver of any prior or subsequent breach. No term or condition of this contract shall be held to be waived, modified or deleted except by a written instrument signed by the parties hereto.

B. LONG FORM CONTRACT TERMS AND CONDITIONS - ROUTINE USE CLAUSES (*)

Routine Use Clauses, identified by an asterisk (*), should be routinely included in any given contract. Routine Use Clauses which are also Standard Clauses (SC) are given in the prior section entitled Long Form Contract Terms and Conditions - Standard Clauses, and not repeated here.

1 *Contracting Parties, Equipment, Software, Services Schedule/Price Schedule

(Used in Contracts: All)

(Comments: Every contract must 1) identify the parties of the contract, 2) show what is being contracted for (through the attachments), and 3) provide for contractual considerations. If the contract results from an RFP or RFQ, it would be appropriate to include a recitation as to the basis for the contract, and where appropriate, included by reference in this section. Any schedules of equipment, software or services to be acquired together with prices/discounts should be included by reference and attached to the contract.)

1.1 The Department of _____ hereinafter called the "Customer", acting as an agency of the State of Washington, hereby awards to _____ hereinafter called the "Contractor," this contract to furnish to the Customer the machines, models, features, accessories (hereinafter called the "Equipment"), services and software, listed and described on Schedule(s) __ attached hereto and by this reference made a part hereof, as though completely set forth herein, at the lease rates, maintenance rates, licensing and purchase prices set forth opposite the description of the Equipment, services and software thereon, subject to and in accordance with the terms of this Agreement. The Contractor further agrees to provide to Customer, as defined herein, any other equipment, services or software from its standard, available offerings under the same Terms and Conditions of this agreement.

1.2 In consideration of the terms, conditions, covenants, warranties, premises, and performance herein contained, the parties do mutually agree as follows:

2 *Advance Payment:

(Used in Contracts: All)

(Comments: To implement State law that no advance payments shall be made to the Contractor.)

No advance payment shall be made for goods or services furnished by Contractor pursuant to this contract. Except as otherwise provided herein, such payments shall be due and payable within thirty (30) days after receipt of such goods or services or after receipt of properly prepared invoices, whichever is later.

3 *Nondiscrimination and Affirmative Action: (Used in Contracts: All)

(Comments: To ensure that the Contractor takes affirmative action with regard to employment, promotion, rates of pay, etc.)

The Contractor agrees not to discriminate against and to take affirmative action to ensure equality of treatment for any client, employee, or applicant for employment or services because of age, race, color, religion, sex, ancestry, national origin, marital status, Vietnam era or disabled veteran status, or the presence of any mental, physical or sensory handicap with regard to but not limited to, the following: employment, upgrading, demotion, or transfer; recruitment or recruitment advertising; layoffs or termination; rates of pay or other forms of compensation; and selection for training, including apprenticeships and volunteers. A vendor in violation of this clause or any applicable affirmative action program may become subject to other penalties as elsewhere provided in Washington State Law.

4 *Alterations and Attachments:

(Used in Contracts: EL IP/LP EM)

(Comments: To establish that alterations or attachments to leased or rented machines may be made upon prior consent of the Contractor.)

4.1 Alterations in or attachments to leased or rented machines may be made upon prior written consent of Contractor, which consent shall not be unreasonably withheld.

4.2 Maintenance credit provisions, as contained in this contract, will not apply if equipment failure is caused by such alterations or attachments not furnished by Contractor and lease, rental or maintenance charges shall continue without interruption.

5 *Anti-Trust Violations:

(Used in Contracts: All)

(Comments: To establish that the Contractor assigns claims for overcharges resulting from antitrust violations to the State.)

Contractor and Customer recognize that in actual economic practice overcharges resulting from antitrust violations are in fact usually borne by the Customer. Therefore, the Contractor hereby assigns to the Customer any and all claims for such overcharges as to goods and services purchased in connection with this contract, except as to overcharges not passed on to the Customer resulting from antitrust violations commencing after the date of the bid, quotation, or other event establishing the price under this contract.

6 *Assignment:

(Used in Contracts: All)

(Comments: To establish that neither party shall assign, sublicense nor transfer its rights, duties, or obligations without written consent of the other party. If Contractor performance or financial condition is a problem, it may be necessary to keep Contractor assignment at the Customer's sole option.)

6.1 With the prior written consent of the Customer which consent may be withheld at Customer's sole discretion, the Contractor may assign this agreement including the proceeds hereof: PROVIDED that such assignment shall not operate to relieve the Contractor of any of its duties and obligations hereunder, nor shall such assignment affect any remedies available to the Customer that may arise from any breach of the provisions of this agreement, its supplements, or warranties made herein including but not limited to, rights of setoff.

6.2 With the prior written consent of the Contractor which consent shall not be withheld unreasonably, the Customer may assign this agreement (and move the equipment/software) to any state agency within the political boundaries of the State of Washington: PROVIDED that such assignment shall not operate to relieve the Customer of any of its duties and obligations hereunder, including the obligation to pay monthly charges when an assignment is made; and provided further that all risks and expenses incurred in connection with such removal and relocation of said equipment including transportation, rigging, drayage, insurance, and installation charges shall be borne by the Customer.

7 *Contractor Correction of Software Malfunction:

(Used in Contract: SL)

(Comments: To establish that the Contractor will provide correction to Contractor supplied software.)

7.1 Contractor shall provide a correction service at no additional cost to the Customer for any error, malfunction, or defect, if any, in the Contractor supplied software which, when used as delivered, fails to perform in accordance with Contractor's officially announced technical specifications or Contractor's proposal and which the Customer shall bring to Contractor's attention. Contractor shall undertake such correction service in a timely manner and shall use its best efforts to make corrections in a manner which is mutually beneficial.

7.2 When Contractor performs services pursuant to this Agreement which require the use of the Customer's computer system(s), the Customer agrees to make it available at reasonable times and in reasonable time increments, and in no event will the Customer charge the Contractor for such system use.

8 *Contractor Commitments, Warranties and Representations:

(Used in Contracts: All)

(Comments: To assure that written commitments by the Contractor within the scope of this contract shall be binding upon the Contractor. It is recommended that specific listing of incorporated documents be included, as well.)

8.1   Any written commitment by the Contractor within the scope of this contract shall be binding upon the Contractor. Failure of the Contractor to fulfill such a commitment may constitute breach and shall render the Contractor liable for liquidated or other damages due the Customer under the terms of this contract.

8.2   For purposes of this contract, a commitment by the Contractor, which must be in writing, includes: (1) prices and options committed to remain in force over a specified period(s) of time; (2) any warranty or representation made by the Contractor in a proposal as to hardware or software performance or any other physical, design or functional characteristics of a machine, software package, system or other product; (3) any warranty or representation made by the Contractor concerning the characteristics or items in (2) above, contained in any literature, descriptions, drawings or specifications accompanying or referred to in a proposal; (4) any modification of or affirmation or representation as to the above which is made by Contractor in writing in or during the course of negotiation whether or not incorporated into a formal amendment to the proposal in question; and (5) any representation by the Contractor in a proposal, supporting documents or negotiations subsequent thereto as to training to be provided, services to be performed, prices and options committed to remain in force over a fixed period of time or any other similar matter regardless of the fact that the duration of such commitment may exceed the duration of this Contract.

9   *Engineering Changes:

(Used in Contracts: EP EL IP EM)

(Comments: To establish both parties' responsibilities for scheduling equipment engineering changes.)

Contractor warrants that installation of such engineering changes as Contractor may from time to time require or recommend shall not cause the performance of the machine modified to be materially degraded below the Contractor's official published specifications at the time of installation of the equipment. If such engineering changes are scheduled to take two hours or less, they shall be installed at a mutually agreeable time during contracted hours of maintenance. Engineering changes scheduled to take in excess of two hours shall be installed at a mutually agreeable time.

10   *Entire Agreement:

(Used in Contracts: All)

(Comments: To establish that the contract constitutes the entire agreement and supersedes all previous discussions, bid processes, and agreements, except as provided in Contractor Commitments, Warranties, and Representations. Specific documentation such as Contractor proposals, equipment and software specifications, communications regarding goods and services to be provided, etc. should be included in the contract by reference or attachment, where Contractor assurances and performance questions are concerned.)

This contract sets forth the entire Agreement between the parties with respect to the subject matter hereof and except as provided in the Provision entitled "Contractor Commitments, Warranties, and Representations," understandings, agreements, representations, or warranties not contained in this Agreement or a written amendment hereto shall not be binding on either party. Except as provided herein, no alteration of any of the terms, conditions, delivery, price, quality, or specifications of this contract will be effective without the written consent of both parties.

11 *Equipment Condition:

(Used in Contracts: EP EL IP)

(Comments: To establish that the Contractor warrants that the equipment is newly manufactured or identified as refurbished.)

Contractor warrants that Equipment acquired subject to this agreement is either (1) newly manufactured from new and serviceable used parts which are equivalent to new in performance, reliability and durability, or (2) identified as refurbished and carries the same warranty as counterpart new equipment.

12 *Installation (Site) Security:

(Used in Contracts: All)

(Comments: To assure Contractor conformance to State premise security regulations.)

Contractor, its agents, employees or subcontractors shall conform in all respects with physical, fire or other published security regulations while on the Customer's premises.

13 *Installation and Delivery Dates:

(Used in Contracts: EP EL IP/LP)

(Comments: To establish the terms, dates, and conditions for equipment delivery and installation.)

13.1 The Contractor shall install the equipment, ready for use on or before the installation dates(s) specified in _____. The equipment shall not be considered ready for use until the Contractor provides the Customer with documentation of a successful system audit utilizing Contractor's diagnostic routines, performed at the Customer's installation site, which demonstrates that the equipment meets minimum design capabilities and after reviewing such documentation the Customer agrees that the equipment is ready to begin acceptance testing and so notifies Contractor in writing.

13.2 Contractor agrees to provide Customer with written specifications for the installation site within

_____ days after the equipment is ordered.

13.3 The Customer agrees to have the equipment installation site prepared in accordance with Contractor's written specifications prior to the facility readiness date specified in _____. The Customer shall provide the Contractor access to the equipment installation site on the installation date for purpose of installing the equipment.

14 *Liquidated Damages:

(Used in Contracts: EP EL IP/LP EM)

(Comments: To establish the general Terms and Conditions for damages because of Contractor performance delays or State site preparation delays.)

14.1 Liquidated Damages - General

14.1.1 Any delay by the Contractor to perform will interfere with the proper implementation of the Customer's programs to the loss and damage of the Customer.

14.1.2 Similarly, delay by the Customer in readying the facility or permitting installation will interfere with the schedule under which the Contractor is operating, thus resulting in damage to the Contractor.

14.1.3 As it would be impracticable to fix the actual damage sustained in the event of any such failure to perform, the Customer and the Contractor, therefore, presume that in the event of any such failure to perform, the amount of damage which will be sustained will be the amount set forth in the following paragraphs and they agree that the Contractor and the Customer shall pay such amount as liquidated damages and not as a penalty.

14.1.4 Amounts due the Customer as liquidated damages may be deducted by the Customer from any money payable to the Contractor pursuant to this contract, the Customer may bill the Contractor as a separate item or the Customer may seek recovery from any performance bond secured in connection with this contract. The Customer shall notify the Contractor in writing of any claim for liquidated damages pursuant to this provision at least 30 days prior to the date the Customer deducts such sums from money payable to the Contractor.

14.1.5 Liquidated damages provided for under the terms of this agreement are subject to the same limitations as provided for in the provision entitled "Limitation of Liability."

14.2 Liquidated Damages - Installation of Equipment

14.2.1 If the Contractor does not install the system and/or machines described in this contract and special features and accessories described in this contract with the system and/or machines, ready for use on or before the installation date set forth _____ the Contractor shall pay to the Customer as fixed and agreed liquidated damages in lieu of all other damages due to such noninstallation, for each calendar day between the agreed installation date set forth _____ and the date such equipment is installed ready for use by not more than one-hundred eighty (180) calendar days, an amount of $100 per day, or 1/30th of the basic monthly lease or rental contract charge, whichever is greater, for all equipment regardless of whether said equipment is rented, leased, or purchased.

14.2.2 If some, but not all, of the machines on order are installed, ready for use by the stipulated installation date, and the Customer uses any such installed machines, the Customer agrees to pay the normal lease rate described in this Agreement for the machines used. If the Contractor provides suitable substitute equipment acceptable to the Customer on or before the stipulated installation date, no liquidated damages shall apply to the ordered equipment. When the Contractor provides suitable substitute equipment acceptable to the Customer, monthly charges shall be the rate for the equipment ordered or the rate for substitute equipment, whichever is less. When a substitute product is replaced with an ordered product, the contracted equipment rate will apply.

14.2.3 Any monthly lease or rental payments made and any purchase option credits accrued for substitute equipment shall be transferred to the ordered product, as if the ordered product had been initially installed.

14.2.4 If the delay is more than 30 calendar days, then by written notice to the Contractor, the Customer may terminate the right of the Contractor to install and may obtain substitute equipment. In this event, the Contractor shall be liable for liquidated damages, in the amounts specified above, until substitute equipment is installed, ready for use, or for 180 days from the installation date, whichever occurs first. The Contractor shall be liable for inbound and outbound preparation and shipping costs for equipment returned pursuant to this provision.

14.3 Liquidated Damages - Delivery of Licensed Programs

The shipment dates for licensed programs will be specified in Schedule _____. If the Contractor does not ship any of the licensed programs listed on Schedule _____ready for use in substantial accordance with Contractor's official published specifications on or before the specified shipment dates, the Contractor shall pay to the Customer for each unshipped program fixed and agreed liquidated damages in the amount of 1/30th of the monthly charges or 1/10th of 1% (.001) of the one-time charges if there are no monthly charges up to a maximum of $100 total for all unshipped programs, for each calendar day between the specified shipment date and the date of shipment of such programs, but not to exceed 180 calendar days, in lieu of all other damages. If the Contractor provides suitable substitution of licensed programs acceptable to the Customer, damages shall not apply, PROVIDED, however, liquidated damages will apply if such substituted licensed programs are shipped later than the specified shipment date.

14.4 Liquidated Damages - Site Preparation

14.4.1 In the event the equipment installation site is not prepared by the facility readiness date specified _____ the Customer shall pay to the Contractor as fixed and agreed liquidated damages, an amount equal to the 1/30th of the basic monthly lease or rental contract charge for all equipment regardless of whether said equipment is rented, leased, or purchased, for each calendar day between the specified facility readiness date and the actual readiness date, but not to exceed 180 calendar days in lieu of all other damages. The charges for any 30-day period shall not exceed the basic monthly lease or rental contract charge.

14.4.2   In the event a change directed by the Customer requires a later installation date of certain equipment and the Customer has failed to notify the Contractor of the delay on or before the change notification date specified _____, the Customer shall pay the Contractor an amount equal to 1/30th of the basic monthly lease or rental contract charge of said equipment, for each day between the scheduled installation date and the new installation date, but not to exceed 180 calendar days in lieu of all other damages. The charges for any 30-day period shall not exceed the basic monthly contract charge.

14.4.3 The Customer shall not be liable for liquidated damages under both paragraphs above during the same period of time with respect to the same equipment.

14.5 Liquidated Damages - Delivery of System Control Programs

14.5.1   If the Contractor does not deliver all the System Control Programs described in Schedule _____attached hereto, ready for operation in substantial conformance with the Contractor's specifications on or before the specified installation dates, the Customer may at its option delay the equipment installation date and the Contractor shall pay to the Customer as fixed and agreed liquidated damages the amount of one hundred dollars ($100), irrespective of the number of System Control Programs undelivered, for each calendar day between the specified installation dates and the date of the delivery of such System Control Programs, but not for more than 180 calendar days, in lieu of all other damages for nondelivery of programming aids. If the Contractor provides suitable substitution of System Control Programs, acceptable to the Customer, liquidated damages for nondelivery of System Control Programs shall not apply, PROVIDED, however, liquidated damages will apply if such substituted software is provided later than the specified installation date.

14.5.2 Liquidated damages for nondelivery of System Control Programs shall likewise not apply for any day on which liquidated damages for noninstallation of equipment accrues.

14.5.3 If the Contractor's delay in delivering System Control Programs is more than 30 calendar days, then by written notice to the Contractor, the Customer may terminate the right of the Contractor to install or may discontinue the equipment immediately in the event it was already installed. In the event the Customer terminates the right of the Contractor to install or the Customer discontinues the equipment, the Contractor shall be liable for liquidated damages in the amount of $100, irrespective of the number of System Control Programs undelivered, for each calendar day for a period of time between the installation date and the date that the Customer terminates the right of the Contractor to install or the date of discontinuance of the equipment, but not for more than 180 calendar days. The Contractor shall be liable for all inbound and outbound preparation and shipping costs for equipment returned pursuant to this provision.

15 *Maintenance of Equipment:

(Used in Contracts: EP EL IP/LP EM)

(Comments: To establish the terms, conditions, and provisions for maintenance of the equipment.)

15.1 Leased Equipment: Contractor agrees to maintain the Equipment to original performance specifications and in accordance with the following maintenance Terms and Conditions during the term, or extension thereof, of any lease entered into pursuant to this Agreement.

15.2 Purchased Equipment: Contractor further agrees that, for purchased Equipment, Contractor will, at the sole option of the Customer, maintain the Equipment to original performance specifications and in accordance with the following maintenance Terms and Conditions for a period of five (5) years from date of this acceptance of any Equipment purchased pursuant to this Agreement, provided that said Equipment has been continuously maintained by the Contractor, or the Contractor's authorized Subcontractor, since its acceptance. Maintenance for purchased Equipment may be discontinued by the Customer upon ninety (90) days written notice to Contractor.

15.3 Maintenance charges are as set forth on Schedule _____.

A. General Provisions

(1) The Customer shall provide the Contractor access to the equipment to perform maintenance service.

(2) Preventive maintenance shall be performed at a time convenient to the Customer within or contiguous with contracted periods of maintenance. The Contractor shall specify in writing, for each machine, the number of hours it requires per month for preventive maintenance and the frequency and duration of such preventive maintenance. From this Contractor supplied information the Customer shall develop and provide to the Contractor in writing the schedule within which the Contractor shall provide preventive maintenance. This schedule may be modified by mutual agreement.

(3) Remedial maintenance shall be performed after notification that Equipment is inoperative. The Contractor shall provide the Customer with a designated point of contact and shall make arrangements to enable a maintenance representative to receive such notification.

(4) Contracted response time is defined as the time, as specified on the Equipment Order, within which Contractor's maintenance personnel must arrive at Customer's Equipment installation site after notification by the Customer that maintenance service is required.

(5) Except for causes beyond the control of the Contractor, if the maintenance personnel fail to arrive at the Customer's installation site within the contracted response period, the Contractor shall grant a credit to the Customer in the amount of 1/200th of the basic monthly lease and maintenance charges for each "late" hour or part thereof (prorated) beginning with the time of notification and ending with the time of arrival. For purposes of response time computations, only hours of contracted maintenance shall be included; except that, if any portion of the Contracted Response Time falls outside contracted periods of maintenance, the maintenance personnel shall arrive at the beginning of the following period of contracted maintenance.

(6) The Contractor shall furnish a malfunction incident report to the installation upon completion of each maintenance call. The report shall include, as a minimum, the following:

(a) Date and time notified;

(b) Date and time of arrival;

(c) Type and Serial Number(s) of machine(s);

(d) Time spent for repair;

(e) Description of malfunction;

(f) List of parts replaced;

(g) Additional charges, if applicable.

(7) There shall be no additional charges for replacement parts.

(8) Maintenance Credit for Equipment Malfunction

(a) If a machine remains inoperative due to a malfunction through no fault or negligence of the Customer for a total of 12 hours or more during any 24-hour period, the Contractor shall grant a credit to the Customer for each such hour in the amount of 1/200th of the basic monthly lease and maintenance charges for the inoperative machine plus 1/200th of the basic monthly lease and maintenance charges for any machine not usable as a result of the breakdown; provided that, for equipment supplied by other vendors the credit shall be as mutually agreed. Downtime for each incident shall start from the time the Customer makes a bona fide attempt to contact the Contractor's designated representative at the prearranged contact point and continue until the machine is returned in good operating condition; PROVIDED THAT, time required, as a result of the malfunction to reconstruct data stored on disks and/or other storage media, shall be considered down time for that equipment required for said reconstruction; and PROVIDED FURTHER THAT, outside primary service areas specified on Schedule _____, downtime for each incident shall be reduced by either the contracted response time or the actual response time whichever is less.

When maintenance credit is due the total number of creditable hours shall be accumulated for the month and adjusted to the nearest half hour.

(b) Exclusive of the provisions of Paragraph _____ above, the Contractor shall grant a credit to the Customer for any machine being maintained by the Contractor which fails to perform at an effectiveness level of 95 percent during any month. The effectiveness level for a machine is computed by dividing the operational use time by the sum of that time plus machine failure downtime.

Downtime shall be defined and computed in the same manner as provided in subparagraph _____ above. The credit shall be a reduction of the total monthly lease and maintenance charges by the percentage figure determined by subtracting the actual effectiveness level percentage from 95 percent. For example, if the effectiveness level for a machine is 82 percent, the credit would be 13 percent. Any downtime for which credit was granted in accordance with Paragraph _____ above shall not be included in the effectiveness level computation.

(c) In the event that a leased machine, or a purchased machine which has been installed less than two years, is inoperative due to machine failure and the total number of hours of downtime exceeds ten per cent (10%) of the total operational use time for three consecutive calendar months, the Customer reserves the right to require the Contractor to replace the machine. The purchase option and/or age depreciation credits for the replacement machines shall not be less than the credits accrued from the date of installation of the original machine, regardless of whether the replacement is made at the request of the Customer or for the convenience of the Contractor.

(9) There shall be no additional maintenance charges for:

(a) Preventive maintenance, regardless of when performed.

(b) Remedial maintenance which was begun during the principal period of maintenance or extension thereof or when the Contractor was notified during the principal period of maintenance or extension thereof of the need for remedial maintenance.

(c) Remedial maintenance required within a 48-hour period due to recurrence of the same malfunction.

(d) Time spent by maintenance personnel after arrival at the site awaiting the arrival of additional maintenance personnel and/or delivery of parts, tools or other required material after a service call has commenced.

(e) Remedial maintenance required when the scheduled preventive maintenance preceding the malfunction had not been performed.

(10)   Malfunctioning equipment must be repaired or a replacement spare installed by the Contractor's maintenance technician no later than the close of business on the work day following notification of equipment malfunction. Failure of the Contractor to comply with this requirement shall be a failure to perform.

15.4 "On-Call" Maintenance

(1) The basic monthly maintenance charges set forth in Schedules _____ shall entitle the Customer to maintenance service during the principal period of maintenance, which is from ____ to ____ times on ____ to ____ days.

(2) The Customer by giving fifteen (15) days written notice to the Contractor, may extend the principal period of maintenance in the time increments, and for the charges as shown in Schedule ____.

(3) The principal period of maintenance or extension thereof may be changed by the Customer upon fifteen (15) days written notice to the Contractor.

4) Should the Customer require maintenance service outside the designated principal period of maintenance or extension thereof on an on-call basis, charges for such additional maintenance service shall be as shown in Schedule ____. Only one maintenance person shall respond to a request for maintenance unless it is mutually agreed that more than one shall is required.

15.5 Replacement Parts

Contractor shall furnish replacement parts for the equipment for a period of seven (7) years commencing with the date(s) of acceptance of the equipment in accordance with acceptance criteria elsewhere in this Contract. After the expiration of said seven (7) year period, Contractor, when requested by the Customer, shall furnish all data necessary to enable the Customer to purchase such replacement parts or have them manufactured elsewhere.

16 *Maintenance Documentation:

(Used in Contracts: EP IP/LP EM)

(Comments: To assure that the Contractor shall provide appropriate documentation for maintenance of purchased equipment upon request.)

For purchased Equipment, Contractor shall upon commencement of performance, provide to the Customer such current diagrams, schematics, manuals, and other documents necessary for the maintenance of the Equipment by the Customer or its subcontractor. There shall be no additional charge for said maintenance documents.

17 *Notices:

(Used in Contracts: All)

(Comments: To define official addresses for formal notifications.)

Any notice required or permitted to be given under this Agreement (except notice of malfunctioning machines) shall be effective if and only if it is in writing and as an alternative to personal delivery sent by U.S. Mail, if to the Contractor (Contractor address), and if to the Customer (agency representative name and address), or to such other address as each party may notify the other in writing.

18 *OSHA/WISHA:

(Used in Contracts: EP EL IP/LP)

(Comments: To establish that the Contractor warrants that its products are designed to meet federal and State safety and health regulations.)

Contractor represents and warrants that its products are designed and manufactured to meet Federal and Washington State safety and health regulations that are in effect at the time of their shipment to the Customer. Contractor further agrees to indemnify and hold harmless Customer from all damages assessed against Customer as a result of the failure of the items furnished under this contract to so comply.

19 *Patent and Copyright Indemnification – Leased or Rental Equipment/Licensed Software:

(Used in Contracts: EP EL IP/LP SL)

(Comments: To establish responsibility of both parties in event of infringement of a U.S. Patent or Copyright.)

19.1 Leased or Rental Equipment/Software

Contractor will at its expense defend the Customer against any claim that machines or programs supplied hereunder infringes a U.S. or foreign patent or copyright, or that the machines' operation pursuant to a current release and modification level of any programming supplied by Contractor infringes a U.S. or foreign patent. Contractor will pay resulting costs, damages and attorney's fees finally awarded provided that:

    a. the Customer promptly notifies Contractor in writing of the claim; and

    b. Contractor has sole control of the defense and all related settlement negotiations.

If such claim has occurred, or in Contractor's opinion is likely to occur, Customer agrees to permit Contractor at its option and expense, either to procure for Customer the right to continue using the machines or programming or to replace or modify the same so that they become noninfringing and functionally equivalent. If neither of the foregoing alternatives is reasonably available, the Customer agrees to return the machines or programming at Contractor's risk and expense upon written request by

Contractor. In the event the product has been installed less than one year, transportation to the initial installation site paid by the Customer shall be refunded by the Contractor. No termination charges will be payable on such returned machines, and the Customer will pay only those charges which were payable prior to the date of such return.

Contractor has no liability for any claim based upon the combination, operation or use of any machines or programming supplied hereunder with Equipment not supplied by Contractor, or with any program other than or in addition to programming supplied by Contractor if such claim would have been avoided by use of another program capable of achieving the same results, or based upon alteration of the machines or modification of any programming supplied hereunder, if such claim would have been avoided by the absence of such alteration or modification.

19.2 Purchased Equipment

Contractor will at its expense defend the Customer against a claim that machines or programming supplied hereunder infringes a U.S. or foreign patent or copyright, or that the machines' operation pursuant to a current release and modification level of any programming supplied by Contractor infringes a U.S. or foreign patent. Contractor will pay resulting costs, and attorney's fees finally awarded provided that:

a. Customer promptly notifies Contractor in writing of the claim; and

b. Contractor has sole control of the defense and all related settlement negotiations.

If such claim has occurred or in Contractor's opinion is likely to occur, Customer agrees to permit Contractor at its option and expense either to procure for Customer the right to continue using the machines or programming or to replace or modify the same so that they become noninfringing and functionally equivalent. If neither of the foregoing alternatives is reasonably available, Customer agrees to return the machines or programming at Contractor's risk and expense upon written request by Contractor. In the event the product has been installed less than one year, transportation to the initial installation site paid by Customer shall be refunded by Contractor. Contractor agrees to grant Customer a credit for returned machines as depreciated. The depreciation shall be an equal amount per year over the life of the machines.

For this section only, the depreciation shall be calculated on the basis of a useful life of six (6) years commencing on the effective date of purchase and shall be an equal amount per year over said useful life. The depreciation for fractional parts of a year shall be prorated on the basis of 365 days per year.

Contractor has no liability for any claim based upon the combination, operation or use of any machines or programming supplied hereunder with equipment not supplied by Contractor or with any program other than or in addition to programming supplied by Contractor, if such claim would have been avoided by use of another program capable of performing the same function or result. Contractor has no liability for any claim based upon alteration of the machines or modification of any programming supplied hereunder, if such claim would have been avoided by the absence of such alteration or modification.

The foregoing states the entire obligation of Contractor with respect to infringement of patents and copyrights.

20 *Payment and Invoice Provisions:

(Used in Contracts: All)

(Comments: To establish provisions for the timing of payments and establish conditions for delinquency and penalties.)

20.1 The Contractor will submit properly certified itemized invoices and/or vouchers in triplicate to the Customer. Invoices shall provide and itemize as a minimum:

(a) Type and description of each Machine or software package;

(b) Serial Number;

(c) Basic monthly charge;

(d) Applicable discounts;

(e) Applicable taxes; and

(f) Total charge.

20.2 The contract and order number must appear on all invoices, bills of lading, packages, and correspondence relating to this contract. All payments to the Contractor shall be remitted by mail. The Customer shall not honor drafts, nor accept goods on a sight draft basis.

20.3 Payment of rental and maintenance service of less than one (1) month's duration shall be prorated at 1/30th of the basic monthly charges for each calendar day.

20.4 Any credits due the Customer may be applied against the Contractor's invoices with appropriate information attached, upon giving of prior notice required herein, if any, by the Customer to the Contractor.

20.5 The Customer shall pay monthly lease charges, monthly installment purchase payments and/or monthly maintenance charges, as well as all other charges provided for herein within _____days of receipt of properly completed invoices. Monthly maintenance charges will commence, as to each unit of Equipment, on the first day of the Successful Performance Period as defined in the provision entitled "Standard of Performance and Acceptance of Equipment." Monthly lease charges and monthly installment purchase payments, which will be invoiced separately, will commence as to each unit of equipment on the first day of the Successful Performance Period.

20.6 The charges do not include, and the Customer assumes the reasonable cost of: (1) supplies; (2) painting or refinishing the Equipment; (3) movement of any unit or part thereof; and (4) repair of damage to the Equipment, including replacement of parts, resulting from the fault of the Customer or causes reasonably within the Customer's control.

21 Price Protection – General

(Used in Contracts: All)

(Comments: To guarantee state agencies the vendors most favored customer prices)

The Contractor agrees all the prices, terms, warranties, and benefits granted by the Contractor are comparable to or better than the equivalent terms being offered by the Contractor to any present customer meeting the same qualifications or requirements as the Customer. Except as otherwise herein provided, if the Contractor shall, during the term of this Contract, enter into arrangements with any other said customer providing greater benefits or more favorable terms, this Contract shall be obligated to provide the same to the Customer.

22 *Relocation (Leased Equipment):

(Used in Contracts: EL)

(Comments: To provide reasonable notice for movement of leased Equipment.)

22.1 Except in an emergency, Equipment rented or leased under this contract shall not be moved from the general location in which installed, unless the Contractor has been given 30 days prior written notice that a move is to be made. For emergency relocation the Customer will provide notification to the Contractor within three calendar days after such relocation.

22.2 Upon 30 days prior written notification to the Contractor, equipment may be transferred from one Customer location to another.

22.3 The Customer shall arrange and pay all transportation, rigging and drayage charges for relocation of Equipment. The Contractor shall provide technical guidance in the relocation, packing and unpacking of Equipment at the Contractor's rates then in effect. Any other relocation costs shall be borne by the Customer. Rearrangement of Equipment on the same site for Customer's convenience shall be at Customer's expense.

23 *Risk of Loss (Purchased):

(Used in Contracts: EP IP)

(Comments: To relieve the Contractor for risks of loss or damage after installation of the Equipment.)

During the period the machines, model changes, or features are in transit or in possession of the Customer, up to and including the date of installation, Contractor and its insurers, if any, relieve the Customer of responsibility for all risks of loss or damage to the machines, including damage caused by the

Customer's negligence, except for loss or damage caused by nuclear reaction, nuclear radiation, or radioactive contamination for which the Customer is legally liable. After the date of installation, the risk of loss or damage shall be borne by the Customer except loss or damage attributable to Contractor's fault or negligence.

24 *Risk of Loss (Lease or Rental):

(Used in Contracts: EL)

(Comments: To relieve the State of responsibility for risks of loss or damage when leasing or renting Equipment.)

During the period the machines, model changes, or features are in transit or in the possession of the Customer and until such time as title is accepted by the Customer, Contractor and its insurers, if any, relieve the Customer of responsibility for all risks of loss or damage to the machines, model changes, or features except for responsibility for (1) loss or damage caused by nuclear reaction, nuclear radiation, or radioactive contamination for which the Customer is legally liable, and (2) loss or damage attributable to the Customer's fault or negligence.

25 *Software Documentation:

(Used in Contracts: SL)

(Comments: To establish that the Contractor will provide appropriate software documentation.)

25.1 Contractor will provide software documentation itemized on schedule, within 30 days after execution of this agreement or as otherwise mutually agreed, in the form of a mutually agreed number of manuals adequate for use of software ordered under the provisions of this agreement. Manual upgrades will be provided on a no-charge basis through the Contractor's local sales and service office.

25.2 For all Contractor programs furnished to the Customer within the scope of this Agreement, the Contractor agrees that in the event it withdraws its support (if supported) from such programs, it will immediately furnish to the Customer, if requested, at no additional cost, sufficient documentation to permit the Customer to maintain, modify or enhance such purchased or licensed programs.

25.3 Contractor grants to the Customer the right to copy or otherwise reproduce manuals and documentation furnished pursuant to this provision, for use within the scope of this Agreement at no additional charge.

26 *Standard of Performance and Acceptance of Equipment:

(Used in Contracts: EP EL IP/LP)

(Comments: To establish provisions for a standard of performance which must be met before any

Equipment is accepted by the State.)

26.1 This provision establishes a standard of performance which must be met before any of the Equipment is accepted by the Customer. It is also applicable to any replacement or substitute machines and machines which are added or field modified after completion of a successful performance period.

26.2 The performance period shall begin when the Equipment is installed and ready for use and shall end when the Equipment has met the Standard of Performance for a period of 30 consecutive days by operating in conformance with the Contractor's technical specifications (or as quoted in any proposal) and at an effectiveness level of at least 95 percent.

26.3 In the event the Equipment does not meet the Standard of Performance during the initial 30 consecutive days the Standard of Performance test shall continue on a day-to-day basis until the Standard of Performance is met for a total of 30 consecutive days. If the Equipment fails to meet the Standard of Performance after 90 calendar days, from commencement of Acceptance Testing, the Customer may, at its option, either terminate the Equipment without penalty, request replacement Equipment, or continue the performance test. The Contractor shall be liable for all inbound and outbound preparation and shipping costs for Equipment returned pursuant to this provision. The Customer's option to terminate the Equipment Order under this Agreement shall remain in effect until such time as a successful completion of the performance period is attained.

26.4 (Lease Only) - Lease and maintenance charges shall apply beginning on the first day of the successful performance period.

26.5 The effectiveness level for a machine is a percentage figure determined by dividing the operational use time of the machine by the sum of that time plus machine failure downtime.

26.6 Operational use time for performance testing for a machine is defined as the accumulated time during which the machine is in actual use.

26.7 Machine failure downtime is that period of time when scheduled jobs cannot be processed on that machine due to machine or Contractor supplied software malfunction.

26.8 Contractor supplied software shall, for purposes of this Agreement, mean standard Contractor software packages released and generally offered to lessees or purchasers of Contractor's Equipment as modified and offered by Contractor from time to time as standard software.

26.9 During periods of machine downtime, the Customer may use operable Equipment when such action does not interfere with maintenance of the inoperable Equipment.

26.10 Machine failure downtime for added, field modified, substitute, or replacement machines after the completion of a successful Performance Period is that period of time when such machines are inoperable due to machine or Contractor supplied software malfunction.

26.11 Downtime for each incident shall start from the time the Customer makes a bona fide attempt to contact the Contractor's designated representative at the prearranged contact point until the machine(s) is returned to the Customer in proper operating condition, exclusive of either contracted response time agreed to by the Contractor and the Customer or actual response time, whichever is less.

26.12 During the performance period for a machine a minimum of 100 hours of operational use time with productive or simulated work will be required as a basis for computation of the effectiveness level. However, in computing the effectiveness level the actual number of operational use hours shall be used when in excess of the minimum of 100 hours.

26.13 The Customer shall maintain appropriate daily records to satisfy the requirements of this provision and shall notify the Contractor in writing of the date of the first day of the successful Performance Period.

26.14 Equipment shall not be accepted and no charges shall be paid until the Standard of Performance is met. The date of acceptance shall be the first day of the successful Performance Period.

26.15 Operational use time and downtime shall be measured in hours and whole minutes.

27 *Taxes:

(Used in Contracts: All)

(Comments: To identify tax liability and exemptions for the contract.)

The Customer will pay sales and use taxes imposed on goods or services acquired hereunder. The Contractor must pay all other taxes including, but not limited to, Washington Business and Occupation Tax, taxes based on the Contractor's income, or personal property taxes levied or assessed on the Contractor's personal property to which the Customer does not hold title.

28 *Term of Agreement:

(Used in Contracts: All)

(Comments: To establish term of agreement, conditions for extensions and termination, and the survivability of certain clauses.)

28.1 The initial term of Agreement shall be _____ year(s), commencing upon the date of its execution by both the parties. The term of this Agreement may be extended by ___ one year periods, PROVIDED: The extensions shall be at the exclusive option of the Customer and shall be effected by the Customer giving written notice of extension to the Contractor not less than thirty (30) days prior to the expiration date of the initial term of this Agreement. No change in Terms and Conditions, increased lease rates or increased purchase prices shall be permitted during these extensions.

28.2 The term of leases executed pursuant to the authority of this Agreement shall be one (1), two (2), three (3), four (4), or five (5) years, at the option of the Customer. The term of said leases shall commence upon acceptance of Equipment in accordance with the terms of the provision entitled "Standard of Performance and Acceptance of Equipment," elsewhere in this Agreement. Upon expiration of the initial lease term, said leases shall continue on a month-to-month basis, at the Customer initial lease price, until terminated by either party by the giving of thirty (30) days prior written notice to the other party; provided Equipment is continuously leased for at least three (3) years; otherwise, the lease rate shall revert to the then-current one (1) year rate.

28.3 All lease or purchase transactions executed pursuant to the authority of this Agreement shall be bound by all of the terms, conditions, purchase prices, and lease rates set forth herein, not withstanding the expiration of the initial term of this Agreement or any extension thereof, for the periods set forth following:

(a) Leased Equipment - for the initial lease term and any extension thereof as may be effectuated by virtue of the Terms and Conditions of this Agreement;

(b) Purchased Equipment - for so long as the Equipment is maintained by the Contractor or the Contractor's authorized subcontractor; PROVIDED THAT, with respect to purchased Equipment, the following clauses shall remain operative for so long as the Equipment remains in use by an agency or political subdivision of the State.

Governing Law

Severability

Waiver

Independent Status of Contractor

Limitation of Liability

Maintenance Documentation

Patent and Copyright Indemnification

Software Documentation

Anti-trust Violations

Entire Agreement

Counterparts

Notices

29 *Title (Purchased):

(Used in Contracts: EP IP/LP)

(Comments: To assure that the Contractor shall convey clear title of purchased Equipment upon completion of acceptance testing.)

Upon completion of acceptance testing, the Contractor shall convey to the Customer good title to purchased Equipment free and clear of all liens, pledges, mortgages, encumbrances, or other security interests, except for any security interest associated with an installment payment agreement between the Customer and Contractor.

30 *Title (Leased):

(Used in Contracts: EL)

(Comments: To establish that the Contractor retains title of all leased Equipment, to assure that Customer does not impair same, and to assure Contractor retains clear title for Equipment with purchase option.)

Equipment furnished hereunder to which the Contractor retains title shall remain personal property and, except as otherwise provided herein, title thereto is retained by the Contractor. The Customer shall keep the Equipment free of all liens and claims and shall do nothing to impair or encumber the Contractor's title or rights nor to remove or obscure the property identification markers of the Contractor. The Contractor shall have the right to inspect the Equipment during the Customer's normal business hours. For all leased or rented Equipment for which the Contractor grants to the Customer an option to purchase, the Contractor shall keep said Equipment free and clear of all liens or other claims.

31 *Signature Blocks:

(Used in Contracts: All)

(Comments: To provide a statement of understanding and agreement followed by signature blocks.)

THE PARTIES hereto, having read this Agreement in its entirety, including all attachments hereto, do agree thereto in each and every particular. In witness thereof, the parties have set their hands hereunto.

C. LONG FORM CONTRACT TERMS AND CONDITIONS - OPTIONAL CLAUSES:

In developing a contract, or a competitive solicitation document, optional clauses should be selected to meet specific contract needs. These clauses are intended to provide a basis for negotiation with the Contractor, not a final set of Terms and Conditions. Not every clause will be required in every contract, nor will these clauses satisfy every contract need.

In a competitive acquisition, any contract requirements should be carefully selected from these listings and other sources as necessary, and then tailored to meet specific functional and operational needs.

1 Table of Contents:

(Used in Contracts: All)

(Comments: To list and identify the provisions contained within the contract.)

(This section, at the beginning of the contract, should contain a chronological list of all the provisions contained in contract with optional page number references.)

2 Attorneys' Fees and Costs:

(Used in Contracts: All)

(Comments: General clause for payment of attorneys' fees.)

If any litigation is brought to enforce, or arising out of this Contract or any term, clause, or provision hereof, the prevailing party shall be awarded its reasonable attorneys' fees together with expenses and costs incurred with such litigation including necessary fees, costs, and expenses for services rendered at both trial and appellate levels as well as subsequent to judgment in obtaining execution thereof.

3 Backup Availability:

(Used in Contracts: EP EL IP/LP)

(Comments: To provide a means for obtaining replacement system Equipment upon a permanently disabling disaster for mission essential Equipment. This or similar disaster recovery requirements should be specified in functional requirements in the solicitation document.)

In the event the computer or telecommunications system or any component thereof is rendered permanently inoperative as a result of a natural or other disaster, Contractor will deliver a replacement system, within ____days from the date of Customer request. In such event, Contractor agrees to waive any delivery schedule priorities, and to make the replacement system available from the manufacturing facility currently producing such Equipment, or from inventory. The price for replacement Equipment will be the then current published price or the price payable under this contract plus ____% per year for each full year between the delivery date of the Equipment hereunder and the request for replacement, whichever is lower. If the inoperability is due to the negligence or fault of the Contractor, replacement Equipment will be delivered at no cost to the Customer.

4 Business or Support Termination Rights:

(Used in Contracts: SL)

(Comments: To give Customer a perpetual license in event of business termination, regardless of term of license.)

In the event that Contractor shall, for any reason, cease to conduct business, or cease to support the software licensed under this agreement, Customer shall have a right to convert the software licenses listed in Schedule ____, herein, into perpetual licenses, with rights of quiet enjoyment, but subject to payment obligations not to exceed the then current rates.

5 Compatibility:

(Used in Contracts: EP EL IP/LP SL)

(Comments: To ensure that hardware, software or other products delivered are compatible with Customer's currently installed systems, or with other hardware, software or products also manufactured and/or available from contractor. This clause should be tailored to Customer's specific operational needs as identified in functional requirements in the acquisition solicitation documents.)

Contractor acknowledges that other products listed in Schedule ___ are available for purchase, lease or license to the Customer, and are similar in function to that being delivered hereunder. Both the products to be delivered and the products in Schedule ___ are data and program compatible with Customer's existing systems, so that Customer's existing data files and applications programs will operate on Equipment contracted for herein without necessity for alteration, emulation or other modification.

6 Compliance with Standards:

(Used in Contracts: All)

(Comments: To cause Contractor to comply with specified hardware and software standards (Customer's, American National Standards Institute (ANSI), International Standards Organization (ISO), or other.)

Contractor represents that all hardware, software, and elements thereof, including but not limited to, documentation, and source code, shall meet and be maintained by Contractor to conform to the standards set forth on Schedule __.

7 Confidentiality:

(Used in Contracts: All)

(Comments: Provides for Contractor maintaining Confidentiality of Customer material.)

7.1 The Contractor acknowledges that much of the material and information which has or will come into its possession or knowledge in connection with this Contract or its performance, consists of confidential and proprietary data, whose disclosure to or use by third parties will be damaging.

7.2 Access to information concerning individual recipients of Customer's services or individual clients shall not be granted except as authorized by law or agency rule.

7.3 The Contractor, therefore, agrees to hold all such material and information in strictest confidence, not to make use thereof other than for the performance of this Contract, to release it only to authorized employees requiring such information, and not to release or disclose it to any other party.

7.4 The Contractor agrees to release such information or material only to employees or other parties who have signed a written agreement expressly prohibiting disclosure.

8 Conflict of Interest:

(Used in Contracts: All)

(Comments: Prohibits Conflict of Interest, and provides for termination upon breach.)

8.1 The Customer may terminate this Contract, by written notice to the Contractor, if it is found after due notice and examination that there is a violation by Contractor of:

    a.   The Executive Conflict of Interest Act, Chapter 42.18 RCW;

    b.   Code of Ethics for Public Officers and Employees, Chapter 42.22 RCW; or

    c.   Any other similar statute involving the Contractor in the procurement of or performance under this Contract.

8.2 In the event this Contract is terminated as provided above, the Customer shall be entitled to pursue the same remedies against the Contractor as it could pursue in the event of a breach of the Contract by the Contractor. The rights and remedies of the Customer provided by this clause shall not be exclusive and are in addition to any other rights and remedies provided by law.

9 Counterparts:

(Used in Contracts: All)

(Comments: To provide for duplicate originals of the contract.)

This Agreement is to be executed in duplicate originals and each duplicate shall be deemed an original copy of the Agreement signed by each party, for all purposes.

10 Covenant Against Contingent Fees:

(Used in Contracts: All)

(Comments: Prohibits contingent fees, permits termination for violation.)

10.1 The Contractor warrants that no person or selling agency has been employed or retained to solicit or secure this Contract:

    a.   Upon any Contract or understanding for a commission, percentage, brokerage, or contingent fee,

    b.   Excepting bona fide employees or a bona fide established commercial or selling agency of the Contractor.

10.2 The Customer shall have the right, in the event of breach by the Contractor, of the above-stated provision, to:

    a.   Annul this Contract without liability, or,

    b.   In its discretion, deduct from the Contract price or consideration or otherwise recover the full amount of such commission, percentage, brokerage, or contingent fee.

11 Cross Guarantees:

(Used in Contracts: All)

(Comments: To ensure that a contract signed by a subsidiary has the support of the parent organization and vice versa.)

By their signatures at the foot hereof, the following companies _____, hereby, jointly and severally with Contractor, guarantee the full and timely performance hereof by Contractor.

12 Definition of Terms:

(Used in Contracts: All)

(Comments: To establish specific definitions for terms used within the contract.)

(This section, near the front of the contract, should contain a definition of any potentially confusing, ambiguous, vague, unique, etc., terms or any other terms that may be appropriate and useful in the contract.)

13 Discounts and Purchase Options:

(Used in Contracts: EP EL IP)

(Comments: To establish any special discounts for volume or long-term lease and define conditions for any lease/rental credits toward purchase.)

13.1 The Customer may purchase all of the items of Equipment specified on Equipment Order at any time during the lease period, or any extension thereof, provided the Customer has complied with the Terms and Conditions of this Agreement.

13.2 The purchase price for any item of Equipment shall be the list purchase price on the Equipment Order less lease credits (based upon net lease payments exclusive of amounts paid for software, maintenance, taxes, and materials) accrued on the basis of the following schedule; PROVIDED THAT, except for Equipment as shown in Schedule __, in no event will the purchase price for installed leased Equipment exceed the list purchase price specified above, less _____ percent (__%) discount:

13.3 In the event the Customer exercises its purchase option, the Customer shall pay all applicable taxes, as provided in the provision entitled "Taxes," if any, imposed on such purchase.

13.4 This purchase option ceases for each Agreement upon its termination unless extended.

13.5 In addition to outright purchase and lease with purchase option, the Equipment listed in Schedule __ is offered by the Contractor under a Time Payment Sale on a monthly payment plan. Monthly payments, excluding maintenance, are shown in Schedule __ and are subject to the provision entitled "Price Protection - Lease Rates/Purchase Prices/Maintenance Rates", of this Agreement. Designation of Time Payment Sale on Exhibit ___ and acceptance of the order by the Contractor binds the parties to the full term specified therein which may not be terminated except as provided by the provision entitled "Non-Allocation of Funds" or by the provision entitled "Termination, Cancellation, and Repossession," of this agreement. At the end of the specified term, the Customer may, upon paying one additional payment take title to the item(s) of Equipment subject to the terms of the Agreement.

13.6 The purchase prices listed in Schedule __ are list prices.

13.7 All Equipment listed in Schedule __ and any other Equipment offered by the Contractor under the terms of this Agreement, except Equipment as indicated in Schedule __ and except cables listed in Schedule __, shall be available to the Customer at a discount of _____percent (__%) for new Equipment. Installed Equipment will be available for purchase as provided above.

14 Disputes:

(Used in Contracts: All)

(Comments: Dispute arbitration clause - optional clause - limits arbitration to determinations of fact. Should only be used if negotiating away a more onerous clause, as it limits agency rights and freedom of action to resolve a problem, by putting the issue in the hands of an arbitration team.)

14.1 Except as otherwise provided in this Contract, when a bona fide dispute concerning a question of fact arises between the Customer and the Contractor, and it cannot be resolved, either party may initiate the dispute resolution procedure provided herein.

14.2 Time is of the essence in resolving disputes. The initiating party shall reduce its description of the dispute to writing and deliver it to the responding party. The responding party must respond in writing within two (2) state working days.

a.   Then, both parties shall have three (3) state working days to negotiate in good faith to resolve the dispute. If the dispute cannot be resolved after three (3) days, a panel of arbitrators may be appointed.

b.   Each party will designate an arbitrator, and those two arbitrators will appoint a third arbitrator to the panel.

1)   The panel will review the written descriptions of the dispute, gather additional information as needed, and render a decision on the dispute in the shortest practical time.

2)   Both parties agree to be bound by the determination of the panel of arbitrators.

14.3 Once formed, the panel of arbitrators shall remain in effect through the performance period of this Contract.

14.4 Both parties agree to exercise good faith in dispute resolution and to avoid arbitration whenever possible.

14.5 The Customer and the Contractor agree that, the existence of a dispute notwithstanding, they will continue without delay to carry out all their respective responsibilities under this Contract which are not affected by the dispute.

15 Equipment Configurations:

(Used in Contracts: EP EL IP/LP)

(Comments: Equipment conformance to specifications. Includes specific listings of Equipment and interface and connectibility requirements, which should be included in acquisition solicitation documents.)

15.1 Each item of Equipment, component, or feature thereof delivered hereunder will conform to the detailed specification of said item, attached hereto as Exhibit __ and herein incorporated by reference, in all respects including, but not limited to, physical characteristics, operating characteristics, space requirements, power requirements, maintenance or warranty characteristics, modularity, comparability, and the like.

15.2 The Equipment, components, or features thereof purchased hereunder, for the purpose of delivery and performance under this Contract, shall be grouped together in one or more hardware configurations as set forth in Exhibit __.

a.   Any such configuration shall be deemed incomplete and undeliverable if any item of Equipment, component, or feature thereof within that configuration has not been delivered, or if delivered, not installed or operational in accordance with the Installation and Delivery Dates Clause of this Contract.

b.   Any such configuration shall be deemed not accepted if any item of Equipment, component, or feature thereof within that configuration is deemed not acceptable in accordance with the Standards of Performance and Acceptance of Equipment Clause of this Contract.

15.3 The Customer shall have the right to connect the Equipment herein contracted for to any Equipment manufactured or supplied by others including other computers, peripheral Equipment, terminal devices, communications Equipment, and the like which interface with the Equipment purchased hereunder.

a.   The Customer shall notify the Contractor at least five (5) state working days prior to any such connection. If the Contractor shall deem it necessary or desirable for proper warranty service, the Contractor shall make or supervise the interconnection, at the Contractor's expense. Any such connection shall not void any herein-stated warranties.

b.   The Contractor shall supply any required interface devices, proprietary to the Contractor, as described in published Contractor manuals at the then current price. Said price shall be subject to the herein-stated Price Protection Clause provisions.

c.   The Contractor warrants that the hereunder purchased Equipment, components, or features thereof are fully compatible with, support, and shall operate and perform correctly with or cause to operate and perform correctly the connected devices as described in the configuration requirements of the solicitation document which is attached hereto and incorporated herein as Exhibit _____.

15.4 If requested by Customer, the Contractor agrees to identify, on all items of Equipment, components, or features thereof supplied under this Contract, all appropriate test points for connecting commercially available hardware monitors designed to measure system capacity, performance, or activity.

16 Equipment Warranties:

(Used in Contracts: EP EL IP/LP EM)

(Comments: To establish specific Contractor warranties for performance of Equipment and software and define remedies in the event of failure of warranted products.)

16.1 The Contractor warrants that the Equipment when installed shall be in good operating condition and shall conform to the Contractor's official published specifications as shown in Schedule ____attached, at the time of installation. The Contractor further warrants that the Equipment when installed shall be free from defects in material and workmanship and shall remain in satisfactory operating condition for the term of any lease, subject to the charges and provisions of the applicable maintenance provisions.

16.2 The Contractor's obligation and liability under these warranties shall be that the Contractor shall either, at its option, adjust, repair, or replace, as promptly as is possible, the defective parts or units of Equipment claimed to cause unsatisfactory operation of the Equipment. The Contractor shall assume the costs for the replacing parts or units and their installation. The Customer agrees that the Contractor will not be liable for any damages caused by the Customer's failure to fulfill any of its responsibilities as set forth herein. The provisions of this clause shall not be exclusive but are in addition to the various rights of the Customer and the overall obligation of the Contractor as set forth in this Agreement.

17 Escrow of Source:

(Used in Contracts: SL)

(Comments: Protects users right to continuity of use and access to source code for package programs. Clause is not intended for routine coverage of all software, rather for mission critical software, where Contractor's business cessation would gravely impact agency systems performance. Should be accompanied by an attached escrow agreement with Contractor, third party and Customer signatures.)

The Contractor agrees to keep, and maintain current, a copy of the source code in escrow with _____, as escrow agent. The escrow agent shall be paid by Contractor and shall be authorized to release the source code in accordance with the provision entitled Source Availability and Access or Contractor's cessation, for any reason, to do business or to support the software that is the subject of this contract, or in accordance with the escrow agreement attached hereto and incorporated herein as Exhibit .

18 Exchange Provisions:

(Used in Contracts: EP EL IP/LP SL)

(Comments: To establish conditions for upgrade, downgrade, trade-ins, etc., for exchange of leased or purchased Equipment.)

(Some Contractors will provide conditions by which the Customer may exchange the unit of Equipment or software being acquired in conjunction with a future upgrade or new release. If an agency determines that such a clause may be important it is usually the responsibility of the Contractor to provide such Terms and Conditions.)

19 Freedom of Use – Software:

(Used in Contracts: SL)

(Comments: To insure that users of a computer service center have the right to use the center's software without interference or additional licenses.)

Contractor understands that Customer provides information processing services to other users that are agencies of state government and other tax supported entities. Software delivered hereunder will be used in the delivery of these services. Contractor acknowledges and agrees that said use of software products is acceptable under the licensing agreements contained herein.

20 Hold-back for Entire Contract Compliance:

(Used in Contracts: EP IP/LP SL)

(Comments: To provide for holdback of payment for products pending performance of entire contract. Other options include per diem liquidated damages for non-completion, or inclusion of a requirement for a Contractor's performance bond to be held in escrow by Customer pending full contract compliance.)

Contractor and Customer acknowledge that certain performance will be required of Contractor subsequent to initial acceptance of products by Customer. Accordingly, _____% of the purchase or license amount otherwise payable upon such acceptance shall be retained by Customer and shall be payable upon performance and acceptance of all tasks described on Schedule ___.

21 Industrial Insurance Coverage:

(Used in Contracts: EP EL IP/LP EM)

(Comments: Requires Contractor to have industrial insurance coverage.)

21.1 The Contractor shall provide or purchase industrial insurance coverage prior to performing work under this Contract. The Customer will not be responsible for payment of industrial insurance premiums or for any other claim or benefit for the Contractor, or any subcontractor or employee of the Contractor, which might arise under the industrial insurance laws during the performance of duties and services under this Contract.

21.2 The Contractor shall be primarily and directly responsible for the payment of all Washington State Industrial Insurance Fund payment of all employer's premiums for all the Contractor's employees engaged in work under this Contract where the work or employees are subject to the provisions of Chapter 51 RCW. The Contractor shall make sure all applicable contributions or premiums for Contractor employees are collected and paid as required by said statute.

22 Installment Financing Provisions:

(Used in Contracts: IP/LP)

(Comments: A clause or set of clauses which contractor may require to help protect its security interests. (NOTE: Any installment purchase, lease with purchase option, or third party financing contract may need prior approval of the State Finance Committee, and/or use of specified Terms and Conditions as may be required by the Committee, the Office of Financial Management, or DIS PPD).)

(Typically required is a clause or clauses covering: default, destruction of Equipment, no prepayment penalty, payment schedules, Customer covenants, remedies available to Contractor, tax liability, etc. This clause is used to protect Contractor's security interests in a third party financing contract. Any proposed provision should be carefully reviewed by an Assistant Attorney General.)

23 Insurance:

(Used in Contracts: EL IP/LP)

(Comments: To establish both parties' insurance responsibilities.)

(In some instances the Contractor may require an agency to obtain insurance on the Equipment being acquired. If this occurs, the agency may wish to acquire insurance - refer to the Risk Management Office of the Department of General Administration for assistance in obtaining cost-effective insurance policies - or convince the Contractor that the State's "self-insurance" is sufficient to cover the risk of loss.)

24 Interface of Equipment:

(Used in Contracts: EP EL IP/LP)

(Comments: To provide assurance that contractor provided products will interface with specified telecommunications Equipment, listed terminals and peripherals, as previously identified in the acquisition solicitation documents.)

Contractor warrants that Equipment provided hereunder will connect without modification or damage to Equipment not provided by Contractor as follows:

a. Voice and data telecommunications Equipment identified in Schedule _____,

b. All terminals identified in Schedule _____,

c. All peripheral Equipment identified in Schedule _____.

25 Licensing Standards:

(Used in Contracts: All)

(Comments: Establishes Contractor's requirement to be licensed in Washington.)

The Contractor shall comply with all applicable local, state, and federal licensing requirements and standards necessary in the performance of this Contract. (See Chapter 19.02 RCW for Washington State licensing requirements and definitions.)

26 Limitation of Authority:

(Used in Contracts: All)

(Comments: Identifies agency Contracting Officer as Customer authorized signatory, provides for other prior written delegation.)

Only the Contracting Officer or delegate by writing (delegation to be made prior to action) shall have the express, implied, or apparent authority to alter, amend, modify, or waive any clause or condition of this Contract. Furthermore, any alteration, amendment, modification, or waiver of any clause or condition of this Contract is not effective or binding until made in writing and signed by the Customer unless otherwise provided herein.

27 Maintenance Surcharges:

(Used in Contracts: EP EL IP/LP EM)

(Comments: To establish costs for extraordinary maintenance situations.)

27.1 Periods of Maintenance

The basic monthly maintenance rates set forth on Schedule __, attached, shall entitle the Customer to maintenance service during a principal period of maintenance which shall be established in the provision entitled "Maintenance of Equipment," subparagraph "'On-Call' Maintenance," and as further provided hereunder. The principal period of maintenance shall be any _____ -hour period between _____and _____ Monday through Friday, excluding Customer observed holidays. The contracted period of maintenance may be extended beyond the principal period of maintenance according to the procedures set forth in provision entitled "Maintenance of Equipment," in the increments and for the surcharges set forth in Schedule __.

27.2 Zone Charges and Contracted Response Times

Contracted Response Time, as defined in provision entitled "Maintenance of Equipment," subparagraph A.(4), shall be as provided for each Zone in the attached schedule __.

In addition to the basic monthly maintenance rates set forth in Schedule __, the Customer shall pay a surcharge, as provided opposite the applicable zone in the attached Schedule __, based upon the indicated percentage of said Basic Monthly Maintenance charge. Zones are based upon existing points of service as set forth in Schedule __, with point of service subject to change of location by the Contractor on sixty (60) days prior written notice to Customer. Such changes shall not result in substantial cost increases to the Customer, or substantial degradation of maintenance service. All zones are defined in one-way shortest route road miles from nearest point of service to installation site.

28 Minority & Women's Business Enterprise Participation:

(Used in Contracts: All)

(Comments: Contracts with Minority or Women's Business Enterprise participation should include specific language covering required participation and remedies upon breach of contract. Contact the Office of Minority and Women's Business Enterprises (OMWBE) for specific language.)

(MWBE specifications for required participation, when part of contractor's commitment, should be included in contract Terms and Conditions, together with language indicating that failure to comply with MWBE requirements is a material breach of contract subject to penalties and other remedies under Washington Law.)

29 Price Protection – Lease Rates/Purchase Prices/Maintenance Rates:

(Used in Contracts: EP EL IP SL EM)

(Comments: To establish conditions for price increases, reductions, escalation, and notices thereof.)

29.1 The Contractor agrees to lease, license or sell the Equipment or software to the Customer at the lease rates, license fees and/or purchase prices set forth on Schedule(s) __, less applicable discounts, which lease rates and purchase prices shall not be increased during the initial term of this Agreement and thereafter only as set forth elsewhere in this Agreement.

29.2 Maintenance rates and surcharges are set forth in Schedule(s) __, attached hereto and by this reference made a part hereof. Said maintenance rates and surcharges shall not be increased during the initial term of this Agreement; thereafter, maintenance rates and/or surcharges, time and material rates and mileage, may be increased by a maximum of ____ percent as to future purchases and leases and for

Equipment then under lease once per State fiscal year (July 1 through June 30) upon written notice to each agency or political subdivision using the Contractor furnished machines pursuant to the terms of this Agreement, subject to the provision in the following paragraph.

29.3 Such written notice shall be furnished not less than 90 days prior to the commencement of the State fiscal year in which such maintenance rate and/or surcharge increase shall become effective. If the Contractor reduces its list purchase prices, lease, or maintenance rates for any of the Equipment during the term of this Agreement, the Customer shall have the benefit of such lower prices for new installations for like terms, conditions, quantities, configurations, and length of lease.

30 Price Protection – General

(Used in Contracts: All)

(Comments: To guarantee state agencies the vendors most favored customer prices)

The Contractor agrees all the prices, terms, warranties, and benefits granted by the Contractor are comparable to or better than the equivalent terms being offered by the Contractor to any present customer meeting the same qualifications or requirements as the Customer. Except as otherwise herein provided, if the Contractor shall, during the term of this Contract, enter into arrangements with any other said customer providing greater benefits or more favorable terms, this Contract shall be obligated to provide the same to the Customer.

31 Protection of Proprietary Information:

(Used in Contracts: All)

(Comments: To establish protection of Contractor's rights and interests in technical information, software products, copyrights, etc.)

(Proprietary information can be defined as any data, information, and programs and usually includes corrections, modifications, revisions, and copies thereof, whether in machine readable or visually readable form, containing information which is the property of and confidential to the Contractor. It is the responsibility of the Contractor to identify such proprietary information and provide appropriate Terms and Conditions in the contract.)

32 Publicity:

(Used in Contracts: All)

(Comments: To establish that the Contractor will not use any advertising, sales promotion, or any other publicity matters wherein the State's name may be specifically stated, implied, or inferred without the consent of the State.)

The Contractor agrees to submit to the Customer, all advertising, sales promotion, and other publicity matters relating to any Product furnished by the Contractor wherein the Customer's name is mentioned or language used from which the connection of the Customer's name therewith may, in Customers judgment, be inferred or implied; and the Contractor further agrees not to publish or use such advertising, sales promotion, or publicity matter without the prior written consent of the Customer.

33 Security Interest – Financed Equipment:

(Used in Contracts: IP/LP)

(Comments: Provides Contractor a security interest in property being acquired under an installment purchase or third party financing contract. (NOTE: Any installment purchase, lease with purchase option, or third party financing contract may need prior approval of the State Finance Committee, and/or use of specified Terms and Conditions as may be required by the Committee, the Office of Financial Management, or DIS PPD).)

33.1 Equipment furnished hereunder pursuant to any financing or installment purchase Terms and Conditions herein shall remain personal property and, unless otherwise provided herein, the Customer grants to the Contractor or its assigns a security interest in the Equipment and in Contractor-supplied substitutions or replacements thereof, and additions thereto, pending the full payment of the purchase price and any accrued and unpaid charges.

33.2 The security interest herein granted shall be governed by the Uniform Commercial Code of the State of Washington, Title RCW. The Customer shall have all the benefits accorded to debtors under said statute unless otherwise provided herein, required by law, or dictated by court rule.

33.3 The Customer shall keep the Equipment free of all other liens and claims and shall do nothing to impair or encumber the Contractor's rights.

33.4 The Contractor shall have the right to inspect Equipment during the Customer's normal business hours.

33.5 The parties hereto agree that in the event the Contractor or its assigns should file for bankruptcy, the Customer has the right, at its sole discretion, to settle its debt hereunder by payment in full, and the Contractor or its assigns shall withdraw all claims and liens thereto.

a. Thereafter the Customer shall have clear title to the property acquired hereunder as provided herein, whether or not billed by the Contractor or its assigns; and

b. Said title shall vest exclusively in the Customer, and the Contractor, its assigns, or their successors in interest have no claim thereto.

33.6 A copy of this Contract may be filed with the appropriate authorities anytime after signature by the Customer as a financing statement in order to perfect the Contractor's security interest. The Customer also shall execute from time to time, alone or with the Contractor, any reasonable financing statements or other reasonable documents considered by the Contractor to be necessary or desirable to perfect or protect the security interest hereby created.

34 Site and Installation Planning:

(Used in Contracts: EP EL IP/LP)

(Comments: To establish responsibility for site specifications and preparation.)

34.1 Site preparation guidelines shall be furnished in writing by the Contractor within _____days after an Equipment order has been signed by both parties. These guidelines shall be in sufficient detail to permit the Equipment being installed to operate efficiently from the point of view of environment and power. Contractor specialists will be available at no cost to the Customer to provide required consultation relative to site planning. When the site is prepared, Contractor Field Engineering will inspect the facilities to assure compliance with published guidelines and approve in writing.

34.2 The Contractor, for each installation, will provide at no cost to the Customer such installation support as is necessary for adequate understanding and operation of the Equipment and software installed by the Customer.

35 Software Ownership:

(Used in Contracts: SL)

(Comments: To warrant that Contractor is the owner of software and/or has unrestricted right to license it to Customer.)

Contractor as Licensor hereby warrants and represents to Customer as Licensee that Contractor is the owner of the software and licensed programs delivered hereunder or otherwise has the right to grant to Customer the license to use the software and licensed programs identified in Schedule _____ without violating any rights of any third party, and that there is currently no actual or threatened suit by any such third party based on an alleged violation of such right by Contractor.

36 Software Maintenance, Upgrade, Enhancement:

(Used in Contracts: SL)

(Comments: To establish the Contractor's responsibility to provide software updates, upgrades and enhancements. Specific requirements should be included in the solicitation document and be reflected in this clause.)

(Software maintenance, upgrade and enhancement can outline several areas of Contractor responsibilities. These may require the Contractor:

- To supply at no added cost updated versions of the software to operate under new releases of the manufacturer's operating system.

- To supply updated versions of the software which encompass improvements, extensions, or other changes which Contractor, at its discretion, deems to be logical improvements or extensions of the original products supplied to the Customer.

- To supply interface modules which are developed by the Contractor for interfacing the software to other software products.

Each of these items may be negotiated independently, depending upon the circumstances, with regard to each party's responsibilities, costs, etc. Refer to provision entitled "Software Documentation" and provision entitled "Contractor Correction of Software Malfunction" for additional information regarding software.)

37 Source Availability and Access:

(Used in Contracts: SL)

(Comments: Provides Customer with source code to programs when Contractor warranty or Contractor maintenance expires.)

The Contractor agrees to furnish to the Customer, upon request and without charge, a single copy of the source code used in the preparation of the software licensed or acquired hereunder , brought up to date to the date of delivery, after the occurrence of any of the following events, provided that, at the time of request, the user is not in default hereunder: (a) expiration of maintenance provisions of this contract; (b) expiration of ____years from the date of installation of the package; or (c) when such source code is made available to other users of the package. Upon taking possession thereof, the user agrees that the source code shall be subject to the restrictions on the software itself.

38 Specifications:

(Used in Contracts: All)

(Comments: To provide for including technical Equipment specifications by reference and attached to the contract.)

Technical Equipment and/or software specifications are listed and described on Schedule ____attached hereto and by this reference made a part hereof, as though completely set forth herein. Contractor warrants that products delivered hereunder shall perform in accordance with these specifications.

39 Termination, Cancellation, and Repossession:

(Used in Contracts: EP EL IP/LP)

(Comments: To establish conditions for termination or cancellation of the lease or purchase contract by either party, and the requirement for appropriate notices.)

The Customer may, upon 14 days prior written notice cancel orders or leases for any unit(s) of Equipment. A lease agreement under the terms of this agreement shall terminate upon cancellation of the last unit of Equipment. The Contractor may elect, without prejudice to any of its other rights or remedies, to cancel a lease or purchase agreement with a Customer and, with or without cancellation, repossess the Equipment if the Customer, upon 30 days written notice, has failed to make payments due hereunder or has failed to perform any other obligation to be performed by the Customer under this Agreement.

40 Termination:

(Used in Contracts: All)

(Comments: Alternative termination clause, with Termination for Default, Termination for Convenience, and termination following arbitration under the optional disputes clause.)

40.1 Termination for Default

The Customer may, by written notice, terminate this Contract, in whole or in part, for failure of the Contractor to perform any of the obligations or provisions hereof.

a.   In such event, the Customer shall thereupon have the right to purchase on the open market the Equipment, software and services hereunder required in lieu thereof, and the Contractor shall be liable for damages as authorized by law. The Customer shall thereupon have the right to deduct from any monies due or that thereafter become due to the Contractor or to require the Contractor to pay the Customer for all additional costs for said Equipment and services including, but not limited to, the following:

1) Any cost difference between the original contract price of Equipment, software, and services and the replacement cost of Equipment, software, and services, and

2) All administrative costs directly related to the replacement contract such as, costs of competitive bidding, mailing, advertising, applicable excess financing charges or penalties, staff time and the like;

b.   PROVIDED, that if it is determined for any reason said failure to perform is without the Contractor's control, fault, or negligence, the termination shall be deemed to be a Termination for Convenience; and

c.   FURTHER PROVIDED, that this provision shall not apply to any Contractor failures to perform that result from the negligent acts or omissions of the Customer.

d.   The rights and remedies of the Customer provided above shall not be exclusive and are in addition to any other rights and remedies provided by law or under this Contract.

40.2 Termination for Convenience

a.   Except as otherwise provided in this Contract, the Customer may,

1) By fourteen (14) days written notice, beginning on the second day after the mailing,

2) Terminate this Contract, in whole or in part, when it is in the best interest of the Customer.

Invocations of the Non-Allocation of Funds Clause are deemed Terminations for Convenience.

b.   If this Contract is so terminated, the Customer is only liable for payment:

1) Required by the terms of this Contract, for

2) Equipment or software delivered and accepted or services rendered prior to the effective date of termination.

40.3 Termination Procedure

Unless otherwise provided by installment purchase or financing Terms and Conditions herein, upon termination of this Contract:

a.   The Customer, in addition to any other rights provided in this Contract, shall require the Contractor to deliver to the Customer all Equipment, software, or services accepted prior to the effective date of termination by the Customer for performance of such part of this Contract as has been terminated;

b.   Unless otherwise provided herein, the Customer shall pay to the Contractor the agreed-upon price, if separately stated, for the Equipment, software, or services accepted by the Customer and the amount agreed upon by the Contractor and the Customer for:

1) Completed services for which no separate price is stated,

2) Partially completed services,

3) Other Equipment, software, or services which are accepted by the Customer and

4) The protection and preservation of property, unless the termination is for default in which case the Customer shall determine the extent of liability;

c.   Under conditions of termination or cancellation by the Customer for default,

1) Subject to a finding of fact by the Dispute Arbitration Panel, convened as set forth in the disputes clause herein, that:

a) The Contractor did not, in good faith, effect a cure or remedy for a failure to perform, non-performance, poor performance, or constructive non-conformance hereunder, or

b) The Customer has other cause of action against the Contractor for a breach hereof wherein the Customer does not waive said breach, and

c) Further resolution requires a decision on a question of law beyond the authority of said panel;

2) The Customer may withhold thereafter from any amounts due the Contractor for such Equipment, software, or services such sum as the Customer determines to be necessary to protect the Customer against loss or liability and to make a reasonable effort to mitigate damages sustained;

d.   The rights and remedies of the Customer provided in this clause shall not be exclusive and are in addition to any other rights and remedies provided by law or under this Contract; and

e. After receipt of a notice of termination, and except as otherwise directed by the Customer, the Contractor shall:

1) Stop work under this Contract on the date, and to the extent specified, in the notice;

2) Place no further orders or subcontracts for materials, services, or facilities except as may be necessary for completion of such portion of this Contract as is not terminated;

3) Assign to the Customer, in the manner, at the times, and to the extent directed by the Customer, all the rights, titles, and interest of the Contractor under the orders and subcontracts so terminated, except for those orders and subcontracts for which the Customer has paid the Contractor and the Contractor has not paid the subcontractor, in which case the Customer has the right, at its discretion, to settle or pay any or all claims arising out of the termination of such orders and subcontracts;

4) Settle all outstanding liabilities and all claims arising out of such termination of orders and subcontracts with the approval or ratification of the Customer to the extent required which approval or ratification shall be final for the purpose of this clause;

5) Transfer title to the Customer and deliver in the manner, at the time, and to the extent, if any, as directed by the Customer any property accepted by the Customer which, if the Contract had been completed would have been required to be furnished to the Customer;

6) Complete performance of such part of this Contract as shall not have been terminated by the Customer;

7) Take such action as may be necessary, or as the Customer may direct, for the protection and preservation of the property related to this Contract which is in the possession of the Contractor and in which the Customer has or may acquire an interest; and

8) Provide written certification to the Customer that the Contractor has surrendered to the Customer all said property.

41 Training:

(Used in Contracts: All)

(Comments: To establish any provisions and Contractor responsibilities for training on Equipment or software.)

(It is the responsibility of the agency to ensure that any training offered or promised is included in the contract.)

42 Transportation:

(Used in Contracts: EP EL IP/LP)

(Comments: To establish responsibility for cost of transportation, transit insurance, risk of loss, and title of Equipment during shipment to the installation site.)

The Contractor shall ship all Equipment leased or purchased pursuant to this Agreement, prepaid, FOB Destination. Upon receipt of properly completed freight bills, the Customer shall reimburse the Contractor for transportation costs. The method of shipment shall be consistent with the nature of the Equipment and the hazards of transportation.

D. PURCHASE ORDER SHORT FORM TERMS AND CONDITIONS:

The Purchase Order Short Form Terms and Conditions are intended for use with State or agency purchase orders.

1 Standard Terms and Conditions, Request for Quotation, Purchase & Field Order Contracts:

(Used in Contracts: SF)

(Comments: Standard Disclaimer and heading for Short Form Purchase Order—includes by reference Washington Law and DIS RCW 43.105 acquisition policy and procedure.)

This purchase order contract includes the following Terms and Conditions and includes, but is not limited to the Request For Quotations, specifications, plans and published Policy and Procedures of the Department of Information Services under RCW 43.105 and the Laws of the State of Washington, which are hereby incorporated by reference.

2 Acceptance:

(Used in Contracts: SF)

(Comments: Integration clause-rejects vendor clauses without prior concurrence in writing.)

This order expressly limits acceptance to the Terms and Conditions stated herein, all additional or different terms proposed by vendor are objected to and hereby rejected, unless otherwise provided in writing by the customer.

3 Anti-trust:

(Used in Contracts: SF)

(Comments: Assigns any overcharges due to anti-trust activity to Purchaser.)

Vendor and Purchaser recognize that in actual economic practice, overcharges resulting from antitrust violations are in fact borne by the Purchaser. Therefore, Vendor hereby assigns to Purchaser any and all claims for such overcharges.

4 Assignments:

(Used in Contracts: SF)

(Comments: Requires prior permission for assignment of proceeds due vendor.)

The provisions or monies due under this order shall only be assignable with prior written consent of Purchaser.

5 Brands:

(Used in Contracts: SF)

(Comments: Provides for Purchaser inspection of alternate products prior to acceptance.)

Special brands, when named, are to indicate the standard or quality, performance, or use desired. Bids on Vendor's equal will be considered provided Vendor specifies brand, model, and the necessary descriptive literature. In the event Purchaser elects to contract for an alternate purported to be an equal by the bidder, the acceptance of the item will be conditioned on Purchaser's inspection and testing after receipt. If, in the sole judgment of Purchaser, the item is determined not to be an equal, the material shall be returned at the Vendor's expense and this order terminated.

6 Changes:

(Used in Contracts: SF)

(Comments: Requires prior written consent to change purchase order conditions.)

No alteration in any of the terms, conditions, delivery, price, quality, quantities, or specifications of orders under this Agreement will be effective without prior written consent of Purchaser.

7 Default and Governing Law:

(Used in Contracts: SF)

(Comments: Combines recovery of attorney fees and governing law in Washington.)

The Vendor covenants and agrees that the Laws of the State of Washington shall govern this order, and in the event suit is instituted by Purchaser for any default on the part of the Vendor, and the Vendor is adjudged by a court of competent jurisdiction to be in default, it shall pay to Purchaser all costs, expenses expended or incurred by Purchaser in connection therewith, and reasonable attorney's fees. The Vendor agrees that the Superior Court of the State of Washington shall have jurisdiction over any such suit, and that venue shall be laid in the County in which the Purchaser's principal offices are located.

8 Delivery:

(Used in Contracts: SF)

(Comments: Establishes that timeliness is of the essence, and makes order subject to termination for late performance.)

For any exception to the delivery date specified on this order, Vendor shall give prior notification and obtain written approval thereto from the Purchaser. With respect to delivery under the order, time is of the essence and the purchase order is subject to termination for failure to deliver on time.

9 Handling:

(Used in Contracts: SF)

(Comments: Prohibits handling charges, unless specified in the order.)

No charges will be allowed for handling, which includes, but is not limited to packing, wrapping, bags, containers, or reels, unless otherwise stated herein.

10 Identification:

(Used in Contracts: SF)

(Comments: Instructions on including purchase order number in shipments, packages, invoices, etc.)

All invoices, packing lists, packages, shipping notices, instruction manuals, and other written documents affecting this order shall contain the applicable purchase order number. Packing lists shall be enclosed in each and every box or package shipped pursuant to this order, indicating the content thereof.

11 Infringements:

(Used in Contracts: SF)

(Comments: Indemnifies Purchaser against patent and copyright, trade secret, or franchising violations on part of the Vendor)

Vendor agrees to protect and save harmless Purchaser against all claims, suits, or proceedings for patent, trademark, copyright, or franchising infringement arising from the purchase, installation, or use of goods and materials ordered, and to assume all expenses and damages arising from such claims, suits, or proceedings.

12 Liens, Claims and Encumbrances:

(Used in Contracts: SF)

(Comments: Assures Purchaser that items are free and clear.)

Vendor warrants and represents that all the goods and materials supplied hereunder are free and clear of all liens, claims, or encumbrances of any kind.

13 Non-waiver by Acceptance of Variation:

(Used in Contracts: SF)

(Comments: Assures that waiver of one term does not waiver other contract terms.)

No provision of this order, or the right to receive seasonable performance of any act called for by the terms shall be deemed waived by a waiver by Purchaser of a breach thereof as to any particular transaction or occurrence.

14 Nondiscrimination and Affirmative Action:

(Used in Contracts: All)

(Comments: Commits Vendor to affirmative action.)

The Contractor agrees not to discriminate against and to take affirmative action to ensure equality of treatment for any client, employee, or applicant for employment or services because of age, race, color, religion, sex, ancestry, national origin, marital status, Vietnam era or disabled veteran status, or the presence of any mental, physical or sensory handicap with regard to but not limited to, the following: employment, upgrading, demotion, or transfer; recruitment or recruitment advertising; layoffs or termination; rates of pay or other forms of compensation; and selection for training, including apprenticeships and volunteers. A vendor in violation of this clause or any applicable affirmative action program may become subject to other penalties as elsewhere provided in Washington State Law.

15 Off-Shore Items:

(Used in Contracts: SF)

(Comments: Off-shore reporting requirement.)

In accordance with Chapter 39.25 RCW, upon completion of this order, Vendor shall furnish a certified statement setting forth the nature and source of off-shore items in excess of $2,500 which have been utilized in the performance of this order.

16 Payments, Cash Discount, Late Payment Charges:

(Used in Contracts: SF)

(Comments: Provides for no advance payment, discounts, and thirty day payment period.)

Invoices will not be processed for payment nor will the period of computation for cash discount commence until receipt of a properly completed invoice or invoiced items are received, whichever is later. If an adjustment in payment is necessary due to damage or dispute, the cash discount period shall commence on the date final approval for payment is authorized. If a discount is made available for this order, but the invoice does not reflect the existence of a cash discount, Purchaser is entitled to a cash discount with the period commencing on the date it is determined by Purchaser that a cash discount applies. Under Chapter 68, Laws of 1981, if Purchaser fails to make timely payment, Vendor may invoice for one percent per month on the amount overdue, or a minimum of one dollar. Payment shall not be considered late if a check or warrant is available or mailed within the time specified, or if no terms are specified, within thirty days. Normally payments to vendors will be remitted by mail. The Purchaser shall not honor drafts, nor accept goods on a sight draft basis.

17 Prices and Price Warranty for Commercial Items:

(Used in Contracts: SF)

(Comments: Combines Price Protection Clause and Price Warranty - or "most favored nation" clause.)

If price is not stated on this order, it is agreed that the goods shall be billed at the price last quoted or paid, or the prevailing market price, whichever is lower. Vendor warrants that prices charged to Purchaser are based on Vendor's current catalog or market prices of commercial items sold in substantial quantities to the general public and prices charged do not exceed those charged by Vendor to other Customers purchasing the same item in like or comparable quantities.

18 Rejection:

(Used in Contracts: SF)

(Comments: Reserves purchaser's right to inspect and reject goods and material for nonconformity to the order and sets a time limit of two weeks on purchaser's rejection.)

All goods or materials purchased herein are subject to approval by Purchaser. Any rejection of goods because of nonconformity to the terms and specifications of this order, whether held by Purchaser, or returned, will be at Vendor's risk and expense, PROVIDED, that Purchaser has notified Vendor of such rejection within a two week period following receipt, or the goods will be deemed to have been accepted by Purchaser. Purchaser shall have no obligation to pay for goods which have been timely rejected.

19 Risk of Loss:

(Used in Contracts: SF)

(Comments: Gives vendor risk of loss during shipment.)

Regardless of FOB Point, Vendor agrees to bear all risks of loss, injury, or destruction of goods and materials ordered herein which occur prior to delivery; and such loss, injury, or destruction shall not release Vendor from any obligation hereunder.

20 Safety and Health Requirements:

(Used in Contracts: SF)

(Comments: Commits vendor to OSHA/WISHA.)

Vendor agrees to comply with the conditions of the Federal Occupational Safety and Health Act of 1970 (OSHA), the Washington Industrial Safety and Health Act of 1973 (WISHA), and the standards and regulations issued thereunder and certifies that all items furnished and purchased under this order will conform to and comply with said standards and regulations. Vendor further agrees to indemnify and hold harmless Purchaser from all damages assessed against purchaser as a result of Vendor's failure to comply with the Acts and the standards issued thereunder and for failure of the items furnished under this order to so comply.

21 Save Harmless:

(Used in Contracts: SF)

(Comments: Indemnification clause protecting Purchaser from person or property damage due to vendor acts or omissions.)

Vendor shall protect, indemnify, and save Purchaser harmless from and against any damage, cost, or liability for any injuries to persons or property arising from acts or omissions of Vendor, its employees, agents, or subcontractors, howsoever caused.

22 Shipping Instructions:

(Used in Contracts: SF)

(Comments: Provides standard shipping instructions.)

Unless otherwise specified, all goods are to be shipped prepaid, FOB Destination. Where shipping addresses indicate room numbers, the Vendor shall make delivery to that location at no additional charge. Where specific authorization is granted to ship goods FOB Shipping Point, Vendor agrees to prepay all shipping charges, route as instructed or if instructions are not provided, route by cheapest common carrier, and to bill Purchaser as a separate item on the invoice for said charges, less federal transportation tax. Each invoice for shipping charges shall contain the original or a copy of the bill indicating that the payment for shipping has been made. It is also agreed that Purchaser reserves the right to refuse COD shipments.

23 Taxes:

(Used in Contracts: SF)

(Comments: Standard tax language, incorporating federal exemption if required.)

Unless otherwise indicated, Purchaser agrees to pay all State of Washington sales or use tax. No charge by Vendor shall be made for federal excise taxes, and Purchaser agrees to furnish Vendor, upon acceptance of goods or materials supplied under this order, with an exemption certificate.

24 Termination:

(Used in Contracts: SF)

(Comments: Provides for termination on notice upon vendor breach.)

In the event of a breach by Vendor of any of the provisions of this order, Purchaser reserves the right to cancel and terminate this order forthwith upon giving oral or written notice to vendor. Vendor shall be liable for damages suffered by Purchaser resulting from Vendor's breach of contract.

25 Warranties:

(Used in Contracts: SF)

(Comments: Vendor warrants conformance to ordinary use, provides for fitness for purpose, when appropriate.)

Vendor warrants that goods and materials supplied under this order conform to specifications herein and are fit for the purpose for which such goods and materials are ordinarily employed; except if a particular purpose is stated, the goods and materials must then be fit for that particular purpose. Vendor and Purchaser agree that this order does not exclude, or in any way limit, other warranties provided for in this agreement or by law.

DOCUMENT 9

Model Request for Proposal, BC Systems Corp.

XX January 1995

Summary of Key Information

- Request For Proposal Definition:

An RFP defines the situation or objective for which the goods and or services are required, how they are expected to be used and/or problems that they are expected to address. Vendors are invited to propose solutions that will result in the satisfaction of the purchaser's objectives in a cost effective manner. The proposed solutions are evaluated against a predetermined set of criteria of which price may not be the primary consideration.

- Closing date for this RFP#00000 is 00 January, 1995 at 2:00 p.m. local time.

- Send three copies of each proposal.

- Please use the above RFP number on all correspondence.

- For further information contact:

Purchasing Manager

BC Systems Corporation

4000 Seymour Place, Victoria, BC   V8X 4S8

- Information offered from sources other than the above is not official and may be inaccurate.
- This RFP is in two parts:

Part A - Administrative Section

Part B - Requirements Section

Table of Contents

Part A - Administrative Section

Introduction

Corporate Mission

BC Systems' mission, primarily in BC, is to provide information technology solutions which assist public sector organizations in B.C. to maintain and fundamentally improve the quality of service to the public.

British Columbia Systems Corporation Overview

The British Columbia Systems Corporation was formed in 1977 as a Provincial Crown Corporation under the System Act (Bill 44). The Corporation's mission is to provide information technology solutions which assist public sector organizations in B.C. to maintain and fundamentally improve the quality of service to the public. We are driven first by our customer's needs and second by technology. We capitalize on the excellence of our people, data centers, networks, and on B.C. companies. We focus on innovations that make a real difference and aim to be the major player in developing the best possible information management infrastructure for British Columbia.

The main shared computer processing complex at 4000 Seymour Place in Victoria provides a leading-edge, highly reliable, low-risk source of computing power for customers across the province. We provide highly reliable, secure data processing and telecommunications services. The use of shared processing frees our customers from the concerns of acquiring, maintaining, supporting and upgrading complex equipment of their own.

The Corporations telecommunications services include both data and voice networks. Through telecommunications, we link over 100 cities and towns throughout the province, with over 35,000 telephone locations, more than 27,000 network connected devices and over 60,000 data processing users.

Professional services are a major part of our business as well. Over 400 highly skilled professionals provide computer systems management and technical expertise at customer locations.

BC Systems is an equal opportunity/equity employer and recognition would be given to bidders who similarly give priority to employment equity.

RFP Terminology

Generally, throughout this RFP the following terminology is used:

• "Mandatory" - a requirement that must be met in a substantially unaltered form. The terms "must", "required" and "will" are also used to indicate mandatory requirements.

• "Desirable" - a requirement has a high degree of importance to the objectives of this RFP. The term "should" also indicates a desirable requirement.

• "Optional" - a requirement that is not considered essential, but for which evaluation credit may be given. The terms "may", and "can" also indicate optional requirements.

Proposal Preparation and Submission

All submissions must conform to the Vendor Response Format and all the Requirements as outlined in Part B "Requirements Section". Bidders are cautioned to read the requirements carefully and follow the response format of this Request for Proposal as any deviation from the format and requirements listed, may be cause for rejection.

Receipt Confirmation Form

Upon receipt, fill out the attached Receipt Confirmation Form (Appendix A) and fax it to the Corporation. All subsequent information regarding this RFP will be directed only to those who return the form with an indication that they intend to submit a proposal

Bidders Meeting

Details regarding a bidders meeting are defined in Part B (Requirements Section).

Closing Date

Three complete copies of each proposal must be received at 4000 Seymour Place, Victoria, British Columbia by 2:00 PM, local time on the date specified in the Summary of Key Information, Appendix B. Addressed to:

Manager, Administration and Procurement Services

Contract Section, British Columbia Systems Corporation

4000 Seymour Place , Victoria, B.C. V8X 4S8

Telephone: (604) 389-3519 · Fax: (604) 360-7007

Proposals should be clearly marked with the name and address of the bidder and the RFP number on the envelope.

Format of Proposal

All three copies of the bidder's proposal should be arranged as follows:

Title Page: showing RFP number, closing date and time, bidder name, address, telephone number, and contact person.

Letter of introduction: one page, introducing the company and signed by the person(s) authorized to sign on behalf of, and bind the company to, statements made in response to this RFP.

Company Profile and Vendor Information: addressing the Company Profile and Vendor Information points documented in Part B, Requirements Section.

Detailed Response: addressing each of the items listed under Evaluation Criteria detailed in Part B, Requirements Section.

Bidders must conform to instructions given regarding proposal requirements as detailed in Part B, Requirements Section.

Mandatory Requirements

Part B of this RFP includes mandatory requirements. Proposals must meet all mandatory requirements.

Terms and Conditions

Inquiries

All inquiries related to this request for proposal are to be in writing to the Corporation as noted on the Summary of Key Information. Information obtained from any other source is not official and may be inaccurate. Do not contact any other person involved. Inquiries and responses will be recorded and may be distributed to all bidders at the Corporation's option.

Notification of Changes

All recipients of this request for proposal who have returned the Receipt Confirmation Form will be notified regarding any changes made to this document.

Changes to Proposal Wording

No changes to wording of the proposal will be accepted after submission unless requested by the Corporation.

Funding

All Corporation capital expenditures are subject to both Executive and Board approval. Therefore, the Corporation reserves the right to discontinue the RFP process if funding is not available.

Ownership of Proposals

All responses to this request for proposal become the property of the Corporation.

Bidders Expenses

Prospective bidders are solely responsible for their own expenses in preparing a proposal and subsequent negotiations with the Corporation, if any.

Contract Solution

The Corporation reserves the right to award a contract in part or in full, or not at all, on the basis of responses received.

Acceptance of Proposals

This RFP should not be construed as a contract to purchase goods or services. The Corporation is not bound to accept the lowest price or any proposal of those submitted.

Liability of Errors

While the Corporation has used considerable efforts to ensure an accurate representation of information in this RFP, all prospective bidders are urged to conduct their own investigations into the material facts and the Corporation shall not be held liable or accountable for any error or omission in any part of this RFP.

Acceptance of Terms

All the terms and conditions of this RFP are deemed to be accepted by the bidder and incorporated in its proposal, except those conditions and provisions which are expressly excluded by the proposal.

Quotes From The Marketplace

The Corporation reserves the right to consider quotes from the marketplace from suppliers other than those invited to respond to this competition.

Payment Holdback

The Corporation will hold back a percentage of the total contract price until the requirements outlined in this RFP have been met. The holdback amount will be decided as part of the contract negotiations, or as specified in the RFP.

Financial Stability

The successful bidder must demonstrate financial stability and any successful bidder who carries on business in British Columbia shall be registered to conduct business in British Columbia.

Negotiation Delay

If any contract cannot be negotiated within thirty (30) days of notification to the designated bidder, the Corporation may terminate negotiations with that bidder and negotiate a contract agreement with another bidder of its choice.

Shortlist

Unless there is a successful bidder based on the responses, the evaluation procedure will be to develop a shortlist based on the stated criteria. The shortlisted bidders may be asked to prepare a presentation and/or provide additional information prior to the final selection.

Debriefing

Upon written request from an unsuccessful bidder, the Manager of Contracts and Purchasing will arrange for a debriefing session. The debriefing is not to be seen as an opportunity to challenge the decision. Once debriefing ends, the RFP process is finished and the RFP will not be discussed further with the bidder at any time.

Electrical Safety

All equipment must be CSA certified or Electrical Safety Branch approved for use intended and must be so labeled prior to delivery or installation. All costs of approval to be at the bidder's expense.

Department of Communications Approval

Any device that will be attached to a communication line must have Department of Communications approval.

Subcontracting

Utilizing a subcontractor (who must be clearly identified) to remedy deficiencies in the prime bidder's product or service is acceptable. This also includes a joint submission by two bidders having no formal corporate links. However, in this case, one of these bidders must be prepared to take overall responsibility for successful interconnection of the two product/service lines and this must be defined in the proposal. Subcontracting to any firm or individual involved in the preparation of this RFP will not be permitted.

Definition of Contract

The Corporation may at its option notify a bidder in writing that its bid has been accepted and such acceptance shall at the Corporations option constitute the making of a formal contract for the services as set out in the bid. Alternatively, the subsequent full execution of a written contract shall constitute the making of a contract for services, and no bidder shall acquire any legal or equitable rights or privileges whatever relative to the services until the Corporation has delivered either a signed notice in writing to the bidder or a fully executed written agreement to the bidder.

Labour Disruptions

Any contract resulting from this Request For Proposal process is subject to the right of the Corporation to postpone acceptance of delivery and payment by the Corporation in the event of any form of labour disruption.

Contract Administrator

A contract administrator will be assigned to oversee the contract awarded to the successful bidder. In addition, the successful bidder will be expected to name a counterpart project manager. The bidder project manager will be responsible for providing scheduled status reports to the contract administrator or his designate.

Compliance With Laws

The contractor shall give all notices and obtain all the licenses and permits required to perform the work. The Contractor shall comply with all the laws applicable to the work or the performance of the contract.

Governing Law

This RFP and any contract entered into between the bidder and the Corporation shall be governed by and in accordance with the laws of the Province of British Columbia.

Confidentiality and Security

This document, or any portion thereof, may not be used for any purpose other than the submission of proposals.

The successful bidder must agree to maintain security standards consistent with security policy of the Corporation. These include strict control of access to data and maintaining confidentiality of information gained while carrying out their duties. The successful bidder will be required to ensure that all personnel employed on the contract, who require access to BC Systems information or facilities, meet the criteria for personal security clearance prescribed by BC Systems.

Suppliers should be aware that pertinent facts relating to their proposals (excluding trade secrets or proprietary information) could potentially be released as soon as 60 days after the selection of the successful supplier.

BC Systems is subject to British Columbia's Freedom of Information and Protection of Privacy Legislation (FOI). Should your submission, to this Request For Proposal, contain "trade secrets", or other information that the disclosure of which could reasonably be expected to be harmful to business interests (Section 23), you must ensure that such information is clearly identified and marked as such. Identification must be specific by item or paragraph.

Marked information will be treated as Confidential Third Party Information. Should marked information be the subject of a request under FOI you may be requested either to consent to the request, or make representation explaining why the information should not be disclosed.

Unpublished information pertaining to the Corporation or its customers obtained by the bidder as a result of participation in this project is confidential and must not be disclosed without written authorization from the Corporation.

General

Subsequent to the submission of proposals, interviews and negotiations may be conducted with some of the bidders, but there shall be no obligation to receive further information, from any bidder.

Any or all proposals shall not necessarily be accepted. The Corporation shall not be obligated in any manner to any bidder whatsoever until a written agreement has been duly executed relating to an approved proposal. The Corporation reserves the right to modify the terms of the RFP at any time in its sole discretion.

Neither acceptance of a proposal nor execution of an agreement shall constitute approval of any activity or development contemplated in any proposal that requires any approval, permit or license pursuant to any federal, provincial, regional district or municipal statute, regulation or by-law.

Pricing

Firm Pricing

Prices quoted in the proposals shall be firm for a period of at least 90 days after the submission deadline.

Currency and Taxes

Prices are to be in Canadian dollars, duty and delivery FOB destination included. Provincial Sales Tax, if applicable must be shown as extra (excluded).

GST Certification

This is to certify that the property and/or services ordered/purchased hereby are for the use of, and are being purchased by the Province of British Columbia, with crown funds, and are therefore not subject to the Goods and Services Tax.

Payment Terms

The Corporation standard payment term is 30 days upon receipt of invoice after services are performed or goods delivered.

Volumes

Prices quoted should reflect the possibility of supplying one or more units to offices at various locations in the province. Guaranteed volume cannot be established to form the basis for discount structures.

Discounts

Prices are requested on nationally published suggested list prices less a fixed percentage discount. The discount may or may not vary between models offered, but must be effective for a minimum of one year after award of contract.

Part B - Requirements Section

Purpose and Scope

Purpose

The purpose of this RFP is to inform the private sector of a potential business opportunity to provide

_____

to the BC Systems Corporation, herein referred to as "the Corporation." Depending on the proposals offered in response to this RFP, one or more contract(s) may be negotiated with bidder(s).

The Corporation anticipates the selection will be completed by _____, 1995.

Requirement Definitions

**** This section is where you identify your requirements. ****

• Indicate what the vendor needs to know about the overall approach you have selected for the project/purchase.

• Narrative of general goals and objectives of the project

• Scope and size of project

• Mandatory requirements

- Outline your requirements in respect of:

  -workplan, resource requirements, deliverables

  -maintenance/enhancement

  -development methodology

  -programming standards

       -experience/past performance/qualifications/capabilities

        expected

  -project management plan

  -progress reporting and meetings

  -structure of project team

Evaluation Criteria

Objective performance standards must be set out in the RFP's inception. The following criteria are examples to be considered when setting out RFP evaluation standards.

- Methodology

- Bidder business and technical reputation

- Financial Stability

- Delivery performance

- Service, including guarantees and warranties

- Pricing (including shipping costs, warranty, etc.)

- Return on investment

- Quality of proposal

- Project team experience.

Bidders meeting

**** You may use either paragraph depending on whether or not a bidders meeting is required. ****

There is no bidders meeting planned for this RFP. Questions relating to this RFP should be directed to the RFP Administrator either by phone, or fax if a written response is required.

A bidders meeting will be held at the time and in the location specified on the Summary Of Key Information. Attendance may or may not be mandatory. A transcript of the questions and answers will be distributed, courier collect, to all attendees and bidders who have returned the Receipt Confirmation Form. Verbal questions will be allowed at the bidders meeting. However, questions of a complex nature, or questions where the bidder requires anonymity, should be forwarded in writing to the Corporation prior to the meeting.

**** If you require a professional recorder to take notes and prepare a transcript, please notify the Contact the Department a week in advance. ****

Vendor Response Format For Pricing and Value-Added Information

The vendor will provide prices (in Canadian dollars) for the items listed below. It is important that vendors outline features of their proposal, such as value-added product(s) and/or service(s), that would not normally be addressed in a pricing evaluation as they are of a non-monetary nature. Indicate volume discount levels if they apply to your product(s). If your organization has a lease or purchase option, or a Cost of Purchase Agreement, explain the terms fully. Where a software license is dependent on certain CPU model groups, and/or number of users, provide a table that explains the situation fully.

Detailed Costs

**** How do you want the Vendor to Quote ****

_ price to quote

_ time and materials

_ list price, discounts

_ purchase, rental or lease arrange

_ options priced separately

_ service, parts and supply

_ per diem/weekly/monthly usually with a "cap"

_ delivery installation, start up

Value-Added Considerations

Describe the relevant services or products that will be provided to the Corporation which are not priced in this proposal, but which enhance the acquisition process.

Company Profile and Vendor Information

• Company Overview.

- Brief (one or two paragraphs). Description of the vendor's business, its history and future plans.

• Vendor Identification

– Corporate name (in British Columbia, Canada and the USA)

- Corporate address (both regional and headquarters)

- Telephone numbers

- Contact person(s)

•   Vendor Size

- If you become a successful vendor you will be asked to provide Corporate financial statements for the most recent financial year-end (if your company is multinational, provide statements for operations and consolidated statements for the parent Corporation)

    - Number of branches and their locations

    - Number of employees

    - Number of support locations in Canada

•   Vendor Stability

- Number of years in business

- Financial viability

- Growth of company over the last five years (revenue, sales, before tax profit)

- Support Staff availability on Vancouver Island (list people, position and location)

Appendix A Receipt Confirmation Form

Re: Request for Proposal for _____ Reference #_____

Please complete and return this confirmation form within 5 working days to:

Manager, Administration and Procurement Services, Contract Section

British Columbia Systems Corporation

4000 Seymour Place, Victoria, B.C. V8X 4S8

Tele. (604) 389-3519   Fax: (604) 360-7007

Failure to return this form may result in no further communication regarding this RFP.

Company Name: _____

Address: _____

City: _____ Postal Code _____

Contact Person: _____

Phone Number: _____ Fax Number: _____

I have received a copy of the above noted RFP.

_____ We will be submitting a proposal

_____ We will not be submitting a proposal

I authorize BC Systems Corporation to send further correspondence that the Corporation deems to be of an urgent nature by the following method:

Courier Collect _____ Mail _____

Signature:_____

Title :_____

If a bidders meeting has been arranged for this RFP, please indicate if you plan to attend: Yes   No

Appendix B - Summary of Key Information

1.   Bidders meeting: _____

2.   Closing date for bidder response:_____, 1995 at 2:00 p.m. local time. Send three complete copies of each proposal.

3.   Interested bidders are advised to fax the enclosed receipt confirmation form (Appendix A) immediately to ensure that they receive further information with regard to this RFP.

4.   Responses to this RFP, and inquiries concerning the RFP process and contractual conditions should be addressed to:

Manager, Administration and Procurement Services, Contract   Section

Reference Number _____

British Columbia Systems Corporation

4000 Seymour Place, Victoria, B.C. V8X 4S8

Tele: (604) 389-3519 · Fax: (604) 360-7007

5.   For further information contact:

Contracts Section

BC Systems Corporation

4000 Seymour Place , Victoria, B.C. V8X 4S8

Tele: (604)389-3807 · Fax: (604)360-7007

Information offered from sources other than the above is not official and may be inaccurate. Do not contact any other Ministries or agencies involved in this RFP.

6.   This RFP is in two parts:

Part A - Administrative Section

Part B - Requirements Section

DOCUMENT 10

Evaluators' Handbook

EVALUATORS HANDBOOK

for the

Electronic Integrated Resource Package

(RFP 46789)

Table of Contents

Page

I. PRINCIPLES

Principle #1

The evaluation process as stated in the RFP cannot be changed.

All proposals will be evaluated by an Evaluation Committee made up of qualified personnel.

Principle #2

Reasonable steps must be taken to eliminate personal biases and differences in individual's style.

Individuals will only evaluate those sections of the proposals which are within the experience and competence of the person. For example, only a financial person will construct and evaluate the life cycle total cost, with assistance from individuals with direct experience in identifying project and life cycle costs. Only a person with intimate knowledge of communications protocols will evaluate the technical merit of a proposed communications strategy. The chair will assign sections of the proposals to each committee member. Each evaluator will perform the identical evaluation on all eligible proposals.

Principle #3

Only information provided with a proposal can be used to evaluate that proposal.

If a company omits a section, or fails to answer a key question, you cannot permit the company to submit new (missing) information.

If a company provides an unclear response, evaluators can seek clarification through the chair of the Evaluation Committee. For example, suppose a supplier proposes to provide a fixed price cost of development for one sub-system and, in a different part of the proposal, indicates that network charges from BC Systems Corp. will be re-billed at cost. It is reasonable in this situation to contact the supplier to clarify this apparent contradiction. Are network charges included in the development cost or in addition to the fixed-cost?

Evaluators cannot seek major new pieces of information which would *materially improve* the proposal. For example, suppose a supplier provides a project plan but with only 4 milestones. You cannot go back to the supplier and indicate that the plan was inadequate and a new, more detailed plan, one with at least 100 milestones must be prepared. If you do this, you must provide all suppliers with the same opportunity. To do this requires that the RFP be re-issued and the submission dates extended.

The evaluation phase will consist of 2 distinct parts:

1. The written response to this RFP;

2. The oral interview.

The Committee will evaluate and numerically score each proposal in accordance with the evaluation criteria described in this section. The purpose of the Evaluation Committee is to assist the chair to reach a decision as to the recommended short-list. Each member of the evaluation committee will be provided with those sections of the proposals to be evaluated, and evaluation sheets. Prior to the evaluation meeting, each member will review the proposals making notes. The scores will be established at the committee meeting by a process of discussion among those responsible for each section.

The Chair of the Committee will submit its results to the Project Authority for review and approval.

Upon completing the evaluation of the submitted proposals, a point total will be calculated for each. Those vendors submitting the highest rated proposals will be scheduled for oral interviews. At the end of the Oral Interview phase, the evaluation of each proposal/vendor will be completed.

The number of vendors invited to attend a presentation will depend on the results of the first step in the evaluation process. The Chair of the Evaluation Committee will provide a list of recommended vendors and reasons to the Project Authority for consideration.

Principle #4

The Evaluation Committee will document all decisions and make these a part of the contract file.

Under the Freedom of Information and Privacy Act, ANY information may be requested by suppliers. Assume that all written material will be subject to public scrutiny.

Principle #5

Each evaluation step shall be performed independent of the others by appropriately qualified individuals.

II. STEPS IN THE PROCESS

Before Starting

1.   Review and approval of the evaluation procedure by the Steering Committee.

2.   Briefing of the evaluation committee (including the financial analyst) by Procurement Officer. Briefing will review the"do's and dont's" and walk through the process.

3.   Identification of specific sections by the Project Director for evaluation by each member of Evaluation Committee.

4.   Release of the proposals by Contract Office to the Project Director.

When Proposals Are Released

5.   Project Administrator to verify and note the contents of each package; copy sections as required;

deliver appropriate sections to Evaluation Committee members, financial analyst, and Procurement Officer.

6. Project Administrator to provide evaluators with guidelines and worksheets as required.

7. Evaluators to review proposals and perform preliminary analysis.

The Formal Evaluation

8. Meeting of evaluation committee.

9. Meeting of Finance group to review costs.

10. Combining of results of steps 8 and 9 by Project Director. Identify those firms which scored highest on the combined scores.

11. Formulation of recommendation and presentation to Project Authority. Invitation to selected suppliers to attend presentations and notification to them of the agenda.

12. Supplier presentations. Finalization of recommendation. Formal presentation and documentation of recommendation to Steering Committee.

Finishing the RFP Process

13. Resolution of any major contract issues which could, potentially, disqualify the supplier.

14. Signing of contract.

15. Notification of all other suppliers.

16. Scheduling and organizing of debriefing sessions.

17. Report by Procurement Officer to the Project Director.

III. A PROPOSED SCORING SYSTEM

Scoring System Summary	
10	Exceptional
9	
8	Exceeds Standards
7	
6	
5	Meets Standards
4	
2	
1	
0	Unacceptable

Now that we have established the complete set of tables for Step I of the evaluation, let's examine how we are going to score each item. What is deserving of a '1'? how do we determine when a subsystem is worth a '10'? how do we eliminate personal bias and take some of the arbitrariness out of scoring?

I propose that evaluators use the following rules:

1.   If a requirement (objective) is particularly difficult to meet and the proposal offers an approach which, *with little or no risk*, will yield a result which *exceeds requirements qualitatively*, the item should score "8", "9" or "10," dependent upon the level of exceptional features offered.

2.   If the requirement (objective) is relatively difficult to meet, the majority of the factors are acceptable, *no major deficiencies or risks exist therein, and the collective approach yields a qualitative benefit to the project beyond that which is minimal,* a score of "6" or "7" should be assigned, dependent upon the benefits to be attained.

3.   If the majority of the factors meet standards, the requirement is not overly difficult to meet, and the factors which are deficient are of a very minor nature or are susceptible to easy correction, the item should be scored "5". A "4" is assigned if the deficiencies are slightly more than "very minor".

The assignment of a score above "5" must reflect some qualitative achievement such as improved ease of maintenance effort through simplicity of design and use of tools.

4.   If a majority of the factors for the item are deficient and their correction, either collectively or individually, poses a serious problem in correction or has a "domino" effect on the other design features, or the approach poses a high risk without means for correction, if the approach fails, a score of "3", "2" or "1" should be assigned, with the lower score indicating a serious or severe condition.

5.   If the major factors of the item are deficient to the extent that a major reorientation of the proposal is necessary, of if the approach taken is undesirable and correction would require a major and material change in the proposal, the item should be scored "0".

Costs (20 points)

The lowest cost proposal will receive the maximum number of points allocated to cost. Points for other proposals will be allocated relative to the total cost.

Lowest Cost Proposal = _____(A)

Proposal From Supplier _____ = _____ (B)

Points awarded = (C) _____ (A/B)x100

IV. EVALUATION CATEGORIES

The evaluation process consists of three steps: written responses (consisting of 2 items), and oral interviews.

The points assigned to each step and grouping are presented below as contained in the RFP.

There are 3 different evaluation categories identified below. **To be considered for Category 3 - Oral Interview, a proponent must obtain at least 70% of the points available in each of the first two categories.**

9.1 Proposal Evaluation Categories

Evaluation of Written Responses

1.	To build the IRP and provide ongoing support	100 points
2.	To be a strategic partner	100 points
	Total Points (1 and 2 only)	200

The Oral Interview

3. Oral Interview	50
Total Possible Score	250

The evaluation process will assign scores to each factor identified above using the evaluation criteria stated in the RFP. In order to standardize the scoring, the following scoring scheme will be adopted. This will ensure a consistent assignment of numerical scores by each evaluator.

V. DETAILED EVALUATION STEPS

This section of the evaluator's handbook describes the detailed steps for establishing a score for each factor, and for completing the Master Evaluation Table.

The evaluation process assigns a score to each evaluation factor identified in the table below. The score, out of 10, is then multiplied by the Maximum Points, the weighting, to determine the Earned Points for that factor.

9.2 Explanation of the Evaluation Criteria

9.2.1. The evaluation of objective 1 - to implement a resource manager will be based on the following criteria, identified as 9.2.1 (a) through (e):

(a) Understanding of the project - 20 points

Proposals will be evaluated against the questions set out below:

(i) Has the proposer demonstrated a thorough understanding of the purpose and scope of the project?

(ii) How well has the proposer identified pertinent issues and potential problems related to the project?

(iii) Has the proposer demonstrated that it understands the deliverables the Ministry expects it to provide?

(iv) Has the proposer demonstrated that it understands the Ministry's time schedule and can meet it?

(b) Methodology Used for the Project - 20 points

Proposals will be evaluated against the questions set out below:

(i) Does the methodology depict a logical approach to fulfilling the requirements of the RFP?

(ii) Does the methodology match and contribute to achieving the objectives set out in the RFP?

(iii) Does the methodology support the time schedule in the RFP?

(c) Management Plan for the Project - 20 points

Proposals will be evaluated against the questions set out below:

(i) Does the management plan support all of the project requirements and logically lead to the deliverables required in the RFP?

(ii) Is accountability completely and clearly defined?

(iii) Is the organization of the project team clear?

(iv) Does the management plan illustrate the lines of authority and communication?

(v) To what extend does the proposer already have the hardware, equipment, software products and licenses to perform the contract?

(vi) Does it appear that the proposer can meet the schedule set out in the RFP?

(vii) Has the contractor gone beyond the minimum tasks necessary to meet the objectives of the RFP?

(viii) Is the proposal practical, feasible and within budget?

(ix) Have any potential problems been identified?

(x) Is the proposal submitted responsive to all material requirements in the RFP?

(d) Experience and Qualifications - 20 points

(i) Do the individuals assigned to the project have experience on similar projects?

(ii) Are resumes complete and do they demonstrate backgrounds that would be desirable for individuals engaged in the work the project requires?

(iii) How extensive is the applicable education and experience of the personnel designated to work on the project?

(iv) Has the firm demonstrated experience in completing similar projects on time and within budget?

(v) How successful is the general history of the firm regarding timely and successful completion of projects?

(vi) Has the firm provided letters of reference, or reference names and descriptions of previous projects

(vii) If a subcontractor is proposed, how well does it measure up to the evaluation used for the proposer?

(e) Costs (20 points)

The lowest cost proposal will receive the maximum number of points allocated to cost. Points for other proposals will be allocated relative to the total cost.

9.2.2 The evaluation of Objective 2 – To be a strategic partner – will be based on the following criteria, identified as 9.2.2 (a) through (h). (100 points)

(a) The proposers ability to identify and provide the required skills, knowledge, and people;

(b) The proposers market intelligence capabilities and how they contribute to the partnership;

(c) The proposers research and development capabilities and how they contribute to the partnership;

(d) The proposers technical depth and breadth as it relates to software products, tools available on the specified networks and its ability to apply this knowledge to the benefit of the ministry;

(e) The proposers approach to commercialization of this product and its experience with similar products. The proposers specific marketing and sales capabilities;

(f) the proposers relationship with software development organizations, software companies, and other computer industry entities;

(g) The practicality of the business plan and the associated revenue/cost generated over the five year period

(h) Proponent's partners ability to work with the education community.

9.2.3 Oral Interview (50 points)

The vendors with the highest rated proposals (as determined by the sum of the points for 9.2.1 and 9.2.2) will be permitted 2 hours in which to present their solution.

The presentation will be followed by a question and answer session. A maximum of 4 hours will be set aside for the presentation and question and answers. The session may be recorded.

Points will be awarded by the Committee for a subjective assessment of

(a) how well the total proposal meets our needs

(b) the knowledge of the vendor about problems associated with similar projects

(c) the proposed project team

Clarifications made during the interview will be included with the written proposal itself.

Rules Governing Competition, State of California

A. Identification and Classification of IFB/RFP Requirements

1. Requirements

The State has established certain requirements with respect to bids to be submitted by prospective contractors. The use of "shall," "must" or "will" (except to indicate simple futurity) in the IFB/RFP indicates a requirement or condition from which a deviation if not material may be waived by the State. A deviation from a requirement is material if the deficient response is not in substantial accord with the IFB/RFP requirements, provides an advantage to one bidder over other bidders, or has a potentially significant effect on the delivery, quantity or quality of items bid, amount paid to the vendor, or on the cost to the State. Material deviations cannot be waived.

2. Desirable Items

The words "should" or "may" in the IFB/RFP indicate desirable attributes or conditions, but are nonmandatory in nature. Deviation from, or omission of, such a desirable feature, even if material, will not in itself cause rejection of the bid.

B. Bidding Requirements and Conditions

1. General

This IFB/RFP, the evaluation of responses, and the award of any resultant contract shall be made in conformance with current competitive bidding procedures as they relate to the procurement of goods and services by public bodies in the State of California. A bidder's Final Bid is an irrevocable offer for 45 days following the scheduled date for contract award specified in Section I. A bidder may extend the offer in the event of a delay of contract award.

2. IFB/RFP Documents

This IFB/RFP includes, in addition to an explanation of the State's need which must be met, instructions which prescribe the format and content of bids to be submitted and the model(s) of the contract(s) to be executed between the State and the successful bidder(s).

If a bidder discovers any ambiguity, conflict, discrepancy, omission, or other error in the IFB/RFP, the bidder shall immediately notify the State of such error in writing and request clarification or modification of the document. Modifications will be made by addenda issued pursuant to Paragraph B-7, Addenda, below. Such clarifications shall by given by written notice to all parties who have been furnished an IFB/RFP for bidding purposes, without divulging the sources of the request for same. Insofar as practicable, the State will give such notices to other interested parties, but the State shall not be responsible therefore.

If the IFB/RFP contains an error known to the bidder, or an error that reasonably should have been known, the bidder shall bid at its own risk. If the bidder fails to notify the State of the error prior to the date fixed for submission of bids, and is awarded the contract, the bidder shall not be entitled to additional compensation or time by reason of the error or its later correction.

3. Examination of the Work

The bidder should carefully examine the entire IFB/RFP and any addenda thereto, and all related materials and data referenced in the IFB/RFP or otherwise available to the bidder, and should become fully aware of the nature and location of the work, the quantities of the work, and the conditions to be encountered in performing the work. Specific conditions to be examined may be listed in the IFB/RFP section on Administrative Requirements.

4. Questions Regarding the IFB/RFP

Bidders requiring clarification of the intent or content of this IFB/RFP or on procedural matters regarding the competitive bid process may request clarification by submitting questions, with the envelope clearly marked "Questions Relating to IFB/RFP _____" (using the IFB/RFP identification on the IFB/RFP title page), to the Department Official listed in Section I. To ensure a response, questions must be received in writing by the scheduled date(s) given in Section I. Question and answer sets will be provided to all bidders without identifying the submitters.

A bidder who desires clarification or further information on the content of the IFB/RFP, but whose questions relate to the proprietary aspect of that bidder's proposal and which, if disclosed to other bidders, would expose that bidder's proposal, may submit such questions in the same manner as above, but also marked "Confidential," and not later than the scheduled date specified in Section I to ensure a response. The bidder must explain why any questions are sensitive in nature. If the State concurs that the disclosure of the question or answer would expose the proprietary nature of the proposal, the question will be answered and both the question and answer will be kept in confidence. If the State does not concur with the proprietary aspect of the question, the question will not be answered in this manner and the bidder will be so notified.

If the bidder believes that one or more of the IFB/RFP requirements is onerous, unfair, or imposes unnecessary constraints to the bidder in proposing less costly or alternate solutions, the bidder may request a change to the IFB/RFP by submitting, in writing, the recommended change(s) and the facts substantiating this belief and reasons for making the recommended change. Such request must be submitted to the Department Official by the date specified in Section I for submitting a request for change. *Oral answers shall not be binding on the State.*

5. Bidder's Conference

A Bidder's Conference may be held, during which vendors will be afforded the opportunity to meet with State personnel and discuss the content of the IFB/RFP and the procurement process. Notification of the time and place of such conference, if held, will be made to all vendors receiving this IFB/RFP for bidding purposes. Written questions received prior to the cutoff date for submission of such questions, as noted in Section I, will be answered at the conference without divulging the source of the query.

The State may also accept oral questions during the conference and will make a reasonable attempt to provide answers prior to the conclusion of the conference. A transcript of the discussion, or those portions which contain the questions and appropriate answers, will normally be transmitted within approximately ten (10) working days to all vendors furnished this IFB/RFP for bidding purposes. If questions asked at the conference cannot be adequately answered during the discussion, answers will be provided with the transcribed data. Oral answers shall not be binding on the State.

6. Vendor's Intention to Submit a Bid

Vendors who have been furnished a copy of the IFB/RFP for bidding purposes are asked to state their intention by the date specified in Section I, Key Action Dates, with respect to submission of bids. the State is also interested as to a vendor's reasons for not submitting a bid; as, for example, requirements which cannot be met or unusual terms and conditions which arbitrarily raise costs. Vendors are asked to categorize their intent as follows:

a. Intends to submit a bid and has no problem with the IFB/RFP requirements.

b. Intends to submit a bid, but has one or more problems with the IFB/RFP requirements for reasons stated in this response.

c. Does not intend to submit a bid, for reasons stated in this response, and has no problem with the IFB/RFP requirements.

d. Does not intend to submit a bid because of one or more problems with the IFB/RFP requirements for reasons states in their response.

If vendors have indicated significant problems with the IFB/RFP requirements, the State will examine the stated reasons for the problems and will attempt to resolve any issues in contention, if not contrary to the State's interest, and will amend the IFB/RFP if appropriate. All vendors who have been furnished a copy of this IFB/RFP for bidding purposes will be advised by the State of any actions taken as a result of the vendor's responses. If after such actions, a vendor determines that the requirements of the IFB/RFP unnecessarily restrict its ability to bid, the vendor is allowed five (5) working days to submit a protest to those IFB/RFP requirements of the State's action, according to the instructions contained in Paragraph E-1 of this section.

Hereafter, for the purposes of the instructions of this IFB/RFP, all vendors who have indicated their intent to submit a Final Bid are called bidders until such time that the bidder withdraws or other facts indicate that the bidder has become nonparticipating.

7. Addenda

The State may modify the IFB/RFP prior to the date fixed for submission of Final Bids by issuance of an addendum to all parties who are participating in the bidding process at the time the addendum is issued,unless the amendments are such as to offer the opportunity for nonparticipating vendors to become participating, in which case the addendum will be sen tot all parties receiving the IFB/RFP for bidding purposes. Addenda will be numbered consecutively. If any vendor determines that an addendum unnecessarily restricts its ability to bid, the vendor is allowed five (5) working days to submit a protest to the addendum according to the instructions contained in Paragraph E-1 of this section.

8. Removal of Names from Prequalified Bidders List

The Department of General Services may remove the name of any vendor from its lists of prequalified bidders under any one or more of the following conditions:

a. A vendor does not respond by bid to three consecutive calls for bids on equipment, software, or service for which such vendor has previously requested opportunity to bid.

b. A vendor's past performance on State contacts has demonstrated a lack of reliability in complying with and completing such contracts.

9. Bonds

The State reserves the right to require a faithful performance bond or other security document as specified in the IFB/RFP from the vendor in an amount not to exceed the amount of the contract. In the event a surety bond is required by the State which has not been expressly required by the specification, the State will reimburse the vendor, as an addition to the purchase price, in an amount not exceeding the standard premium on such bond.

10. Discounts

In connection with any discount offered, except when provision is made for a testing period preceding acceptance by the State, time will be computed from date of delivery of the supplies or equipment as specified, or from date correct invoices are received in the office specified by the State if the latter date is later than the date of delivery. When provision is made for a testing period preceding acceptance by the stated date if delivery shall mean the date the supplies or equipment are accepted by the State during the specified testing period. Payment is deemed to be made, for the purpose of earning the discount, on the date of mailing the State warrant or check.

Cash discounts of less than 20 days or less than one half of one percent will not be considered in evaluating offers for award purposes unless otherwise specified by the State in the bid invitation; however, offered discounts of less than 20 days will be taken if payment is made within the discount period, even though not considered in the evaluation of offers.

11. Joint Bids

A joint bid (two or more bidders quoting jointly on one bid) may be submitted and each participating bidder must sign the joint bid. If the contract is awarded to joint bidders, it shall be one indivisible contract. Each joint bidder will be jointly and severally responsible for the performance of the entire contract, and the joint bidders must designate, in writing, one individual having authority to represent them in all matters relating to the contract. The State assumes no responsibility or obligation for the division of orders or purchases among the joint bidders.

12. Air or Water Pollution Violations

Unless the contract is less than $5,000 or with a sole source contractor, Government Code Section 4477 prohibits the State from contracting with a person, including a corporation or other business association, who had been determines to be in violation of any State or federal air or water pollution control law. Government Code Section 4481 requires the State Water Resources Control Board and the Air Resources Board to notify State agencies of such persons.

Prior to an award, the Department shall ascertain if the intended awardee is a person included in notices from the Boards by reference to notices. In the event of any doubt of the intended awardee's identity or status as a person who is in violation of any State or federal air or water pollution law, the State will notify the appropriate Board of the proposed award and afford the Board the opportunity to advise the Department that the intended awardee is such a person.

No award will be made to a person who is identified either by the published notices or by advice, as a person in violation of State or federal air or water pollution control laws.

13. Fair Employment and Housing Commission Regulations

The California Government Code Section 12990 requires all State contractors to have implemented a Nondiscrimination Program before entering into any contract with the State. The Department of Fair Employment and Housing (DFEH) randomly selects and reviews State contractors to ensure their compliance with the law. DFEH periodically disseminates a list of vendors who have not complied. Any vendor so identified is ineligible to enter into any State contract.

14. Exclusion for Conflict of Interest

No consultant shall be paid out of State funds for developing recommendations on the acquisition of EDP products or services or assisting in the preparation of a feasibility study, if that consultant is to be a source of such acquisition or could otherwise directly and/or materially benefit from State adoption of such recommendations or the course of action recommended in the feasibility study. Further, no consultant shall be paid out of State funds for developing recommendations on the disposal of State surplus EDP products, if that consultant would directly and/or materially benefit from State adopting of such recommendations.

15. Follow-on Contracts

No person, firm, or subsidiary thereof who has been awarded a consulting services contract, or a contract which includes a consulting component, may be awarded a contract for the provision of services, delivery of goods or supplies, or any other related action which is required, suggested, or otherwise appropriate as an end product of the consulting services contract. Therefore, any consultant who contracts with a State agency to develop formal recommendations for the acquisition of EDP products or services is precluded from contracting for any work recommended in the formal recommendations. (Formal recommendations include, among other things, feasibility studies.)

16. Disclosure of Financial Interests

Proposals in response to State procurements for assistance in preparation of feasibility studies or the development of recommendations for the acquisition of EDP products and services must disclose any financial interests (i.e., service contract, OEM agreements, remarketing agreements, etc.) that may forseeably allow the individual or organization submitting the proposal to materially benefit from the State's adoption of a course of section recommended in the feasibility study or the acquisition recommendations. If, in the State's judgement, the financial interest will jeopardize the objectivity of the recommendations, the State may reject the proposal.

In addition, should a consultant establish or become aware of such a financial interest during the course of contract performance, the consultant must inform the State in writing within 10 working days. If, in the State's judgement, the newly-established financial interest will jeopardize the objectivity of the recommendations, the State shall have the option of terminating the contract.

Failure to disclose a relevant financial interest on the part of a consultant will be deemed grounds for termination of the contract with all associated costs to be borne by the consultant and, in addition, the consultant may be excluded from participating in the State's bid processes for a period of up to 360 calendar days in accordance with Public Contract Code Section 12102(j).

C. Bidding Steps

1. General

The procurement process to be used in this acquisition is composed of at least one phase of bid development. Refer to *Section I to determine which phases and steps are included in the IFB/RFP. References in this Section II to steps not included in Section I are not applicable to this IFB/RFP.* There is always a Final Phase, which may include a Draft Bid and revisions, and will always include a Final Bid. Prior to the Final Phase, there may be a Compliance Phase. The possible steps of the Compliance Phase are a Conceptual Proposal, Detailed Technical Proposal and revisions of either or both. A description of these phases and their steps follows.

The Final Bid is a mandatory step for all bidders; all other steps are optional. However, all bidders are strongly encouraged to follow the scheduled steps of this procurement to increase the chance of submitting a compliant Final Bid. *Cost submitted in any submission other than the Final Bid may preclude the bidder from continuing in the process.*

2. Compliance Phase

The Compliance Phase is an iterative, conversational mode of proposal and contract development. It requires the State, working together in confidence with each bidder, to assess and discuss the viability and effectiveness of the bidder's proposed methods of meeting the State's needs as reflected in the IFB/RFP. It is a departure from the rigid "either accept or reject" philosophy of traditional competitive bidding, yet it is highly competitive in nature. It provides the flexibility needed for the bidder to test a solution prior to formal submittal of the Final Bid, and it facilitates the correction of defects before they become fatal to the bid. The steps may include the submission of a Conceptual Proposal and/or a Detailed Technical Proposal by the bidder, Confidential Discussions of the bidder's proposal(s) and written Discussion Memorandum as to the correction of defects and the State's acceptance of such changes.

a. Conceptual Proposal

The Conceptual proposal may be included for the purpose of allowing each bidder to provide a general concept of a proposal with just enough detail to enable the evaluators to determine if the bidder is on the right track toward meeting the functional requirements as stated in the IFB/RFP; and if not, where the bidder must change a concept. This step invites the bidder to be as innovative as the IFB/RFP requirements allow in eliminating unnecessary constraints.

b. Detailed Technical Proposal

The Detailed Technical Proposal may be included for the purpose of allowing each bidder to provide a detailed technical description of its proposal to determine at an early stage whether the proposal is totally responsive to all the requirements of the IFB/RFP, and if not, which elements are not responsive and what changes would be necessary and acceptable.

c. Evaluation of Proposals and Discussion Agenda

Upon receipt of the Conceptual and Detailed Technical Proposals, the evaluation team will review each proposal in accordance with the evaluation methodology outlines in the IFB/RFP section on Evaluation for the purpose of identifying areas in which the proposal is non-responsive to a requirement, is otherwise defective, or in which additional clarification is required in order that the State may fully understand the ramifications of an action proposed by the bidder. As a result of this evaluation, the evaluation team will prepare an agenda of items to be discussed with the bidder, and will normally transmit the agenda to the bidder at least two working days before the scheduled meeting. The agenda may also include, in addition to the identification of discovered defects, a discussion of the bidder's proposed vendor support, implementation plans, validation plans, demonstrating plans and proposed contracts, as appropriate.

d. Confidential Discussion with Each Bidder

In accordance with the discussion agenda, the evaluation team will meet with each bidder for the purpose of discussing the Conceptual Proposal or Detailed Technical Proposal (as the case may be) in detail. The bidder may bring to the discussion those persons who may be required to answer questions or commit to changes. As the first order of business, the bidder may be asked to give a short proposal overview presentation. To the maximum extend practical, the bidder will address the major concerns of the evaluation team, as expressed in the Discussion Agenda, and should be prepared to answer any questions that may arise as a result of the presentation. The participants will then proceed to discuss each of the agenda items.

The State will not make counter proposals to a bidder's proposed solution to the IFB/RFP requirements. The State will only identify its concerns, ask for clarification, and express its reservations if a particular requirements of the IFB/RFP is not, in the opinion of the State, appropriately satisfied. The primary purpose of this discussion is to endure that the bidder's Final Bid will be responsive.

If any contractual items have a bearing on, or are affected by, the content of the proposal, such matters may be discussed in an effort to reach agreement. (As a concurrent activity, the bidder and the State will have been working together to negotiate the proposed contract(s) which will become operative if the bidder's Final Bid is accepted by the State. Further discussion of the contractual aspect of this procurement is contained in paragraph D., Contractual Information.)

e. Discussion Memorandum

Throughout the Confidential Discussion, a written record will be kept of all items discussed, their resolution, and any changes the bidder intends to make and the State's acceptance of such changes. If the bidder's proposal, with the agreed-to changes, is acceptable to the State, such acceptance shall be noted. If agreement has not been reached on all matters during the initial discussion, such will be noted with a specific plan for resolution before the next step. These resolutions and agreements will be prepared in final form as a Discussion Memorandum (which will be the official State documentation of the discussion), and will be mailed to the bidder normally within two work days of the discussion. If the discussion is not completed in one meeting and is continued in subsequent meetings, the Discussion Memoranda will follow the meeting at which the discussion is concluded. If a bidder discovers any discrepancy, omission, or other error in the memorandum, the bidder shall immediately notify the State of such error in writing and request clarification or correction. *Oral statements made by either party shall not obligate either party.*

f. Rejection of Bidder's Proposal

If, after full discussion with a bidder, the State is of the opinion that the bidder's proposal (Conceptual Proposal or Detailed Technical Proposal, as the case may be) cannot be restructured or changed in a reasonable time to satisfy the needs of the State, and that further discussion would not likely result in an acceptable proposal in a reasonable time, the bidder will be given written notice that the proposal has been rejected and that a Final Bid submitted along such lines would be nonresponsive.

g. Submission of Amended Proposal

If, at the conclusion of the Confidential Discussion, the State determines that required and agreed-to changes can only be fully confirmed through the submission of an amended proposal (Conceptional Proposal or Detailed Technical Proposal, as the case may be), the State may require the submission of an addendum consisting only of those pages which were in doubt or a complete resubmittal. Similarly, if the bidder wishes confirmation that the changes the bidder intends to make, in accordance with the Discussion Memorandum, are acceptable to the State, the bidder may request and receive permission, if the time permits, to submit such addendum within a reasonable time after the conclusion of the Confidential Discussion. In either event, the State will advise the bidder as to the acceptability of the amended proposal, or may schedule another discussion period, if in the State's opinion, such a discussion is desirable.

3. Final Phase

The purpose of the Final Phase is to obtain bids that are responsive in every respect. This phase may include a Draft Bid and will always include a Final Bid, as described below:

a. Draft Bid

The purpose of the Draft Bid is to provide the State with an "almost final" bid in order to identify any faulty administrative aspect of the bid which, if not corrected, could cause the Final Bid to be rejected for ministerial reasons.

The Draft Bid should correspond to submittals and agreements of the Compliance Phase, if required, and must be complete in every respect as required by the IFB/RFP section on Proposal and Bid Format, except cost. The inclusion of cost information in the Draft Bid may be a basis for rejecting the bid and notifying the bidder that further participation in the procurement is prohibited.

Review of the Draft Bid by the State may include confidential discussions with individual bidders and will provide feedback to the bidder prior to submittal of the final proposal. If no such discussion step is included in the key action dates then the review of the Draft Bid does not include any assessment of the bid's responsiveness to the technical requirements of the IFB/RFP. regardless of the inclusion of a confidential discussion, the State will notify the bidder of any defects it has detected in the Draft Bid or of the fact that it did not detect any such defects. Such notification is intended to minimize the risk that the Final Bid will be deemed defective; however, *The State will not provide any warranty that all defects have been detected and that such notification will not preclude rejection of the Final Bid if such defects are later found.*

If the State finds it necessary, the State may call for revised Draft Bid submittals, or portions thereof. The bidder will be notified of defects discovered in these submittals as well. Again *the State will not provide any warranty that all defects have been detected and that such notification will not preclude rejection of the final bid if such defects are later found.*

b. Final Bid

The Final Bid must be complete, including all cost information, requires signatures, contract language changes agreed to in writing and corrections to those defects noted by the State in its review of the Draft Bid. If required in the IFB/RFP section Proposal and Bid Format, cost data (as identified in the above referenced section) must be submitted under separate, sealed cover. Changes that appear in the Final Bid, other than correction of defects , increase the risk that the final bid may be found defective.

4. Confidentiality

Final Bids are public upon bid opening; however, the contents of all proposals, Draft Bids, correspondence, agenda, memoranda, working papers, or any other medium which discloses any aspect of a bidder's proposal shall be held in the strictest confidence until notice of intent to award. *Bidders should be aware that marking a document "Confidential" or "Proprietary" in a Final Bid will not keep that document from being released after notice of intent to award as part of the public record, unless a court has ordered the State not to release the document.* The content of all working papers and discussions relating to the bidder's proposal shall be held confidential indefinitely unless the public interest is best served by an item's disclosure because of its direct pertinence to a decision, agreement or the evaluation of the bid. Any disclosure of confidential information by the bidder is a basis for rejecting the bidder's proposal and ruling the bidder ineligible to further participate. Any disclosure of confidential information by a State employee is a basis for disciplinary action, including dismissal from State employment, as provided by Government Code Section 19570 Et Seq. Total confidentiality is paramount; it cannot be over emphasized.

5. Submission of Proposals and Bids

The instructions contained herein apply to the Final Bid. They also apply to the Conceptual Proposal, Detailed Technical Proposal, and Draft Bid, except as noted.

a. Preparation

Proposals and bids are to be prepared in such a way as to provide a straightforward, concise delineation of capabilities to satisfy the requirements of this IFB/RFP. Expensive bindings, colored displays, promotional materials, etc., are not necessary or desired. Emphasis should be concentrated on conformance to the IFB/RFP instructions, responsiveness to the IFB/RFP requirements, and on completeness and clarity of content.

As stated above, the State's evaluation of Conceptual and Detailed Technical Proposals is preliminary, and the review of Draft Bids is cursory. Therefore, bidders are cautioned to not rely on the State, during these evaluations and reviews, to discover and report to the bidders all defects and errors in the submitted documents. Before submitting each document, the bidder should carefully proof it for errors and adherence to the IFB/RFP requirements.

b. Bidder's Cost

Costs for developing proposals and bids are the responsibility entirely of the bidder and shall not be chargeable to the State.

c. Completion of Proposals and Bids

Proposals and bids must be complete in all respects as required by the IFB/RFP section on PROPOSAL AND BID FORMAT. A Final Bid may be rejected if it is conditional or incomplete, or if it contains any alterations of form or other irregularities of any kind. A Final Bid must be rejected if any such defect or irregularity constitutes a material deviation from the IFB/RFP requirements. The Final Bid must contain all costs required by the IFB/RFP sections on Cost and Proposal and Bid Format, setting forth a unit price and total price for each unit price item, and a total price for each lump sum price item in the schedule, all in clearly legible figures. *If required in the IFB/RFP section Proposal and Bid Format, cost data (as identified in the above referenced section) must be submitted under separate, sealed cover. Draft Bids must contain all information required in the Final Bid except cost.*

Exhibit II-A at the end of this Section II entitled Competitive Bidding and Bid Responsiveness emphasizes the requirements of competitive bidding and contains examples of common causes for rejection of bids. Bidders are encouraged to review this exhibit.

d. False or Misleading Statements

Bids which contain false or misleading statements, or which provide references which do not support an attribute or condition claimed by the bidder, may be rejected. If, in the opinion of the State, such information was intended to mislead the State in its evaluation of the bid, and the attribute, condition, or capability is a requirement of this IFB/RFP, it will be the basis for rejection of the bid.

e. Signature of Bid

A cover letter (which shall be considered an integral part of the Final Bid) and Standard Agreement Form 2, or a Bid Form shall be signed by an individual who is authorized to bind the bidding firm contractually. The signature must indicate the title or position that the individual holds in the firm. *An unsigned Final Bid shall be rejected.*

The Draft Bid must also contain the cover letter and Form 2, or Bid Form, similarly prepared, including the title of the person who will sign, but need not contain the signature. The Conceptual Proposal and Detailed Technical Proposal need not contain the cover letter and Form 2, or Bid Form.

f. Delivery of Proposals and Bids

Mail or deliver proposals and bids to the Department Official listed in Section I. If mailed, use certified or registered mail with return receipt requested.

Proposals and bids must be received in the number of copies stated in the IFB/RFP section on Proposal and Bid Format and not later than the dates and times specified in Section I and in the individual schedules provided the bidders. One copy must be clearly marked "Master Copy." All copies of proposals and bids must be under sealed cover which is to be plainly marked "Conceptual Proposal," "Detailed Technical Proposal," "Draft Bid," or "Final Bid" for "IFB/RFP _____" (use IFB/RFP identification number from the IFB/RFP title page). Also, the sealed cover of all submittals, except the Final Bid, shall be clearly marked "Confidential," and shall state the scheduled date and time for submission. Proposals and Draft Bids not submitted under sealed cover will be returned for sealing. Final Bids not received by the date and time specified in Section II or not sealed, will be rejected. If required in the IFB/RFP section Proposal and Bid Format, all cost data (as identified in the above referenced section) must be submitted under separate, sealed cover and clearly marked "Cost Data." If cost data is required to be submitted separately sealed, and is not submitted in this manner, the bid will be rejected. Proposals and bids submitted under improperly marked covers may be rejected. If discrepancies are found between two or more copies of the proposal or bid, the proposal or bid may be rejected. However, if not so rejected, the Master Copy will provide the basis for resolving such discrepancies. If one copy of the Final Bid is not clearly marked "Master Copy," the State may reject the bid; however, the State may at its sole option select, immediately after bid opening, one copy to be used as the Master Copy.

g.   *Withdrawal and Resubmission/Modification of Proposals and Bids*

A bidder may withdraw its Conceptual Proposal, Detailed Technical Proposal or Draft Bid at any time by written notification. A bidder may withdraw its Final Bid at any time prior to the bid submission time specified in Section I by submitting a written notification of withdrawal signed by the bidder authorized in accordance with Paragraph C-5-e, Signature of Bid. The bidder may thereafter submit a new or modified bid prior to such bid submission time. Modification offered in any other manner, oral or written, will not be considered. *Final Bids cannot be changed or withdrawn after the time designated for receipt. except as provided in Paragraph 7d of this section.*

6. Rejection of Bids

The State may reject any or all bids and may waive any immaterial deviation or defect in a bid. The State's waiver of any immaterial deviation or defect shall in no way modify the IFB/RFP documents or excuse the bidder from full compliance with the IFB/RFP specifications if awarded the contract.

7. Evaluation and Selection Process

a.   *General*

Proposals and bids will be evaluated according to the procedures contained in the IFB/RFP section on Evaluation Special instructions and procedures apply to Conceptual Proposals, Detailed Technical Proposals, and Draft Bids.

b.   *Evaluation Questions*

During the evaluation and selection process, the State may desire the presence of a bidder's representative for answering specific questions, orally and/or in writing.

c. Demonstration

This procurement may require a demonstration of the bidder's response to specific requirements (including benchmark requirements) before final selection in order to verify the claims made in the bid, corroborate the evaluation of the bid, and confirm that the hardware and software are actually in operation; in which case prior notice will be given. The bidder must make all arrangements for demonstration facilities at no cost to the State. The location of the demonstration will be determined by the bidder; however, its performance within California is preferred and will be attended at the State's expense. Demonstration outside California will be attended only if the bidder agrees to reimburse the State for travel and per diem expenses. The State reserves the right to determine whether or not a demonstration has been successfully passed. See Section on Demonstrations for additional information.

d. Errors in the Final Bid

An error in the Final Bid may cause the rejection of that bid; however, the State may at its sole option retain the bid and make certain corrections.

In determining if a correction will be made, the State will consider the conformance of the bid to the format and content required by the IFB/RFP, and any unusual complexity of the format and content required by the IFB/RFP.

(1) If the bidder's intent is clearly established based on review of the complete Final Bid submittal, the State may at its sole option correct an error based on that established intent.

(2) The State may at its sole option correct obvious clerical errors.

(3) The State may at its sole option correct discrepancy and arithmetic errors on the basis that if intent is not clearly established by the complete bid submittal the Master Copy shall have priority over additional copies, the bid narrative shall have priority over the contract, the contract shall have priority over the cost sheets, and within each of these, the lowest level of detail will prevail. If necessary, the extensions and summary will be recomputed accordingly, even if the lowest level of detail is obviously misstated. The total price of unit-price items will be the product of the unit price and the quantity of the item. If the unit price is ambiguous, unintelligible, uncertain for any cause, or is omitted, it shall be the amount obtained by dividing the total price by the quantity of the item.

(4) The State may at its sole option correct errors of omission, and in the following four situations, the State will take the indicated actions if the bidder's intent is not clearly established by the complete bid submittal.

(a) If an item is described in the narrative and omitted from the contract and cost data provided in the bid for evaluation purposes, it will be interpreted to mean that the item will be provided by the bidder at no cost.

(b) If a minor item is not mentioned at all in the Final Bid and is essential to satisfactory performance, the bid will be interpreted to mean that the item will be provided at no cost.

(c) If a major item is not mentioned at all in the Final Bid, the bid will be interpreted to mean that the bidder does not intend to supply that item.

(d) If a major item is omitted, and the omission is not discovered until after contract award, the bidder shall be required to supply that item at no cost.

(5) If a bidder does not follow the instructions for computing costs not related to the contract (e.g., State personnel costs), the State may reject the bid, or at its sole option, recompute such costs based on instructions contained in the IFB/RFP.

If the recomputations or interpretations, as applied in accordance with this section, subparagraph d, result in significant changes in the amount of money to be paid to the bidder (if awarded the contract) or in a requirement of the bidder to supply a major item at no cost, the bidder will be given the opportunity to promptly establish the grounds legally justifying relief from its bid.

IT IS ABSOLUTELY ESSENTIAL THAT BIDDERS CAREFULLY REVIEW THE COST ELEMENTS IN THEIR FINAL BID, SINCE THEY WILL NOT HAVE THE OPTION TO CHANGE THEM AFTER THE TIME FOR SUBMITTAL.

(6) In the event an ambiguity or discrepancy between the general requirements described in Section IV (Proposed System) and the specific technical requirements set forth in Section VI (Technical Requirements) is detected after the opening of bids, Section VI, and the bidder's response thereto, shall have priority over Section IV, and the bidder's response thereto. Refer to Paragraph B-2 regarding immediate notification to State contact when ambiguities, discrepancies, omissions, etc., are discovered.

8. Award of Contract

Award of contract, if made, will be in accordance with the IFB/RFP section on EVALUATION to a responsible bidder whose Final Bid complies with all the requirements of the IFB/RFP documents and any addenda thereto, except for such immaterial defects as may be waived by the State. Award, if made, will be made within forty five (45) days after the scheduled date for Contract Award specified in Section I; however, bidder may extend the offer beyond 45 days in the event of a delay of contract award.

The State reserves the right to determine the successful bidder(s) either on the basis of individual items or on the basis of all items included in its IFB/RFP, unless otherwise expressly provided in the State's IFB/RFP. The State reserves the right to modify or cancel in whole or in part its IFB/RFP.

Unless the bidder specifies otherwise in its bid, the State may accept any item or group of items of any bid. The State reserves the right to modify or cancel in whole or in part its IFB/RFP.

Written notification of the State's intent to award will be made to all bidders. If a bidder, having submitted a Final Bid, can show that its bid, instead of the bid selected by the State, should be selected for contract award according to the rules of Paragraph C-7, the bidder will be allowed five (5) working days to submit a protest to the Intent to Award, according to the instructions contained in Paragraph E-l of this section.

9. Debriefing

A debriefing may be held after contract award at the request of any bidder for the purpose of receiving specific information concerning the evaluation. The discussion will be based primarily on the technical and cost evaluations of the bidder's Final Bid. A debriefing is not the forum to challenge the IFB/RFP specifications or requirements.

D. CONTRACTUAL INFORMATION

1. Contract Form

The State has model contract forms to be used by State agencies when contracting for EDP or Telecommunications goods and services. The model contract(s) appropriate for the specific requirements of this IFB/RFP are included in the IFB/RFP.

2. Specific Terms and Conditions

In traditional competitive bidding, the contract to be awarded is included in the solicitation document in its final form, and any alteration by a bidder will result in rejection of its bid. The State recognizes, however, that the various suppliers of EDP goods and services have developed pricing structures and procedures that differ from each other, and that, if the State were to specify the exact language of the contract to be executed, it could result in firms being unwilling to do business with the State of California because of contract statements which are incompatible with their business methods. In recognition of the above, the form of the contract(s) contained in the attached Appendices permit, where appropriate, the substitution and/or insertion of vendor-specified language by the bidder. *All such substitutions and insertions must be approved by the Department of General Services.* The Department of General Services may request the Department of Finance's concurrence on the approval of changes involving significant issues. Terms and conditions which do not comply in substance with all material requirements of the IFB/RFP, which are contrary to the best interests of the State, or which are in opposition to State policy will not be accepted.

The State will prenegotiate repetitively used terms and conditions with vendors at their request. These prenegotiated terms and conditions will be kept on file and bidders may refer to them as their proposed contract language for individual solicitations.

3. Approval of Proposed Contract

To comply with the requirements of competitive bidding procedures, the contract must be fixed prior to the submission of the Final Bids; no negotiation is permissible after that time. It is required, therefore, that any vendor who intends to bid on this IFB/RFP submit its proposed contract to the State in accordance with the schedule contained in Section I. If a bidder has prenegotiated language with the State, the bidder may indicate that this is the language-proposed and submit only changes to any language that has not been prenegotiated. (For a particular IFB/RFP it is possible that prenegotiated language will not be acceptable due to special circumstances. The State will notify the bidder if this is the case and will renegotiate that language for this procurement.) For language that has not been prenegotiated, the proposed contract, or portions thereof, must be submitted in the form of the prescribed model(s), and deviations from the exact language contained in the model(s) must conform to the guidance therein stated. The proposed contract must contain all proposed terms and conditions, and with all blanks filled in, but it must not contain (other than in sample form) any identification of proposed goods or cost data. (Note, however, that the Draft Bid must contain the approved contract with all the blanks filled in except for cost data, as specified in Paragraph C-3 above.) The proposed contract must be clearly labeled "Proposed Contract" with the IFB/RFP identification from the IFB/RFP title page. The State will notify the bidder as to which, if any, terms and conditions are not acceptable to the State and will arrange an appropriate meeting at a mutually satisfactory time to resolve any differences.

Each appendix contains a set of instructions to guide the bidder through a step-by-step procedure to develop proposed new language or changes to model contract language, negotiating contract language and securing State approval. Proposed contract language which is not prepared in accordance with these instructions may be returned to the bidder without review by the State.

IT IS ESSENTIAL THAT THE BIDDER'S PROPOSED CONTRACT BE ACCEPTABLE TO THE STATE PRIOR TO THE FINAL BID SUBMISSION DATE. SUCH ACCEPTANCE DOES NOT RELIEVE THE BIDDER OF PROVIDING OTHER NECESSARY INFORMATION REQUIRED IN THE CONTRACT. IF A BID CONTAINS UNAPPROVED CONTRACT LANGUAGE, THE POTENTIAL FOR BID REJECTION IS SUBSTANTIALLY INCREASED.

APPROVED CONTRACT LANGUAGE FOR THIS PARTICULAR IFB/RFP WHICH IS NOT PROPRIETARY TO THE BIDDER WILL BE AVAILABLE TO ALL BIDDERS SHORTLY AFTER THE LAST DAY TO NEGOTIATE CONTRACT LANGUAGE.

PRENEGOTIATED TERMS AND CONDITIONS ARE AVAILABLE AT ANY TIME.

4. Term of Contract

The State intends to retain the required goods and services for at least the period specified elsewhere in this IFB/RFP. Ideally, the term of the contract will be for the specified period. If the State requires the contract to be terminated during the contract period, such a requirement will be specified in the IFB/RFP section on ADMINISTRATIVE REQUIREMENTS. The State will accept a contract for a longer period than specified if, at the sole option of the State, the contract may be terminated at the end of the period specified with or without the payment of termination charges. Such termination charges, if any, must be included in the evaluated cost of the bid.

E. OTHER INFORMATION

1. Protests

Before a protest is submitted regarding any issue other than selection of the "successful vendor," the bidder must make full and timely use of the procedures described in this Section II to resolve any outstanding issue(s) between the bidder and the State. The procurement procedure is designed to give the bidder and the State adequate opportunity to submit questions and discuss the requirements, proposals and counter proposals before the Final Bid is due. The protest procedure is made available in the event that a bidder cannot reach a fair agreement with the State after exhausting these procedures. In such cases, a protest may be submitted according to the procedure below. Protests regarding any issue other than selection of the "successful vendor" will be heard and resolved by the Deputy Director of the Department of General Services Procurement Division whose decision will be final.

If a bidder has submitted a bid which it believes to be totally responsive to the requirements of the IFB/RFP and to be the bid that should have been selected according to the evaluation procedure in the Section on EVALUATION and the bidder believes the State has incorrectly selected another bidder for award, the bidder may submit a protest of the selection as described below. Protests regarding selection of the "successful vendor" will be heard and resolved by the State Board of Control whose decision will be final.

All protests must be made in writing, signed by an individual authorized under Paragraph C-5-e, Signature of Bid, and contain a statement of the reason(s) for protest; citing the law, rule, regulation or procedures on which the protest is based. The protester must provide facts and evidence to support the claim. Protests must be mailed or delivered to:

Street Address:

Deputy Director

Procurement Division

1823 14th Street

Sacramento, CA 95814

Mailing Address:

Deputy Director

Procurement Division

P.O. Box 942804

Sacramento, CA 94204-0001

All protests to the IFB/RFP or protests concerning the evaluation, recommendation, or other aspects of the selection process must be received by the Deputy Director of the Procurement Division as promptly as possible, but not later than the respective times and dates specified in Section I for such protests or the respective date of the Notification of Intent to Award, whichever is later. Certified or registered mail must be used unless delivered in person, in which case the protester should obtain a receipt of delivery.

2. News Releases

Any publications or news releases relating to a contract resulting from this IFB/RFP shall not be made without prior written approval of the Department Official listed in Section I.

3. Disposition of Proposals and Bids

All materials submitted in response to this IFB/RFP will become the property of the State of California and will be returned only at the State's option and at the bidder's expense. The Master Copy shall be retained for official files and will become a public record after the date and time for Final Bid submission as specified in Section I, KEY ACTION DATES. However, confidential financial information submitted in support of the requirement to show bidder responsibility will be returned upon request.

4. Contacts for Information

Bidders may contact the Department Contact listed in Section I for visits to the physical installation for purposes of familiarization and evaluation of the current processes. Visits shall be made by appointment only, during normal business hours, and will be limited to the Department Contact listed in Section I or the Contact's designee. Visits shall be permitted to the extent that they do not unduly interfere with the conduct of State business.

Oral communications of department officers and employees concerning this IFB/RFP shall not be binding on the State and shall in no way excuse the bidder of any obligations set forth in this IFB/RFP.

EXHIBIT II-A
COMPETITIVE BIDDING AND BID RESPONSIVENESS

The purpose of competitive bidding is to secure public objectives in the most value-effective manner and avoid the possibilities of graft, fraud, collusion, etc. Competitive bidding is designed to benefit the public body (the State, in the present context), and is not for the benefit of the bidders. It is administered to accomplish its purposes with sole reference to the public interest. It is based upon full and free bidding to satisfy State specifications, and acceptance by the State of the most value-effective solution to the State's requirements, as determined by the evaluation criteria contained in the IFB/RFP.

Competitive bidding is not defined in any single statute but is more in the nature of a compendium of numerous court decisions. From such court decisions, the following rules have evolved, among others:

1. Invitations for Bids must provide a basis for full and fair competitive bidding among bidders on a common standard, free of restrictions tending to stifle competition.

2. The State may modify the IFB/RFP, prior to the date fixed for submission of bids, by issuance of an addendum to all parties who have been furnished with the IFB/RFP for bidding purposes.

3. To have a valid bid, the bid must respond and conform to the invitation, including all the documents which are incorporated therein. A bid which does not literally comply may be rejected.

4. For a variance between the request for bids and the bid to be such as to preclude acceptance (the bid must be rejected), the variance or deviation must be a material one.

5. State agencies usually have the express or implied right to reject any and all bids in the best interests of the State. Bids cannot, however, be selectively rejected without cause.

6. Bids cannot be changed after the time designated for the receipt and opening thereof. No negotiation as to the scope of the work, amount to be paid, or contractual terms is permitted.

7. A competitive bid, once opened and declared, is in the nature of an irrevocable option and a contract right of which the public agency cannot be deprived without its consent, unless the requirements for rescission are present. All bids become public documents.

8. Bids cannot be accepted "in part," unless the invitation specifically permits such an award.

9. Contracts entered into through the competitive bidding process cannot later be amended, unless the Invitation for Bids includes a provision, to be incorporated in the contract awarded, providing for such amendment.

Since competitive procurement became the required method for securing certain EDP goods or services, the State has received a number of bids which were deemed to be nonresponsive to the Invitation for Bids or which could not be considered as valid bids within the competitive bidding procedures. Nonresponsive bids or bids which contain qualifications must be rejected. Many of the causes for rejection arise from either an incomplete understanding of the competitive bidding process or administrative oversight on the part of the bidders. The following examples are illustrative of the more common causes for rejection of bids. These examples are listed to assist potential bidders in submission of responsive bids.

1. A bid stated, "The prices stated within are for your information only and are subject to change."

2. A bid stated, "This proposal shall expire thirty (30) days from this date unless extended in writing by the _____ Company." (In this instance award was scheduled to be approximately 45 days after bid submittal date.)

3. A bid for lease of EDP equipment contained lease plans of a duration shorter than that which had been requested in the IFB.

4. A personal services contract stated, "_____, in its judgment, believes that the schedules set by the State are extremely optimistic and probably unobtainable. Nevertheless, _____ will exercise its best efforts..."

5. A bid stated, "This proposal is not intended to be of a contractual nature."

6. A bid contained the notation "prices are subject to change without notice."

7. A bid was received for the purchase of EDP equipment with unacceptable modifications to the Purchase Contract.

8. A bid for lease of EDP equipment contained lease plans of a duration longer than that which had been requested in the IFB with no provision for earlier termination of the contract.

9. A bid for lease of EDP equipment stated, "...this proposal is preliminary only and the order, when issued, shall constitute the only legally binding commitment of the parties."

10. A bid was delivered to the wrong office.

11. A bid was delivered after the date and time specified in the IFB.

12. An IFB required the delivery of a performance bond covering 25 percent of the proposed contract amount. The bid offered a performance bond to cover "x" dollars which was less than the required 25 percent of the proposed contract amount.

13. A bid did not meet contract goal for MWDVBE participation and did not follow the steps required by the bid to achieve a "good faith effort."

14. A bid appeared to meet contract goal for MWDVBE participation with the dollars submitted, but the vendor had miscalculated the bid costs. When these corrections were made by the State, the vendor's price had increased and the dollars committed for MWDVBE participation no longer met goal. The vendor had not followed the steps to achieve a "good faith effort."

Model Request for Proposals, State of Alaska

STATE OF ALASKA

DEPARTMENT OF TRANSPORTATION
and
PUBLIC FACILITIES

REQUEST FOR PROPOSALS

FOR

AUTOMATED MANAGEMENT SYSTEM(S) FOR THE
ALASKA STATE EQUIPMENT FLEET (SEF) AND
FOR THE ALASKA INTERNATIONAL AIRPORT SYSTEM (AIAS)

TABLE OF CONTENTS

SECTION 1 - GENERAL PROPOSAL INFORMATION

1.01 INTENT

The State of Alaska, Department of Transportation and Public Facilities (DOT&PF), Information Systems Division is seeking proposals for the purchase, modification, and installation of an Automated Equipment and Facilities Management software/hardware package that will meet the needs of both the State Equipment Fleet (SEF) and the Alaska International Airport System (AIAS). SEF has a requirement for an automated Equipment Management System which we will refer to hereafter as an EMS. AIAS has a requirement for an automated Facility Management System, or FMS.

Although we are asking for proposals which address the needs of both SEF and AIAS, the respondent needs to clearly understand that these are two separate divisions of DOT/PF and although their needs are similar, their specific requirements mandate that each entity has their own system in terms of operational control. Any shared software or hardware between the two systems must be organized so as to be transparent to the individual user groups in their day-to-day activity.

In essence, we are looking for two systems: one for SEF and one for AIAS. But to the degree that a contractor can propose economy of scale by taking advantage of commonalities of functions between the two divisions, a common data base management system or shared hardware is permissible as long as a separation is maintained between the two systems We are seeking an overall system approach to our requirements. This system approach has been divided into four primary areas within the RFP General System Requirements, EMS Functional Requirements, FMS Functional Requirements and Technical Requirements.

This system shall:

A. have a history of successful applications in organizations with a vehicle fleet greater than 2,500 individual pieces of equipment or attachments distributed across a wide geographic area;

B. have a history of successful applications in facility management within an airport environment or similar campus type organization of buildings, grounds, special structures, and equipment;

C. cost effectively accommodate change;

D. provide cost modeling capability essential to management of a fleet of vehicles and to facility management;

E. be a mainframe, IBM 3084Q or IBM 4381, data base management system (DBMS) solution or

F. be a minicomputer or microcomputer software/hardware, RDBMS solution to the problem and

G. System of software must be of fourth generation type (4GL).

The RFP and its Appendices contain administrative and procedural information, instructions for preparing and submitting proposals, and terms and conditions to be included in any contract awarded as a result of this RFP.

These instructions prescribe the format that proposals shall follow and describe the approach for the development and presentation of proposal data. They are designed to ensure a complete submission of information necessary for an equitable analysis and evaluation of submitted proposals. There is no intent to limit the content of proposals.

Proposals that merely offer to conduct the task or provide the product in accordance with the requirements of the Statement of Work shall be considered non-responsive to this RFP and shall not be further considered. To be found responsive to this RFP the respondent shall submit a definitive description of the methodology, time phases, and the respondent's resources to be committed to delivery of the Automated Equipment and Facilities Management software/hardware system and services to be purchased under this RFP.

1.02 LEGAL AUTHORITY

Authority to purchase professional service is found in Alaska Statute (AS) 36 30 200 - 260; Alaska Administrative Code (AAC) 2 AAC 12; and Alaska State Administrative Manual, Section 8104.

1.03 ISSUING OFFICE

This Request for Proposal (RFP) is issued for the State of Alaska, Department of Transportation and Public Facilities by the Information Systems Division. The Information System Division (ISD) Director and the (ISD) Data Processing Manager are the sole points of contact in the state for this RFP.

CONTACTS:

Project Procurement Officer: Mr Tom Kluberton

Director, Information Systems Division

Department of Transportation and Public Facilities

MS 2500, P O Box Z, Juneau, Alaska 99811

Telephone (907) 465-2889 · Fax (907) 586-8365

Project Manager: Mr Duane Horn

Data Processing Manager, Information Systems Division

Department of Transportation and Public Facilities

MS 2500, P O Box Z, Juneau, Alaska 99811

Telephone (907) 465-2889 · Fax (907) 586-8365

1.04 ACKNOWLEDGEMENT OF RFP

Each respondent interested in submitting a proposal shall acknowledge receipt of this RFP not later than the date set for the preproposal conference. See paragraph 1.06. Acknowledgement shall be confirmed in writing, but may be informally made by telephone. The confirmation must be sent or delivered to the project manager designated in paragraph 1.03.

1.05 PERIOD OF PERFORMANCE

Any contract resulting from this Request for Proposal (RFP) shall be submitted to the Commissioner of Administration for approval. If approved, it is effective the date of approval.

It is anticipated that the Automated Equipment and Facilities Management Software/Hardware System Contract will be awarded in 1990. The state expects the offeror elected to commence work within five (5) working days following the issuance of the Notice to Proceed. The offeror will be expected to implement the system within six months after contract award and be willing to maintain an on-site presence for ninety (90) days following implementation and acceptance of the system.

1.06 PRE-PROPOSAL CONFERENCE

A formal pre-proposal conference will be held at 1:30 p.m., Alaska Daylight Savings Time on June 11, 1990, in the DOT&PF Headquarters building, room 340, at 3132 Channel Drive in Juneau, Alaska. The purpose of this conference is to discuss with the prospective offerors the work to be performed and to allow them to ask questions arising from their initial review of this RFP. Questions and answers shall be transcribed and sent to attendees as soon as possible after the meeting.

All prospective offerors must attend the pre-proposal conference. Proposals from offerors who do not attend the conference will be rejected.

1.07 INQUIRIES

Questions that arise subsequent to the pre-proposal conference shall be submitted in writing to the project manager shown in paragraph 1.03. Questions and answers thereto shall be provided all prospective offerors who send representatives to the pre-proposal conference; however, the name of offerors submitting questions shall not be disclosed. All questions shall be received not later than 10 days prior to the response date in paragraph 1.09.

1.08 ADDENDA TO THE RFP

In the event it becomes necessary to revise any part of this RFP, addenda shall be provided to all offerors who send representatives to the pre-proposal conference. Additional material (correction, modification or withdrawal) submitted by respondents as a result of addenda to the RFP, or to the question/answer transcripts shall be received by the project manager shown in paragraph 1.03 no later than the response deadline stated in paragraph 1.09 and in the cover letter.

1.09 RESPONSE DATE

To be considered, proposals shall be received by the project procurement officer shown in paragraph 1.03 at or before 3:00 p.m., Alaska Daylight Savings Time, July 3, 1990. Offerors mailing proposals should allow ample mail delivery time to ensure timely receipt of their proposals. It is the offerors' responsibility to ensure that the proposal arrives prior to the deadline. In no event will a proposal be considered if it is received after 3:00 p.m., Alaska Daylight Savings Time, July 3, 1990.

1.10 PROPOSALS

To be considered, proposers must submit a complete response to this RFP, using the format provided in Section 3. Each proposal shall be sealed and submitted in seven (7) copies to the project procurement officer listed in paragraph 1.03. No other distribution of proposals shall be made by the proposer. Proposal shall be signed by an official authorized to bind the proposer to its provisions as detailed in this RFP. For this RFP the proposals shall remain valid for at least one hundred eighty (180) days from the proposal receipt deadline. The state shall reject all proposals which do not follow the format outlined above. All proposals and other material submitted become the property of the state and may be returned only at the state's option. Proprietary information should not be included in the proposal or supporting materials. The issuing office shall retain all proposals, both successful and unsuccessful, as part of the contract file for at least three (3) years.

1.11 REJECTION OF PROPOSALS

Proposals should be submitted initially on the most favorable terms which the respondent can propose from both a price and technical standpoint. The respondent shall submit its proposal with the understanding that the proposal shall become a part of the official contract file as required by Alaska Statute 36.30.510. The Issuing Office reserves the right to reject any proposal that does not address all the material requirements of this request. In addition, the state may reject all proposals at any time, negotiate separately with any source(s), or make the award without further discussion on any grounds provided by law. Any proposal which includes a debarred or suspended offeror shall be rejected.

1.12 ACCEPTANCE OF PROPOSAL CONTENT

Offerors shall carefully review this solicitation, without delay, for defects and questionable or objectionable matter. Questions, objections, or comments shall be made in writing and received by the project procurement officer identified in paragraph 1.03 no later than ten (10) working days before the response date in paragraph 1.09. This allows issuance of any necessary amendments in order to prevent the opening of a defective solicitation upon which award could not be made, but which would result in the exposure of offeror's proposals. Protests based upon any omission, error, or the content of the solicitation shall be disallowed if not made in writing prior to the response date in paragraph 1.09. Comments should be forwarded to the project procurement officer identified in paragraph 1.03 and a copy sent to The Commissioner, Department of Administration, P.O. Box C, Juneau, AK 99811-0200.

The successful proposal shall become an integral part of the contract The final contract shall not be limited to the terms and conditions stated in this RFP or the successful offeror's proposal, but shall also include terms and conditions later negotiated.

The state reserves the right to use any of the ideas presented in any reply to the RFP Selection or rejection of the proposal does not affect that right.

1.13 INCURRED COSTS

All cost incurred in the preparation, submission, and/or presentation of a proposal responding to this RFP, including, but not limited to the respondent's travel expenses to attend a pre-proposal conference, oral interview, demonstration of the proposed software/hardware package in Anchorage, and proposal negotiation session, shall be the sole responsibility of the respondent and shall not be reimbursed by the state.

1.14 CONFLICT OF INTEREST

Each proposal shall include a statement indicating whether or not the firm or any individuals working on the contract has a possible conflict of interest (e.g., employed by the State of Alaska, etc.) and, if so, the nature of that conflict. The Commissioner of Administration reserves the right to cancel the award if, in his sole discretion, any interest disclosed from any source could give the appearance of a conflict or cause speculation as to the objectivity of the program to be developed by the offeror. The Commissioner's determination regarding any questions of conflict of interest shall be final.

1.15 DISCLOSURE OF PROPOSAL CONTENTS

Alaska Statute 36.30.230 requires proposals to be opened in a manner to avoid content disclosure to competing offerors until the Notice of Intent to Award is issued A register of proposals containing the name and address of each offeror shall be prepared in accordance with regulations adopted by the commissioner. The register and the proposals are open for public inspection after the Notice of Intent to Award a contract is issued. All proposal and other material submitted become the property of the state and may be returned only at the state's option.

1.16 SUBCONTRACTORS

All respondents shall include in their proposal the subcontractor information outlined in paragraph 5.08 of this RFP, including the type and percentage of work they will be providing, corporate and individual resumes, and the information outlined in Section 3 of this RFP. In addition, within five (5) working days after the identification of the most advantageous proposal, the offeror shall provide a list confirming the subcontractors the proposer intends to use on the contact. The list shall include a minimum of the name, location of the place of business for each subcontractor, and evidence of the subcontractor's valid Alaska business license.

Relations between the proposer and subcontractors shall be in accordance with Alaska Statute 36.30.115.

1.17 NONCOLLUSION CERTIFICATION

By their signature on their proposal, proposers certify under penalty of perjury that the price submitted was independently arrived at without collusion.

1.18 PROPOSER'S NOTICE

By signature on their proposal, proposers certify that they are complying with (1) the laws of the State of Alaska; (2) the applicable portion of the Federal Civil Rights Act of 1964; (3) The Equal Employment Opportunity Act and the regulations issued thereunder by the federal government; and (4) all terms and conditions set out in this RFP. If any proposer fails to comply with (1) through (4) of this paragraph, the state reserves the right to disregard the proposal, terminate the contract, or consider the contractor in default.

1.19 AVAILABILITY OF ADDITIONAL TECHNICAL DATA

The Department of Transportation and Public Facilities, Information Systems Division shall make available in its Headquarters Building at 3132 Channel Drive, Juneau, Alaska, a library of reference materials regarding the current equipment management system. The information is for reference purposes only. It may be viewed by appointment, but will not be distributed. Appointments can be arranged through the project manager. The library includes documentation in the areas summarized below.

INPUT FORMS - A collection of the most frequently used input source documents are provided.

REPORTS - A summary of all reports generated by the current system including a sample page from each report, distribution and frequency information provided.

INTERFACES - This includes a description of all interfaces including file references, file characteristics, and frequencies.

STATE STANDARDS - This includes "The State of Alaska, Division of Information Services, User' Guide" and "The Information Systems Division Application Procedures and Guidelines document."

ALASKA STATUTES - A copy of the applicable Alaska Statutes is provided.

1.20 PROPOSED PROJECT FUNDING

The contract resulting from this RFP is subject to the availability of appropriations for the purpose of the contract. Total funding for the project is $558,000. $400,000 is being funded through a FY91 state capital appropriation and $158,000 is being funded through the international Airport Revenue Fund. Proposals in excess of $575,000 will be considered non-responsive. System changes resulting from initial legislative action or executive action arising after the initial contract date will be negotiated as contract amendments with funding dependent upon available sources. All other costs associated with this project are to be included in the scope of the initial contract and borne by the contractor. No price adjustments after the formation of a contract shall be allowed.

1.21 NEWS RELEASES

News releases pertaining to this RFP or the project to which it relates shall not be made without prior approval of the Commissioner of Administration, and only in coordination with the Issuing Office.

1.22 LOBBYING

Any lobbying efforts by proposers as a result of this RFP, or its award, are prohibited.

1.23 PROPOSED PAYMENT PROCEDURES

The state proposes to make periodic payments based upon a negotiated schedule. Each billing shall consist of an invoice and progress report. No payment shall be made until the progress report and invoice have been approved by the project manager and the clients, the SEF manager and AIAS manager. The state shall pay 90% of all invoices after the required approvals. The remaining 10% shall be withheld until completion of the contract, including the acceptance of all deliverables and services. The final payment shall be based upon acceptance of the system by the state, a final progress report, and a final invoice submitted by the contractor and approved by the project manager and the clients.

1.24 MULTIPLE OR ALTERNATE PROPOSALS

In accordance with 2 AAC 12.830 multiple or alternate proposals shall be considered non-responsive.

1.25 RIGHT TO INSPECT PLACE OF BUSINESS

The state may, at reasonable times, inspect the part of the place of business of a contractor or subcontractor that is related to the performance of a contract awarded a a result of this RFP. If an inspection is made in the place of business of a contractor or subcontractor, the contractor or subcontractor shall provide without charge all reasonable facilities and assistance for the safety and convenience of the person(s) performing the inspection or testing.

1.26 REPORTING OF ANTI-COMPETITIVE PRACTICES

When for any reason collusion or other anti-competitive practice are suspected among offerors, a notice of the relevant fact shall be transmitted to the state attorney general by the person who suspects the collusion or other anti-competitive practices.

1.27 ON-SITE INSPECTIONS

The state reserves the right to conduct on-site visits to evaluate the operation of installed software packages at the locations provided as references by the offeror.

1.28 PRE-AWARD AUDIT

Interested respondents agree to the following. When deemed advisable by the project procurement officer, and before any contract is awarded, The Department of Transportation and Public Facilities, Information Systems Division, Division of Administrative Services and the Alaska International Airport System reserves the right to cause an on-site pre-award audit to be made by staff of the department or by outside auditors selected by the state to determine the respondent's ability to meet the terms and conditions of the RFP.

SECTION 2 - MINIMUM OFFEROR'S QUALIFICATIONS

2.01 LICENSES

Any successful offeror shall be required to hold a valid Alaska business license and the necessary applicable professional licensed required by Alaska Statute. For more information on these licenses, contact the Department of Commerce and Economic Development, Division of Occupational Licensing, P.O. Box D, Juneau, Alaska, 99811.

AS 36.30.210 (a) requires that offerors submit evidence of a valid Alaska business license when submitting offers in response to proposals. This evidence is not required to be submitted with the proposal, but shall be submitted prior to the project procurement officer's determination of responsibility and award of the contract.

Acceptable evidence that the offeror possesses a valid Alaska business license may consist of any one of the following:

A.   copy of the Alaska business license;

B.   certification on the proposal that the proposer has a valid Alaska business license and has included the license number in the proposal;

C.   a canceled check for the Alaska business license fee;

D.   a copy of the Alaska business license application with a receipt stamp from the State's business license office;

E.   a sworn notarized affidavit that the proposer has applied and paid for the Alaska business license;

F.   other forms of evidence acceptable to the Department of Law.

2.02 MINIMUM FINANCIAL REQUIREMENTS

In order to be considered responsive, a responding offeror shall meet the following minimum financial standards.

A.   The offeror shall provide audited annual financial statement for the past three (3) years.

2.03 PRIOR EXPERIENCE

The successful offeror shall have prior specific experience in all aspects of computerized equipment and facilities management deign, development, testing, implementation, and operation in organizations with a vehicle fleet greater than 2,500 individual pieces of equipment or attachments (preferably governmental organizations). Also the offeror shall assign personnel to the project who have experience with the proposed software/hardware package and are knowledgeable in its installation. All personnel assigned to the project shall document their experience and background using the resume format in Appendix C.

2.04 INSURANCE REQUIREMENTS

The successful respondent shall carry satisfactory insurance coverage, including workers' compensation, as required by the Department of Administration, Division of Risk Management. Failure to provide evidence of adequate coverage is a material breach and grounds for termination of the contract. Please review Appendix B, indemnification and insurance provisions, for details on required coverage.

2.05 BID BOND AND PERFORMANCE BOND

BID BOND

The bid bond shall be payable immediately if the respondent is properly selected and fails to negotiate or fails to deliver a fully executed contract within fourteen days of receipt after the completion of successful negotiations with the issuing office. The amount of the bid bond is $10,000.00. Proposals unaccompanied by such a bid bond shall be rejected.

PERFORMANCE BOND

The amount of the performance bond shall be equal to the total amount of the proposal through the term of the contract. The respondent shall enclose a letter of commitment from a bonding company for the performance bond with his/her proposal. This bond shall be obtained within thirty (30) days of the award of the contract. Irrevocable letters of credit may be substituted for the required bond at the discretion of the Commissioner of Administration, State of Alaska.

SECTION 3 - PROPOSAL PROCESS AND INSTRUCTIONS TO OFFERORS

3.01 GENERAL INSTRUCTIONS

The following subsections provide detail on how to respond to this RFP. All responses must be in the prescribed format and include the ten response items listed in paragraph 3.04.

3.02 PROPOSAL SUBMITTAL

Submission of Proposal Copies. One original and six (6) copies of the proposal shall be submitted in a sealed package to the project procurement officer:

Mr. Tom Kluberton

Director, Information Systems Division

Department of Transportation and Public Facilities

3132 Channel Drive, Room 250, P O Box Z, Juneau, Alaska 99811

3.03 AMENDMENTS TO PROPOSALS

Amendments and/or withdrawals of proposals shall be allowed only if the amendment is received prior to the response date in paragraph 1.09. No amendment, corrections or withdrawals shall be accepted after the response date and time for any reason.

3.04 PROPOSAL INSTRUCTIONS

Proposal responses are to be organized and submitted in accordance with the instructions in this section. Responses should be organized into the following Response Item sections and submitted in an indexed binder.

Response Item

1. Transmittal letter

2. Acknowledgement of Amendments

3. Offeror's Qualifications

4. Proposed Software/Hardware

5. Response to System Requirements

6. Pricing Proposal

7. Project Management Plan

8. Subcontracted Work

9. Financial and Bond Requirements

10. Other Information

Elaborate or unnecessarily voluminous proposals are not desired. Respondents are encouraged to take care in completely answering questions and proposal requirements and to avoid submitting extraneous materials that do not show how the respondent intends to meet requirements.

Requirements for each Response Item are detailed below:

RESPONSE ITEM 1. TRANSMITTAL LETTER

A Transmittal Letter on the offeror's letterhead shall be submitted and at a minimum include the following:

a. The signature of a person authorized to commit the offeror to the extent of work and financial obligation included in the proposal shall appear on the transmittal letter.

b. It shall identify all material enclosures being submitted in response to this RFP.

c. A summary of the respondent's offering and a brief statement of the offeror's qualifications to meet the needs of the state.

d. A cross reference from each RFP requirement to the corresponding area of the respondent's proposal shall be included.

e. If the proposal deviates from the detailed specifications and requirements of this RFP, the transmittal letter should identify and explain these deviations. The state reserves the right to reject any proposal containing such deviations or to require modifications before acceptance.

RESPONSE ITEM 2. ACKNOWLEDGEMENT OF AMENDMENTS/ADDENDA

A statement identifying all amendments/addenda to this RFP issued by the Information System Division and received by the respondent shall be included. If no amendment/addenda have been received, a statement to that effect should be included.

RESPONSE ITEM 3. OFFEROR'S QUALIFICATIONS

The offeror may include any additional material he or she wishes the state to consider in selecting an automated equipment and facilities management software/hardware package. Suggested optional items include evidence of the market acceptance of the proposed package, track record in meeting promises to customers, new features in development or planned releases, or area not addressed by specific sections of this response item.

The following minimum information must be provided in this section.

a.   Evidence of an Alaska Business License, (see paragraph 2.01);

b.   Resumes for all project personnel, including subcontractors if any, (see format in Appendix C and paragraph 5.08);

c.   Statement of Terms and Conditions Affirmation (see format in Appendix D); and

d.   Describe the company, its age, organization, number of full time employees, and product specialization.

e.   If awarded this contract, from where would support services be provided? How many personnel are located at this location, and what is their specific experience with the proposed package?

g.   List a minimum of three (3) customers with an equipment fleet greater than 2,500 individual pieces of equipment or attachments (preferably governmental organizations) who are currently utilizing the proposed package, and are willing to allow an on-site visit by members of the proposal evaluation committee (PEC). Answer the following for each reference.

(1)   When was the package installed at the specified location?

(2)   Approximate size of the organization and geographical distribution of the equipment fleet, parts depots, facilities and repair shops.

(3)   Provide the name and telephone number of a person knowledgeable of the package that can be contacted as a reference.

RESPONSE ITEM 4. PROPOSED SOFTWARE/HARDWARE

In this response item, the offeror should provide information relative to the packaged software and hardware proposed as a solution to the State's needs. Your response must include the following:

a.   The offeror shall provide a description of each module, including its functions and capabilities.

b.   A comprehensive narrative and/or pictorial description including all files and programs of the proposed packaged software shall be presented. Included in this narrative shall be:

(1)   a listing of all hard coded tables and their location;

(2)   an estimate of the number of system programmers required to support the system operations after installation;

(3)   an estimate of the number of application programmers required to support system operations after installations and

(4)   an estimate of the number of central office operations administrative staff required to support the system after installation.

c.   Required Changes to Packaged System. In this part the offeror should identify changes required in the packaged system to meet the specific requirements of the state automated equipment and facilities management software/hardware system. Ensure each change is referenced to a specific requirement contained in the Statement of Work, Section 4 of the RFP.

d.   State And Offeror Responsibilities. This part should contain the offeror's understanding of the specific responsibilities of the State and the offeror for each part of the project.

e.   Assumptions And Constraints. In this part the offeror should identify any assumptions and constraints which affect the anticipated scope of work.

RESPONSE ITEM 5. RESPONSE TO SYSTEM REQUIREMENTS

In this response item please address each of the items required in Section 4, Statement of Work.

The response shall be in five parts. The first part is to provide your response to the General System Requirements, the second to the Equipment Management Functional Requirements, the third to the Facilities Management Functional Requirements, the Fourth to the Technical Requirements (the hardware environment your proposal will use, mainframe, mini or micro), and the fifth to provide any additional information you may wish to include relative to how your proposed solution addresses the Statement of Work.

Your answer shall be numbered to correspond to the item number in the RFP and explain how the requirement is met. Each item in this part shall tell how:

(a)   the proposed package is capable of fully meeting the requirement;

(b)   a modification to the proposed package currently under development will enable it to fully meet the requirement within the project schedule; or

(c) the proposed package shall be modified with unique code to meet the requirement; if so explain the extent of the change.

RESPONSE ITEM 6. PRICING PROPOSAL

In this item, please provide your response relative to pricing of your proposed solution. Address each of the specific sections and include any additional information that may be pertinent to the pricing of your proposal

It is the state's intent that this should be a fixed price contract. Price adjustments after the formation of a contract shall not be allowed.

The following information must be provided in this section.

a. A statement as whether or not the offeror desires to be considered for the Alaska Vendor Preference. If a preference is requested, attach the required documentation to support the claim authorized under AS 36.30.170(b). See also section 3.10.

b. A statement that the offeror certifies, and in the case of a joint proposal, each party thereto certifies as to its own organization, and in connection with this procurement:

(1) the prices proposed have been arrived at independently, without consultation, communication or agreement, for the purpose of restricting competition, as to any matter relating to such prices with any other respondent or with any competitor; and

(2) unless otherwise required by law, the prices quoted have not been knowingly disclosed by the respondent prior to award, directly or indirectly, to any other respondent or to any competitor.

c. Cost Schedule. A comprehensive schedule of all costs shall be submitted for the cost of the software/hardware package and for modifications and installation. A separate schedule shall be submitted for the software/hardware package costs.

(1) The software/hardware package cost schedule shall include the proposed prices, fees, and rates for the software/hardware package, including the supporting services offered.

(2) The modification/installation schedule shall use the following cost categories:

(a) Personnel - The respondent shall list all labor categories for all personnel performing services during the modification/implementation phase as described in the technical proposal project management plan, see response item 7. The number of units shall be expressed in hours and the unit price shall be the price per hour for services to be provided. The sum of costs for each position (unit price multiplied by the number of units) shall equal the proposal costs for personnel. The unit price shall include all travel related costs, overhead, general and administrative, and profit. Costs associated with training and technical assistance should be itemized in sufficient detail to permit realistic projections

(b) Equipment - All equipment not supplied by the state shall be listed and the amount charged for such equipment shown.

(c) Facilities - All facilities not supplied by the state shall be listed and the amount changed for such facilities shown.

(d) Training - All costs of developing training materials except personnel costs shall be listed.

(e) Office Supplies - All office supplies not provided by the state shall be listed by quantity and type and the amount changed for supplies shown.

(f) Printing and Photocopying - The quantity and type of all printing and photocopying not provided by the state shall be listed in detail and the amount charged shown.

(g) Freight and Postage - All freight and postage not provided by the state shall be listed in detail and the amount charged shown

(h) All other costs, including the cost of securing the performance bond, should be itemized in full detail. There is no need to show a separate listing for overhead, general and administrative, or profit. Those shall be included in the rates quoted in each direct cost category.

(3) Wage Rates. The wage rates used in the cost schedule shall be the rates charged by the contractor for all work accomplished under change orders/amendments issued to the contract resulting from this RFP. The offeror shall include a statement (including the restatement of these wage rates) to this effect as a required part of the cost proposal. Proposals that do not contain this statement shall be rejected.

(4) Maintenance Agreement Prices. Specifically identify the prices of any maintenance agreements for maintaining and enhancing the software, providing updates to standard software offering, and conforming to governmental standards and labor agreements during the implementation phase.

d.   Fixed Price Contract. The contract resulting from this RFP is intended to be a fixed price contract, thus quotations should include all changes accompanying the proposed package. All items shall be F.O.B. Juneau, Alaska, unless otherwise specified. No price adjustments shall be allowed.

The state shall not be responsible for any costs not included in the proposal or agreed upon during contract negotiations.

e.   Progress Payment Schedule. The offeror shall include a proposed schedule of progress payments. This schedule shall include the total costs and be divided into two parts as follows:

(1) All costs shall be scheduled over the life of the contract with payments based upon achievement milestones included in the project management plan; and

(2) the final payment shall be withheld until completion of the contract, including the acceptance of all deliverables and services. Also see paragraph 1.23. The timing of this payment shall be based upon acceptance of the system by the state, a final progress report, and a final invoice submitted by the contractor and approved by the project manager and the two client managers.

RESPONSE ITEM 7. PROJECT MANAGEMENT PLAN

The offeror shall provide a project management plan that includes:

a.   Project Management Approach. The offeror shall describe its project management letter approach including:

(1) the method used in managing the project; and

(2) the project management organizational structure including reporting levels and lines of authority.

b.   Project Control. The offeror shall describe its approach to project control including details of the methods used in controlling project activities.

c.   Project Schedule. A chart of project progression from beginning to completion that includes the achievement milestones upon which progress payments shall be claimed.

d.   Status Reporting To The State. The offeror shall describe its statue reporting methodology including details of written oral progress reporting. The state requires a minimum of weekly oral progress reporting and a minimum of monthly written progress reporting.

e.   Interface With The State. The offeror shall describe its interface points with the state including types of interfaces, level of interface, and level of personnel who may commit the contractor and to what extent.

RESPONSE ITEM 8. SUBCONTRACTED WORK

At a minimum, this response must include the following:

a.   A statement indicating the exact amount of work to be done by the prime contractor and each subcontractor, as measured by price shall be included.

b.   If the use of subcontractor(s) is proposed, provide:

(1) evidence of a valid Alaska business license (see paragraph 2.01) for subcontractor; and

(2) a statement on the subcontractor's letterhead shall be appended to the transmittal letter signed by

an individual authorized to legally bind the subcontractor and stating:

(a)   the general scope of work to be performed by the subcontractor;

(b)   the subcontractor's willingness to perform the work indicated; and

(c)   that they do not discriminate in their employment practices with regard to race, creed, color, age sex, national origin, marital status, pregnancy, parenthood, or disability.

RESPONSE ITEM 9. FINANCIAL RECORDS AND BONDS

This response must contain the following information.

a.   A certified copy of a corporate resolution granting the signing officer the power to bind the respondent to any contract resulting from their proposal. The corporate seal shall be affixed to the copy of the certified resolution which shall bear the original signature of an officer of the corporation and one other person authorized to execute the contract.

b.   The bid bond in the amount of $10,000 as specified in paragraph 2.05.

c.   A letter of commitment from a bonding company for the performance bond as specified in paragraph 2.05.

d.   Copies of audited financial statements for the past three (3) years.

RESPONSE ITEM 10. OTHER INFORMATION.

a.   A statement as to whether or not the offeror has been involved in litigation within the last five (5) years or has pending litigation arising out of contract performance. Exclude routine interpleader action, garnishments, and similar routine matters that do not reflect on contract performance. List all such contracts, reference number, contact persons and telephone numbers for the other parties, and a brief description of the facts surrounding each incident.

b.   A statement as to whether or not the offeror or principals has ever been involved in any kind of bankruptcy proceedings. Give a summary of all proceedings.

3.05 ORAL PRESENTATIONS AND INTERVIEWS

The proposal evaluation committee reserves the right to require elected offerors to make an oral presentation of their proposal and/or independently interview respondents. Such presentations/interviews provide the offeror with an opportunity to clarify the proposal and to ensure a mutual understanding of its content. The presentation may be scheduled at the convenience of the evaluation committee and shall be recorded.

3.06 SYSTEM DEMONSTRATION

The proposal evaluation committee reserves the right to require one or more selected offerors to provide a demonstration of their proposed solution in Anchorage Alaska. Requirements of the system demonstration are outlined in the discussion on Evaluation of Proposals which follows.

3.07 EVALUATION OF PROPOSALS

All proposals shall be evaluated by an Evaluation committee made up of qualified personnel. The committee shall evaluate and numerically score each proposal in accordance with the evaluation criteria shown below.

The evaluation phase will consist of three distinct parts:

1. The written response to this RFP;

2. The oral interview;

3. The live system demonstration.

Upon completing the evaluation of the written responses to the vendor proposals and application of the 10% Alaska vendor preference, a point total will be calculated for each proposal. Those vendors submitting the highest rated proposal will be scheduled for oral interviews. At the end of the Oral Interview phase a determination will be made if the vendor will move on to the final stage of the evaluation process, the live Demonstration.

The Evaluation Committee shall document all decisions in writing and make these a part of the contract file.

3.07.1 Proposal Evaluation Criteria

Step One. Evaluation of Written Responses

1.	Alaska Vendor Preference	250
2.	General Requirements	250
3.	Functional Requirements	500
	- SEF Requirement (375)	
	- AIAS Requirements (125)	
4.	Technical Requirement	100
5.	Project Approach and Plan	50
6.	Qualifications Experience	100
7.	Cost Proposal Evaluation	250
	Total points	1,500

Step Two. The Oral Interview

8.   Oral Interview   300

Step Three. The Live Demonstration

9.   Demonstration   700

     Grand Total Possible Score   2,500 points

3.07.2 - Explanation of the Evaluation Criteria

1.   Alaskan Preference - Refer to paragraph 4 04 for the
     explanation on Alaska Preferences   250 points

2.   General Requirements Evaluation   250 points

The general requirements will be evaluated based upon the following:
-   demonstrated understanding of the stated general requirement.
-   capability of proposed solution to satisfy all required general requirements.
-   The quality of the solution to the general requirements.

The total 250 points will be distributed in the following manner;

- System Support	25 points
- Data Base Management	45 points
- Report Writer	35 points
- User Friendly Screens	20 points
- System Security	25 points
- Data Integrity	20 points
- Ease of Customizing	20 points
- Connectivity	20 points
- Documentation	25 points
- Capacity	15 points

3.   Functional Requirements Evaluation   500 points

Functional Requirement will be evaluated on a checklist to determine completeness. They will be evaluated on the following set of criteria;

- demonstrated understanding of the stated functional requirements.

- capability of proposal to satisfy all required functions stated in the RFP.

- the quality of the solution to the functional requirement.

The total 500 points possible will be distributed in the following manner:

Equipment Management	375 points
- Manage Equipment Inventory	40 points
- Replace Equipment	15 points
- Analyze Equipment Statistics	40 points
- Manage Equipment Maintenance	65 points
- Manage Inventory	55 points
- Analyze equipment, parts, maintenance, costs	55 points
- Manage equipment billing and Accounts Receivable	60 points
- Audit SEF Activity	30 points
- Maintain Master Tables	15 points

Facilities Management	125 points
- Manage Equipment inventory	10 points
- Manage Building Inventory	15 points
- Manage Airstrips, taxiway, roads, and grounds	15 points
- Manage Maintenance of assets	20 points
- Manage parts, fuel, and Supply inventory	10 points
- Scheduling and tracking of staff time	20 points
- Analyze equipment, parts, maintenance and operations costs	20 points
- Audit AIAS activity	10 points
- Maintain Master Tables	5 points

4. Technical Requirements   100 points

The proposal will be evaluated on the technical merit of the total proposed System Evaluation. Factors will include, but not be limited to the choice of programming language, data base, system capacity, hardware proposed. Proposals will be expected to meet a minimum technical level to be considered responsive. The following technical items are critical issues that may cause a proposal to be considered non-responsive:

- Use of programming languages such as OS/VS COBOL, NATURAL 1 2, PL/I for a mainframe solution;

- The absence of a database management system for a mainframe solution or a relational database management system for a mini or micro solution;

- The lack of capability to distribute printed reports to remote locations using the State SNA/SDLC network.

- The lack of capability to use existing terminals, PCs and printers already tied into the State SNA/SDLC network.

5. Project Approach and Plan   50 points

The project plan will be evaluated based upon the following:

- The plan's completeness. It should include all the details of time, tasks and resources needed to implement the automated equipment and facilities management software/hardware system.

- The plan's reasonableness. The committee will review the plan to determine if the tasks outlined can reasonably be expected to be accomplished in the time frames proposed.

- The clarity of the respondent's discussion of the objective of each work task identified in the work plan and the logical relationships of each work task to the objectives of the project.

6. Qualifications & Experience   100 points

The firm's qualifications will be evaluated on the following:

- The past experience of the respondent in projects of a similar nature and magnitude.

- The quality of references and the content of their responses.

- Experience with Equipment and Facilities Management.

7. Cost Proposal Evaluation

Cost proposals will be rated as follows:

Price of Lowest Cost Proposal x 250   = total points
Price of Proposal Under Consideration

Note - Cost proposals from Alaska Vendors will be reduced by 5% for this calculation (reference Alaska Statute AS 36.30.250).

8. Oral Interview   300 points

The offerors with the highest rated proposals will be required to present a 60 to 120 minute description of their solution at the DOT/PF Headquarters, 3132 Channel Drive, Juneau, AK. Arrangements for necessary media equipment such a projector, video equipment, etc. should be coordinated through the project manager named in paragraph 1.03 of this RFP.

The presentation will be followed by a question and answer session. A maximum of 4 hours in duration will be set aside for this session.

Points will be awarded by the committee for a subjective assessment of:

- how well the total proposal meets our needs.

- the knowledge of the vendor about equipment and facilities management

- The quality and knowledge of system software implementation displayed by the proposer.

Clarifications made during the interview will be included with the written proposal itself.

9. Demonstration   700 points

At the conclusion of the oral interview a time and location will be arranged for the live system demonstration(s). The offeror with the highest rating after the oral interviews will advance to the third and final phase of the evaluation process. This demonstration must take place in Anchorage within 10 working days after the interview date.

The selected finalist(s) will present a two (2) day demonstration of their system in action. The demonstration will consist of three steps:

The point to be awarded or each section based on the following evaluation criteria:

A. Day One   300 points

Structured examples of system transactions will be performed. The specific steps to be performed will be provided by SEF. The vendor will be required to perform a set of transactions. Batch processing will be run, and a bill produced. No deviation from the structured performance will be allowed at this time. Questions from state observers will be held to a minimum. The points will be awarded based on the following criteria:

- can the software perform the assigned tasks.   100 points

- how well the task is performed by the software.   100 points

- subjective assessment of general overall system; 100 points
  ease of use, logic in format and design.

B.   Day Two   100 points

Prepared Demonstration by the Vendor. The vendor will be given 90 minutes to demonstrate key features of their application in any format they desire. No questions from State observers will be allowed during this phase.

Points to be awarded on the basis of how well demonstrated features apply to this RFP's requirements and the State's need in facilities and equipment management.

C.   Day Two   300 points

Question and Answer period, with hands on use of system by state observers. State personnel may address questions to the vendor at this time relating to function of specific application features. The availability of multiple terminals during this phase is desirable.

In order to minimally impact the on-going work of DOT&PF employees, the demonstration shall take place in an environment outside the DOT&PF facilities. The vendor shall schedule the demonstration in Anchorage. The vendor shall make all necessary preparations in advance. The vendor should plan on up to 30 observers and should ensure adequate seating and viewing capabilities.

3.08 CONTRACT NEGOTIATIONS

Upon completion of the evaluation process the preferred offeror shall be notified of being selected for contract negotiation. Contract negotiation will be held at The Department of Transportation and Public Facilities, Headquarter Building, 3132 Channel Drive, Juneau, Alaska. All parties involved in the negotiation of State contracts shall act in good faith in accordance with Alaska Statute 36.30.880.

3.09 FAILURE TO NEGOTIATE

If the selected offeror fails to provide the necessary information for negotiation in a timely manner, fails to negotiate in good faith, or cannot perform the contract within the amount of budgeted funds available for the project, the state may terminate negotiation and negotiate with the next highest-ranked offeror, or terminate award of the contract.

3.10 ALASKA PREFERENCES

3.10.1 ALASKA VENDOR PREFERENCE

In determining whether a proposal is advantageous to the State, the proposal evaluation committee and project procurement officer shall take into account, in accordance with regulation of the commissioner, whether the offeror qualified as an Alaska Vendor under Alaska Statute 36.30.170(b). The Alaskan Vendor's Preference consists of a 10% overall evaluation point preference and 5% price based preference.

An "Alaska Vendor" is a person who:

A.   holds a current Alaska business license;

B.   submits a proposal for goods or services under the name as appearing on the person's current Alaska business license;

C.   has maintained a place of business within the state staffed by the offeror or an employee of the offeror for a period of six months immediately preceding the date of the proposal;

D.   is incorporated or qualified to do business under the laws of the state, is a sole proprietorship, and the proprietor is a resident of the State or is partnership, and all partners are residents of the State; or

E.   if a joint venture, is composed entirely of ventures that qualify under A - D of this subsection.

3.10.2 ALASKA PRODUCT PREFERENCE

The Alaska Product Preference referenced in As 36.30.332 is not applicable to this RFP.

3.11 NOTICE OF INTENT TO AWARD CONTRACT

After completion of the evaluation process and contract negotiations and at least ten (10) days before the formal award of a contract, the Department of Transportation and Public Facilities shall issue a Notice of Intent to Award a Contract to all respondents. This notice shall contain the names and address of all respondents including the intended recipient of the contract.

3.12 AGGRIEVED RESPONDENTS

3.12.1 PROTESTS

An interested party may protest the award of a contract, the proposed award of a contract, or a solicitation for professional services by an agency. The protest shall be filed in writing with the Project Procurement Officer, Information Systems Division, Department of Transportation and Public Facilities, P.O. Box Z, Juneau, Alaska 99811, within ten (10) days after a Notice of Intent to Award the contract is issued and include the following information:

1.   the name, address, and telephone number of the protester;

2.   the signature of the protester or the protester's representative;

3. identification of the contracting agency and the solicitation or contract at issue;

4. a detailed statement of the legal and factual ground of the protest, including copies of relevant documents; and

5. the form of relief requested.

The project procurement officer shall issue a written decision containing the basis of the decision within the statutory time limit set out in AS 36.30.580. A copy of the decision shall be furnished to the protester by certified mail or other method that provides evidence of receipt.

3.12.2 APPEALS

An appeal from the decision of the Project Procurement Officer on a protest may be filed by the protester with the Commissioner, Department of Administration, P 0 Box C, Juneau, Alaska 99811-0200. An appeal shall be filed within five (5) days after the decision is received by the protestor. The protestor shall also file a copy of the appeal with the issuing office. The appeal shall contain the information required in paragraph 3.12.1; as well as:

1. a copy of the decision being appealed; and

2. identification of the factual or legal errors in the decision that form the basis for the appeal.

If necessary, a hearing shall be held to determine whether the award of the contested contract was made in accordance with statute and prescribed procedures. The hearing shall be limited to the evaluation and solicitation process used in this Request for Proposals.

SECTION 4 — STATEMENT OF WORK

4.01 INTRODUCTION

This section of the RFP is intended to provide the prospective offeror with the information necessary to develop a competitive proposal. It begins with the requirement for the new system. This is followed by a subsection identifying system requirements. Final subsections identify State provided resources and offeror obligation. A final subsection describes the hardware environment option and SEF and AIAS statistics. The successful offeror shall provide all effort necessary to purchase, modify, and install an automated equipment and facilities management software/hardware package that meets the state's needs and provides flexibility for future growth.

Editors Note: Sections 4.02 through 4.06 containing New System Requirements, some 47 pages in length, have been deleted.

4.07 OFFEROR OBLIGATIONS

The successful offeror shall provide all effort necessary to purchase, modify, and install an automated equipment and facilities management software/hardware package that meets the state's needs and provides flexibility for future growth. This shall include, but not be limited to:

A. ALASKAN PRESENCE

The offeror must be willing to maintain an on-site presence for ninety (90) days following implementation and acceptance of the system.

B. PROJECT MANAGEMENT

The offeror shall perform all management functions for the project including, but not limited to responsibility project personnel management, project team organizational structure, controlling project activities, project tracking including the achievement milestones upon which progress payments shall be claimed, status reporting to the state and other interfaces with the state.

C. COMPLIANCE WITH STATE STANDARDS

The offeror shall comply with state standards as detailed in "The State of Alaska, Information Resource Management User's Guide" for installation of a mainframe solution. The offeror shall also comply with the Information Systems Division Application Procedures and Guidelines document if unique code must be developed for a mainframe solution.

D. SOFTWARE/HARDWARE ACQUISITION

The offeror shall be responsible for acquisition of the software/hardware package being proposed in response to this RFP.

E. SOFTWARE/HARDWARE INSTALLATION

The offeror shall be responsible for installation of the proposed software/hardware package. This includes all tasks necessary to achieve the performance objectives outlined in this RFP. Limited computer availability may require offerors to schedule their staff to work between the hours of 5:00 p.m. and 7:00 a.m. if necessary.

F. SOFTWARE MODIFICATION

The offeror shall be responsible for all software modifications needed to successfully implement their proposed system in compliance with the specifications of the RFP. The state will not accept any modifications that require reinstallation of changes each time a new release of the system is installed. In those cases where RFP requirements cannot be met without writing unique code and the use of a current state subsystem is determined to be more cost effective the contractor shall incorporate the subsystem into the new system.

G. CONVERSION

The offeror shall be responsible for developing a plan for conversion of all master files in the existing system to the data base management system needed for the new system. State personnel from ISD, SEF and AIAS will perform the actual conversion. A file or files will be produced in the format ready to be loaded into the DBMS or RDBMS.

H. TRAINING

The offeror shall provide on-site training for all aspects of the system as installed. This includes the offeror's standard software offering as well as modification and additional features installed in compliance with the State's requirement. Training shall be provided for programming staff, system administrators and all and users. Training of ISD, AIA and FIA programming staff, and SEF management analysts shall be provided prior to the testing phase.

The offeror shall provide appropriate course materials including user manuals. This shall be accomplished at a minimum of three (3) locations, Anchorage, Fairbanks and Juneau after all testing phases have been completed.

I. CHANGE ORDERS

The offeror shall use the procedures contained in section five (5) of this RFP for accomplishing all contract change orders.

J. MAINTENANCE

The offeror must be willing to provide system maintenance for software and modifications made for the state's unique needs for a maximum of ninety (90) days following implementation and acceptance.

K. DOCUMENTATION

The offeror shall provide current and complete user and technical documentation, including a glossary of all data elements used by the system. Updated documentation shall be provided with all changes/updates to the software. Quantities to be delivered shall be determined during project installation.

L.   CONSULTING SUPPORT

The successful offeror shall provide consulting support in Juneau or project planning, project review, specifications, coding, testing and other consulting activities related to the project.

M.   ACCEPTANCE TESTING

The ISD, SEF and AIAS staff shall have up to 90 days to conduct detailed testing on the production system after implementation in a test environment which shall mirror production. Final acceptance will not be and until the completion of test steps. Vendor will maintain a presence to answer any questions resulting from questionable test results and/or to fix any identified product malfunctions discovered during the test/acceptance phase. The system shall not be moved to a production environment until the testing phase is complete.

SECTION 5 - GENERAL CONTRACT INFORMATION

5.01 CONTRACT APPROVAL

Any contract resulting from this Request for Proposals shall be submitted to the Commissioner of Administration for approval. If approved, it is effective from the date of approval. The state assumes responsibility for work done, even in good faith, prior to approval of the contract by the Department of Administration.

5.02 PROPOSAL AS PART OF THE CONTRACT

The successful proposal shall become an integral part of the contract. It shall not, however, be considered the total binding obligation for the contract. Any and all proposal conditions may be included, at the discretion of the project procurement officer, as a part of a final negotiated and approved contract.

The contract awarded as a result of this RFP may incorporate the following documents:

1.   The RFP, a amended.

2.   Written Bidder's questions and answers.

3.   Transcript of Contractor's oral presentation to the State.

4.   The proposal.

Should there be any conflict among the documents, the following order of precedence shall govern the resolution of conflict:

First, the contract document.

Second, the RFP as amended or as modified by the State's written answers to bidders' questions.

Third, transcript of Contractor's oral presentation.

Last, the proposal.

5.03 ADDITIONAL TERMS AND CONDITIONS

The state reserves the right to include additional terms and conditions during the process of contract negotiations. These terms and conditions shall be within the scope of the original RFP and contract document, and shall be limited to cost, clarification, definition, and administrative and legal requirements.

5.04 STANDARD CONTRACT PROVISIONS

The successful respondent shall be required to sign the Standard Agreement Form for professional services, for 02-093(see Appendix A). A copy is included for your reference. The contractor shall be required to comply with the general contract provisions of Appendix A. Any alteration of these general provisions shall be approved by the Department of Law before the contract can be accepted by the project procurement officer.

5.05 ADVANCE PAYMENTS

The state shall pay only for services rendered, reviewed and accepted by the project manager. No advance payment shall be authorized.

5.06 LIQUIDATED DAMAGES

The state reserves the right to include liquidated damages in the contract to ensure the contractor's performance of all contract provisions in a timely manner.

5.07 FUNDING CONTINGENCIES

The State reserves the right to cancel a contract negotiated as a result of this RFP at any time due to lack of appropriated funds. In addition, the State may terminate the contract at any time when it is in the State's best interest as specified in Appendix A, Article 5, of the state standard agreement form.

5.08 CONTRACT PERSONNEL

All contractor project personnel, including all subcontractor, shall be identified with a resume (see format, Appendix C) in the proposal document. Each person's role in the project must be identified and documented. The state reserves the right to approve or disapprove any change in the successful respondent's project team members whose participation in the project is specifically offered in the respondent's proposal. This is to assure that persons with vital experience and skill are not arbitrarily removed from the project by the prime contractor.

Any change in contractor personnel shall be submitted in writing to the State for the State's review and approval before the change is made. Contractor personnel changes which impact the work in any manner may be cause for the State to terminate the contract.

The state reserves the right to request that contractor or subcontractor personnel be removed from the project at any time.

5.09 STATE PROPERTY

Software written as a result of the project shall be transmitted to the state in source code form, with complete and acceptable documentation, as it is completed or acquired. Any software that might be used (either written or acquired) shall be approved by both the State and the contractor in writing before being used. Any software so approved shall be delivered to the State as stated herein.

All products, software, reports, data, flow charts, and equipment, etc , developed under this contract become the sole property of the State and shall be transmitted to the state promptly upon completion or termination of the contract.

Software provided to the contractor by the State as a result of this contract remains the sole property of the state. The contractor does not have the right to retain copies of any product, software, report, data, etc , developed or acquired as result of this contract either for further use or for purposes of resale.

All copyright of materials produced under any contract or subcontract awarded as a result of this RFP shall be retained by the State.

5.10 STATE PROVIDED RESOURCES

A. WORK SPACE

Except for specific tasks identified by the contractor in advance of accomplishment and approved in writing by the project manager, all work related to the General and EMS requirements shall be performed at the Department of Transportation and Public Facilities, Headquarters Building, located at 3132 Channel Drive, Room 250, Juneau, Alaska. Work related to the FMS requirements shall be performed at the Anchorage International Airport, 5000 West International Airport Road, Concourse C, Room SC2850, Anchorage, Alaska.

Work space, computer terminals as required, and furniture shall be provided by the state. Necessary supplies shall be subject to negotiation at the time of the contract.

B. COMPUTER RESOURCES

If the package selected is a mainframe solution the Information Systems Division shall be responsible for securing the computer resources needed for installation, testing, and operation of the proposed system.

This shall include the required computer time, disk space, tape drives, technical services, data base services and data control support. All project requirements shall be coordinated and approved through the project manager far enough in advance to facilitate scheduling.

C. TELECOMMUNICATIONS NETWORK

The existing statewide telecommunications network shall be available to the offeror for the purposes of this project. Requirements shall be coordinated and approved by the project manager.

D. PROJECT COORDINATION

The state project manager shall be the primary contact point between the contractor and State. All reports, billings, and problems shall be routed through him .The daily supervision of project personnel shall be the responsibility of the contractor's project manager and not the responsibility of the state's project manager.

E. STAFF SUPPORT

State staff allocated to the project on a full time basis from beginning to completion shall be limited to an Analyst/Programmer from the Information System Division, an Analyst/Programmer from each of the Anchorage and Fairbanks International Airport and a Management Analyst from the State Equipment Fleet staff.

5.11 OWNERSHIP OF DOCUMENTS

In addition to Article 10, Appendix A, of the standard agreement form, all form of data generated as a result of this contract shall be delivered to the State at the direction of the Director, Information Systems Division, or his/her authorized designee. During the period of performance, the information may not be disclosed to third parties, except as expressly provided in the contract, without the written permission of the Director, Information Systems Division.

5.12 PAYMENT OF TAXES

Potential contractors in arrears on any state taxes shall have the payment provisions of the contract approved by the State of Alaska, Department of Revenue, prior to contract award.

5.13 STANDARDS

Unless otherwise agreed to in writing by the state, all work performed shall conform to state and Department of Transportation and Public Facilities standards, requirements and criteria.

5.14 SYSTEM CHANGES (MAINFRAME SOLUTIONS)

The State shall notify the contractor of data center hardware and software system changes that affect this contract and shall allow the contractor up to 30 days to adjust.

5.15 REIMBURSEMENT TO STATE FOR UNACCEPTABLE DELIVERABLES

The contractor is responsible for quality, accuracy and completion of all work identified in the contract. All work shall be subject to evaluation and inspection by the state at all times to assure satisfactory progress, to determine quantities of work performed for progress payment purposes, to be certain that work is bring performed in accordance with contract specifications, terms and conditions, and to determine if corrections and modifications are necessary. Should such inspections or the state audit indicate substantial failure on the part of the contractor, the state may terminate the contract for default. Furthermore, the state may require the contractor to reimburse any monies paid (pro rata based on the identified proportion of unacceptable product received) and any associated damage such as, but not limited to, state facilities and other resource used, and direct expense incurred.

5.16 PAYMENT OF INTEREST

Under no condition shall the state be liable for interest payment on any unpaid balance owed the contractor for any reason under a contract awarded as a result of this RFP.

5.17 TERMINATION FOR DEFAULT

If the contractor refuses or fails to perform the work, or any separable part thereof, with such diligence as shall ensure its completion within the written contracted time frame, the state may, by written notice to the contractor, terminate the right to proceed with the work or such part of the work as to which there has been delay. This clause does not restrict state termination rights under the general contract provision of Appendix A, Article 5, Termination.

5.18 CONTRACT CHANGES

During the course of performing the work required by this contract, the contractor may be required to perform additional work within the general scope of the contract. At such time when additional work is required, the state shall forward to the contractor a description of the work to be accomplished and request that a proposal be offered within a given period. No work shall commence by the contractor without prior written authorization from the state. All labor costs for additional work shall be baed upon rate specified in the contractor's cost proposal.

5.19 RIGHT TO AUDIT

The state reserves the right to audit the books and records of a contractor or a subcontractor to the extent that the books and record relate to the performance of the contract or subcontract whenever it is deemed appropriate. Books and records shall be maintained by the contractor for a period of three years after the date of the final payment under the prime contract and by the subcontractor for a period of three years after the date of final payment under the subcontract. These audits may be performed by state personnel, or by outside auditors elected by the state.

5.20 RETENTION OF BOOKS AND RECORDS

Books and records that relate to a state contract or subcontract shall be retained in such a manner that all actual costs related to the contract or subcontract can be easily determined.

5.21 CONTRACT CONTROVERSIES

A contractor shall file a claim concerning a contract awarded as a result of this RFP with the project procurement officer in accordance with Alaska Statute 36.30.620. If the controversy assorted by the contractor cannot be resolved by agreement, the project procurement officer shall, after receiving a written request by the contractor for a decision, issue a written decision.

5.22 APPEAL ON A CONTRACT CONTROVERSY

An appeal from a decision of the project procurement officer on a contract controversy may be filed by the contractor with the Commissioner of Administration. The appeal shall be filed within 14 days after the decision is received by the contractor. The appeal shall contain a copy of the decision being appealed and identification of the factual or legal error in the decision that form the basis of the appeal.

5.23 JUDICIAL APPEAL

Any dispute arising out of this agreement shall be resolved under the laws of Alaska. Any appeal of an administrative order and any original action to enforce any provision of this agreement or to obtain any relief from or remedy in connection with this agreement may be appealed to the superior court in accordance with the Alaska Rules of Appellate Procedure. A final decision of the Commissioner of Administration under AS 36.30.630(b) may be appealed to the superior court for a trial de nove.

5.24 PRIME CONTRACTOR RESPONSIBILITIES

A written determination of responsibility of a prospective contractor shall be made by the project procurement officer. Factors that may be considered in determining whether a prospective contractor is responsible include, but are not restricted to whether the prospective contractor:

    A.   has a satisfactory record of performance;

    B.   is qualified legally to contract with the state;

    C.   has supplied all necessary information in connection with the inquiry concerning responsibility.

The selected contractor shall be required to assume responsibility for all services offered in his/her proposal whether or not (s)he produces them. Further, then state shall consider the selected contractor to be the sole point of contact with regard to contractual matters, including payment of any and all charges resulting from the contract.

5.25 WITHHOLDING OF CONTRACT PAYMENTS

Notwithstanding any other payment provisions of this contract, failure of the contractor to submit required reports of deliverables when due, or failure to perform according to the work schedule or deliver required work, supplies, or services shall result in the withholding of future payments under this contract unless such failure arises out of causes beyond the control of and without the fault or negligence of the contractor. The project manager shall promptly notify the contractor of any intention to withhold any payments.

5.26 COPYRIGHTS TRADE SECRETS AND CONFIDENTIAL TECHNICAL DATA

All proposals shall be open for public inspection after the Notice of Intent to Award a contract is issued (AS 36.30.230). Offerors should not include proprietary information in proposals, if such information should not be disclosed to the public.

Proprietary information which may be presented during negotiations shall be held to be confidential if expressly agreed to in writing, in advance by the contracting agency.

All copyrighted materials used by the offeror in any contract resulting from this RFP shall be protected in accordance with federal and state laws.

5.27 NOVATION OR CHANGE OF NAME

A contract resulting from this RFP may not be transferred or otherwise assigned without the prior written consent of the chief procurement officer or the project procurement officer.

If the chief procurement officer or the project procurement officer determines it is in the best interest of the state, a successor in interest may be recognized in a novation agreement in which the transferor and transferee agree that:

    A.   the transferee assumes all of the transferor's obligations under the contract;

    B.   the transferor waives any and all rights it has under the contract a against the state;

C. the transferor guarantees performance of the contract by the transferee; and

D. the transferee furnished satisfactory performance and payment bonds, if required by the project procurement officer.

If a contractor requests to change the name in which it holds a contract with the state, the project procurement officer responsible for the contract may, when it is in the best interests of the state, enter into an agreement with the requesting contractor to effect the change of name. The agreement changing the name shall specifically indicate that no other terms and conditions of the contract are changed.

5.28 FRAUD OR BAD FAITH BY THE CONTRACTOR

Upon finding that a solicitation or award is in violation of law or that the recipient of the contract acted fraudulently or in bad faith, the contract shall be declared void.

5.29 GUARANTEE OF ACCESS TO SOFTWARE

The state shall have full and complete access to all source code, documentation, utilities, software tools, and other similar items that are used to develop/install the proposed automated equipment and facilities management software/hardware or that may be useful in maintaining or enhancing the equipment and facilities management software/hardware system after it is operating in a production environment. For any of the above mentioned items which are not turned over to the state upon completion of the installation, the contractor must provide a guarantee to the state of uninterrupted future access to, and license to use, these items. The guarantee must be binding on all agents, successors, and assignees of the contractor and subcontractor. The state reserves the right to consult legal counsel as to the sufficiency of the licensing agreement and guarantee of access offered by the contractor.

5.30 PRODUCT WARRANTY

The State requires a product warranty of one year from date of final product acceptance. Warranty shall include all labor and travel costs incurred by the vendor to correct errors identified by the State in the software application. The vendor shall have 10 days to correct identified errors.

Editors Note: Appendices A, B and C have been deleted.

APPENDIX D - STATEMENT OF TERMS AND CONDITIONS AFFIRMATION

The following terms and conditions represent an integral part of our proposal and we accept them without any reservations or conditions.

1. We agree to all of the provisions, terms and conditions of the RFP without exception. All the

contract terms and conditions contained in the RFP are considered and included in our proposal.

2.   We are organized as a _____ (corporation or other legal entity) under the laws of _____ (state).

3.   All subcontractors are identified in our proposal.

4.   Our proposal contains a statement indicating the exact amount of work to be done by the prime contractor and each subcontractor, as measured by price.

5.   No attempt has been made or will be made by us to induce any other person or firm to submit or not submit a proposal.

6.   We are an affirmative action employer and do not discriminate in employment practices with regard to race, creed, color, age, sex, national origin, marital status, pregnancy, parenthood, or disability.

7.   No cost or pricing information has been included in any part of the proposal except the cost proposal.

8.   The system proposed will meet the specifications set forth in the RFP.

9.   The transmittal letter identifies and explains all proposal deviations from the detailed specification and requirements of this RFP. The state reserves the right to reject any proposal containing such deviations or to require modifications before acceptance.

10. The prices contained in our proposal are binding for 180 day following the proposal due date.

11. We certify that the prices proposed have been arrived at independently, without consultation, communication, or agreement, for the purpose of restricting competition, as to any matter relating to such price with any other respondent or with any competitor.

12. We certify that unless otherwise required by law, the prices quoted have not been knowingly disclosed prior to award, directly or indirectly, to any other respondent or to any competitor.

13. We agree to pre-award audits, on-site audits and on-site inspections as described in the RFP.

14. We agree to secure the insurance coverage required by the Department of Administration, Division of Risk Management.

15. We agree to secure the bid and performance bond as described in the RFP.

16. We agree to retain books and records that relate to a state contract or subcontract in such a manner that all actual costs related to the contract or subcontract can be easily determined.

17. We agree to guarantee to the state uninterrupted future access to, and license to use, all source code, documentation, utilities, software tools, and similar items not turned over to the state upon completion of the installation. The guarantee shall be binding on all agents, successors, and assignees or the contractor and subcontractor.

18. We certify that we are complying with the laws of the State of Alaska; the Federal Civil Rights Act; the Equal Employment Opportunity Act and the regulations issued thereunder by the state and federal

government; the Fair Labor Standards Act; Copland Anti-Kickback Act; Contractor Work Hours and Safety Act; Patents; Date and Copyright Act; and the Examination of Contractual Records Act.

19. The person signing this affirmation and the accompanying proposal is the same and certifies that s(he) is the person in the respondent's organization responsible for, or authorized to make, decisions as to the prices quoted and work to be performed.

Editors Note: Appendices E through I, some 37 pages in length, have been deleted.